KU-016-262

Leeds Metropolitan University
17 0166740 4

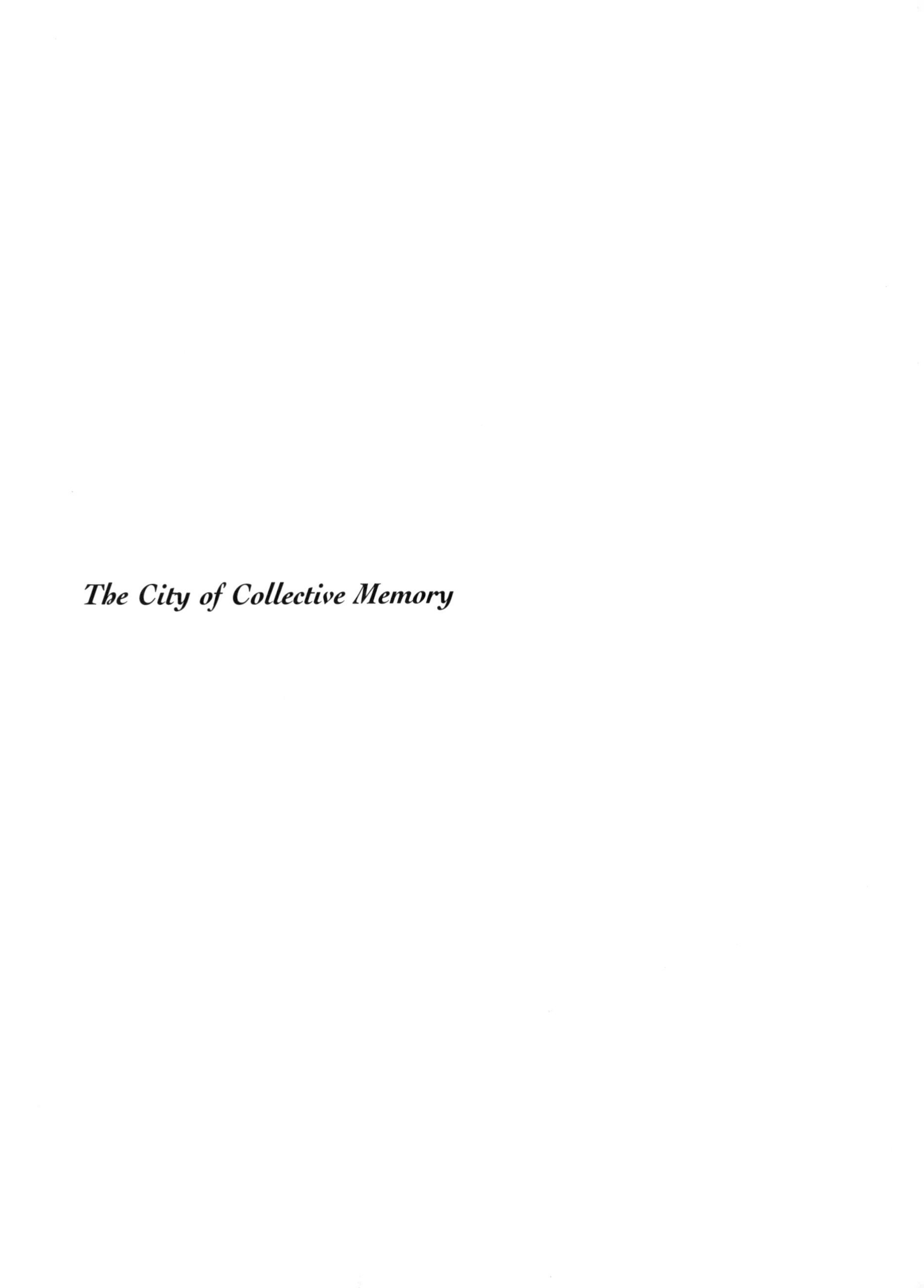

The City of Collective Memory

M. Christine Boyer

The City of Collective Memory

Its Historical Imagery and Architectural Entertainments

The MIT Press
Cambridge, Massachusetts
London, England

First MIT Press paperback edition, 1996

This book was set in Cochin by DEKR Corporation and was printed and bound in the United States of America.

Library of Congress Cataloging-in-Publication Data

Boyer, M. Christine.
The city of collective memory : its historical imagery and architectural entertainments / M. Christine Boyer.
p. cm.
Includes bibliographical references and index.
ISBN 0-262-02371-7 (HB), ISBN 0-262-52211-X (PB)
1. City planning—Psychological aspects. 2. Architecture—Aesthetics. 3. Urban beautification. 4. Architecture and society.
I. Title.
NA9031.B72 1994
711'.4—dc20 94-10041
CIP

Contents

Acknowledgments

This book began in the mid-1980s as a critique of the practices of historic preservation, urban design, and postmodern architecture. It was instigated by their unacknowledged complicity with real estate forces and government economic development policies focusing on redeveloping the centers of American and European cities during the 1970s and 1980s. As the book evolved, however, the work turned to explore the larger issue of how images from the nineteenth century have been translated into contemporary views of the city, how the restoration of former architectural and neighborhood traces forged a hybrid layering of architectural sites and a constant migration from one time period to another. This layering recoups many urban scenes for commercial or civic intent, situating the spectator between official narrations and more personal experiences or memories of city places. There is a constant oscillation established between any conventional and imaginary urban vision, a shimmering that produces both pleasurable and disturbing experiences. Thus this work offers both a look at phantasmagorical urban visions and a critique of economic and social practices that have captured these displays and used them for more commercial and political purposes.

Deepest gratitude is owed to the support of the Graham Foundation for Advanced Studies in the Fine Arts and to a Rockefeller Foundation Humanities Fellowship that allowed for necessary travel and research establishing the base from which this work developed.

There are many who have contributed significantly to the development of the argument of this book. Parts of chapter 8 evolved from discussions with Michael Sorkin for a chapter I wrote for his edited volume entitled *Variations on a Theme Park*. Special thanks should be offered to Christina Spellman, Richard Sennett, and Tony Vidler for their helpful comments drawn from a close reading of an earlier version of this manuscript. Thanks should also be extended to Melissa Vaughn and Jeannet Leendertse of The MIT Press for careful editing and thoughtful design of the book. And gratitude is due to Yasmin Ramirez for her help with visual materials. In addition there are numerous students to thank for exploring the visual imagery of cities in classes taught at The Chanin School of Architecture, The Cooper Union for the Advancement of Science and Art and The School of Architecture, Princeton University. Finally I want to express my deep gratitude to archivists and librarians of Avery Library, Columbia University, New York; Bobst Library, New York University, New York; The Gennadeion Library, Athens; The Guildhall Library, London; The Historic New Orleans Collection, New Orleans; The Library at the Architectural Conservation Program, ICCROM, Rome; The Library at The Royal Institute of British Architects, London; The Library at the Section Française de l'ICOMOS, Paris; The Library of Congress, Washington, D.C.

Introduction

o n e

The Place of History and Memory in the Contemporary City

Postmodern Ambiguities

This work investigates representational images and architectural entertainments of present-day cities. By doing so, it attempts to critique the practice of architecture, city planning, and historic preservation in a specific manner. It recognizes that these arts still carry within their visual imaginations the influence of nineteenth-century procedures and representational views of city building. Perhaps unconsciously, often explicitly, they reach back to manipulate architectural fragments and traces formulated as expressions of nineteenth-century problems and needs, but then they insert these fragments into contemporary contexts that are controlled by vastly changed circumstances and desires. Engulfed and enframed by a set of new constraints forged in contemporary times, these fragments from the past appear denigrated by nostalgic sentiments that fuel their preservation or reconstruction, while our collective memory of public places seems undermined by historicist reconstructions. When juxtaposed against the contemporary city of disruption and disarray, the detached appearance of these historically detailed compositions becomes even more exaggerated and attenuated.

Consequently, the role of history and memory and the concepts of space and time in our contemporary arts of city building need to be reconsidered when they rely too explicitly on constructs and models formulated in earlier periods. If these arts borrow nineteenth-century fabrications such as museumlike cities and travels in time, the trompe l'oeil wall painting and the tableau vivant, scenographic stage sets and civic spectacles, to cite only a few examples, then we need to understand both the historical organization of these visual genres in their original spatial and temporal contexts as well as their insertion and meaning within aestheticized cityscapes of today. Differing in visual and articulable qualities, these forms cannot be transferred from one age to another without making adjustments in the parameters of representability or accounting for changes in the social, political, and historical field of vision.

This book will argue that the shift of view from the present to the historical, from the modern to the traditional, from twentieth-century to nineteenth-century city forms, leaves many questions unanswered and not even posed. Designers of urban projects, especially in the 1970s and 1980s, seemed intent on arranging and detailing ornamental places of the city until a matrix of well-designed fragments appeared. In these compositional nodes, they called on history or local and regional traditions to specify through design codes and regulations the ambience and styles of particular places until an aestheticized aggregate prevailed.[1] But the matrix of places that results encourages partial, piecemeal vision pushing interstitual spaces out of its view. The deindustrialized and deterritorialized, displaced and disadvantaged, have no seat in this constructed array. As spectators or designers of these city scenes, we have allowed our visual imaginations to project this matrix with its apparent intervals and disconnected places onto a seemingly unified image of the city. In this illusionary totalized view, it is paradoxically the question of linkages and totality that matrices suppress: those that question how the past, the present, and the future are related; those that examine contemporary inversions that privatize public space and publicize private space; or those that might admit the maligned but necessary idea of community, of public space, of a collective project to bind us together in harmony.

Matrices are a ploy in the postmodern war against totalities; their tactics are those of erasure and interruption. As opened-ended aggregates of details and differences, they never congeal into universals, always deferring closure that concepts such as "the public sphere," "the city plan," or "collective memory" by necessity require. To "totalize," on the other hand, is to yield to the modernist's desire to master and dominate city space, or to experience the city in a coherent and integrated manner. In our current negation of totalities, we no longer dare, as Sartre once said, to draw even a partial summing up of the historical and social situation to guide our future actions, to judge our collective project, or to prescribe necessary social transformations.[2] Adrift in a sea of fragments and open horizons, our postmodern position is ambiguous. We cannot speculate or reflect on a more rational and equitable form for the city, for fear of erecting perspectival wholes and illusionary totalities that might exclude or homogenize what we believe must remain plural and multiperspectival. Confronted with an all-too-totalizing system of late capitalism with its global reach and administrative rationalizations, however, the indeterminacies and undecidabilities of our postmodern stance offer no virtuous solutions with which to confront contemporary crises, nor allow us to oppose and resist the increasingly uneven development of our cities and nations. The aestheticized matrix with which we cover the city becomes a screen that allows us to perfect only partial attachments—to this local community, to that particular history, to these traditions. It displaces an engaged commitment, making us ambivalent about whether oppositional critics can effect any change. In other words, the pictorialization of space and time, which this book will explore within the contemporary arts of city building, shatters our place in the city and forbids us to envision a social order that we can reform. Although this pictorialization may amuse, lull, or even entertain us, it does not alienate, nor hold us accountable, nor sustain our resistance.

If modernism blew apart the relationship between history and the city, destroying the perception of architectural illusions that the nineteenth century put into place, then architecture in the 1970s and 1980s attempted to restore the public realm of the city, to reweave the shredded urban fabric, and to reconstruct a sense of collectivity and cooperation. But this gesture was fraught with paradoxical positions. Because inherited notions of good city form or any mention of "collective" entail a totalizing perspective, there are women, minorities, gays, and marginals, in particular, who have opened these forms of closure and exclusion to enable different voices and other positions to find expression. Yet something gained has also meant something lost: broken totalities that deconstruct the voice of paternalism and Western rationality come along with other things we don't necessarily want. We have lost a moral public sphere in this sea of plural voices; the better argument wields no collective weight, actually enabling the public sphere to be dominated by private voices selling fictional styles of life and imaginary behaviors.

By extension, we may see contemporary architectural expressions as vertical slices cutting across a matrix of plural styles and intertwining artistic expressions, rather than holding onto an Enlightenment or nineteenth-century view where even architectural styles, it was argued, followed a progressive and linear development. But if we do, then here too we have lost any authoritative voice that might orchestrate our civic spaces, any normative design that might bind our spirits together. Yet our desire for authentic memories and city experiences reveals an empathy for lost totalities, even though no one actually speaks out in favor of a unified city. Paradoxically, we seem to recognize that struggles over good city design are always multistructured, requiring alternative viewpoints and spectator positions, and we do seem aware of the exclusions our matrix engenders, but then we allow dominant voices to impose their meaning and to control the politics of representation. The contemporary arts of city building are derived from the perspective of white, middle-class architectural and planning professionals who worry in a depoliticized fashion about a city's competitive location in the global restructuring of capital, and thus myopically focus on improving a city's marketability by enhancing its imageability, livability, and cultural capital. Since the early twentieth century, architecture has been a commodity as well as a form of publicity, but now in the triumphant culture of consumption, designer skylines and packaged environments have become vital instruments enhancing the prestige and desirability of place. Due to these paradoxical positions, we need, consequently, to examine our contemporary ambivalence that both desires yet rejects a view of the city as a constructed totality.

Another postmodern ambiguity that depoliticizes and neutralizes our critical awareness of contemporary city form lies in the manner in which we reference "history," and this too has to be reexamined. As being "modern" in the early part of the twentieth century meant, among other things, being self-consciously new, blowing up the continuum of tradition, and breaking with the past, the contemporary arts of city building, by returning to traditions established in the nineteenth century, explicitly jump over the city of modernism, hoping to drive that representational order out of their sight. In a conscious attempt to eradicate modernism's oppositional or critical stance that aimed to disrupt the hierarchical authority and official heritage that the nineteenth century bourgeoisie succored within their own set of historicizations and eclectic views, contemporary reevaluations of "history" have crushed any redeeming sense of tradition. By now, traditions have been so thoroughly "invented" or homogenized, and "history" so absolutely marketed or commodified, misrepresented, or rendered invisible, that any oppositional potential rooted in collective memory has been eclipsed completely. We need, therefore, to be reminded of Walter Benjamin's claim that all history writing is a story of the triumph of bourgeois values and represents the posthumous reconstruction of fragmented events according to a completely fabricated architecture. Benjamin felt that random historical objects from the past such as the debris to be found in flea markets or discrete historical events such as the construction of the first arcades must be allowed to violently collide with others, so that the present may achieve insight and critical awareness into what once had been.[3] In a similar manner, our memory of the city, of pictorialized space and time, must be revitalized by reexamining the writing of history as representation and by reawakening utopian involvement invested in architectural and urban forms.

In jumping over modernism's sense of history, however, contemporary historicizations are no different from any writing of history that aims to separate a present time from a past, to break with and differ from everything that has occurred just before and up to the present dividing line. This new discrete time period recognizes that everything in the recent past must be forgotten, eradicated, repressed, or treated as dead and unthinkable, in order to establish a new representational form. So Michel de Certeau claimed, every new time finds its legitimation in what it excludes. Yet this new time nevertheless welcomes the existence of earlier pasts, specified by earlier ruptures before the time of the current division—it even builds its representational forms out of materials from these accepted pasts, reorganized by conflicts and interests formed in the present.[4]

Consequently it is not surprising to find that the refuse and remnants of nineteenth-century architectural and urban traditions have been rescued by the avant-garde of contemporary times, although such salvage operations often appear to be enigmatic quotations and awkward supplements. If modernists were preoccupied with the present or current time, then architects and designers of the 1970s and 1980s grounded their own obsession on refiguring the past. Yet in these gestures they reaffirmed its perishability and death. The past, being over and done with, now falls prey to our invention. It is resuscitated or resurrected in partial or ironic refigurings, subsequently reinforcing our sense of loss and detachment. The City of Collective Memory, with its quasi-archeological presentations and stagings, bears witness again and again that something has vanished from our present-day cityscapes that we seek to regain and to review. Artistic forms and representational logics borrowed from the nineteenth century seem to hold sway over contemporary imaginations, becoming perniciously ideological when they are misrecognized as natural constructs and rational decisions. We should be suspicious of their control on our perception and how they insinuate their way into representational forms of the city, for representations always mediate between the spectator's perception of reality and what might be reality: they are supplements or substitutes standing in for the "real," never establishing a perfect fit nor a mimetic relationship. To regain oppositional awareness in the contemporary city—an awareness sustained by a critical sense of history—we need to study the generative forces influencing their representational forms.

The Inversions of Public and Private Space

In the City of Collective Memory, we are interested particularly in the creation of meaningful and imaginative public spaces. Yet perhaps one of the most maligned constructs of today is the misrepresentation of the word "public" when applied to city places. A fresh look at the history of public space might sharpen the issue. Before the end of the eighteenth century, "public space" was usually designed as an honorific place celebrating the power of the king, queen, or aristocracy and used to recall and to invigorate their sovereign conduct and responsible actions. Think, for example, of the ceremonial city of late medieval and Renaissance times, whose important junctions and public spaces were marked at special times of the year with stages and scaffolds holding aloft theatrical tableaux vivants. As the royal procession paraded through the city from site to site, these dramatic tableaux revealed not only the terms by which royal authority was accepted, but also reflected the city's self-image of its own obligations. Eventually transcribed in stone, a memory system of public monuments and places arose, rearticulating these communal covenants and rehearsing their sovereign pledges.[5]

The great political revolutions of the eighteenth and nineteenth centuries transformed this ritual conscription of city space into the democratic public sphere. Here the meaning of public space was extended to include places of public debate and gatherings where the rational voice of the people could be heard. Now public authority was linked to a system of norms and regulations, and these in turn were publicly known, debated, and discussed until a consensus arose over their legitimate and rational application.[6] The space of the city became the model of this rational bourgeois public sphere. By the end of the eighteenth century Paris, for example, had been divided into twenty districts, and these subdivided into twenty sections; each section contained twenty houses, and each house numbered, its floors divided and all doors assigned a letter. Subsequently each individual residing in the city could be known and represented by their rational coordinates within this Cartesian grid; anything irrational and threatening disorder could be expelled from sight. Thus hospitals, cemeteries, poorhouses, and prisons were banished from the center of the city to reappear at marginal sites on the outskirts.[7]

Thoughout the nineteenth century, as the working class rose up in protest and the uneducated and illiterate grew in numbers, the public sphere of the city was reconceptualized in terms of the rich and the poor. The "irrational" and repressed demands of the working and dangerous classes returned to haunt the streets and disturb the spaces of the city. Unreason was unleashed within the heart of the city, endangering and undermining the bourgeois foundations of order. Attempts were made to rout out this dangerous disease by piercing large boulevards through the slums and insalubrious areas of the city, but in the end these reforms only produced more riots, unrest, and anxiety. Because the rational demands of the poor were now met with irrational suppressions, "reason" could no longer legitimate the bourgeois public sphere, so its meaning began to evaporate.[8] When the state tried to guarantee social order by promising to fulfill needs that the private sphere had long neglected, such as housing, transportation, education, and health services, then the concept of the public was transformed once again into the more abstract public sphere of the welfare state. Electoral reform and public education seemed to lie at the heart of this new public sphere, a rearrangement in which the topographical sites of the city could be readily employed. At the turn of the twentieth century, cities in the Western world underwent a revitalized period of civic improvement that embellished in an ad hoc manner municipal buildings, public libraries, railroad stations, public parks and parkways, bridges, and statuary, trying wherever possible to establish civic spaces of beauty and order. So a New York City Municipal Art Society Committee Report of 1905 proclaimed:

> The inculcation of love for the city in which one lives, being only an enlarging of the love for home, is an end that should meet with response from the newest recruit to American principles. It is a form of patriotism that can appeal to all people who come to this country. . . . Adequate, dignified, beautiful governmental buildings will produce an effect on the governed which mere holders of office as individuals cannot do.[9]

Once again, in the last few decades there has been a restructuring of concepts: the "public" has become a negative concept connoting unruly bureaucracies, corrupt officials, inefficient management, regulatory impositions, and burdensome taxations. Meanwhile, "private" has been refurbished with an exalted image: the freedom of the market and the freedom of choice and style of life that commodities and wealth can provide.[10] As the importance of public space in the center of cities has waned—in part the result of explosive privatization that both the rise of suburbs and the media revolution have engendered—then private space becomes more valued than public places. Most civic improvement schemes and inner-city spatial recyclings play on this inversion of values—creating private preserves for the wealthy that are then transformed into "public amenities" by allowing a select group of people to stroll unimpeded along their corridors and spaces of power. Yet even this contemporary reference to the public is a universalizing construct that assumes there is a collective whole, while in reality the city's public is fragmented into marginalized groups, many of whom have no access to or voice and representation in the public spaces of our revitalized and gentrified cities.

The public realm of the City of Collective Memory should entail a continuous urban topography, a spatial structure that covers both rich and poor places, honorific and humble monuments, permanent and ephemeral forms, and should include places for public assemblage and public debate, as well as private memory walks and personal retreats. Having lost this understanding, the spatial form of the contemporary city reveals a patchwork of incongruous leftover pieces alongside a

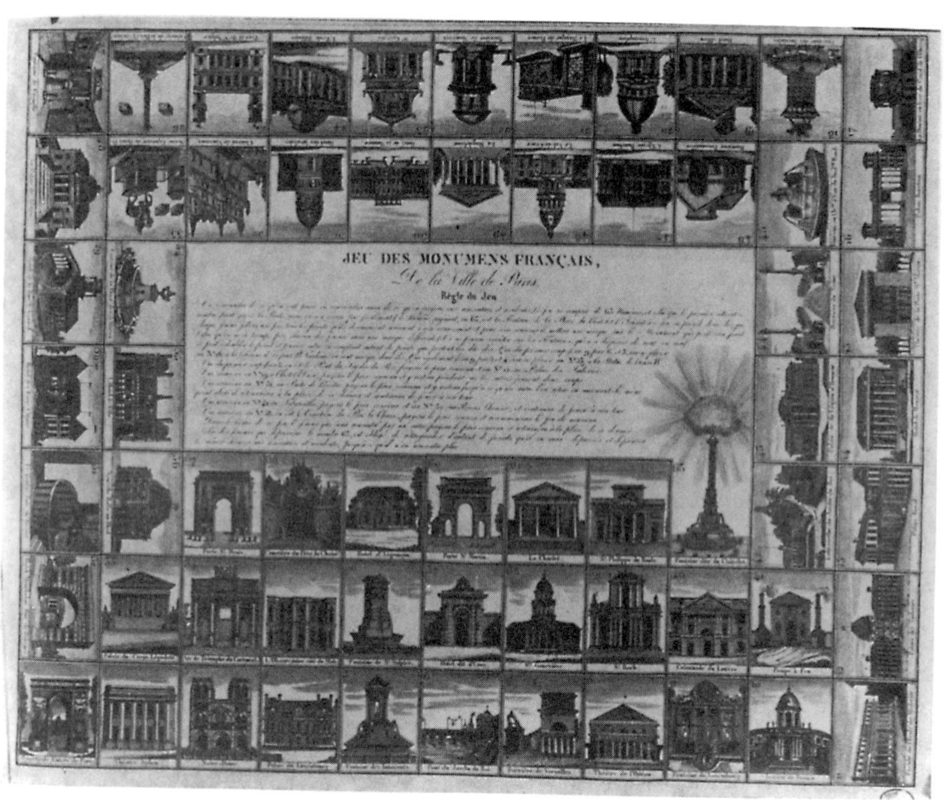

Game of Chance, "Jeu des monuments français de la Ville de Paris," (1810).

set of artfully designed compositions. Even though "the public" may be referenced in these well-designed nodes, not one of these places actually addresses the metropolitan whole nor recollects what the city totality requires. Instead, designers formalistically draw on nineteenth-century manuals of civic art that prescribe an order and harmony for each inserted enclosure, but then fail to link these sites together or relate them to the layers of history and people that the city actually presents. The result is the city matrix that we explored above, an instrumental symbol of order that Stephen Tyler has called the "ultimate thought picture of Western desire."[11] Instrumentally imposed on the surface of the city by the developer, the planner, the preservationist, or urban designer, it is the web of space that defines the city as an array of well-defined or historically preserved places. But this array entraps and inhibits our desire to explore what resides outside of the grid, or to understand what must be done to obtain an open and just society. This latter project requests that we reconceptualize and reformulate banished theories of the public sphere and how this affects contemporary constructs of urbanism or the process of planning the city.

The Generating Powers of a City Plan

If the contemporary city suffers from an inadequate and misguided process of planning, then perhaps a reexamination of some of the latter's historical roots might awaken forgotten intentions. A sense of urbanism or a process of city planning was one of the procedures by which the Enlightenment aestheticized absolute power—parceling and redistributing it through a utopia of rationalized space. Those who held Enlightenment ideals projected that scientific and technical instruments of rationality would control chaotic urban form and provide an emancipatory public sphere and an improved quality of life for all citizens in newly formed democratic states. Behind every city plan and architectural project lay the wildly utopic belief that society was progressing toward a better future, that industrial production when harnessed by collective desires would erase want, eradicate disease, and supplant revolution. An architectural regime that controlled the behavior of individuals belonged to this instrumental rationality: believing that architecture itself could effect and reform social behavior. If the masses, housed and fed by meager allowances and expanding in number within the working-class districts of nineteenth-century industrial cities, presented a dangerous threat to social stability, then how better to discipline their behavior and instill democratic sentiments and a morality of self-control than through exemplary architectural expression and city planning improvements?

Michel Foucault explained how disciplinary procedures were developed during the nineteenth century to produce efficient, well-behaved, and productive individuals; how norms of good behavior and rationality were internalized through education and training.[12] But the development of disciplinary structures transforming individual behavior also implied that a utopian image of a well-governed and comely arranged city must first be developed. This idea was based on the assumption that an exemplary model was antecedent to perception and only secondarily produced the normative behavior expected of each individual. If the self could be constructed, its identity specifically shaped by educational experiences, then for each individual to willingly blend into a collective totality and to enable the spirit of the whole to prevail, it was necessary that a harmonious arrangement of society be represented, its organizational rules learned, remembered, and applied. Georges Canguilhem, in his work entitled *The Normal and the Pathological* (1966), found "the social order [to be] a set of rules with which the servants or beneficaries, in any case, the leaders, must be concerned. The order of life is made of a set of rules lived without problems."[13]

Many treatises written in the mid-sixteenth and seventeenth centuries and once again at the end of the eighteenth century and early nineteenth century, so Foucault described, outlined the art of governance—accounts that taught not only how a citizen should conduct himself and be spiritually led, but how as well the sovereign ruler should govern the state, what were her/his moral duties and obligations to her/his subjects, and how the sovereign's own behavior should be ruled by rational forces, not the persuasion of might. The sovereign was like a wise head of the family carefully supervising his household economy for the common good of all its members. Intelligently governed, the state or household economy produced the greatest wealth; it operated efficiently without waste, it created sufficient means of subsistence, and so its members multiplied and prospered. This was the positive art of governance, a pastoral model in which the leader positively ensured, sustained, and improved the life of each individual. It supplanted the model of brute force and hierarchical privilege negatively imposing laws and sanctions. The pastoral model implied that a ruler must have sufficient knowledge to judge wisely, and must know the needs of the subjects and the state of the nation, its markets and trade, its territory and property. But it also implied that subjects were well educated, obedient, and acted responsibly so that they too partook of the art of governance. To ensure acts of self-governance, citizens were presented with visual models to internalize, remember, and apply.

Consequently, if a wise leader were to follow these directives, she or he would architecturally embellish a capital city to visually demonstrate what the order and organization of a well-governed state or society should be. This sovereign would place a conceptual diagram before each subject that outlined the city's collective infrastructure and networks of communication, its provisions for public hygiene and edification, and its arrangements for private housing.[14] We can turn to a little known reformer of Paris in the mid-nineteenth century, A. Perreymonde, to examine how a sovereign might establish such a relation between a unified perceptual image of the city and the moral governance of its citizens. Commenting on the state of Paris in the 1840s and hoping to augment the grandeur and power of Louis Philippe, Perreymonde noted that the city had disintegrated into a series of autonomous residential quarters and had lost its formal coherence and dominating influence over its citizenry. The core of Paris, he proclaimed "must be ONE, STABLE, CENTRAL, and ACTIVE BY ITSELF," and so he emphasized that the grand crossing of routes at the center of the city must be strengthened.[15]

Designing a new plan for Paris, Perreymonde highlighted only the significant streets, reducing the rest of the fabric to neutral background. Against this backdrop he dramatized important buildings, and by creating a series of major new streets he not only specified the location of the three symbolic centers of government, school, and the city—the Louvre, University, and Hôtel de Ville—but he as well gathered what had become a series of autonomous residential quarters into one large district by enclosing them within a newly formed network of streets. The residential instability of Paris, accentuated by its numerous insalubrious quarters, so Perreymonde believed, was an abnormal state of affairs and led to moral and material decay. These districts must be regularized and pierced by large straight routes so that the population could be stabilized and begin to prosper. Finally, Perreymonde stressed the role of history in unifying the city totality: creating new squares surrounding significant churches and historic structures, which set them off from the rest of the city. A new representational order was imagined for Paris: an expansive amd majestic panorama that drew the totality together, outlining only its significant sites for public embellishment and inspiring its citizens, through the contemplation of its sublimity and grandeur, to be rational and orderly in their public affairs.[16]

Both Napoleon I and Napoleon III understood this art of governance that embellished and beautified cities. Envisioning themselves to be the spiritual fathers of their nation, they both desired to represent the collective spirit and social harmony of their sovereign responsibility by turning nineteenth-century Paris into a universal museum containing a collection of historic artifacts and monumental structures. Building on the classical art of memory, which associated specific ideas with unique locations within an imaginary structure and then linked these ideas through a memory walk from place to place, Napoleon III in particular conceived of the architectural promenade not only to bind his city of Paris into one cohesive unit, but to act as a memory walk through the historic monuments and grandiose architectural facades that represented the heroic accomplishments and communal responsibilities of his directorship. It was assumed that the ties that bound the city of Paris to its history were revealed to the spectator through its architecture, while "history" so embodied in the fabric of the city represented an ordering structure enabling each spectator to understand its heroic and virtuous lessons and the progress and stewardship its shaping revealed. Not only was the city with its collection of monuments expected to be a source of inspiration, but monumental buildings were as well theatrical backdrops for dramatic representation and enduring civic display.[17]

César Daly, an architectural critic, embellished these nineteenth-century desires for a unified and monumental city by using his *Revue Général de l'Architecture et des Travaux Publiques* as an instrument of both architectural and social reform. As early as 1843, Daly already perceived that vistas and aerial views articulated a unity and urban order that could not be gained by a viewer traveling through the city along its rude labyrinthian streets. A bird's-eye perspective offered the spectator not only an outline of the circulation scheme that ordered the city, but it also revealed the relative importance of specific buildings and gardens to the degree that each stood out from the whole. So he wrote

> Nothing is so beautiful as great horizons, immense landscapes, perspectives whose extent one's eye cannot seize. Great spectacles reinvigorate man's forces, stir his heart and seduce his imagination. It is only from on high that one apprehends the masses of great monuments, reads their true dispositions and real character, and recognizes the general arrangement of their parts. . . .[18]

As Daly outlined, a visual and unified city could be achieved through a program of public works. In his view the plan of streets, along with canals and railroads, became the ordering structure of the city linking together different sites, both historic and contemporary, and thus became the generating device for its civic inspiration. Simultaneously the collection of civic structures in the heart of the city reinforced the center's position as an object of public admiration and spiritual elevation.[19]

These ideas outlining a memory system for the nineteenth-century city still influence contemporary architects and planners, albeit in a submerged and unconscious manner. The last two decades in particular have been concerned as well with the problem of time: of permanence and discontinuity, of generation and rupture. We want to know what aspects of the city plan resist change and which do not, or what structures or forms have evolved slowly and collectively over time? And just how does the city become the locus of collective memory and not simply an outdoor museum or a collection of historic districts? Although we are no longer interested in the ties that bind sovereign to citizen nor the creation of a totalistic perspective over a unified city, yet there is a dormant desire hidden behind many of our contemporary historicizations that the chance survival or willful preservation of architectural remnants and monuments within the city retain the visible marks of the passage of time and enable them to symbolize or encapsulate a culture of place. And although we may no longer be deluded by a naive Enlightenment belief that architecture can reform behavior or that moral norms can be deduced from architectural expressions, and we hardly place much faith in the architectural promenade as a narrative journey that controls our perception of or unifies the city, nevertheless we still want public spaces to penetrate our aesthetic sensibility and offer spiritual and pleasurable experiences. And like architects of the nineteenth century, we too in contemporary times recognize the importance of history to our sense of place and well-being. Daly proclaimed, "To neglect history, to neglect memory, that which is owed to our ancestors, is then to deny oneself; it is to begin suicide."[20]

One link between past and present urban memory systems, which translates these desires into contemporary forms, lies in the work of Marcel Poëte, Professor at the University of Paris from 1914 to 1948, and before that director of the Bibliothèque des Travaux Historique de Ville de Paris. Poëte keeps cropping up in this book in surprising places—as a collector of Atget's photographs of forgotten byways and passages in Paris at the end of the nineteenth century or as an influence on the urban theories of Aldo Rossi in the 1960s. Poëte believed the urbanist to be a doctor who treats the city as a living being that is born, evolves, acts and reacts, is modified and expands, declines and dies. As doctors of cities,

Poëte warned, we must collect all the visual symbols of this urban being—all the evidence of its pathologies and normalities, gathering and storing all the memory tokens from bygone times, so that in our present time we can arrive at an equilibrium between the urban being and its material environment. It is the play of functions that explains the arrangement of life in the city—functions such as a market or a theater that confer a soul or personality on their surrounding districts. The quarter becomes the essential element of the city to study, for the city complex is composed of quarters, each with its own characteristics and each part related to the whole, thus defining the urban totality. In addition, Poëte noted that across historical periods there exists a certain constancy of themes discernable in a city's monuments, pattern of streets, and fragments of the original plan that persist over time. In fact, Poëte argued, the plan becomes both the real and abstract generator of subsequent urban form, and by studying this plan a spectator can understand the spatial arrangement of the city itself.[21] Cities tend to hold to their original pattern, yet still grow and evolve, deform or transform their inherited shapes. It is these permanences that mark the difference for Poëte between the contemporary and historical city: they are the artifacts that give meaning to and constitute our memory of a city.[22]

These nineteenth- and early twentieth-century urban theorists expected that a city's formal structure and material appearance could signify its civic prowess, historical achievements, and wholeness of being. They demanded that places and monuments transfer meaning and knowledge across generations, indeed that these artifacts actually generate memory and inscribe civic conduct. But simultaneously this opened up the possibility that city forms could fail to generate meaning and memory, that partial structures could cause memory loss by disrupting signification and decentering the spectator. It seems that Poëte was pointing at this when he called the urbanist a doctor of cities who read and interpreted the normal and pathological signs of the city. And indeed two discourses did arise in the nineteenth century that focused on improving the material form of the city from these different perspectives. Architects outlined the rules and regulations that would produce an ideal state of good city form, unifying diversities and eradicating differences. Following Canguilhem we call this "normal space," and however you carve it up it is centered, mappable, and manipulable space never allowing for visualizable gaps. It is above all else exclusionary space incapable of articulating or making sense of much of the paradoxical and irrational world, and hence allows neither unrealized possibilities to happen nor unexpected events to take place. On the other hand, nascent planners of the nineteenth century set their gaze on the deviances and abnormalities that defined the pathological city. To restore the city to an assumed normal or healthy state and to recompose its ideal form, they summoned up a body of statistics, legal regulations, and cause-and-effect instrumental controls, aiming to correct these abnormalities. In their attempt to heal the ills of the city, they disavowed its physical form, treating the space of the city like the body of a woman, who also in the nineteenth century was envisioned as a site of excess, of hysterias, of illnesses and exclusions.

We still have this inheritance today: architects hoping to heal the image of the city brutalized by modern intrusions though contemporary incremental insertions, contextual additions, or figured zoning, trying in this manner to retie "knots" in the unraveling city fabric, reintroducing a human scale, a sense of place and tradition that the modern city destroyed. And city planners remain even more disturbingly abstract than their nineteenth-century forebears, manipulating policies that ride high above the city's physical form, breaking the syntax that enables them to speak about bodies and buildings in space. Whether from a normal or pathological perspective, it seems today that we still are ruled by a latent desire for a perfectly ordered and rational city, excluding everything that does not fit into this utopian mold. We still look to civic architecture to legitimate state interventions and help us remember exemplary actions. We long nostalgically for public spaces and monumental architecture in which the spirit of the city or the grandeur of a nation can be expressed. And in contested terrains, it is still a fragile issue of how to tie the obligations of citizens to state directives. Often it is suggested through monumental gestures and architectural displays. After the bright white nothingness of modernity, once again we expect to draw forth from the urban terrain hidden meanings and unconscious memories that we believe lie buried in the material form and generating structure of the city: meanings and memories that offer the pleasure of recognition and collective well-being.

The Writing of History and Memory Crises

This book about memory in the city is also about architectural entertainments and the pleasure that spectators find in, or at least expect from, architectural expressions. In the City of Collective Memory, we find that different layers of historical time superimposed on each other or different architectural strata (touching but not necessarily informing each other) no longer generate a structural form to the city but merely culminate in an experience of diversity. Especially in the last few decades, these architectural residues from earlier times have become important sites of pleasure. Perhaps it is the elusive quality of these outmoded places or their precarious state of existence that offers the spectator pleasure. Or pleasure might be found because these fragments reawaken forgotten memories that have long been dormant, or because their original function and purpose have been erased, allowing the viewer to substitute invented traditions and imaginary narrations. Maybe it is only that these traces from the past interrupt the normal fast-paced tempo of city life and as countercurrents and back eddies in the flow of events momentarily subvert the traveler's directions and plans. Whatever it is, these fragments and remnants cause an unexpected shift of attention, allowing a reappraisal of their presence in the city.

To fully appreciate or be able to read this cityscape as text, however, spectators are required to look at the city not only in formal and functional terms, but in figural or interpretive ways as well. Yet the pure vision imposed by modernist theories of urban space destroyed any relationship that might have existed between form and figure, or a rational and subjective view. By erasing historical references and linguistic allusions, the modernists constructed a disciplined city of pure form that displaced memory and suppressed the tug of the fantastic. They relied too

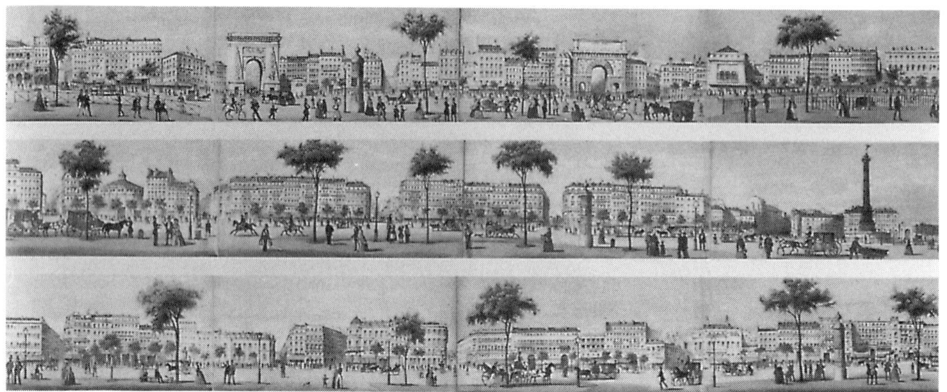

Panoramic Wallpaper, "Les Grands Boulevards de Paris," (c. 1855).

heavily on the power of science to reduce perception to that which could be conceptualized or visualized. By following the path of scientific methodology and assuming their role to be that of social engineering, they sought an absolute correspondence between the exterior city reality and its truthful and purified representation. On the other hand, to read across and through different layers and strata of the city requires that spectators establish a constant play between surface and deep structured forms, between purely visible and intuitive or evocative allusions.[23]

We might begin to build a passage between the two, and reestablish a linkage between objective and subjective views, by reconsidering how we write and read "history," because that is what we are trying to evoke in the City of Collective Memory: a better reading of the history written across the surface and hidden in forgotten subterrains of the city. Throughout this book we will encounter two liminally conjoined spaces: that of history/memory, or that of objective thought/subjective testimony. In each of these pairs, however, a line is drawn separating one from the other such that the continuity of movement between the two is inhibited if not forbidden. The writing of modern "history"—a term coined in the eighteenth century—seemed to have established itself as the guardian of this threshold, for it banished subjective storytelling, eliminated the dangers of otherness, and eradicated lived traditions so that it could substitute instead a fictional order of time progressing toward the future, ever improving upon the past.

Thus modern Western history was established on an act of repression and separation: repressing archaic spectacles and mythical appearances and separating the time frame of the present from that of the past.[24] If ancient history had been the collection of great lessons and exemplary accounts to guide action and persuade thought in the present, or if people's actions were believed to be tied to the terrestial influence of the stars and interventions of God's will, then modern history attempted instead to narrate a true and objective picture of how the past must have been. The modern age wanted cold clear facts, not mythical narrations or religious significations. The experience of constant change and revolution in the late eighteenth and nineteenth century spawned a widespread awareness that time was constantly changing, and that past, present, and future time periods were categorically distinct. History's didactic role and its lessons that endured across the ages were transformed. Instead, "history" seemed to be constructed by individuals, the present plannable and future outcomes predictable. "History" established a linear sequence of cause and effect; it belonged to science and the present, not rhetorical persuasion or didactic illustration. Thus the past as a separate period of time was to be critically analyzed and instrumentally reconstructed in order to achieve for the present an independent and critical awareness of things.[25]

Consequently, history writing throughout the nineteenth century, and again in the contemporary arts of city building, meant an increasing instrumentalization of the past, substituting a framed space contrasting with the thickness of reality, replacing the teller of tales with the narrator of history. Baudelaire would criticize this instrumentalization in his prose poem "Windows," claiming that

> he who looks in from the outside through an open window never sees as many things as he who looks at a closed window. There is no object deeper, more mysterious, more fruitful, more shadowy, more dazzling, than a window lit by a candle. What one can see in the sunshine is always less interesting than what goes on behind a pane of glass. In this black or lighted hole life lives, life dreams, life suffers.[26]

The narrator of history, in Baudelaire's poem, has substituted a preoccupation with reality and truthful representation for experiential knowledge and imaginary musings.

Walter Benjamin would reiterate this substitution of experience with factual accounts, noting in modern times that

> experience has fallen in value. And it looks as if it is continuing to fall into bottomlessness. Every glance at a newspaper demonstrates that it has reached

> a new low, that our picture, not only of the external world but of the moral world as well, overnight has undergone changes which were never thought possible.[27]

This diminution of experience in the early decades of the twentieth century could be witnessed in the proliferation of information whose quantitative ascendance was matched step by step with its qualitative decline. "Every morning," Benjamin noted, "brings us the news of the globe and yet we are poor in noteworthy stories."[28] Journalistic accounting of events was intentionally divorced from everyday experience and its very brevity, its newsworthiness and its juxtaposition, column by column, with other random events only enhanced this feeling of separation.[29] When storytelling was alive, Benjamin felt, experience was still embedded in tradition and connected with historical memory. Thus storytelling always contained some useful advice or conventional moral from the past; it conveyed experiences that were still meaningful within the shared communal life of its listeners. But modern life had transformed collective experience into a series of fragmented and privatized events. When the worlds of memory replaced themselves in rapid succession, as they did in the nineteenth century, then the continuum of tradition was ruptured irrevocably.[30]

Benjamin went even further, exploring within the modern metropolis this degraded nature of experience with its ensuing loss of memory. The city, or so Benjamin thought, once offered pleasurable streets and phantasmagorical visions, beckoning the stroller to explore. But as the familiar patterns of experience declined throughout the nineteenth century, the modern metropolis met the spectator's gaze with "shock experiences." The swelling crowd in large cities, for example, buffeted the spectator about, subjecting her or him to traumatic collisions and abrasive noises. Inevitably for sheer survival, the spectator's conscious awareness withdrew from such negative experiences, while a veil descended protecting the viewer against such attacks. Thus memory traces, once recorded as experiences in a direct and natural manner, failed to register at all. Consequently the continuum of traditional experience and remembrance embedded in spatial forms, once thought to be the ordering structure of the city and the generating device for memory, was impoverished beyond recognition. This continuum could only be resuscitated synthetically and unnaturally in frozen city landscapes where memory had fallen asleep, lulled by the comfort of "once upon a time."[31]

For Benjamin, writing in the early decades of the twentieth century, the present must be awakened from the phantasmagorical spell of nineteenth-century images that still dazzled and controlled awareness and memory. As "history" now seemed to be composed of these images or snapshots, not narratives or stories, a voyage into the deep structure of these memory images must precede reawakening. Hence Benjamin became a collector of out-of-date artifacts, seemingly disparate memorabilia of bygone times, which he subsequently used to develop new perception and substitute for the loss of memory taking place in the present. The disgarded and ruinous arcades, souvenirs, street signs, railroad stations, winter gardens, and panoramas were collective dream images carried over from the nineteenth century whose psychic force, Benjamin believed, still held sway over a spectator's subconscious and inhibited anything new from occurring. By placing these objects in unique contexts and configurations, they became a new form of "shock experience" used to reawaken memory. They enabled the spectator to think through dream images and to achieve a critical awareness of the present.[32]

"Memory" and "remembrance" seemed to be in crisis throughout the late nineteenth and early twentieth centuries.[33] Finally the act of remembrance, having severed its ties with everyday experience, was driven out of sight and into the unconscious at the very moment when the metropolis seemed to threaten the psychological stability of the spectator, when totalistic vision and the ability to represent collective reality were reduced to analyzing leftover fragments and outmoded scraps, when the acceleration of time seemed to open up a void, closing off any meaningful access to the past. A panoramic flow of unstable visions offered a new accounting of memory disturbances: those of amnesia, paramnesia, hypermnesia, for example, all narrate not only an increasing medicalization of memory disturbances at the end of the nineteenth century, but reveal as well a growing anxiety and need to establish a normal relationship between the present and the past. How much memory was good for the present, both reaffirming our connection with the past and enabling the transmission of moral values that guaranteed social stability? Where should memory tokens be stored lest they burden the present with unnecessary remembrances? And what were the techniques by which forgotten memories and hidden traces could be recalled to conscious narration?[34]

Of course, Sigmund Freud contributed considerably to the internalization of this memory crisis. He believed that the recollection of repressed memories was a partial reconstruction, a fictional retelling that actually took the place of personal histories now lost from sight.[35] Delving into the deep structure of dreams and concealed forms of expression that condensed, distorted, or displaced the real materials of life, Freud aimed to impose or to narrate a connected story from these underlying and fragmentary meanings and thus restore continuity to the patient's everyday life. Henri Bergson also focused on memory, consciousness, and duration in the late nineteenth century. Reality, for Bergson, was always a composite collection of things—a representation that became problematic only when individuals lost their ability to discern that representation contained two different presences, one of recollection and one of perception. By mixing these together, individuals often projected outside themselves states that were purely internal. These two different lines of external observation and of internal experience, however, must converge for recollection to insert itself correctly into perception. And memory was the key to the restoration of perception.[36] When we search for a recollection that escapes us, Bergson claimed,

> We become conscious of an act . . . by which we detach ourselves from the present in order to replace ourselves, first in the past in general, then in a certain region of the past—a work of adjustment, something like the focusing of a camera. But our recollection still remains virtual; we simply prepare ourselves to receive it by adopting the appropriate attitude. Little by little it comes into view like a condensing cloud; from the virtual state it passes into the actual . . .[37]

A student of Bergson, Maurice Halbwachs, would elaborate on and revise these theories in the 1920s and 1930s, making them more available to planners and architects. Halbwachs claimed that collective memory was rooted in concrete social experiences and associated with temporal and spatial frameworks. Forgetting, he felt, was not necessarily caused by obstacles that had to be removed, as Freud and Bergson had professed, but instead was the result of vague fragmentary impressions producing inadequate stimuli to prompt awareness.[38] Memories, Halbwachs suggested, were recalled by time periods, by recollecting places visited and by situating ideas or images in patterns of thought belonging to specific social groups. Memory was essentially social, for Halbwachs claimed, "a man who remembers alone what others do not remember resembles somebody who sees what others do not see. It is as if he suffers from hallucinations."[39] Thus memory orients experience by linking an individual to family traditions, customs of class, religious beliefs, or specific places. Halbwachs rejected Bergson's claim that memory was individualistic, represented by a horizontal series or flow of perceptions. Instead, for Halbwachs, memory was based on lived experience, something that reached out of the past and seized the individual in the manner of naive and immediate knowledge. Memory had to be linked to lived experience; otherwise it was reduced to "history," becoming abstract or intellectualized reconstructions, debased or faked recollections. Diverting the flow of perceptions, memory made the rememberer aware of time and offered a perspective on the past that membership in a group provided. And memory always unfolded in space, for when memories could not be located in the social space of a group, then remembrance would fail. Consequently, the activity of recollection must be based on spatial reconstruction.[40]

So it seems that at every rupture point between the moderns and the traditionalists there occurs a memory crisis—at the end of the nineteenth century and once again in the last few decades of the twentieth century—a problematization of the normal relationship of the present to the past. A memory crisis is provoked, perhaps, by the very desire to establish a rupture, to break with recent traditions, to slay the father as the modernists did and the postmodernists propose. As every memory crisis recognizes that something is lacking in the present, a desire develops to collect tokens from the past, to store them in museums and collections lest these items be allowed to slip from our view, be forgotten in the dust of time, or be free to roam at will and thus disturb the road to the future. But then there arises a new problem of where to put our memory tokens and what should be the appropriate balance between the present and the past, for collecting can be obsessive, repeating over and over the desire to recapture a vanished past, to restore that which is lacking and gone from the present until one—like John Ruskin in the nineteenth century—loses one's mind.[41] And like the last half of the nineteenth century, we too have experienced a "frenzy of the visible": a memory crisis of too many images, too phantasmagorical, too commodified, that inhibit the recall and recollection of images stored in the mind.[42]

Recognizing this crisis, an attempt was made in the late nineteenth century to medicalize memory disturbances and to classify disorders that blocked a patient's normal access to the past. And so it seems today. Zones once silenced and rejected as marginal territories now loom into view as what the past lacked and what must be brought back into memory: madness, carnivals and festivals, the masquerade and the melodrama, women's studies and black studies, subaltern cultures and, of course, the City of Collective Memory become frontiers of new exploration.[43] And once again it is a matter of subjective interpretation, not of objective and rational science. In the modern age, it was assumed that individuals could know with certainty what was true and what was false, what was normal and what pathological, what was rational and what irrational. But there was always a tug from below mediating the truth of the world, turning its arrogant confidence back on itself, destroying any account of the way we represent the true and the normal.[44]

As Gilles Deleuze has noted in his commentary on Michel Foucault,

> The unthought is therefore not external to thought but lies at its very heart, as that impossibility of thinking which doubles or hollows out the outside.[45]

> The folding or doubling is itself Memory: the "absolute memory" or memory of the outside, beyond the brief memory inscribed in strata and archives.[46]

> To think means to be embedded in the present-time stratum [the outside] that serves as a limit: what can I see and what can I say today? But this involves thinking of the past as it is condensed in the inside, in the relation to oneself (there is a Greek in me, or a Christian, and so on). We will then think the past against the present and resist the latter, not in favour of a return but "in favour, I hope, of a time to come" (Nietzsche), that is, by making the past active and present to the outside so that something new will finally come about, so that thinking, always, may reach thought.[47]

Remembering and recollection today have achieved new importance as the contemporary metropolis becomes a source of constant exchanges in and relays of information, and represents a physical site in which images and messages seem to swirl about, devoid of a sustaining context. Recall no longer refers exclusively to psychological memory—our ability to recollect forgotten experiences and retie then to conscious awareness. Nor is memory considered to be collective, in the sense that it is linked to the social and physical space of a people and related to the transmission of values and traditions. The presence of interpretative systems that translate memories and traditions into meaningful contemporary forms have vanished once and for all. Our memory crisis seems to be based on our need to establish counter-memories, resisting the dominant coding of images and representations and recovering differences that official memory has erased. If the purities of modern urban planning have left us face to face with displacement, disengagement, and disenchantment when it comes to the urban experience; if the visualizations of multinational capitalism present an array of oppositions juxtaposing homelessness and luxury spaces, soup kitchens and haute cuisine, smells of decay and obsession with perfume—a montage of images that confuses us and makes us question still further our place in the city—then today's memory crisis seems to rest on our need to interweave disjunctive and noncommensurable images to establish connections across the city and reappropriate its utopian promise.[48] We are compelled to create new memory walks through the city, new maps that help us resist and subvert the all-too-programmed and enveloping messages of our consumer culture. But how can the arts of city building attend to the city of tradition and memory without limiting its horizons to conciliatory conclusions and foreclosing zones of uncertainty and complexity, without imposing unjustifiable control over the city and exercising unwarranted authority over others? This is the contemporary challenge that the arts of city building must wield against postmodern furies.[49] Can we, like Walter Benjamin before us, recall, reexamine, and recontextualize memory images from the past until they awaken within us a new path to the future? This too is the task of the City of Collective Memory.

t w o

City Images and Representational Forms

In the City of Collective Memory, the fundamental relationship between architecture, urban form, and history is questioned, for the city is the collective expression of architecture and it carries in the weaving and unraveling of its fabric the memory traces of earlier architectural forms, city plans, and public monuments. Although the name of a city may remain forever constant, its physical structure constantly evolves, being deformed or forgotten, adapted to other purposes or eradicated by different needs. The demands and pressures of social reality constantly affect the material order of the city, yet it remains the theater of our memory. Its collective forms and private realms tell us of the changes that are taking place; they remind us as well of the traditions that set this city apart from others. It is in these physical artifacts and traces that our city memories lie buried, for the past is carried forward to the present through these sites. Addressed to the eye of vision and to the soul of memory, a city's streets, monuments, and architectural forms often contain grand discourses on history.[1]

Not only does the city structure shift with time, but its representational form changes as well. As an object studied by architects, planners, and those involved with historic preservation, the city has been re-presented in different ways: that is, different structural logics—call them aesthetic conventions—have been imposed for various reasons and at separate times upon the city's imagined (imaged) form. Every discourse sets up a spatial order, a frozen image that captures the manner in which the transitory present is perceived. Momentarily arresting disruptive and energetic forces, representational forms become succinct records of what we consider to be present reality. These aesthetic models transform our sense of the real, for the image of the city is an abstracted concept, an imaginary constructed form.

But architecture in the city is not only a spectacle shaped by the representational order of planners and architects; it involves the public as well. Composed city scenes are designed to be looked at and the spectator's amazement and memory evoked by their figural images. As spectators, we travel through the city observing its architecture and constructed spaces, shifting contemporary scenes and reflections from the past until they thicken into a personalized vision. Our memory of the city is especially scenic and theatrical: we travel back in time through images that recall bits and pieces of an earlier city, we project these earlier representations forward into recomposed and unified stagings. This is a book about these images of the city, fixed scenes that for a moment reflect significant fictions about the city, smoothed-over appearances that set up imaginary or hoped-for order. The spectator's city experience is inseparable from these representational images, for they either help to or fail to produce a personal perception and view of the city whose physical form actually is changed and rearranged in constant and bewildering succession.

Suppose we assume that three different aesthetic conventions represent the image of cities in the traditional, modern, and contemporary time periods. These are the City as a Work of Art, the City as Panorama, and the City of Spectacle. Next we ask how these models have been constituted and how they participate in what is taken to be reality. We want to ask what role they offer the spectator and how they have influenced the strategies and tactics of architecture, city planning, and historic preservation. Representational forms are metonymic figures in which one element is taken for the whole: hence the picture frame stands for traditional society, the panorama for the modern, and the cinema or television screen for the contemporary. Through a process of inversion, these figures of a static order, a totalizing gaze, and a decomposed image become an accepted way of seeing, knowing, and representing the city.

In this synthesizing act, however, we must never lose sight of the fact that these representational models are impositions upon a flow of events. By binding up forces that threaten to explode beyond their boundaries, and excluding elements that fail to fit into their determining mold, these logics reduce a complex of events into a generalized representational scene. To the contrary, the production of urban space is always a battlefield of contending forces, while the language of architecture and planning a struggle among waging discourses. Shifts in the political economy, technological procedures, legal maneuvers, community oppositions or client preferences, spectators' attitudes and aspirations, and the desire for planned order or the need for release from its rational control simultaneously configure both the discourses and representational forms of the city.

The City as a Work of Art

Until the end of the nineteenth century, builders of modern industrial cities were absorbed with picture making, a practice in which the picture frame became emblematic of a closed and unified spatial order. The essence of a bounded work of art was this self-containment, a gesture that augmented the unity of the picture as much as it centered the eye and set off the work of art from extraneous detractions.[2] The picture frame defined narrative space as well, for there was an urban story to be told within its bounded frame. Constellations of pictorial images and their theatrical stage sets acted as stimuli for reinforcing ceremonial decorum and for recalling memories of triumphal acts and heroic deeds. Historical monuments and civic spaces as didactic artifacts were treated with curatorial reverence. They were visualized best if seen as isolated ornaments; jewels of the city to be placed in scenographic arrangements and iconographically composed to civilize and elevate the aesthetic tastes and morals of an aspiring urban elite. This was an architecture of ceremonial power whose monuments spoke of exemplary deeds, national unity, and industrial glory.

The concept of "society" was a newly forged idea in the early nineteenth century, and architectural embellishments were utilized to strengthen the fragile and synthetic links that gathered people together in collective unity. The art of government entailed an efficient and harmonious order of things and people, an arrangement that could be represented symbolically and directed at the citizenry through architectural compositions harmoniously and rationally disposed.[3] Iconographical ornamentation could teach and reinforce the spirit of thoughtful guidance that the state instilled, underscoring its careful management of the nation's great wealth and resources, its scientific and technological advancements, its shared customs and common ends. The art of government needed as well to outline what the collective form of the city might be and how it supported the well-being of its citizenry. Architects were called on to adorn the surface of the city with ceremonial structures and promenades, with collective facilities and tranquil retreats, until the city revealed through its compositional forms the mechanism of a well-regulated and rationally guided state. For concern with the City as a Work of Art was also an attempt to fulfill cultural and aesthetic needs destroyed in the turmoil of progress, political revolution, and pestilence that the nineteenth century unleashed. A desire arose for entertainment, pleasure, and fantasy in the realm of aesthetics, standing apart from the sphere of labor, work, and politics, disease, overcrowding, and filth.[4] The spectacle of entertainment in public spaces had just begun to recompose certain zones of the city into scenic arrangements for leisure and play.

Perhaps it is Jacques Ignace Hittorff whose architectural and urban projects exemplify this nineteenth-century art of ceremonial embellishment and public picture making.[5] As Paris expanded toward the west in the early decades of the nineteenth century, its new center became the Place de la Concorde, although this roofless atrium was no more than an unruly and haphazard arrangement. When the city was given control over this space and the Champs-Élysées in 1828, it was charged with the task of embellishing these spaces within five years. Consequently the conception arose that the Place de la Concorde could be turned into a centripetal composition that would not only establish the focal point of the city, but celebrate the national unification of France as well. In 1833 Hittorff was asked by Rambuteau, the prefect of Paris, to create such a ceremonial composition. Believing that architectural embellishment progressed from ephemeral forms to monumental and permanent arrangements, and that the art of government displayed both rational and pleasurable arrangements of things, Hittorff extended his ceremonial vision westward down the Champs-Élysées, hoping to create in the 1840s a new public zone for popular entertainment and promenading and finally in the 1850s extending this view from the Place de l'Étoile to the Bois de Boulogne, with a majestic new boulevard connecting the two. Paris already had the ornaments with which to composed this new ceremonial arrangement. Lenôtre in 1670 had given the Tuileries a noble axial perspective and the Champs-Élysées extended from the Rond-Point to the Place de l'Étoile by 1765. The monumental Arc de Triomphe had begun to rise on its site in 1806, although it was not completed until 1836, and even the Place de la Concorde, as the renamed Place Louis XV became known, had been ceremoniously composed in 1753 by G. A. Gabriel.

To Hittorff fell the task of creating a brilliant new scenic composition out of these disparate ornaments, a work to be accomplished between 1836 and 1840. As the symbol of concord and national unity, Hittorff in a daring and innovative gesture located a politically "neutral" 240-ton Egyptian obelisk—a "gift" from the viceroy of Egypt to the people of France—in the center of the wide-open square instead of placing there the common equestrian statue of royalty and surrounding it with enclosing walls in the usual manner of design. This centripetal point of focus was then counterbalanced by centrifugal views extending down two major cross-axes, which terminated in a monument to royal power to the east (Tuileries) and

View of the Place de la Concorde after the edges were filled in and the obelisk erected by J.-I. Hittorff.

to military triumph on the west (Arc de Triomphe), to the Church and National Government on the north (Madeleine and Chamber of Deputies) and the Seine and its bridge leading to the ministry of the Navy to the south. In addition, this modern pageant of civic unity glorifying the genius of France, her resources and progress, was further encoded by statuary and fountains iconographically celebrating the triumph of industry, agriculture, and transportation, and praising eight regional cities of France chosen not for their virtues of sovereign allegiance as heretofore commonly practiced, but for their prowess in commerce and industry.

In particular, the iconography of the fountains stressed the communication network that maritime and river activities established and the ship of state whose leaders guided the boat, its cargo, and sailors safely to port. The Place de la Concorde with its centripetal/centrifugal arrangement thus symbolically represented the secular map of France held in place by the triumph of technological and economic progress. Clearly royalty had been displaced by references to the state. Indeed, even the raising of the monolith was planned as a civic spectacle to demonstrate publicly through the use of a newly developed steam engine that technology under the guidance of the state now truely enabled man to conquer nature.[6] Never one to slight the festive aura of decoration, Hittorff included in his scheme elaborate gilding and polychromed decor, outlining in relief the symbolic figures and representational ornaments against the background of bronze and the granite and marble bases of columns, statues, and fountains.

As an appendage to the Place de la Concorde, on the northwest quadrant of the Rond-Point, and continuing his theme of public embellishment, Hittorff built in 1839 a unique structure for entertainment, The Panorama (demolished in 1856); in 1841, as the Champs-Élysées was being transformed from a wooded and dangerous area into an elegant new park and entertainment zone for all sorts of balls, concerts, restaurants, and spectacles, he located there a Summer Circus for equestrian displays (demolished in 1900). The Panorama, analogous to the Roman Coliseum in form, was a circular rotunda capped with a conical roof, whereas the Summer Circus, a sixteen-sided polygon, emulated Roman arenas in decor and iconography. Brilliant polychromatic displays of blue, red, yellow, and gold clarified sculptural details and offered an air of festivity and richness for this circus of equestrian pageantry and ephemeral illusions. By the mid-1840s, private concessionaires had opened restaurants and lemonade stands, lecture halls and cafe-restaurants along the Champs-Élysées, and Hittorff continued to embellish the place with other rotundas and spectacular structures such as a "Georama" in the form of a globe (designed in 1843 but never built), a "Neorama" for the display of famous interiors such as Saint Peter's in Rome (1847), a National Theater (1848), and finally, for the Universal Exposition of 1855, the iron and glass Palace for Arts and Industries (1852/1854).[7]

In 1852, when Napoleon III became emperor, he requested that Hittorff refurbish the Place de la Concorde, for it had failed to educate the urban populace and instead was still being used as a focal point for mass demonstrations. It remained a constant reminder that the site had been the execution spot of Louis XVI and Marie Antoinette. He was ordered as well by Baron von Haussmann, the new prefect of Paris, to remove the monolithic obelisk from its center, where it was felt to be the cause of traffic congestion and the site of frequent accidents. Hittorff refused to comply because the obelisk was the center of focus for his closed perspectival views and the icon of concord in his ceremonial display—a decorous design diametrically opposed to the long axial perspectives that Haussmann preferred as his tribute to centralized power. Next came a bitter struggle over the composition of the Champs-Élysées. Haussmann demolished Hittorff's Panorama in 1856 only to erect another close by, generally replanted and relighted the Champs-Élysées, and completely defaced his polychromatic decor.

There was also a battle over the redesign of the Place de l'Étoile and the plans for the route to the Bois de Boulogne. Haussmann was transforming Paris into a modern city of circulation and flux; he was not one to endorse a closed and bounded view. The monuments of the city were an impediment to his idea of modernity, and wherever possible they were to be isolated from their context, no longer allowed to stand as organic elements of the city's compositional form.

Caizac, L'Érection de l'Obélisque.

Consequently Haussmann, wanting to emphasize the Arc de Triomphe as a form around which circulation ebbed and flowed, decided to regulate the avenues randomly springing from the place and increase their number to twelve. He thus rejected Hittorff's earlier scheme. Hittorff had planned a ring of low houses with a unifying arcade one story in height arching over each avenue. This enclosure would offset the new boulevard planned as a greenway leading westward to the Bois de Boulogne. But more important, this ringed arcade would have acted as an enclosing balustrade around the Place d'Etoile and so would have guaranteed that the Arc de Triomphe rose far higher than the encircling houses and thus continued to terminate the axial view from the Place de la Concorde. Haussmann threw out this scheme, for it would have severely limited the flow of traffic and marred his plan for triumphal perspectival views and monuments isolated in grand open spaces. Before Haussmann could act, however, Hittorff and another architect quickly erected in 1856 two four-story houses flanking the Avenue du Bois de Boulogne (now Avenue Foch), and thus established by decree the general appearance of the rest. Haussmann was furious with Hittorff for ignoring his request for monumental structures, and subsequently planted a row of trees to mask Hittorff's puny display. Hittorff's design for the Avenue du Bois de Boulogne already had been set aside by Haussmann in 1852, for it too was only a modest gesture—a simple tree-lined carriageway with parallel bridle and pedestrian paths. By now the battle had heightened, a struggle Haussmann won by creating a scheme three times the size of Hittorff's suggestions, thereby creating a neo-Baroque triumphal way from the Place de l'Étoile to the Bois de Boulogne and completely eclipsing Hittorff's enframed ceremonial views.[8]

The City as Panorama

In a few more decades, the modern metropolis of the early twentieth century would seem to be an anarchic visual arrangement. Now the city appeared as an open and expansive panorama, ruled by the transformation of space and time that modern modes of travel engendered. The new experience of moving through the city tended to erase the traditional sense of pictorial enclosure as the cityscape was transformed into a series of fleeting impressions and momentary encounters. One's attachment to place or milieu dissolved into a kaleidoscopic arrangement of images and forms. This dissolution of fixed content and monumental gestures was an expression that reached across different aspects of art and architecture, for fragmentation was also involved in the erasure of traditional values, in the disruption of iconographic connotations, and in the general degradation of historical meaning. The pictorial image of the City as a Work of Art was replaced and in its stead stood the City as Panorama, the city of soaring skyscrapers and metropolitan extension; a spatial order when seen from a bird's-eye perspective that requested deciphering and reordering.

Railroad travel in the nineteenth century already had annihilated the old continuum of space and time by erasing the perception of in-between space. As travel by train both reduced the time it took to cover the space between known points on a map and drew remote places of the world into closer proximity, it thus created a new panoramization of space. The landscape through which the train traveler was projected suddenly turned into a vast screen unrolling its fleeting tableaux. As these indiscriminate views in quick succession passed by the eye of the spectator, space simply became a series of continously changing scenes. Mobility in space thus enabled a juxtaposition—even a collision—of disparate but sequential images. So too the city was no longer seen from a static frontal perspective, or as a centered and composed picture, but as a multidimensional traveling view that was itself a new spatialization of time.[9]

Now add to this a unique prospect: that of viewing the city from a towering structure or looking down at the world from an airplane. Gertrude Stein gives us some insight into the shift in representational form that this twentieth-century perspective proposed. Speculating upon the Cubists' breakup of traditional space, of traditional ways of seeing, where the eye was drawn outward to the boundaries as much as to the center of a painting, she believed that Picasso knew without ever having been up in an airplane that space in the twentieth century was not the same as that in the nineteenth century, and inevitably he drew it as different. When Stein was in America she traveled by airplane for the first time, and there she said she looked out of the window and saw all the Cubists' abstractions, their reduction of depth, their elimination of detail, their compositions with simplified forms, their simultaneous unifications of the whole picture surface—how odd, she mused, for not one Cubist yet had been up in an airplane.[10]

Sigfried Giedion clearly perceived this new formation of space and time that the twentieth century developed, for Giedion's architectural history was a depiction of shifting spatial sensibilities. As he noted, the first space conception came from Egyptian, Greek, and even early Roman architecture, which depended upon the creation of space-emanating volumes. So the pyramids and the Parthenon stand as structures set in unbounded fields. The Pantheon, subsequently, became the second perception of space, the instant when hollowed-out forms modeled by light and shadow attained architectonic expression. From that moment until the end of the nineteenth century, interior space received constant elaboration. In the twentieth century, a transparent perception arose in which the interpenetration of inner and outer space was juxtaposed against volumes in space and hollowed-out forms establishing new interrelationships. Gustave Eiffel, with his soaring open latticework of the Eiffel Tower, this empty and transparent monument of 1889, had produced the prototype for the dissolution of boundaries between exterior and interior forms, and for the fluctations between solids and voids.[11] Seen from every corner of the panorama of Paris, it was an image that changed with every point of view: a stiff and towering needle if viewed from the horizon, yet within its interior it seemed to be a lacy network of iron. Blaise Cendrars wrote a futurist essay on the Eiffel Tower in 1913 that celebrated these changing perceptions, this simultaneity of representational images. From a distance, he thought, the tower tended to dominate the spectator, but as he drew near it bent over him; from the first platform it twisted beneath him like a corkscrew, and from the top of its needle it seemed to collapse under its own weight.[12] Used as an antenna after 1904, this pylon of steel broadcasting incessant radio waves in all directions became the emblem of modern technology's conquest of the world, a symbol truly rupturing the traditional boundaries of space and time.

Yet no matter how many times space and time seemed fragmented into isolated and conflicting views, the modern architect and city planner reached out in panoramic control to impose a uniform composition upon the whole. Le Corbusier knew the visual sensation of limitless panoramic space and the correction it imposed upon spatial arrangement. Ascending the Eiffel Tower he felt was a solemn moment, for little by little as the horizon rose, the mind was projected onto a wider screen. When the eye took in the urban panorama, optimism reigned and there the imagination conceived of vast new arrangements of space.[13] This aerial perspective implied a new way of seeing and knowing—by analysis, comparison, and deduction.[14] From this vertical perspective, Le Corbusier noted, the eye sees clearly, the mind makes wise decisions, and the city planner knows what to do.[15] So Le Corbusier claimed, a new consciousness was born from this aerial view, for we were plunged into realism from which we dared not escape. From the moment of its birth, the eagle eye of an airplane could penetrate into the misery of traditional urban form, returning with photographic evidence for those not brave enough to see for themselves.[16]

The vertical bird's-eye view thus called for a new organization of the city, making it apparent that this wasteful treatment of space cried out for readjustment. No longer could the traditional meandering streets dominate the material order of the city, for the automobile had turned the ad hoc pedestrian town into an antique and stifling form; nor could the theatrical street scene framed by parallel rows of houses and drawn from a uniform point of perspective remain the representational model for the city of modern mobility.[17] Le Corbusier assumed that there existed a distance between the view that he projected and the spectator's eye, and he continually slips and slides between these two positions. Because a modern panoramic vision occurred from a detached perspective, it consequently enabled the spectator to reassemble or project a completely different scene in her or his imagination, specifically the site as Le Corbusier thought it ought to be arranged and

Robert Delaunay, Eiffel Tower *(1910–1911).*

corrected. Educated by the plethoric illustrations and publications of Le Corbusier, the spectator's rational gaze would lead in time to the actual transformation of both the city and the region into a coherent and uniform order. Thus the panorama of Algers as it unfolded its horizontal forms to the spectator who stood on the bridge of an approaching steamship reappears in Le Corbusier's drawings, as a linear town conforming to the topography's contours. Rio de Janeiro from the eagle-eye perspective of an airplane is reassembled into a gigantic viaduct city, or the perspective from a resident's window becomes a spectacular view out over the Radiant City, turning greenery, sunlight, and space into a permanent extension of one's home.[18]

This new visual sensibility depended upon a traveling eye, a cosmic reordering of the world that inverted the interior and exterior and presented in strange juxtapositions fragmented and paradoxical views. The world, Le Corbusier argued, had been transformed by the elevated highway, which opened up a wider perspective and enabled housing to be concentrated in residential towers and nature to touch the base of every building. The public space of greenery consequently became a privatized view from one's room, and the higher one lived the more spectacular the panoramic view.[19] In a similar manner, the traditional street, having been killed by the motorway, reappeared as an internalized private space. Along the rue corridor of these residential towers were located all the necessary collective services as well as the entry to each housing cell.[20] But the inversions don't stop there: the stately urban square, that quiet oasis in the traditional city acting as a theatrical stage set for monumental architectural views, became transformed in the modern city into ramps, stairways, and elevators, points of exchange between public and private space.[21] Even past traditional architectural forms were privatized in their own ceremonial space. Appropriating traditional urban spaces, this modern panoramic view was to be judged by the standards of the present: those of efficiency, functionality, and optimality without the permanence and continuities of history or the imposition and weight of past models. Le Corbusier noted that the past had lost its fragrance, for mingling with the new now placed it in a false environment. Instead tokens and relics from the past should be enclosed within their own scenery of trees and woods, "for material things too must die, and these green parks with their relics are in some sort cemeteries carefully tended, in which people may breathe, dream and learn. In this way the past becomes no longer dangerous to life, but finds its true place within it."[22]

In this vast urban place, if one followed the dictates of Le Corbusier, space itself became a focus of social concern and an object of investigation and control. Everywhere the architect and city planner cut the fabric into discrete units and recomposed them into a structured and utopian whole: disorder was replaced by functional order, diversity by serial repetition, and surprise by uniform expectancy. These cuts and insertions, by imposing their ideal model of scenic unity in which solids dematerialized into transparent and interpenetrating forms and structures filled in or hollowed out space, decomposed the city into a random array of homogeneous sites, emptied of historic reference and ignorant of building types and city places specific to each location. Because this was a city where there was no need for tradition, only for documentation, history books were banished from architectural lessons, the picturesque urban schemes of the nineteenth century were ridiculed, and the cruel beauty of orthogonal grid-iron street patterns, elevating glass skyscrapers, and shocking modern mobility was celebrated. And so proliferated in the disciplined City as Panorama the mirroring curtain-wall skyscrapers in which today we see reflected the City of Spectacle.

The City of Spectacle

By the 1980s, the transformation of the material world by invisible bands of electronic communication encircling the globe, by computer-simulated visual environments, and by theatricalized image spectacles seemed by extension to have decomposed the bits and pieces of the city into an ephemeral form. An art and architecture based on the recomposition and recombination of borrowed imagery appear to make reality and representation equivalent references in infinitely mirrored reflections. Coherent urban places, even those modern sculptural arrangements of solids and voids, are said to be historic constructs at a time when Los Angeles is celebrated as the prototypical contemporary place.

It is not surprising then to find that the organizers of an exhibit entitled "The Immaterial" at the Pompidou Center in Paris during the spring of 1985 felt that a new space-time perspective was required for its museum installation. When one travels from San Diego to Santa Barbara in a car, they witnessed in the catalogue for the show, the only evidence of transformation or progression in this large conurbation is the constant shifting of the radio dial as the car exits from and enters into the invisible zones of broadcast emissions.[23] There is no longer any opposition between the center of the city and its periphery, no distinction exists between the built and natural environment that marks the passage. Los Angeles fails to offer the traveler a series of city tableaux, framed sites ruled by the lines of perspectival space. A nonplace, existing in a state of constant flux and interfaces, becomes a new synthetic space-time, a contemporary assemblage of nonmaterial electronic forms, serial arrays of representations and messages that transport the viewer across visual thresholds to separate places and other times.[24]

Of course the representational model for this new urbanism of perpetual movement in which fatuous images and marvelous scenes slide along in paradoxical juxtapositions and mesmerizing allusions is the cinema and television, with their traveling shots, jump-cuts, close-ups, and slow motion, their exploited experience of shock and the collisions of their montage effect. This contemporary city is pure spectacle, culling a programmed and projected look. For this is the reaction against order: to break apart the dominating unity that prevailed for so many years in the City as Panorama. The utopic disruptions of rational town planning, the boredom of their pure crystalline forms, produced in their wake the City of Spectacle, a city in which appropriations of historical styles and restaged scenographic allusions now become bounded nodes within an urban composition criss-crossed by highways and invisible electronic circuitry. Simulated environments, the spreading out of designed milieus, posed and theatrically staged compositions, the blown-up chromolithographs of billboards and mesmerizing advertisements dazzle in front of our eyes as pure visual displays. Through simulations we manipulate space and time, traveling nostalgically backward through historic reconstructions, projecting our vision forward in futuristic travel adventures.

A sense of theatricality has returned to the City of Spectacle in images that confront the spectator by juxtaposing high and low art forms or by the deliberate posing of pictorialized views and constructed tableaux. There is an immediate visual contact with this city based on the revitalization of traditional building typologies or the construction of new compositions that relate contextually to the urban morphology and resuscitate sensuous colors and tactile building materials. Yet often, it is argued, this material reappropriation or restoration of the images of the city presents us with a bracketed look devoid of iconographical meaning or symbolic conception. There may not be an underlying text to which this grafting of disparate images refers, nor ironical twistings that read out a message. Our contemporary encyclopedia of illusionary forms and historical imagery seems to be a gigantic list of entries, constantly being rearranged in odd juxtapositions, fantastic compositions, and imaginary associations as if we were manipulating pattern languages and sets of serial imagery.

This erosion of meaning in the representationl images of the city and the play of pure signs that it posits is evident across many contemporary forms of artistic expression and can be historicized.[25] In one of his descriptions of montage, the juxtaposition of two images that combine into a third, Sergei Eisenstein used the streets of New York as an example. Eisenstein found numbered—not named—streets difficult to remember. Consequently it was necessary to assemble a set of characteristics belonging to each street, so that "42nd Street," for example, became distinct from "45th Street." When "45th Street" was subsequently called, its characteristic images would slowly come to mind, but it was only later after several repetitions that these elements began to fuse into a single spontaneous view. Montage, Eisenstein explained, involved the spectator in this same two-stage process: first recognizing the separate elements, the discrete scenic spaces, and then experiencing the dynamic process by which they were assembled into an image.

Paul Citroën, Metropolis *(1923).*

The early twentieth-century artists had developed a new awareness of time, realizing that what was changing was the manner of viewing and understanding the dynamic process by which both the emergence and assembly of compositions were formed. This new aesthetic of temporality, Eisenstein said, could be found in jazz, in modern poetry and Cubism, and by extension, in the modern urban landscape. Noting that Roman squares and villas, or Versailles's parks and terraces, were "prototypes" for the structure of classical music, so Eisenstein claimed,

> The modern urban scene, specially that of a large city at night, is clearly the plastic equivalent of jazz. . . . The nocturnal sea of electric advertising knock out all sense of perspective, of realistic depth. . . . these lights tend to abolish all sense of real space, finally melting into a single plane of colored light points and neon lines moving over a surface of black velvet sky.
>
> Headlights on speeding cars, highlights on receding rails, shimmering reflections on the wet pavements—all mirrored in puddles that destroy our sense of direction (which is top? which is bottom?), supplementing the mirage above with a mirage beneath us, and rushing between these two worlds of electric signs, we see them no longer on a single plane, but as a system of theater wings, suspended in the air, through which the night flood of traffic lights is streaming.[26]

This absence of perspective in the contemporary cityscape, Eisenstein argued, is an image that belongs to the early twentieth century and formed a part of the reasoning of anyone who lived in that time, a period of decadence, he maintained, that allowed the normally centripetal movement in representational form to turn into a centrifugal gesture hurling apart all unifying tendencies that were incompatible with an epoch that stressed the importance of the individual.[27]

Although montage and the aesthetic of temporality derived their structure from the visual form of the early twentieth-century metropolis and left their mark on modern literature, painting, music, and film, it is only the City of Spectacle that utilizes simultaneous stage settings, juxtaposing multiple perspectives and spatializing separate times, as intentional compositional arrangements. The contemporary arts of city building are self-consciously aware of the ruptured and fragmentary status of city space including the endless flux of combinatorial forms that they decoratively disperse across its broken surface. There appears to be no center to this city, no subject responsible for its arrangement, no motive force behind its accepted fragmentation.

To the contrary, the modern city, as exemplified by Le Corbusier, anchored both the subject and the horizon of city space: enabling man at the center of this static whole to reach out in panoramic control. Three-dimensional space, the checkerboard grid and skyscraper towers, objects depicted in precisionistic order and clear light, all of these separated and framed images in rigid functional and geometrical distinctions. The figurative poetics of motion and time would be a latecomer to the representational forms of architecture and planning. Not until the City of Spectacle does the pedestrian travel across a sequence of disparate sites whose decor and composition intentionally allude to different places and other times, whose complex montage annihilates the in-between space, whose superimposed and inserted scenery and pictorial tableaux work by benign neglect against any rational order. As we shall see, however, each one of these compositional units has a well-coded and -motivated theme, a play within the play so to speak, intentionally staged to lure the spectator's gaze by the pure visibility of the show while veiling the appearance of a fragmented and damaged image of the city taken as a whole.

Now the spectacle, or so Guy Debord argued in 1967, is capital accumulated to such a degree that it actually becomes an image.[28] And not surprisingly we shall find that the City of Spectacle, the city reduced to the play of pure imagery, has developed intimate tie-ins with the logic of consumption and the selling of leisure-time lifestyles. The spectacle is, after all, always a show, and going to the theater part of a holiday or time off from everyday life. At such times and in such places, the spectator hopes to see a festival of lights and glittering pageantry, ludic demonstrations and exuberant ornamentations, both on the stage and among the audience. The modern view of the city, stripped of fatidic and spontaneous gestures and emptied of lyrical and poetical values, produced an incredible void within its heart. Even the pedagogues of modern architecture and city planning recognized this fault by the 1950s. Turning to focus on the reconstruction of historic centers of cities that were detroyed by or blighted after World War II, they recognized a need that the City as Panorama had missed. The man in the street, they surmised, had been pushed around by the automobile long enough. He felt alienated and lost in the public realm of nihilistic forms and crystalline structures. He desired new gathering places, new open-air markets, and spaces for spontaneous celebration, for he wanted to participate in the wondrous spectacle of urban life, not just remain a passive bystander.[29]

In redefining the heart of the city as a new meeting place for the arts, Le Corbusier believed that people needed new settings to act out their own dramas, what he called "spontaneous theatres" erupting out of the collisions and contact that might occur between different events and groups. So he wrote, "Architecture is judged by eyes that see, by the head that turns, and the legs that walk. Architecture is not a synchronic phenomenon but a successive one, made up of pictures adding themselves one to another following each other in time and space, like music."[30] If Le Corbusier and his admirers had emptied the city's public realm of historical references, privatized the view of greenery and parks behind walls of glass, and replaced the public streets along which pedestrians might wander with interior corridors, then in contrast the continuity between architecture, history, and the city would become a new debate in postwar city reconstructions. The poetry of visual form would return to the public realm contrived as a spectacle: through new covered passageways and markets, the reappearance of articulated places and blocks, the reevaluation of vernacular architecture and ornamented styles, and the improvisational recyclings of urban junk and city wastelands.

Perhaps there is no better example of these postwar places than the heart of Paris, the hole in the ground where once stood the cast-iron market sheds designed by Victor Baltard in the 1860s and known to Parisians as "Les Halles." At the great crossing of two axes, the 100 acre site is not only the exact center of Paris, but has been a market place since at least the twelfth century. In 1946, however, the municipal authorities decided to transfer the noisy and cumbersome food markets outside of Paris to a more efficient location. Yet no group was formed to decide if Les Halles were demolished, what would be erected in place of these great monuments of functional architecture. By 1964, it seemed clear to the authorities that the center of Paris—and most particularly they meant the area surrounding Les Halles—was filthy, diseased, and overcrowded; it should be transformed into a modern space of greenery and lagoons with submerged parking lots below. But if Les Halles were displaced, it was also clear that another animated activity, one that operated around the clock, must be substituted for the markets and their nighttime activity of cafes, restaurants, and brothels. Les Halles, the authorities argued, must become a cultural district dedicated to information, housing, and the tourist industry, surrounded by antique shops, art galleries, artists' studios, libraries, cafes, and restaurants. A place rendered at first only by modernist urban designs, within a few years the restoration and rehabilitation of the most important historic structures in the surrounding zone had been secured as well. Nevertheless the historic market sheds, in spite of a huge public outcry, were demolished in 1971, and in their place spread a great subterranean forum of shops, cinemas, parking lots, and metro stops. The surface level, the upper town of this labyrinth, became a grand pedestrian plaza with its own set of shops, hotels, and housing both historic and reconstructed, while the Plateau Beaubourg to its east was redesigned as a piece of industrial machinery, called the Pompidou Center, housing a great art museum, public library, and media center.[31]

Redevelopment projects such as Les Halles taking place in historic centers soon revealed a new paradox: the look of the traditional city with its vernacular styles of architecture, the fabric of its enclosed squares and picturesque streets, its civic and ecclesiastical monuments suddenly appeared to contrast sharply with the representational insertions of open spaces and cool abstractions appearing in the reconstructed city of modernism. At a moment in history when urban renewal was destroying more of the city's historic patrimony than war and neglect had done, architectural ruins and ornamental styles held out a seductive and nostalgic allure. Yet life, and by analogy the city, has change as its very essence. To conserve, to stop the flow of development, appeared at first to be an almost impossible gesture; it meant sacrificing vital growth and valued production. The historic centers so badly in need of reconstruction in the 1950s and 1960s could not await the slow and contradictory process of preservation. There seemed to be no point of dialogue between the old and the new, until a special vocabulary developed in the 1960s and 1970s that spoke of districts, ensembles and fragments, of insertions, recyclings and reuses, making preservation appear to be compatible with new compositions. Slowly, bit by bit, forgotten waterfronts, underutilized manufacturing areas, downtrodden inner-city neighborhoods, the parts of the city that modern architects and planners had neglected or simply overlooked, were placed behind regulatory boundaries, their architectural patrimony entrusted to protection societies and their aesthetic appearances constantly rehabilitated and revitalized. Like statues and paintings torn from their original location in palaces and churches and then placed within the guarded walls of a museum, these restored city streets and districts turned parts of the city into new visual spectacles and revitalized theatrical decors.

But historic preservation projects were not the only pictorial additions to be inserted into the modern urban landscape in the center of the city. The profusion of urban junk and the wastelands of city space gave rise as well to a set of strangely constructed compositions and popular decors that in their turn completely transformed the modernist's panoramic arrangements of pure objects in space. Way back in the 1950s, the English architects Alison and Peter Smithson described their idea of the city as people and objects in constant motion and change: this was to be the stuff and decoration of a new urban scene.[32] If Jackson Pollock had created a new pictorial ordering, an *n*-dimensional multivocative space, then the Smithsons asked, should not the overlaid imagery of American advertisement be taken seriously as the source for the contemporary visual climate and the start of a new way of looking

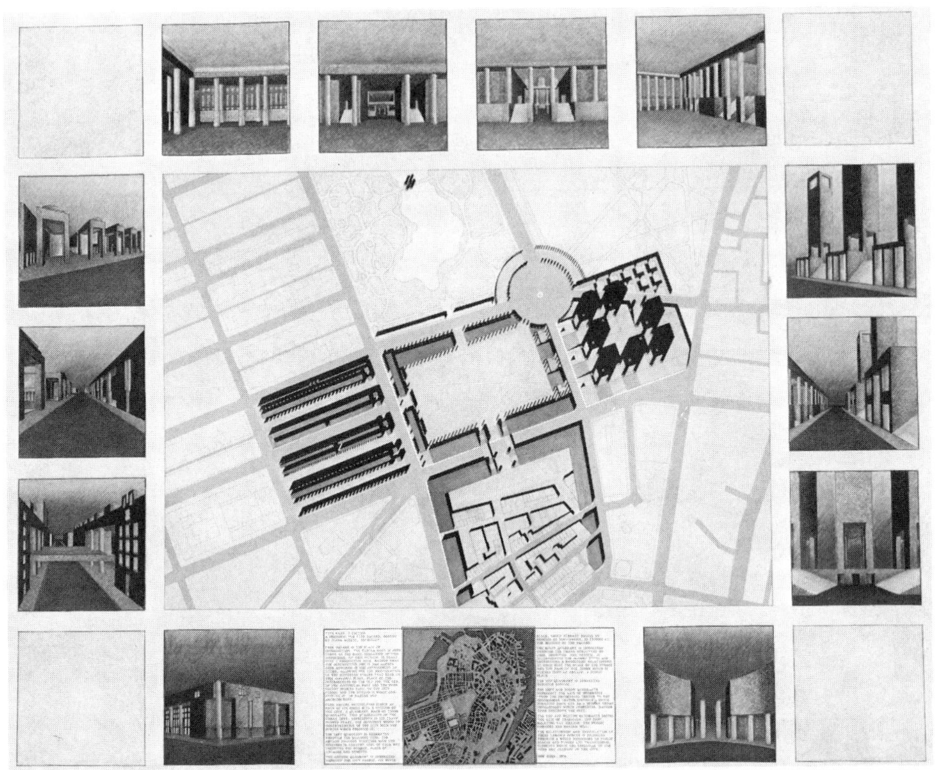

Diana Agrest, Type Wars: A Fiction. Proposal for Park Square Boston—site plan with old and new typologies defining public space *(1978).*

at cities? Everyday objects, like the fabulous fin-tailed Cadillac convertible seen in the pages of *Life* magazine, or the throwaway items and obsolescent parcels of urban debris, should be recontextualized and elevated to high art, for "Things need to be ordinary and heroic at the same time."[33] Together with members of the Independent Group that formed in 1952 at the Institute for Contemporary Arts in London, the Smithsons worked to combat the purities of modernism and the City as Panorama by exploiting the images found in science fiction landscapes taken from the mass media, combining these with urban rubbish and bombed-out spaces, consumer clutter and the waste of affluence disgarded along every city side street.[34] A strong visual influence came directly from the commercial advertisements found in the American mass media, but as transferred to England in the 1950s, America was the fantasy land of unadulterated luxury displaying the seductive glamour of Hollywood, the faraway and unreal world of comics and westerns—in short all the dreams that money could buy and that rationing in postwar England did not yet allow.

One of the members of the Independent Group, Reyner Banham, explained that the mingling of commercial forms with architecture during the 1950s was a natural event because architecture after all was a commercial art and a branch of advertising as well. But add to this the 1950s' love affair with mass-produced commodities and disposable items, and this spelled trouble for the modern aesthetic. The fin-tailed automobile of the late 1950s, which the Smithson's elevated to art, was a great sign of planned obsolescence and a foil against the purities of modernism: it was an antifunctional design mixing speed, sex, and pleasure, which delighted consumers. So Banham believed, this powerfully decorated mobile box was a rich three-dimensional overlapping composition just like Jackson Pollock's drip paintings, offering the spectator a new visual order devoid of frontal perspective.[35] From there it was a simple step to consider the commercial clutter and kinetic forms of the city as the start of a new visual sensibility. Because constant change was now built into the picture, future images must start from the present.[36] And this new visual awareness could find no better source for inspiration than the junk culture or throwaway material of cities collected in garbage bins, attics, gutters, vacant lots, and garbage dumps. This junk obtruded into space with the aim of achieving maximum intimacy where "proximity and participation replace distance and contemplation as the communicative style of the object."[37]

In turn, this new aesthetic of popular landscapes, fictive and real, collectible or discarded, filtered back to America where it influenced in the late 1960s Robert Venturi and Denise Scott Brown. They both suggested that the analysis of popular culture—the hybrid Las Vegas strip and the commercial signs on billboards and roadside advertisements—offered the architect a formal design vocabulary relevant to diverse needs and tastes. They argued that forms found in the popular landscape and mass media were just as important to designers in the 1970s as the structures of Imperial Rome had been to the Ecole des Beaux-Arts, and as the shapes of Cubism and machine technology were to early moderns.[38] Americans, Venturi believed, do not like piazzas and public places; they prefer to stay home and watch television. So they advised, if designers were to regain the spectators that modernism's purities had alienated, then let them study the nouveau riche environments of Hollywood of the 1920s and 1930s, Las Vegas of the 1970s, the people's environments of Levittown or Society Hill for popular imagery; or let them look as well for physical backgrounds in the mass media, movies, soap operas, pickle and furniture advertisements. Madison Avenue, they noted, had a good idea of what was homey, what would sell, what was convincing to the popular taste. Because these fictive and real environments were untouched by the modern aesthetic, they consequently offered the designer the only source for the symbolic and communicative aspects of architecture. A picture, Venturi argued, "in the landscape of the auto age. . . . is worth a thousand forms."[39]

This documentary interest in the popular and vernacular landscape, the commercialized sign and communicating image, eventually reduced itself to an ornamental and decorative style and in the end became—no more no less—than bracketed moments of pure theatricality inserted at random points into the City of Spectacle. When pure forms of modernism were replaced by popular forms of mass consumption, Venturi and Scott Brown proposed that judgment be deferred, allowing a new visual sensibility to arise from these everyday forms before they were subjected to criticism and devalued as visual inspiration.[40] But this regrounding of the image of the city in hybrid and contradictory forms was a strategy that turned against itself: aiming to be truly popular and critically transformative, it merely achieved the status of ornament and became one more language game for the architect to manipulate.

Popular scenes drawn from the *n*-dimensional forms of commercial advertisments or the throwaway and obsolescent objects found in the urban environment took their place among the repertoire of images and landscapes underwriting the compositional forms of the City of Spectacle. The architectural historian and writer of illustrated guidebooks added to this visual archive, propelling the spectator's imagination to radiate outward across the city from a safe and elevated perspective.[41] They taught the viewer quite a lot about architecture, but not necessarily city form, for these architectural histories spoke of the refined urbane place dressed in formal attire. Sequestered within the pages of a book, they slowly turned this city view into an open-air imaginary museum as devoid of popular tastes and memorable ceremonies as high art ever could be. Observed through a window or displaced metaphorically in the pages of illustrated guidebooks, the architectural historian described a city that was cool, detached, and mannerly, not immediate, melodramatic, and threatening. Yet every traveler along city streets when they leave behind the guided tour, every frequenter of the low road and meandering byways, knows a less perfect look. The serene city of the architectural historian is just as much a figurative tableau as are the trompe l'oeil historic or popular landscapes set up before the spectator's eyes. In all of these views, the disarray of everyday life is marked as the threatening other, the forbidden difference that gnaws away at puristic illusions. Then suddenly around the corner there appears a parade that disrupts this order, turning it inside out: open-air markets that take hold of leftover remnants, the homeless that wander about, the chromolithographs and billboards that blast out another aesthetic, the excessive tearing down and throwing up of new buildings—these constantly exploding images seem to travel through the city, adding motion and violativity to what the trompe l'oeil depicts as a static and inflexible mold.

The Politics of Representational Forms

Because every economic formation or structure engenders a cultural form or an aesthetic convention, it can be expected that the representational forms of the City as a Work of Art, Panorama, or Spectacle reflect different stages of capitalism.[42] The very term "work of art," for example, implied that there existed a market for these "works," that art was a commodity for sale and no longer sponsored or protected by aristocratic or royal patronage. This nineteenth-century art market, however, was compromised: the bourgeoisie and the rearguard ancien regime, the old aristocrats and academicians, still ruled over popular taste.[43] Under their influence, historicism reigned for the plundering of old styles such as the Gothic, Baroque, or Classical could all be used to cover over changes wrought by political revolutions, industrialization, urbanization, even the rise of the bourgeoisie with their materialistic aspirations and blatant pretentions. The battle of styles and the City as a Work of Art were consequently nothing other than a backward-binding gesture: trying to secure the turbulent present by tying it to the great artistic inheritance of the past, and mirroring through stylistic references the security and traditional order of pre-industrial and pre-revolutionary times. Consequently more liberated artistic expressions were at once critical of yet helpless when faced with the virile popular taste of the bourgeoisie with its love of show, its tendency toward self-aggrandizement, conformity, and mediocrity, its delight in pure entertainment and fashionable styles. Some artists and architects felt held back as well by the conservative control of official academies and the latter's collusion with governmental authorities who had recently gained responsibility for adorning the city with displays of ceremonial architecture. Not surprisingly then, the new opera houses, theaters, governmental office structures, universities, museums, libraries, and city halls—even the new railroad stations with their massive hotel complexes—found themselves decked out in historicist garb.

Drawing a distinction between high art and popular tastes, the avant-garde artists saw the invasion of the market economy into artistic production as a debasement of pure authentic expression that called for an act of defiance or a stance of autonomy against the impregnation of the commodity in culture. But this was a lonely and alienating gesture that erupted only within isolated spots in a general climate of aesthetic conservatism. Artists no longer had a sponsored position outside of the market economy from which to resist. With few obstacles placed in its path, therefore, the nineteenth-century city became an array of leisure-time entertainment zones for its bourgeois residents. Even if unwillingly, artists turned to this new audience of luxury consumption not only for economic support, but the subject matter of their paintings began as well to depict the promenading bourgeoisie on their boulevards and recreational sites, their domestic interiors and fashionable attire. And needless to say, architects became the orchestrators of these entertainment sites, turning the nineteenth-century cityscape into a work of art by designing new parks and promenades, huge department stores and theaters, phantasmagorical exhibition halls and luxurious hotels, monolithic railway stations and majestic banks and offices. The interiors of the newfangled apartment houses and suburban villas became the showcases for new consumer commodities, crammed with layers of plush velvet and overstuffed furniture, bric-a-brac and trifles. The profusion of these ornamented interior styles made it ever apparent that the bourgeoisie held an insatiable desire for novelty and expressed an irrational taste for the exotic that subsequently tainted the production of every "work of art."

As traditional aristocratic and royal patronage was supplanted slowly during the nineteenth century with the artistic programs and plans of the modern bureaucratic state, the latter became the center of focus in the early decades of the twentieth century and rationalized or administered art a new fear. The invasion of art by politics, by governmental bureaucracies with their interest rooted in the status quo and their legitimation based on continuing traditions, was a new threat, for it was believed that only a compromised art could result, an art that no longer revealed the traces and shadows of its alienation. Popular culture, because it was accessibile to the masses, or so Theodor Adorno warned, must be seen not as the liberator but as the social bad conscience of autonomous modern art. The latter, or so the avant-garde's myth proclaimed, must remain aloof and exclusive if it was to be critical and oppositional. "Both [high and low art, Adorno declared] bear the stigmata of capitalism, both contain elements of change . . . Both are torn halves of an integral freedom, to which however they do not add up."[44]

A modern art and architecture of abstract formalism, the City as Panorama, would try to radically separate itself from popular culture, although as in the nineteenth century it would never in practice be so clear. In the beginning of the modernists' program, high art, the other of popular culture, would be inspired by and contaminated with lesser visual forms: the circus, billboard advertisements, the reflected images from shop windows, as well as the machine aesthetic, the speed of automotive travel, and the power of electricity were all sources from which the visual sensibility of modernism drew sustenance. Aesthetic reform, as preached at the Bauhaus and by Le Corbusier, was expected to result in meaningful new social relations, following the belief that totally redesigned everyday environments—from teapots to prefabricated housing utilizing the latest industrial products and technological innovations and maximizing organizational efficiency—would liberate society from its wants and inequities. But this was a naive conception, and instead the purities, whiteness, and distinctions of high modernism and the City as Panorama eventually prevailed. The architecture and morphology of the city were as coolly analyzed as the abstractions of geometry, and reassembled in rational forms as precise and clear as crystal. In the end modernism became an aesthetic response removed and repelled by the ludic gestures and primal necessities of everyday life; it offered an urbanism of empty scenic spaces and alienating imagery actually turned against the visual realities and spectacles that metropolitan existence produced.

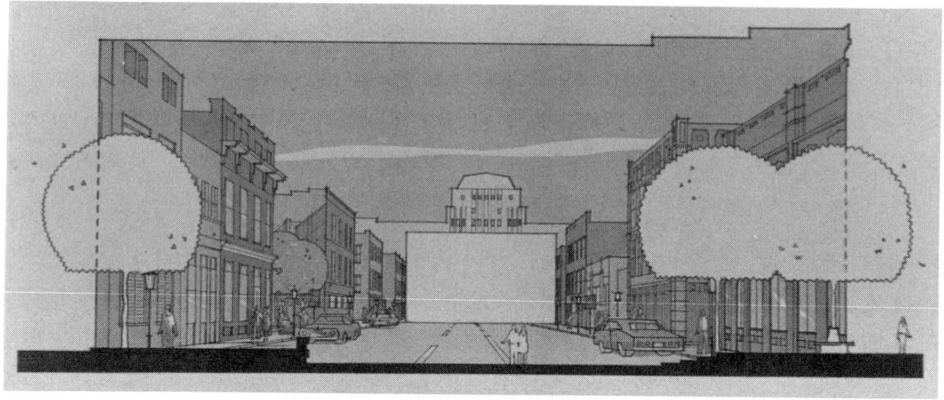

Venturi, Rauch & Scott Brown, Galveston Development Project, View of the Strand *(1974)*.

In time, however, the oppositional and unassimilated nature of modern art and architecture, in spite of their pretense of autonomy and authenticity, were canonized by mass culture: in the museums of modern art, in the advertising images of modern lifestyles, in the design of everyday objects and habitats, in the uniform city plans of urban renewal and redevelopment. The actual aestheticization of everyday life and its forms of visual communication, which the modernist doctrine proclaimed, distilled into one more style propelling the long march of the commodity through culture. Now we find that the modern aesthetic resides among a plurality of compositional forms and styles, each one posing a distinct set of images and staging a set of goods and alternative lifestyles. And these image sets and atmospheric milieus, far from being oppositional and authentically pure as modernism proposed, have become the normal background for our contemporary mode of consumption in the City of Spectacle.

Sometime in the 1960s and early 1970s, the city landscape and its leisure-time activities began to be circumscribed by the sensuous structures of consumption, until its terrain overflowed with upscaled marketplaces and commodities for sale. The modernist line supposedly separating high art from popular culture was renegotiated because the spectacle of capital and accelerating consumerism no longer appeared to impose an alienating threat. Every consumer's identification and pleasure seemed linked instead to a series of alternative lifestyles showcased and staged in advertisements and scenographic segments of the city. This city of consumption, reveling in its own imagery and display, blocked any awareness of a reality that might differ from this spectacle of pure forms and play of consumer choices. A whole complex of looking was held in place by the force of pure entertainment, by the very act of showing, which kept the gaze focused on surface appearances and constructed sets of images. Shop windows, packaged goods, billboards, architecture, historic preservation, television displays, came to the same focal point—the theatricalized City of Spectacle.

By the 1970s and 1980s, consequently, bureaucratic or administrated art was no longer a central issue. Because the state by then responded directly to the imperatives of consumption and production and the commodity had totally saturated the cultural terrain, the existence of an autonomous oppositional art and architecture appeared to be a questionable point of view. Having pulled away from both directly subsidizing urban redevelopment and underwriting the urban poor, the state with its free-market ideology began to treat urban growth and decline, empowerment and impoverishment, as natural events responding to market demands that recycled and revalued parts of the city or displaced and recentered different residential groups. Because many cities had lost or were losing their manufacturing base, while their white-collar employment was increasing, these cities experimented with new coalitions of public–private investment to produce residential, work, and leisure-time spaces in order to support and expand this white-collar base. In consequence, the state offered lucrative but generally invisible tax incentives to private developers and property owners to help them restore undervalued areas of the city, to spur on the gentrification of inner-city neighborhoods, and to invest in new leisure-time spaces and tourist attractions such as convention centers, sports arenas, and upscaled marketplace complexes. And in the competition among cities for white-collar businesses and middle-class citizens, every city turned to advertising their fine features and benefits: specifically drawing on their history, safe neighborhoods, good shops, excellent education, and progressive governments.[45]

Now it appears in this narration of representational forms of the city that the City as Panorama was an anomaly and that the City of Spectacle was supposedly the natural inheritor of traditions originally displayed in the City as a Work of Art. Such an argument, however, when facilely made is intended to eradicate awareness of the social programs and utopian ideals embedded within the modernist view. By making an allegiance with nineteenth-century representational forms, the contemporary postmodern position denies that artists and architects can change the world. By celebrating the commodity's successful invasion into all spheres of cultural expression, it completely ignores the modernists' opposition to conservative market-based values. Because global satellite communication and computerized information processing systems under private market control have become all-pervasive in the 1970s and 1980s, they have produced a nexus of information and cultural expressions dominated by corporate values and marketing dictates.[46] Corporations now sponsor museum exhibitions, theatrical performances, sports events, national celebrations, and of course media entertainment and the news; they control many architectural spaces of the city, theme parks, and shopping malls—in short they have underwritten the very sites of cultural expression. But who raises a voice in opposition to this corporate organization of culture? If modernism once kept up a lively critique of the commodity, of the increasing commercialization of culture, holding the entanglements of government and monopoly capital to be the enemy, then postmodernity has eradicated this stance and accepts the corporate-cultural enterprise as a new totalizing system.

These new technologies of cultural production and consumption have saturated the City of Spectacle with an array of images. The art of selling now dominates urban space, turning it into a new marketplace for architectural styles and fashionable lives. If highly adaptable production techniques can create products and services upon demand, then consumer tastes must be constantly manipulated to desire whatever is new. Images become aestheticized commodities representing livable cities for sale, placing products in lifestyle stage sets, turning museum exhibitions and cultural entertainments into events for corporate enhancement. Postmodernity thrives within the fantasy realm of these image spectaculars, refusing to articulate a critical stance and mistrusting the value of art to speak of utopian potentials. Here is where the real failure of postmodernity lies: in denying the power and control of cultural enterprises that silence oppositional voices and dismantle resistant positions. Having too much fun in the City of Spectacle spawns historical amnesia and false reconciliations. It does not allow for critical perspectives grounded in values formed outside of the marketplace, beyond the grip of the image, in opposition to the aestheticization of everyday life.

The Scenic Spaces of Memory

Global electronic media have changed the relationship of collective memory, history, and city spaces as well, for memory now consumes the past as a set of reconstructed images manipulated and rearranged at random. What results is a solipsistic aesthetic involved in the repetition of already known patterns and formal sets. In this mimicking of computer algorithms, pattern languages generate fragmented parcels of city space as autonomous elements that say nothing about the city as a whole. This recursive mentality is serial, mass producing city spaces across the western world reproduced from already known patterns or molds. Because a pattern language is ornamental, these places tend to be dedicated to entertainment and play. Being solipsistic, this recursion circles back upon itself, forbidding a critical distance.

The Italian cultural critic Umberto Eco called postmodernism an "aesthetics of seriality," suggesting that the era of electronics places an emphasis on the repeatable, the cyclical, and the expected.[47] Intermittent viewing audiences, going about their everyday domestic routines or absentmindedly traveling along city streets, search for relaxation and light amusement. Indifferent to the content, they relish the repetition of well-known themes that draw on their recorded memory and cleverly highlight important information. Recycling or recasting processes depend on knowledge of past forms and styles, and they consequently exhibit a renewed interest in borrowing and quoting from commonly shared cultural codes and traditional legends.

Just at the point when computer electronics appeared to be disturbing the spectator's perspective of geographical space and historical time, there was in the 1970s and 1980s a reversion to the art of memory based upon well-established city views and architectural imagery inserted into the city's compositional form at random places and sites. Yet the French sociologist Maurice Halbwachs claimed as long ago as the 1920s that to the contrary, collective memory exists only as long as it is part of the living experience of a group or individual, but when that continuity with the past is ruptured, history comes into play.[48] History fixes the past in a uniform manner; drawing upon its difference from the present, it then reorganizes and resuscitates collective memories and popular imagery, freezing them in stereotypical forms. Utilizing its distance from the past, history sets up a fictional space manipulating time and place, and re-presenting facts and events.

Memory, Halbwachs argued, stands opposed to this narrative history, for memory always occurs behind our backs, where it can neither be appropriated nor controlled. Collective memory, moreover, is a current of continuous thought still moving in the present, still part of a group's active life, and these memories are multiple and dispersed, spectacular and ephemeral, not recollected and written down in one unified story. Instead, collective memories are supported by a group framed in space and time. They are relative to that specific community, not a universal history shared by many disparate groups. History on the other hand gives the appearance that memory persists in a uniform manner, being handed down from one period of time to another and passing successively from place to place.[49] Disrupted from its original time and historic place, the past then reappears as a historical theater, presenting its voice to the spectator through a series of images. Because this past is fragmented, it can be rewritten and recomposed into plays and theatrical scenes. Such a historical theater acts out the past, little by little extending its power over the spectator's memory, slowly turning former events into an imaginary and fictional museum.[50]

Postmodern art and architecture assumed that images and artifacts bear the record of the past; they either speak their historical role or relay memories to the present. But history and memory, as Halbwachs accounted, are actually opposing terms, the one manipulable and re-presentable in a play of lost significance, while the other is plural, alive, and cannot be appropriated. Consequently the construction of meaningful urban compositions that escape the stench of nostalgia and turn aside the longing for centered stability and structured communication, this effort to articulate the City of Collective Memory through theatricalized and representational forms, whether drawn from the repertoires of high art or popular vernaculars, has most often been both troubled and distorted, as we shall see.

Every memory, Halbwachs reminds us, unfolds in a spatial framework. It is above all scenic, and it is here in the arrangement of cities and places that remembrance will reemerge.[51] But it must be kept in mind that memory, as opposed to history, responds more than it records, it bursts upon the scene in an unexpected manner, demanding an alteration of established traditions. Operating only in fragments, memory is an art that connects disparate events; it is formed on the tactics of surprise, ruptures, and overturnings that reveal its true power and its grip over the spectator's imagination. Memory is above all an antimuseum and not localizable, certainly not appealed to through revisionary historic and popular landscapes proposed in the City of Spectacle.[52] The figural forms of memory and allusion involve us instead in the open possibility of displacement and difference, a play that draws many absences into the present. Memory traces then become the remaining marks of historical moments; images that are metaphorically and metonymically displaced onto different contemporary contexts.[53]

In the City of Collective Memory, the architect, city planner, and spectator must begin to move beyond the will to instrumentally formulate historical unities. This gesture requires accepting the inadequacies of both the City as Panorama, with its rational scientific models based on describable pasts and predictable futures, and the City of Spectacle, with its commercially contrived and theatricalized stage sets. What will become fascinatingly rich in the City of Collective Memory will be the play of oppositions, the existence of randomness, disturbances, dispersions, and accidents. New city forms and spaces will depend as well on the creation of innovative tactics and plays to deal with uncertainty and disorder in this city of lost narrative forms and decomposed centers. The City of Collective Memory will require a double reading of nineteenth-century memories and late twentieth-century forms, recovering stories heretofore silenced or misrepresented and nurturing spaces that once appeared stereotyped and rhetorical. This program guides our travels in *The City of Collective Memory:* as we wander through the record of historical constructions and muse upon the collection of representational forms and monumental places that once bore meaningful messages.

Representational spaces of the city contain both conceptual and material strategies engendering imaginary and real effects. The awareness not only of the material forms of representation but the conceptual processes that inform them will be our consideration. In this book on city imagery and architectural pleasures, we want to explore the manner in which these representational forms are structured and modified, how they repress or reveal our perceptions and memories of the city, and how they influence our view of the city whose shape is rearranged constantly. The function of the image, which we seek to historicize, is to record the material form and look of the city, and to present it to the beholder through staged or posed views, instantaneously or artfully narrated. The art of the city is often one of vicarious travel and imaginary explorations. We have learned to gaze upon the city as artifact through illustrated portfolios and architectural guidebooks that have their own procedures for characterizing place and tradition. We often find city forms to be a theatrical art of scenographic composition, resurrected on an imaginary stage where its vanished architecture and ruins are given new life and arrangement. Even the city landscape itself can be theatrically composed, carrying the projected view of various representational schemes and involving the spectator through repeated devices and framed encounters.

History and memory become variable elements in the art of preservation and restoration. Often invented for specific purposes, history always stands against memory, the one as a constructed or recomposed artifice, the other a lived and moving expression. We travel backward in time through memory and through the recorded imagery of paintings, photographs, the cinema, and architecture. Collected in archives, museums, encyclopedias, and memory theaters, these visual icons once stored and classified are available for the appropriations and recylings of later generations. These collections bracket history from their own point of view, recomposing the artifact's context through a network of references and comparative rereadings that resituate the past in the present. Cutting across this art of travel and the theater, of history and memory, lie the contaminated intertwinings but distinct classifications of high art and popular entertainment, didactic illustrations and designed commodities, the oppositional aesthetic and the compromised, the pure or pleasural forms of architecture. These are the ways in which we frame the city, visually imagining its form and materially reconstituting its structure: by travel, in the theater, at the museum, from the cinema, through its architectural compositions.

PART

Historical Precedents for the City of Collective Memory

ONE

three

The City and the Theater

It is in the city that one learns to be a citizen. There people acquire valuable knowledge, see many models to teach them the avoidance of evil. As they look around, they notice how handsome is honor, how lovely is fame, how divine a thing is glory.

LEON BAPTISTA ALBERTI[1]

And among all the dreams that the architect has laid upon the earth, I know of no more lovely things than his flights of steps leading up and leading down, and of this feeling about architecture in my art I have often thought how one could give life (not a voice) to these places, using them to a dramatic end. When this desire came to me I was continually designing dramas wherein the place was architectural and

> *lent itself to my desire. And so I began with a drama called "The Steps".*
>
> EDWARD GORDON CRAIG[2]

How many times have the city, its architecture, and the theater been intertwined, for the theater is often a foil for the representations of public life, and public space frequently is arranged as if for a theatrical performance. Both the theater and urban space are places of representation, assemblage, and exchange between actors and spectators, between the drama and the stage set. Finding their roots in the collective experience of everyday life, they are ordering experiences of that chaos. The Greek word "theatron" means literally "place for seeing"; argued analogically then, theatrical and architectural space are both cultural prisms through which the spectator experiences social reality, viewing mechanisms that metaphorically spatialize reality, establishing the scene as authentic and truthful, or fanciful and spectacular.[3] As perspectival devices, the theater and architecture impose coherent meanings and illusory representations that determine what we call a well-made performance. Scenographic theatrical arrangements are mirrors held up to society. Often reflecting the perfected image of a well-ordered city, these stagings are really civic portraits intended to be remembered. And architectonic forms of the stage inserted into urban space establish these theatrical compositions as focal points, a kind of artificial memory device not only for spectators at random, but for citizens of the nation, the region, and the city itself.

Until the end of the nineteenth century, the city as a work of art carried a sense of moral order within its aesthetic forms, bringing the memory of a harmonious society to public review. This ideal reached back to fifth-century Athens, when the theater assisted in the reenactment of individual and collective deeds and tragedies, when drama was intended to instruct the spectator by recalling the customs, values, and laws of the city, hoping by recollecting the past to inspire perfected acts in the future. The city and the theater were fused: not only did the drama reach out to instruct its audience, thus enfolding them within its message, but this act of containment was reinforced by the semicircular amphitheater enclosing its spectators, while the drama and theater, in turn, were bounded by the geographically defined and ideologically delimited city.[4]

The classical theater compelled the spectator to take part in a dialogue, one that questioned the meaning of the drama, judged the logic of its events, and investigated its moral significance. The drama came from some place and was directed at someone. In the contemporary city of spectacle, all that remains of the drama of architecture and the city is pure visual form. We no longer question the performance, for there is no moral argument, logical narration, or centered community to link the drama and the spectators in dialogue. Visually enthralled, we submit to the theatricalized show, suspending critical judgment. The agon of contested terrains that pits the play against the audience, the space of the theater against the city, has been eclipsed in the centerless sprawl of the contemporary city. Advertising dramaturgies and architectural scenographies in the contemporary theatricalized city draw us close to the condition that Jean Baudrillard describes where "the seduction of the signs themselves [becomes] more important than the emergence of any truth."[5]

The theater contains contested terrains within its aesthetic, be they utopian views, resisting positions, redemptive solutions, or conservative ploys. It is a prism through which the spectator looks to envision reality. As the essence of the theater is to reveal and to conceal, this prism necessarily distorts or deflects through its imaginary representations. The theater is inherently ambiguous: it can emancipate by liberating passions and imaginations or by creating a community out of its spectators, but it can also subjugate and control an audience through the devices of distance and internalization. If there is a continual change in the nature of the theatrical and its order of vision in contemporary cities, then we need to ask what kind of rupture the city of spectacle entails, what forms of the theater have been discarded and which does it contain? And most of all we need to explore in this history of the theater and the city the riddle of community. For if we are to be critically involved with the agon of the city, this implies that we try to obliterate the distance that separates art from reality, the form of the city from political morality, the fragmented public from a collective ideal. If the theater and the city came into being together, perhaps we can understand the city's deconstructed and invisible nature by questioning theatrical forms.

Let us begin with Vitruvius, who described in *De Architectura* what must have been the classical theater of Augustan times, its performance space and scenic forms. This theater was a total architectural scene encompassing the stage, the spectator, the amphitheater, and the landscape. There was no curtain separating the audience from the actors, and no lighting immersed the spectators in dark while highlighting the stage. And the city, receiving the drama's instruction, could always be viewed beyond the theater, for the performance took place in the daylight. It appears that the scena or backdrop of the platform stage were double doors decorated to resemble those of a great palace, and to their right or left were doors of the guest chambers. These formed a flat backdrop to the stage and served as entrances and exits for the performers. Beyond were the *periaktoi,* niches set aside for what may have been three-sided prisms decorated with three different scenes, which revolved by mechanical means. These scenes—a tragic, a comic, and a satyric setting—were used to provide theatrical atmosphere. Tragic scenes were decorated with columns, pediments, statues, and other ceremonial objects, while the comic scene was entirely different, filled with images of private dwellings, balconies, and rows of windows. Silvan scenery such as trees, grottoes, and mountains decorated the satyric scene.[6] Hardly offering scenic illusion, however, conventions seemed to have determined the change of location: revolving one of the *periaktoi* meant a shift of scene within the same town, while revolving both meant a move to another place; entering from one side of the stage implied that one came from town, the other side from the country.[7] The classical theater did not pretend to scenographic illusion, but lent itself to imaginative suggestion or wonderment. The dialogue remained the most important theatrical event and the scenery of minor embellishment.

Although confusion reigns with respect to the classical stage, Vitruvius does seem to give evidence that the art of scenography, that branch of optics which has to do with the representation of pictorial illusion, was known to the ancients. Depicting an accurate representation of space, or projecting a view as if the spectator were actually there, depends on understanding the principles of linear perspective. Both architectural and stage illusions rely on these rules enabling the eye to travel backward through spatial recession into the illustrated scene. So Vitruvius wrote in volume 7 of his works,

> . . . Agatharcus in Athens, when Aeschylus was bringing out a tragedy, painted a scene, and left a commentary about it. This led Democritus and Anaxagoras to write on the same subject, showing how, given a centre in a definite place, the lines should naturallly correspond with due regard to the point of sight and the divergence of the visual rays, so that by this deception a faithful representation of the appearance of buildings might be given in painted scenery, and so that, though all is drawn on a vertical flat facade, some parts may seem to be withdrawing into the background, and others to be standing out in front.[8]

Forgotten in the dust of time, the optical laws of perspective outlined by Vitruvius and essential to the art of scenography and architectural composition would be rediscovered along with Vitruvius' texts in 1414. Although his treatise was maimed by age and full of omissions and imperfections, it influenced a long line of new architectural compendiums. Leon Baptista Alberti's *De re Aedificatoria* was the first to be based on Vitruvius' work and was printed without illustrations in 1485, although it had circulated in manuscript form since 1452.[9] Borrowing lessons learned from the Greeks, the Renaissance humanists of the fifteenth century tried to instill a sense of composition and clarity into the chaotic disorder of their urban environments by projecting illusions of harmony and moral significance onto its fabric.

Thus Alberti conceived of an ideal city as an imaginary theater of tragic scenery whose streets were paved and perfectly clean, lined with two identical rows of houses or arcades and porticoes of uniform height. As a harmonious work of art, this ideal city was arranged such that all of its parts had their proper place, number, proportion, and order.[10] In the city center, Alberti placed a library representing textual consciousness and civic intactness, for following the Greeks he too believed that without memory of its origins and the principles of continuity, a city would tend toward destruction.[11] Focusing on his city's squares, really theatrical stages surrounded by multistoried arcades, he gave each one a specific function such as a market or a place of exercise, and turned them into building types designed according to the rules of proportion.[12] Since man was the measure of all things, the proper relative height of a square should be one-third, or at least no less than one-sixth, of its breadth and thus stand within the range of a spectator's angle of vision.[13] He wrote of his ideal city filled with these theatrical squares that

> Glory springs up in public squares; reputation is nourished by the voice and judgments of many persons of honor, and in the midst of people. Fame flees from all solitary and private spots to dwell gladly in the arena, where crowds are gathered and celebrity is found; there the name is bright and luminous of one who with hard sweat and assiduous toil for noble ends has projected himself up out of silence, darkness, ignorance, and vice.[14]

Alberti's ideal and real worlds led separate existences, and he remained pessimistic about how one could actually change reality and attain unrealizable harmony. Nevertheless, a good painter, by following the rules of perspective, could create the illusion of unity and thus infuse humanist ideals into a resistant world. And a well-trained architect could design ideal city stages and insert them at random into the heterogeneous mixture of urban forms, instilling the illusion that harmonious order controlled chaotic and unruly reality.[15] This was the vanishing point toward which all of Alberti's theories strove: the miraculous linking of the perfected humanist world with reality, of the spiritual with the temporal and by extension, theatrical ideals reordering the soul of the spectator.[16] Thus his imaginary city became a pictorial stage for the representation of significant actions, a theatrical milieu of power and status, of counterdeception and stability, dignity and glory taking place in a deceiving and turbulent world. Town planning was established as the highest expression of virtue and rational purpose, upholding the illusion of a perfectly harmonious world and maintaining the myth of its intactness.

Alberti advised the painter that he could bring the image and reality closer together by following the laws of perspective through the use of a camera obscura. A painter, he wrote,

> made some incredible things to be closed up in a small box to be seen through a small hole. Vast planes could be seen here, spreading around a huge sea, and far-off regions lost in the distance. He used to call these things demonstrations. They were such that the learned and the unlearned would affirm that they could not recognize it as having been made with a brush, but as true to nature.[17]

The laws of perspective enabled an artist to solve mathematically the problem of diminuation in size with distance and thereby produce a pictorial space that was centrally focused and uniformly scaled. Buildings and monuments were the objects in space that the artist formally analyzed and compared for their proportional relationships in order to imitate what the eye perceived. Then this ideal architectural landscape was projected onto a plane or a veil in a gesture that reduced the difference between building and painting to one of medium. Thus linear perspective paintings contained architectural and theatrical settings, recreating the city's squares with their arcades, cornice lines, and windows retreating toward the vanishing point.[18] Consequently both painted and real architecture were approached in a similar manner: along a central axis from which the imaginary or actual beholder gazed upon a series of objects proportionally arranged and retreating in ratio into the background. And both painter and spectator looked through the same perspectival view toward the same vanishing point.[19]

Giulio Carlo Argan has underscored these figurative and architectonic interests of the Renaissance artists by describing Brunelleschi's panels in the Baptistry and Palazzo della Signora.[20] To view the first panel, a spectator had to look at its reflection in a mirror seen through a hole cut in the back of the panel. The mirror was placed at a distance proportional to the distance that the artist had actually stood from his work, while a background of burnished silver reflected the sky with its clouds in motion. The second panel was too large for this reflective act, so Brunelleschi cut out the structures by following the outlines of their rooftops and then placed this work against a real background of sky.[21] Argan suggests that Brunelleschi resorted to such visual maneuvers to demonstrate the laws of symmetry and proportion that a good painter should follow. By conforming to the laws of linear perspective the artist arrived at proportion, but if the single point of view from the eye of the painter to the picture plane was not accurately followed, then the reversed image in the mirror would be unsymmetrical and its defects more apparent in this unaccustomed view. Such a demonstration allowed the spectator to establish the correctness of the painter's calculations and the exactness of his illusion of reality. But second, Argan argues, in neither painting did Brunelleschi paint the sky, for he wished to demonstrate that the artist should be interested only in depicting objects in space that could be known by measuring and comparing. Architecture by its very finiteness gave definition to the space in which it was located and could be measured, but the sky, being limitless, consequently was unmeasurable. An exact knowledge of space had become for the Renaissance artist a supreme demonstration of man's domination over reality.[22]

This rational perspective with its illusion of deep space begins to open up a distance that separates the spectator from the image, the subject from the object. Whether in Brunelleschi's experiments or Alberti's camera obscura, where the realism of the represented view revealed the painter's control over the aesthetic correctness of the image, or in the constructed effect of the dramatic narrative intended to morally educate and socially control the observer, boundaries divorce the perceiving subjects from the represented object. The framed pictorial view and unified compositional theme excluded extraneous elements and peripheral subthemes from sight and reflected the presence of an all-seeing and all-knowing authority controlling the scene. But this representational scene also included the spectator as the theatrical audience. The visual axes radiating from the focal point of an urban piazza or square were mirror reflections of the axes converging in the eye of the spectator and hence as Normal Bryson writes in *Vision and Painting,* "Albertian space returns the body to itself in its own image, as a measurable, visible, objectified unity. . . . it solidifies a form which will provide the viewing subject with the first of its 'objective' identities."[23]

Coterminously, the development of perspectival projection depended on techniques of surveying and mapping that could accurately locate and scale objects in three-dimensional space and represent them on flat planar surfaces. There thus existed a reciprocal relationship between the development of Renaissance perspective and cartography. In medieval maps, cities were symbolically represented as a collection of typical but isolated monuments. These maps were never intended to offer an accurate sense of scale nor reflect the measured distance between two objects. The Renaissance sought a system to collectively and rationally display the order of monuments and significant places in the city, and simultaneously to realistically represent the topography of urban space. They sought a new spatial and symbolic totality. Both congealed in methods of mapping and visualizing the city's terrain. Hence the city was submitted to a radial order of axial streets converging on focal points and regularized squares. This system of axial roads, moreover, was abstracted above the existing city fabric and became a generating device for a new symbolic and spatial totality that drew together the walled city and its surrounding region. In Alberti's view, framed axial routes became the major structuring device, and they were of course processional routes flanked by parallel rows of buildings of uniform heights, porticoes or rows of trees directing the spectator's view toward the focal point or culminating square.[24]

Inigo Jones, Roman Atrium.

Alberti's interest in optical laws and topographic space combined with his desire to render more precisely the imagery inspired by the antique. Haunted by the memory of ancient Rome and aware that the fifteenth-century city was a pile of ruins and broken fragments, that the classical city actually lay buried beneath the contemporary town, Alberti began an exhaustive study of all the known facts about Rome's monuments and urged their immediate restoration. Developing a method based on the use of polar coordinates, he set about measuring the Aurelian walls and submitting his findings to a scaled map of the city. Each building was placed by two measures, one taken from a radius that ran through the building to the center of the city established as the Capitolium, and the other from a similar radius to a point on a circular horizon.[25] By determining accurate distances and the location of important monuments, a new topographical composition of the city totality emerged in which the walls and gateways, the river, temples, and public buildings, the historic monuments and civic and ecclesiastical buildings gained primary significance. Hoping this morphological and syntactical analysis would be a visual key to the eventual restoration of ancient Rome, Alberti intended to offer the spectator a ceremonial and theatrical experience of the city, and consequently he developed a systematic guide to its ancient ruins and Christian monuments.[26]

Rationally measured architectural space depicted in perspectival view was transferred to the theatrical stage in the work of Sebastiano Serlio, whose illustrated volumes of *Architettura* began to appear in 1537. Marking a departure in architectural publication, Serlio intended to have illustrations be the major point of his work, juxtaposing his commentary, which drew heavily on the work of Vitruvius and Alberti, on one page opposite an illustrated page.[27] Serlio established stage design as a by-product of architecture, describing in his second volume (published in 1545) the laws of perspective that turned the stage into a scenographic cube, an act from which it has seldom escaped. His scenic illustrations—borrowed from the Vitruvian tragic, comic, and satyric views—recreated on the illusionistic stage the architectural settings, public squares, and street scenes already represented in perspective by Alberti and other Renaissance painters. In a semicircular amphitheater based on the classical pattern, but enclosed and elongated for rectangular sites, Serlio eliminated the palace backdrop of the classical stage and substituted instead both a flat forestage where the action took place and a sloping section behind it. This section enabled a perspective picture to be arranged using three different pairs of frames alligned on an angle, some of which were three-dimensional and others flat.[28] As his woodcut illustrations described, Serlio embellished the Vitruvian scene: in the tragic architectural stage, for example, the spectator saw palaces, temples, triumphal arches, obelisks, pyramids, and other buildings, spacious squares and long vistas of avenues with intersecting streets, all arranged parallel to the picture plane but receding in an identical manner toward the painted backdrop whose perspectival view carried the eye still further in depth.

Serlio's drawings, however, failed to capture the marvels of illumination that accompanied these scenes: pieces of colored glass or containers of colored liquid reflecting lights from behind were carefully arranged in small openings along the cornices and architraves of the perspectival view. Dissolving the static architecture of the classical stage, Serlio offered instead a brilliant atmosphere of light, a scene that glittered as if adorned by the sparkling luster of precious stones.[29] More important, Serlio's perspectival scene established a new relationship between the spectator, the actor, and the pictorial stage, for the lines of perspective were composed around a central vanishing point drawn perpendicular to the sovereign's seat. Distinquishing itself from the classical theater, which enfolded the entire audience within its amphitheater and figurative point of view, in Serlio's theater both the sovereign's eyepoint and the scenery's vanishing point were located opposite the center of the stage and were raised above the rest of the audience. The royal seat was either on a platform or cut into the Vitruvian rows of seats in the amphitheater, and it was from that perspective only that the pictorial scene was well formed.[30] In addition, this perspective stage—under the guise that it was a wonderful spectacle commanded by the architect—became part of the princely display of power and control. A framed picture show, offering an illusion of real public space that only the sovereign saw clearly, was as well a mirror of social and political instruction. The seating arrangement reflected the centralized order and social hierarchy of reality, for the closer in power one stood to the sovereign and the higher one's social rank, then the nearer one sat to royalty and to the centering of the perspectival view. One's position determined one's clarity of view, yet none challenged that of authority. But Serlio noted still further that the more elaborate the performance and the more costly the spectacular effects of machinery, the higher in esteem the spectators placed the prince. A stable and consistent image underscored by sudden tricks of the eye called into mind the imaginary composition of the whole, for it was sovereign power alone that controlled the view and arranged the mirroring image.[31]

These perspective theaters, located within one of the rooms of the many princely palaces in Italy, in the beginning were simply festive entertainments. The point of amusement where spectacular events were fully developed were called "intermezzi," and their entire visual environments were dependent on the talents of architects who had to be great machinists and painters, marvellous decorators and builders. The "intermezzi" were really allegorical episodes displayed between acts of the drama, and the marvels of their stage settings included not only painted scenery that quickly changed, glittering candle lights, and reflective mirrors, but ghosts and devils that sprung out of trap doors, brilliant clouds that descended with hosts of people, rainbows and thunder storms, and beautiful cloths for curtains until, as Joseph Furttenbach the Elder wrote in his *Civil Architecture* of 1628, "the spectator is so overcome with wonders that he scarcely knows whether he is in the world or out of it."[32]

The new court society of Europe, those dukes, cardinals, and princes who were rich and powerful enough to create an aristocratic audience, quickly grasped the basic relationship between theatricality and the fixed eyepoint of power. Not only did regal spectacles seem to mysteriously hold their subjects in awe, but perspectival scenery enabled the transforming ideals of the new humanists and scientists to embellish sovereign authority. Thus the powers of vision were theatrically combined, with "cheats of the eye" being equally as important as mathematically exact illusionary scenography. But now the distance between the spectator and the theatrical show begins to widen: Serlio, for example, not only devised an elongated stage to enhance perspectival depth, but he placed the central point where acting took place in front of the proscenium frame. This central point was removed from the scenic background as well as from the audience. Thus analogically argued, the action perceived to reflect the sovereign's power took place under the gaze of a spectator but one removed by distance, by respect, or by awe. Kernodle has argued that "the modern theater grew out of the desire to see and hear with living actors the historical rulers, romantic stories, and allegorical fancies already portrayed by the painters—out of the desire to enhance the personalities and events of the present by endowing them, through a dramatic re-enactment, with the glamour of history and the approval of allegory."[33] But this desire for a pictorial image theater begins to silence the audience or fails to call on the audience's reciprocal involvement, for a theater devoted to images and symbols conveying meanings difficult to state diminishes dialogue. In addition, the spectator begins to deny his/her role of questioning what is not visually apparent, allowing sovereign power to be legitimated or at least accepted through this genre of entertainment.

There were still other developments that brought changes to the theater. With the rise of a stable monarchy in sixteenth-century England, for example, theater became a crown monopoly, and acting companies were banned unless they operated under royal licensing and patronage. But such theatrical control and political censorship created elite and stultifying audiences and actually opened a breach between the theater and the general populace and gave birth to a new public theater based on a mixture of popular and learned traditions. London, whose population swelled on the tide of commercial capitalism, was the first city to offer (from 1570 until the 1640s) the economic and demographic conditions supportive of a permanent, public, and commercial playhouse, a theatrical form increasingly secular in orientation and providing separate roles for the investor, actor, playwright, and audience.[34]

As the theater began to reflect the mentality of an increasingly commercial society, the nature of "theatricality" achieved new importance. In the expanding and increasingly abstract marketplace, social signs and symbols had become so thoroughly "staged" that every human act had to be scrutinized for what it both represented and misrepresented.[35] Jean-Christophe Agnew has argued in *Worlds Apart* that the changing relationships between market and theater were encapsulated in the shifting meaning of the metaphor of "theatrum mundi"—viewing the world as a stage. Since antiquity, "theatrum mundi" had been used to call to mind the vanity of human achievements in a world where God was the ultimate stage manager. This meaning shifted in the sixteenth century to refer not only to the world stage but to an individual's ability to see him or herself as an actor on stage, assuming different roles and postures.[36] It no longer was the relationship between the individual and the sovereign [or God] that held the essence of theatricality, but secular life. In the world of the market as well as the stage, one judged by appearances not words, where close observation of posturing and posing were keys to successful performances.[37] The theater became an essential vehicle rehearsing and repeating new social roles and exchange relations that a market society demanded; it was also an instrument revealing the lost transparency of ordinary acts.[38] And brooding about the theater's theatricality, its posings and posturings, simulations and dissimulations, enabled the theater to withdraw from the conventional rituals and staged ceremonies established in medieval town life. By distancing itself, the theater could then hold a mirror up to society and become an experimental staging for the agonistic relationship of buyer and seller—spelling out new conditions of representation.

Shakespeare's "Merchant of Venice" (1596) can be viewed as such a rehearsal of playing and pretense. Not only do extraordinary events require characters to wear disguises and cause mistaken identities, but this play, by integrating the bourgeoisie into aristocratic society and revealing the precariousness of aristocratic privileges and exclusions, acts out a new social configuration. Evoking English fears of capitalism and Venice's procapitalist stance, the play also strives to achieve acceptance of new economic relations and accommodation to new market behaviors. On the other hand, the failure of traditional social codes meant that uncertainty, insecurity, and reversals of fortune constantly confronted the actors, and these too could be seen as an "acting out" of new social arrangements.[39] In addition, these experimental public playhouses withdrew spatially from the city of London, locating outside its walls in no-man's land called the "Liberties." Here they were surrounded by other marginal spectacles such as gaming houses, taverns, marketplaces, and brothels, but they were also freed from the crown's direct authority and only weakly controlled by the city. As Steven Mullaney explains in *The Place of the Stage,* "Neither a part of nor fully apart from the city, the 'Liberties' served as a kind of riddle inscribed in the cultural landscape. The riddle was one of community, its limits and its threshold, and up until the second half of the sixteenth century it was the citizens of London who could correctly parse its message, and so reconstitute and define themselves as a community, through a ritual process of interpretation."[40]

Marking the advent of the commercial theater run for private profit, James Burbage erected a public outdoor playhouse in the "Liberties" in 1576 that he called "The Theater." For the first time since antiquity, the theater had an architecture built expressly for performance, and by the end of the sixteenth century London was ringed by such playhouses poised strategically at the portals of the city. By locating the theater beyond the crown's and city's control, Mullaney argues, a critical distance opened offering Elizabethan playwrights and actors a decentered vantage point and a space in which they could criticize and comment on the contradictions and transformations of their culture and time. But this was an eccentric perspective that confused categories, counterfeited roles, and threatened the social order.[41] As one critic of the theater noted in 1582, "If private men be suffered to forsake their calling because they desire to walke gentlemen like in sattine & velvet, with a buckler at their heeles, proportion is so broke, unities dissolved, harmony confounded, that the whole body must be dismembered, and the prince or heade cannot chuse but sicken."[42]

Inigo Jones, A Great City: In the Sky the Clouds with Deities.

More conservative and aristocratic Renaissance spectacles of power and authority simultaneously found their way to England in the early seventeenth century through the court architect Inigo Jones. Reviving the art of court masques, Inigo Jones and Ben Jonson, who collaborated and quarreled for twenty-five years, offered idealized stage settings and theatrical fictions that reiterated the realities of power and politics, the protocol of the court and its aristocracy. Revolutionary for England, because of Jones's scenic use of single-point perspective with its centric rays emanating from the royal throne, the masque was really a mingling of different theatrical forms. The spectators were courtly masquers and dancers, never actors or performers, hence this combination helped to erase the boundaries separating the real from the imaginary, the rational from the fantastic, and established the masque's representational form. These Renaissance artists were determined to reveal the deeper truth, the cosmic order and structure of harmonic relations that lay behind the world of appearances—hence their interest in hieroglyphics and in emblem books that united words, images, and reality. Thus Jones's scenographic compositions borrowed from the architectural and theatrical heritage of illustrated folios and recombined these images in fanciful and fictive arrangements. These stage pictures to delight the eye were coated with moral messages; as a controlled staging of architectural imagery they contained symbolic ideas made visually apprehensible.[43]

Inigo Jones expressly sought to establish the autonomy of theatrical architecture and the dominance of visual imagery over the literary meaning of a play with its poetical stage illumination of virtuous roles. The triumph of Inigo Jones's fictive architecture over Ben Jonson's poetical texts marked the ascendence of the modern spectacle in which an excessive taste for the purely visual, for facades and masks, decor and style dominate theatrical space.[44] By dividing his stage into two sections, an upper part for celestial visions and a lower for the main play, Inigo Jones actually turned the stage into a forceful machine as clouds descended to the floor, thrones ascended to the sky, and curtains flew up. These suddenly shifting pictures or scenic spectacles became the major theatrical action.[45] And this theatrical machine he carefully turned into a visual representation, an analogical projecting apparatus, celebrating and confirming the formation and wonder of Great Britain unified under the Stuarts. Thus these masques were actually celebrations of kingly power: low comedy or the turmoil of earthly pursuits were their staple form to be banished from the scene by visions of royal harmony and peace.[46] Here was the illusionistic world of the perspectival theater developed to its height as an ideal instrument for educational reform! The King cleverly knew that to control the manner in which the audience viewed the monarch was to control their responses to his policies as well. The power to project these images and the realism of their perspectival views involved the power to direct both the spectators' imaginations and the way they looked at reality. But more, these masques were magical mirrors reflecting back to the monarch in perfected form how he wished to view himself and his reign—a devine order in an otherwise chaotic world.[47]

Eventually, however, these courtly masques as elaborate spectacles of royal power found that their allegorical parts were at odds with the concept of role playing being rehearsed on the public stage. Tensions began to develop between the aristocratic and public theaters that reflected both deepening social and political struggles and realignments of power. In the early decades of the seventeenth century, England embarked on its course of colonization bringing in its wake the rise of a gentry and a merchant class and the decline of the court, the peerage, and the clergy. Masques were really a form of court hieroglyphics, as Ben Jonson referred to them, a kind of court propaganda that turned increasingly inward upon itself. As a closed theatrical form, the masque protected itself against both the theatricality and commerciality of the public theater, while its architectonic vision of the world's unity and the spectator's position within it allowed neither challenge nor dialogue. Indeed in the early Tudor masques, courtly players refused to speak their parts, preferring to wear significant words embroidered on their costumes.[48] By the time of Ben Jonson and Inigo Jones, speaking parts were performed by professionals in what was called the "antimasque" where the world of disorder and vice was presented. The ideal world portrayed in the main courtly masque was intended to struggle against but finally overcome and replace this "antimasque." Such idealizations were in actuality elaborate analogies of the responsibilities and glory of royal power, for as Queen Elizabeth said, "We princes, I tell you, are set on stages, in the sight and view of all the world duly observed."[49]

The Crown also feared the oppositional voices that arose from the public theater, and by 1605 it increased its monopoly control over the theater by restricting patronage to members of the royal family. Although this reduced the number of theatrical troupes, it did allow those that survived to do so with greater financial security. And so the public theater thrived and even expanded until 1614, when its profits began to decline. Economic survival in the end caused actors and playwrights to shift more of their theatrical activity toward the court and the aristocratic stage. In the wake of this defection, the brief flowering of the public theater of Marlowe and Shakespeare—an oppositional, open, and questioning theater—began to wither, and with the outbreak of Civil War in 1642 Parliament closed both private and public theaters, sealing the fate of this nascent public theater.[50]

It was not until the eighteenth century that a liberal bourgeois public sphere began to emerge, carving out a discursive space of enlightened criticism and rational judgment and negotiating a refined terrain between the waning authority of the court and the waxing spectacle of the crowd. While the illusionistic trompe l'oeil picture stage would remain the dominant scenographic form until the end of the nineteenth century, theater architecture and its role in the city begin to shift. Public entertainment and expressive modes of architecture defined and controlled a new urban scenography in which the theater became a permanent building type and a culminating civic expression of good taste and rational restraint. Because spectators wanted places for theatrical display, these new urban theaters were designed with many entrances and exits, imposing facades and arcades, stairways and lobbies, adjacent shops and cafes. They came to dominate the development and character of their surrounding districts. As Jacques François Blondel explained in 1771, "To build a theater means first and foremost erecting a public building in a city; secondly

Facade of the Grand Theatre at Bordeaux, *Victor Louis, Architect (1773–1780).*

it means finding adequate accommodation for spectators within this building and, finally, preparing a show to put on in front of them."[51]

As the city grew in population, however, inserting these large monumental structures into districts of the city where a great number of theatergoers could gather was no longer an easy event. So often theaters were sited in new districts of the city, where they became priviledged monuments, their entire structure set off by open plazas or set at the end of grand perspectival views. This gesture not only enhanced the structure's theatrical imagery, but offered the city a civic monument around which traffic and pedestrians could converge and flow while simultaneously minimizing the hazards of fire.[52] The Théâtre de l'Odéon in Paris, designed by Charles de Wailly and Marie-Joseph Peyre (1779–1782) is illustrative of the theater's new position in the city. At the converging point of three major axes emphasizing the lines of perspective that drew the city, the theater, and the stage together, the Odeon was a grand national monument and a magnificent gesture in civic pageantry. Raised to the rank of a temple, so Quatremère de Quincy praised, ". . . from the point of view of architecture it is still the only theatre worthy to be called a monument. The space surrounding it, the regularity of the square in which it stands, and of the adjacent streets, above all its isolated position—makes it worthy of admiration and no theatre can be compared to it as far as easy accessibility and circulation go."[53]

The popularity of illusionistic stage settings combined with the spirit of the French Revolution, however, may have brought yet another reform pushing the theater's interior design toward accoustical and optical perfection. Aware that the vision of perspectival stage scenery was distorted in the commonly designed Italian theater with its tiers of boxes and galleries, and desiring absolute scenographic realism, democratic reformers of the late eighteenth century called for a return to the ancient theater, hoping to reconcile the bourgeois illusionistic box stage with the semicircular amphitheater of the Greeks. Defending his unusual choice of a curving auditorium for the Odeon, de Wailly wrote "let us observe people when they are trying to see and hear a speaker in a square: first they form a semicircle in front of him and he will more or less represent the center of its radii: if the radii become longer, new spectators will push in at the sides of the speaker, thus increasing the circumference and finally forming three quarters of a circle. . . ."[54]

As the aristocracy begins to disappear from the political stage and from the audience, to be replaced by the stable bourgeoisie, scenographic taste shifts as well. Rather than projected imagery and tricks of the eye employed to enchance the spectacle of sovereign authority, now realistic sets and visual tableaux become the common theatrical expression reinforcing and underscoring middle-class morality and democratic social reality.[55] Raymond Williams seemed to think that "realism" as a form developed in the drama of the eighteenth century can be characterized by a concentration on secular (not religious) values, action in the contemporary world (not the historical or legendary past), and utilizing subjects whose social rank was equivalent to that of the spectators.[56] Diderot appears to have encapsulated these changes in his preference for the silent theatrical tableau over the abrupt changes of narrative pace, reversals of fortune, and spectacular revelations that had heretofore been theatrical stock. His play "Le Fils Naturel" (1756) was a domestic drama reenacting life's events, a realistic form he found suitable for middle-class audiences.[57]

Diderot proposed that playwrights consider themselves to be painters and look for real tableaux, scenic compositions that were visually pleasing to the audience, static in nature, and instantaneously comprehensible. A play would then consist of a series of these pictorial tableaux reinforced by realistic stage sets across which actors moved.[58] Already with Diderot the sentimental spectacle and the immediacy of the visual stereotype have entered the theater, beginning to demonstrate their universal appeal. Pictorial effects and gestures held in the mind's eye, repeatable because they were memorable, were deemed more important than words. Now what linked the spectator to the tableau was a state of enthrallment or contemplation, not authoritative and didactic ties binding the public to the sovereign. Instead the theatrical tableau urged the beholder to emulate its model by internalizing the moral values and middle-class rationality it repetitively re-presented: sacrifices made for virtuous causes, the discipline it took to achieve a goal, the sentimental relations between parent and child. The spectator's eye moving slowly across these visual pictures, with their realistic scenographic displays and atmospheric effects, was assumed to be absorbed in moral contemplation inspiring a love of virtue and a horror of vice. Diderot sought to solicit the active participation of the spectator in this visual theater of the imagination; to project through aesthetic means a wholeness that was increasingly absent from reality. In this manner, Diderot's tableaux helped to mediate the transition from a highly stratified society marked by authoritative and didactive controls to functionally differentiated, increasingly abstract, secularized, and urbanized modern life requiring new modes of socialization and discipline.[59]

The theater responded to these changes by presenting a visual display of social and aesthetic values, or theatrical scenes that directly confronted and spoke to the beholder. More realistic stage settings (as if the scenes were drawn from nature) garnering local color were among they ways to engage the viewer. In the middle of the eighteenth century there was a turn to historical accuracy in theatrical presentations and a desire to recapture on stage the pictorial records of famous events. First appearing in costumes, this taste soon spread to scenery and decor in an effort to accurately represent historic and topographical places. In 1779 Philippe-Jacques de Loutherbourg created a landscape scene for the theater from sketches he actually made in Derbyshire, and William Capon undertook detailed surveys of old buildings in London in order to anchor his Shakespearian scenery in accurately depicted periods of time.[60] Diderot found much to praise in de Loutherbourg's spectacles of light and shadow performed at his Eidophusikon (translated as "Representation of Nature"). Here Diderot believed the viewer learned to regard the effect of art as that of nature, and nature as that of a scene.[61]

As the theater became obsessed with historical illusion, the stage decorator became no more no less than a restorer of historic monuments composing illusionistic settings from a mere glimmer of a historic detail, anecdote, or time period as archeological imagination was allowed full reign. On this dubious record of visual facts, the stage designer literally recreated a totalistic decor, a representation of an actual locality or the atmosphere of an epoch now called to be a witness pointing out the scene where dramatic events had occurred. The scenographer's focus fell on the ornamental detail, not the architectural structure. His was the work of the copiest or the reproducer, for he was valued for the universality and extravagance of his vision: the representation of all the decorative styles, all the flora and fauna, all the habitats of man from around the world.[62] In the past, it was noted, all that was required for a stage designer was knowledge of the laws of perspective and the mechanics of theatrical devices. But now the designer must be a learned man, arranging sets that would please painters, archeologists, sculptors, architects, even botanists and natural scientists. This interest in realistic settings, more precise than reality and more pleasing to the eye, would absorb the theater until the end of the nineteenth century. This picture theater, however, enclosed the spectator within its visual delights, and by its very literalness stopped the imagination, diminished the expressive power of the actors, and established the primacy of illusion.

Therefore when Karl Friedrich Schinkel's theater designs were published in Berlin in 1819, astonishing the audience with their degree of historic and environmental accuracy, they simultaneously introduced a radical simplification of the scenic ensemble and a return to classical order not to be repeated again until the work of Edward Gordon Craig in the early twentieth century.[63] Like de Wailly and Peyre's designs for the Odeon, Schinkel's perspectival scenes were themselves a commentary on architecture in the city; they were representations meant for the stage as well as the town. As it was impossible to find work as an architect due to the Napoleonic Wars of the first two decades of the nineteenth century, Schinkel instead designed scenery for the theater and for panoramas and dioramas. Culling ideas already developed in pen-and-ink drawings produced while on a trip to Italy in 1803–4, his landscapes and cityscapes, drawn from a high prospect overlooking the view, were often panoramically spread over two pages of his sketchbook.[64] Taking Serlio's three scenes as a point of departure, Schinkel developed his own form of theatricalized landscapes, arranging and rearranging their forms into a

Karl Friedrich Schinkel, The Burning of Moscow Panorama *(1812).*

pleasing stage set that emphasized depth and the horizon, as well as the architectonic nature of volumes and forms. These panoramic views he then transferred to the stage. One of his most popular panoramas, "The Burning of Moscow by Napoleon in 1812," was overwhelming in scale, as it stood 15 feet high and 90 feet long. From this dramatic effect engulfing the viewer, Schinkel learned the art of composing huge public spaces through which the spectator moved, allowing the eye to shift constantly from spatial voids to structural wholes.[65]

In 1815, at the time Schinkel became the official architect charged by Friedrich Wilhelm III to embellish Berlin, he found a city devoid of a plan, its appearance a motley collection of disparate buildings and ill-arranged networks of canals and streets. In the center of the city was the island of Coln, where the royal palace and cathedral stood near a barren and ugly parade ground whose edges were lined with a string of warehouses, factories, shops, and vending booths. It was this island that Schinkel would transform into a theatrical stage set for leisure and living. Through a series of designs for churches, city squares, a civic theater and new museum, warehouses and residential structures, Schinkel turned the center of Berlin into a series of pleasing vistas and perspectives, varying in scale and orientation.[66]

Beginning with his designs for the Royal Theater (Schauspielhaus) in 1818, Schinkel revealed his scenographic approach to the city. The theater was the focal point of an already existing square, flanked on either side by two churches whose architectural forms Schinkel's work carefully echoed and reiterated. On opening night in 1821, Schinkel designed a theatrical backdrop that explained his idea of a totally composed architectural setting, for his architectural monuments were never meant to be seen as isolated objects of art, but as part of a totally balanced and organized urban scenography. The audience looking across the stage of the theater in which they were sitting saw a panoramic view of the new theater framed by the proscenium columns and projecting the point of view outside of the theater toward the city. So Schinkel noted, ". . . . If the scenography must have a more elevated character, then the proscenium should increasingly acquire the essence of the fixed scene of ancient times and therefore be the distinct frame for the entire theatrical representation, a frame within which the action, coming out of the scene as a focal point projected to the outside, represents the most luminous spot of all representation."[67]

A play of vistas, the interior one's inverting the exterior's, demonstrated Schinkel's control over the theatrical setting and visual experience of architecture in the city. By treating the actual cityscape as a panoramic sequence of structures, Schinkel enabled the spectator to perceive these scenes as a theatrical arrangement of vast new urban spaces in which buildings of uniform height receded into the distance.[68] Simultaneously, Schinkel referred to the ancient theater stage as a converging lens concentrating the action into a single point, therefore distancing itself from the surrounding reality. And this distancing, in contrast to Diderot's absorption, was essential to Schinkel's theatrical effect for "The wonderful illusion of an apparent removal of the scene itself, [was the] illusion that consists in the fact that the spectator imagines the action as taking place very far away from him, while he, instead, is seeing it with the clarity afforded by true closeness."[69] For Schinkel, this was the only way to create true illusion: providing a single, big painted backdrop and allowing the spectator's imagination and critical powers to fill in the rest.

Schinkel's 1822 design for a new museum built on the north side of the Lustgarten (pleasure garden) continued to emphasize his urbanistic skills at varying vistas and composed public ensembles. On the opposite side of the garden from the Royal Palace, Schinkel raised his museum on a platform, thus providing a better foil for the Palace and enabling its colonnade when viewed from a distance to be comprehended as a unit. The third facade of the garden was formed by a dense screen of trees with a church in its center. Statues on pedestals stood in front of this screen and were related to statues on the palace bridge in the opposite direction. In this panoramic scene arranged from an ideal point of perspective, openings were balanced against masses, while vistas were alligned with their focal points. From a semi-enclosed vestibule of the museum on the second floor, for example, the

Karl Friedrich Schinkel, Stage Backdrop for opening night in the Schauspielhaus, Berlin *(May 26, 1831).*

spectator looked back through a double screen of columns, in an oblique perspective that placed the museum against the city's panorama as a backdrop.[70] This was a landscape created by man, offering an ordered and stable vista in which the rhythmic movement and the distancing of the eye from close-ups to long-shots, in scanning and traveling views, played important new roles. In Schinkel's work the perspectival stage had reached its ultimate achievement: the scenographic arrangement of the modern city.[71]

During most of the nineteenth century, however, a more elaborate taste for spectacular stage effects, realistic reconstructions, and pageantry was the dominant aesthetic value of the rising bourgeoisie. Their love of ornamentation, exuberant decor, eclecticism, and pastiche became prominent in theatrical settings for the stage as well as the city. Decorative luxury took many forms: in the plush of the seats, in their colors and gilding, in the elaborate staging of stairways, in audacious two-point scenic perspectives, in the grandiose or monumental reconstructions of exotic architecture on stage. The verisimilitude of this scenic imagery became more studied and known than reality. Its illusionistic quality, or the trompe l'oeil visual effects that literally recreated a pictorial scene before the spectators' eyes, may have dulled their literary imaginations and killed the value of the play, but as good imitations and exacting copies this spectacular decor masked the failures of drama and enabled the spectators to become armchair travelers to faraway places or vicarious examiners of a city's physiognomy. The theater could easily display this taste for spectacle and luxury, but it became as well a place for special social rites. Once again the center of focus returned to the ensemble—not just the scenic stage but now the auditorium, the balconies, lobbies, and elegant stairways played specific roles in the bourgeois spectacle of commerce and enterprise. Expecting to be entertained and hoping to escape the problems of reality, the bourgeoisie went to the theater to be seen, to show off their new wealth displayed in their costumes and jewels, to promenade and strut about with their marriageable daughters, to arrange their business affairs and prepare their intrigues. Although the seats of the aristocracy were now occupied by the nouveau riche, social hierarchy was held in its place by the price of tickets, and inequality still remained, condemming the cheapest seats in the upper galleries to a partial view of the stage, and sometimes placing them beyond the range of voices as well.[72]

The epitome of the bourgeoise theater, its culminating act so to speak, was the Paris Opera designed by Charles Garnier in 1861. Emblematic of the transformations Baron von Haussmann was strategically employing throughout Paris, the Opera stood astride new axial boulevards carving their way through the remnants of the medieval city. As a monumental traffic island its electic facades commanded the view from every direction. Its location was visually strategic in yet another manner: it was the centerpiece of Haussmann's drama separating the old Paris from the modern. Located in the new district for pleasure and business, between the new residential districts of the bourgeoisie to the west and the working-class sections to the east, it represented, as Theophile Gautier claimed, "a sort of mundane cathedral of civilization where art, wealth and elegance celebrate their most beautiful rites."[73]

Garnier created a virtual stage for the performance of social rituals by providing a series of entryways, vestibules, foyers, and staircases. These showcase places actually filled a space as large as the stage itself. Interested in offering the spectator a variety of perspectives and theatrical experiences, Garnier actually made actors of the public, adding their own ornamentation to the show: crowds ascending and descending stairways, spectators leaning over balconies, brilliantly clothed spectators mingling in the foyers and lobbies. Entering the vestibule, the theatergoer could linger leisurely, surveying the ticket booths, the axial entries to the auditorium, and the magnificent stairway of honor. The latter, Garnier claimed, were "one of the most important dispositions of theaters, not only because they are indispensable to the ease of movement and circulation, but also because they produce an artistic motif which can be developed broadly, and which can contribute to the beauty of the building."[74] Garnier's intent was to provide the viewer with a series of flat two-dimensional tableaus receding in space, a layered perspectival composition through which the spectator moved changing the picture as his or her position shifted: first through the flat facade, followed by the vestibule, then a sequence of screens, arches, and columns, next the great cupola of the auditorium, followed by the great roof of the stage forming the background to the theatrical tableau.[75]

Toward the end of the nineteenth century, however, the constraints of this theater of spectacle appeared to be insupportable. An expanding middle class produced a mass audience that constantly demanded new forms of entertainment not coded with the status quo of bourgeois morality. Because this middle class desired more uniformity in the arrangement of seats with increased visibility, new theater designs responded to these pressures and consequently became less elaborately appointed, with fewer balconies or boxes, and more communal in organization. Social instability, the crowd in the street, urban chaos, metropolitan growth, and the shift toward corporate and bureaucratic administration all spelled out conditions in which the individual increasingly felt alienated from everyday life. Escape from an overwhelming sense of helplessness fostered by urban estrangement and isolation was one demand placed on the theater. But the advent of theatrical lighting, however, had the opposite effect, tending to augment the spectator's isolation by suddenly submerging the auditorium in a sea of darkness and highlighting the action on stage, taking place over there beyond the viewer's control or participation. The stage was becoming an autonomous space of its own while the spectators were reduced to being mere shadows in darkness.[76] As the integrity of the theatrical whole diminished, the ties binding the audience and the actors were severed: the chairs that once were arranged at the edge of the stage were removed, the audience was no longer allowed to interrupt the performance, nor the actors to repeat sections of the play. Carrying the stigmata of alienation, a theater of separateness, displaying a highly formalistic modern aesthetic, was beginning to emerge.[77]

By the end of the nineteenth century, Emile Zola was teaching the value of naturalistic decor as a new representational mode. Decor, he claimed, should not represent an actual place but should be suggestive of a milieu, a mise-en-scène that

Bibiena Theatrical Design. Inauguration of the Theatre Royale in Turin (December 26, 1740). *Painted by Pietro Domenico Olivero.*

acted with force on the turn of events. Since actions of men were affected by the ambience of a place, its genius loci or atmosphere, so the stage decor should create the visual equivalent of the spirit of a play, establishing both a mood that actors may not throw off and a dramatic space that determined the nature and flow of a drama.[78] Following these instructions, Zola believed, the theater would once again become a place of dreams and a play of analogies. Furthermore electric lighting, essential in establishing this new atmosphere of the stage, actually destroyed the effect of perspectival illusion. Light appeared to be abstract in form and motion, and actors seemed to be caught helplessly in its enframement. While actors increasingly related to and were constituted by the milieu created on stage, the drama grew in depth and its meaning increased in opaqueness. So, it has been argued, the play taking place on a lighted stage now needed to be explained and interpreted to an audience that remained in the dark. And acting needed to be reformed until the actor's personality was removed and she or he held a subordinate (more naturalistic) role, submitting to the overall unity of the production. Consequently, the theatrical director arose, imposing his interpretation on the audience, the actors, the decor, the theater space, and the play until he composed a new work of art, the unified ensemble of lighting, space, motion, and music. Theater and urban life now seemed to offer related experiences, for didn't going to the theater mean placing oneself under the control of the director, subordinating one's will to his interpretation, allowing his totalized vision to substitute for the wholeness so absent from urban reality?[79]

Besides submerging the audience in darkness, and lighting up the stage in an abstract manner, electricity brought other reforms to the theater. Of course it lent itself to the projection of scenic illusions, but it offered new possibilities for motion and rhythm as well. By quick transformations, electric lights at one moment could highlight a part of the stage and then suddenly shift to another part, dramatizing and constantly remodeling space. As a result, the scenographic cube disintegrated, no longer controlled by the laws of perspective nor by static architectural constraints. And sound was as effective in shaping this space, projecting voices and music in back of an actor, to the side of or even next to a spectator. Finally the cinema added its impact by transforming the manner in which spectators perceived the space within which a narrative unrolled. Multiple points of view, close-ups and long-shots, the traveling shot suddenly fragmented the unified perspective of traditional narrative form. The visual setting took on a life of its own, as a succession of images, mobile and fluctuating, now appeared to be taking form outside of the spectator's position, as if events were being projected from a distant point.[80]

Democratic reforms cried out in the early twentieth century for a truly popular theater open and accessible to crowds, one that drew on collective rites and rituals that the public all shared. And as these reforms were met, the theater, or so Adolphe Appia declared, would become "the cathedral of the future"—an entertainment for the masses inspired by both religion and sports.[81] Appia seemed to be the first to note the major scenic reallignments taking shape in the early years of the twentieth century, as well as to understand the new tension and contact created between actors and spectators. Appia claimed these reforms were the result of a new interest in sports and the revival of the Olympic games in 1896, the sculpture of Rodin and the dancing of Isadora Duncan, all arts that placed a new emphasis on the unadorned living body and the unalloyed beauty of natural movement.[82] So, he mused, the theater would become the new harmonious art of time and space, and it would compensate for both the alienation of modern existence and the failure in contemporary times of moral persuasion and traditional bonds on which the contemplative tableau had relied. "Our modern art, destined for spectators imprisoned within themselves, can never serve as an example nor as a norm. Our touchstone will be our experience of beauty—an experience made in common."[83]

Appia wanted rhythmic spaces sculpted out of simple architectural forms, dramatically scored by naturalistic bodies and illuminated by moving light, to be the essential ingredients of his expressive theater. He had experimented, as early as the 1890s, with the use of projections: milieu-creating photographs, shapeless rhythmic tones, and special effects such as clouds, fire, or water.[84] In collaboration with Emile Jaques-Dalcroze, Appia created a totally abstract stage architecture as the appropriate scenery for rhythmic movements. Dalcroze was developing a new rhythmic gymnastics of movement and sculptural body gestures that sought not only to internalize musical rhythms but to express in space and time the body's innermost feelings. Dalcroze wrote

> We can judge a work of architecture only in relation to the space in which it is constructed; and similarly, musical rhythms can be appreciated only in relation to the atmosphere and space in which they move. In other words, musical rhythm can be appreciated only in relation to silence and immobility. . . .[85]

In Dalcroze's system, Appia found the perfect means to exteriorize music and to liberate the body from its clumsy movements.[86] Moreover, his architectonization of the stage ensemble was supposed to represent the physical feelings, movement, and expression of the typical man of the times—the sportsman and the athlete. Because of their prowess, Appia argued, the spectator had become sensitive by extension to the rhythmic articulation of movement involved in all architectural creation.[87] Hence the actor was to the space of the stage, as the architect was to the space of his or her building: both lived in the ambience created by their imaginations. Architectural and scenic language were similar: they were languages of gesture—the lift of the column, the spring of the vault, the rhythmic return of the meander.[88] The scenographic cube, with its illusionism and trompe l'oeil scenery, the stage with its sentimental morality and normative exemplars, had exploded into bits and pieces under modern sensibilities, as space and time, form and movement, gestures and rhythms became the emotive elements.

Edward Gordon Craig would push this architectonic scenery still further, for under his hands stage decoration would become a form of architecture. He believed that the illusionistic stage had to be banished once and for all because it created disharmony among the architectural design of the theater, the painted scenographic picture and the volumetric nature of bodies moving on stage. A single characteristic element appearing on stage, such as a balcony, a portico, a chair, or a fountain, Craig preached, was sufficient to express the whole modern mise-en-scène. Having studied and compared more than 250 models of various habitations from around the world, Craig rejected every element not found in the others until he reduced this habitation to the universal components used by all mankind since the beginning of time. All that remained were the floor, the ceiling, and the walls. From this distillation he made just one scene, arguing that scene-making was an art and not a toy factory, that "the artist is to speak to the spectators through scene, he is not to display a large doll's house for them."[89] All that was needed in addition to this scene was an effective system of lighting, for it alone could change the theatrical mood, enfolding or repelling the actors. Scene and light were to be like two dancers or singers in perfect accord. Never still, lighting flooded the stage or trickled down the walls; it cut or caressed.[90]

After studying classical drama and medieval spectacles, Craig decided that their basic form, so different from the illusionistic stage, was architectural. They were able to call forth spiritual forces deeper than realistic scenography ever could do; they were visual theaters taking advantage of spectacular architectural enclosures. Whether in an amphitheater or a church, the entire setting was the stage, and it was this genuine place and its simple architectonic qualities that he wished to reproduce. Movement was also important in Craig's theatrical reforms: he proposed that a stage in which walls and shapes rose up and opened out, unfolded or retreated in endless motion could become a performance without any actors. Once again someone in search of theatrical reform turned to praise de Loutherbourg, the late eighteenth-century creator of spectacles showing cities aflame and ships in storm without so much as one actor appearing on stage. De Loutherbourg's Eidophusikon was actually an illusionistic spectacle of light and shadow, but Craig saw it as the forerunner of his abstract movable stage, which he called "Scene"—a place that might have been Athens, Rome, or contemporary London, it might have been a mud hut, a palace, or a shop, but it represented for Craig the place in which an untold number of dramas might occur. The link between Craig and de

Loutherbourg lay in the fact that movement and change made the scenery an active agent in the dramatic event. Craig dedicated his 1906 engravings of "Scenes" to Johann Sebastian Bach, for it had been musical rhythm that freed Craig from the clawing grasp of the illusionistic theater and helped him develop his theater of color, light, mobile cubic shapes, and varying spaces that underlined the phases of a drama as music underscored movement. Craig wrote, "The scene also has what I called a face. This face expresses. Its shapes receive the light, and inasmuch as the light changes its position and makes certain other changes, and inasmuch as the scene itself alters together as in a dance—insomuch does it express all the emotions I wish it to express."[91]

Craig was stimulated as well by Serlio's perspectival views of the stage; they seemed the perfect direction to follow if the stage was to be cleared of all its decorative and pictorial clutter yet remain a purely architectonic space. Serlio's illustration of a chessboard stage inspired Craig to conceive of a modern stage of plain flat walls with mobile parts. Sections of the checkerboard could be raised or lowered at the will of the director, moving screens could descend from the ceiling or move in all directions at any tempo. The stage thus became a device to receive the play of light rhythmically, creating an endless variety of mobile cubic shapes and varying spaces.[92] Deep wells, stairs, open spaces, platforms, or partitions created a stage of complete mobility, which Craig believed appealed to the imagination. In his most ideal schemes, Craig conceived of the proscenium as a movable part, like the lens of a movie camera. Without breaking the action, it could quickly create a close-up view by contracting until an actor was able to touch all four corners of the scene, or suddenly it could expand so that it panoramically encompassed a huge crowd.[93]

After studying the masques of Inigo Jones and Ben Jonson, Craig realized that their highly stylized patterns and ceremonial processions could also be used to reform the theater. Against all illusionistic and photographic realism, the ritual of masques and the mysterious appearance of masked actors gave the theater a new magical and spiritual force. Craig felt that the face was separate from the body and could no longer be used to offer realistic forms of expression. Instead it must portray enigmatic and spiritual aspects of life. He even suggested that actors be replaced by marionettes, which he felt erased an actor's unnecessary expressions of emotion and personality. Placed completely under the control of the director, marionettes could mirror more accurately than actors his will and intention. "The mask must only return to the stage to restore expression—the visible expression of the mind—and must be a creation, not a copy."[94] Proposing many different masques between 1905 and 1910, Craig's "Masque of Hunger," for example, revealed a figure of a man with a hideous mask of grief surrounded by a falling black rain. The man's amplified breathing symbolically expressed overwhelming emotion and material deprivation.[95]

With Appia and especially Craig, a symbolic not an imitative theater develops where "that which cannot be known but only hinted at takes precedence over what can be grasped and compared. . . . the general, the representative, the unspecific, is gaining in authority over the 'merely' imitative."[96] Craig, however, would be totally unsuccessful in promoting his theatrical reforms, a failure that John Peter in *Vladimir's Carrot* claims was the result of being ahead of his time, the first real advocate of a closed theatrical form before such a drama had really been created. In Craig's work, the illusionistic perspective stage was transformed into a quest for something limitless and beyond representation: movement in the abstract, rhythmic sounds devoid of signification, visual images without disclosure. Even though Craig advocated a return to popular art forms, he proposed nevertheless an elite theater of the imagination; perhaps even a monological theater without an audience. It was a closed theatrical form that Peter defines as being a total statement of what it was trying to say, a drama not open to questions.[97]

In the manner of its inaccessibility, closed to questioning and dialogue, Craig's art foretold of the intentions of modern architecture, which would insert scenic voids and silent places into the dense visual display of the city. Mies van der Rohe's elegantly frozen glass towers silently composed around Alexanderplatz (plan of 1928) are exemplary of these modernist forms. Perhaps the city could be viewed through the open spaces that lay between the equivalent slab structures formally aligned around the circle, but nevertheless this urbanistic scheme proposed no real dialogue with the city; it commented on neither the visual nor historical form of Berlin. By decomposing the city and substituting instead an immobile and abstract composition, such a pure arrangement of forms inevitably denied the presence of an audience.[98] Craig's work reflected other modernist movements as well. Kasimir Malevich being an obvious comparison, for he too sought to rupture the binds of realism that held the audience to a work of art and instead allow the artist to move into a higher reality, the prophetic beyond where he claimed, "I have destroyed the ring of the horizon and got out of the circle of objects, the horizon ring that has imprisoned the artist and the forms of nature."[99] Or in closer comparison to Craig, Malevich described his "Black Square" in the following manner: "Any painterly surface is more alive than any face from which a pair of eyes and a smile protrude. A face painted in a picture gives a pitiful parody of life, and this allusion is merely a reminder of the living. But a surface lives; it has been born."[100]

Advocates for art forms that existed on the cutting edge, on the threshold of the new, obviously influenced the Futurists' attempts to electrify the theater. Flinging their manifestos against the static nature of painted backdrops and scenic architecture, which they too felt inhibited visual and emotional flights of imagination, they praised instead a new theater of rapid pace, of mechanical movement and clockwork precision—lessons they drew from the modern drama of electricity and urban dynamics. Following Craig, they argued that the stage should be transformed into a huge electromechanical architecture, a luminous stage bathed in multicolored assemblages of light and motion.[101] But instead of closed theatrical forms, the Futurists wanted to establish a new relationship between the actors and the audience. They turned their would-be luminous stage into a performance of exuberant improvisations, outrageous provocations, and inventive condensations. Marinetti believed that people flocked to the theater seeking laughter and an escape from daily routine, not a reminder of the drag of reality. The source of theatrical excitement, he considered, lay in the spectacles of the variety theater, the circus, and burlesque. Through a clever use of parody and ridicule and in a constant flow of colors, simultaneous action, music, mechanical effects, and condensed spectacles or performance pieces, the Futurist theater hoped to undermine traditional forms of the bourgeois drama. In the confusion produced by illogical surprises, mocking effects, and clowning absurdities, the spectator did not always understand the reason for every action, yet felt the direct impact of its sensory appeal. To reduce the distance between the actor and the audience, suddenly a spectator turned into a clown planted in the audience, acrobats undertook daring feats that spoke directly to the viewer's emotions, and hilarious entertainment controlled the show.[102] The Futurists claimed, "reality vibrates around us, hitting us with bursts of fragments with events amongst them, embedded one within the other, confused, entangled, chaotic."[103]

In the work of the Futurists both theatrical performances and scenographic views of the city were infected by a new visual awareness. Not only did they rise up against the bourgeois forms that separated art from life, but they proposed as well to destroy the realistic theater by turning it inside out, allowing material from life to enter the stage and the performer to reach out to shock the spectator. An instinct of play, of transfigurative gestures, of electrifying movement and improvised compositions, "theatricalized" both the stage and reality.[104] Leaving room for surprise and accidents, Marinetti wrote, "Our Futurist theatre jeers at Shakespeare but pays attention to the gossip of actors, is put to sleep by a line from Ibsen but is inspired by red or green reflections from the stalls. WE ACHIEVE AN ABSOLUTE DYNAMISM THROUGH THE INTERPENETRATION OF DIFFERENT ATMOSPHERES AND TIMES."[105] Their visual sensibility, far from searching for closed and abstract theatrical forms as Craig had advocated, pushed each spectator toward a cinematographic view by disrupting the contemplative quality of art and emphasizing visual effects.[106] With their hoped-for but seldom realized kinetic theater, the Futurists wanted to "win the race with cinematography" by paralleling on stage cinematic effects such as variable frames that opened and closed, or split screens and cross-cuttings that interwove simultaneous actions.[107]

Eventually the influence of the cinema on theatrical forms had to be directly addressed. Sergei Eisenstein undertook some of these experimentations. Wanting to create a theater in which material-practical images could be juxtaposed with fictitious-descriptive forms, he brought the theater to the edge of the cinema. He tried different procedures such as close-ups, double and multiple exposures, superimposing images and running two parallel lines together, but these cinematic practices were too strong for the theater to bare. He never achieved on the stage the unity he desired to forge out of actuality and theatricality. Wanting to visualize the maelstrom of the stock market, the dizzy tempo of city streets, the astonishing sea of lights that the big cities of capitalism represented, for example, Eisenstein suggested the idea of "running scenery" when he directed a play written by Pletnev called "Precipice." To capture the drama of an inventor who either raced or was chased through city streets, and who felt trapped in the merciless web of the city, Eisenstein proposed that pieces of buildings and architectural details be carried about the stage by actors on roller skates. Two bankers would hold the stock exchange, the policeman's costume would be decorated with streets, trucks, streetcars, and automobiles, and other actors would transport a blaze of streets lights and electric signs. This double exposure of images in transition, the dynamic intersection of man and the city milieu, was expected to fuse into an expressive whole. Although Eisenstein never produced this play nor designed its scenery, he nevertheless was hinting at the core concepts of film montage: two images when juxtaposed, that is, the double exposures of moving actors and parts of buildings, combining into a new concept expressing either the dizzying tension and changing perspectives of the city of capitalism, or the urban experience of plodding through crowded streets and being lost in astonishing places.[108]

Like the Futurists, Eisenstein wanted to create theatrical works permeated with life, works that prodded the spectator to become bored with "Art" and to prefer instead the drama of reality. He actually staged his production of Tretiakov's "Gas Masks" in a Moscow Gas Factory, hoping to underscore the real-life aspects of the drama. By observing the reactions of spectators, however, Eisenstein realized they were affected far more by the turbines, workers, and smells of reality than by the illusions of fictional representation. Inevitably theater was instilled with artifice, and it thus looked ridiculous in the midst of a real factory. Eisenstein had pushed the theater beyond its limits, to the point that actuality negated its fictional make-up. Consequently Eisenstein turned away from the theater and toward the cinema, where he believed shots of reality could then be edited to produce the emotional sequences and the montage experiences he wanted the spectator to assemble and realize.[109]

Longing for art forms that were coterminous with life, constructions that revealed the layering manner in which the world was put together, artists under the spell of this visual theatricality began to look at the city as if it were a fluctuating and mobile stage setting. The reality of the city as a spectacle began to influence its representational forms. Fernand Léger was one of the earliest artists to see the city from this perspective, viewing it as an industrial landscape composed of still lifes, long-shots, and close-ups reassembled in an imaginary jump-cut space.[110] Modern art, Léger advised, should glorify the industrial object, following the example already set by commerce and industry that showed the artist how to interpret these objects, how to display their scenic and alluring qualities in a manner suitable for the stage. It was the small shopkeeper with the art of window dressing who had turned the city streets into a permanent spectacle of infinite variety.[111] Objects in the city asserted their autonomy through their very proliferation and movement: lights, colors, mannequins, billboards, and buildings were all mobiles visually commanding attention. Consequently the city landscape was rich with common and everyday objects displaying theatrical potential: "To talk about spectacle," Léger wrote in 1924, "is to imagine the world in all its daily visual manifestations."[112] Speed was the essence of an urban age, compressing all the images and objects of a city into a rapid series of hypertropied views colliding with one another, cutouts asserting themselves for a moment before being replaced by a contrasting view. Following this new sensibility to city imagery, Léger declared, the theater of spectacle was formed out of light, color, and moving images.[113] Just look at the city streets, and there one could find the origin of the modern performance! Two men carrying gigantic letters in a wheelbarrow just removed from the marquee of a theater, for example, turned the city streets into a spectacle that everyone stopped to watch: this was a witty city of pulsating energy and rhythm, contrasting and incongruent views, a totally man-made environment, alive and vital.[114]

The Bauhaus was also involved with this visual revolution and in the reforms affecting theatrical presentation and scenographic views of the city. Laszlo Moholy-Nagy believed that the traditional theater was a disseminator of centered action, a kind of eyewitness report that subordinated visual illustration to narrative or propagandistic forms. Modern theater instead ought to be new assemblages of sound, color, motion, space, and form developing away from a verbal context and moving toward explosive action. He too turned to the circus, the operetta, and vaudeville, praising these arts for their spectacular feats and simultaneous actions. Envisioning a new theater of suspended bridges and drawbridges piercing the stage in diagonal, horizontal, and vertical lines—where platforms rotated and disklike areas and movable stages brought some actions close up and kept others in the background—Moholy-Nagy saw the total stage action as a great dynamic-rhythmic process in which man and the background achieved total harmony, in which theatrical and urban space interpenetrated one with the other.[115] "The new space [he wrote] originates from free-standing surfaces or from linear definition of planes (wire frames, antennas), so that the surfaces stand at times in a very free relationship to one another, without the need of any direct contact."[116]

Moholy-Nagy would talk in 1936 about creating a monumental architecture of light—actually huge light displays in the open air. By utilizing special materials and reflectors, he felt it would be possible to project light onto clouds and other gaseous substances, which then would be seen as one flew by in an airplane or walked through its mist.[117] "With light," he wrote, "architecture itself can be changed. With light one may pull together walls and windows or break them down into small units. With neon or other lights a completely different building outline can be created overnight in place of the actual structure. In the future, light . . .

will play an essential part in architecture."[118] Simultaneously architectural form was altered by motion: once the frontal axial view had dominated its arrangement, but with the advent of the balloon and the airplane, Moholy-Nagy claimed, architecture could be viewed as well from the sides, from above, even from below. "Architecture appears no longer as a static structure, but, if we think of it in terms of airplanes and motor cars, architecture must be linked with movement. This changes its entire aspect so that a new formal and structural congruence with the new element, time, becomes manifest."[119] Consequently a pedestrian's and a driver's visual experience of objects differs: from a moving vehicle objects come into new relationships with each other, for which the pedestrian has no eye. This new space articulation in architecture, Moholy-Nagy believed, would bring about a better relationship between land and buildings as well. Already the huge undivided glass windows of modern structures enabled nature to penetrate the interior of the structure; while different space and time configurations were brought together by the reflections and mirrorings of shop and automobile windows. "Mirroring means in this sense the changing aspect of vision, the sharpened identification of the inside and outside penetration."[120]

Transformations within the early modern visual perception, which involved not only the theater and cinema but the city and architecture as well, enables comparison with the City of Spectacle, for once again in contemporary times there is a preoccupation with the formal and the visual, with kaleidoscopic flux and change, illogical patterns and non-narrative themes. Like the early moderns, the City of Spectacle takes the visual effects of form as the objects of its analyses. The question remains to be asked, however: by focusing so narrowly on visual perception and the representational play of forms, what has been ignored? As Peter noted in *Vladimir's Carrot,* artistic expressions that overwhelm the spectator with visual spectacles and fantastic environments are, at the same time, not open to dialogue and questioning. "Art of any kind is, or we think it is, the creation of other worlds with which we can have a dialogue. And if we are engaged in a dialogue we can neither suspend judgement nor simply submit, not even in delighted recognition or a feeling of identity."[121]

Siegfried Kracauer was aware of some of the negative aspects of the early modernists' admiration of and enthrallment with spectacle. He called all visual forms structured by a rapid flow of discrete fragments and short-term events "ephemeral phenomena": forms such as city streets, the circus, sports events, and theatrical revues. Kracauer felt that these entertaining image spectacles, far from renewing perceptual sensibilities and forging new political associations, were instead the surface ornamentations of the twentieth century, which bound the spectator to a world of passive visual entertainment. Leisure time was a new phenomenon for urban workers in the early decades of the twentieth century, and theater for the masses became simply an artful diversion of time. Mass audiences were thrilled by replications of themselves in decorative patterns: whether in the geometric precision of dancers in revue, gymnasts in formation, or crowds on parade. Perhaps these collective and routinized forms, what Kracauer called "mass ornaments," were but a parody of the linear assembly line and the efficiency of Taylorized body movements, their alienating forms transcended through a pleasurable mirroring of their figural patterns. But ornamental patterns, he insisted, only observable from a distant or aerial view, effaced the presence of the individual in the organized fabrication of the mass. More than this, they focused the spectator's attention on the visual flow of discrete events.[122]

Because modern city life, Kracauer explained, was routinized and depersonalized, pleasure was envisioned as an imaginary escape from repetition and boredom into a world of pure play and artifice. For this reason, interiors and facades as glamorous and superficial coverings simulating various architectures became popular constructions: the Vienna Room, the Bavarian Room, and the Jazz Room of the Haus Vaterland in 1920s Berlin, for example, were scenographic recreations inspired by the lyrics of popular songs, but painted in painstaking detail.[123] But one step away from the real thing, these aesthetic surface coverings enabled everyone to experience momentarily the feeling that they were indeed rich and famous.

Presenting exotic and hypnotizing pictures of faraway lands, these simulated environments conjured up the distractions and absentmindedness of travel, diverting attention away from the monotony and ugliness of everyday life. A flight of images, the killing of time, an emptying out of all meaning—these Kracauer noted were offered as the perfect illusory escape for white-collar urban workers.[124] Entertainment in the early twentieth century, a time when so many processes were left unexplained or invisible to the naked eye, was confined to surface appearances, delighting in the easy recognition of identifiable visual icons and emblems. Just like postmodern times, these artificial environments, Kracauer claimed further, reflected an increasingly fragmented world, a globe divided into discrete geographical units, but then reexperienced as a uniform surface through a combinatorial montage of coexisting but distinct scenic spaces so tightly recomposed into a glamorous unity that not a contradictory image could squeeze through the covering.[125]

Kracauer believed that an overstimulating flow of vivid images constantly buffeted the pedestrian about in the labyrinthine streets of the modern city. These visual shocks and fragmented experiences were subsequently rearranged by the spectator into a comprehensive unity, albeit in a distracted and sonnambulant manner. Far from being a new visual sensibility as the early modernists declared, the fragmentation of everyday life enabled the superficial to insinuate itself into the modern metropolis, Kracauer found, producing only mild astonishment by its unintentional but assertive pose.[126] The city actually became a mechanism for diversion, exemplified in the architectural and decorative splendor of the 1920s' Berlin movie palaces. These theaters were sustained at great profit by the urban mass's addiction to distraction. Within the palace's darkened and stylized interior, a dreamlike atmosphere enveloped the spectator who passively absorbed the visual panorama unfolding on the screen. Building on modern visual sensibilities, these theaters kept the audience's eye trained on the peripheral, and subsequently veiled from consciousness the fact that the show actually failed to produce significant meanings or develop awareness of the social injustices taking place outside the theater's walls.[127]

In turn the visual experience of city streets, the shock of their constantly changing and shifting imagery, was translated in cinematic form into a fearful and impenetrable place. Represented as a corrupt and dangerous threat to life, the modern city set its snares to trap the unassuming visitor or to entangle the well-intentioned hero. The individual had to struggle as best as she or he could in this crowded jungle, where traffic and pedestrians ebbed and flowed in indifferent and uncaring waves. Fire engines and police were filmed as they rushed through its streets or gave chase to fugitives and thieves. Overwhelming insecurity, the inversions of fate, and menacing adventures were the early cinema's stock manner for depicting metropolitan existence and for distracting the public in playful constructions. Kracauer thought the essence of modernity was captured in these expressive images of the metropolis. Sometimes dreamlike, often evasive and empty as mere ornamental facades and city streets could be, city images were fleeting, ever changing, simultaneously full of nervous anxiety and astonishing nuances. Whatever their ambiguities and threats, their exhilarations and promise, they gave evidence of visual sensibilities and modes of experiencing reality that constituted the essence of a modern aesthetic.

Like it or not, the spectacle entranced the viewer through its stunning theatricality: its very nature was to put on a show by posing and provoking, outwitting and revealing. Assuming a stage presence, the theatrical longed for a roomful of spectators that it tried to lure through a panoply of visual tricks—through quotations of historical forms, by repetitions that reduced the image to a formal pattern, by luminous projections, scalings, layerings, and superimpositions. Michael Fried has written in an essay entitled "Art and Objecthood" (1967) that a war exists between the pictorial arts and the theater, a war in which the visual arts can be the winners only as long as they remain self-contained or closed compositions relating only to their own materials and genre. But when a painting is posed, when it exhibits itself in front of a public, that is when art is concerned with how its look affects spectators' perception; then art degenerates into the theatrical.[128] Following Fried's claims against the theatrical, the pictorial arts should remain closed works of art, not open to questions or dialogue. Yet as we have seen, the line separating theatrical forms from self-sufficient works is never so clearly drawn. Welcomed or not, the performative and spectacular mode intrudes into the aesthetic of the city, the theater, and art—a simple twist of perspective reveals their presence. Just how to evoke audience involvement, to open the theater to everyday life or represent civic and moral values on stage, to reveal something spiritual beyond the reach of formal expression: these questions have always been the other side of every attempt to establish works of art as autonomous, pure, and exclusive.

As the historical record has shown, the theater has at times constructed, intentionally or not, a social model of the city. Richard Schechner calls these models "cities-as-production" and notes that they are sometimes harmonious, but oftentimes fractious. He claims "there may be ritual unity or contentious dialectics at the heart of a community. But in either case the City is an arrangement, a negotiation among parts."[129] Sometimes, however, the theater retreats from this ideal situation, sliding back into easy formulas, passive audiences, and apolitical texts. Schechner adds, "What's left is what we have in so many of the [postmodern] solo works: brilliant, but not enough; personalistic rather than concerned with the polis, the life of the City, the life of the people. . . . What's missing is a heart for the City as such. The work does not weep for, or be in a rage for/against, the life of the people. And no matter how we want to avoid social issues, politics, the life of the people in its collective manifestations, the City—as tragedy, satire, celebration, farce—is not only what theatre is about but its chief glory."[130]

Of course we can blame modern architecture in the 1920s for abandoning the "city-as-production" and replacing it with an "essential" form stripped of anything that reeked of theatricality. Instead of glorifying the metropolis for the spectacle that its noise, its motion, its chaotic visual montage created, modern culture was in an orthogonal state of mind begging to reorganize this fragmented jumble of views. So Le Corbusier believed a new dignity would be brought to the city if the architect imposed a pure geometrical configuration upon the existing city, a rational cartesian grid that ruthlessly separated functional areas, allowing the straight line and the right angle to dominate.[131] Decomposed into pure forms and rigid classifications and dedicated to machine efficiency and technological progress, the modern city would be stripped of any scenographic compositions or theatrical gestures that beckoned the beholder. This was as silenced and mute a city as ever could be!

Of course the pure, crystalline images of modern architecture always engendered the less pure pleasure of looking, for architecture as a visual theater was the city observed, the city on stage, and this as we have seen always entailed a less perfect and often ambiguous look. The visual spectacle is the lure of sensuality and excess living off of the delirium produced by seeing and being seen. Its play of signs, the total richness of its imagery, which modernism could never completely erase, actually undermines the coherence of its overall form. These tendencies were already apparent in the Hollywood musicals of the 1940s and 1950s. "On the Town" (1949), for example, presents New York as an elaborate artifice, one gigantic montage of sites through which the actors sing and dance. But this staging of city space is inherently an ambivalent form, and so it has been suggested, the song "New York, New York it's a wonderful town. The Bronx is up and the Battery down. . .", a device repeated throughout the movie, actually becomes a cue, keeping the actors from getting lost in the confusion of sites and threatening experiences of big-city life. The post–World War II city had become a place of open-ended happenings and ambiguous stories, in which the combinatorial possibilities surpassed the narrative plot.[132] Once again, city space was typified as the site of signs and a flux of symbols, although its visual richness and plenitude presented an illusion that change was only a matter of transforming symbols and signs, rearranging them in new patterns and combinatorial motifs.[133]

Thus the postwar city reentered the theater bracketed by quotation marks, a show-within-the-show that enabled a pause in the narrative flow but did not project a believable image of reality. This theater of imagery inherently problematized the presence of actors and the reception of audiences as it engendered a split between display and reference, between things and meanings. A unified audience had become an allusion, a figure that had disappeared slowly since the times of Inigo Jones. In that theater it could be assumed naturally that the spectators, drawn as they were from an aristocratic elite, understood the visual messages of sovereign authority and civic harmony that the theatrical setting encoded. But the cinema, and the postmodern theater of proliferating images, must assume instead that a plurality of viewing publics exists, entailing fractured and multiple points of view. Postmodern performance is based on the very rejection of shared experience and narrative form, those magnets that held together the bits and pieces of a play or a picture in a centered and comprehensible whole. Instead the postmodern spectacle is an ongoing composition, and the city or the play a negotiated arrangement of scenes. Its very theatricality lies in the experience of what is being projected and in the flow of its fragments, its startings and stoppings, repetitions and redoublings, slowdowns and speedups.[134]

Robert Wilson's "CIVIL warS" is prototypical of the contemporary theater, for this interwoven complex of images and sounds has been developed not only in disjointed fragments and unfolding segments, each one performed in a different part of the world, but in this traveling panorama there is no centered view, no coherent message, no enframed perspective. The show is itself a projection of images and symbols of indeterminate meanings, which recycle and return, are enlarged or diminished, posed or transposed, so that multiple themes at play are linked in sequence and carried along by a single flow of rhythmic motion.[135] Each spectator is left to follow the cues that the stream of instantaneous views provides without assuming that everyone has read the same history books, been told the same myths, overheard the same fragments of conversation, or retained the same memories. Meaning floats above or below or alongside of this ambiguous and open-ended sequence of images, only hinting at coherence in fragments and traces. In this imagery theater, flow and mobility have once against scattered all contextual reference while literary or rhetorical forms have exploded into the visual, alluding to offstage messages and visual traces, of solipsisms, ellipsisms, and intertextual referentiality and refractions that the spectator must connect despite their indecipherable nature. This pastiche of borrowed imagery problematizes more than ever the spectator's presence and threatens her or his comprehension of meaning and form.

The problematic presence of a collective audience and the failures of architecture as a narrative gesture were also the dilemmas around which architecture in the city seemed to falter during the early 1970s. A nostalgic urge drove architects at first to call for a return to a symbolic order and to iconic messages tied to the realities of everyday experience, hoping in this manner to be purged of the alienating purities and abstract formalisms of modernism. Referring to the tragic and comic scenery of the Serlian stage, they contrasted and compared these views in a reworked manner that made a distinction between past and present scenographic arrangements. The tragic stage was assumed to be that of princely authority, Alberti's ideal city formally composed and orderly arranged, a scene from which urban architecture and urban scenographic compositions continuously drew succor. The comic stage, on the other hand, represented the chaotic and boisterous medieval city, more of an everyday scene to be transformed by the architect into a more dignified and tragic whole.[136]

Robert Venturi referred to these stages as the tragic scene of high modernism and the comic of popular art, the one an aristocratic view, the other a vulgar form.[137] But this was a false comparison, for both stages as we have seen are perspectival views, frontally composed, enframed and bounded. Both represent scenes that exist prior to their staging, and encompass a method by which to project and accurately copy their views. Because no one really believes the myth of representational verisimilitude, that the actual and the ideal are one, the visual image necessarily becomes a conflictual view seen from multiple perspectives. But the Serlian ideal stages assumed to the contrary the presence of a universal viewing public to which their imagery was directed and imposed. They admitted both a narrative format and an integrated community that shared the same point of view. Whatever disagreed, whatever challenged, whatever was marginal to the tragedy or farce was banished from the stage, therein erasing the contradictory status of representation. Those who draw a false dichotomy between the tragic and the comic stages imply in addition that the tragedy of classical art ignored the ludic, the improper, the ordinary, indeed all forms of popular culture in order to establish its utopian world of eloquent and reserved decorum far removed from the banalities and vulgarities of everyday life. Yet the boundaries between high and popular art are never so clearly separated nor carefully maintained. The witty and the vernacular, or the mannered and the decorous, have always been contaminated by imitations and translations stolen from each other. One is hardly more ideal and the other more real as has been presumed. By maintaining the mythology and overestimating the purities of high modernism, architects of the 1970s and 1980s hoped that lost traditions would be regained, that history and everyday visual reality once rejected could be reinscribed in new projections of the comic theatrical stage. But something else has destroyed our visual perspective of city scenes, our shared memories that enliven representational views. In this current age, the cinema, television, and video have a capacity for organizing our visual pleasure that lies far outside of the architecture of perspectival views; long ago they have taught us to view the city as a gigantic spectacle of contradictory, paradoxical, and ambiguous scenes explicitly constructed and posed.

If this killed that, as Victor Hugo wrote, the book killing architecture, then Venturi has been shrewd enough to surmise that television has killed the book. Therefore he proposed that architecture should draw its solace from the mass media, accepting a role as a marginalized social force yet gaining in return from popular appeal.[138] The Strip, the American Main Street, the linear corridor of motion and messages were quintessentially, or so Venturi and Scott Brown argued, the conventional and commonsense cityscape and the reality of everyday life that should configure American architecture. Here, as in advertisements and graphic design, one finds lettering as ornament, hybrid and contradictory images of pure visibility, the theatrical pose and the hype. But the real problem with the return to narrative architecture lay with the message, not with the forms as Venturi suggested, because the fragmentations and successive redoublings of the mass media prevent the spectator from comprehending reality as a coherently organized totality. The images of architectural environments presented to the viewer on television, from overblown billboards, by advertisements, and in the movies are stereotypical forms taken from a set of fictional representations. Their pleasure, produced by the quick recognition of picture recall, is hardly the effect of a deep structured symbol system or an architecture parlante meant to communicate. Graphically designed for consumer appeal, these images work on our emotions because they are ordinary and anonymous views, and then repeated again and again they become formal patterns abstracted and closed off from any critique.[139]

As architects increasingly reduced their work during the 1970s and 1980s to just another form of merchandise, judgment about popular taste was deferred, for their art became merely a commentary about codes of representation and the theatrical devices of the artifice and its presentation. It was neither a discourse about symbolic meanings nor urban reality.[140] A certain passivity prevailed, urging the spectator to accept the city as it appeared and to forget about one's civic obligations, humanity's sufferings, or the construction of perception and social connectedness. Fragments taken from architectural history books, bits remembered from American streetscapes, images drawn from the mass media and then reassembled and transposed in overlapping and interlacing forms are no other than a hermetically sealed pattern language or a syntactic play of images devoid of semantic content. Supposedly the reality of the popular environment was revealed in the theatrical way that it looked, but city images reduced to formalistic devices became the City of Spectacle: scenographic compositions arranged for a silent and unquestioning spectator. The tendency to hide behind a purely visual facade constantly undermined, as Kracauer explained, a more critical attempt to have architectural form and the total theater of the city highlight contemporary attitudes and aspirations. The artifice and ornaments of conventional architecture and everyday forms deny that art can instruct through pleasure and please through instruction. Devoid of a social or critical framework, most architects of the 1970s and 1980s remained unconcerned about how the space of the city was produced or what economic, social, aesthetic, and legal controls influenced its form. Symbols and signs do not produce their meaning alone. It is not their visible form that conveys the message, but the codes by which they are produced and the social context that configures their expression. As closed dramatic forms, both architecture and the theater in the 1970s and 1980s completely eclipsed this relationship to the city-as-theatrical-production.

four

The Art of Collective Memory

The little Aphrodite, with her connexions, her antecedents and references exhibiting the maximum of breakage, is no doubt as lonely *a jewel as ever strayed out of its setting; yet what does one quickly recognize but that the intrinsic lustre will have, so far as that may be possible, doubled? She has lost her background, the divine creature—has lost her company, and is keeping, in a manner, the strangest; but so far from having lost an iota of her power, she has gained unspeakably more, since what she essentially stands for she stands for alone, rising ineffably to the occasion.*

HENRY JAMES[1]

. . . the true museum of Rome, which I am talking about, is composed, it is true, of statues, colossi, temples, obelisks, triumphal columns, baths, circuses, amphitheaters, triumphal arches, tombs, stuccoes,

frescoes, reliefs, inscriptions, fragments of ornaments, building materials, pieces of furniture, implements, etc., but it is no less composed of the places, sites, mountains, quarries, antique routes, of the respective positions of ruined towns, of geographic connections, of the mutual relationships of all objects, of souvenirs, local traditions, of still extant uses, of parallels and comparisons which can only be drawn within the country itself.

QUATREMÈRE DE QUINCY[2]

The Paradox of the Museum

For many who lived in its whirl, the nineteenth century represented a world of ruins and fragments, emptied of meaningful traditions and authentic memories that once connected the present to the past. In such a world, everything seemed to be collectible: treasures transferred to the museums of culture, reprints and copies relocated as souvenirs in domestic interiors, city views and architectural monuments reconstructed and preserved as the landscapes of heritage. Walter Benjamin believed that a deep and pervasive memory crisis haunted the nineteenth century. Memory after all was a regressive gesture, holding onto a past that had been torn asunder by the hurricane winds of progress emanating from the nineteenth century's political, industrial, and urban revolutions. Benjamin thought in contradistinction that memory springing from the natural chains of tradition should be like an epiphany, flashing up in ephemeral moments of crisis, searching to exhibit at that particular time the way of the world in order to direct one's pathway toward the future. In the nineteenth century, however, this natural, traditional sense of memory was forgotten, replaced by a constructed linear series of events, a continuum of time, entitled "official history."[3] This God's-eye view of history, Benjamin argued, was built on a false memory or dream from which the twentieth century must be awakened. For Benjamin believed that historical insight was like a scale, one side weighted with the past, the other with the present—many insignificant and unobtrusive events might be assembled on the side of the past, but the present should be weighted with only a few graspable and important events. If not evenly balanced in this manner, as happened in the nineteenth century, then historical insight would be biased by neohistoricist empathy.[4]

So today we might say that the pervasive appearance of historic districts in our Western cities, the nostalgically designed theme parks and historically coded styles of life, have tilted the scale toward a contemporary form of memory crisis. Ripping fragments of buildings or artifacts from their original contexts and then collecting and preserving them in nineteenth-century museums is not that distinct an act from attempts to transform our present-day cities into outdoor museums whose architectural streetscapes and spatial stratas become privileged landscapes to explore in pleasure or dismay. If the nineteenth century sought stabilizing roots and permanent values in rare and treasured works of art, hoping to quell the explosions of progress and revolution; if the material value of these artifacts was enhanced as monetary value dematerialized in that century's creation of newfangled credit systems and speculative stock markets, then this act of collecting and retaining remnants from the past in face of increasing change and immateriality only added to that century's pervasive sense of flux and uncertainty. Because the museum's collection is built on this essential paradox—both closure and openness—it produces more anxiety than it absorbs. Thus our contemporary memory crisis with its attendant rash of commemorative acts may be based less on the production of synthetic memories that the migration of history into advertising and the nostalgia industry seems to affect and more on the paradoxical assumptions embedded within the methodology of curatorship and the ideology of the collection.[5]

The museum's paradox stems from the nineteenth century and is cleverly outlined in Michel Foucault's famous comparison: "Flaubert is to the library what Manet is to the museum. They both produced works in a self-conscious relationship to earlier paintings or texts—or rather to the aspect in painting or writing that remains indefinitely open. They erect their art within the archive."[6] So, Foucault believed, Flaubert was the first author of the nineteenth century to realize that imagination grew out of reading, among signs, from book to book stored within a library [fiction's labyrinthian web of textuality], while Manet's "Déjeuner sur l'Herbe" or "Olympia" were the first paintings to be visualized in comparison to the network of paintings organized into periods and styles within the museum's collection. By internalizing the external world within the storehouse of the library or museum, these nineteenth-century institutions focused on the reader or spectator rather than the essential meaning of books or works of art in themselves.[7] They inverted what Hegel called the aim of art "to strip the world of its inflexible foreignness . . . to make it into something the mind can recognize as its own product, its own image, so that man can enjoy in the shape of things an external realization of himself."[8]

Librarians and curators dream of complete collections even while they acknowledge that every act of totalization can only be partial, a fragment of universal knowledge or a part of the history of art. Because the collector's series can never be closed—there is always another book to be written, another object of art to examine—the series necessarily opens an endless desire for an imaginary collection where all series of objects will form complete sets, a perfect representation, starting with their primitive origins and advancing to their final stage of mature development. Within the confining walls of the museum, in particular, the spatial juxtaposition of heterogeneous and arbitrarily associated artifacts is miraculously transformed into a carefully studied and ordered display. It assumes that the curator can create a rational organization of works of art that are simultaneously deprived of their spatial and temporal contexts and estranged from their origin and function. This is the fiction on which the museum is built: by asking that a fragment stand in for the whole or that a set of series produce an adequate representation of the history of art, it demands that the spectator cover over the voids left out of the imagined totality. Take away the fabulations of the curator and the museum's collection may simply disintegrate into a random display of bric-a-brac and assorted objects. Thus the paradox becomes apparent as it is acknowledged that the museum may at best be only a memory device based on fictional images drawn up by museum directors, art historians, archeologists, and antiquarians.[9]

The museum offers the viewer a particular spatialization of knowledge—a storage device—that stems from the ancient art of memory. Since classical times, as Frances Yates explained, the art of memory depended on developing a mental construction that formed a series of places or "topoi" in which a set of images were stored: images that made striking impressions on the mind. Using this device, an orator trying to remember a speech, for example, located specific images as cues to parts of his speech in the rooms of his imaginary place system. The formation of the sequence of spaces, like the rooms of a house or the streets and places of a city, was essential, for the same set of places would be used repetitively as a memory prompt for different material. To recall specific facts, or to remember the parts of a speech, the orator visited the imaginary rooms, passing through the house in sequence and demanding of each location its specific contents.[10] By the nineteenth century, the museum had become such a memory device: its rooms or "topoi" were places to stop and to look around, to visually observe the common and contrasting features, the arbitrary analogical relationships that arranged the history of art into self-enclosed periods, schools, and styles. The path through the sequence of rooms narrated the evolutionary development of history and simultaneously walled in the heterogeneity of time.

Thus within the museum's paradox there is as well a fundamental distinction to be made between history and memory that neither the collector, the archeologist, nor the antiquarian appears to address. Maurice Halbwachs drew a distinction in his writings on "Collective Memory" in the 1920s, noting that where tradition ends, history begins.[11] As long as memory stays alive within a group's collective experience, he argued, there is no necessity to write it down or to fix it as the official story of events. But when distance appears, conferring its distinctions and exclusions, opening a gap between the enactments of the past and the recall of the present, then history begins to be artificially recreated. History divides the continuum of time into static periods and didactic stages, when in reality time

John Blaeuw, Italie . . . oud en Nieuw Rome, *Frontispiece,* Views of Rome *(1724).*

exhibits undemarcated and irregular boundaries. History whips a disparity of details and fragments into a unitary whole, relocating these within newly erected frameworks. And these frameworks in turn enable the historian to establish comparisons and contrasts, thereby recomposing the variety of times and places into a uniform pattern of thematic shifts and minor variations, while leaving a range of inquiry outside of its posited mold. With this illusory structure, however, a universal history or a summary vision of the past is erected, tipping the scales toward historicism as it did in the nineteenth century.

Authentic or Reconstructed History

Yet as Walter Benjamin noted, revolutionary classes always believe they are exploding this linear continuum of time and this false sense of historicism. As a consequence, they immediately inaugurate a new calendar functioning as "a historical time-lapse camera," where flashes of memory are supposed momentarily to arrest the flow of time, leaving behind blank spaces as days of remembrance or handles on memory. Blank spaces enabled a community to withdraw from their activities of work, allowing them time to relax and to focus attention on rituals and traditions. "They [the blank spaces, the heterogeneous fragments of time] are days of recollection, . . . not marked by any experience . . . They are not concerned with other days but stand out from time."[12] Nevertheless, these collective days of remembrance, Benjamin found, had been quickly secularized in the nineteenth century, becoming leisure events: the melancholic empty time of public holidays and dreadfully boring weekends. All the monuments and marks of memory, just like the days of celebratory remembrance, were hollowed out of lived experiences and loaded instead with wishful dreams and anxious moments.[13] What Benjamin called that whore, the eternal "once-upon-a-time" residing in "the brothel of historicism," erased every trace of authentic experience, seducing random and scattered events into its universalizing panorama. Experience became fragmented and the unity of community irretrievably lost.

Side by side with these recreations and reconstructions of history emptied of meaningful experiences and felt remembrances, Benjamin observed, the very landscape of the nineteenth-century city had restructured the spectator's visual perception. The great collective experiences of that century—that is, the glass arcades, department stores, industrial exhibitions, and even the promenades and passageways of the city—had all been transformed into antiquarian gestures artificially resuscitating, neutralizing, and trivializing every lived event and actuality. For Benjamin, this was the absolute death of the phantasmagoria of history, and the erasure of all the fire and revolution of the street, because these artificial stagings of the nineteenth century actually put the city on display. City landscapes and diversionary architecture became matter-of-fact reality in the nineteenth century, beckoning to the beholder with a posed theatricality and a universal familiarity. They hid all the mysteriousness and indecipherability of social reality behind their glittering and contrived masquerades.[14]

So closely linked were the city landscape and the architecture of entertainment—both designed for consumption and display—that one became the necessary perceptual and visual shift that enabled the other to rise. The culprit was machine production, or so Benjamin argued, for commodities serially reproduced from identical molds or a city of architectural objects composed in repetitious manner were both deprived of all uniqueness and devoid of the customs of craft. Having lost their aura, their ability to return the gaze of the spectator, a detachable nimbus was transferred to the copy, the reprint, the reproduction, a nimbus that greatly augmented the sense of the similar and familiar. And novelty, the darling of every epoch's fashionable taste, turned the historical past into something inherently passé. Thus a great storehouse arose filled with antiquated relics, forgotten idols, and misplaced memories waiting patiently to be reappropriated by the dictates and modes of fashion.[15] Consequently, within the spatial composition of the nineteenth-century city, the aestheticized past reappeared as a gallery of images and serial reflections, a condition in which the eye of the city traveler inevitably became insensitive to and easily distracted by this visual array. "Architecture," Walter

Benjamin wrote, "has always represented the prototype of a work of art the reception of which is consumed by a collectivity in a state of distraction."[16]

Benjamin believed that a work of art should communicate something to the viewer, and thus arose his melancholy lament as he saw the visual experiences of architecture and city landscapes fall in value and felt tradition being excluded from the unfolding panorama of historicism. When signs refer to things in an indifferent manner, they signify a loss of aura and a lapse into historicism. For Benjamin historicism was "a methodical exercise in oblivion, condemned to perpetuate the Fall [from Paradise, from the pure state of language] it innocently ignores . . ."[17] Subsequently all self-perpetuating acts of forgetting take the form of "distractions," never allowing the essence of a thing to penetrate perception.[18]

Yet city spaces and architectural landscapes often have been the active systemizers of memory. How did they suddenly become in the nineteenth century such passive retainers, such plastically arranged panoramic vistas concealing heterogeneous reality from view? When Maurice Halbwachs first visited London, for example, he took walks around the city literally and figuratively with different companions. An architect taught him how to look at the arrangement of streets and the style of buildings; an artist drew his attention to the color and lines of the city, its shadows and lights; a historian pointed out historical spots and noteworthy places. These memories and views shared in common, Halbwachs asserted, were the cues that helped him to recall and to stay in contact with the memories he retained of his visit to that city. Halbwachs felt that city spaces that surround our everyday life often appear to be constant and unchanging even, and perhaps specifically, in the face of great wars, national calamities, and political upheavals, for every collective memory always is embedded in a spatial framework.[19]

> Now space is a reality that endures: since our impressions rush by, one after another, and leave nothing behind in our mind, we can understand how we can recapture the past only by understanding how it is, in effect, preserved by our physical surroundings. It is to space—the space we occupy, traverse, have

> continual access to, or can at any time reconstruct in thought and imagination—that we must turn our attention. Our thought must focus on it if this or that category of remembrances is to reappear.[20]

In opposition to Halbwachs, Benjamin found that it was precisely associative structures of remembrance, no matter how spatial they might be, that the hurricanes of tumult and revolution in the nineteenth century had torn into tatters and shreds. Abetted by photography, the concept of an organic city totality—one that gave rise to involuntary memory—died and in its place rose a new visual perception, an archival consciousness that focused on details, on the recollection of past images, on the comparison and contrast of similarities and differences. The photograph was an excellent recorder of the past; it offered greater control over what could be termed "historic." But simultaneously, it was a destroyer of tradition. From the camera's viewpoint, the past was a pile of rubble and the present a chaos of information; both offered a thousand views to be appropriated and recorded. Thus it was from out of the debris produced in the wake of modernity that the collector of photographs appeared like a ragpicker rummaging among fragments.[21] For the photograph ripped an image out of its traditional context and brought the view so close that unassimilated details and hidden features entranced and distracted the eye. The authentic experience of viewing a building, of visiting a city, of exploring a milieu declined as the photographic journal and pictorial press, a new form of image writing, exploited reproducible exposures and vicarious travels. The look of the world was being reduced in the nineteenth century to the flat photographic surface of collapsed time and transported facsimiles.

There is a corollary to the shift of visual sensibility found in Benjamin's crisis of memory that arose in the nineteenth century, and it lies within the development of a curatorial conception of monuments and artifacts. As the photograph opened a gap between the moment of looking and the time of recording, similarly the museum isolated, collected, and transported cultural treasures from one period and context to another time and place. So cloistered, it was an obvious step to

Reinagle and Barker, Panoramic View of Rome from the Tower of the Capitol *(1804).*

compare and contrast this heterogeneous albeit sensuous collection of artifacts merely by the manner of their surface appearance. Under the rational gaze of the art historian, objects in the newly established museums were sorted and shifted about until they began to fall into evolutionary and developmental periods and styles. The photograph was the perfect companion for a curator's mentality that sought either to distinguish schools, styles, and periods of paintings by examining details or to establish the attribution of works of art by inspecting the authenticating marks of an artist.[22]

The curatorial model, however, posed yet another problem. Once artifacts had been retrieved from the ravages of time and the neglect of communities, safeguarded within the protected walls of a museum, how might their fragmented and damaged appearance be restored for the viewing pleasure of successive generations? As every act of conservation or restoration must necessarily be a translation of the work of art and a displacement of its original intent, it necessitates a critical perspective. Historicism erected a false continuum of history, covering up ruptures and interferences, and often turning works of art into lewd collections of patrimony amd heritage. It was against these catastrophes of translation and transmission oppressing "the past" that Benjamin continually struggled. The idea of a universal history that museums and historicism possess, for Benjamin, depends on the prior acceptance of a universal language, a false synthetic language that can be easily understood.[23] But as Benjamin stated in the opening of his essay on "The Task of the Translator": "[i]n the appreciation of a work of art or an art form, consideration of the receiver never proves fruitful. . . . No poem is intended for the reader, no picture for the beholder, no symphony for the listener."[24] As a work of art always contains something unfathomable, in Benjamin's view, it has to be the task of the critical historian to direct his translation to the afterlife of a work of art, considering the intentions underlying language as a whole. There always remains something that cannot be communicated as sheer information, something that symbolizes or something symbolized.[25] And hence a work of art, a literary text, a narrative history must be blasted out of the false continuum of history so that it can live on in an unfathomable manner.[26]

The instrumental methodology of curatorship that developed in the nineteenth century is the cause of Benjamin's complaint. It aimed at a universal history, as we have seen in the paradox of the museum, a perfect and purified collection rendered accessible to and receptive by the viewer. But might its acts of translation simultaneously been ones that attempted to contain the primal cult of artifacts, to repress the auratic and ambiguous forces that works of art possess? As the basis of collective memory and the storehouse of a nation's treasures, official language like the museum preserves what it desires to record, and a priori arranges what can be represented and recalled. Yet in insignificant places and unnoticed ways, Benjamin noted in drawing a comparison between language and history, "the past has left behind in literary texts images of itself that are comparable to the image which light imprints on a photosensitive plate," and these illuminations must be recognized again and remembered.[27]

Looking for an alternative to the writing of universal histories and the development of curatorial models, Benjamin expressed great interest in the late nineteenth-century Austrian art historian Aloïs Riegl.[28] This interest arose because the latter emphasized the importance of insignificant details and border regions of officially recognized art, attempting to revalue minor art forms that had been degraded and marginalized by the more classical canon. But Benjamin valued Riegl especially for his belief that all art possessed intentionality, transparently expressing the collective will of a period and age.[29] If we look at the urban landscape that Benjamin so carefully attended to, we find these themes in place: the collective whose experiences he valued over the bourgeoisie's, the detailed images of public space that impress themselves with physic force on involuntary memory, the insignificant fragments and disgarded ruins that spur on imagination and flights of fantasy:

> The collective is an eternally alert, eternally moving being that witnesses, experiences, perceives and devises as much between the house walls outside as individuals within the protection of their own four walls. To the collective, the shining enameled signs of a store or company are just as good as or better than the decorative oil paintings on the wall of the bourgeois salon. Walls with the sign *Défense d'Afficher* are the collective's writing desk, newspapers stands its libraries, mailboxes its bronze sculptures, benches its bedroom furnishings, and the cafe terraces are the alcoves from which it looks down at its home. Where the asphalt worker lets his coat hang on the railing, that is the vestibule. And the gateway, leading out into the open from multiple court yards, is the long corridor which frightens the bourgeoisie; but is to them the entrance into the chambers of the city.[30]

Modern historiography locked inside official salons and museums, where it could breathe only the air of elevated values and universal forms of high art, was devoid of authentic memories reflecting the collective life and time of a people. Nor could it account for shifts in visual perception and attention to marginal details that greatly affected the spectator's imagination and the collective's unconscious.[31] Instead, Riegl wrote, "To grasp the *Kunstwollen* [the collective will or artistic volition] of a past epoch whose taste may be completely alien to our own there is no other way open to the historian than to view the stylistic phenomena genetically, to reconstruct their genealogical tree, and to find out their ancestors as well as their offspring."[32] Trained in philology, but working as a curator of textiles and rugs for the Vienna Museum of Applied Arts in the 1880s, Riegl was concerned with how even minor art forms mirrored their period and time, expressing unconscious desires. This meant tracing insignificant details and ornamental patterns such as plant motifs on carpets back to their roots in antiquity and outlining the grammatical laws of change and rhythmic developments they had followed ever since.[33] Art like language developed in a continuous and evolutionary manner, but it revealed a process of fragmentation away from its original unity, bringing accidental and unexpected forms into play. Hence it could be only subjective taste that called these accidents decadent forms or deviants from the classical norm.[34]

More to the subject of preservation, however, Riegl found that historic monuments, in a manner similar to the evolutionary history of decorative arts, had a constantly changing role in culture as their value and appreciation shifted with time. But what would be the fate of the cult of monuments in modern times, when historic revivals and nostalgic yearnings for past architectural styles seemed to have little use in a period that valued innovation and change? Riegl thought the controvery surrounding restoration work on the giant western portal of St. Stephen's Cathedral in Vienna—a controversy that brought an end to the work in the 1880s and again in 1902—reflected the different ways a monument might be valued in modern times. He believed there would be less trouble enveloping every restoration attempt when the history and significance of these values were carefully told. He argued that if the monument of St. Stephen had been esteemed solely for its "original style," then restorers would have stripped away the Gothic portal, allowing its Romanesque ruins to be revealed; but if the monument was evaluated for the signs of time that had passed across its face, including changes wrought by the hand of man, then restorers would have rejected any attempt to remove additions or add anachronistic improvements, allowing the monument to remain as it was. But which value should have priority—its authenticity as a work of art or its melancholic reminder of the passage of time?[35]

In a manner that resembled his history of the decorative arts, Riegl outlined a classification scheme for the evolutionary history of monuments. Like different styles of art, history had generated different types of monuments, valued at different periods of time for different reasons. He described in a 1903 essay, "On the Modern Cult of Monuments," three types of values that concerned historic monuments: memorial value, historical value, and age value.[36] Dividing the history of monuments into two large classes, Riegl found that the earliest class contained intentional monuments designed egotistically by their makers to be memorials recalling specific moments in time, commemorating the greatness of a nation's past, or leaving a lasting testimony for succeeding generations. They, like Halbwachs's collective memory, continued to be memorials as long as the conditions that brought them into existence remained alive, but when these conditions died, these intentional monuments were usually destroyed. All of antiquity and the Middle Ages, Riegl claimed, had known only intentional monuments. The Italian Renaissance, however, began to revalue artifacts from the past and to preserve their forms because they were believed to be images reflecting a golden age of history and thus revealed universally valid norms. These Riegl called unintentional monuments, originally built for other purposes then abandoned or ravaged by time; they received their monumental status artifically when an epoch bestowed on them the value of history. Finally there was the age value of a monument. Although a monument might contain nothing of value for a historian of art or of culture, it might be valued because as a ruin or fragment it moved the spectator in mysterious ways. Having endured the weathering of ages or the destructive reshaping of man's own hand, or because it was evidence of the primordial passage of time from birth to maturity and death, it might be subjectively valued for its age. Age value, an invention of the nineteenth century, concerned vision more than touch: changes to the surface, the patina of colors, the damage to angles and corners. It appears that if one valued age, no one had the right to intervene or spoil the degradation that nature inevitable wrought. These monuments of age, valued on their visual appearance alone, contained universal appeal reaching beyond the province of historians and conservators. They were, or so Riegl believed, the most democratic and altruistic monuments of all.

It was the nineteenth century, however, that pervasively annointed monuments with historic value, reaching out with the power of the state or the museum to isolate and protect them from further destruction and annul the degradations of time. That century placed the artifacts of history in direct opposition and conflict with the values of age. Historic monuments were respected because they represented a particular style, period, or school and valued because of their original state. Any alterations or additions consequently play a perturbing role when the restorer

Restored Colosseum.

desired the original. Hence the historic monument represented an authentic document that contained at least remnants of its original form, and thus any restoration work must return the momument as close as possible to its original state, and any stabilization work must be made apparent to the eye for generations to come. The twentieth century, on the other hand, was not yet ready to give up its right to deal as it might wish with old objects from time. It needed the value of history to teach the value of age; it required the presence of museums and preservation societies to defend against memory loss that the nineteenth century had caused. Historic research and conservation studies were necessary preludes—so Riegl argued—affecting the transformation from egotistical to altruistic values, and hence were essential steps toward a society that would accept all works of art, monumental and marginal, and ultimately all nature as well, as a vital part of their well-being and quality of life.[37]

The Wonder of Images

On the basis of this compromise, the twentieth century has shown little interest in shaking the custodial customs that perpetuate our sense of history. Of course the boundaries that define the terrain of collectible art have been extended over time to include marginal forms and degraded genres, and the social practices and material conditions that illuminate the production of a work of art have often been exhibited as well, but the museum remains at its core inception a Western cultural institution that still bears the stigmata of its imperialistic and colonial origins. Monuments and artifacts of every kind have always been the loot of the victorious, the treasures of war or the spoils of political and economic turmoil transported home by private and public collectors. They subsequently formed odd and wonderful bounty, displayed primarily to show off the pleasure of possession. Over time, with the democratic shifts of the eighteenth and nineteenth centuries, however, this great papal, aristocratic, and military plunder became the center around which nascent national museums were organized. And here the sensuous and eclectic displays of antiquarians were rearranged for didactic purposes. Now a new tension became apparent, pitting the sheer wonder that objects possess against their exhibitionary qualities emphasized by pedagogical displays. In the muffled museums of art, often the mysterious aura of images and objects was dampened if not silenced when the works, stripped of their contexts and the rubble cleared away from their pedestals, reappeared as idealized versions of themselves.[38] Yet this unresolved tension between the auratic mystique of art and its more distancing exhibitionary potential always enlivens the best museum displays because there is a deep-rooted mystique that surrounds every object of art. There are either ambiguous Ur-forms that relay primitive emotions and deep-structured pathos to the spectator, as Aby Warburg believed, or like Aloïs Riegl's genealogical studies of art they reveal the mentality and spirit of its age, or they are Walter Benjamin's "luminosity" and "aura" that every text and object of art contained.[39]

Gottfried Semper argued in the middle of the nineteenth century that

> [a]rt has its particular language, residing in formal types and symbols which transform themselves in the most diverse ways with the movement of culture through history, so that in the way in which it makes itself intelligible, an immense variety prevails, as in the case of language. Just as in the most recent research in linguistics, the aim has been to uncover the common components of different human linguistic forms to follow the transformation of words through the passage of centuries, taking them back to one or more starting points where they meet in a common Urform . . . a similar enterprise is justified in the case of the field of artistic inquiry.[40]

Like the quest that established Sanskrit as the initial source, the "lost origin" of all Indo-European languages, so the museum curator searched for the artifact's origins, reconstructing an imaginary visual tableau to narrate the temporal development of art from its archaic beginnings to its more advanced stage of modernity. Thus the desire arose for museological reasons to establish the origins of Western art in

Classical Greece, hoping thereby to impose a set of stable values and a coherent order over continuous progress and the evolution of time.

The monuments of antiquity have often been held on high for their exemplary value, underscoring the contrast between historical events and lived traditions, the art of duration and the ephemeral. The curator of high art fears the debasing influence on culture and society of the undifferentiated mass and the sea of mediocrity that whirls around him as much as he fears the auratic—perhaps sexual—mystique of art, and thus he cries out for an eternal system of order. At the end of the eighteenth century and again at the beginning of the twentieth, an appeal to classicism rang out the alarm. As the virtuosi of the eighteenth century, the collectors of coins and fragments stored in their cabinets of curiosity began to compare their findings with the romantic legends and poems of antiquity; they began to reappraise the art of the past and reformulate their aesthetic taste. Simultaneously a few scholars in Germany began to dislike the corrupting influence so-called purile and falsely urbane French taste held on the supposedly more rigorous Germanic culture, thus setting the scene for a call to order. In particular, Gotthold Ephraim Lessing in *Laocoon,* written in 1766, attacked Horace's famous simile "as is painting so is poetry," and instead tried to reestablish the clear boundaries and sharp distinctions that he believed separated not only the genre of poetry from painting but defined the autonomy of other genres as well.

The nineteenth century would have none of this purity, and instead wantonly mixed rational thought with ideal perception, utility with romanticism. So once again in 1910, Irving Babbitt in *The New Laocoon* drew the circle closer around the classical ideal. After a hundred years of free expression and revolt, what Babbitt referred to as Eleuthoromania [i.e., the craze for freedom], society was once again bereft of restraint, clearly effeminate and childish.[41] To control the whirl in the streets and "the mere buzzing of the romantic chimera," the classical heritage of the West was once again to be re-collected and reinstalled as the pedagogical norm.[42] All art, Lessing had claimed and Babbitt repeated, was an imitation of ideal human action in which every detail of representation, its symmetry and proportion, was subordinated to a unified and recognizable end. So Babbitt affirmed, "The neo-classicists were right: the highest law is the law of concentration, a law of unity, measure and purpose."[43] The public taste of the nineteenth century had descended into the fog of sentimentality and the eclectic mixing of genres and crossing of disciplinary boundaries, a depth from which it seldom emerged. Siegfried Giedion referred to this downward tendency of public taste as a tragic rift between methods of thinking and methods of feeling so that judgments of quality were lost, enabling the public to call instead for an art and a literature that allowed them to bask in misty images and romantic daydreams.[44]

The power of images to seduce, whether through dangerous cross-breedings of genres or eclectic pictorial allusions, has often been thought to be a fearful ability that must be tamed. The world was a work to be observed, its artifacts accumulated in museums and encyclopedias composed as memory theaters, with systematic cross-references and interconnections. Meaning was generated and controlled in this system by linking fragments, and consequently the encyclopedia, the library, as well as the museum and guidebook were connecting nodes in the labyrinthine array of information enveloping modern man, yet rationally recomposed in this manner. Efforts to tame the power of images have deep historical roots. Athanasius Kircher had dreamed of an "ars combinatoria" as early as the seventeenth century, a memory calculus by which he could generate new concepts from established ones and thus gain control over knowledge that had become so wildly prolific it could no longer be retained through mnemonic devices. He proposed, but of course never built, a box in which all extant tabulae were to be placed and spatially coordinated like a computer so that this arrangement would enable combinatory crossovers among different ideas and facts.

To implement this scheme, Kircher searched to discover a pictorial basis among the primal and archaic layers of language, a vast hieroglyphic system that might unlock the secrets of the world and serve as memory devices.[45] His experimentations with imagery and emblems led to the creation of a magic lantern, a mechanism by which he might exhibit with the aid of light and shadow the "wonders of nature." In the beginning this simple device projected letters onto a transparent taffeta screen placed between the lantern and the viewer. By holding a candle in front of a concave mirror into which slides of silhouetted letters were inserted, all of a sudden handwriting appeared on the screen, without anyone apparently writing. A second more elaborate machine involved either a strip of glass or a revolving wheel on which silhouettes of pictures were painted. As the strip moved or the wheel turned, the images changed so that a viewer suddenly saw one animal blend into another, fire erupting then diminishing, and numerous fantastic enlargements and manipulations. These image shows obviously bordered on the occult and the magic of vanishing appearances, of shadows and reflections, and gave Kircher the fearful reputation of being a sorcerer.

But Kircher's 1645 treatise "The Great Art of Light and Shadow" (Ars Magna Lucis et Umbrae) revealed how deeply his fascination with tricks of the eye lay, as he illustrated this work with different kinds of optical devices and magical shows, sketching instruments, magic clocks and sundials, telescopes and lenses, a camera obscura, and a large cabinet called a catoptric theater or peep show, in which many mirrors were hidden. In his picture theater in Rome, moreover, Kircher assembled every kind of scientific and antiquarian object, hieroglyphics from Egypt and curiosities from the new world, remarkable amber stones with mysterious imagery, stuffed animals and fish, and whatever he found that pertained to writing in pictures. Such was the passion of this collector, this "Doctor of a Hundred Arts," that his assembled array bordered on the chaos of plethoric and uncontrollable artifacts. No matter what their scientific pretension as aids to memory and to the establishment of universal knowledge, these hallucinating images conjured up the mysterious sources of archaic emblems and the secret codes of decipherment. They ushered in the upside down and phantasmagorical world of the camera obscura, a world of conjuring images that mystified both perception and representation instead of clarifying the path toward rational thought.[46]

Neoclassical theories of decorum wanted instead an immutable world, they feared these "wild parings without a priest."[47] As traditions were erased and the spatial system of memory eroded throughout the long process of industrialization and urbanization, the ruins of antiquity were held out time and again as the only coherent survivors of the classical age that could control and uplift man's knowledge and taste. "Greece" became an ideal place, an invention of the Eurocentric mind. So, for example, Johann Winckelmann in the mid-eighteenth century, although he never visited the land, defined the order and serenity of the Hellenic (Ancient Greek) ideal. He believed

> [t]here is but one way for the moderns to become great, and perhaps unequalled; . . . by imitating the ancients. . . . It is not only *Nature* which the votaries of the Greeks find in their works, but still more, something superior to nature; ideal beauties, brain-born images.[48]

Winckelmann's neoclassical art metaphorically involved the use of a concave mirror, not a flat reflecting surface, because the former created a concentrated image serving the immobile and uniform center.[49] Consequently, artists were to present an ideal, to generalize and transpose their images based on archetypical representations, not literal imitations of nature.[50] Supposedly the best of ancient Greek art had already been transported to Rome; although today we see them as derivative or Romanized copies, they represented for Winckelmann the epitome of ideal beauty. To be inspired by Greek forms, or so he assumed, led to the highest standards of moral life, and hence Greek art was an ideal model for structuring the temporal world, for teaching noble restraint and individual discipline.[51]

Winckelmann commanded of the generation to succeed him that "Hellas [Greece] is the inexhaustible source in which all artists must steep themselves to attain an ideal of noble simplicity and grandeur."[52] But the energies of popular taste could not be restrained; they imitated and misquoted wherever they could. No matter how high ancient Greek sculpture might be held as the exemplum of perfected nature, a taste for thoughtless copying and historical verisimiltude, with their ludic and picturesque mixing of genres, broke through the constrained surface of the neoclassical age. Phantasmagorical antiquity, as it slowly emerged in the newly discovered ruins and monuments of Greece, was the site where the archaic and modern would merge. A kaleidoscopic rearrangement quickly occurred, turning past into present, historical into fictional time, as the nineteenth century blended the authoritative and didactic Greek ideal with a haunting sympathy for the ruinous landscapes of Greece and a love for freedom drawn poignantly into focus by the Greek War of Independence (1821–1833). Here on this site of Greek antiquity the orderly and masculine forms of classicism meant to discipline and to cultivate taste commingled and merged with romantic dreams of foreign places and picturesque landscapes, which took wing on the desire for escape into exoticism and sensuous inner experiences.

The Memory of Classical Athens

The collective memory of Western cities clearly reaches back to ancient Athens and her reknowned Acropolis, inciting both admiration and imagination. But would nineteenth-century Greece be a site of learning or a place of fantastic dreams? Was it to be a member of European culture as the birthplace of Western civilization and democracy, or was it a marginal land, a border protecting the West from "barbaric" incursions that came from the East? Was Greece an exotic other or a case of arrested development along the universal path of progress?[53] The uncanny aspect of nineteenth-century Greece arose on this split, revealing a deep ambivalence that recognized on one hand an archaic Ur-Europa, yet disavowed on the other the presence of its marginalized and degraded modernity. Would Greece be allowed to represent itself and write its own history, or would its representation and national identity be forged by external powers?[54] The story can be told by looking at the manner in which its art and artifacts were valued, and the method that imposed a new town plan on the so-called cradle of liberty.

The Western world is indebted to Athens, for so it has been claimed time and again, "[a]ll the nations of Europe have at their best epochs gone directly to her for instruction."[55] Since the Renaissance, Italy and Rome had yielded up their

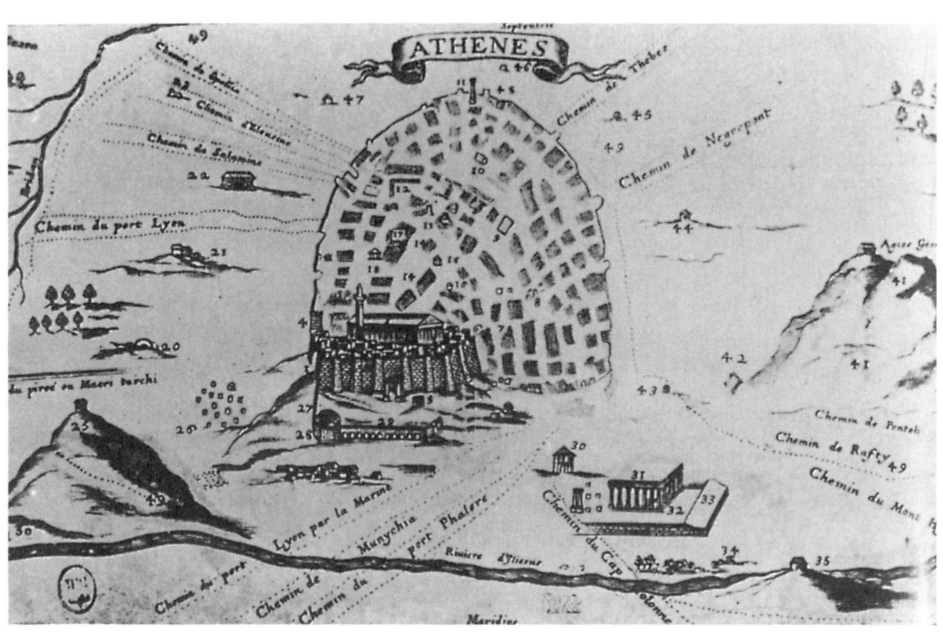

Plan of Athens by Spon *(1676)*.

remains to cultivated men. From that time arose the fashionable art of studying the traces of vanished civilizations. Humanism was established on this taste for antiquity, combining a thirst for classical knowledge with the need to discover and trade with new lands. But Greece, or the Levant as the eastern Mediterranean was called, was under Turkish domain and remained relatively unexplored and unchartered. In the seventeenth century, agents had been sent by the French court and the English aristocracy to explore the East; they brought back the first souvenirs such as coins, small sculptural pieces, and inscriptions that embellished many a collector's cabinets of curiosity. The Earl of Arundel and the Duke of Buckingham were among the earliest private collectors establishing the fashionable attributes of "taste" and igniting a veritable hunt for antiquities.[56] The Earl of Arundel in 1620 had amassed at least 600 Italian paintings, 200 objects of art (mostly of Roman origin), and an array of Greek antiquities.[57] These were chaotic collections, however, valued for their documentary or historical evidence rather than for their aesthetic appeal. But with the appearance of Johann Winckelmann's *History of Greek Art* (1764), which used "style" to discriminate between different periods of Greek sculpture, a more systematic and chronological arrangement of antiquities began to be made. Curiosities and questionable souvenirs were weeded out from works appreciated as art, and these were subdivided into developmental stages revealing their supposed perfection or decadence.[58]

Although all voyagers to the Levant in the seventeenth and eighteenth centuries had as their goal to visit the Acropolis, this was not an easy achievement. The Turks had fortified the Acropolis, and visitors were at the caprice of the *voivode* and *disdar* who commanded or controlled the citadel. Even if access was gained, these visitors never attempted to measure accurately nor understand correctly these monuments' historical importance. And so until the 1750s, accounts of the ruins were impressionistic and full of mistakes, based on erroneous assumptions or misconstrued hypotheses.[59] Most studies of Greek art, including that of Winckelmann, were based on sculptures and monuments to be seen in Rome. Up to this time, no architect had ever bothered to study the Greek temples, either at Paestum in southern Italy or Segesta in Sicily; in fact the taste for antiquity seemed entirely spent on coins, inscriptions, and small sculptures.[60] The only precedent for the study of Greek architecture was the Viennese architect Bernhard Fisher von Erlach, who tried in 1721 to delineate the major stages of architectural history and included as illustrations in his work the Temple of Olympian Zeus, the Parthenon, and the Acrocorinth, as well as mythical wonders like the Colossus of Rhodes, the Pharos of Alexandria, and the Labyrinth of Crete. So it was quite enterprising for two among the colony of apprentices in Rome, who assembled to draw and study her monuments, to propose a scheme in 1748 for producing and publishing measured drawings of the architectural plan, elevation, and ornamental details and decorations of the Acropolis and other antiquities to be found in Athens. Thus the young engraver James Stuart, with his companion the painter Nicholas Revett, set off for Athens in 1750, arriving there in early spring of 1751.

As we have seen, classical culture had affected the imaginations and sympathies of cultivated men for generations—the visual arts of antiquity being prized especially because only they, or so it was believed, could instill and transmit the ideals of the classical age to the present day. In 1734, the Society of Dilletanti was formed, bringing together a group of English noblemen and gentlemen for the purpose of toasting "Grecian taste and Roman spirit" and retelling over and over their Italian travel tales. Enthralled with the "ideal of Greece," however, their attention shifted from travel stories and legends to archeological sites and architectural ruins. The society began to sponsor travelers, charging them with the task of collecting information about and sketching the antiquities that survived in the East. Elected to the Society in 1751, Stuart and Revett were given the mission of recognizing, measuring, and accurately drawing the antiquities of Athens.[61] Obviously the Society hoped that accurate drawings based on the original monuments would restore some integrity to the stylistic expression of the classical orders and quell the contemporary tendency to distort their compositional structure and misapply their ornamentation. But the Society was not above political causes as well,

The Acropolis d'Athènes, *Typ. J. Clary.*

for they hoped these accurately measured drawings would overthrow the neo-Palladian architecture favored by the governing Whigs.[62]

Stuart's and Revett's drawings and plan of the Acropolis attained a precision unknown for the time; their grand folios of engravings and prints comprising *The Antiquities of Athens* appeared in 1762, 1788, 1794, and 1814. (Richard Chandler's and Revett's *Ionian Antiquities* was published in 1769 and 1797.) Even though five hundred subscriptions were sold before publication, Stuart and Revett feared that the austere look of the simple Doric order might jar popular taste, so they began with a volume on more decorative and picturesque ruins such as the Roman Tower of the Winds and the Lantern of Demosthenes.[63] Soon after the publication of Volume One, however, models of Doric details and temples began to appear in England, decorating buildings and parks. This would soon be abetted by Lord Elgin's collection of marbles, which he carted away from the Acropolis and sent home to England in 1805. Greece began to achieve eminence over Rome as "Grecian Gusto" became a fashionable craze.[64] Richard Chandler's *Travels in Asia Minor* (1775) and *Travels in Greece* (1776) established the style for subsequent guidebooks and whetted the apetite for more information. Following Chandler's customs, a writer would first establish the history of a place before describing its present condition, making full allowances for contemporary accounts, and finally lapsing into the adventures of travel.[65]

Lest the English appear the only villains plundering the marbles of Greece and the only country flaming the candle of liberty, the French consul Louis Fauvel was instructed as well to pillage and remove from the Acropolis and Athens all of the stones that he could.[66] Furthermore, the French, by claiming themselves to be the most complete and civilized nation,[67] placed a double bind on the damaged relic of Greece. Pierre Augustin Guys described the modern Greeks in his *Voyage Littéraire de la Grèce* (1771) in the following manner: "What difference between the Greeks and ourselves! They tread undeviatingly in the footsteps of their forefathers; while we exert our utmost ingenuity to recede as far as possible from the usages, modes, customs, and even manners of our ancestors."[68] Thus an imaginary time gap seemed to separate the people of Europe from those of Greece, and although the latter might be the living ancestors of Europe upholding the role of Ur-Europa, they were simultaneously blamed for being immature and backward children held down by their ancient past.[69] This placed nineteenth-century Greece in an impossible position: it was to be the standard of civilization in the abstract sense, but judged in reality to be a humiliated Oriental vassal clearly inferior to—and in the end dependent on—the more modern Europe. This bind, moreover, served Eurocentric purposes and legitimated the plundering of Greece's past.[70]

Stuart's and Revett's folios illustrated the novel Doric order and popularized the Ionic. They opened up an unquenchable desire for accurate information and authentic reports on the antiquities of Greece, which only augmented the plunderer's quest. Heretofore the profiles, entabulatures, and ornamental details of the orders considered to be the distinctive marks of antique architecture had been copied from Roman buildings, and followed the more splendid and elaborate Corinthian form.[71] The admiration of "authentic" Greek architecture soon became an inseparable mark of taste and knowledge in art. George Aberdeen wrote in his introduction to William Wilkin's 1812 English translation of Vitruvius' writings that the intellectual associations emanating from Greek art exist only among men of knowledge and learning, and appear highest among those whose taste is the most cultivated and whose science is the most extensive.[72] "Athens," Aberdeen claimed, "still presents to the student the most faultless models of ornamental architecture," for the Greeks had no concept of the picturesque or of delighting the imagination through visual appearances.[73] A style aiming at the picturesque, Aberdeen criticized, attempts to connect the building to the landscape surrounding it, and in this manner makes the eye of the painter as indispensable as the science of architecture. In this picturesque style, all the precepts derived from the simple and regular structures of Greece remain totally inapplicable. In Greek architecture, he argued, the symmetrical proportions of the building and the fitness of ornamental parts are both indispensable to the sensation and aura of its beauty.[74] Columns were the chief feature in ornamentation and should preserve the harmony and proportion of the building, thereby creating a conformity with use and presenting a powerful display of shadow and light. But a row of columns, which popular taste allowed to be composed as a screen supporting only an entablature, so Aberdeen noted, detracted from the idea of the whole and suggested to the mind of the viewer the image of a ruin or that of an unfinished work. A slice of pilasters applied to a facade, twisted columns or broken pediments, also destroyed the repose and simplicity of surface that the Greek models from antiquity revealed. Ornamentation ostentatiously displaying a desire for splendor was becoming offensive to the well-trained classical eye. Now that the pure forms of Greek architecture had been rediscovered—forms that had been unknown to or not recognized by previous generations—Aberdeen believed that "henceforth, these exquisite remains should form the chief study of the architect who aspires to permanent reputation; other modes are transitory and uncertain, but the essential qualities of Grecian excellence, as they are founded on reason, and are consistent with fitness and propriety, will ever continue to deserve his first case."[75]

Not everyone would try to distill the ideal of Greek architecture to this "new square style."[76] The Romantics would elevate the symbolic memory of Athens over the rigors of classical form, raising perhaps a false nimbus to replace momentarily the authentic one they believed was lost forever. Antiquity became an escape: into adventure, into the exotic other, into the marvelous. It offered the compensation of "once-upon-a-time" to mollify the flat and repetitive present. Ideological voyages into the Orient also arose on the not very innocent power relations swelling between the East and the West.[77] Evoking the mystical source or mythical origin of Western culture is but a metonymy for the act of appropriation: in plundering the sculptures of Greece, in the act of measuring and documenting the Athenian marbles, in the gesture of planning a modern new city as the cradle of democracy reborn, the West imposed its representational order onto a dominated and colonized East. Because it was commonly believed that the Greeks, even with their newfound liberty and freedom from the Turks, were unable to preserve the symbolic heritage of the West, it immediately instilled the obligation for others to appropriate wherever they could.

The stones of Athens were mute and the East, supposedly unconscious of their value, remained powerless to preserve them in situ. The cradle of the West became inevitably the pillage of the more educated aesthete.

Edward Dodwell displayed this eye of appropriation when he painted the marbles of the Acropolis and the city of Athens in the early 1800s. By reducing that spectacle to a passive and ordered panoramic view, turned symbolically upside down by his camera obscura, his paintings metaphorically subdued the exotic and threatening East. Dodwell had trouble attaining permission in 1801 and 1805 to enter and reenter the Acropolis to observe and to draw its monuments. By plying the disdar with presents he apparently obtained the necessary access, although other problems immediately ensued. Dodwell executed his paintings with the aid of a camera obscura, following the outlines of the reduced image in order to measure accurately the proportions of the Parthenon marbles. But this scientific apparatus also gave him a magical aura that thrilled the disdar. As Dodwell described the situation:

> I was one day engaged in drawing the Parthenon with the aid of my camera obscura, when the Disdar. . . . asked with a sort of fretful inquietude, what new conjecture I was performing with that extraordinary machine? I endeavoured to explain it, by putting in a clean sheet of paper, and making him look into the camera obscura; he no sooner saw the temple instantaneously reflected on the paper in all its lines and colours, than he imagined that I had produced the effect by some magical process.

Pestered relentlessly by the curious disdar and his soldiers, Dodwell finally resorted to trickery: if they would not leave him alone to paint at his will, he would put them into his camera's box and find it difficult to release them again. From that point onward, every time that Dodwell appeared on the Acropolis to paint and to draw, the disdar and his soldiers left him quite solemnly alone.[78] The East, after all, was but an ignorant and backward place, dependent on the help of others. When gratitude was not forthcoming, the people were treated as amusing or disobedient children.

In general during the early nineteenth century, the topography of ancient Greece was admired romantically for its ruinous features and for the meaning these exercised on the viewer's imagination. It was the era to travel into the past, to gaze on the history of ancient times and meditate upon the grand and melancholy spectacle as it remained isolated within the present. Every traveler to the city of Athens in previous centuries had recounted the emotions evoked by the ancient site and told of celebrated images rooted in classical soil. And still in the very early years of the nineteenth century one arrived at Athens through an olive grove and stood before the spectacle of a thousand ages without guide or witness except for the monuments in stone. The view across the village, an almost deserted field, contained for the Romantic viewer nothing that was not Greek and heroic, nothing that might distance the suppliant pilgrim's first impressions of Attica; no obstacle rose to stand between history and the voyager's eye.[79] Even though it could be argued that Athens was damaged by Turkish barbarians, retaining deep imperfections in its Hellenic mirror, still it was a shrine for pilgrims' thoughts and feet, longed for and to be attained if possible.[80] There across the plains, as one entered the town of Athens, arose the Acropolis to meet the voyager's eyes, described as the most beautiful ruin of the world, a little like a fortress with its cyclopean walls, an ensemble frightening yet sublime.[81]

During the Greeks' struggle for freedom from the Turks and their seige of Athens in 1826 and 1827, most of the city was burned and destroyed and many of the monuments on the Acropolis ruined. Preparing for battle, the Turks demolished the walls enclosing the paved way to the first gate of the Acropolis and removed many houses on the upper slopes of the town. The marbles on the Acropolis were mutilated by bullets and canon balls; the Erechtheion suffering the worst damage as its southern wall was almost completely destroyed, its portico beam felled, its roof blown away, and only three out of six of its caryatids left intact. Lamartine wrote in 1832 that he finally attained the town of Athens after fifteen minutes of wandering among an inextricable labyrinth of rocks and marbles thrown pell-mell, of crumbling walls and broken columns.[82] In the same year Christopher Wordsworth recalled his impressions: "the town of Athens is now lying in ruins. The streets are almost deserted, nearly all the houses are without roof. The churches are reduced to bare walls and heaps of stones and mortar."[83] In this state of "modern desolation" the grandeur of the ancient monuments appeared even more striking and their preservation more sublime. "It makes an abstraction [so Wordsworth continued] of all other features, and leaves the spectator alone with Antiquity. In this consists, particularly at the present period, the superiority of Athens over Rome, as a reflection of the ancient world."[84] "If we may use the illustration, the ancient characters impressed on the Roman soil, are only descried [sic] with great labour through the modern surface of the classical manuscript. Athens on the other hand, though a very tattered manuscript, is not yet like Rome, a Palimpsest."[85] The city and its 1,650 houses, 129 churches, 12 religious buildings of the Turks, 21 fountains, and a few administrative buildings were in ruins, and all of its 150,000 olive trees on its western plains burned to ashes. Yet its stones remained the source of fascination, pleasure, and memory.[86]

Thought to have been both liberated by the Philhellenes of northern Europe and subsequently dependent on them, modern Greeks were deemed unfit for self-rule and liberty. So it was said in 1820, "[i]n the same way as the Jews expect the Messiah, so do the Greeks look forward to independence: liberty would, however, alight in vain on these shores, once her noblest domain. This nation would no longer comprehend her divine language, which would be confined exclusively to ignorant caloyers [monks]."[87] After years of deliberation by the allies and as the price extracted for "offering" them independence, the presumedly chaotic and immature Greeks were given a simplified and morally enlightened social organization in the form of a Eurocentric monarchy.[88] Othon, the prince of Bavaria, was selected to be King of Greece in 1829, and his father, King Ludwig I of Bavaria, was instrumental in choosing Athens as the site for the modern capital of the new nation. Now a full-blown Hellenic purity would be constructed in imaginary and architectural plans. Sentiment and a lively interest in preservation led King Ludwig I to listen to the teachings of his court architect Leo von Klenze, and to the architect of his brother-in-law Friedrich Wilhelm IV of Prussia, who was none other than Karl Friedrich Schinkel. Ludwig followed their directives, for he believed no other city in Greece could compare with Athens either in its striking name, in the wealth of its antique monuments, or in the sentiments it aroused in the hearts of men.[89] His love for ancient Greece would command the subsequent development of modern Athens. Stamatis Cleanthes (1802–1862) from Macedonia and Eduard Schaubert (1804–1868), both former students of Schinkel, were the first to draw up a plan for Athens in 1832.

"In accordance with the glory and beauty of the ancient city of Athens," they developed a triangular plan that turned all perspectives toward the Acropolis yet refrained from encircling its girth. The base of the triangle, named Ermou, was drawn across the old Turkish town, placing what would become the new bourgeois city to its north and leaving the so-called polluting place isolated to its south. Clearly modern Athens was a disgraceful sight to be reconstructed, with its Eurocentric focal point drawn on the enlightened times of antiquity. But its contemporary form was tarnished by the Turks and therefore full of imperfections, ranging from their architectural remains to their influence on the spoken language. On each side of the Turkish bazaar, located on the ruins of the Roman agora and the Hadrian library, the new city planners drew two parallel streets named Aeolu and Athenas at right angles to the base of Ermou. The two boulevards joining the base at either end were Piraeus and Stadiou, meeting in an apex where the King's Palace was to be located, on the site of current-day Omonia Square. The south side of the triangular base was planned as a large archeological park containing the ruins of the ancient shrine, and it was even proposed that all new structures should be built with cellars in order to facilitate the excavation and preservation of ancient remains that might be buried on their sites.[90] Violent opposition arose from landowners who protested that the plan took too much space for public squares, for wide boulevards, for the archeological park, and for a green swathe of land to encircle the city.

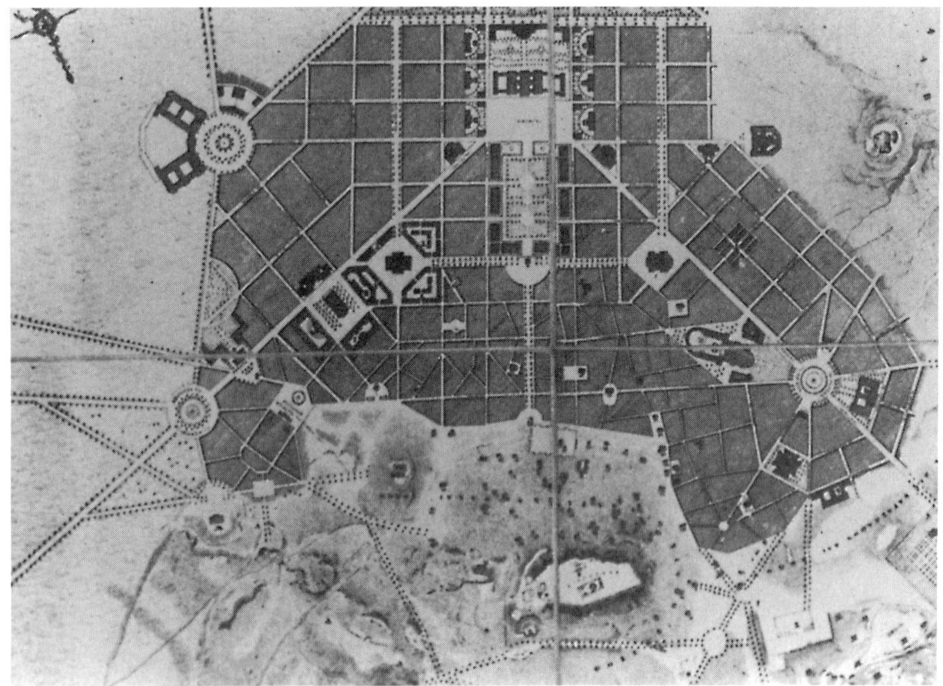

Plan of Athens by Cleanthes and Schaubert *(1833)*.

Consequently Leo von Klenze devised a second plan in 1834, and although it was based on the same triangular form and eventually implemented in part, he limited the amount of land to be taken for streets and for parks, altogether abandoning the earlier theme of a garden city of antiquity.[91]

King Ludwig also asked Schinkel to prepare a restoration plan for the Acropolis and to design a royal palace at its vacant eastern end. As Ludwig's consuls owed the architect a considerable sum of money, it was hoped that this commission would take care of those debts. Schinkel decorated the Parthenon with a court of honor filled with gardens and flowers for outdoor gatherings. By separating the apartments and galleries from the ancient monuments, none of the new structures was allowed to visually dominate the treasured archeological ruins. Deftly shifting the levels of his sunken gardens and terraces, Schinkel used staircases and walls to overcome the irregular terrain of the Acropolis and formally organized the whole through an interrelated series of cross-axes and opened and closed spaces that provided dramatic vistas over the plains of Attica.[92] But King Othon's advisers had other ideas: rejecting this scheme they suggested another palace be designed by Leo von Klenze (later modified by Friedrich von Gartner). Having slept in every quarter of the city, these advisers decided that the healthiest spot was the Boubounistra, because it was there that they awoke with lighter heads and more energy. Hence that spot, at the head of Ermou, where present-day Syntagma Square lies, became the site for the new palace. After its location a new boulevard named Panapestimiou (University) was laid parallel to Stadiou, and another called Vassilissis Sophias extended toward the west.[93]

In spite of all this effort expended on town planning, however, land speculation reigned, and houses sprang up faster than they could be regulated, appearing in the middle of vaguely outlined streets and blocks. So it was said of Athens in those years that "it is a city where there is not yet a road, and where one begins by constructing a palace, a faithful image of a country where one has just made a king, before being assured of a people."[94] Consequently some sections of the city stood with ruins, pieces of columns, fallen capitals, and broken parts of statues

Karl Friedrich Schinkel, Plan for the Acropolis Palace *(c. 1833).*

strewn about, while new construction in other districts utilized these fragmented parts as new building materials. The only tentative urban order appeared along Athenas and Aeolu streets; but all the rest was disordered and confused, full of gaps where once there had been a hope for planned development. Hardly any paving existed, little vegetation developed, and to orient oneself in this labyrinthine layout one constantly had to find the Acropolis.

It appeared that the ancient ruins were being destroyed and the ancient town obliterated as quickly as a new Bavarian town was being erected. Of the 129 churchs counted in 1821, only 24 were in a state that could be reused. The others were destroyed by opening roads or by those who plundered for building materials. Some of the ruins on the Acropolis fared no better. The German archeologist Ludwig Ross arrived in Athens in 1832. He found that the city walls hastily erected by Hadji Ali in 1778 were still intact, although they would be demolished three years later. Shortly after Independence, Ross was appointed the Conservator of Antiquities with Schaubert and Hansen as his assistants, and twelve wounded veterans as custodians. Although it was agreed by everyone that no modern buildings should be erected on the Acropolis, still it was generally feared that the foreign archeologists would destroy "all the picturesque additions of the Middle Ages in their zeal to lay bare and restore the ancient monuments."[95] And indeed, they set about removing the corruptions of time (Riegl's age value) such as the Turkish mosque used as a military garrison, the Frankish Towers, and the various fortifications that polluted the Acropolis display of Hellenic purity.

The first small but significant move toward restoring the antiquities of Athens began in 1834, when Othon arrived in Athens with Leo von Klenze and in a ceremonial gesture replaced one barrel of a column belonging to the northern colonnade of the Parthenon.[96] It was here that restoration work would begin, for this northern site was visible from the city and was beloved for its picturesque effect.[97] Money was set aside for the future restoration of the Acropolis, with the first task being the removal of debris scattered about its surface. But conservators were either not willing to spend money on the removal of rubble or hoping to proceed at a much faster pace toward the total restoration of the Acropolis, for they allowed many blocks of marble and mutilated stone to be pushed over the walls of the citadel where they could be carted away as building material. Beginning in 1833, the Propylaea were disengaged from encumbrances, but no documentation was kept on this work. The mosque that stood in the middle of the Parthenon was demolished in 1842, serving at first as an archeolgical museum, but work on restoring the Parthenon itself had to wait until the 1890s and the early twentieth century.[98]

Archaic images merged with the modern, or so Charles Bracebridge described his view of the new city in 1839:

> The Theseion, Parthenon and Erechtheum, carry back the mind to the earliest times of history, verging on fable; while the mass of modern buildings standing on the rubbish of successive cities, from twelve to twenty feet deep, remind us that the Cities of Theseus, Pericles, Augustus, Hadrian; of the Normans, the Italians, and the Turks, have all in turn yielded to destruction; and been at length replaced by a town partly German, partly Levantine; where the Moslem cupolas, the Frank tower, the Italian belevedere, are intermingled with the huge masses of ruined walls, vaulted Greek churches, light wooden structures in the Constantinople style, and solid rectangualar houses,in which green paint and whitewash proclaim the ultra-mundane taste of the builders.[99]

It was commonly felt that the Bavarian regime pursued an anti-Greek policy, rooting out every indigenous plant, the national mode of dress, the picturesque Asiatic style of house, and supplanting these with European forms, erected from different architectural systems and cast in different compositional molds.[100] But in fact many Greeks helped to spread the taste for neoclassical forms and to eradicate the existing diversity. Their own self-image was compromised: having fallen from a state of classical purity, they accepted the Eurocentric assumption that their heritage had been flawed by Turkish influence. These allegedly disfiguring marks in language, customs, architecture, and music had to be rooted out and corrected by classically structured codes. Such reforms, established and championed by educated Greeks, comprised a double means of self-liberation. Eventually a purified language based on classical Greek (Katharevousa), for example, offered freedom from Turkish influences that remained within their spoken language (Demotic), while it simultaneously made then independent from European condescension that they were culturally incomplete. Educated Greeks wanted to be admitted into European society as cultural and political equals.[101] Architecture was another area in which Greeks could attempt to recover their classical past, for every neoclassical facade visually conveyed itself to be a symbol of Hellenism.[102]

Cloaked in the mantle of classical respectability and uniformity, Greek cultural expression was denied individual diversity, indeterminancy, and unpredictability. Where once the imagination soared freely above the plains of Attica, now each corner of the earth was named, every marble called a monument, and the eye and the mind restrained to focus only on the Acropolis. Modern houses lined the route without plan or symmetry belonging to another century and another country, for a mass of strangers had descended on Athens to exploit it, to sell its ruins in fragments until all that once was authentically antique nearly vanished from sight.[103] The marbles of the Acropolis became a modern museum, a marvelous out-of-doors place, but a museum nevertheless. So one nineteenth-century voyager complained, it evoked less of history than of familiar objects to be seen in the art galleries of any other European capital. To resuscitate this dead architecture, to recall its meaning that had been lost across the centuries, archeologists began to document, to explain, to reconstitute the past, but they were unable to arouse the indifferent beauty that the Acropolis had held for centuries. They could scarcely reclaim as works of art or treasured religious icons objects that had lost their aura and emotional spirit. It seemed to displease the erudite and the aesthete traveler from the West to see in these Eastern antiquities anything other than curious documents or architectural spectacles from the historical past. Surrounded by the antiquities of Greece, these Neo-Hellenes erected a cult image, a Greek fantasy from a lost golden age. The sanctuary of their religion, the Acropolis, became their new idol. It was called the cradle of human reason and the font of aesthetic expression, becoming by 1850 the superlative model of Greek perfection.[104]

The new city of nineteenth-century Athens took only its name from antiquity: far from being confined to the cult of the past, it would extend itself into the future. As one moved away from the Acropolis, the geometric uniformity of its districts and streets discouraged the imagination. Bourgeois neoclassical houses spread out on the plain toward Patissia or held to the foot of Lycabettus Hill. Distributed along straight roads and large avenues where the sun, wind, and dust raged all around, the modern Athens, as one visitor complained, scarcely lent itself to the *flaneur*.[105] "The modern city," another gentleman noted in 1879, "is a little German market town, and has a trim rectilinear, raw military air about it."[106] Modern Athens had been planned as an analogical extension of the ancient city, but the nineteenth century was too eager to appropriate its heritage, too quick to document its ruins, too fascinated with idealizing and purifying its classical antiquities, so instead a neoclassical monument arose to commemorate the memory of ancient Athens. The architects of this new Athens felt it to be a sacred duty to employ the architecture of classicism when they built adjacent to the ancient relics of Greece. Consequently all of its public and institutional buildings and large private houses were designed in the neoclassical mode. Two cities arose side by side: a new Athens that borrowed from everywhere and came to resemble nowhere, and the scenographic illusions of ancient Athens, ephemeral as a dream.[107]

Classicists often hope to erect a transcendental history, to find security in the illusory ideal of antiquity. But every reconstruction must be a repetition of past events, of historical time, and of necessity can be only a provisional rewriting, the re-presentation of a recounting.[108] The memory of classical Athens was rooted in a sentimental desire to return to the origin of Western knowledge, to reappropriate the rightful patrimony of northern Europe, and to reform the present based on the highest and purest accomplishments of the past. As Chateaubriand had said, however, the only reason for traveling to Athens was to search for some images, some impressions of history, and that was all.[109] But these were impressions nevertheless that lay heavily on the modern mentality. Von Klenze had written in 1830, even before he had traveled to Greece:

> Never has there been, and never will there be, more than one art of building, namely, that which was brought to perfection at the epoch of the prosperity and civilization of Greece. . . . Grecian architecture alone is marked by universal propriety, character and beauty, although any mode of architecture is capable of effecting us, and has a certain value of its own when it is a really national style. . . . Grecian architecture can and must be the architecture of the world, and that of all periods; nor can any climate, any material, any difference of manner prove an obstacle to its universal adoption.[110]

And so, the picturesque classical ruins of Athens were copied and imitated by northern architects time and again. Because the solid Doric order appeared heavy and ungainly, at first more picturesque schemes of miniature temples, arches, and towers as a playful assortment of curiosities appeared in English gardens. But Gotthard Langhans was brave enough in 1789 to base his monumental design for the Berlin Brandenburg Gate on the Propylaea, although he added a base to the shockingly barren Doric columns and placed demimetetopes at the end of his friezes.[111] But the architect who seems to have best understood the imagery that the Acropolis conveyed and how it commands our visual imagination and memory was Frederich Gilly. In an amazing tour de force for its time, one that greatly influenced the later work of both Schinkel and von Klenze, Gilly designed a monument for Frederick the Great in 1797, placing a pure Doric temple on a pediment raised high enough so that it dominated its environment. Just as the abstract geometry of the Parthenon controls the plain of Athens that spreads out from the foot of its Acropolis, so Gilly imagined that a viewer who ascended the steps of his Grecian temple would gaze over the plaza below, with its ceremonial obelisks, and then beyond to the panoramic landscape of Berlin, the royal city that

The Erechtheion, view from the West
(1862). Typ. J. Clary.

Frederick had created.[112] Here lay the Romantic ideal that Athens bestoyed on the imagination: a classical monument in its landscape setting.

Continuing this tradition, Le Corbusier would note in the 1920s:

> In actual fact a birds'-eye view such as is given by a plane on a drawingboard is not how axes are seen; they are seen from the ground, the beholder standing up and looking in front of him. The eye can reach a considerable distance and, like a clear lens, sees everything even beyond what was intended or wished. The axis of the Acropolis runs from the Piraeus to Pentelicus, from the sea to the mountain. The Propylaea are at right angles to the axis, in the distance on the horizon—the sea. In the horizontal, at right angles to the direction that the architectural arrangement has impressed on you from where you stand, it is the rectangular impression which tells. This is architecture of a high order: the Acropolis extends its effect right to the horizon. The Propylaea in the other direction, the colossal statue of Athena on the axis, and Pentelicus in the distance. That is what tells. And because they are outside this forceful axis, the Parthenon to the right and the Erechtheum to the left, you are enabled to get a three-quarter view of them, in their full aspects. Architectural buildings should not all be placed upon axes, for this would be like so many people all talking at once.[113]

Every allusion to the story of Babel and the mixture of tongues serves as an allegory of the cost of internal cultural diversity in disobedience to an idealized national unity. Here as elsewhere, however, the ideal of neoclassical purity remained unattainable by the Greeks except through European translation.[114]

The Analogous City

There is another way to look at the monuments of classicism that presents a more contemporary reconstruction of the city. It was assumed in the 1960s and 1970s that the city could be treated in an analogous manner to structural linguistics. Thus it was expected that the duality of its architectural language, a system of comparisons and contrasts, of selections and orderings, would produce new figural arrangements. Under these considerations, the city text became writerly rather than readerly, allowing the compositional model of its spaces and the twists and turns of its poetical imagery to construct an "analogous city." In the confrontation between constituent components of the city and the memory or imaginative elements they evoked—that is, in the play between the syntax and poetics of city space—it was hoped that a new interlacing would arise between spatial form and representational meaning, or a new cross-breeding would take place between the geometry of the city and its perceptual imagery. As we have learned from classical rhetorics, the memory of a city develops out of its monuments and artifacts; the forms we want to remember having been collected in inventories, archives, and encyclopedias as emblems of recall. Writing becomes the device of memory that depends on the interweaving of dozens of citations and fragments taken from the inventories it mimes. A walk through this metaphorical memory space is a transformational displacement, never coalescing into an illusionistic totality but relying instead on flashes of unconscious recall, that like the pieces of a kaleidoscope suddenly appear in new compositions and visual constructions.

The writerly codes that generate the artifacts and artifices of this city of memory are fabricated by selecting different entries from the encyclopedia of images and organizing them into new ornamental or grammatical patterns and thereby transforming our geometrical and perceptual experiences of the city into new representational forms. These new city spaces drawn from our memory archive are a re-presentation of past forms; they flow back to the point where they were originally constituted. Consequently they reflect either a desire, as we have seen among the nineteenth-century neoclassicists who dreamed of classical Athens, to solidify and present a totalizing image banishing every ill-formed and unpresentable part from within their centered and enclosing frames, or they remain only provisional and imaginary reconstructions cutting across the sedimented layers of history where different time series and personal memories break into each other, creating new patterns and forms. Although the distinctions never are outlined so clearly, either memory steps back from reality to reassemble the past exactly as it might have been "once-upon-a-time" in an eternal return to an illusionary original form, or memory gives way and plunges forward into new compositions, exploiting the polysemic ambiguity of its imagery and artifacts.[115]

Architectural writing relies on imagery and artifacts, visual tropes that form the basic elements of its selective and combinatory system. An "analogous city" text, not quite a real city nor entirely a fictitious one, is a composition of images produced by two kinds of generators: concrete images drawn from a memory archive of architectural types, or imaginary figures and archaic symbols retrieved from the deep structure of memory. City texts consequently are visual constructions overlapping and superimposing architectural images that contaminate and bleed into each other. This visual montage of real and imaginary objects relies on the viewer to round out the whole, to make the necessary associative links between fragments and layers that both lead back into the text as well as outward toward other works and external reality. We can begin to explore this "analogous city" by looking at two prototypes: the imaginary views of Antonio Canaletto (1697–1768) and the fantastical scenographic perspectives of Giovanni Battista Piranesi (1720–1778).

Beginning in the Renaissance, a particularly Roman tradition of city views developed that were fanciful reconstructions of ancient monuments and spectacular scenes of how the city once might have appeared. By the sixteenth century more rigorous drawings were made to document and record ruins, and accurate topographic views of the city were composed to honor the city's glory. Within another century, these ruins no longer appeared merely as backdrop to the city's landscape, but had become the major focus of display, and now these views tried both to capture the present state of Rome's moldering decay and to lament the memory of her lost antiquity.[116] A few years more and stage designers began to combine these ruin paintings with imaginary scenographic views. They were inspired by one of the most influential scenographers of the early eighteenth century, Ferdinando

Galli-Bibiena, who developed fantastical stage sets with cross-axial perspectives that exploded the stage's architectural space by abandoning a central or single focal point and by encouraging the spectator instead to view architectural compositions from a variety of angles and overlapping layers of scenery. In these popular stage sets, the spectator became an imaginary traveler who moved through ruinous landscapes and imaginary terrains, thrilled by illusory spectacles and the memory of unfathomable voyages.

In the early years of his career as a painter, Canaletto worked for his father, a famous Venetian scene painter knowledgeable of Bibiena's craft. Although Canaletto abandoned scenography after a few years, his composite and detailed views of Venice and other cities utilized many of the scenographer's devices. In Canaletto's fantastic tableaux, the city view became an analogous stage set where real and imaginary architectural scenes were combined with antique inscriptions and decorative motifs gathered from different places and times. Recomposed into lyrical and improved representations, Canaletto's city views fused memory with imagination, the real with the reconstructed. These were intended to be visual mementos for tourists, who in turn were enchanted by these souvenirs instilling the hope for future adventures into unknown and fanciful places, yet simultaneously reminding them of scenes that had given them pleasure.[117]

Piranesi also borrowed the devices of Baroque scenographers, heightening the impact of his fantastical compositions of Rome by twisting and turning their viewpoints, creating a confused montage of fragments and spaces, of exaggerated proportions and depth. If Greek architecture was the epitome of purity and restraint, then Roman architecture, so Piranesi surmised, had been erected by plunderers and despoilers, and its compositional forms were not only eroded by time but compromised by choice. Roman ruins were exceptions to the ideals of purity, existing beyond any order that classicists might impose. Their mysterious allure resided instead within irrational and archaic realms. So Piranesi, a bricoleur in search of new orders and new inventions, turned away from those who poked around for the origins of architecture among its ornaments and stones and reached

G. B. Piranesi, Veduta del Piranesi con l'Olmata.

beyond the contemporary zeal for restoration. He moved instead into an arbitrary, utopian, and entirely imaginary sphere of subjective experience. Fantasy holds an essential role in any "analogous city" view, for fantasy is the mediator between an archeologist's mind bent on exploring the roots and remnants of antiquity and a creative imagination that quotes and remembers only arbitrary and unrelated fragments and traces. Through incongruous recombinations and imaginary superimpositions, Piranesi diverted architectural symbols from their original meaning. He played an enigmatic game of architectural writing in which reality and the imaginary are confused.[118]

Drawing closer to contemporary times, we find that forty years ago the School of Architecture in Venice was concerned with developing both typological inventories and grammatical structures by which to compose or write "analogous city" views. Carlo Aymonino and Aldo Rossi were two of the architects who in the 1950s began to study the relationships between architecture and the city, history and memory. If modern architecture had lost its meaning by failing to communicate with either its urban surroundings or its spectators, then perhaps to quote one of the fathers of structural linguistics, it was because "[m]eaning is the translation of a sign into another system of signs" and architecture had failed to develop its system of signs.[119] Thus Aymonino and Rossi asked two fundamental questions borrowed from structural linguistics: how is the city formally composed of signs, and as a formal system, how has it been physically structured and transformed over time? They surmised that architecture in the city was analogous to language, patterned by constituent units following certain rules and conceptual schemes. Thus related questions could be drawn from this model of linguistics: how might a typology of basic building elements be developed, how were the codes that governed the structural or morphological patterns of the city determined, and how could the transformational rules that generated new uses and forms over time be discovered?

Aymonino and Rossi were concerned with the form of architectural discourse and the constructing aspects of architecture in the city. Writing the "analogical city" meant developing a better lens through which the eye could analyze the artifacts of the city, discern the elements of which it was composed, and uncover its structure. Theirs became a self-contained dialogue, however, constrained by formal properties of the architectural project, ruled by perception not expression, of signification not communication. Yet only if their questions could be answered, or so Aymonino and Rossi proclaimed, would architecture in the city become a rational science freed from subjective motivations and stylistic intentions. The realization of universal distinctive features and logical codes of structure—although they never clearly defined just what these features or codes might be—would determine new urban interventions. It appears that Aymonino and Rossi never questioned the validity of the linguistic model they borrowed unconsciously, nor examined whether meaning in architecture could be reduced to a system of signs; they simply followed the belief that laws of signs prescribe all productions of the "unconscious mind," whose activity in turn involved imposing form on content.[120]

Aymonino and Rossi might have found further support for their "analogical city" in the work of Michel Foucault, for he had shown the critical value bestowed on language in the nineteenth century when suddenly it became the medium for all scientific knowledge. Turning language back on itself, so Foucault explained, linguists during that century began to search for the deep structure of language, a set of a priori or preconceptual rules by which not only to understand all that could be expressed within this language system, but to develop as well a structural formalization that could generate all that could be said.[121] The type of history that Foucault wrote throws further light on the "analogous city," for his was a history of ruptures, interruptions, and discontinuities, a history that searched among the strata and layers of time for the points where concepts were displaced and transformed, or the moments where history was moved. Rather than pursuing an intellectural history of concepts that assumed a progressive refinement of terms as they became increasingly rational and abstract in nature, Foucault looked instead for the field in which these concepts were constituted, the rules that governed their use over time, and the theoretical contexts in which they developed and matured. For Foucault, it was the architectonic qualities of a language system that drew his attention, as well as the internal coherence of statements, the deductive connections in a discourse, the compatibilities of what could be said and what was prohibited.[122]

Discourse and its nonlinguistic structures such as institutions, laws, social manners, and political events, as Foucault outlined, were practices that swirled around and engendered the objects of which they spoke; they created the space from which various forms emerged and the place wherein they were continuously transformed. In a similar manner, Aymonino and Rossi assumed that ruptures and discontinuities explained the history of architecture, that the language of architecture, moreover, was dependent on its social, legal, and institutional contexts. On the level of discourse, moreover, architecture in the city takes on the characteristics of being influenced by a historically a priori order or a collectively discursive system of customs that condition its existence, even though this order or system may remain rather vague. Clearly there is no cause and effect posited here, no proof of ruptures or breaks, no empirical methodology that tells us how the customary system is developed.[123] We are left with indeterminant specifications that can lead to a misinterpretation of facts and feverish speculations.[124]

In their search for a logic that would govern the building types of a city, a logic freed of the specifics of style and the architect's intentions, the Venice School began by reassessing universal types first established by the neoclassicists. The concept of "type" representing an ideal imitation and not a model of reality goes back to the theories of Winckelmann, who espoused ancient Greek sculpture as the epitome of beauty informing an ideal type. A too-faithful imitation of nature or reality following the dictates of a model, he argued, would offer only an illusion of verisimilitude, whereas the "type," defined as an ideal imitation, an incomplete resemblance or an archetypal representation, was an image perfected in the mind of an artist yet simultaneously reflecting collective analysis and thought.[125] Following the conventions of an ideal type, the artist or architect created works that were quite dissimilar, whereas from the rules specifying a concrete model the artist could only repeat or imitate the prescribed form. Developed for specific needs and in quest of beauty, building types, Aldo Rossi agreed, formed the very basis of architecture and have always been found in architectural treatises and histories.[126] As Rossi defined the concept of "type," however, it became something "permanent and complex, a logical principle that is prior to form and that constitutes it."[127] In every "type," Rossi argued, following his linguistic analogy, there resides a logical rule or a structural principle that is clear to the senses and to reason, and it can be found in the analysis of every architectural object.[128] Thus Rossi posited the existence of universal norms or conventions that articulate an architectural object for the spectator in a manner sympathetic with the time and the place.[129]

The aim of the School of Venice, however, was to break with the autonomy of "types" that the classical ideal assumed in order to bridge the gap separating the technical from the historical arts, the material forms of architecture from their actual production in space. They intended to articulate the conditions surrounding the art of building in the city. Thus building types were not to be characterized as if they existed outside of their material or concrete application to site and to place. "Types" were the primary irreducible elements of architecture and of the city—the language of architecture's constitutive units—but they also were mediators between the individual and the collective characteristics of a building.[130] Here is where the city and architecture were joined in a reciprocal relationship, the one forming and being formed by the other. Just as walls and columns formed the compositional elements of buildings, so buildings were the elements that composed cities. Architecture could not be separated from the formation of the city: it was a collective process constructed slowly over time, and hence architecture was not to be analyzed for its autonomous styles or ornamental structures, but was at one with the stratified space and layered time of the city.[131] Thus "type" became a constant and analyzable element, elementary forms in an *ars combinatoire* to be manipulated in an open-ended manner in the production or writing of new city spaces. Yet "type" also entered into a dialectical relationship with construction techniques, with the functions and styles of building, with the collective nature of city compositions and the autonomous aspects of the building as artifact. Far from the ideal types espoused by Winckelmann, the School of Venice formed a different conception of typology,

G. B. Piranesi, The Pyramid of Caius Cestius.

consisting of an archive of building types and a set of rules for their combination and cross-references. Their "type" was a mold or mental image whose internal structure and deep geometry developed out of simple typological elements and whose compositional conventions were both conserved and transformed over time.[132]

Carlo Aymonino began to differentiate the distinctive features of building types by suggesting the following contextual conditions: first the singleness of purpose or theme of a structure, then the architectural effects of its regulatory or building codes, and finally both its relative indifference to the urban context and the self-reflexive nature of its own plan.[133] If Aymonino had started by classifying architectual and urban functions as most typologists had done, then Rossi felt he would have posited "type" erroneously as the organizing model for the city: static forms that function as patterns for apartment houses and commerical structures, or codified structures to be utilized in the design of industrial towns and cultural cities. These "types" would tell us nothing about how a city actually was composed and how it had been transformed over time, for architecture in the city was far from being a set of arbitrarily associated forms.[134] Instead a building typologist must analyze the block and lot morphology of a city, the persistence of its plan and its monuments, the influence of economic factors and real estate practices, social concerns and historical conditions. These contextual studies enabled both the architect and the spectator to pursue a continuous reading of the architectural form of the city as it had developed historically over a prolonged period of time.[135] Thus typological studies based on historical analysis revealing both the morphological structure and the formal persistences or variations within each city were the mediating conventions by which the architect wrote and the spectator read the collective forms of the city.[136]

Aymonino offered a dialectical concept that incorporated all the visual elements of the city, its street walls and plans, its gardens and courtyards, its block and lot morphology, classified according to their period of development. The built parcel then became a combinatory system that integrated a series of open spaces within its boundaries, yet was structured simultaneously by precise spatial forms already in evidence in the city. An ensemble of such parcels, the elementary organizational form of the city, was constructed at a particular period of time by incorporating a series of public spaces within its compositional arrangement. This composition revealed a specific density within its internal configuration; it was affected by the location and directional force of the city's monuments and by potential linkages with other forms in the city. Then finally the characteristics of the city took shape as a combination of ensembles affected by the trace of earlier city walls, the contour lines of topography, the location of squares and monuments, and the generative force of the original city plan.[137]

To write the "analogous city," it must never be a question of having a fixed image of the city frozen at a given historical moment. Instead the focus must rest on changes in space and time, seizing on the ruptures or origins around which the modern city was formed. Such rupture points might be the moment when the city burst beyond its encircling walls, thus transforming the traditional boundaries between the inside and outside of a town into the contradictory relationship between the center city and its periphery; or the point when industrialization destroyed the scale of a city and eroded the links tying a place of work to a place of residence; or yet another rupture point was located at the moment when architectural interventions were no longer at the level of the building lot, but took place on assembled parcels. Assuming that these rupture points reflected major shifts in the compositional form of a city, Aymonino concentrated on the analyses of European cities up to a historical cutoff point: the moment when the modern movement of architecture literally ruptured the continuity of built form and destroyed the spectator's perception of recognizable building types. Never claiming that urban or architectural history was evolutionary, a linear process moving toward perfection, the School of Venice in general pursued a history of ruptures and breaks, searching for those points where the urban fabric had been cut and transformed, or leftover fragments that now offered opportunities for imaginary and innovative interventions sympathetic to more traditional forms of the city.

Along with a typological archive and morphological compositions that rule the well-defined city, there must also be a grammatical structure governing permanencies and changes in the "analogical city's" architectural form. Monuments of endurance played a particular role in this transformational game. Viollet-le-Duc in nineteenth-century Paris, facilitated a few years later by the work of Baron von Haussmann, had developed a unique manner of creating a monument by isolating it from its original urban fabric, destroying its original functions, erasing its heterogeneous supports, and then placing this context-free object in a completely redesigned scenographic space, recomposing it as an ornamental fragment, or reconfiguring it as the focal perspective point of new axial boulevards. Viollet-le-Duc's theories of preservation were scientific and historical, if somewhat radical. After adequate research had located the building in its appropriate stylistic context, and after sufficient analyses in situ had recorded the history and vicissitudes of its constructional record, then a conservator under the sway of its historic value might have sufficient information by which to restore the monument to its supposedly ideal form. Any artful creation suggesting a stylistic or scenographic context for a given structure such as Viollet-le-Duc intended, however, was diametrically opposed to the concept of monument and the persistences and invariants of a city plan and its streets that Rossi proposed.

Context is what historic preservation is interested in, creating through its facade restorations and reconstructions the illusion that these architectural compositions are merely stage designs or backdrops for theatrical dramas. Rossi claimed that these static representations preserved city spaces as if they were museum artifacts and were consequently opposed to the very concept of monument as the generating or inhibiting force influencing a city's structural formation.[138] Contextual artists interpreted buildings and city forms as functional containers to be filled with any suggestable use. Rossi's monuments of the city had another value. Take for example the Roman Forum as his most illustrative urban artifact, a space that contains the origin of the city, yet is a field transformed again and again with the passage of time.[139] In 1811 the prefect of Rome, Count de Tournon, offered a plan

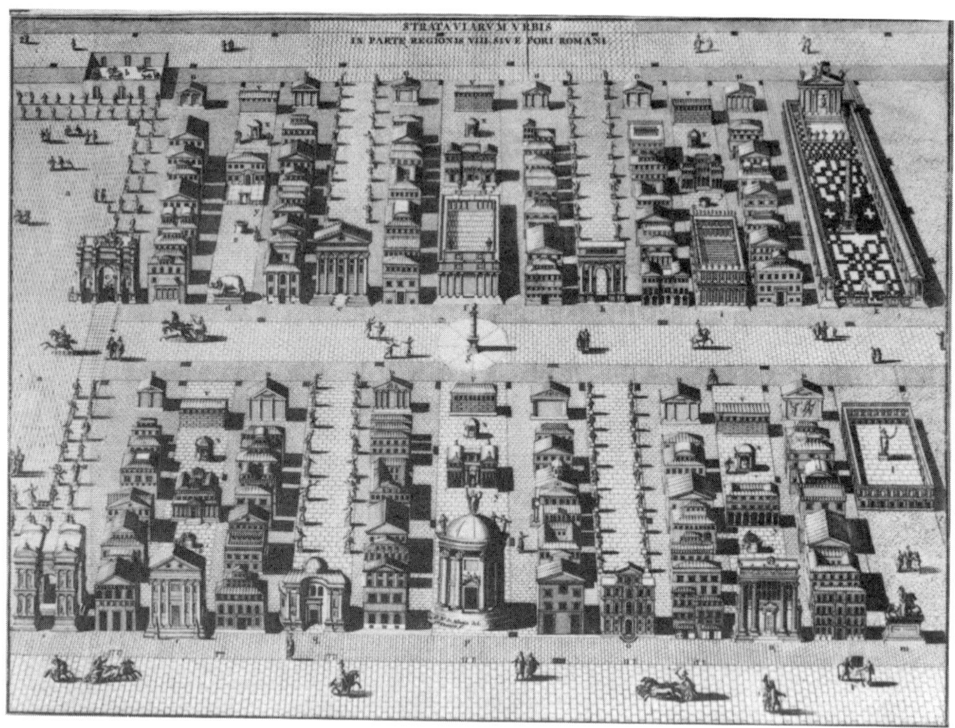

G. W. D. Hennin, Reconstruction of the Roman Forum in the form of a regulated plan *(c. 1700).*

for its restoration that would have freed the ruins from the dirt that covered their lower parts and would have linked them together by an irregular passageway, thus turning them into an accessible spectacle. The Palatine Hill, where the ruins of Caesar's palaces stood, was to become a planted garden picturesquely enclosing its remaining stones and monuments.[140] If such a restoration plan for Rome's most outstanding monuments, or any of the subsequent preservation ideas that had plagued the city over the centuries, ever had been executed even in part, then, Rossi argued, most of the city's monuments and ruins would have been destroyed long ago. The city must never be thought of as a series of isolated fragments and monuments that could be transformed or reconstructed at will, as Viollet-le-Duc had proposed and whose mandate contextual artists had followed every since. Instead the "analogical city" must be understood as a historical text whose continuities, in the form of persistences as well as transformations, resided in the deepest layers of its urban structure. In this sense, the city's history was never reproducible nor restorable to a "once-upon-a-time" except as a flattened two-dimensional account or a narration of mythical proportion.

In the "analogous city" of memory that Rossi proposed, the concepts of permanence and change were revealed in the grammatical structure of the city. Monuments became primary elements of the city persisting through time; built forms such as the trace of an original street plan, the impression of a city's pre-urban nucleus, or the material evidence of its neighborhoods, streets, bridges, and arcades. Uncovered in the study of a city's history, these mental images impressed themselves on the spectator's or architect's mind; they formed both the memory of each city and created a formal unity out of all of its parts. They were the past we still experience in the present, and they enabled us to read the city in a contiguous manner. But these primary elements or monuments could either propel or inhibit our understanding of the city: as visual summarizations they could suddenly enable us to grasp the city's totality, or as formalistic artifacts they could stand in complete isolation tenuously linked to the whole. A propelling monument thus remained a focal point throughout time, and although its functions may have changed, it still was a primary element conditioning the form in which the city grew and was transformed. Pathological elements appeared as anomalies and exceptions; they were unmodifiable artifacts whose dynamic linkage with the rest of the city had been severed, yet they too remained constituent elements of the city's memory and form. These primary elements or monuments and the city's morphology were linked in a moment of formation as stable structures that underwent continual change. Because the city's texture was composed out of its public and private spaces, the monuments or primary elements being public and collective, the residential private, then primary elements became the fixed points around which the residential and anonymous parts of the city waxed and waned; they were really the generating elements of a city's form. Consequently the special configuration of each city at any moment in time depended on how both these public and private spaces interrelated as nuclei or crystallized forms.[141]

No matter how Aymonino and Rossi might have tried to focus on the imaginary analogies and collective meanings of city form, the material reality of the city, the formal pattern of architecture in the city, its visual syntax and grammar described entirely in terms of observable relations, prevailed over any conditions of use, shared traditions, or subjective expressions that give significance to form.[142] It privileged the position of the analyst and the definer of codes over lived experiences and subjective conditions. Because perception, memory, and imagination, however, depend on the imprint of mental images—not material signs manipulated by the language of architecture—it therefore makes the analogy between architecture and language quite problematic. Writing the "analogical city" requires a specific training, an expert who knows how the system of mental constructs are connected into visual patterns and spatial schema. It defines an enclosed system much like the museum's interior that cannot escape its presuppositions.[143] Objects in a museum enable the spectator to admire their formal characteristics, but they are objects spatially and temporally deprived of their originating conditions and signifying rituals. The museum and the "analogical city" are gestures that stand in for reality, they re-present the past through their strategies of writing.

Perhaps for this reason, Rossi turned toward another kind of spatial generator, a form of visual poetics that could mediate between the real and imaginary forms of the city. As every city carries within it the landscape and architectural remains of other cities, and as a memory image is a fragment of a deep-seated notion or an archetype, might the irrational call and untranslatable message of archaic symbols be utilized to disrupt the linear codes and rational conventions of language? This system of assembling—really reassembling—incompatible city images searches through the deep layers of a city's fabric for unconscious and absent figures pressing to be expressed, images drawn from a meta-encyclopedia or meta-guidebook that create nodes of turbulence and entanglement. As Yuri Lotman describes, ". . . the deeper the abyss of untranslatability between two languages, the more acute is the need for a common metalanguage to bridge the gap between them by creating equivalences."[144] The closed system of structural linguistics can be met, therefore, with semantic indeterminacy and analogical modes of thought expressed through rhetorical figures or tropes such as metaphor and metonymy. "A trope," Lotman defines, "is a figure born at the point of contact between two languages, and its structure is therefore identical to that of the creative consciousness itself."[145]

On the basis of a perceived connection between deep and surface features, substitutions work their way upward through the method of collision and collage. Fusions and figurations, citations and reinscriptions thus become the sensed but imaginary inspiration, visual and spectacular creations, to be used in both fanciful and real designs of the city. Each image that coalesces, each association of memory, produces a studied and deliberate reconstruction of pictorial traces from the past. To continue with Lotman's description: "Herein lies the specificity of tropes: for they are in part both irrational (because they make elements that are known to be non-equivalent and totally disparate equivalent), and hyper-rational (because they include a conscious construct directly into the rhetorical figure)."[146] We can think of Federico Fellini's films of Rome to understand how rhetorical figures can be used to construct sound and optical images that give meaning of great complexity.

Viollet-le-Duc, Entrance of Ionian House.

Fellini denies the incompatibility of subjective memory and everyday experiences by effacing the distance between the spectacle and the spectator. So he claims, "[w]e are constructed in memory; we are simultaneously childhood, adolescent, old age and maturity . . ."[147] Thus his films are wandering spectacles, giant Luna Parks that weave together images from childhood and school years, circuses and spectacles, nightmares and poverty, emptiness and solitude. As Deleuze describes Fellini's *Roma,* "The only unity of Rome is that of the spectacle which connects all of its entrances. The spectacle becomes universal and keeps on growing, precisely because it has no object other than entrances into the spectacle . . ."[148]

Thresholds of the city invite us to travel into the subterranean world of symbolic dreams and ancient myths that have been banished from modern cityscapes. They bring us full circle, back to the writings of Walter Benjamin, who saw the topography of Paris filled with these entry points: the arcade, the railway station, the old river bed of the Seine were thresholds to an archaic subterranean world that lay underneath its modern appearance. To exacavate, to follow the path that led downward across such thresholds, was also for Benjamin an act of remembrance. By recognizing that antiquity resided within modernity, by drawing unconscious thoughts to the surface, Benjamin was tracing lost fantasies and studying the prehistory of contemporary times, but simultaneously he was trying to awaken the present-day from the phantasmagorical spell of these dream images by placing these memory accounts in contemporaneous contexts and constellations. Benjamin was a collector—perhaps a ragpicker, to use one of his own emblems—who rescued objects from oblivion not in order to use them for some utilitarian purpose, investment, or prestige but to place them in a historical constellation and thus reveal how seemingly disparate things were necessarily connected. But Benjamin's collector is distinct from a curator, for the former wanted to save objects from being placed in false contexts established by the dictates of tradition or located in museums where they inevitably died.[149] Objects were collected to transform perception, and in this manner Benjamin wrote:

> one observes the Parisian arcades as if they were possessions in the hand of a collector (Thus, one might say, the collector basically lives out a piece of dream-life. For in the dream too, the rhythm of perception and experience is so transformed, that everything—even the apparently most neutral element—thrusts itself towards us, affects us. In order to understand the arcades in their fundament, we sink them into the deepest layer of dreaming, we speak of them as if they thrust themselves towards us.)[150]

Ancient cities like Rome or Paris present us with such a polysemous contamination of memories and relics. The history book of what these cities have become, of all that they might have been or once were, have been blended and shuffled by time into changing patterns that always contain a trace of their otherness. Consequently it is only through a deep-structural reading of secret insights into a city's topography, a downward voyage into their archaic underworld, bringing back to the surface only what is essential, pleasurable, or memorable that the starting point for writing an "analogical city" can be found. To the contrary, museum cities such as Venice or Florence, or historic districts such as Le Marais in Paris or London's Westminster areas, to cite a few European examples of modern preservation, present the spectator with tragic stage sets revealing an antiquarian's taste for the dead past in which the transitions of time and heterogeneity of chance events and experiences have been reduced to the normality of visual scenography properly ordered and maintained. It is modernity that must be criticized for taking a wrong turn, causing societies to lose all connection with the nature of objects and any fascination with the transformative quality of things. Stripped of all sensuous associations and devoid of origins, the alienated and reified objects of modernity unleash only the nostalgic desire for experiences and memories that never can be fulfilled.

The past lies beyond the reach of the intellect, or so Walter Benjamin taught, to be regained in brief flashes and fragmented moments that arise like an epiphany from the presence of some material object or through the sensations and memories an image or object evokes. Recounting Proust's inability to recall his childhood, Benjamin remarked that it was only on dipping a madeleine into his tea that suddenly visions from his past came forward.[151] Ackbar Abbas explains that Benjamin found "certain practices of collecting, like certain textual practices, [to be] alternative means of laying hold of experience in modernity."[152] Through the images a writer uses or by viewing objects in a collection, the reader or spectator might find their way back to experience. A writer's "image does not fix experience but allows it to unfold, as memory itself is unfolded."[153] This can be compared to a collector's passion for material objects that extends to objects of no value, ruins and forgotten items that she or he subsequently uses to confront the distortions of cultural history and to allow repressed stories once again to be told. Thus the collector places lost items back into conscious awareness where they cannot be forgotten, "for a true collector the whole background of an item adds up to a magic encyclopedia whose quintessence is the fate of his object," how an object was produced and how it was received, forgotten, and remembered.[154] A collector stands opposed to the reification of objects, the isolation of things within the interior of a museum, the burden of patrimony and inherited tradition. Instead collecting is a way of transmitting experience through objects, allowing their stories and fate to unfold.[155]

In contrast to the controlled thirst for the past that the museum ensured, Benjamin juxtaposed the psychic force of images in the street and the latent mythology embedded within architectural forms. To be immersed in things, to follow the illumination of significant details, or to study "the physiognomical aspects of visual worlds where dwell the smallest things, meaingful yet covert enough to find a hiding place in waking dreams,"[156] these Benjamin believed could arrest memory loss and restore experience within modernity. Applying the principle of montage to history and allowing the material to speak for itself, Benjamin hoped to effect "a critical 'dialectical' transition from myth to history, prehistory to actuality."[157] In a similar manner Rossi blends the real and the imaginary, alluding to the metaphysical paintings of de Chirico in the early 1900s and to the magic realism

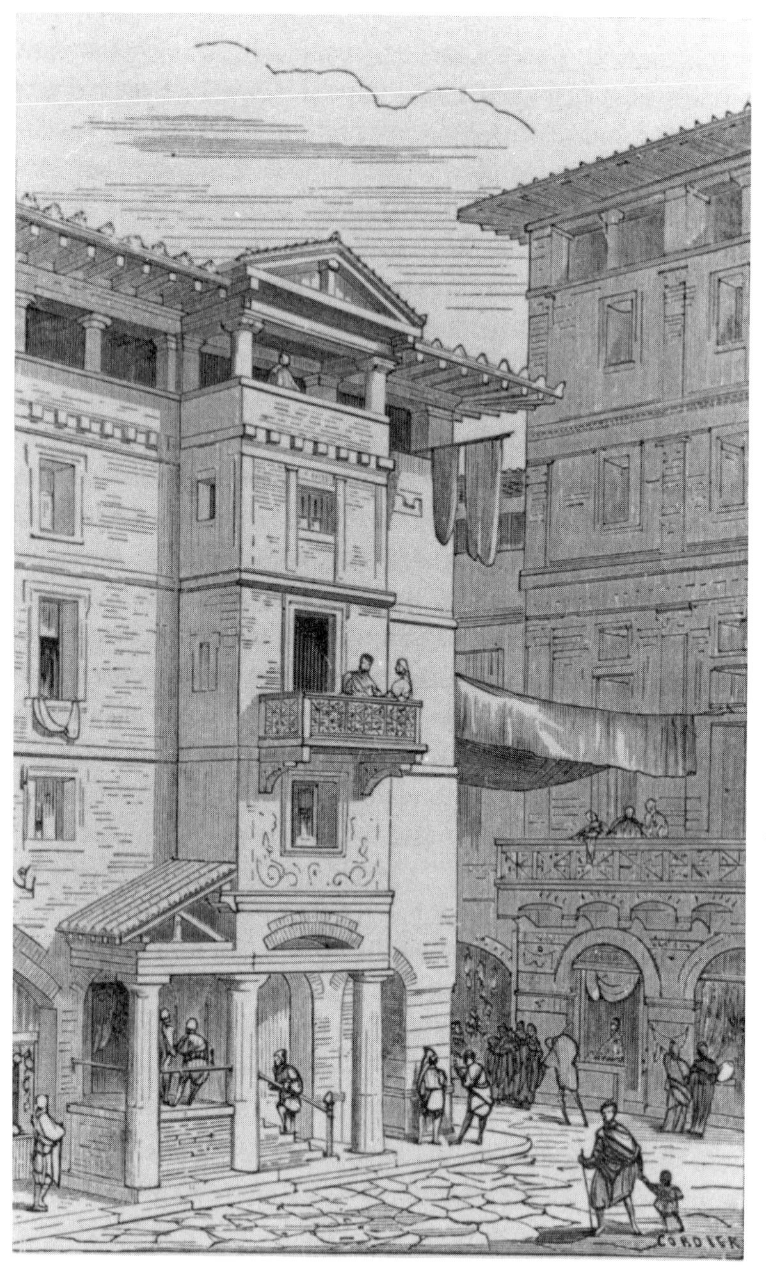

Viollet-le-Duc, Scene in Old Rome.

of Magritte and Hopper. These enigmatic art forms juxtapose discordant thoughts and objects, enabling the spectator to experience the deferred sensations and uncanny strangeness of their surprising, often illogical, collisions. Through frozen images of the city, a timeless array of objects, or by the vibrations established by contrary things, the spectator is being taught how to read the city text not as a picture framed and bounded, but as an oscillating dialogue between the repetition of past forms and the process of continual and indeterminate change. What Benjamin called puzzling constellations and correspondences between situations and things, Rossi defines as analogical links: "Perhaps a design is merely the space where the analogies in their identification with things once again arrive at silence. . . . Not in purism but in the unlimited contamination of things, of correspondences, does silence return. The drawing can be suggestive, for as it limits it also amplifies memory, objects, events."[158]

There are other parallels that can be drawn between Benjamin the collector and Aldo Rossi the architect and writer, for both were disenchanted with the modern world and both looked back through history to find traces of an otherness not yet completely erased. To save the past, to turn it inside out, is simultaneously to rescue the present from alienation, boredom, and distraction.[159] Both Benjamin and Rossi were vigilant by way of memory expressing an obsession with stopped time, and consequently the clock attains symbolic importance for both of them. Commenting on the fact that nineteenth-century revolutionaries in Paris destroyed the city's clocks in the full light of day, Benjamin claimed they did so not because they wanted to step outside of historical time, but in order to stop mechanical time, homogeneous and empty time, the time that caused forgetting and somnabulant unawareness.[160] Rossi's clocks in the campanile of his empty squares perhaps bear witness to this vigilance against forgetfulness and the dangers of boredom and neglect. He too follows Benjamin here, finding material objects to be the way back to experience, to memory, and awakening.[161] And as Lotman outlined, Rossi arranges these objects and images in a meta-encylopedia where the gap between imagination and reality is bridged. As Rossi wrote in *A Scientific Autobiography*:

> Perhaps the observation of things has remained my most important formal education; for observation later becomes transformed into memory. Now I seem to see all the things I have observed arranged like tools in a neat row; they are aligned as in a botanical chart, or a catalogue, or a dictionary. But this catalogue, lying somewhere between imagination and memory, is not neutral; it always reappears in several objects and constitutes their deformation and, in some way, their evolution.[162]

Fascinated with the psychic and imaginative impact of material objects and primitive forms, Rossi makes the allusion to Benjamin explicit:

> . . . the object, whether part of the country or the city, is a relationship of things. There no longer exists purity of design which is not also a recompositioning of all this, and in the end the artist can write, in Walter Benjamin's words, "Therefore I am deformed by connections with everything that surrounds me here."
>
> The emergence of relations among things, more than the things themselves always gives rise to new meanings.[163]

Rossi, like Benjamin before him, also sees the architectural event as the unfolding of a story, what the image and the object reveal.[164] An uncanny and enigmatic power of things, be they archaic objects that resist change or primary forms such as the triangle, pyramid, cone, and cube, move the spectator and thus become the locus for collective memory. Stairs and courtyards, columns and windows, barrel vaults and galleries, fisherman's huts and farmhouses, coffee pots and bottles, lighthouses and silos appear again and again throughout Rossi's work, becoming universal forms that relay personal and collective myths. They are like Benjamin's arcades, street signs, railroad stations, department stores, and so many other urban artifacts real and imaginary, which nourish myths and somnambulism. Yet the trace of history upon things also can have a liberating potential and awaken the spectator from sleep. Rossi claims that his interest in objects, instruments, and tools always led him to confuse "the thing itself with the word through a kind of ignorance, or prejudice, or even through the suspension that this would give to the meaning of a statement or a drawing. . . . I came to regard architecture as the instrument which permits the unfolding of a thing. I must say that over the years this awareness has increased my interest in my craft, especially in my latest projects, where I have tried to propose buildings which, so to speak, are vehicles for events."[165]

Perhaps the theater is Rossi's most important emblem, one that draws together many different aspects of his work, for Rossi's theaters are places of suggestion and recreation, and like the anatomy theater a place of experiment as well. Thus Rossi likens his architectural projects to the fixed scenery of theatrical stage sets, silent and mysterious before the unfolding of human events.[166] Asking how architecture might evoke the mystery of the theater, its public rituals, and its private moments, how it could recall the enigmas of theatrical imagery wherein dwells the space and time of the imaginary, Rossi sets up a series of analogical links between architecture, cities, and theaters.[167] Although theatrical performances were temporary events out of step with normal time, they were definitely in tune with life and thus held great lessons for architecture. Elusive sites, the theater transformed every situation in their recreations and repetitions, but like architecture they had their rituals and events that must be performed. Without events there was neither theater nor architecture, but events could pass by in succession and disappear with time, perhaps to return at some other place or time, while architecture, the fixed scene of human events, remained behind. "[T]he theater must be stationary, stable, and irreversible—but this seems true of all architecture."[168]

Rossi ". . . linger[s] in these places, trying to grasp the possibilities of the architecture, measuring the spaces, noting the placement of the atrium, the stairs, the stages, which become modified in the various expansions or compressions of the distances between the parts. Scarcely do we experience a sense of largeness than we realize the deception of the proportions, just as we comprehend that the

Aldo Rossi, Perspective View of Plan for Mantua *(1981).*

different elements in the work are woven strangely together, illuminating one another. Perhaps the magic of the theater especially resides in this mixture of suggestion and reality."[169] Theatrical visions, Rossi found, were true architectural projects articulating stages as isolated and bounded scenes, yet alluding to the theatrical totality. Here too the city might be critically reconstructed through bounded yet theatrical fragments full of allusions and transpositions. In turn the bounded theatrical scene was inseparable from its stage sets and its architecture: recomposed worlds where typologies interbreed (i.e., amphitheater, stairways, galleries, and stages), where images contrasted and combined to produce a magical metamorphosis.[170] Referring to Raymond Roussel's "Theatre of Incomparables," Rossi plays with the figures of joining and discovery in the theater/city of the imagination, a process where repetition, imitation, and reinvention become the means by which to join so many incompatible or different images, where the identity or meaning of separate scenes is found in their transposed duplicates, in their vanished pasts, or in the secret of their origins.

Underneath the universal appeal of basic geometrical elements, such as the sphere, cone, and cylinder or the galleries, squares, and courtyards, lurks the archaic tug of these images and architectural forms, the visual theatrical play between optical and associational meanings. We come back full circle again and again to question how images are stored in the archive of memory, how they return from the past to affect the present. Aby Warburg in the 1920s warned that images were charged with a mnemonic energy that could overpower the artist if not handled with care. Memory was the mechanism by which the energy of images not known to the conscious world were preserved and transmitted over time. Charged with negative or positive potential, the selective will of an age turned the untamed energies of these ancient relics to harmful or creative advantage.[171] So he wrote, "Between the two [magic and art] extends the realm of the imaginative life, the realm of speech and metaphor, of empathy and art. All these partake in some measure of both the magic and the rationalist attitude."[172] And it is memory above all that mediates between the primitive and the scientific, between the orgiastic and the contemplative, between the elevated and the debased, being both the storehouse of mythical and elementary images and the container of named and rationalized experience. Thus it is the combinatory effect of language and images, the rational and the archaic, that forms the components of our collective memory and gives rise to artistic expression.[173]

This wonderful contamination and these primitive analogies are precisely what museums neutralize or try to suppress through their representational models and structural patterns. The curator's dream is to rationally master ambiguous forms, to inventory, classify, and arrange all the works of art and historical objects into series and periods. But such a totalization can only be momentary, for the heterogeneous nature of objects will quickly escape their determined positions, and rational control cannot always contain the vivid impressions and imaginative forces that escape from between the fold of any official narration. As Benjamin and Rossi noted, curators are always battling with time, seeking to arrest its course and make it stand still in a frozen panorama. But works of art, Aby Warburg argued, contain their own source of energy preserved within their images and symbols. These charges filled with tension blast an object out of the false continuum of history and momentarily enable the viewer to recognize the present retrospectively in the past as they come together in new constellations. Collective memory is formed on such ruptures and breaks. The difference between the museum and collective memory, therefore, lies in the method by which the museum keeps an object's subterranean attractions within well-defined limits, which memory seeks inevitably to explode. Can material objects and verbal images give up their role as muffled actors and speak out, project, touch, surprise the spectator? Are these objects and images allowed to point self-critically to their own exhibitionary qualities? "The German word 'museal' ["museumlike" as Adorno defined it] . . . has unpleasant overtones. It describes objects to which the observer no longer has a vital relationship and which is in the process of dying. They owe their preservation more to historical respect than to the needs of the present. Museum and mausoleum are connected by more than phonetic association."[174] Yet no matter how false their modes of presentation might be, we cannot do without museums, for without their acts of preservation a culture would lose all relationship with past tradition. Across their willful selections, separations, and exhibitions, museums can be sanctioned by spectators who leave their naivete at the door and contemplate in deadly seriousness both art and reality that stand "under constant threat of catastrophe."[175]

f i v e

Topographical Travelogues and City Views

Antiquity had been a civilization of spectacle. [Quoting N. H. Julius, who wrote of the Panopticon in 1831, Foucault continued] "To render accessible to a multitude of men the inspection of a small number of objects": this was the problem to which the architecture of temples, theatres and circuses responded. With spectacle, there was a predominance of public life, the intensity of festivals, sensual proximity. In these rituals in which blood flowed, society found new vigour and formed for a moment a single great body. The modern age poses the opposite problem: "To procure for a small number, or even for a single individual, the instantaneous view of a great multitude." In a society in which the principal elements are no longer the community and public life, but, on the one hand, private individuals and, on the other, the state, relations can be regulated only in a form that is the exact reverse of the spectacle: . . . . Our society is one not of spectacle, but of

> *surveillance; [or documentation] . . . . We are much less Greeks than we believe. We are neither in the amphitheatre, nor on the stage, but in the panoptic machine, invested by its effects of power, which we bring to ourselves since we are part of its mechanism.*
>
> MICHEL FOUCAULT[1]

Spectacular and Descriptive Modes of Mapping

We grasp the immediacy of city life through its imagery. Sometimes thrilled by the imposed vision and power of the sovereign spectacle, we are as well mesmerized by the visual facticity of everyday sights. If scenographic forms of the city most often present exceptional and phantasmagorical views that lie outside of the ordinary, then there is another look, a more disciplined observing eye, that catalogs the minutiae and facts of everyday life.[2] Alberti's topographical analysis of the sites and monuments of Rome already reveals this crossover focus from ideal scenographic compositions to the rational development of accurate maps. In the historical roots of topographic views of the city, we find the same primacy of the visual and pictorial, combining the spectacle with documentation; placing the spectator inside the panoptic machine, intensifying in a blackened room, through a peep box, a camera obscura, or urban observatory, the experience of an isolated viewer gazing upon the many fascinating things presented on the urban stage, but a gaze that classified, categorized, and judged the verisimilitude of the projected imagery.

In the rise of a disciplinary attitude toward the city in the nineteenth century, a shift occurred in the spatial configurations of the city and in the visual arrangement of knowledge that would constitute this view. This was a shift that mixed the image as a spectacular or theatrical form with the image as a descriptive and rational depiction of reality: what Svetlana Alpers describes as the difference between the Albertian and Keplerian use of the camera obscura. In Alberti's camera, the world is viewed through a window, becoming a theatrical stage on which figures enact significant roles. Kepler's concern with the camera obscura lay with the picturing eye, that is, with knowledge obtained through the eye as the description of realistic appearances. In these two images of the camera obscura we find that the spectacular and the documentary, or the subjective and the objective modes of representation, are differentiated—the former concerned with the symbolic and wondrous, the latter with the authority of the outline or the designating index of the thing itself.[3]

Yet in reality, a binary differentiation between these views was never so easily attained. Travel, for example, is both a vehicle for pleasure and escape into unknown lands and imaginary worlds, in addition to being a metaphor for exploration and economic conquest, for the collection of information and goods that implies mastery and control. Even here binary distinctions cannot be maintained, for imaginary worlds are places that cannot be visualized, they must rely on discourse for description and hence they involve selections, representations, stereotypical images, and mappings—all aspects of instrumental control used to adjust the reader's sight to new modes of existence, new cultural customs, new forms of apprehension.[4] Besides, travel for pleasure often gives way to the desire to systematically arrange the sites, architectural artifacts, landscapes, and cityscapes into a formal guide linking places and names, designating the relationship between objects, instructing and directing those who will follow. A universal methodology of guidebooks eventually is the result. The opposite side of this bifurcation, that of instrumental control over a given terrain—whether for military, religious, or economic purposes—cannot suppress or eradicate the emotional and imaginary effects of wondrous landscapes, the grandeur of architectural marvels, the curious customs of peoples and habits of place. New knowledge continually challenges older perceptions and assumptions, giving rise to resistances and disavowals before change and adjustment. So we find that the real and the imaginary coexist side by side; to disavow their complicity is to foreclose on the multiplicity of places and peoples, to erect stereotypes and universal histories, to assimilate the unknown to familiar frames of reference. Instead the result must be a continuous process of constructing and reconstructing topographical views.

Because maps are visual apparatuses through which we view or describe the world and are essential instruments of travel, we can begin to explore this mixture of real and fictitious imagery as it relates to our visual memory of cities by considering two different methods of mapping that combine the spectacular and the descriptive. In the medieval world, for example, maps were often imaginary or fanciful and towns were usually arranged in lists, highlighting only those features of interest and enabling the sequence of such to simply denote the order in which they were to be seen. These maps were all foreground, a landscape of symbols rather than facts, multidimensional and experiential in form.[5] A similar classification of space depicting multiple events and simultaneous views existed in the medieval street pageants, which combined a series of show pictures or show architecture with a processional tour of the town. As the visiting royalty or her or his emissary entered the gates of the town, she or he passed by a series of triumphal arches, fountains, bridges, and a number of tableaux vivants. Copied from tapestries or illuminated manuscripts, these borrowed images and street shows were then displayed on the walls of the town, the facades of its buildings, or raised on platforms located either within a public square or to the side of a street. Built by the hundreds in the fourteenth to sixteenth centuries, such street architecture often contained living actors who pantomined a historical picture or an allegorical grouping. In addition to their celebratory and festive intent, these tableaux vivants were used as well to remind the noble visitor of the city's loyalty, generosity, and military strength, as well as to underline and clarify the sovereign's duties and pledges to the town. As the visitor and the processional party slowly toured the city, making their way from the city gates to the castle, these picture shows suddenly opened in a dazzling display of color and light, music and architectural decor, banners and inscriptions.[6] This was truly the city viewed as a spectacular performance, its architectural forms and urban composition literally transformed into a series of stages didactically addressed to the sovereign's gaze, yet emblematically arranged to stress through allegorical means the reciprocal arts of sovereign allegiance.[7]

Medieval vision had special properties quite separate from our own. Its apprehension of reality, for example, often was configured by dream visions, by extraordinary appearances, or by supernatural messages—reminders of the many wonders of the world that God had created. So for example a thirteenth-century treatise on the science of geography quite surprisingly incorporates an *imago mundi* manuscript (world image) within its folders describing a journey through time of three Mesopotamian monks who traveled to find the end of the earth. It is an account of the known and speculative geography of the entire world, established through exploration and hearsay. On the extremities of the known world or in the far-flung corners of the earth lay places of unseen truths and fanciful perceptions, terrains full of anomalies, marvels, and voids. So the narrative recounts, three monks set off to find the place somewhere in the east where heaven and earth were joined, a place from which no known person had ever returned. On their journey they passed through Persia, then India, before moving into uncharted lands. Here they met dragons and unicorns, followed by a region of perpetual darkness, and then a monument to Alexander the Great. Forty more days of travel brought them to a poisonous lake full of snakes in which the faithless were condemned to drown, for after all, these imaginary worlds actually tested the reader's faith. The monks continued on their travels, coming to a land where speaking birdlike animals continually prayed to God; a hundred days more and they finally found themselves in a land of tiny people, where they met an old man named St. Marcarius. He told them that he too had tried to find the end of the earth, but had heeded the warning of an angel that appeared to him in a dream and told him not to complete his journey although he was only twenty miles away from his goal. And so obediently the three monks listened to the old saint's warning and faithfully turned around to retrace their journey, going back to their monestary without having reached the end of the world.[8]

The simultaneous depiction of the real and imaginary, known and magical spaces, whether in geographical accounts, symbolic maps, or tableaux vivants, eventually gives way to a different representational order without eradicating a

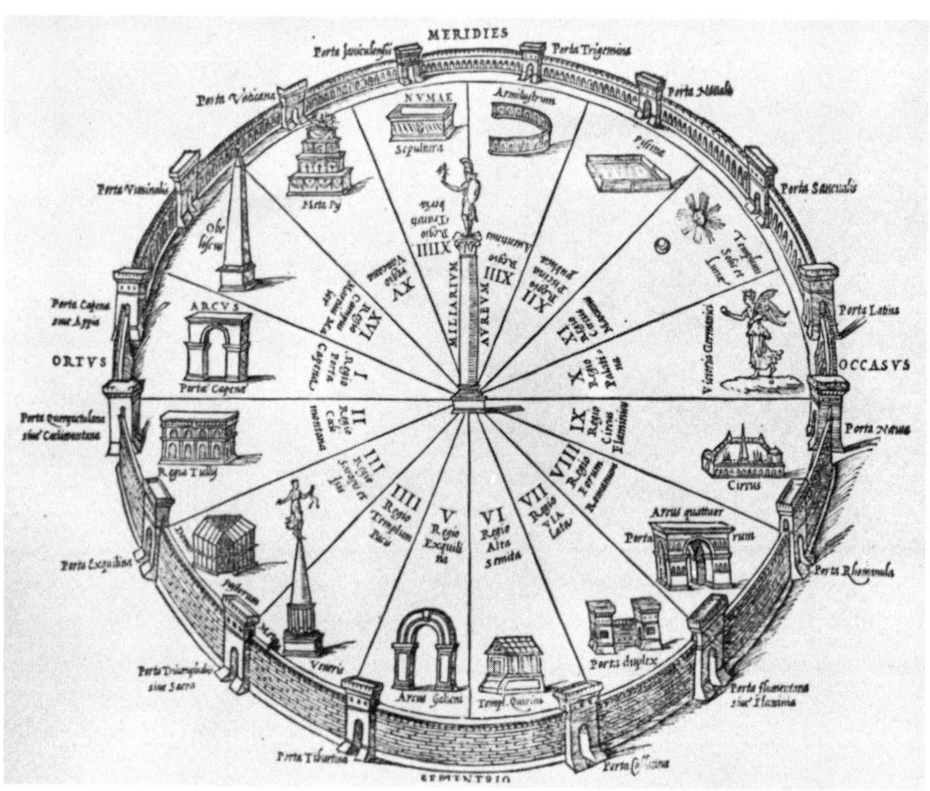

M. F. Calvo, Map of Rome in the time of Augustus *(1527).*

sense of wonder and surprise. By the sixteenth century, mapmaking passed out of the hands of the speculative artists and moved into the territory of the surveyor, where mathematical and optical laws governed its form. Here the Renaissance obsession with the laws of perspective could no longer govern the pictorial view, or else buildings in the foreground of the map would seem to be larger than background ones, and distances between parts of the city would appear distorted and out of proportion. Instead, the city was conventionally represented by a planar surface, a horizontal trace observed from an infinite number of viewpoints all drawn perpendicular to the plane of the ground.[9] Now the map became a world describer, and on its surface mathematically measured information was arranged and displayed. Leonardo da Vinci anticipated these developments in his early map of Imola in 1502, which revealed both his concern with scale, city outline, and plan as well as his experiments with instruments of measurement.[10] In between the eye and the representational form of the image there was placed a translating device to bridge the gap between information obtained through direct optical observation and its subsequent graphical abstraction, for each polygonally shaped three-dimensional object now had to be oriented and measured before being transposed to the surface of the planar map. Leonardo's transit with which he produced this abstract city view was a circular diallike instrument divided into eight sections representing the winds, with a magnetic compass and a movable sight located at its center.[11]

Maps collapse both space and time so that the most remote places, once measured and rendered as information and fixed on a planar map, can be brought home and viewed right before one's eyes. Thus maps offered the pleasures of vicarious travel and imaginary explorations for those who stay at home.[12] Suddenly the accounts of scientific voyages and adventures began to rival and sometimes displace the love for the picturesque, with its spectacular treatment of nature as a a series of extraordinary scenes. Consequently another realm revealing the competition between the spectacular and the descriptive image can be found in the eighteenth-century's taste for travel and exploration. Barbara Stafford has outlined in *Voyages into Substance* the theatrical arrangements of picturesque English gardens, with their shifting scenic visions and composed landscapes intentionally arranged as objects of light amusement.[13] With the advent of the microscope and the telescope, she argues, this picturesque landscape of the world stood ready to be explored in minute detail, rendered by scientific observation and pierced by a penetrating gaze. By the mid-eighteenth century, the definition of discovery would incorporate that of travel and would engender an altered vision or "a finer optic." Scientific voyages demanded a detailed procedure for gathering facts, beyond what either amusing passages through picturesque scenes or an inattentive gaze traveling quickly over the surface of things could provide. Accuracy in the description of flora and fauna, the geological stratification, and primordial environments of distant lands was matched by the architectural detailing and accurate measurement of ruins and monuments now confirmed by firsthand accounts and archeological renderings. The powerful language of visual observation came to rule the observer's perception, because the purpose of these scientific travel reports was to display before their audience, as graphically as possible, the greatest range of precise information culled from every spot in the world.[14] No matter what the scientific intent, however, and in opposition to "a finer optic," the phantomlike aspect of nature, the magical and primal contact with the universe, the romantic thrill over moldering ruins and fragments of antiquity, always gave rise to a belief that somehow these spectacular visions could be materially represented: not just tamely in scientific illustrations and accurately depicted maps, but in exaggerated scenography and through the marvellous replication on stage of sunsets and sunrises, storms and conflagrations which de Loutherbourg's Eidophusikon so readily captured. The phantasmagorical and the sentimental, the symbolic and the imaginary, no matter how they much they were banished from an objective and rational view, nevertheless stood side by side, often mingling with (and sometimes transforming) the purities of scientific vision.

If we turn to the modern roots of measuring and mapping the city's terrain, we will find the same contamination of the marvellous and the rational. The anthropologist Victor Turner believed that there are and always have been two moods of the city, one subjunctive and one rational, both hopelessly intermingled under the surface of its drama. It is the rational or realistic device representing the way things and events actually appear as facts or evidence that has dominated the narration of modern city development. But there is as well a subjunctive wish that things might possibly be different, that alternative choices exist, that peoples and places can be improved and reformed. Turner claimed that ritual, carnival, festival, theater, and film, all types of visual performance, tend to possess the subjunctive mood expressive of desires and possibilities more frequently than they contain rational accounts of facts and events.[15] Using the term "liminality" to define a betwixt-and-between condition, Turner linked cultural subjunctivity to both a retreat from and a reaggregation of the facticity of everyday events. Liminal propositions, or what Turner also called "frames," are "privileged spaces where people are allowed to think about how they think, about the terms in which they conduct their thinking, or to feel about how they feel about daily life."[16] These frames place the spectator outside the system of instrumental propositions and objective measures used to conduct daily life. They recognize that other scrutinizing and evaluating procedures, really meta-languages, are required to talk about the system itself. At times the space of the city takes on this sense of liminality, it becomes a text to be read or a space to enter in order to retreat from and subsequently reflect on the social order and cultural significance of its architectural passages and transformations. The development and management of city spaces displaying paradoxical and ambiguous problems often require this decentering and estranging device in order for the spectator to gain an exterior vantage point from which to judge its successes and failures, especially during moments of transition. As things change, as a new order arises, a review of all objects, a survey or listing of all events, spectacles, and spaces that used to take place in the city, often supplements the more paradoxical and ambiguous developments. Although these accounts appear to be gripped by nostalgia or seized with an instrumental intent to control, they are just as often aware that a vanishing order of things must be accounted for before they disappear from awareness. A passage through the city thus becomes a listing and surveying process, one that may appear to retreat from the marvelous and enchanting mixture of objects and events while yielding momentarily to an instrumental arrangement of things in order to comment on and to judge the points of transition.[17]

Sir Patrick Geddes seemed to exemplify this liminal vision, being one of the first in the late nineteenth century to propose that the industrial city, experiencing massive upheavals and pains of transition as it took on the appearance of the gigantic metropolis of modern times, might be controlled by developing comprehensive city surveys and scientific city plans. These in turn could be developed by studying, cataloging, and reorganizing the visual phantasmagoria on the surface of ordinary city life and by understanding the underlying geological factors that seemed to have produced this morass.[18] Geddes proposed an even larger optical survey to accompany each city survey, for he conceived that the regional environment was a visual archive, which if placed metaphorically under a microscope would reveal an ongoing evolutionary process. A scientific gaze projecting out over the landscape, piercing and recording every substance and strata, would exhume the history of its formation and lead the way forward to future change. This optical voyage in both breadth and depth was to be a new method of direct observation in the field and outside of the confines of academic libraries and lecture halls; it was, moreover, an optical gaze that struggled to depict the hidden operations behind every evolutionary step that created the transformational potential of the earth, the region, and the city.

Geddes's Outlook Tower, which he opened in 1892 in Edinburgh, was such a pictographic record or visual encyclopedia. His graphical-visual sensibility stemmed from the fact that while on a trip to Mexico as a young man, he was confined to darkness for several months under pain of losing his eyesight. There in total darkness day after day, he tried to keep his mind active by projecting all of his acquired knowledge through visual symbols onto the screen of his imagination. So he reasoned, if the sciences such as mathematics, biology, and chemistry were based on and communicated through graphical notations, then why could not the other branches of knowledge be graphically displayed and arranged on an abstract landscape of maps and globes?[19] Aided by the matrix of panes in the windows of his darkened room, which his hands could feel, he developed the framework for his Index Museums and his Encyclopaedia Graphica.[20] Organizing his ideas around the "Place, Work, and Folk" scheme of Frederic Le Play, these Index Museums allowed Geddes to propose that new linkages between ideas emerge by constantly placing the squares of the matrix in new constellations and arrangements.[21]

Developed as an experimental laboratory, the Outlook Tower constituted a global graphic encyclopedia and formed the basis for the regional survey and town planning exhibits that Geddes later promoted. Here were brought together two worlds: the artificial and the natural, or the outlook of both the arts and sciences, in a synthetic and illustrated representation of the universe. Geddes referred to this place as a museum of museums or an index of encyclopedias, showing how to study the city, the region, the nation, or the universe, by spreading a widening view concentrically in superimposed, ever-enlarging and penetrating rings of knowledge. The eye was to dominate whatever fell within its gaze and thus to reveal a deep structural understanding that would illuminate the path to the future. Geddes believed that a smashing of conflicting ideas and artifacts would result in the vital production of new knowledge. But more than this, he actually was combining three traditions in which Edinburgh had excelled during its golden age of the eighteenth and early nineteenth centuries: the publishing of encyclopedias (from 1808 to 1830), the printing of cartographic views with the establishment of the Bartholomew firm in 1797, and the excellence of its university. His Index Museum, really an imaginary conception in which the Outlook Tower played only a fragmentary role, was to be a visual encyclopedia of all knowledge graphically illustrated and labeled, extending from the local plane to the level of the universe. Consequently, the Outlook Tower condensed a series of artistic views with the many looks of the sciences: the images of the camera obscura, the vantage point of the balconies, the inspections of the telescope, the bird's-eye graphical views, the drawn panoramas, the measured maps, and constructed globes. But the Index Museum also implied a procedure to guide the traveler through its array of visual information by following its graphical map.[22] Call it an Index Museum or an Encyclopaedia Graphica, Geddes assumed it would one day be the cultural center in every city and region.

The previous owner of this Outlook Tower had already built a camera obscura on the top of the building: its viewpoint could be moved around the horizon, enabling various images to reappear as projections on a white table placed beneath it. This optical device presented the region up close for minute examination, causing the remote to be suddenly immediate. Out on the balcony, the open roof prospect enabled the viewer's gaze to scan the horizon and to focus on those aspects of the scenery that drew his or her attention. Geddes personally pointed out details to be examined more attentively, thereby bracketing the infinitely open arrangement. A cell of meditation stood just inside the prospect, where one could reflect on the outlook and its mirrored reflections and detailed studies. Here, Amelia Defries wrote, "is where one's picture is conceived, not copied, from nature. It is the room of the Weaving of Dreams."[23] Inside, a world survey was arranged as a prototype of the Index Museum. Its charts, diagrams, friezes, and instruments depicted the universe as seen from the point of view of Edinburgh. In the octagonal room below, astronomical charts and appartuses demonstrated the orbit of the earth among the heavenly bodies. The apparent movement of stars was visualized from within a hollow celestial globe that the spectator could actually enter. Outside this room on the parapet stood a telescope where a system of arrows incised on stones and located within the field of vision guided the eye to features of importance. In the Scottish room, the evolution of Edinburgh and Scotland were traced graphically through a great floor map, which provided a key to those geographical factors that had aided their social development. Still lower floors contained surveys of Britain, the Empire, Europe, and other countries. And finally the World Room contained two great globes, one in relief and the other depicting the world's vegetation. These globes as well as the celestial globe were designed by Paul Reclus, the nephew of the French geographer Élisée Reclus.[24]

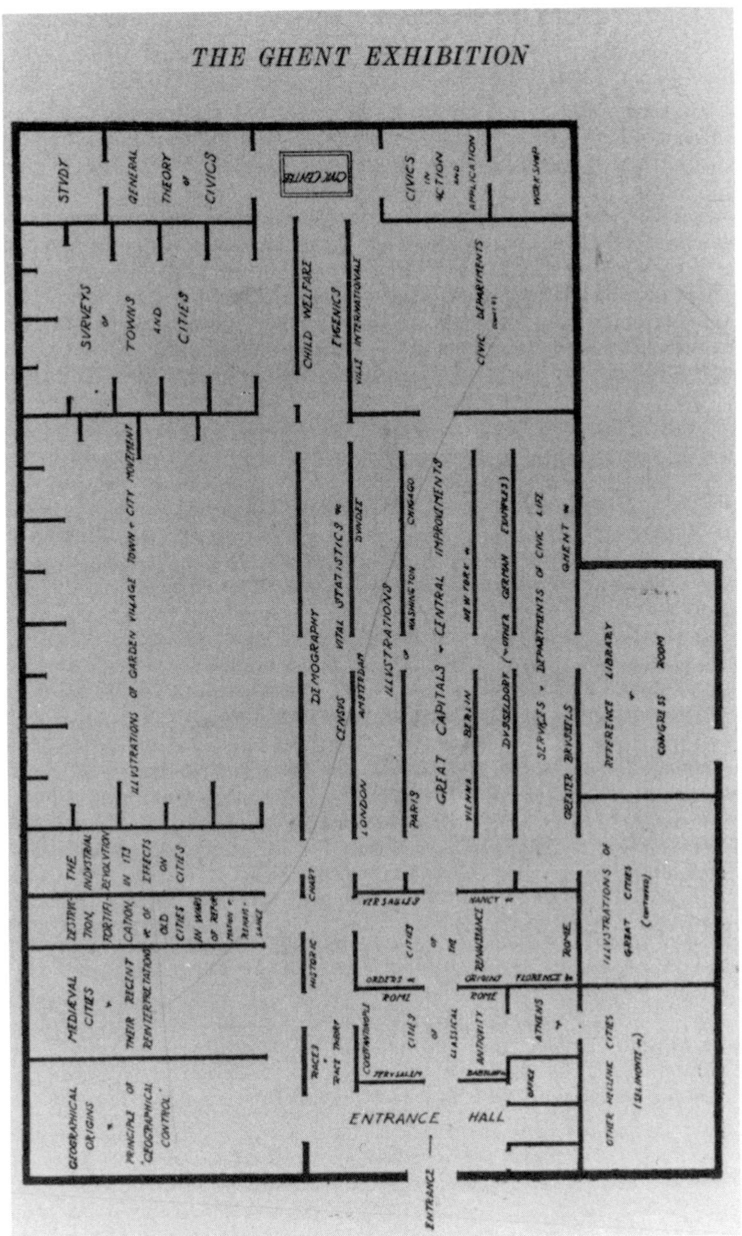

Sir Patrick Geddes, Floor Plan of The Survey of Cities at The Ghent International Exhibition *(1913).*

Continuing his obsession with optical knowledge, Geddes also proposed a slide series for the Outlook Tower, dissolving views of Edinburgh projected so that one image melted into another, thus revealing both the historical construction of the city and the perfection of certain landscapes.[25] Three stained-glass windows placed on the landings of the Tower's stairs underscored Geddes's visual sensibility. In the first, called the Arbor Aesculorum or the Tree of Life, two sphinxes guarded a tree whose roots lay in the fire of life, and whose branches represented the succesive ages of man. Smoke curled upward through the branches, symbolizing how the previous ages had been blinded to the thought and work of their ancestors. Emerging out of the smoke at the top was the phoenix of man's renewed body and the butterfly of humanity's immortal soul. Lapis Philosophorum or the Philosopher's Stone was the second window, displaying the reintegration of art and science. The third window called the Valley Section represented a typical regional view from mountain to sea, with its various occupations. Geddes professed that only by understanding the origin of city professions (those that lay in mining, forestry, hunting, sheep herding, farming, and fishing) and how these created the urban iron and steel foundries, timber and paper merchants, furriers and woolen mills, bakers and greengrocers, breweries and ports—that is, only by descending from source to sea, or following the downward-looking and penetrating gaze, could we comprehend the development of civilizations from their simple origins to their complex forms and eventually arrive at an understanding of the morass of the emerging metropolis.[26]

Élisée Reclus inspired the work of Geddes in innumerable ways: his elaborate cartographic schemes were one influence, but in addition Geddes and Reclus both shared the idea that men must not use the earth wantonly, destroying and desecrating it as they pleased but instead must constantly improve it through the benefits of science and technology. From one of Reclus' books, *The Story of a Brook* (1869), Geddes took his "Valley Section," the panorama of history unfolding as one descends from river to sea.[27] So Geddes later claimed, as surveyors of cities and regions we must read the evidence of their past, and clarify their heritage from their concrete origins to their ambiguous present. Their crafts must be reconstituted from fragments, and so too their words from wall scribbles and popular songs, from mighty literature and theatrical shows.

> Thus, knowing and confessing its many evils and meannesses since now plainly seen and undeniable, [the people of each city and region] cannot but think and strive towards purging it anew. . . . What Pompeii, as re-excavated more and more skillfully, does for later and modern Naples, that we may have to do everywhere, so far as may be, for every city—in itself and in its ancestry direct and remote. Thus the Florence of Giotto's Tower and the Florence of Medicean palaces should be reconstructed, not merely to the historian's imagination, but also as friezes in our civic galleries, as models in our museums (as indeed has already been done in Rome and elsewhere today). These should be combined with their vital literature; Dante's supreme presentation of the good and evil of Florence, into which converges and in which culminates, well nigh the whole Middle Ages; and then again the literature of the great humanists, and artists also, from whom radiated the Renaissance, in whose decline we moderns for the most part live today, despite all that our industrial and other advances have given or lost.[28]

All of this should be re-collected, not it seems as models of replication, but as rites of purification and revision.

Geddes tried to organize a company to publish a series of panoramas, maps, and synoptic charts and to manufacture Élisée Reclus's designs for relief globes. If enough of those artifacts could be sold, Geddes hoped that a huge globe 80 feet in diameter would be built with the proceeds and displayed at the 1900 Paris Exhibition.[29] This was to have been his panorama of panoramas, and though never built, it was projected to be a huge iron structure with a spiral staircase enabling spectators to contemplate the globe from every latitude and longitude. Geddes believed that the nineteenth-century industrial exhibitions were the greatest curators of everyday life, graphically displaying the most recent acquisitions of human knowledge.[30] But instead of their random arrangement of items, he suggested that an Index Museum must be compiled to turn these expositions into productive machines. Consequently Geddes developed an information center as an interpretative annex to the Paris Exposition of 1900. Here he proposed to orient visitors to the separate displays, which for the first time were organized by "types" of exhibitions rather than by national demonstrations as had been the custom of previous shows. He wanted each spectator to be able to interpret these views in relationship to each other and thus develop a comprehensive picture of the major tendencies in Western knowledge and technological achievement.[31] Geddes was fascinated by the many geographical illustrations from almost every portion of the globe that were present at the exposition, especially the panoramas of all possible types, from unrolling views to vast tableaux the size of an entire exhibition hall. He believed that these views achieved such a remarkable synthesis of artistic and mechanical skill that geographical truth and landscape beauty were stunningly combined in views of mountain ranges, sea voyages, and climate and atmospheric effects; the many relief displays of public architecture, Geddes felt, taught the popular mind more about the need for their protection than many a preservation society had every attained.[32]

In 1904 Geddes was asked by the Carnegie Dunfermline Trust to development a plan for the town's preservation. In this work of reconstruction Geddes decided to utilize the many fascinating optical displays he had seen at the Paris Exposition. He felt that a new class of exhibitions and museums had been rolled into one wherein the explorer and the geographer, the trained artist and the simplistic visitor, country folk and child could alike find keen and active pleasure and genuine and enduring education. He greatly lamented that these great panoramas were scattered to the winds after the exposition, in spite of his efforts to find them a permanent home. So in Dunfermline, Geddes proposed to draw on the knowledge, skill, and experience that had produced these panoramas. Let the curator of the museum, which Geddes proposed to be the center of his restoration of Dunfermline, be one of these geographical artists, and then the completion of each new panorama would be at once an educational and artistic event in both the town and the region! The growing collection would not only command the attention of geographers and intellects in Scotland and beyond, but they would attract and educate the spectacle-loving visitor of every class and age.[33]

Geddes also directed and scenographically composed "The Masque of Learning," another visual experimentation performed in Edinburgh by 500 masquers in 1913, and replayed by 900 to 1,200 performers in London the following year. Instead of facts about great heroes, royalty, and wars, the masque visualized the important events from past ages, offering tableaux vivants of poets, inventors, discoverers, and students of nature. Friar Bacon in his cell, Columbus pleading for money to support his voyages, composers from Burns to Beethoven, all gave visual witness to the evolution of human knowledge and to the sacrifices made for the sake of its advancement. The masque depicited the progression of European cultural ideals from preclassical (i.e., the fall of Rome) to modern times, opening onto the future as the torch from past ages was passed to those in the present. In the last episode of the masque an array of social types representing the creation of modern occupations was displayed: and there among them stood the modern aviator as the new messenger of peace.[34]

When the Town and Country Planning Act became law in 1909, it was proposed that the Royal Academy of Art create a town planning exhibit to demonstrate the virtues of planning. Who else but Geddes should be called on to provide material from his Index Museum, although it was no more than a hotchpotch of picture postcards, newspaper clippings, crude woodcuts, stange diagrams, and archeological reconstructions, causing critics to proclaim that this heterotopia was a lowly assault on the academy's aesthetic traditions. Yet the record shows that many viewers of this exhibit were shocked by their own ignorance with respect to the complex factors that had gone into the development of cities and the multiple causes of their misery.[35] Geddes rearranged this eclectic demonstration into a giant Survey of Cities at the Ghent International Exhibition in 1913. Here was a massive survey, the dull grey view of the penetrating and exacting gaze aimed at the unification of studies both contemporary as well as historical, geographical and economical, anthropological, demographic, and eugenic.[36]

This was an exhibition of Geddes's "politography" and "politology" in which visitors saw and felt the profusion and confusion of the subject. Hence in the Entrance Hall a medley was hung of old and new things, pictures, plans, architectural and civic views—each image interesting but without any obvious association with the next. This was the presentation of the confused beginnings of the development of cities. From there one entered the gallery of "Modern Civic Administration," again with little systematic arrangement, being alphabetical at best in the prosaic manner of city fathers. Next the spectator saw the alternative to this rough and ready arrangement as she or he moved into the room of Classic Cities, which illuminated the glory of Athens and the grandeur of Rome. Then came the gallery devoted to "Towns and Cities of the Renaissance." A few of these cities had survived in the struggle for existence, and now were called the "Great Capitals of Europe." From these few examples many colonial towns had derived their physical form, and hence a larger gallery was devoted to these capital cities. Here the viewer could see the spectacular results of centralized power, of triumphal wars, of the rise of railway and telegraph systems, of administrative and economic concentrations. The spectator graphically witnessed how imperial power had determined the town planning of Berlin in the 1800s, Paris in the 1860s, then Rome or Vienna, and Washington and London. But she or he saw as well how another process counteracted this centralizing tendency, the centrifugal energy of industry, culture, finance, and education. Thus the "Great Capitals" gallery ran directly into the "Central Improvements" exhibit, which was displayed around the walls and moved from city to city revealing exactly how architects and planners had resolved the same problems in different locations. Now the spectator was ready to enter the final gallery, the most unfinished of all, which displayed the nascent science of civics and illustrated future alternatives. Between the last two exhibits stood the ancient model of a City Cross, a symbol of the return of civic idealism. And behind this symbol stood a miniature model of the Outlook Tower, a reminder of the importance of the civic observatory and the urban graphical laboratory. The spectator was now prepared to return to the entrance hall and begin again to review the material with the knowledge of what had already been learned from the galleries of classical cities and great capitals; those of race, population and child welfare (which seemed to have been located in adjacent corridors); and that of the geographical and historical origins, surveys, and developments of towns and cities; and try once more to make sense out of this clashing of compelling views and images.[37]

Treasures are to be found in the artifacts of cities, in the deep structures that configure their form. These Geddes claimed were the real reasons for preserving a city's architectural history—not because some notable person slept there or a historic event occurred in the town, but instead because these possessions revealed the city's social and physical formation.[38] Obviously the phantasmagoria of material facts and visual imagery fascinated Geddes on their own, but this labyrinthine world in abundance had to be mapped and structured in some manner if this plethoric accounting of details was to be intelligible; this need led him to base his Encyclopaedia Graphica, with its matrix of cross-references and free associations, on the earlier eighteenth-century work of the great encyclopedists Diderot and d'Alembert. Their work had contained an exhaustive survey of the mechanical arts, codified and drawn in exact representation. Hoping to defend the value of manual labor, Diderot placed these images carefully in the pages of his folios before they were replaced in reality by more industrialized arts. In this manner the past lived on in the visual archive of the Encyclopedia. Likening the organization of an encyclopedia to that of a city of streets, whose buildings should be designed by different architects lest the viewers become bored, Diderot knew that the ordering of such a vast outpouring from different "architects" required a system of cross-referencing. He used basically two different systems of organization: the first was similar to linking a branch to the trunk so that the tree of knowledge contained connected pathways from the source to its nodes; and second, his system depended on opposition, contrast, and comparison. But third, a man of genius like Diderot himself—or obviously Geddes—could cross-reference through new analogical comparisons, giving rise to innovations and speculative truths.[39] Like Geddes after him, Diderot assumed that the viewer's gaze was an actively exploring and interpreting stare that upset and refuted known findings before it established new knowledge. For both, the encyclopedia assumed the role of memory for a people, guiding them and overseeing their path to the future.[40] Images on which comparisons were made acted as the stimulus to memory, resurrecting past ideas through resemblance. Didactic as well, these images aroused enthusiasm on their behalf by operating directly on the senses.[41]

Geddes's Encyclopeadia Civica, or his Index Museum at the Ghent Exhibition, cleverly called on images for arousal to civic action and city planning. But the plethora of details, the circling route of the spectator designed to link all the displays together, continuously broke down in confusion. The representation of facts that had given rise to the physical form and chaos of cities, a relaying of views once known but now lost from sight, failed to come to the surface. It was a kind of knowledge that relied on the eye, but the eye alone could not grasp this world in its entirety, nor render its spectacular effects an exact and meticulous grey. Geddes's pictorial displays, museums, and masques foregrounded the visual; as setups they offered the beholder direct confrontation with nature and art. Although sight may be a strong provocator of memory, images unaided do not establish a language; they convey inherently ambiguous expressions. The relationship between two indices in a matrix, or two juxtaposed views such as panoramas and globes, the vertical overlapping of successive perspectival views or the serial layers of underlying images, were supposed to designate the unity and order of the world. Through a variety of optical instruments, Geddes reached out to confront the massive amount of data the modern and archaic world ejected. These tools were a necessary first step along the path leading toward an instrumental control over the future form of a city or the preservation of what was left of its past. But a visual sensibility oscillating between memory and reality, the phantasmagoric and the scientific, necessarily opened on an infinity of interpretations not to be enclosed within the museum, the encyclopedia, or the pictorial record. Using visual imagery, the subjunctive mood embedded in the optical theater and displaying the liminal terrain where one questions the system of one's own inscription brought into focus a different kind of perception and alternative sensiblities, which the rise of twentieth-century modernity would completely suppress.

The Architectural Archive

Michel Foucault claimed that the nineteenth century discovered an imagination that the preceding century had forgotten. It was the meticulous detailing and scholarly passion of the archivist who found that his imagination leaped out of the void between the pages of his book and the light of his lamp. To dream, the scholar must read the pages of a book, the text of a city, or the stones of its architecture, comparing these images, following their shifts and amended positions, staring at the torn and battered fragments of their monuments. In between these sources, in the voids they present, the imaginary took flight not in opposition to the real but in an entirely different manner.[42] Geddes has enabled us to begin to fathom this imaginatory voyage, for his was a traveling, scanning eye, a probing and comprehensive gaze, displayed and rearranged for our view. But let us move further into the depths of the nineteenth-century imaginary, backward to its fascination with travel, wherein every journey became the start of another, every step taken the pretext for the next. The encyclopedic mind was such a traveling vision, a horizontal cross-referencing of facts and details scattered across the earth. This was a invitation to compare and combine according to the index provided, which kept the plethora of details and chaos of things from disintegrating into disorder.

John Ruskin was another like Geddes whose visual imagination resided within the tight enclosure of the book, the library, and the museum. As a literary architect, he turned the pages of his books into a gallery of images and optical memories, reconstructing views and contemplating details that he felt his contemporaries were intent on destroying. Architectural sites and cities were places to travel to and to read about, things in the world around which a spectator formed his or her visual sensibilities, and objects beheld from which imagination took flight. Yet nineteenth-century Venice lay in ruins, and elsewhere, or so it seemed to Ruskin, the ecstasy of Gothic architecture was being wantonly crushed in countless instances by the artless hand of restorers, while the century's revolutions and the rise of the bourgeoisie were spreading a numbing pall over the past. Fearful of the political upheavals of 1848, Ruskin intended in *The Seven Lamps of Architecture* (1849) to establish the manner wherein architecture expressed its meaning and moral atmosphere, to demonstrate how architecture could become an instrument of social stability. Between the lamp and the book, the architectural imagination of a nation would spring forth if it followed the guidebook Ruskin provided.

Modern society bent on progress and development, Ruskin proclaimed, forced most people in the nineteenth century to live in cities shut away from gardens and fields where they might reflect on the quietness and primordial powers of nature. Thus it was the role of architecture to fill this void, to speak of the deep relationships that bound the beholder to his or her natural environment.[43] Because devotional and memorial architecture were generous gifts that benefactors made to society, they became instruments of social harmony through the very spirit of that sacrifice. The Lamp of Sacrifice thus expressed itself in the costly labor expended on carvings and embellishments, and especially in the variety and mysterious forms of ornamentation drawn from nature. Such acts of sacrifice stood opposed to the modern mode bent on producing the largest result for the smallest cost. So, Ruskin preached, a nation must learn to sacrifice if it was to offer architectural monuments for future generations to revere and remember. To be lasting, however, the spirit of architecture must be honest, hence the Lamp of Truth was necessary to guide the architectural imagination away from deceit and shams in the materials it used, in the ornamentation it inscribed, in its display of technical virtuosity. The Lamp of Power, on the other hand, spoke of how an architect could emulate the awesome and sublime expressions of nature through a play of light and shadow, in the bold expanses of unbroken surfaces, in color and tintings. But forms and images not derived from natural objects were judged to be ugly, hence the Lamp of Beauty must spread its light over organic colors and natural shapes, guiding the hand of the architect. Because the selection of an architectural style was a matter of life and death, the fate of a nation being written in the stones that it erected, the Lamp of Life showed the path toward national posterity and honor. A Lamp of Memory also was essential if a nation was to remember its history, for without architecture a society had no record of its past achievements. Hence this Lamp spread its light over the duties of an architectural imagination, rendering the architecture of the day historical and preserving as faithfully as possible for generations to come the architectural inheritance of the past.[44] And last was the Lamp of Obedience, the restraints and sacrifices needed if a nation's architectural imagination was not to be dissipated in the building of railway tressels and tunnels, in the production of superfluous luxuries and pleasures. Even though Ruskin thought the nineteenth century to be an era exalting in rapid-fire progress, he believed there was a way to resist the advancing shadows of change by reuniting technical and imaginative elements, and by following the noble laws and truthful reality of nature.[45] Crossovers between architecture and nature, passages between the text and the image, were supposed to open vistas in the mind of the spectator-reader, guiding every architectural imagination toward the future.

Architecture, for Ruskin, was not an issue of aesthetics but one of moral reform, and required an exacting study of nature and a belief in an ideal society. He found support for his position in the work of Thomas Carlyle. Ruskin professed that he owed much to Carlyle, reading and rereading his works until their mode of expression became his own second nature.[46] In *Past and Present* (1843), Carlyle posed an antithesis between the medieval organic society, stressing its familial and social connectedness, and the modern frenzy of fragmentation and disconnectedness. As a reformer, Carlyle struggled to save contemporary society from its absorption with material goods and its enslavement to industrial processes, turning back nostalgically to the simpler ways and purer times of the medieval past, hoping they would transform contemporary minds and social arrangements.[47] If Carlyle had used the past and present comparative approach to point out contemporary needs for reform, then Ruskin used the Crystal Palace, erected in 1851, as a central figure in his comparative method, a metonym representing the dementia of his age. The Crystal Palace, what Ruskin called a greenhouse larger than ever a greenhouse had been built before, was clearly the product of architects from the Royal Academy, artists from the government schools of design, and engineers from the railway companies.[48] It was they who had separated art from nature, labor from design, and function from beauty at the very moment when Ruskin wished to establish a synoptic view of these categories.[49] Their pride of progress spread a mute white blankness before the observer, making it impossible either to read a historical legend in its glossy white reflections on glass or to understand natural beauty and organic ornamentation in its massive and repetitive forms.[50] This monumental building in glass, or so Ruskin believed, killed the ability of architecture to speak to the emotions or memory of an observer. In the engineering bravura of this gigantic structure, architectural technique had been separated from both expression and aesthetics, fracturing the power of contemplation.[51] To the contrary, Ruskin professed that it was the duty of noble architecture to speak precisely, to act as if it were a book of history and express its story well.[52] But a building of white enameled opaqueness was a building of forgetfulness: its novelty erased all the monuments of the past, enabling a new people to arise without a record or trace of their history.[53]

The Crystal Palace, Ruskin complained (as it was relocated near his Herne Hill home in 1854) blocked his view and kept him, metaphorically speaking, from thinking about the great ends of architecture and from studying the past as it cast its shadow on the present. It snuffed out each of his seven lamps of architecture. Drawing a comparison between the industrial arts of the nineteenth century and medieval art, and calling the former material pollutants that drew a dry black veil over the Gothic ruins of the past, Ruskin like Carlyle before him returned to celebrate the moral values medieval society confirmed.[54] Architectural choices displayed a life-and-death drama, for Ruskin could read in the stones and textual details of a nation's buildings the strengths and weaknesses of its soul and spirit.

In the Gothic cathedral Ruskin found pure and unpolluted compositions of architecture, an architecture that organically rose from its environment and freely and naturally developed its ornamentation and form.[55] But a few years hence, when the novelty of the glass greenhouse should have subsided, how, asked Ruskin, could a people still admire fourteen acres covered by the glass of the Crystal Palace when the true and noble Gothic architecture of the past was being destroyed recklessly by Napoleon III, in his ambitious reconstructions of Paris, and by the wanton zeal of conservators more fatal to monuments than fire and revolutions ever had been?[56] Once upon a time, or so Ruskin believed, the Rouen Cathedral had been the finest flower of Gothic art, but by the mid-nineteenth century its upper part had been restored and cleaned to what he called "the white accuracies of novelty," and the lower structures flanking its approach were closer in comparison to the "handsome fronts" of the modern-day American hotels and offices than any of its historic precedents.[57]

The age value of ruins with their stern, patient endurance spoke of the past, but restorers all over Europe were destroying what time and weather could never undo. In addition, every city scene was jarred by modern improvements, and the day was not far away, so Ruskin thought, when the character of Venice, Florence, or Rouen would be transformed into lifeless imitations of Paris and Birmingham.[58] When all the monuments of the past have been erased in the path of progress, Ruskin wondered whether nations would look around and subsequently with pride—because they were freed from precedent and the entanglement of memory—thank the fathers of progress, "that no saddening shadows can any more trouble the enjoyments of the future—no moments of reflection retard its activities; and that the new-born population of the world without a record and without a ruin may, in the fullness of a phemeral felicity, dispose itself to eat, and to drink, and to die?"[59] We shall, he believed, eventually learn to discern what is great and to preserve and possess what is precious, but it will be too late.

> We shall wander througn our palaces of crystal, gazing sadly on copies of pictures torn by cannon-shots, or casts of sculpture dashed to pieces long ago. We shall gradually learn to distinquish originality and sincerity from the decrepitudes of imitation and palsies of repetitions; but it will be only in hopelessness to recognize the truth, that architecture and painting can be 'restored' when the dead can be raised,—and not til then.[60]

Passages through the City

The nineteenth century displayed a passion for traveling as the primary means to learn about history, while simultaneously perceiving travel narratives, history books, historical painting, and architectural ruins to be modes of vicarious travel through time and space.[61] Travel for Ruskin in particular was a perceptual as well as a literary device, moving the spectator/reader through a succession of views and a sequence of details. His observer of architecture and cityscapes was simultaneously a traveler before unfolding scenery and a stationary beholder of details and fragments.[62] In Ruskin's writings, "history" seemed to unroll from site to site, being frozen in fragments plucked from a moment in time. Once again relying on comparison, Ruskin drew distinctions between past and present modes of perception, pointing to the disastrous effects on imagination that modern modes of travel by train had wrought. The speed by which a train propelled a viewer through the passing landscape overtaxed and dulled imagination because the traveler now was compelled to see too much in too quick a succession.[63] Ruskin thought the train was therefore a foolish modern device for killing space and time, for making the world seem smaller, when it was the visual perspective on time and distance as a slowly unfolding panorama that a wise traveler cleverly sought.[64] The fury and vulgarity of modern life was encapsulated in this inability to examine the details of nature, "the loss of the wish to gather a flower in travelling."[65] Pleasure, Ruskin claimed, came from visual observation, the slow uncovering of details and artifacts affecting the imagination and memory. The testing of place against its representational forms, this Ruskin equated with a former style of traveling, one in which the traveler experienced something more to be anticipated and remembered in the entry places to a new city than the glass roofing and iron girders of a railroad shed.[66] Carving its way through virgin landscape and plunging deeply into the heart of a city, the railroad was a personal assault on Ruskin's sensibilities, steeped as they were in the art of memory garnered from earlier excursions.[67]

Ruskin's *Stones of Venice* (1851–1853) can be read consequently as both a travel epic celebrating the rise and fall of Gothic architecture and as a method of perceptual reform and reeducation of aesthetic taste for those vicarious observers who read about architectural cityscapes from the comfort of their living room armchairs. This of course had its polemical and moral side: to call for better schools of architecture and to sponsor the building of expressive monuments in whose stones subsequent beholders would read the spirit and greatness of nineteenth-century England.[68] Ruskin always drew the comparison between the past and present state of architecture and subsequent visual sensibilities, for he feared that the industrial revolution has pushed England into a decadent and moribund stage. As Ruskin commands the reader before describing a small English cathedral town,

> Think for a little while of that scene, and the meaning of all its small formalisms. . . . Estimate its secluded, continuous, drowsy felicities, and its evidence of the sense and steady performance of such kind of duties as can be regulated by the cathedral clock; and weigh the influence of those dark towers on all who have passed through the lonely square at their feet for centuries, and on all who have seen them rising far away over the wooded plain. . . . And then let us quickly recollect that we are in Venice. . . . there rises a vision out of the earth, [that of St. Mark's] and all the great square seems to have opened from it in a kind of awe, that we may see it far away;—a multitude of pillars and white domes, clustered into a long low pyramid of coloured light; a treasure-heap, it seems, partly of gold, and partly of opal and mother-of-pearl, hollowed beneath into five great vaulted porches, ceiled with fair mosaic, and beset with sculpture of alabaster, clear as amber and delicate as ivory,—sculpture fantastic and

> involved, of palm leaves and lilies, and grapes and pomegranates. . . . Between that grim cathedral of England and this, what an interval![69]

Traveling, visiting museums, studying maps, gazing upon architecture, and even observing a city's plan, were all optical means by which the beholder organized his mind and his visual memory. Ruskin placed "looking" in clear parallel to reading, just as collecting or storing in a museum or archive was analogous to a mode of contemplation and a style of memory.[70] Fixated with museums and libraries, Ruskin as the passionate collector and curator of artifacts and illustrated views became obsessed with developing the syntactical and indexical structure that would realize a perfectly organized and cross-referenced visual archive. Once again Ruskin used his central trope—the Crystal Palace of 1851—as an emblematic device, this time demonstrating the manner in which the nineteenth century had destroyed the hierarchies and centralities of taste that any good museum as a collosal collection of visual materials must provide. The public, especially the working classes, so Ruskin felt, needed places of entertainment not like schools but more like museums, where they could obtain useful information and improve their manners. They flocked to the Crystal Palace for such mind-expanding experiences, but what did they receive in this new cathedral of modern faith when it reopened in 1854? Down the vista of its main aisle, a huge pantomine clown with his mouth and eyes opening wide then closing shut was all the pleasure that mechanical means could provide, but no one, least of all Ruskin, seemed to laugh at this gawkish apparition.[71] By trying to combine an art school with a place of entertainment, the Crystal Palace, Ruskin claimed, had destroyed both. The plethoric array of white plaster-cast statues dampened every observer's amusement, while its indiscriminate borrowings from good and bad works of art were miscolored, misinterpreted, and misplaced until the unsuspecting viewer, whose mind and eye had been debased beyond redemption, demanded visual relief from all this chaos and found it only in steam wheelbarrows and mechanical toys.[72] Places of public amusement, argued Ruskin, should be instead pretty places with good prints and pictures, well catalogued, arranged, and exhibited.[73]

Establishing the Guild of St. George in the 1870s, Ruskin used this half-utopian, half-realistic model of a preindustrial agricultural and educational community not only as an example of how to reclaim neglected farmlands of Europe, but as a procedure perfecting his view of how museums could be educational institutions for simple people and for children.[74] It was a mistake, Ruskin felt, for the public to think that the British Museum was partly a place for seasonal entertainments, partly a lending library, and partly a parish school. The public should have a clear idea in their mind that a national museum was a place for treasuring and not for educating. Access to its sanctum should be based on a higher privilege. Thus the British Museum became the center of Ruskin's collection, where only rare and unique books would be stored. The rest of its books and art works were to be dispersed to local lending libraries containing their own collection of illustrations and casts easily viewed and decorously presented.[75] Thus a museum with everything in its place, with nothing crowded, puzzling or bizarre—in fact, an arrangement perfectly complete and thoroughly explained—would educate the disorderly and rude populace about elegance and manners.[76]

The first educational guild museum, established by Ruskin near Sheffield in 1875, was arranged for the iron workers of Derbyshire. Here a synthesis of art, science, and history took place in simply but intelligently coordinated displays, much like the ideas and artifacts later promoted by Geddes. The foundation of the museum was a storehouse of plaster sculptural casts, for these Ruskin felt were most effective in educating the eye. Next came a demonstration of natural history illustrating the geology and flora of the region surrounding Sheffield.[77] Every painting, book, and illustration was chosen to exemplify historical and literary themes of the region and the nation. And each item in the collection was in turn related to the publications of the Guild of St. George. So complex was this synthesis of beautiful images and words that not only was art linked to nature and nature to art, but cultural to moral history, the education and training of the hand to draw and the eye to observe, and in the end the collection was less a systematic classification than an assemblage of moral and aesthetic paradigms to aid the teaching by visual example. But beyond this collection lay Ruskin's concern that beautiful objects in the world were being destroyed, restored beyond recognition, or removed from the visual record of mankind. Hence his museum must contain as many records as could be gathered of beautiful images, buildings, and scenes in danger of restoration or destruction. Employing many craftsmen to record these objects, Ruskin sent Arthur Burgess to photograph the details of Rouen Cathedral before its restoration, and then placed his collection of negatives in the museum; casts of Venetian sculptures were obtained before their restoration; and paintings that told of the true record of Venice's national monuments and scenery were also collected.[78]

Certainly the new schools of art, located within the art galleries and museums that the nineteenth century was developing, would bear fruit in time, but Ruskin felt it would be too late, and so the reform of old schools was essential if the arts were to be made available to a wider audience. In England, Ruskin complained, the public taste was destroyed by artists either educated in the neoclassical manner at the National Academy or in the technical routines of government schools.[79] Thus Ruskin proposed a School of Drawing at Oxford in the early 1870s, to train the power of both the eye and the mind, to recombine art and design, technical and critical skills in an attempt to make art education as inclusive as possible. His objectives in establishing this school were twofold: creating a school of art and developing a critical apparatus so that educated men would arise able to criticize and patronize art wisely, and to observe intelligently and record accurately all that they saw. As teaching aids, Ruskin developed a series of illustrations, framed images that slid in and out on grooves made in their storage cabinets.[80] Like his series of books or Bibliotheca Pastorum that he proposed every household should have, this series of illustrations was intended to be as perfect and complete a collection as possible. For the curator Ruskin, a museum or a collection of beautiful objects was "neither a preparatory school, nor a peep show; but it may be more delightful than either."[81] Arranged in four series, his collection of wonders and ways of teaching was in fact never comprehensively nor systematically arranged.[82]

Picturesque Travel

Now Ruskin obviously bound images to sight, and history to travel, borrowing from the devices already established in the travel literature and topographic paintings produced in the eighteenth and early nineteenth centuries. But a shift occurred in his perspective away from a purely textural, sequential, and unified description of landscape. Instead of the traditional view extending from a prospect out over the landscape below, in which the eye scanned from near to far until it reached the horizon, Ruskin moved toward a visual description that focused in addition on the observing eye, juxtaposing and superimposing images, comparing and detailing views, finding that pleasure now lay in the experience and associations culled in the act of gazing itself. This same shift from factual objective accounts to perceptual, subjective experience—the latter entailing a deeper or penetrating view into the geological, historical, and emotional strata of the architectural or natural landscape—occurred as well in the travel literature written during the last half of the eighteenth century, a literature with which Ruskin was quite familiar. One of the most popular literary forms of the eighteenth century had been the unvarnished travelogue, gaining readers' interest in parallel with a world progressively revealed by explorers who returned to tell of marvelous new lands and unbelievably exotic peoples. No longer a mixture of fact and fiction, this genre, almost scientific in nature, was an instructive depiction of place mixed with a modicum of style and pleasure. But no matter how scientific or objective their intention, the mere presentation of bizarre and wondrous materials and strange and remote lands and people—plus a curious combining of text with images, as these accounts by the end of the eighteenth century tended to be illustrated by voyaging artists—both enthralled and transformed contemporary culture. The imaginary or real thrill of adventure and escape from daily routine, plus the promise that the reader/traveler

Panoramic Wallpaper, "Les Combat des Grecs," manufactured by Zuber, designed by J.-J. Deltil (1827).

Panoramic Wallpaper, "Les Combat des Grecs," manufactured by Zuber, designed by J.-J. Deltil (1827)

could revel in exotic realms and majestic views, became the major attractions of this new genre of travelogue.

In the first half of the eighteenth century, rather rigorous conventions seemed to have governed the format of travel literature: written most often in journal or in letter form, the author/researcher never appeared in first person. Providing accurate descriptions of places visited plus a detailed itinerary of the trip, these travel accounts generally were indexed and portable, in a masterful attempt to give order and clarity to a world appearing more complex and varied with every exploration. Their popularity depended solely on the presentation of novel content such as the discovery of new places and countries or the description of new flora and fauna. After 1750, Spain, Portugal, Russia, and even the more remote rural regions of England and France became topics of curiosity, as did unusual subject matter such as the description of antiquities, sculpture, and paintings, or agriculture and mineralogy. A few decades later, "manners and customs" of people and places were fascinating additions to the genre. Then in 1792 a thrilling new class of travel books developed after the appearance of William Gilpin's "Three Essays: On Picturesque Beauty; On Picturesque Travel; and on Sketching Landscape." Nature, Gilpin advised, was now to be viewed "like a picture," and picturesque travel was to be seen as a form of entertainment in which the traveler felt, absorbed, and experienced rather than surveyed the surrounding terrain. Descriptions of the beauty of nature soon arose, playing on the reader's emotional response to natural environments and geological descriptions. Believing that the dominant pleasure of travel was that of pursuit, Gilpin noted that the tourist was thrilled at finding the truly novel place or artifact, or was enthralled by minute varieties and the examination of details that had gone unrecorded.[83] The picturesque traveler was a nomad wandering through the landscape in search of scenery in which "the eye may lose itself, and the observer may be absorbed into and transformed by the observed."[84] The epitome of this genre was H. B. de Saussure's volumes of *Voyages dans les Alpes,* published in 1779, 1786, and 1796.[85] Saussure's *Voyages,* which contained a panoramic description of the Alps, focused on the depiction of each contributing peak and described their actual appearance, heretofore unknown to be great triangular shapes or peculiar clumps.[86] These volumes, which intently compared and contrasted individual aspects of Alpine scenery, intending to reveal in the end nature's inherent lawlike order, were Ruskin's favorite geology books and deeply informed his own methods of observation, comparison, and classification.[87] Here lay the roots of Ruskin's and later Geddes's traveling eye, scanning across the earth's surface on the way to the horizon, yet probing deeply into the strata of geological layers and naturalistic forms to render pictorially the hidden, the past, and the remote as observable, present, and near.[88]

After the end of the Napoleonic Wars in the second decade of the nineteenth century, the pleasure tour became an increasingly common experience for the middle classes, or a habit they cultivated vicariously. Travel literature and illustrated landscape and architectural folios, now abetted by the development of wood engravings and the invention of lithography after 1799, expanded to fill the demand created by the rise of this beholding imagination. Following the author or illustrator in his travels meant emotionally experiencing the unfolding of scenery before one's eyes, the sequential arrangement of views, even the exploration of detailed studies of rocks, flowers, sculptures, or paintings.[89] By now the eighteenth-century conventions of travel literature had been left far behind, for the travel account had become personalized, offering the reader (who it was assumed would eventually travel) explicit information and opinions of what to see and how to find places, what to expect of local denizens and customs, and what to remember about historical events and artifacts.[90] Perhaps the tradition began with Mariana Stark's two volumes of *Travels in Italy,* the first published in 1800 and the second after the Napoleonic Wars. Stark developed a personalized series of exclamation marks that underscored her suggestions about travel and places to see and included in her guidebook directions about how to mail a letter, what prices to expect, or where to find a doctor. Karl Baedeker of Leipzig published his first guidebook, beginning with the town of Koblenz, in 1829. He too offered the traveler advice on where to find things and what to expect in strange places, developing his own star system of rating landmarks as the extraordinary (**), the noteworthy (*), and the merely attractive (no *), and thus initiated travel as a star-gazing event.[91] The first edition of *John Murray's Guidebooks,* written by Sir Francis Palgrave for travelers in northern Italy, however, changed completely the tone of this advice when it appeared in 1842: now the reader was told what she or he ought to see, not what might be seen, assuming the traveling beholder was in search of heightened emotional experience to be found in classical statuary and natural environments.[92]

Among the most important lithographic travel folios of the early nineteenth century were the twenty or so volumes of the *Voyages Pittoresques et Romantiques dans L'Ancienne France* by Baron Isidore Taylor and Charles Nodier, the first volume of which was printed in 1821 and the last in 1878. Guidebooks since the mid-eighteenth century had utilized the terms "Voyage Pittoresque" to specify large-folio volumes of illustrations that offered the pleasures of vicarious travel, and the composite term had slipped into English art theory to refer to attractive views and pleasurable scenes that fell outside of the canons of neoclassical taste.[93] As early as 1810, Baron Taylor had the idea of making a visual record of the monuments and scenery of France, hoping to catalog all the stones of antiquity, the middle ages, and the Renaissance by the new and inexpensive means of lithography. Waiting until the Napoleonic Wars were completed, Taylor and Nodier felt that by rediscovering and documenting France's glorious architectural and colorful historical past, they could reconquer a spiritual empire that war and time had vanquished. Theirs was to be a work appealing to the imagination's associative powers, where history and architecture conspired with the viewer's emotions and memories. At the time of Taylor's conception, France was a relatively unexplored country, and so Nodier wrote in the introduction to Volume One:

> It is not as scholars that we are crisscrossing France, but as travelers curious to find interesting sights and avid for noble memories. Shall I say what inclination, easier to sense than to define, has shaped this journey through the ruins of old France? A certain melancholy disposition of thought, a certain involuntary

> predilection for the poetic customs and the arts of our ancestors, the sentiment I know not what mysterious correspondence of decay and misfortune between these old structures and the generation which has passed.[94]

This was a typical disclaimer for picturesque travelers searching for alluring scenes and arresting exposures over which they waged no control but unto which their gaze lay open to multiple and diverse visual and emotional effects. It was the assemblage of many-sided perceptions and suggestions, an open-ended and detailed view, that provided the most intense pleasure.[95] Yet Taylor and Nodier also held the desire to expand the knowledge of little-known regions of France by means of accurate drawings rendered on the spot. Tinged with nostalgia for the past, with the romantic view that held architecture in the consoling embrace of nature, this topographic project was enthusiastically waged as an urgent albeit tragic campaign to record buildings and scenery province by province before their inevitable destruction by neglect and industrial progress. Using the best landscape and history painters of the day, artists who specialized in topographic views, by the end of the project the architecture and scenic views of nine different provinces were visualized in nearly 3,000 lithographic plates.[96]

The *Voyages Pittoresques* were the first expression in France of a new archeological spirit, which would give rise to the historic preservation movement. Being the first serious study of architectural ruins and monuments, these documents stressed the accurate depiction of place as well as the preservation of any accompanying documents. Inspired by this effort, the historian François Guizot believed in 1830 that one of the projects a government should sponsor was the writing of national history from unpublished and little-known sources—relying, no doubt, on the power of the eye to weld regional differences and local details into a unified national landscape. Consequently he helped to create the Commission des Lettres, Philosophie, Sciences, et Arts, whose Subcommittee on Arts and Monuments began to inventory all the endangered monuments of France, establishing a supervisory group to oversee their conservation and promoting a group in each province to try to accomplish the work of restoration. In 1837, the Commission des Monuments Historiques was formed, with Prosper Mérimée as its chief and including Baron Taylor among its members. Under its direction the Mission Héliographiques was set up in 1851, an experimental attempt to send photographers such as Henri Le Secq, Hippolyte Bayard, and Edouard-Denis Baldus on missions to record 120 specific monuments and sites throughout France.[97]

In the rise of the nineteenth-century's visual imagination, even the newly emerging towns of France and the cityscapes of turmoil and revolutionary change captured the fascination of that century's lithographers and photographers. Jean-Jacques Berger, the prefect of Paris for a brief four years just before Baron von Haussmann was appointed prefect in 1853, began to instill Napoleon III's image of modernity on Paris by eradicating the rookeries that existed between the Louvre and the Tuileries, extending the Rue de Rivoli in a straight arcaded line, and clearing away the buildings that crowded the foot of important monuments such as the Tour Saint-Jacques. The photographer Henri Le Secq followed Berger's path of improvement in 1851, turning his camera's eye on the picturesque scenes and crooked lanes about to be destroyed. Le Secq captured the melancholy mood and sublime stillness of those ancient relics of medieval Paris as they waited in silence for the wrecker's ball, almost without a witness. Utilizing long exposure times, playing on light and shadow, focusing on the abstract nature of architectural details, and composing his views devoid of people, Le Secq's photographs offered a nostalgic but fleeting memory of a city about to be radically transformed.[98]

By the 1860s, as Haussmann was driving his boulevards relentlessly through the fabric of Paris, he commanded both Charles Marville as the official photographer of the city of Paris and Jean Charles Adolphe Alphand as his inventor of landscapes to record the victories of modernization. With no nostalgic sentiment in mind, Haussmann established the Trauvaux Historiques in 1865 and gave it the task of writing a general history of Paris. Inverting the dictums of Carlyle that Ruskin so avidly pursued, Haussmann believed the past would vindicate the present by making evident the superiority of his transformations. Thus Marville, who informally photographed the rebuilding of Paris in the early 1860s, officially joined Haussmann's team of historic researchers. His charge for fifteen years was to photograph clinically, in before-and-after shots, those districts of the city that straight new boulevards eventually would pierce. Focusing on an imaginary trajectory that each new street would follow, Marville's low camera angle presented a view of the intransient city fabric through which Haussmann would plow.[99] Alphand's task, on the other hand, was to illustrate his artifically constructed parks and promenades (1863–1873). Nature in the city of Haussmann was hardly a picturesque bucolic scene, but a mechanically contrived and technically organized urban space. The engravings in Alphand's *Les Promenades des Paris* illustrate the beauty of hydraulic machines that pumped water to the parks, of drills that sank the wells, of machines that transported trees sometimes as tall as thirty feet so they could line the new boulevards in exact and regularized heights—in short, all the technological instruments required to salvage the leftover and often unhealthy spots of the city and transform them into beautiful parks and hygienic walks. Metal was Alphand's preferred material for his urbane kiosks, pavilions, railings, benches, and gratings, the perfect formal accompaniment to Haussmann's regularized and modernized city.[100]

By 1870, the year Haussmann was dismissed in disgrace for his unorthodox financial maneuvers spun to pay for the lavish rebuilding of Paris, the medieval walls surrounding the city were gone, a comprehensive citywide system of parks and squares, sewers and drinking water, new boulevards and widened streets had been created, and row upon row of uniform apartment facades had risen in rigorous homogeneity. More improvements would follow: the decade of the 1890s alone saw 171 new streets introduced, an underground rapid transit system developed, several new railroad stations constructed, and six- or seven-storied residential structures the predominant commercial venture. Already in 1885, alarm at the continual and rapid pace of modernization had seen the creation of the Société des Amis des Monuments Parisiens, with Charles Garnier as its head and Victor Hugo its honorary president. By the next decade publications documenting the medieval

Marville photograph, Old Street of Glatigny, before piercing for new boulevard took place *(c. 1885).*

remnants of Paris began systematically to appear. Keeping alive the nineteenth century's belief that the spirit of an age could be read in its architectural forms and ornamental motifs, A. de Campeaux wrote a series of articles on the decorative ornamentation of "Old Paris" architecture, published in the *Gazette des Beaux-Arts* between 1890 and 1895. Only two years later the Muncipal Commission of Old Paris was established to keep a watchful eye over the medieval remnants of the city, and so popular had views of "Old Paris" become that the 1900 Paris Exposition included a model reconstruction of medieval Paris. By this time, many Parisian neighborhoods had their own local preservation groups, reflecting a general interest in surveying and protecting the city's vernacular environments. Into this scene of evident reawakened nostalgia for "Old Paris" architecture—with its renewed passion for ornamental details now almost completely destroyed or forgotten where they existed in out-of-the-way neighborhoods—entered the photographic documenter Eugène Atget, who made his first large sale of 100 "Old Parisian" photographs to the Bibliothèque Historique de la Ville de Paris in 1899. The chief librarian of the Bibliothèque, Marcel Poëte, who was also an ardent resuscitator of Marville's photographic recordings of Paris, eventually bought over 3,000 of Atget's architectural and topographical views, whose subjects ranged in age from medieval times to the pre-Haussmann era.[101]

Atget was as intent a documentor and classifier of visual material and as mysterious a contraster of past to present as either Ruskin or Geddes had been. In Atget's case, his concern was the characteristic imagery of Parisian architectural heritage overlooked by the modern cult of the fashionably new. Hence he set out to record its old streets, courtyards, and squares; its shop signs and facades, its parks and trees, fountains and sculpture, bridges and quays, its civic and religious architecture, its hotels and monuments.[102] In this inventory of building types and topographical views of "Old Paris," no people or activity surround the isolated scenery and mute structures in stone. Historical buildings, ornamental motifs, and vernacular streetscapes were for Atget merely surface images devoid of a symbolic or ritualistic context. These empty stage sets were to be viewed as desolate relics and transitory landscapes, in a manner that drew on the nineteenth century's nostalgic taste for recording the forgotten and perishing past witnessed in the *Voyages Pittoresques* and all of the topographic views that it had spawned.[103] By juxtaposing, in his photographic compositions, objects against empty space, stressing contrasts between black and white, the three-dimensional and the flat, the curved and the straight, Atget continually set up a melancholic play between the present and the past, the intangible and the real, the timeless and the transient. He consequently utilized all the characteristic elements of the topographical tradition established throughout the nineteenth century.[104] Reminiscent of Ruskin's cataloging mania, Atget organized his photographic images into thirteen series, five of which were major categories. He began this pictorial and archeological museum with landscape documents; by 1899 the two categories of "Picturesque Paris" and "Art in Old Paris" had taken shape, two years later he moved out into the suburbs or "Environs of Paris," returning by 1907 to focus on the "Topography of Old Paris." Like any good creator of an encyclopedic work, Atget was a cross-referencer, providing editorial albums of approximately sixty selected prints taken from his entire opus but rearranged for different purposes.[105]

An Education through the Traveling Eye

Let us return for a moment to review the history of simulated travelogues and architectural recreations. Until the mid-eighteenth century, topographical or view paintings were imaginary scenes admired for their pictorial unity of time and place, and instantaneously recognizable for their association with significant actions or historical events.[106] In the Salon of the 1750s and 1760s, however, a peculiar series of monumental topographical views appeared, painted by Joseph Vernet and entitled "The Ports of France"; they provided the viewer with documentary evidence and characteristic vignettes from each locale. Aimed to delight the eye as well, they included realistic effects of sunlight and sunsets, storms and clouds. These realistic landscapes were painted from nature according to an itinerary established by Vernet's patron, the Marquis de Marigny, and few took them seriously, for they seemed to depend solely on the viewer's interest in the replicated scenery and failed to provide the usual imaginative and pictorial idealizations. Yet a few years later Diderot, in his commentary on the Salon of 1767, referred to the "Vernet promenade" as a simulated travelogue, whose powerful emotional effect was one of passionate involvement. So expressive and sensational were these realistic views, or so Diderot claimed, that the beholder was mesmerized by the sentimental memories of travel, metaphorically entering the landscape and being carried away on the wings of imagination.[107] The boundaries that neoclassicism carefully maintained between art and reality, or the imaginary and the real, were crumbling as these scenographic paintings of picturesque nature on a truly majestic scale reached out to halt and to touch the observer with the exactitude and detailing of accurately depicted places.

By the late eighteenth and early nineteenth century, topographical views held another function: they provided Europeans with credible evidence of the variety of people, places, and manners that existed throughout the world. Typical landscapes and views of natives played a role as well in the theory of evolution, becoming "scientific evidence" of Europe's superiority in the "survival of the fittest" and legitimation for establishing Europe as the norm against which the progress of other nations and colonies could be compared and judged. It took considerable time and extensive reportage, however, before European culture accepted that the universe was a hierarchical order of things ruled by the laws of nature. Only slowly did they give up the ancient conception that monsters and curious beings resided in the antipodes of the northern hemisphere, and even when they did, Eurocentric biases and prejudices still ruled their view.[108] As most voyages of discovery between 1750 and 1850 carried recording artists as part of their team, or scientists and officers trained in the arts of empirical observation, these illustrators began to accurately record the wide variety of landscapes, geological formations, climate zones, and the different effects of light and atmosphere that existed in the world at large. This plethoric variety of nature seen in the depiction of correct "habitats" and typical vegetation, animals, and climate can be counted among the many reasons that neoclassical taste in landscape painting, which delighted in an imaginary unity of mood and expression, began to dissolve. These new and more realistic landscapes were not always faithful representations, however, for the exotic and the curious lurking just beneath their surface appearance readily lent themselves to picturesque and entertaining interpretations.[109]

William Hodges was one of the painters traveling with Captain Cook on his second voyage to the South Pacific in 1772. He was particularly interested in rendering the pictorial effects of atmosphere on landscape painting, transforming accurately detailed coastal views into dramatic statements of light and shadow. A world traveler before this voyage, Hodges believed that landscape paintings might challenge the supremacy of historical painting, if their views were based on the accurate depiction of the history and customs of various countries.[110] Publishing his pioneering aquatint drawings in *Select Views in India* in 1786 and *Travels in India* in 1793, Hodges introduced Europeans to the delights of Indian art and architecture, and taught them that a unique relationship developed in each part of the world between the needs of men in their everyday lives and the manner by which they controlled their climate through different building forms and materials. Their art and architecture must thus be judged by their own artistic standards and conventions. In an obvious diatribe against the sanctity of Greek architecture with all of its purity, simplicity, and unity, which had gripped neoclassical architects and artists for several decades, Hodges extolled the beauty and magnificent embellishments of Egyptian, Hindu, Moorish, and Gothic modes as alternative architectural arrangements.[111] So he wrote

> but why should we admire it [Greek art and architecture] in an exclusive manner; or, blind to the majesty, boldness, and magnificence of the Egyptian, Hindoo, Moorish and Gothic, as admirable wonders of architecture, unmercifully blame and despise them, because they are more various in their forms, and not reducible to the precise rules of the Greek hut, prototype, and column? Or because

> in smaller parts, perhaps accidentally similar, their proportions are different from those to which we are become familiar by habit.[112]

Constantly changing and picturesque views of travel became a new source of visual pleasure, whether observable in folio form and travel narratives or through specially designed landscape gardens, where bits and pieces of exotic architecture were intimately related to their environmental settings in new and entertaining ways. Such were the recreations of Kew Gardens in London, where a Turkish mosque stood capriciously cheek by jowl with a Chinese pagoda and a Moorish structure—and all were embedded in a veritable hothouse of exotic vegetation. These curious juxtapositions became a major force behind the nineteenth century's impulse and curiosity to travel by actual or vicarious means. Seeing the world as landscape or illustrated picture was a visual and mental experience, one that moved from vista to vista, viewing objects from different perspectives. "Travel" became a way to escape the tedium of everyday life, projecting oneself into an exotic milieu; it was as well a telescoping experience, drawing the faraway background as a place full of mystery and adventure into the foreground, where it could be minutely detailed and studied.[113]

Therefore it is not surprising to find that travel tableaux became popular theatrical entertainments in London by the late eighteenth century. In 1784 a new pantomime of John O'Keefe's appeared at Covent Garden entitled "Omai, or a Trip Around the World" which was really a series of pictorial tableaux Philippe-Jacques de Loutherbourg created for his Eidophusikon. This was the most elaborate travelogue ever simulated on the London stage, whose scenes were taken directly from official accounts of Captain Cook's three voyages published that very same year, and thus relied on the thrill of re-presenting images of places already explored vicariously by the audience in folio form. Drawn from authentic sources—and consequently claiming to be exact representations of foreign lands and customs—the pantomine was praised for being the highest of rational entertainments, a spectacle "which must fully satisfy not only the mind of the philosopher, but the curiosity of every spectator."[114] Yet the tableaux were also criticized for not being strong enough to support a masque, that is, not able to offer its spectators a moral message. Instead these tableaux offered the viewer simple images of the world presented on stage, a visual "look" to be explored and understood, not a didactic arrangement to instruct and sermonize. Vicarious travel was used as a metaphorical device for spatial perception: a world made visible, measured, recorded, and then transported like a photograph back home to be shown to London audiences. Every voyage was linked to the next in series: its charted maps and bestowed place names established the background for future adventures and scientific explorations. This manipulable world was meant to be documented and then read, to be made familiar through vicarious travel, while the visual tableaux were a metaphorical device indicating the slow but steady journey of man's enlightened and rational steps toward the scientific understanding of the observable world.[115]

The illustrations compiled from Cook's three voyages, the last taking place in 1776, affected the European visual imagination in other ways as well. The text of Cook's third voyage, published in 1784 with sixty-one engraved illustrations by John Webber, was exceedingly popular. Translated into all the main languages of Europe, for fifty years it continued to be published, expanding into special editions and supplements. These illustrations of exotic natives in colorful costumes and local habitats constructed in strange and bizarre styles gave rise to costume encyclopedias and the production of exotic wallpapers. St-Sauveur's *Encyclopedie des Voyages* published in 1795–6 was the first of the costume books, and even influenced a series of South Sea panoramic wallpaper views produced as "decorative divertissements" by Josef Dufour in 1804. It was not just the South Seas that captured the European imagination, but travel illustrations in general were popular devices demonstrating the great diversity of picturesque scenery existing in the world from Italy to India, from South to North America.[116] Like the talented nineteenth-century illustrators Thomas and William Daniell, who searched the Indian subcontinent for picturesque monuments in landscape settings, the intention of every picturesque voyager "was to take part in 'guiltless spoilation' in the interests of knowledge and to 'transport back picturesque beauties of those favoured regions'."[117]

Yet no matter how the art and architecture of the world was opened to examination and depiction, they never dislodged the primacy of norms established in the Western world, nor the belief that only Europe was theoretically knowable.[118] This new art might be entertaining—certainly it was a matter of curiosity—but most cultural products of the non-Western world were judged to be backward, decadent, or childish, carrying the stigmata of irrationality and being frozen in time. When compared to the more advanced nations of the Western world, other nations were judged to reveal incomplete or inadequate stages of evolutionary development, or else contained inscrutable customs and incomprehensible ways. Thus Hegel noted in the early nineteenth century,

> . . . as we enter for the first time the world of ancient Persian, Indian, or Egyptian figures and imaginative conceptions we experience a certain feeling of uncanniness, we wander at any rate in a world of *problems.* These fantastic images do not at once respond to our own world; we are neither pleased nor satisfied with the immediate impression they produce on us; rather we are instinctively carried forward by it to probe yet further into their significance, and to enquire what wider and profounder truths may lie concealed behind such representations . . . Nations . . . even in their childhood, require as the food of their imaginative life a more essential content; and this is just what in fact we find in the figures of Indian and Egyptian art, although the interpretation of such problematical pictures is only dimly suggested, and we experience great difficulty in deciphering it.[119]

Since the time of Winckelmann, climate had been associated with a nation's artistic genius, and ancient Greece with its gentle weather allowing for little clothing and encouraging exercise in the nude was placed at the apex of cultural achievement.[120] By the nineteenth century, the idea was generally accepted that each nation exhibited a distinct style of architecture not only adapted to its natural landscape and its climate, but reflecting the mind and spirit of the nation as well. This idea came to influence Ruskin when he began to write about the poetry of architecture in 1837/38. Studying the architecture of cottages and villas found in various European countries, Ruskin showed how each type of building was an embellishment to its physical setting when it followed simple laws of nature. Because the English countryside offered the viewer miniature or snug little scenes, he conjectured, its typical cottages reflected this sheltered form as well and were seldom visible from a distance. England being a country undergoing constant change and improvement, its cottages were never built once and for all time, but as impermanent structures were often torn down and rebuilt over again. The French countryside, to the contrary, was large scale and hence its cottages were gigantic, often isolated, structures. Since its population was either pedigreed aristocracy who preserved without restraint or modern revolutionaries who wantonly destroyed, France's cottages were either protected with infinite care or were ill-treated and disfigured beyond recognition.[121]

All Western landscapes, Ruskin argued, possessed one of four distinct characters: being either woody, green countries; cultivated blue countries; wild, grey countries; or hilly, brown countries. Consequently each landscape instilled distinctly unique emotions in the viewer's imagination. Green countries, mixing views of parklands, pasture, and varigated forests, never presented an unbroken vista unless from a height or prospect. This scenery of duration and antiquity imposed a melancholic and venerable look upon the cottage, demanding it to be grotesque in form and definitely old-fashioned in style.[122] On the other hand, grey regions, like those of northern France, offered a landscape of open fields and undulating hills, which called for cottages massive in scale and dull in color. In blue countries, which were largely agricultural landscapes where the eye stretched out to the horizon, not a single object was useless, frivolous, or nonsensical. In these open stretches the cottage must be cheerful, neat, and scarcely ornamented, reveling in the utilitarian demands of everyday life. In the hilly brown countries, the primary architectural concern was the position or location of its cottages, enabling them to appear natural not artificial additions to the landscape.[123] In *Modern Painters* (Vol. 5, 1860), Ruskin further divided the world into five different climatic zones responsible for what he defined as their artistic genius. Accordingly he judged tropical forest lands typical of the Indian subcontinent and characterized by humid and enervating heat as not conducive to the production of a truly noble art. Even though he allowed that "the Chinese and Indians, and other semi-civilized nations, can colour better than we do, and that an Indian shawl and China vase are still, in invention in colour, inimitable by us," still he argued perjoratively that it was necessary that a nation be half savage and ignorant of all rules of art "in order to obtain power of colouring. . . ."[124] Later he would malign even this bit of generosity by noting that "the pure colour-gift, when employed for pleasure only, degrades in another direction; so that among the Indians, Chinese, and Japanese, all intellectual progress in art has been for ages rendered impossible by the prevalence of that faculty."[125]

There were other changes, closer to home within European cities of the nineteenth century, that perturbed the traveler's view. Attaining an elevated prospect overlooking the scenery, as Ruskin had done, or standing on the bridge of a boat, even dangling from the sky in a balloon, were points from which a traveling observer could obtain a panoramic view over a landscape, cityscape, or seascape. For a moment the horizon framed this expansive view, holding the cottage and its landscape, or the city and its territorial space, in a precarious balance. By the end of the eighteenth century, however, both landscapes and cityscapes were rapidly transformed as cities began their long expansion, turning themselves into modern metropolises by bursting open their surrounding walls and spilling out into their countryside. As they did, the unifying view holding in place the city center, its architectural compositions and pattern of streets and promenades, and then juxtaposing this scene against the enveloping landscape, was an image torn beyond repair. The traditional city with its unique views and known pathways was being transformed by urbanization and industrialization before its citizens' eyes, faster than they could psychologically adjust to these widespread developments. This new city, expanding in size with no end in sight, could no longer be visually recorded in its entirety, but only in disorderly fragments and pieces. These were changes to the traditional townscape so absolutely incomprehensible that one longed to rewitness them in order to achieve an objective understanding, and consequently there developed a fascination in the late eighteenth and nineteenth centuries with the art of verisimilitude and the world of tautology.[126] Mirrors, along with the appearance of doubles and inner duplications, became fascinating devices reflecting the desire to see the world reappear in a form that was rapidly disappearing or as an image that was other than reality. The art of reconstituted urban landscapes, as city views or panoramas, was among the spectacles of verisimilitude that enabled the viewer to travel instantaneously and metaphorically through space and time to other cities and distant lands. In that moment of time, the fragmented city of multiple views was recomposed into a unified image, positioning the spectator in its center. The shock of immediacy was apparent in these city views and panoramas, while the devices of reconstruction remained imperceptible, heightening the overall experience in a phantasmagorical flash.[127]

An all-embracing view painted on a cylindrical canvas, the panorama or diorama became popular in London and Paris during the last decade of the eighteenth century. They were logical extensions of pictorial journalism, a form of instant historical painting of contemporary epic events that became the sensational chronicles of Napoleonic times. They soon were housed within specially designed amusement halls in which the tricks of illusion inverted the inside and the outside, or the represented and the real. City images appeared to be divorced from everyday life as if they stood outside the events of history. As nothing unpleasant or disturbing could be found in their view, they were perfect reflections of a new sense of pride among the bourgeoisie, who marveled at the decorative and scenic look of their city they now claimed responsibility for embellishing. So for example, when scaffolding was erected in 1821 to repair the dome of London's St. Paul's, this also enabled the painter Thomas Horner to climb to its top and, aided by telescopes and a camera obscura, to make a graphic record of the city's entire panorama. It was not long afterward that a special Colosseum was designed in Regent's Park to house this immense circular canvas, encompassing 46,000 square feet. When the Colosseum opened to the public, visitors climbed an elaborate scaffolding, which simulated that originally erected around St. Paul's dome, and peered out upon the circular room. The experience was so accurate that spectators believed they were indeed atop St. Paul's dome and not inside a building some three miles away; they were peering out on the actual cityscape of London, and not onto a circular canvas wall. The heart of the panorama's novelty for the nineteenth century lay in the special precautions taken to erase all evidence that detracted from its illusion. If the picture had discernible edges, if it had been a flat not a circular form, if it had not been so gigantic and overpowering, it would not have been mistaken for the real.[128]

This art of the double—London contained within London, for example—inaugurated the age of mass entertainment where authentic ceremonies and rituals, real historical and political events would be replaced by controlled and regulated performances. The panorama turned cityscapes into pictures like those that hung in art galleries, a series of encircling spaces that contained their spectators, regulated their pleasures, and focused their gaze. The real city, never actually displayed, gradually disappears from view: its chaos, its class distinctions, its snares and vices, all of these lay outside the circular frame beyond the horizon that dominated the spectator's gaze. In the nineteenth century, the panorama became the mirror image of the Panopticon: spectators observing from a central tower a surface that revealed everything and said nothing. The act of showing a city's image was becoming the spectacle itself. There was no need for narrative in this view, nor authentic collective experiences, for in the panorama the spectator was being isolated and her or his perspective privatized, trained to view the surrounding environment as a disciplined order of things. This art of verisimilitude lay with the repetition of the familiar, in the pleasure of viewing from a distance. It consequently reinforced a new urbane look, slightly bored, certainly disinterested, a gaze that accepted the world of appearances without particular challenge.[129]

View of a simulation of St Paul's Tower and the Panorama of London inside the Colosseum, Regent's Park.

View of a simulation of St Paul's Tower and the Panorama of London inside the Colosseum, Regent's Park.

Moving panoramas were soon employed to exploit the pleasures and adventures of travel. One of the largest of this type was produced by John Banvard, who painted a canvas three miles long depicting at least thirty-six different scenes of the Mississippi River stretching from the Missouri River to New Orleans. It was an unprecedented commercial success: Banvard claimed that his Mississippi Panorama, which unrolled in a downstream direction for one show and rolled back upstream for the next, attracted 400,000 in New York City in the late 1840s and reportedly earned him a sum of $200,000. To gain such notoriety, the travelogue was offset with live entertainment and accompanied on the pianoforte with specially composed songs, the sheet music for which was also on sale. When this gigantic American panorama appeared in London, *The Illustrated London News* commented that it "has excited what would appear to be insatiate taste for that class of artistic production in our own metropolis. Strange it is that we should have received such a hint from a nation by no means distinguished for its school of painting; and we suspect the explanation will be traceable to certain broad effects which alike characterize Transatlantic scenery and manners."[130]

An American reaction to the delights of Banvard's show was described in the *Boston Journal* of 1846, when the panorama was first shown in that city. The *Journal* claimed, "with a very slight stretch of the imagination, the spectator can fancy himself travelling over this mighty 'Father of Waters', and beholding the beautiful scenery that lines its shores . . . all represented with a truthfulness which delights as well as astonishes the beholder."[131] Longfellow was reported to have composed his "Evangeline" after viewing Banvard's show, and certainly Mark Twain's "Life on the Mississippi" directly borrowed its startling pictorial set pieces, their colors, lights, and shadows, from the panorama's paintings.[132] Americans were proud of the sublime expanse of primitive wilderness that rolled across the West and of their country's gigantic waterways. The Mississippi River was a particular focus that underscored the mightiness and antiquity of these places, leading Audubon to locate and record its native birds and Henry Lewis to boat along its entire length, drawing traveling shots of its scenery, towns, rivercraft, and

Indians.[133] At least eight different Mississippi River panoramas were designed, countless entertainments exploited the marvels of Niagara Falls, and numerous panoramas followed the pioneers as they rolled westward. The Romantic impulse to glory in the sublimity of the American landscape, the desire to retell the saga of its frontier and bask in the spirit of a rising democracy, lent themselves again and again to pictorial reenactment. The panoramic eye was a peculiarly nineteenth-century product, combining a taste for spectacular illusion with the thrill of documentary realism. Although most spectators may have searched for the sublime or awe-inspiring elements in a depicted landscape's vistas, they were as well provided with a pair of binoculars to enhance the detailing and veracity of the effect.

Perhaps the epitome of "rational entertainment"—the visual melange of the spectacular and the scientific—lies in the organizational heart of the great nineteenth-century exhibitions that turned the industrial world into one immense picture show. These eclectic jumbles of artifacts and bazaars of movable tokens from many of the world's nations offered the spectator a series of tableaux heterogeneously juxtaposed one against another. A ramble through these fairgrounds of the nineteenth century was no different from the visual experience received by turning the pages of an illustrated "Picturesque Voyage," or scanning the random juxtaposition of news columns, illustrations, and advertisements in the popular press. Spectators simply compared one image to another, contrasting the difference between nations and gauging the distance between the past and the present, the so-called developed and the backward. In these exhibition halls where commodities were displayed, the tactile qualities of production and craftsmanship, the perception of vernacular settings and traditional manners, and the social relationships among men and things were replaced by a sequence of optical tableaux, an accumulation of weightless and fantastical images that floated about in a dream world.

The newly industrialized world, which seemed to be structured completely by things, suddenly created an environment in which the individual's autonomy was lessened as she or he too became subordinated to the objects consumed or admired.[134] In this new milieu of things, the eye had to learn to observe a piece of goods as merchandise, whereas a promenader's look attached itself to the obvious, because the surface image was all that really could be gauged before an item was replaced by the next one that quickly came into view. As spectacles of capital and in order to teach about this new environment of things, the industrial exhibitions required appropriate settings—theatrical stage sets that held in place the virtuoso performance of commodities while transfixing the spectator's awareness to the absolute and wondrous present. This spectacle was a theater without precedence, enabling a viewer to revel in its make-believe and its myth-making force.[135] Each exhibition was a sheer bravado of architectural expression, for this was the manner in which the new industrial age chose to give its drama a shape. Planned to be both sensational and educational, as well as the handmaiden of commerce, these living encyclopedias, the industrial exhibitions of all nations, were as well simulacra of industrial technology—a vast list of appropriations and a gigantic assemblage of serial processes.[136]

Mixing education with entertainment could often be a risky affair producing strange concoctions and weird illusions. For example, when the Crystal Palace in 1854 was moved to Syndenham after its completion as a world's exhibition hall and remodeled into an overblown version of itself, Owen Jones and Digby Wyatt were given the responsibility for some of its new interior decorations. They arranged in its elaborate courtyards their view of a universal history of architecture and the decorative arts. Addressing this exhibition directly to the eye of the spectator, they intended to teach the viewer how to delineate the separate forms and different styles of architecture by seeing porticos of buildings arranged side by side as if in a continuous line of Western historical development. A portico from each historical age had been selected, supposedly modeled on accurate drawings done on the spot in Egypt, Greece, Spain, and Italy. Already in 1847/8, Owen Jones had published a book on the Alhambra, and subsequently he wrote *Grammar of Ornament* in 1856. In both these books he aimed to educate the public in the decorative arts by illustrating the many different forms of beauty and diverse ornamental styles to be found in the world. At the Crystal Palace of 1854, Jones particularly hoped that the public—especially upholsterers, weavers, and calico printers—might give up their unpleasant habit of copying styles from whatever period was currently fashionable if they were taught the true relationships that bound style and place together, and if they came to understand what was truely eternal in architecture and ornamentation. So Jones proclaimed, "Art is the patrimony of all, but it is the more necessary that it should be regulated. . . . [so that] public and patrons shall judge wisely. . . ."[137] But his educational intention was reversed in the melange represented by the reconstituted Crystal Palace, and his historical reconstructions found their location adjacent to a menagerie of stuffed birds, beasts and fowls, models and tableaux of various races and ages, a prehistoric marsh with life-size monsters, and thousands of garden curios, grottoes, and mazes.[138]

Like all collections and encyclopedias, the exhibitions of the nineteenth century required a map or a structure enabling the public to perceive some organizational and educational arrangement behind the productive extravaganzas of the industrial age. But how was it possible to travel through the maze of celebratory structures that adorned these fairgrounds and form one's reflective opinion amid the plethoric outpouring of objects and exhibits? It is no wonder then that these exhibitions actually became simulated travelogues, guidebooks to the world of exotic places and encyclopedias of appropriated treasures. Every site became the focal point of other places, every location was the start of a series of possible routes passing through other nations. Traveling across the fairgrounds was literally a panoramic shot of goods and places, constantly provoking a dilemma of how to link one fragmented scene to the next. At both the Crystal Palace of 1851 and the subsequent Paris Exhibition of 1855, the products of all nations were classified as belonging to one of four separate categories: industrial, fine arts, agricultural, or horticultural. A more sophisticated arrangment was developed for the 1867 Paris Universal Exposition, when a vast elliptical hall designed by Gustave Eiffel was composed of concentric oval compartments spreading out from an interior central garden.

Frederic Le Play was Commissioner-General of this 1867 Exposition, and following the suggestions of Napoleon III that a grid system be employed with nations arranged along one side and exhibition categories along the other, he designed the following map of information for the display of objects.[139] The first gallery in this elliptical structure moving outward from the central garden was a thematic show, entitled "The History of Work," and was Le Play's visual preface to the entire exhibition, comprising a comparative historical display of tools and crafts from the Stone Age to the turn of the nineteenth century. Next came the Gallery of Fine Arts, followed by a Corridor for Liberal Arts with an eclectic display ranging from scientific instruments to a patented rocking chair. A corridor for Furniture, a corridor for Textile Fabrics, and a subgallery for Raw Materials followed. The largest gallery and the farthest away from the center was reserved for the Machinery Hall, and finally on the outside ring were restaurants serving food from different nations. Each country was allocated a wedgelike display space radiating out from the center of the exhibition hall. Consequently if a spectator traveled around one concentric oval, then she or he visited the exhibits of different countries, always viewing and contrasting the same category of objects arranged along the elliptical aisles. By a double-entry cataloging procedure, however, a spectator moving from center to periphery could cross-reference all the sets of objects in each category displayed by one nation alone. Never ignorant of sensational effects, Gustave Eiffel designed a hydraulic lift that raised viewers to the roof of the exhibition hall so they could gain a prospectival view across the range of exhibits.[140]

As each country's display inevitably differed in size, the unifying system of classification was all but destroyed because no one nation occupied the same sized spatial wedge. Consequently the Universal Exhibition, the Philadelphia Centennial of 1876, borrowed the classificatory scheme of Le Play, but now this encyclopedia—really a miniature pictorial globe—called for a deeper systematization, for year by year the industrialized world was growing more complex and the number of items exhibited bursting in abundance. Le Play's seven major classificatory sets

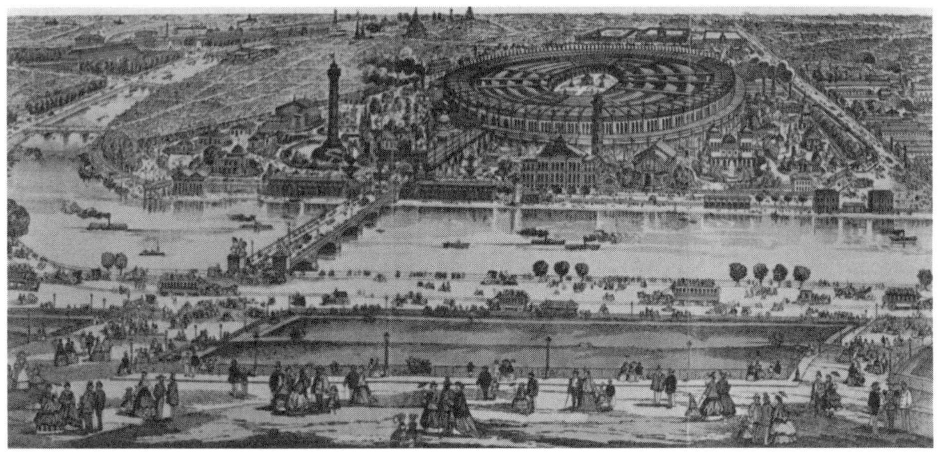

Bird's-eye view of the Exposition Universelle of 1867, Paris.

were refined: mining and metallurgy, manufacturing, education and science, were all displayed in the Main Building, while the arts, machinery, agriculture, and horticulture were located in their own separate structures. These seven sets, subsets, and sub-subsets were cataloged by a system that borrowed from the newly developed Dewey Decimal System used for cataloging books.[141]

Not just educational performances, these exhibitions were entertaining shows as well. Fantasy was inscribed in the space of the fairground as a voyage, and the spectator could choose from many varied itineraries. In an eighty-one acre Pleasure Garden designed by Alphand to surround the elliptical Exposition Hall of the 1867 Fair (a park usually reserved for horticultural and botanical displays), for the first time countries were invited to erect exemplary architectural models of their own choosing: thus a Swiss chalet, a Chinese pagoda, a Moorish mosque, an Eyptian palace—in other words, habitats from around the world—were scattered about in picturesque confusion, although no one pretended that these represented national styles.[142] A spectator could travel back in time to visit a New England log cabin, a hundred-year-old facsimile reconstructed at the Philadelphia Fair in 1876 and filled with furniture that might have arrived on the Mayflower—or maybe it only from Danvers, Connecticut, in 1776. This display was called "a glimpse of history in itself," a pleasing view of life in New England in the preceding century.[143] "Ancient dames [a contemporary wrote] in flower gowns are spinning and performing other domestic duties. In the open fire-place is a spit with a turkey slowly turning and roasting for a Thanksgiving dinner. There are shelves of crockery, plain-fashioned furniture of that time, and on one of the tables an old clasped Bible. Herbs and other stores of the careful housewife are hanging from the rafters, and in the room adjoining is a canopied bed with a patchwork quilt, and alongside a little old cradle."[144] This log cabin was contrasted to a modern kitchen, and the mode of cooking and manner of serving likewise compared so that the viewer could ascertain progress in the culinary arts made over the centuries.[145]

By the 1878 Paris Exposition, these popular displays had taken the form of the Rue des Nations, one gigantic streetfront along which participating nations erected facades according to their architectural preference. An American observer to the Exposition felt that the best national reconstruction was that of Belgium, which copied the Hôtel de Ville at Antwerp; England had three different houses, all noteworthy specimens of early Elizabethan houses; Sweden and Norway provided rustic houses based on that country's ancient wooden compositions; while Japanese primitive houses, a Moorish facade from Spain, and other imaginary styles paraded along the route.[146] These so-called travel exhibits were always didactic demonstrations, pouring a thinglike world into selective inventories. Underscoring the linear progression of time with epic ambitions, they sought to frame a static universal picture of the habitations of mankind in a world fluctuating and palpitating with change. It was assumed that the house constituted the basic environment that influenced all men and was in addition a vessel to hold and to display the objects of industry. So, it was argued, the mentality of a nation was best explained, its cultural intellect, instincts, and habits fairly exhibited through typical scenes and interior arrangements of domesticity.[147] By now, however, it was not just the comparative view of a nation's progress that was at issue, but the origins of societies, the relative age of their monuments and works of art, and the historical roots and generative development of their stylistic traditions.

Eugene Emmanuel Viollet-le-Duc, the ardent restorer of France's monuments, agreed to join this search for the origins and many filial derivations defining the habitations of mankind. By simulating a dialogue between hypothetical travelers in his book *The Habitations of Man in all Nations* (1863), Viollet-le-Duc offered the reader his interpretation of the methods of construction and the evolution of different architectural forms found in the world. If architects were to improve contemporary dwellings, Viollet-le-Duc reasoned, they must understand the elementary nature of habitation; they must study the past to gather inferences about humanity, the means by which mankind in different ages expressed their thoughts, their taste, and their genius.[148] Housing may have stemmed from simple origins, responding to different needs and climatic conditions, but over time it was altered by unique imaginations, resulting in complex and varied expressions. Through rational analysis, comparison, and classification of a supposedly universal history of habitation, a wise architect could unravel the evolutionary route of their forms. As in geology, or so Viollet argued, the architect could not understand a single deposit if it was isolated from its context. She or he had to examine the strata that lay above and beneath it.[149] Thus the duty of the nineteenth-century architect was to analyze, contrast, and appropriate the traditional forms of architecture, but to be wary of imitating or recombining these elements in bizarre and false compositions. So Viollet-le-Duc advised, the architect must look to the pictorial memory of early forms as authentic archives of human progress, and by informing her or his reason and understanding through comparative study she or he would thus be able to wisely fulfill contemporary needs.[150]

The habitations of mankind became a popular architectural motif of the fairs. Perhaps the desire was actually to represent in model form the lessons derived from the writings of Viollet-le-Duc, and consequently we find that Charles Garnier, the architect of the Paris Opera, was given the task at the Paris Fair of 1889 to exhibit typical examples of housing from around the world.[151] Like rings of an onion that wrap around a core, Garnier presented a synthetic panorama of the "History of Human Habitation" surrounding the Eiffel Tower. Through analogical comparison and contrasts of forty-four types of houses, the spectator could witness how different people and their architects had struggled over the centuries to answer the need for shelter, and how they had modified these forms from century to century. Garnier divided his circular tableaux into two divisions: those structures from the prehistory of habitation and those from more recent albeit historical times, stressing a unilinear evolution of types.[152] As if raising up forms of housing that had died and disappeared long ago, Garnier presented the spectator with the charm of exhumation supposedly rendered exact through archeological study. But his work, a critic noted, was not what it appeared to be, and the reading not that accessible to the spectator. Quite mysteriously, Garnier's models revealed an unbelievable fidelity to the principles of construction guarded by certain Western people, without offering archeological evidence or theoretical hypotheses.[153]

Charles Garnier, Illustration of Assyrian and Phoenician Houses constructed on the Champs de Mars for the Paris Exposition of 1889.

If this piece of fantasy at the 1889 Exposition was not sufficient, one could voyage to Egypt along La Rue du Caire without ever leaving the fairgrounds. Reconstituted in "scrupulous verite," twenty-five houses were reproduced as exact copies of old houses once found in Cairo but now replaced by European styles. M. Delort was responsible for this "apparition" by saving the best Arab houses from destruction and transporting them piece by piece to the fair. So a contemporary noted, Delort was a magician who evoked with apparent pleasure an exquisite vision of the Orient. It was difficult for an architect to reproduce the samples of foreign art without introducing their own conceptions, correcting and embellishing as they wished instead of faithfully copying earlier works. But so it was explained, Delort had lived among "the natives" for twenty-five years as the First Deputy of France. Supervising all the construction himself, he carefully recomposed even the slightest details from the local mise-en-scène: fifty donkeys accompanied by boys in costume promenaded around the exposition, while along La Rue du Caire itself the sounds of Arabia—its music, dances, boutiques, and bazaars—completed the scene.[154]

The ultimate fantasy of travel at the 1889 Exposition was located in the Panorama Building of the General Transatlantic Company, where a spectator could embark vicariously from Le Havre or Marseille to ports around the world. Although the eleven dioramas and one vast panorama were in truth gigantic advertising posters for the travel and shipping company, they nevertheless offered a complete and believable travel illusion. One boarded the steamboat La Touraine at Le Havre, finding it surrounded by sixty-two company vessels saluting its departure. The first sight of Algiers, a reporter described, was attained from one of the dioramas, and if the viewer became melancholic after realizing that the old picturesque Orient had lost much of its charm since becoming a colony of France, never mind: she or he could be compensated by knowing that Western "civilization" had gained the Mediterranean only a half a century before, and consequently the sea still remained the least secure and offered the most adventuresome travel.[155] Underscoring the nineteenth century's fascination with travel, Rosalind Williams has noted in *Dream*

Charles Garnier, Illustration of Byzantine House constructed on the Champs de Mars for the Paris Exposition of 1889.

Worlds that at the 1900 Exhibition, of the thirty-three major entertainment exhibitions, twenty-one involved some simulated experience of travel. Classified according to the technology providing that illusion, there were ensembles in relief, moving panoramas, panoramas in which the spectator moved, panoramas in which both moved, and moving photographs.[156]

Perhaps the theatrical apex unifying architectural splendor with the marvels of industrial production was reached on the edge of Bohemia at the Chicago World's Fair in 1893, where the power of machines and engineering turned the wasteland shores of Lake Michigan into a make-believe fairyland. Dressed in neoclassical garb and shimmering in white stucco, the main structures of the White City were sited around a Court of Honor and separated from the lake by a monumental peristyle. In contrast and contradiction to this fair White City there arose another, the Midway Plaisance, as remote in style and location from the neoclassical city as it possibly could be. If the White City represented the collaborative climax of architects, landscape gardeners, artists, and sculptors, then the Plaisance, where pleasurable rides and exotic amusements reigned, was the competitive bazaar of modern capitalism.[157] As reconstructions or models of housing types had been popular events since 1867, here too at the Chicago World's Fair state exhibitions provided an ensemble of fanciful fairlike architecture: New York's pavilion, for example, was a villa from the Italian Renaissance; Idaho's building was a modified Swiss chalet; Pennsylvania provided a reproduction of Independence Hall; Massachusetts copied the old John Hancock residence; and Virginia reproduced Mount Vernon.[158]

Spectators who flocked to these nineteenth-century industrial fairs were being transformed slowly into modern consumers. No longer shopping for items that met specific needs or practical uses, these viewers sought instead pure visual entertainment and the thrill of marvelous machine productions not part of their everyday lives. In these exhibitions, commodities of the world were artfully displayed and visually made accessible through the penetrability of both the open floor plans of their display halls and their glass and iron facades. This diffusion, moreover, helped to blur the distinction between functional and desirable goods. Even the pleasure of "just looking," which these exhibitions deliberately flaunted, was derived from the mingling of fantastic architecture with peculiar and innovative commodities, and this too began to erase in the eyes of the viewer the boundaries between culture and commerce, necessities and goods.[159] The spectacle spun by these fairs as simulated travelogues, panoramic visions, even fictional cities, took disparate architectural images and modern amusements and drew them into a simultaneous aesthetic expression of architectural unity that the city had already lost.

It would not take long for cities, however, to understand the lessons that these exhibitions had taught, and soon they too turned their architecture and public spaces into visual delights where just looking at theatrical arrangements of architecture, the aura reflected in shop windows, and the vitality of people and vehicles in flux became a desirable pastime and an end in itself. But the architectural setting of the city and the fluctuating scenery of its streets would offer the spectator more than just entertainment. There were to be found in its streets material evidence of a dying past, of a traditional city being rapidly covered over by the winds of progress that blew against its face. The visual difference between the estranged artifacts from the past and the unsatisfactory constructions of the present gave rise to the desire to respectfully record and to artfully preserve or restore these old buildings and streets, not just as simulated spectacles for exhibitions and fairs, but reappropriated in situ as public property belonging to a common heritage.[160]

Pilgrim Voyagers

Traveling backward in time was a nineteenth-century reflex that tended to idealize the past glories of ancient Greece or the pure spirit of the Middle Ages, even the urbanities of the Renaissance, and then to raise these forms as the standards by which to measure the present. Ever since entering the modern era and witnessing its attending crises of political revolution, urbanization, industrialization, and the rise of a consumer society, a nostalgic lament had been heard calling out for a lost primordial past, a cry that often tried to retie the broken surface of the nineteenth-century city to the vanishing traces of historical times. The architectural ruin in the mid-nineteenth century became a highly significant symbol of this loss and decay. So too, the fabric of the city containing visual remnants of its history was reevaluated, because changes to its physical appearance, while apparent, were actually slower than the rush of modernization, and overlapping traces still remained of earlier architectural styles and morphological structures. The city's topographical arrangement guided the collective memory of its past, the context within which new spatial forms, architectural styles, and functional uses found their formal expression. A critic has recently written about architectural revivals:

> For the serious architect the past exists not as a legacy to be possessed through self-conscious act of the 'modern' will, but as an enduring fact, an ineliminable part of an extended present. From Vitruvius through the Renaissance to the Gothic revival, responses to architecture have been at one and the same time practical and backward-looking. . . . And the pervasiveness of this respect for the past is only confirmed by the hysterical nature of recent attempts to break with it.[161]

The words "'modern' will" and "hysterical attempts" unknowingly point toward rival positions concerning the correct procedures for preserving or safeguarding architectural and urban heritage; an opposition whose roots grow out of the nineteenth century when it first appeared. Many in that century clearly valued the city for the traces it retained of its historical past, but this hold of tradition simultaneously represented a moment of danger, a tendency to be overthrown if an architecture reflecting the spirit of the times and the modern metropolis was to be born. The nineteenth-century city produced opposite reactions to the same dilemma of modernity. For one group, the encroachments of urbanization, technological progress, and the democratic levelings of popular culture created an antimodern reaction: art and architecture must be salvaged from these democratic levelings.

This was a backward, binding vision revealing a preoccupation with the tastes and prestige of an elite historical tradition. On the other hand, the tyranny of the past had to be muffled if a rational architecture was to take form. Standing on the edge of history, groping forward toward the future, these architects eagerly accepted the linear and evolutionary development of history and the progressive promise of science and technology.

Perhaps the nineteenth-century Gothic Revival in its separate English and French forms is exemplary of these polar reactions to the proliferating complexities of modern urban life. Because places of worship as well as museums provide synoptic visions of what a culture wishes to preserve and what to efface, it is not surprising that the Gothic Revival, a discourse on the catholic procedures of ecclesiastical restoration, coincided with the nineteenth century's enthusiasm for museums. In both the piety of museums and Christian worship we find directives telling us what to do with old things and buildings, how to honor and to preserve them. In the early decades of the nineteenth century many architectural historians devoted themselves to the architecture of the English middle ages, surveying and measuring these buildings, dating their styles and origins as accurately as possible. Included among the devotional was Augustus Welby Northmore Pugin, who in 1817 published *An Attempt to Discriminate the Styles of English Architecture, from the Conquest to the Reformation.* In this book Pugin established the categories of the "Early English," the "Decorated," and the "Perpendicular" styles, terms that would become touchstones for the English Gothic Revival.[162] Pugin believed that the restoration of English churches was a deeply religious gesture: "As it is, everything glorious about the English churches is Catholic, everything debased and hideous is Protestant."[163] In an attempt to overthrow the dictates of neoclassical architecture, Pugin proclaimed those forms to be pagan and unreal, a borrowed antique art that was alien to England. Gothic forms on the contrary were Christian, being spontaneous expressions of the people: they truthfully expressed their structural and functional purposes and in addition were ornamented beautifully in emblematic codes.[164] The compositional order of Gothic architecture should be studied, or so Pugin advised, in order that the soul and spirit of earlier work could be recaptured and subsequently imitated and revived.[165]

In the English advocates of the Gothic Revival, particularly Pugin and later John Ruskin, we find a mode of typological thinking that oscillates between reality and the imagination, calling on the ideal world of expression to restore some significance to a rapidly deteriorating world. Ruskin called architecture "a science of feeling more than of rule" because it impresses itself on men's minds.[166] Likening architecture to poetry, music, and painting, the Gothic Revivalists clearly abandoned the well-guarded neoclassical boundaries that maintained distinctions between genres. Because architecture in modern times must play the role for city dwellers that nature once held, subsequently an architect should imitate nature as truthfully as possible. In this manner, or so Ruskin claimed, buildings became landscapes of the mind—the details of a cathedral with its sculptured processions and hierarchical ordering of historic forms were really painted scenes whose very diversity of expression and abundance of irregularity guided the viewer to contemplate correctly the most worthy objects. Being immersed in such a visual world of splendor inspired the viewer's mind to wander as if she or he were contemplating the sublimity of a natural landscape.[167]

The French version of the Gothic Revival as expounded by Viollet-le-Duc was an expression based on an understanding of comparative linguistics. Recognizing the uniqueness of every object and form, the French strove to arrange them in classifications, generalizing and abstracting from the specifics that they felt fluctuated with time. In the third volumne of his *Dictionary* Viollet-le-Duc called "restoration," both the word and the act, "modern," for no other people or civilization had understood the term in the manner the nineteenth century proposed.[168] Only then did man begin to analyze, to compare, to classify, searching for the true history of a monument, following vicariously step by step the way it outlined the route, the progress and the transformations of humanity. These steps were fancifully reinvented and simulated at the nineteenth century's industrial exhibitions, but the same steps could be applied to the art of restoration. Following the comparative anatomical and geological research of Curvier, philologists discovered that the origins of all European languages stemmed from one root. In a similar fashion, the archeologists comparing, discussing, and classifying artifacts only recently discovered in India, Egypt, and even in Europe sought to uncover their origins, their filiations, and their classifications according to universal laws of change and development.[169] Mulling over this information, Viollet-le-Duc proclaimed that "restoration" must not be restricted in meaning to the preservation of a monument, but might represent a far wider sense. It could subsequently mean that a monument be "returned" to a state of perfection that may never have existed before, but that could be ascertained through comparative and genealogical study, tracing the lines of its development back to an ideal root. Like other research based on comparative linguistics, a nation's architectural heritage must be studied, analyzed, and understood not in order to replicate these ancient forms, but rather to make a new composite synthesis, a unity of styles, using the best of modern materials and serving the needs of modern times.

Consequently, Viollet-le-Duc believed that each building or architectural element ought to be restored in the style that belonged to it not only in appearance but in its structure as well.[170] Few buildings ever were built in one stage, or if they had been they usually were modified over time. Therefore it was always necessary before any restoration work be attempted to establish the exact age and character of each part and to compose out of these a kind of verbal synthesis that borrowed from documents written and inscribed. The architects in charge of restoration must know the former styles and construction methods of each period of art, and they must be knowledgeable as well of the specific styles and methods belonging to different schools and regions. Even better, the restoration architect should know the exact structure, its anatomy, its temperament, penetrating into all parts of the building as if she or he had been the original designer, in order to perceive several routes to pursue in the work of restoration. Many times a monument had been restored by an architect who lacked this knowledge, so some of the building's restored elements might stem from the original scheme while others might have been modified dramatically. The act of restoration, as Viollet-le-Duc prescribed, was always a question of reestablishing a unity of style that no longer existed, or may never have existed, but one that reflected the spirit and time in which the monument was originally conceived.[171] In this manner a composite picture, an appropriate style based on scientific study and rational thought, was substituted for the incrustations and additions of time marring its "ideal" beauty.[172]

Ruskin would never agree with Viollet-le-Duc, for "restoration," he warned as early as 1849, meant just the opposite.

> It means the most total destruction which a building can suffer: a destruction out of which no remnants can be gathered: a destruction accompanied with false description of the thing destroyed.* [*False, also, in the manner of parody,—the most loathsome manner of falsehood. (1880 addition)] Do not let us deceive ourselves in this important matter; it is *impossible,* as impossible to raise the dead, to restore anything that has even been great or beautiful in architecture. That which I have . . . insisted upon as the life of the whole, that spirit which is given only by the hand and eye of the workman, can never be recalled.[173]

We had no right, Ruskin felt, to touch the architectural heritage of our past.

> They are not ours. They belong partly to those who built them, and partly to all the generations of mankind who are to follow. . . . What we have ourselves built, we are at liberty to throw down; but what other men gave their strength, and wealth, and life to accomplish. . . . It belongs to all their successors.[174]

Then Ruskin turned to open the floodgates of the modern dilemma, for he could see that the vital forces of all nations were crowding in upon city gates, that modern life would be acted out upon the urban stage. The only influence that could possibly offer the healing inspiraton of wood and field from which these urban crowds had fled would be the "power of ancient Architecture." Gravely he warned: "Do not part with it for the sake of the formal square, or of the fenced and planted walk; nor of the goodly street nor opened quay. The pride of the city is not in these. Leave them to the crowd."[175] The glory and memory of every building, Ruskin noted, lies in its age. Architecture must be the cornerstone of history, a document to be read, a memorial to our Christian faith, and so it should be honored and respected. "We may live without her, and worship without her, but we cannot remember without her. How cold is all history, how lifeless all imagery, compared to that which the living nation writes, and the uncorrupted marble bears."[176]

Both Ruskin and Viollet-le-Duc sought a visual mode of communication, treating architecture as an optical memory theater. Theirs was after all the age of the daguerreotype, which offered itself, or so it was supposed, as a neutral recording device, an unposed vision addressing itself directly and truthfully to all who had sight. The external world was drawn close to the photographic eye, details in space and time became known and experienced directly. Not surprisingly a taste for reality, for truth, for the recorded trace as an exact resemblance of naturalistic lines and authentic colors developed alongside the spread of photography in the nineteenth century. The surface plane of a painting, a book, or architecture was to be a truthful reflection of reality as varied as the events of life. Ruskin believed "the greatest thing a human soul ever does in this world is to see something, and tell what it saw in a plain way. Hundreds of people can talk for one who can think, but thousands can think for one who can see. To see clearly is poetry, prophecy, and religion—all in one."[177]

Ruskin's optical vision was enthralled with appearances: of textures, colors, perspectival viewpoints, and details. The photograph for him became the handmaiden of art, affecting a greater naturalism and truthfulness in form. Leaving ruins where they lay, focusing on selective details of architecture, his optical vision imposed an instantaneous synchronic frame as if in a daguerreotyped world, freezing the linear series of images constantly progressing in time. Ruskin turned everything he surveyed into mummified objects of the past, every city he visited into a museum. He searched to keep the gap between the past and the modern world open as wide as it could be. Worried over how the century would present itself or look to future generations, he was a pilgrim traveler studying the visual formations of cities and stones, but leaving them untouched in his wake as authentic reminders for others to view.[178] Clearly something was wrong with the modern world, yet Ruskin failed to step forward and offer a reforming hand. His was a regressive move into the Gothic past, an interiorized self-defense against the forces of change.

Offering an opposing stance, Viollet-le-Duc placed his faith in the documentary technology of the photograph, a tool to preserve and enrich the best of the past. Thus he found that the photograph provided the exactitude of a verbal and graphic process that referenced the "actual state" of a monument. Searching for the traces that the work of restoration often masked, the photograph enabled the architect to be more scrupulous in his respect for the remnants from former times and to account more clearly for the monument's structure, which the naked eye unaided might overlook.[179] Viollet-le-Duc invented his restorations by combining both materials and recorded architectural forms within the restraining framework of a monument's structural order. The language of restoration for him lay self-contained within a specific monument; it was a play of images and forms that the architect's interpretation deliberately created. If the ruin, speaking directly to a beholder's imagination and memory, was Ruskin's true delight, then Viollet-le-Duc's gaze fell on the external surface and the structural language that the monument disclosed.

Victorians loved the study of fossils, of paleontology—no doubt it was an emblematic gesture for a century concerned with its self-image, of its place among the objects in the museum. Buildings were fossils of the world to be reconstructed by a New Zealander, the pilgrim of ages to come.[180] The universal history they so desperately sought in their panoramas and exhibitions, encyclopedias and museums, catalogues and folios, depended on the prior existence of a universal language, not the babble of eclectic tongues that architects most often spoke. Architecture in the nineteenth century, or so it was believed, held a didactic role—the moral development and improvement of all social classes—and therefore the best architectural examples were sought whether from antiquity, the middle ages, or modern times. "Styles and orders with the careful study and knowledge of their details, the effects they have and the modifications they are capable of," an architectural critic of mid-century wrote, "are as important and indispensable to architects, as the study of words in language to linguists."[181] Buildings after all were monuments of the mind; in their landscapes a nation's talent and genius could be read. The French, for example, had a love for centralization, so that even their art radiated from one ideal, upholding the sanctity of the ensemble or the unity of design. Vary the parts, they might say, but let not the parts be foreign to the whole![182] English architecture, on the other hand, was individualistic, too diverse in its appearance to offer future generations a lasting effect. Many an English church, it was complained, had been spoiled by architectural restorers who unwittingly mixed their styles, until the church became a "museum of architectural metamorphoses." Often restorers destroyed the original plan of a church, its structure or decoration, effacing historical objects and ornaments originally intended to illustrate its meaning. These architects indulged in their own desires and opinions without any regard to the embellishment the structure would be to the city if properly restored and completed according to the intentions of its original designers.[183] As Edward Barry lectured the Royal Academy in 1879:

> When a public feeling for art is weak, [as it is in England] the wealth of a nation is diverted rather to selfish gratification than to public gain. . . . With us, artistic taste has been more a matter of individual education and culture in the case of a few, while it has been neglected as an element of national prosperity. . . . Art has been cultivated by . . . the French, not from inborn taste, but also from calculated policy. . . . Perhaps it may at length dawn upon some of our rulers that an educated national taste may even be a matter of commercial importance.[184]

The ideal of a universal architectural language, even with manifold means of expression, one that might educate and reform the Victorian crisis in taste and eclectic preference, remained an ephemeral wish. National schools of design were established, books of style and ornamentation written, and museums of design promoted: these all helped to reform the industrial and decorative arts, but architecture, considered to be the chief of all arts, still basked in illusionistic virtuosity. Dwelling on the moral inspiration and sublime effects of Gothic architecture and forms drawn from nature that Ruskin believed a nation must encourage, he thought "[y]ou will find that the art whose end is pleasure only is pre-eminently the gift of cruel and savage nations, cruel in temper, savage in habits and conception; but that the art which is especially dedicated to natural fact always indicates a peculiar gentleness and tenderness of mind."[185] Viollet-le-Duc's concern, on the other hand, helped to move the nineteenth century toward a more forward-looking spirit. He wanted to uncover the explanatory links or logic that connected different parts of an architectural monument, in order to assimilate this knowledge in the work of reconstruction. Pointing away from those who gathered spectacular inspiration from the picturesque and sublime, he mounted what might be termed an inquisition into the mysteries and deep structures that lay beneath his gaze. The inspector Viollet-le-Duc resembled the detective, another product of the nineteenth century, who reconstructed a crime and provided missing explanatory links.[186]

Finally, before drawing these travelogues to a close, we should turn to unexplored territories closer to home than the Gothic past or the exotic East that also captivated the inquiring mind of nineteenth-century pilgrims. Henry Mayhew, in the preface of *London Labour and the London Poor* (1851–2), explained:

> As supplying information concerning a large body of persons, of whom the public has less knowledge than of the most distant tribes of the earth . . . and as adducing facts so extraordinary, that the traveller in the undiscovered country must . . . until his stories are corroborated by after investigations, be content to

> lie under the imputation of telling such tales, as travellers are generally supposed to delight in.[187]

All of a sudden the topography of the great cities of Europe appeared to contain two different nations of Rich and Poor. Perhaps it was the French Revolution of 1789 that first unleashed "the savages [who] entered and remained in the city."[188] But who were these nomads who wandered the streets of London and Paris as vagabonds and drifters? What did they do and where did they go? In his novel *Sybil, or The Two Nations* (1846) Disraeli began to describe and represent this new division of nations:

> Two nations; between whom there is no intercourse and no sympathy; who are ignorant of each other's habits, thoughts, and feelings, as if they were dwellers in different zones, or inhabitants of different planets; who are formed by different breeding, are fed by different food, are ordered by different manners, and are not governed by the same laws.[189]

Because the Gothic Revival was not primarily an architectural reform, but basically a literary movement inspired by the romantic tales of Sir Walter Scott and the city of weird hauntings and dreadful intimacy depicted by Charles Dickens, Gothic was also the favored literary form for portraying the poor and working class. London itself blended in an excessive manner realistic and fantastic imagery, nurturing the taste for this genre—for London after all was a kaleidoscope of images, ungraspable and fleeting as any array of instantaneous poses. This city became the Victorians' "matériaux mémoire," offering tokens to be recollected from its past, afterimages and reprints of empirical life. They formed lists and catalogs of the city's virtues and vices, guidebooks and exhibitions to its physiognomy.

London, one architectural critic complained in 1872, was a filthy city, its buildings blackened by smoke, its mouldings and cornices choked with soot, its monotonous rows of brick-built houses every tint of dirt. A haze hung over the horizon of London; smoke belching forth in hydralike fashion from its hundreds of thousands of furnaces. London might have many fine architectural specimens around Hyde Park, or in its Pall-Mall clubs, yet they were hidden in narrow streets and darkened courts, or isolated in style and character from their neighboring structures. No wonder Americans came to London out of a duty to see its major sites, but then rushed off to Paris where they spent the bulk of their time and money. To walk through London was a fatiguing strain on the nerves, while in Paris it was a pleasure to stroll along fine broad boulevards lined with trees. In Paris nothing was hidden nor seemed monotonous to this particular reviewer, everything gleamed in fresh light, basking in the whiteness of its stone facades. So he continued, London failed completely from the artistic point of view. It had an utterly confused town plan, more like a collection of small towns and disparate slums rather than a unified whole. Even Regent Street, the only London passage of any architectural pretension, was pieced together in sections more reminiscent of a crooked stovepipe than a magnificent boulevard of pleasure.[190]

The English Gothic Revival, however, turned this shady obscure London light with its grotesque shadows and indefinite forms into an advantage, finding its ugliness a moment of the sublime. And the sublime also found its way into the terror of the city's magnitude, in the undulation of the viaduct arches that tunneled through the city, in the vast array of warehouses endlessly repeating their recessed bays and giant hoists down the East End quaysides.[191] London was a city of nomads extruded from its darkened interiors. They gathered around the gigantic new railway stations and huge wholesale markets, many slept underneath its bridges and viaducts or crowded into back alleys and blackened courtyards, and hundreds appeared at midnight soup kitchens and common lodging houses. The great improvement plans of midcentury London, the railway and street clearance schemes, continually unsettled the city, displacing whole sections of the town and adding to its desperate congestion.[192] After Henry Mayhew turned his probing eye in 1855 upon this phantasmagoria of urban life, exposing and documenting the life and lot of these strange people who populated the heart of the city, other reformers would follow so that slowly the public space, the streets, back courtyards, and even the darkened stairways were open to the reformers' inquiring gaze.

Out of this darkness and haze appeared two travelers with the same disclaimer as any innocent picturesque voyagers, or so Blanchard Jerrold wrote of Gustave Doré and of himself. "We are Pilgrims—not Historians; travelling by the same highway as that by which the Potters of London, and the Dinantars of Dinant on the Meuse, carried on their commerce six hundred years ago, we approach London."[193] "We are Pilgrims: not I repeat, historians, nor antiquarians, nor topographers. Our plan is to present London in the quick to the reader—as completely as we may be able to grasp the prodigious giant and dissect his Titan limbs, the floods of his veins, the iron beams of his muscle!"[194] The journalist Jerrold and the illustrator Doré sought to perpetuate the memory of London by reducing its Gothic murkiness and doom-laden reality to a series of gallery images, to a linear sequence in a chain of events. Groping their way in the light and shadows of the great city, even escorted on their nocturnal perambles by two plainclothes policemen, they became modern chroniclers and illustrators, relaying their travels to future voyagers in time. Like obsessive detectives silently wandering through the rubbish heap of the great city, they collected fragments of information, probed for new evidence in the depths of its underworld cauldrons, and then reassembled their views into a synthetic account once they returned to their studios.

In its final form, *London, A Pilgrimage* (1872) was a fragment of what Jerrold and Doré had originally planned as a much vaster scheme that aimed to be a complete description of the entire social complex of London: an encyclopedic study of the labor, commerce, politics, and places where Londoners lived, worked, and were entertained. Although they were fascinated by the extreme contrasts in London of abject misery and abundant luxury, the two nations that Disraeli had outlined, Jerrold and Doré's offering was limited instead to a series of "pilgrimages" to the more eccentric parts of the city: its nightly haunts, the London docks, the Thames Embankment, its modes of transportation. They hoped to present in a quick manner an amazing and emblematic "gallery of types" and to record the look of the present.[195] Jerrold's turgid narrative and Dore's 180 engravings, however, were distilled to enumeration and their recounting to counting so that their book reflected the same collecting and retentive gestures as did the nineteenth-century museums and exhibitions. Denying the pull of the underworld and of the archaic, the mysterious world that so fascinated their contemporary, Baudelaire, as he wandered the streets of Paris, their chronicle was instead a sublimated epic: a pile of souvenirs displaying false comforts and distorted representations transformed by their hands into a melancholic reminder of the catastrophe called "London"—a story that could no longer be written in epic form but was not yet available as universal history.[196] *London, A Pilgrimage* was a Victorian parlor-table book to be leafed through absent-mindedly between sips of tea. Doré's sweeping illustrations, so-called pictures for the people, made a genre painting out of Gothic London, distilling its views to a series of arresting vignettes. Meant to appeal instantaneously to the viewer, his showy performances were specifically designed to engage the distracted eye. By exploiting theatrical gestures and poses, dramatic lighting and moods, Doré's calculated views played on a series of mental associations and symbols of human oppression that the viewer could easily grasp. Closely resembling the pictorialism avidly dispelled in the illustrated press, Jerrold and Doré offered their audience a "slice of life"—an arrested historical moment grasped as if the spectator was actually there.[197]

Walter Benjamin reminds us that "newspapers appeared [for the first time in the nineteenth century] in mass circulation. No reader so readily has at his disposal the stories someone else might want to hear him tell. Historically, the various forms of communication competed with one another. The replacement of older narratives by information, and information by sensation, reflects the atrophy of experience."[198] Jerrold and Doré captured this investigatory tone: although the stuff of their reportage were the unknown haunts of the dangerous classes, they reduced the marginal and nomadic to statistical types, dispatching the look of cool disinterested data. Their work drew on a long list of precedents. At least 10,000 copies of E. Chadwick's report on the sanitary conditions of the working class had

Street Advertising, *photograph by John Thompson (c. 1877).*

been distributed free of charge in 1849, and Henry Mayhew's report of *London Labour and the London Poor,* which began weekly publication in 1855, was also an entertaining—not just reforming—survey. Mayhew, a journalist turned social investigator and one of the founders of the magazine *Punch,* knew how to capture the reader's imagination through visual caricature and illustrated maps. Posed as the very antithesis to moral propriety, loyalty, and restraint, this "spectacle of filth" nevertheless both fascinated and repelled its reading audience: the English middle class.[199] Twenty years later, the genre continued when a serial edition of *Street Life in London* (1877) was published in twelve monthly additions, with a text written by the journalist Adolphe Smith (whose real name was Adolphe Smith Headingly) and photographs by John Thompson; to be followed within the next decade by Charles Booth's encyclopedic seventeen-volume study of the *Life and Labours of the People in London* (1889–1903).

This investigative and topographic spirit has an intimate link with the development of lithography. Invented by Alois Senefelder in 1796, lithography was a quick and inexpensive method of printing, and by the 1820s its popularity had spread from Munich to England and France. As superintendent of lithographic printing from 1809 until 1827 in the Kingdom of Bavaria, Senefelder undertook an experimental survey, preparing detailed maps intended to regulate the apportionment of land, to denote its ownership and its rate of taxation. This experiment enabled him to test his lithographic mapping procedures.[200] His invention and its use in maps coincides exactly with the era of canal building, when demands from engineers for accurate surveys of geological and underwater tables gave rise to an outpouring of easily reproducible lithographic maps. Within a few years lithographic surveys began to include social and moral data. One of the earliest statistical maps was Baron Charles Dupin's map of France in 1827, symbolically depicting the number of boys in school in each regional department of the country. Many different social problems were soon explored in depth and the information transferred to maps: statistics on crime, pauperism, "improvident marriages" (i.e., marriages of boys under twenty-one years of age), the location and virulence of epidemics and their accompanying environmental conditions such as polluted water and sewage, and eventually even the production and distribution of goods.[201]

The great legacy of nineteenth-century London improvement schemes, however, lies in mapping the topography of invisible fields, many quite literally underground or unexplored. These fields focused on sanitation and circulation problems—the flow of air, water, goods, and people—and became essential ingredients in the nascent processes of city planning. Investigative reporters turned the dense, dark, and diseased corners of London toward the sunshine, opening their unknown ways to the cleansing influence of air and water so that everything could circulate, so that the indeterminate and swarming mass of people could be documented, located, and mapped. Michel Foucault in *Discipline and Punish* described the topographic albeit utopian procedures developed near the end of the seventeenth century when plague appeared in a town.[202] First of all the town was cordoned off from the countryside, its gates guarded by the militia and its inhabitants forbidden to leave under pain of death. Then the entire town was partitioned into districts, each governed by an attendant and each street, as well, placed under the surveillance of a guard who was sentenced to death if he dared leave his post. Each street guard locked the doors belonging to his houses, keeping the key so that no one could exit from their homes. These keys in turn were deposited with the guard of a district, who held them until the quarantine was over. Every house was required to have sufficient provisions to last through the quarantine; and a system was devised to enable each resident to receive rations of bread and wine, fresh meats, and fish while never contacting the suppliers. Space in this town under quarantine was absolutely frozen and constantly surveyed. The only moving elements were the guards and the "crows," those people of little substance who carried and buried the dead or cleansed the infected. Inspection was a continuous affair: every day a survey of the residents was made, every person's presence noted, and their actions observed to see if they suffered disease. Failing to appear at a window spelled the presence of plague, causing the entire house to be placed under special surveillance. In addition each house, one by one, was purified by a perfuming

Street Doctor, *photograph by John Thompson (c. 1877).*

process: its inhabitants required to leave for a few hours, their furniture and possessions piled in one room and the entire house sealed while the disinfectant worked its charm. This was the paradigm, the spatial tableaux for a disciplined and perfectly controlled space: here the disorder and chaos of the plague were met by a perfect rationality, an order that dealt with confusion by making distinctions between the pure and the contaminated, sunshine and darkness. Against the threatening plague bred on wanton mixings and illicit contacts, discipline brought its analytic powers: the constant gaze of surveillance and a strict visual and topographic division.[203]

This surveying gaze became the spatial tableaux by which the nineteenth-century improvers tried to enact their own theater of discipline. Circulation was an essential ingredient, the remedy for a city sick with disease, with putrifying smells, with the chaotic and unruly threat of the crowd. If the city was to be divided into clearly defined and surveyed spatial districts, if different functions were to be segregated (i.e., the cemeteries, the smelly glue factories, the gasworks, the noisy pumping houses were to be banished to the periphery of the city along with the extruded and displaced working class), then circulation between different parts of the disciplined city became an essential component of the surveying mechanism. Circulatory space determined the rate of flow among static units; it analogously defined the unity of the city. The efficiency of this flow was an indicator of health: pedestrian flows, the flow of traffic and merchandise, the deployment of troops in revolutionary times, the cleansing flow of water and of sewers, the liberating aspects of gas or electricity that lit darkened and threatening streets at night. To channel flow is to distribute it, but this act presupposes that there are places from which and districts to which the flow is directed: thus an abstract spatial order is imposed on the city between the center and its periphery; among sections of the city; and vertically above and below ground. All interferences, all blockages of this circulatory and curative flow were to be eradicated: bridges and tunnels built no matter what the cost in money or life, sewer and subway systems and gas and electric networks carved through the underground, and purified water systems flowed through their pipes without stoppage.[204]

With all this construction work aiding the flow of circulation, London soon became a city of nomads, as thousands were displaced or extruded from the slums of the city by these great improvement schemes. Obviously the modernization and industrialization of the city was a triumphal adventure, but it was marked as well by the lowly and improvident whose visible presence became increasingly apparent. Once again we find a fascinated gaze focused on these outcasts, these others of middle-class society, as they were photographed, labeled, and discussed over and over again until they no longer seemed to be threatening, but merely documentary evidence of change. Failing to achieve either the status of an eyewitness report of social injustice or a picturesque and romanticized portrait of lowlife, the photographic essay *Street Life in London* (1877), for example, marginalized these nomads, rendering them as alien victims of the passage of time. Yet another example of the nineteenth century's penchant for distanced reportage, one that refused to be touched personally or contaminated by the subject, this photographic essay drew a cool account of London's refuse: its nomads, public disinfectors, the "crawlers," the tinkers, the cabmen and watermen.[205] A running commentary directed the viewer, typifying and generalizing the portraits. The value of its photographic record, or so Victorians thought, was its "truthfulness" and that of its commentary, normalization. London nomads, as the portrait of William Hampton was described, not only were defiant of education and moral propriety, they were "improvident" and "unable to follow any intelligent plan of life."[206] Still lower were the "crawlers": mostly old women "reduced by vice and poverty to that degree of wretchedness which destroys even the energy to beg," becoming in the end so lethargic that death would be a better condition.[207] Then there were the "public disinfectors," those boundary maintainers who constantly faced death in order to save society from the perils of pestilence. Although the sanitary laws required that those who suffered infectious disease must be taken to a hospital or isolated in their rooms, there were many cases concealed from the authorities' gaze. The law must be changed, the commentary read, so that entry to houses may be forced if disease was suspected.[208] And there were portraits of those who found employment along the streets such as "swags," who sold goods directly from their carts; and second-hand furniture dealers, who inhabited "unwholesome, overcrowded thoroughfares" marked for demolition and improvement.[209]

Walter Benjamin defined a storyteller to be someone who came from afar, a real or imaginary traveler of foreign countries and past traditions who returned with something to say to those who stayed at home or those who lived in the present. But storytelling as a spatial art of travel or tradition, he continued, had been replaced in the nineteenth century by more authoritative and plausible accounts, that is by the news and by documentary information. Its disappearance was part of the atrophy of experience in the modern world. Storytelling takes over, remembers, and repeats the narrated course of events and thus "creates the chain of tradition."[210] Often borrowing from the imaginary and the miraculous and hiding from any intent at explanation, stories allowed the reader or listener to reminisce and to conjure up his or her own astonishment and conclusions. By drawing on common experiences, stories integrate these into the experiences of a community of listeners; they actually structure the community. But community and experience in modern times were fragmented and to the contrary, information had become directed communication aimed at verifying the pure essence of the thing; it neither transmitted lived experiences nor called on the practice of memory.[211]

And so we come back full circle to a shift in the nineteenth century's perspective on history and memory, a threshold Michel Foucault envisioned as the replacement of sovereign spectacles of authority by disciplinary structures spreading horizontally on the tailcoats of a professionalized gaze. Gathering strength as it obsessively detailed, documented, and accumulated visual and statistical evidence, this disciplinary mentality compulsively stored all of its outpourings in encyclopedic and systematized archives. As we have seen, the city in all of its phantasmagorical appearance did not escape this disciplinary probe: from urban observatories or outlook towers, in national galleries and exhibition halls, in folios and travelogues, in sunshine and darkness books, its surface was surveyed and inscribed in topographical views. The chaotic appearance of large nineteenth-century cities, their failure to contain disease by carefully demarcated and regulated districts, the unruly mixing of social classes on thoroughfares and public conveyances, constantly gave rise not only to the fear of contamination but to a preoccupation with the marginal and the migratory, those without evident roots, identity, or location.[212] And here too the mechanisms of sight came into play, as the photographic record was called on to document, to expose to view, to register and inventory the insalubrious types and putrifying topography of the swarming and inchoate masses, to reflexively theorize about the internal limits of society.

The modern topography of the city was a world of fragments and broken images, perceived by Benjamin to be the cause of general malaise and the decay of experience in the present. Yet utilizing the metaphoric instantaneity of a photographic snapshot, he surmised "the historical articulation of the past does not mean representing the past 'the way it really was' but rather is the attempt 'to seize hold of a memory as it flashes up at a moment of danger.'"[213] Robert Alter believes that Benjamin at the end of his life may have envisioned tradition as a dynamic process that struggled against its own boundaries and limitations. Alter writes "If tradition, including the tradition deemed canonical in the proper theological sense of the term, is actually [viewed by Benjamin to be] a dynamic response to history, daring and at times revolutionary in the treatment of its antecedents, commentary is no longer a delusion but a constantly available vehicle for innovation in a cultural system of overarching continuity."[214] This is the task of the historian and of the transmitter of tradition: to interpret fragmentary and fleeting images and thus illuminate the unconsciousness of a cultural era, to uncover what may have been suppressed or marginalized but bears urgently on the present, "to define the wonderful architectonic structures that man's imagination erects over against, or upon, the abyss of mortality and the dissolution of value that underlies human existence . . ."[215] This means, as well, that the spectator of city scenes must pay attention to the subjunctive mood of the city, the archaic tug from the abyss of signification, the spectacular pull of the fantastical as the subjunctive, archaic, and spectacular resist closure, interpretation, and control.

six

Invented Traditions and Cityscapes

. . . our scholar postulates an Atlantic civilization that expended its entire energy in the making of photographs. . . . Briefly described, it consisted in nothing less than the synthesis, through photographic representation, of an entire imaginary civilization, together with its every inhabitant, edifice, custom, utensil, animal. Great cities were built, in full scale and complete to the minutest detail, by generations of craftsmen who dedicated their skills to the perfection of verisimilitude: these cities existed only to be photographed. . . .

HOLLIS FRAMPTON[1]

If in all ideology men and their circumstances appear upside down as in a camera obscura, this phenomenon arises just as much from their

> *historical life-process as the inversion of objects on the retina does from their physical life-process.*
>
> KARL MARX[2]

The Fascination of Images

The camera obscura is a machine that produces inverted images, and as Marx pointed out, so too does ideology, the model of false understanding. Knowing how well the image fascinates, Marx explored the illusionistic and fantastic quality that attached itself not only to ideas formed by the human mind but as well to desires magically instilled by material objects called commodities. In the dream world of nineteenth-century capitalism, ideological fantasies imprinted themselves on the commodity, but desires and visions stimulated by these commodities impressed themselves equally on the minds of women and men. Both were fetishistic idols of the mind, phantasmagorical images, to use a term so often repeated in the nineteenth century, produced in the black box of a camera obscura but magically transferring themselves to objects and thoughts. The camera's photograph in its early years of development was believed to be an exact copy of nature, produced by scientific instruments according to optical laws. The commodity, on the other hand, appeared as a natural object produced to satisfy individual needs. Both the photograph and the commodity paraded under this banner of realism, meanwhile concealing whatever was not apparently visible. Capitalism, just like the camera obscura, projected a radical metamorphosis between two things: the image and the object, politics and economics, ideology and the desires of women and men.[3]

There exists two visual principles intertwined in the fascination with images. One belongs really to an antivisual bias that is afraid of imagery, finding it to be the false idols and magical apparitions of the camera obscura that intervene between thought and language and confuse the minds of women and men.[4] Consequently many believed that if one could appropriate a people's imagery, one could control their actions; if one could make familiar the unknown by mapping it, documenting and visually portraying it, one could dispell its powers and extend control over its domain. In this dream of making everything visualizable, the "new world" of America was used as a metaphor for the Enlightenment perspective that held man as the measure of all things, the explorer who appropriated and took control of all he surveyed.[5] This faith in science restricted the eye to the observable and banished the magical and the occult. The print, the copy, the facsimile gained exhibitionary value, for they demonstrated mechanical and scientific control over the auratic.[6] The other visual principle involved in the fascination with images lies in the realm of the pure pleasure to be garnered from pictorial illusions, in the world viewed through an enchanted glass, in ephemeral spectacles that flash like fireworks and quickly dissolve. To conceal and to reveal is the heart of theatricality, and the naive eye does not question by what means the apparition appears nor why it has the power to fascinate; it simply delights in the image's surface appearance. Pleasure in the spectacle itself restrains the look from probing behind the mysterious veil; instead the viewer remains mesmerized by the realistic impression of "how things must have appeared."

Perhaps these two strains of visual perception reach back as far as Sir Francis Bacon in the seventeenth century, for not only was he interested in developing a scientific discourse that would demystify and deconstruct older forms of knowledge, but he was intrigued as well by the language of signs such as aphorisms, hieroglyphs, ideograms, and gestures. As words contained ambiguous meanings and often maintained false allusions, Bacon wanted a new code to dispel the tenacious hold of old structures of knowledge in order to liberate the mind for scientific observation and rational thought. But Bacon's new system for scientific classification depended on the classical art of memory as well, for he believed that memory governed invention and judgment, and thus held the key that could unlock the door inhibiting the expansion of scientific knowledge. The art of memory, however, was based on visual recall and thus led Bacon to appreciate the power of pictures to impress themselves upon the mind. And he wondered whether a deep-structured pictorial basis for language might exist, a universal code that could rid the mind of shifts in meaning and false appearances that words naturally engendered. The world, Bacon argued, could be a vast hieroglyph whose secrets might be unlocked step by step, like a metaphorical exploratory voyage, until enlightenment was finally achieved.

Bacon based his art of memory on two concepts: the prenotion and the emblem. To recall an idea one must have a prenotion of what is sought, some method by which to set boundaries on the infinite expanse of ideas though which the mind could wander, and thus limit the space of inquiry to a narrower passage. But ideograms or emblems were necessary as well to make words and things visible and thus memorable. A picture language had a secret way of clarifying the object being discussed and impressing itself on the reader's memory and imagination.[7] Diderot would share Bacon's belief in both the occult and the realistic power of images. The great mastermind of the "The Encyclopedia" (1751–1780) clearly perceived the world as an object to be looked at, observed, and recorded. He worked to reassemble an image of that world, an analogical memory theater or a universal language whose meaning could be communicated instantaneously and unambiguously through the medium of word pictures or hieroglyphs. And Aby Warburg, whose library formed the beginnings of London's Warburg Institute in the 1930s, was astonished at what he perceived to be the latent energy and pagan associations that charged symbols and images with frenzy and revelry. Hence he warned that pictorial and symbolic images must be handled with care lest the viewer or artist succumb to their archaic mentality, causing human expression to break down in chaotic representations. Yet kept at a safe distance, the magic of images in which our memories and traditions lie, he supposed, could give rise to imagination, metaphor, empathy, and art.[8]

Bordering on the aura of the supernatural, the occult and fetishistic, the photographic image captivated the popular taste of the nineteenth century. It intrigued through its apparitions: the illusion of presence and absence, substance and shadows, for the trick of all optical illusions lies in never revealing exactly how they are produced. Visual form seemed to be severed completely from the recording of the material object, for the photograph directed attention to its surface appearance, to details that surprised, to what could be seen but not demonstrated. This is what Roland Barthes referred to as the "punctum" of photography in *Camera Lucida*: some symbolic meaning and pleasure that lingered after a photographic image had been absorbed, or some eruptive detail that unintentionally reached out to touch the spectator, prick the imagination, and give rise to involuntary memories. The photograph becomes a concrete tie with the past, a memory prompt for what has been forgotten as it referenced the clothes and style of another era, the setting of a forgotten trip, or the face of a friend who was gone.[9] The photograph participates in the spectral with its disturbing images from the past and its ability to stop time: for as Barthes said, "photography is a kind of primitive theater, a kind of *Tableau Vivant,* a figuration of the motionless and made-up face beneath which we see the dead."[10]

As a deliberate collector of the exotic and the heterogeneous, the photographic album or folio became a vast *combinatoire,* projecting in miniaturized and transportable form fabulous and imaginary worlds. It exploited an inherited taste for the spectacle, that special theater of illusions called magic lantern spectral shows, for its phantasmic imagery was compelling.[11] The spectacle required nothing more than the act of looking at its intentional theatricality; it was after all, a posed and bracketed moment of time set outside of ordinary experience. Consequently both the immediacy and instantaneity of the photograph and the spectacle produced a shift in the visual sensibility of the nineteenth century: they substituted a complex of surface looks for in-depth analysis, and scenographic arrangements for cooler and more distanced observation. The city, the industrial exhibitions, the pictorial press, the popular musical hall, and vaudeville entertainments of the nineteenth century were infused with the visual spectacle. But just behind these compelling image shows, which unrolled like a constantly moving tableau, stood the inverted culture of the commodity. The spectral shows of the magic lantern were after all commercial ventures, mounting considerable fortunes for the more inventive producers. The exhibitionary and theatrical surface of the city and its array of visual entertainments became linked invariably with the discourse of supply and demand. Enticing the eye of the passerby and selling goods, just looking at cities and shop windows; these became inseparable events in the new theater of capitalism that nineteenth-century cities represent.[12] Yet behind either the commodity or the camera obscura stood the frightening threat of "the alienating spectacle imposed from without"[13] or "that state of neurasthenic excitment in which images whirled chaotically before the inward eye, impressing on the seer an overwhelming sense of their vividness and spiritural truth."[14]

Just think how littered with visual signs the public domain of a nineteenth-century city actually was. The walls of buildings were plastered with advertisements, the inside and outside of omnibuses were similarly covered, while advertising carts and sandwich boards circulated throughout the streets. By the last quarter of the century, poster advertisement resorted to all sorts of optical illusions to attract attention. In 1876, for example, a magic lantern projected enlarged images of existing posters onto a screen located on the second story of a London building. This show of dissolving images in rapid succession gave the passerby quick advice of where to buy the best hat or sewing machine, where to dine, or where to find the latest edition of a popular magazine.[15] By 1893 even Nelson's Column in Trafalgar Square and the National Gallery had become backdrops for such projected shows. Obviously nineteenth-century advertising artists knew how well consumption depended on persuading people to desire potentially useful and valuable goods. They could see that in the gap between reality and fantasy, desire took flight.[16] Thus city streets where the indifferent pedestrian came face to face with advertising images represented the domain where desire was displayed and recorded. A shop window that city travelers quickly passed by suddenly reached out to arrest their vision through its idealized allusions and entertaining tricks of the eye, and subsequently unleashed a host of imaginations and yearnings. Temporarily absorbed by the remarkable sights that the public space of the nineteenth-century city extruded—even knowing these images to be unreal—these pedestrians moved

Large Woven Picture of Chicago World's Fair (1893).

on to experience the desire instilled by other visions and enticements, enveloped yet entertained by this world of visual fantasy and theatrical artificiality.[17]

There is an analogy to be made relating the rise of this visual sensibility to the political economy in the nineteenth century, by following the case of music explored by the French economist Jacques Attali. He claims that music is the true avant-garde of social and cultural change; in its forms and procedures one can find a rough sketch of changes that eventually will invade the rest of society and culture.[18] Music is one of the sites where social transformations first appear, where the roots of aesthetic rationalization and bureaucratization lie. Born out of the noise and violence of murder, before it was tamed and controlled, music remained the simulacrum of ritual sacrifice and a powerful attribute of religious and political ceremony. As music was transformed into a commodity, however, it was deritualized still further and its subversive and ecstatic aspects completely repressed. Other transformations in the eighteenth and nineteenth centuries turned music into the representational instrument of the bourgeoisie. As their mode of cultural expression, music came to reflect their desire for universal harmony and order, and as such it became both a means of power and a form of entertainment. Harmony wielded a pacifying effect on musical form. Eliminating all natural noise, it subsequently imposed a constructed and rational order over sound. By channeling violence into accepted forms, music muffled a people's ability to interpret their own history and to manipulate their own culture. Just entertaining and pretty, music was no longer attached to any particular meaning. As a spectacle to be listened to, it moved into the enclosure of the concert hall, where established modes of public behavior controlled the crowd. Entrance fees were charged and the players were paid a wage, while publishers and entertainment entrepreneurs began to organize the selling or marketing of sound. Utilizing the latest production techniques of the popular press and illustrating the covers of sheet music with entertaining chromolithographs, the mass production of sheet music had a lot to do with the decline of the popular street ballad singers and the disappearance of broadsheet publication. Inevitably the commodity form thoroughly penetrated all aspects relating to the production and distribution of music.[19]

By the beginning of the twentieth century, Attali claims, music, having reflected and represented the harmonious and well-ordered bourgeois world of the nineteenth century, was itself transformed by the serial processes of reproduction and repetition now promised by the newly invented phonograph. With this development, music could be stored in a stockpile of records and its performance repeated at some later date. Once recorded, a live concert could now be mass produced as a record. The mold became more important than the representational qualities of a performance. Attali wrote: "Reproduction, in a certain sense, is the death of the original, the triumph of the copy, and the forgetting of the representational foundation: in mass production the mold has almost no importance or value in itself; it is no longer anything more than one of the factors in production, one of the aspects of its usage, and is very largely determined by the production technology."[20] The economics of repetition required that greater amounts of capital be allocated to the production of consumers and to the stimulation of demand. The technology of recording, on the other hand, was perfected—making even the spectacle of a concert illusionary. Hence musical concerts appear today as simulated events, composed by cutting and replaying bits and pieces of sound, but erasing the errors and noise of a genuine performance.

Eventually architecture and the production of scenographic city space would follow the lead of music, becoming susceptible to the needs of consumption, and they too would allow the mold to become more important than original styles and authentic scenes. In this sense the preservation of nostalgic forms of architecture or the reproduction of stereotypical urban scenes in illustrated views, album cards, stereopticon photographs, and picture postcards—all commercial exploits of the nineteenth century—offered the spectator a packageable and consumable manner of looking at cities.[21] Plain postcards, for example, seemed to have been issued by governments as early as the late 1860s and early 1870s, but picture postcards were first popularized by the international expositions. Souvenir picture postcards could be purchased, written on, and mailed from the top of the Eiffel Tower during the Exposition of 1889, while the first official American picture postcards were published at the Chicago World's Fair of 1893. This right to make a profit out of a supposedly public view was awarded to Charles W. Goldsmith, who subsequently was permitted to manufacture view cards of the fair and to sell them in packages of two for a nickel from vending machines dispersed about the grounds. An act of the American Congress in 1893 extended the right to private publishers to print picture cards that could be sent through the government's mail. And in England too, the post office recognized this market by 1894 allowing printed postcards to be sent for a half-penny stamp.[22] Distilled into set pieces, a kind of tableau vivant, architectural and city views along with patriotic places and heroic men soon became the stereotypical forms and illusionistic spaces into which traditions and memories were poured, as if into so many molds.

Merely looking at architecture and urban spaces for their visual excitement, just viewing them as pure decoration and backdrop illustrations, became a spectator habit within the visual imagination of the nineteenth century, nurtured further by the plethoric outpourings of the illustrated press, the photograph, and theatrical displays. Excursions to cities with their streets full of history or landmark sites and picturesque landscapes were part of this response, exploiting a formula that already worked. Besides, excursions could be thought of as adventure and pleasure time, standing outside of ordinary experience, but a time that could be commodified. As incomes of both the middle class and working class began to expand in the last half of the nineteenth century, and as the modern weekend at least for salaried workers seemed likely to be a reality, leisure time was linked to consumption, and travel became its new stimulus. Entrepreneurs quickly learned that "time out" put people in an expansive mood in which they were likely to spend more for food and recreation then they normally did, and that this so-called free time might be programmed and planned for commercial advantage.

Railroad companies quickly grasped the commercial value of excursions, and by the 1880s and 1890s inexpensively packaged trips had become ordinary fare. Once again the Great London Exhibition of 1851 brought these events into dramatic focus, for after that event excursions were common features of every world's fair. In 1851, the railways brought at least 750,000 travelers from the north of England, who paid for the pleasure of just looking at the remarkable sights and fascinating objects displayed in the Crystal Palace; Thomas Cook, the enterprising travel agent, organized some 165,000 people on excursions to the fair from Yorkshire alone.[23] Sir Joseph Paxton must have viewed the Crystal Palace as a key figure in his promotion of railways, and he must have understood the kind of development railroads could foster. At first he petitioned the directors to allow the Crystal Palace to remain in Hyde Park as a permanent Winter Garden for thousands to enjoy, but finding this to be an unpopular idea, he formed instead the Crystal Palace Company in 1852 in order to buy the structure and move it outside of London to Sydenham. In this new site, where it could be integrated with a vast system of railways, Paxton planned extravagant new interior designs and elaborate parks, gardens, and water displays, intentionally hoping to outrival Versailles as a tourist attraction. In addition, Paxton proposed (but never found the financing) to construct four colossal hotels linked to the Crystal Palace by glass passageways and connected in turn to the railways.[24]

Excursions were often driven by nostalgia, enabling the sightseer to travel vicariously into the past where she or he could experience forgotten places and ruins. Souvenirs such as stereotypical illustrations, picture postcards, and stereopticon views as generators of memory built on this nostalgia and relied on a spectator's desire to see visually re-presented her or his favorite sights and attractions. The nostalgic mood was above all an expressed desire to be connected with the past, even if fictionalized in legendary form and stylized in visual imagery. It was called a backward- and inward-looking "disease," which the nineteenth century suffered from acutely, yet the ailment was actually invented in the late seventeenth century. Named after the Greek words for return and sorrow, "nostalgia" at first afflicted only mercenaries sent to foreign lands and peasants recently transplanted to the city. It was a fatal ailment, in fact suicidal, whose only cure was a return to

Official Postal Card of Manufactures and Liberal Arts Building (1893).

one's native surroundings. By the nineteenth century, however, this disease took on more imaginative forms, penetrating even the educated classes, so that many feared to travel for extended periods. Vicarious travel was as obvious a solution to the problem of nostalgia as was the invention of traditions.[25] Thus "nostalgia" in the nineteenth century might have meant the longing for a past that had never existed or had ceased to exist, or it might have reflected the desire to return to an imaginary place from which one felt estranged. In either case, the past or place now distant or nonexistant was repossessable only in appropriated and stylized form; hence interest arose in restoring a nation's heritage by collecting and preserving artifacts and tokens from its past, then inventing histories and reconstructing lost places in an effort to diminish the power the present held over the imagination, and thus be able to reintegrate the stricken with their lost milieu. Yet the desire and longing that nostalgia evoked could not be stilled by the restoration of material objects or the retelling of mythical stories, for it was the very loss of this mythical past or the absence of this imaginary place that generated and sustained both the longing and the desire.[26]

The image of a past preserved internally within our collective memory and connected with certain stylized images and legendary visions is an alluring ideal: it keeps alive our native myths, our quest for origins, and offers us assurance that we control our patrimony. In particular this ideal helps to establish collective fictions: the self-conscious narratives and distilled views of New Orleans as recounted by Lafcadio Hearn, for example, or stories from the old Southwest as told to us by Charles Lummis, the images of Paris collected by Marcel Poëte,[27] or the American Civil War visualized in the silent film by D. W. Griffith. As reified and arrested illustrations, these paradigms and anecdotes, which seemed to have developed and spread during the nineteenth century, appealed directly to the visual imagination of middle-class spectators and built on their desire to see projected in repeated and expected form favorite places, picturesque scenes, and well-known and recognizable characterizations.[28]

Lafcadio Hearn was one of the first folklorists to describe the peculiar culture of Creole New Orleans in the late nineteenth century. Hearn was fascinated by the hawkers, quarrelers, talkers, and mere passersby whom he saw in the streets of New Orleans; by the language heard in the poorer sections of town, which the Americans pejoratively called "gumbo"; by the curious customs of medicine, voodoo, and foods, and the peculiar habit the Creoles had of talking to themselves. So he described:

> . . . if New Orleans has any special mania which distinguishes it from other cities, it is the mania of "talking to one's self." It were useless to deny so widely recognized a fact as the propensity of people in New Orleans to perambulate their native streets conversing only with themselves. . . . [What they talk about] God only knows! But they do talk either to themselves or to viewless beings or to the sleepy shadows that fling jagged bits of darkness across the streets on sunny days.[29]

Analyzing Creole dictionaries and newspapers, grammars and books of legends, in addition to roaming the streets of New Orleans, Hearn made a study of the dialect, of its proverbs, songs, and street cries. He was fascinated by the sounds of fruit peddlers and meat-peddlers that arose from the streets with the sunrise, the musical tones of "straw-BARE-eries!" or "Black-BREES!", "Ap-pulls" and "Cantel-lope-ah! Fresh and fine. Jus from the vin, Only a dime!"; and the undecipherable shout "A-a-a-a-h! She got!" and a rival retort, "I-I-I-I want nothing!"[30] Or the poetry of the charcoal drivers, who called out "Black—coalee-coaly!" "Pretty coalee-oh-le!"[31] So he wrote, "[t]he collection of tradition, superstitions, legends, fairy tales, goblin stories, impossible anecdotes, supernatural romances . . . . leave a prodigious influence upon the use of language and the formation of style."[32] Keenly aware of the exotic effect the Creole patois had on the everyday ordinariness of New Orleans culture, Hearn lamented nostalgically that as these sounds died, nothing from the present would remain so remarkable. He was, as one biographer has noted, testing the unstable nature of the boundary that supposedly existed between those considered to be "civilized" and those malignly called "savages."[33] And though he wrote that he collected in the Vieux Carré only "scattered petals of folklore, few entire blossoms," still he came across mothers who taught their children "the old songs—heirlooms of melody resonant with fetich words—threads of tune strung with *grigris* from the Ivory Coast."[34] Hearn was critical of so-called highly organized civilization and he constantly struggled against its aggressive nature. "The higher the social development [he wrote] the sharper the struggle. One feels this especially in America,—in the nervous centers of the world's activities."[35] For this he would decry, "Civilization is a hideous thing. Blessed is Savagery! Surely a palm 200 feet high is a finer thing in the natural order than seventy times seven New Yorks."[36]

Bits and pieces of a decaying culture to be collected and recorded, cataloged and classified in essays and almanacs, reflect similar interests expressed wherever change in the nineteenth century was swift and irreversible, one that eradicated folk customs and popular traditions representing centuries of cultural expression. Among the earliest manifestations of cultural regionalism, for example, was a group of young poets who pledged in 1854 to revive the mother tongue and linguistic diversity, local traditions, and customs from the region of Provence. Calling their school the Felibrige, these modern-day troubadours protested the centralization and standardization of institutions taking place throughout France, a national effort intended to reform popular manners, erase archaic dialects, and break up local traditions.[37] The first theorist to outline the importance of language in national development, however, had been Giambattista Vico in *New Science* (1724), who claimed that each nation progressed from a divine stage when they organized their relationship to reality through mute ceremonies and rituals, then moved on to a heroic stage of gestures and signs, before finally emerging at the human stage of language. "Language is then, positively, a distinctively human opening of and opening to the world: not a distinguishable or instrumental but a constitutive faculty."[38] Vico suggested that "truth is constructed"[39] and its grounds were to be found more in poetic metaphors than in rational concepts, in works of art not authoritarian histories, in popular customs not official laws. Thus a critical historian must endeavor to understand a nation's poetic history, retrieving muffled voices negated by official histories yet preserved in the poetic images of language, orchestrating the diverse voices that not only compose a text but generate a cultural configuration.[40] Etymologies, moreover, could be used oppositionally to disturb theoretical legitimations and scientific hierarchies, especially those universalizations claimed by a nation-state, and to place instead the formation of concepts and meanings in primitive origins and relative social experiences.[41] Thus cultural regionalism based in local linguistic traditions belongs to what Michel Foucault called "subjugated knowledges": information disqualified as inadequate or naive, incapable of achieving unanimity. These knowledges, he allowed, are often insurrectional, opposed to the effects of a centralizing discourse that hierarchicalizes and orders a body of theory in the name of some scientific or truthful knowledge.[42]

There is a note of warning, however, hidden behind the assumption that asymmetrical distinctions can be made between regional and national cultures. Michael Herzfeld calls this "a vestigially survivalist thesis—that is, an argument that treats the values of local societies as relatively simple features surviving from a prestatist era."[43] "Survivalism" is a nineteenth-century doctrine that belongs to that theory of national development that labels local cultures cases of "arrested development" and allocates the nation-state, with its governing laws and conventions, to the highest achievable place.[44] Herzfeld continues: "European peasants appeared to validate the survivalist thesis in two complementary ways: first, by demonstrating the persistence of traits from the childhood of the human race even in the most civilized countries; and second, by showing that only the intellectual independence of the educated classes could achieve final escape from the burden of superstition and ignorance."[45]

Myths of the nation are necessary, however, for in the words of the social anthropologist Bronislaw Malinowski, "myth acts as a charter for the present-day social order; it supplies a retrospective pattern of moral values, sociological order, and magical belief, the function of which is to strengthen tradition and endow it with a greater value and prestige by tracing it back to a higher, better, more supernatural reality of initial events."[46] The rise of nation-states in the eighteenth and nineteenth century is inseparable from the creation of imaginary communities and invented traditions. Eric Hobsbawm writes, in *The Invention of Tradition*: "It is also clear that entirely new symbols and devices came into existence as part of national movements and states, such as the national anthem (of which the British in 1740 seems to be the earliest), the national flag (still largely a variation on the French revolutionary *tricolour*, evolved 1790–1794), or the personification of "the nation" in symbol or image, either official, as with Marianne and Germania, or unofficial, as in the cartoon stereotypes of John Bull, the lean Yankee Uncle Sam, and the "German Michel"."[47] The symbolic images of liberty caps, tricolours, and carnivals invented during the French Revolution were "intended, as Abbé Grégoire put it, to penetrate the soul and mould the national character."[48] "Analogies tie the field of national stereotypes together, to help form a culture."[49]

Clearly architecture and city monuments can become artifacts and traces that connect the past with the present in imaginative and inventive ways, and help to build a sense of community, culture, and nation. J. B. Jackson, in *The Necessity for Ruins*, claims that after the Civil War in America there arose a new mood not aimed at preserving monuments, artifacts, and momentos from the past as didactic reminders of important events. Instead these objects were collected and cataloged because of their association with a particular phase of our more recent past. They were reminders of past domestic life and the built context in which that daily life took place. He uses as exemplary the attempt to reconstruct the battlefield of Gettysburg, not as a monument commemorating the event, but as a celebration of American's vernacular past through a sense of place that encapsulated "the way things used to be" or might have looked, so that one could understand the very unfurling of the Civil War battle. Such a view of history, which searches to rescue a usable past from the neglected ruins of our cities, towns, and countryside, assumes that there is a severance or disjunction between the past and the present. The "necessity for ruins," Jackson argues, occurs because only they act as prompters or signs poking our sense of responsibility to return to our origins, which began in the 1860s and 1870s, a time different from our own when life was thought to be simple and genuine.[50] It is precisely this gap in our experience of history from which nostalgia grows, enabling us—just like the inversions in the camera obscura and the phantasmagorical conjurings that float up from an image—to invent, puff up, or imagine all sorts of tall tales, anecdotes, traditions, and places. And America, as we shall see, was especially prone to the invention of traditions and the creation of visual stereotypes.

The invention of tradition, Eric Hobsbawm tells us, never develops or preserves a living past, but instead occurs for three distinct purposes: to establish social cohesion within a group; or for the purpose of socialization—instilling a series of values, beliefs, and behaviors within different members of a society; or finally, to legitimize or to establish the authority of a sovereign or a nation.[51] In America, invented traditions have been made primarily to establish a sense of cohesion among the disparate members and colonies that originally formed the United States, and later to socialize or assimilate to the American way the immigrants who followed. The invention of American traditions is hardly a static process, but has undergone constant change, expansion, and development over time. Take for example Yankee Doodle, the fife-playing revolutionary citizen-soldier. This image derives from a more than two-hundred-year-old popular tune of that name, whose own patrimony is highly debatable. Some claim the ditty was composed by a British officer in the Revolutionary War, others say that it stems from a Hessian military march, still another source believes it to have been a peasant song popular in England before the time of Charles I, and yet another assumes it was composed during Cromwell's reign to criticize the protector.[52]

Whatever its origin (probably a composite source), it was in the beginning a song used by the British to ridicule the good-hearted and patriotic New England rustic. But the Americans quickly appropriated the melody and its words, and by esteeming the tune as warlike as any a grenadier's march, they turned its song against their enemy. The delightful "macaroni" in Yankee Doodle's hat no doubt referred to the English dandies and aristocratic fobs who, having traveled to Italy around the 1760s, soon garnered a taste for continental foods and fashions. This "macaroni" became an excellent ploy for the parodic foil of the yeoman soldier. A British officer wrote in 1777: "After our rapid successes we held Yankees in great contempt, but it was not a little mortifying to hear them play this tune [Yankee Doodle] when their army marched down to our surrender."[53] One century later, by 1876, the representational image of a fife playing "Yankee Doodle" had become a commercial success repetitiously embellishing the trade cards, album cards, and advertisements of almost every department store and luxury retail shop celebrating the country's centennial. Even more successfully, "Yankee Doodle" as a chromolithograph was distributed by the thousands on the streets surrounding Fairmount Park, the site of the Philadelphia Centennial Exposition of 1876. Archibald Willard was the original painter of this genre scene: the representation of martial music and the extravagantly determined and pretentiously patriotic citizen-soldiers having by this period less to do with the spirit of 1776 than the industrial might and pride of 1876. Willard's work was copyrighted and chromolithographed by a Cleveland entrepreneur James F. Ryder, who simultaneously carried out an extensive advertising campaign developing a distributional network across the United States to promote and sell the print during the centennial year.[54]

Lithographic city views as repeatable pictorial statements captured the same nostalgic sentiment as did the popular panoramas. They both hoped to transform the transitoriness of the world into an ideal fixity, focusing on the fugitive images of cities as they underwent rapid industrialization.[55] Exploiting the desire among mass audiences for immediate visual experience, printable pictures quickly became a lucrative trade. In America after the Civil War, billions of mass-produced color lithographs were sold, turning this country into what E. L. Godkin pejoratively called the "chromo-civilization." These cheap and popular pictures spread a culture already packaged and ready for purchase, so that many critics professsed they were a debasement of fine art and should have been banned. The famous New

York lithographers of Sarony, Major, and Knapp advertised in the 1860s that they printed "show cards for manufacturers, views of cities and hotels, book plates, architectural drawings, music titles, maps, plans, labels and Commercial Work of every description."[56] Currier and Ives rose to fame on the fact that their illustrations captured a sense of the news with pictures of disasters, fires, "dastardly acts," Civil War events, the California Gold Rush, and images of faraway places. They as well documented historical events, celebrating the centennial year of 1876 with a series of prints emblematic of America's colonial past.[57]

Louis Prang, one of the most successful nineteenth-century lithographers, experimented with new uses for these printed materials. Suddenly after publishing a map of the Charleston Harbor in April 1861 that depicted its channels, shoals, and fortifications, he became an instant chronicler of the Civil War, selling over 40,000 copies of this print alone. Building on the sensationalism of "being there" that the visual image allowed, another commercial success was his map of Virginia, which sold over 100,000 copies. This map enabled the viewer to locate the various seats of war and to mark their shifting positions as reports of these battles daily unfurled in the press. When map sales flagged, Prang substituted illustrated card portraits of famous generals and a montage of fifty such "celebrity" heads on a single illustrated sheet.[58] Adding color to the American landscape and culturescape, Prang's chromolithographs soon became the popular "brush and pallet [sic]" of the nineteenth century.[59] So a contemporary journal proclaimed: "If chromolithography is not an art, it is in one sense better, since it goes where pure Art can not go, [into]. . . . popular aesthetic culture. . . . Mr. Prang has made possession [of art and places] an easy sequence of desire. For ten dollars the working man may glorify his house with one of Correggio's masterpieces; for the same sum he may delight his eyes and his soul with the harmonious richness of Bierstadt's 'Sunset in California'; he may warm his patriotism and feed his ambition by contemplating 'The Boyhood of Lincoln'; or he may renew his youth in gazing on the inimitable portrait of Whittier's 'Barefoot Boy'.[60] Visual facts and memory tokens seemed to be more important in a young developing nation than aesthetic ideals: America was learning about its past and its landscape through pictures, and then slowly fitting these pieces together until they formed the image of a gigantic puzzle."[61]

To create a stereotype, one must have the power to force an image into a mold, systematically exploiting the facts until they become a euphemization. Subsequently a stereotype can be instrumentally transformed into a salable commodity.[62] The lithographic prints and chromolithographs of the nineteenth century established many of America's national icons that are still popularly cited in city tableaux of today. The legitimating fictions of these stereotypes searched for the mythic origins of America; they repetitively reinforced a sense of solidarity as good citizens. No one had to believe that these were truthful narrations of America's past; instead in societies of visual domination, public order was based on a tacit agreement that these fictions protected its citizenry from more barbaric modes of control.[63] America was a country that based its memory on associative pictures, finding its sense of "history" through conventional comparisons, in images drawn from history books, from city views, from mythical stories. Americans in the nineteenth century craved a history: a mythology to counter its vastness and visual symbols to crystalize its individual states into the form a sovereign nation should take.

The invention of traditions relied on the ability to formalize and ritualize the past through repetition. Parson Mason Locke Weems, for example, established the romantic formula that many would copy for creating national symbols out of ordinary citizen-soldiers and elected officials. Relying on the moral teachings of late eighteenth-century behavior books, which taught the universal values of honesty, virtue, and thrift through stereotypical characters such as "Miss Betsy Allgood" and "Master Billy Bad Enough," Weems created in 1800 a virtuous model of George Washington, turning him into the guardian angel of America, an icon personifying the nation's titanic struggle against a despotic and greedy king. Filio-pietism, it was assumed, would remain a matter of consensus, a bulwark protecting the unity of the nation against divisiveness and tyranny.[64] A reincarnation of George Washington slowly took place: a tall and upright man of noble stature with classical Roman features, a man of dignified demeanor and judicious character. Another historical

Grant Wood, Parson Weems' Fable *(1939).*

nimbus arose around the mythical nature of Christopher Columbus, especially after the Civil War, when Americans renewed with vigor their musings on the nation's past as a basis for reunification. In Columbus, the world finder, a faultless image arose epitomizing the dauntless explorer and exemplifying what human genius and enterprise could accomplish.[65] Several decades later, the great Russian film director Sergei Eisenstein would claim that everyone's stereotypical image of Abraham Lincoln had been synthesized in the American nicknames associated with him during and after his lifetime: "The Great Emancipator, The Martyr Chief, The Sage of Springfield, . . . Honest Old Abe, Father Abraham, . . . The Rail-Splitter. And there were the hostile names given him by the South: The Tyrant, Spindleshanks, The Crow. . . ."[66]

In step with the development of a visual culture, scenic spectacles were as well the stock ingredient of the early American theater. Being slow to develop a native drama in the nineteenth century, America nevertheless encouraged innovation in scenic effects. Before 1820, however, such displays were seldom integrated into the drama itself, but were offered for their own spectacular force. Americans reveled in their taste for the striking and the thrilling, in the magical deceptions of the theatrical arts. The stage was simply a spectacle with water, fireworks, lighting and thunder, battle scenes, ocean voyages, and train rides all making their appearance.[67] Each vivid picture show, repetitiously replayed, became part of the developing collective memory that established an elaborate American iconography. One of the first theatrical celebrations of the Fourth of July, for example, took place at the John Street Theater in New York City during 1786; a custom that reoccurred for many decades and influenced many other pictorial memorials. So the tableau has been described:

> Hallam and Henry exhibited on the stage a piece of painting representing two Corinthian columns, one on each side of a monument. On the monument were inscribed the names of Warren, Montgomery, Mercer, and Wooster. Under these was a spread eagle with a sword in one claw and thirteen arrows in the other.

From his beak issues the label LIBERTY, inscribed with the names of Washington, Greene, Knox, and Wayne. At the top of the monument were two angels, and a flame issuing heavenward—at the foot on each side were placed the genii of Agriculture and Liberty, and in the center between them were thirteen stars in a circle. At the foot of the pedestal on the right were three sheaves and on the left a ship in full sail.[68]

After the 1860s, visual spectacles began to be used as background scenery and dramatic settings. Because travel by train for nineteenth-century Americans was a thrilling adventure, the transcontinental railroad being completed only in 1869, train scenes appearing on stage were sure to thrill the audience. In 1867 Augustin Daly's "Under the Gaslight" offered a sensational melodrama soon to become a stock ploy for many a western film. In his play, the hero was tied helplessly to the tracks as an approaching train was heard in the distance and its headlights began to beam across the stage. Meanwhile the heroine, locked in the train station, was unable to save him. Suddenly, as tension mounted, she gathered supernatural power and flung open the doors, rushing to pull the hero to safety as a thunderous train of cars roared across the stage.[69] Nothing ever excelled the "punch" of the onrushing train, and when motion pictures arrived the new medium utilized this pictorial sensation. One early cinema enterpreneur played on this fascination with travels by train. Producing "George C. Hale's Tours and Scenes of the World" in 1903, Hale created a way to transport the audience into the midst of his travelogue. By showing films of spectacular vistas shot from the cowcatcher or observation platform of moving trains and by arranging his theater like the interior of a railway carriage, with seats rocking back and forth as the train appeared to round a corner, Hale exploited the thrill of pictorial illusion. He even simulated the end of the train carriage on his theater's facade and dressed the ticket collector in a conductor's uniform. Perhaps Hale had based his work on H. G. Wells's earlier attempt to patent a motion picture simulating travel through time and space. Wells placed his audience on a raised platform that swayed back and forth and moved toward and away from the screen, on which were projected scenes from his celebrated "Time Machine." Or Hale might have known about or seen Raoul Grimoin-Sanson's Cineorama at the Paris Exposition of 1900. This visual spectacle simulated a balloon flight sailing over the Parisian countryside. The audience standing on a raised platform gazed down over ten synchronized projectors that threw hand-colored views drawn from life onto a gigantic circular screen—actually 330 feet by 30 feet in size. Forced to close after two days because of the dangerous level of heat produced by the projectors, nevertheless this feat was so visually thrilling that even the *Scientific American* reported on the event.[70] In the early days of the movies, just the realistic illusion of movement and traveling was sufficient to thrill audiences. There was consequently no need at first for a narrative story line, for the sensational showing resided completely in simulated and illusory effects.

In an innocuous introduction then, almost without celebration, the great visual recorder and fantasy projector of the twentieth century was presented to its spectators. The first public vitascope exhibition of Thomas Edison's moving pictures took place in 1896 at Koster & Bial's Herald Square Theater. As the *New York Times* relayed the news, "the ingeneous inventor's latest toy is a projection of his kinetoscope in stereopticon fashion, upon a white screen in a darkened hall. In the center of the balcony of the big music hall is a curious object, which looks from below [like] the double turrent of a big monitor. In the front of each half of it are two oblong like holes . . . The white screen used on the stage is framed like a picture. The moving pictures are about half life size."[71] There were many scenes of movement for the camera to record: crowds on Broadway, a carriage and bicycle parade through Herald Square, a blizzard, travels to exotic climes—sites that had already been located in the collective archive as the subject of picture postcards or as anecdotal illustrations in the pictorial press or as theatrical scenes.[72] Many early films simply exploited the camera's ability to explore space, allowing horizontal and vertical panoramic shots to structure the visual experience. An early (1903) one-minute Biograph film, for example, offered the uncanny feeling of déjà vu, as the camera eye became that of a pedestrian craning his or her neck to get a view of the top of the Flatiron Building in New York City.[73] The variety of skipping, flickering, marching pictures was unending: news events, "actualités" (as the Lumiere brothers called them), historical reconstructions, and travel films had already been presented by the pictorial press and theatrical panoramas, and they now found an eager audience among moviegoers.[74] The Spanish-American War (1897–1900) and military action in the Philippines (1899) suddenly turned motion pictures into visual newspapers. Edison for a time even nicknamed his projector the "Wargraph" machine.[75] To demonstrate how closely the early film depended and built on visual stereotypes already known to the audience, in 1903 the Kline Optical Company, for example, offered a film-slide-lecture show entitled the "Lights and Shadows of a Great City," an exact—but now moving—facsimile of late nineteenth-century illustrated city books of the same name. Building on a successful format, this film offered views of the Tenderloin, ten-cents lodging houses, an arrest for thieving, the transactions of a pawnshop, a police patrol wagon, plus panoramic views of a ghetto.[76]

Fascinated by pictures, the nineteenth century developed a stock of icons and simulated experiences, establishing a base from which visual entertainment in the twentieth century still draws. When D. W. Griffith, for example, filmed "The Birth of a Nation" in 1914, the first nostalgically reconstructed theme movie, he already had an archive of Civil War images to draw on to help project his story: the blue and gray uniforms of the north and south, the parapets from which soldiers fired, troops leaving for war, a typical northern and southern family divided emotionally and physically by the war, and photographic coverage of the types of warfare authentic to that period of time. But the theme, as Griffith described it to *The New York American* in 1915, was uniquely twentieth century: "The Civil War was fought fifty years ago. But the real nation had only existed the last 15 or 20 years, for there can exist no union without sympathy and oneness of sentiment. . . . The birth of a nation began . . . with the Ku-Klux clans, and we have shown that."[77] Far from being unique components of storytelling, Griffith's characterizations were instead visual icons already known and recognizable, events repetitively illustrated by the press or drawn from photograph albums or theatrical representations.[78] But "The Birth of a Nation" was also a commercial spectacle, drawing on all the lessons that simulated events already had taught. To lend authenticity, costumed Confederate and Union soldiers hung about a theater's lobby while female ushers, so-called Griffith Crinoline Girls, were not only dressed in "authentic" Civil War costumes, but their services were obtained through nationwide talent scouts. A special orchestral accompaniment was composed by Joseph Breil, who selected and arranged melodies from popular songs of the 1860s. And drawing dramatic attention to the spectacular event, railroad excursions were advertised as "The Birth of a Nation Limited" or "The Birth of a Nation Express," bringing spectators to view the film.[79]

Pictorial images cannot be left alone—they fascinate or they repell, they please and entertain, or they weaken minds. Like the commodity, visual entertainment protrudes into culture, turning art and the theater, even the cityscape, into yet another consumable item. Pictorial and spectacular images cross barriers, reflecting a coercive power or grip on the mind; they nevertheless are illusory and ephemeral. A pure projection like a snapshot photograph, the image becomes a framed shot, a still, a hieroglyphic moment of time and action that lies beyond the realm of language. It is that moment when every detail comes together for an instant, congealing into a frozen unified form.[80] And so a nexus of looks was held loosely together in the visual imagination of the nineteenth century. The simplest strain lay in the mysterious excitements of the spectacle, the pure visual enjoyment that rose up from illuminated shows and fireworks and turned the darkness of city streets into marvels of light. Ephemeral shows, these punctuating celebrations of sovereign and national power, were public events intended to dazzle the crowd with the greatness of an empire and the glory of a nation. Another theme crossing this visual imagination occurred in the wonderful pictures of cities, repeated again and again in lithographs and panoramas that placed the spectator in direct confrontation with the real city as the latter was rapidly transformed and replanned. These popular shows and illustrations were a duplication of and substitution for urban reality, one that presented only the look of its surface appearance. It was this double that split the images of the city into either imaginary or realistic forms. As representational setups in stereotypical form, they articulated in grand and minute precision the visualized details and dramas of the past projected onto the present. As immortalized mirages of the way things might have appeared, these wonderous images of cities became entertaining and commercialized ends in themselves.[81] And travel of course, simulated or real, extended this panoramic view beyond the city's horizons to exotic lands and foreign towns. Documentations of the present, the meticulous collection and portrayal of images of everyday life, could on one hand calm the anxieties that economic, political, and urban revolutions unfurled. But they could just as well release an unsettling fear that the crowd being entertained and promading about were just looking aimlessly, just wandering about without a sense of history or roots. And so the task of fabricating mental pictures of heroic events, of nostalgically collecting souvenirs or memorable views seemed to slide into place along with all the other elements of this visual repertoire. Viewing audiences were predisposed toward stereotypical repetitions that lent a constructed coherence to historical development and urban compositions. And soon the moving pictures joined the show, exploring the space of the city, tabulating its parades and newsworthy events, drawing on yet adding to the stock of stereotypical images and tokens.

The visual imagination of the nineteenth century exhibited a sincere delight in borrowing and quoting from commonly shared cultural codes and well-established images. Indifferent to the stories being told, relishing instead the repetition of well-known themes and commonplace views, the spectator was fascinated with the verisimilitude, amazed by how closely the copy reproduced reality, and focused on the manner in which small variations embellished well-known visual anecdotes. An aesthetics of seriality arose, never questioning the process of production because repetition enabled many objects to be reproduced from a single photographic negative, one lithographer's stone, or a specific industrial mold.[82] The illusion of just looking at cities, only gazing at their wondrous and magical mirage, depended on the work of concealment that lay at the heart of the phantasmagorical. It spirited away the hand of production; it entertained and amused with incredulous tricks of the eye. As a complete fabrication, casting a magical spell like the camera obscura, it set itself up as an authentic experience and covered over all the contradictions of reality it failed to include. This was the art of the spectacle, the city space and urban compositions that the visual image controlled. In the twentieth century, the spectacles of light and fireworks would become illuminated billboards and electric signs; the industrial expositions and habitats from around the world as display cabinets for commodities and styles of life would find themselves replicated in contemporary city tableaux and architectural reconstructions; and the theatrical thrill of travel and the fascinating allure of exotic places would become the dazzling entertainments of simulated travelogues, nostalgic films, and historicist architectural compositions. The increased importance of the unreal and the nostalgic in contemporary times, their inspiration and illusions, draws sustenance from the visual imagination engendered and nurtured during the nineteenth century and stored in its catalogs and archives.

Vernacular *Topoi*

There are many ways that city space has been imprinted with historic traditions. Vernacular landscapes rooted in a sense of place and local customs have often been preserved or re-created from the longing and desire that nostalgia emits; or spectacles and ceremonies that mark the calendar days of popular festivals have left their traces on a series of celebratory public places—these we might call the popular or vernacular *topoi* of the city that stem from the needs of the people, that mark local and everyday events. They are the landscapes that form the inscapes of local identity.[83] But there are rhetorical topoi as well, those civic compositions that teach us about our national heritage and our public responsiblities and assume that the urban landscape itself is the emblematic embodiment of power and memory. These are absorptive city tableaux, dramaturgical setups and rehearsals that shape and articulate the cityscape through their monumental and mnemonic constructions.

When either topography is established, however, it is because living traditions are fading away and their experienced enactment a weakening memory. It becomes essential then to mark these traditions down, settle them in time, collect their evidence, and write their stories before they are scattered by time. Whipping them into a unified mold, the many voices and shapes of the vernacular in particular are stilled as an officially recreated history takes form. Even though wise spectators may never doubt that at every step of their historical recreation these formalized reenactments of vernacular forms provide evidence that the past has died, nevertheless these re-constructions attract and hold the spectators' attention.

Architecture and city places, as we have seen, give particular form to our memories; they are the mnemonic codes that awaken recall. Christian Mertz writes of the cinema's code: "Every code is a collection of reworkings; of double repercussions. . . . And this set of reworkings is itself, over time, constantly reworked, like a monument—Monumentum: memory, trace, relic—a monument which is being restored but which must have been restored in every phase of its history; and which can have known no other 'condition'; . . . ."[84] So it is of the city: its topographical landscape has been constantly restored, replaced, and renewed from epoch to epoch. Yet the name of a city's streets and squares, the gaps in its very plan and physical form, its local monuments and celebrations, remain as traces and ruins of their former selves. They are tokens or hieroglyphs from the past to be literally reread, reanalyzed, and reworked over time. Images that arise from particular historic circumstances come to define our sense of tradition; they literally manage our knowledge of the historic.

One American city, above all others, holds a central place in the invention of American traditions and in the development of cultural tourism that the nostalgic art of historic preservation has spurred. This is the city of New Orleans. We might argue that the preservation of the Vieux Carré, as the original center of New Orleans is called, began the moment when Jefferson annexed Louisiana, the moment the French territory became American. But this "Carré," this Cartesian square carved out of the wilderness of the New World, has captured the fascination of travelers since the early eighteenth century. And like all travel narratives—and the tales spun around Creole New Orleans were no different—they traced the structure of an adventure story replayed in the panoramic image of the city that first unrolled as the voyager's ship sailed upriver, or gathered together in the unfolding of a lithographic bird's-eye view meant to spur on a viewer's desire for travel and adventure.[85] Once Louisiana became the territory of America, the Vieux Carré became a condensation point: enclosing within its margins the remnants of a Creole culture that wanted to withdraw from the process of Americanization taking place across the spatial void in the plan of its streets, a gap produced by the so-called "free land" of the old Canal that literally separated the French from the American parts of town. The Vieux Carré turned inward upon itself, blatantly ignoring the forces of modernization.

By the 1870s it had become a melancholic symbol of ruin and decline for both the antebellum south and the Creole culture. An *Illustrated Visitors' Guide* to the city in 1879 offered this image as it spoke about The Old Citizens' Bank, which had become

> A shell: in all save the front; which is, after all, but a classic ruin. A ruin gloomy in sunshine: ghostly, in the moonlight, but through all, giving, somehow, a remembrance of older temples and pagan shrines. . . . A shell: in those enlarged lamp-flames, that in this silence of desolution, are as sightless as the eyes of the dead. . . . A shell: in that big iron door, now closed forever, through which have so often passed, with heads high, capitalists with money within their closed purses; and suppliants, with heads bent low, and nothing in their pocket-books save 'promises to pay'. Read that closed iron door aright! And who will not see in it a great fall? . . . . Nothing is behind that classic shell, save Nothingness.[86]

A peculiar miniaturized image is offered to the reader by this guidebook, a view of the French Quarter withdrawing into the mouldy corners of a romantic ruin, of the Creole culture being eclipsed by American manners, of the south undergoing

Old Citizen's Bank as Ruin, New Orleans, *J. Curtis Waldo, photoengraver (c. 1880).*

a painful reconstruction. Yet this nostalgic mood actually enabled the restoration of "Creole New Orleans" to begin and its traditions to assume their anecdotal form. Inverting Penelope's labor of remembering and work of forgetting, the weaving of tales had first to be countered by unraveling what existed. Thus the "nothingness of the past" presented the tourguide with a blank screen, enabling her or him to become the inventor of dreams and narrations and to project onto the petrified features and contours of the physiognomy of "Creole New Orleans" her or his own fantasies and imaginations. In the end these inventions and narrations reveal more about the interpreter than the interpreted.[87]

The Vieux Carré would become the quintessential historic district and the prototypical nostalgic form from which all American cities would borrow. New Orleans had its waterfront, its warehouse district, its old town plan, its public markets and specialized foods, and its local celebrations and carnivals, which captivated nineteenth-century travelers and still tantalize tourists today. But it was not until 1884 that these artifacts, foods, and customs were presented to the public for exhibitionary display. 1884 was the year of the New Orleans Cotton Centennial, and that was the year which William H. Coleman decided to publish three books: *La Cuisine Creole: A Collection of Culinary Recipes,* written by his friend Lafcadio Hearn; Hearn's story of *Gombo Zhèbes: A Little Dictionary of Creole Proverbs*; and Coleman's own *Historical Sketch Book and Guide to New Orleans and Environs,* to which Hearn contributed, including his "Scenes of Cable's Romances." These books (actually published in 1885) represented the first collection of Creole stories, the first cookbook of Creole cuisine, and an updated architectural guidebook. They became the exemplar of nostalgic manuals.

There already was a nationwide audience for these books, for the collective imagination of Americans had been fascinated by stories of New Orleans written by George Washington Cable that appeared nationwide in both *The Century Magazine* and *Scribner's Magazine.* These narrations had popularized the aura of local color hanging over New Orleans' architectural atmosphere and had diffused the sharpness of its imagery in picturesque and ruinous forms. Creole residents of the Vieux

Carré, however, complained by the 1890s that tourists were walking up and down the streets of the district with copies of Cable's books in their hands, trying to identify the picturesque locales and characters of "Romantic Old New Orleans" that his stories had fabricated. Following Cable, their guided tour included such noteworthy landmarks of the Vieux Carré as the Old Absinthe House of 1790, Sieur George's House, Lafitte the pirate's blacksmith shop, Madame Laturie's Haunted House, and the Napoleon House. All of these invented landmarks remain today staples of every guided tour of the Vieux Carré, but the appeal of romance abetted by culinary and architectural tastes had spawned their offspring tourism as long ago as the nineteenth century.[88] And yet the French Creole detested Cable, thinking him an outsider who exaggerated their dialect and glorified "free men of color" at their expense. And Cable returned their venon by narrating over and over the caricatures of laziness, arrogance, backwardness, and complacency that defined his Creole stereotype.[89]

Lafcadio Hearn, on the other hand, was an avid collector of voodoo myths, of Creole expressions, street cries and songs, of folk medicine, food, and stories from people's memories. He wrote for a New Orleans newspaper *The Item* between 1878 and 1881, and then for the *Times-Democrat* for another six years. Although a newly arrived resident of the city, he helped to construct an awareness within some parts of New Orleans of the traditions and culture encapsulated within the boundaries of the Vieux Carré. His main literary device was to dwell on cumulative "recurrences," not the movement of successive events, for he sought to develop the reader's visual impression of New Orleans. This city, Hearn felt, did not display an evolutionary development of stages and epochs, but revealed instead the passage of time in layers and traces. One had only to peel away each layer to find beneath age-old stories, sounds, architecture, and traditions that still impressed themselves on local culture.[90] As Hearn wrote in *The Item* of March 23, 1879,

> The city of New Orleans really contains within itself several little cities, which have preserved their individuality for generation after generation. The old French

> town proper is as much isolated from the rest of New Orleans as though it still wore the ancient girdle of rampart and moat. We know of people living there, and who have lived there for fifty or sixty years, who know little about the district south of Canal Street as though it were a portion of Tibet or Patagonia. . . . Meanwhile the American population strives to spread beyond the barrier, and domicile itself in France; but it makes slow progress, and infinite are the discouragements opposed to it. In the old days when the neighborhood of the French theatre was one blaze of coffee houses, restaurants and billiard rooms, etc., it used to be somewhat unsafe for American strangers to enjoy themselves in that quarter. . . . But the times have changed.[91]

Even though Hearn wrote with sympathy about New Orleans he remained an outsider, finding the world of the white Creole's of Spanish or French descent to be impenetrable. This separate world was his own construction, for he set it up to be the antithesis of the American material world by absolutizing relative differences between the cultures, and stereotypically defining the Creole as defiant of modern traditions.[92] Writing about a "Creole Courtyard," he explained:

> Like many of the Creole houses, the facade presented a commonplace and unattractive aspect. The great green doors of the arched entrance were closed; and the green shutters of the balconied windows were half shut, like sleepy eyes lazily gazing upon the busy street below. . . . But beyond the gates lay a little Paradise. The great court, deep and broad, was framed in tropical green; . . . . Without, cotton-floats might rumble, and street-cars vulgarly jingle their bells; but these were mere echoes of the harsh outer world which disturbed not the delicious quiet within—where sat, in old fashioned chairs, good old-fashioned people who spoke the tongue of other times, and observed many quaint and knightly courtesies forgotten in this material era. Without roared the Iron Age, the angry waves of American traffic; within one heard only the murmur of the languid fountains, the sound of deeply musical voices . . . . Without, it was the

> year 1879; within, it was the epoch of the Spanish Dominion. . . . And yet some people wonder that some other people never care to cross Canal Street.[93]

What Hearn defined as an enclosed landscape, Coleman's architectural guidebook attempted to open to the eye of the stroller and the collector of nostalgic minutiae. He pointed out that most visitors had "done the city" when they had seen the Mardi Gras carnival, Lake Ponchartrain, had a fish dinner, visited the Metairie cemetery, and been to Carrollton, the Jockey Club, and the French Market. But this, he added, was the visitor's mistake and therefore the rationale for his guidebook because the French Quarter, the Vieux Carré, had many more sights:

> . . . odd little balconies and galleries jut out from the tall, dingy, wrinkled houses, peering into each other's faces as if in eternal confab. There, queer little shops are to be found, apothecaries' and musty stores where old furniture, brasses, bronzes and books are sold, bird stores innumerable, where alligators are to be purchased as well—all these lying in a sort of half doze.[94]

One notable old house stood on the corner of Royal and St. Peter's Streets.

> Three months ago it stood there, a tall Venetian-looking four-story edifice of peculiar architecture and more sombre appearance. Of a dull, faded, blue color, with splotches on its front like a convalescent small-pox patient, it gave evidence of its age, and showed how the weather of all those years had made its inroads on the once smooth stucco. Silent and rather forebidding it stood there, a gloomy reminder of days when prosperity and wealth made our city the Damascus of the South, whither the gay and rich voyaged for the nepenthe of revelry and pleasure. . . . A fresh coat of stucco has obliterated now all the work of weather, and the house stands in its new garb as bright and attractive as it did sixty years ago.[95]

Old Absinthe House, Vieux Carré, New Orleans (c. 1930).

The Vieux Carré was an interior landscape, a peculiar spatialization of historical time, and like Walter Benjamin's street images from Berlin, Naples, Moscow, or Paris, those from the Vieux Carré were used against the grain of "the structuring boundaries of modern capitalism."[96] Long forgotten and aging images rose up from shops and streets to confront the wanderer with involuntary memories and reminiscences, plunging the traveler into a universe of hieroglyphics and displaced significations. Nevertheless, this atmosphere of old New Orleans was under seige: an intangible, ephemeral, and fragile substance, its history was being preserved and its aura vanquished with a fresh coat of paint. A decade or so before the Vieux Carré was pronounced to be a historic district in 1937, Guy Manners spoke of the atmosphere of New Orleans in a different, more instrumental manner: "The all American Atmosphere of strength, beauty, and historic value begins at the Place d'Armes, reaching out until its delicate fingers rustle the royal red velvet memories of a three-century-old history of kings, queens, potentates, pirates, letters of marque, love, romance, adventure, plot, counter-plot, intrigue, the deuello—wondrously beautiful women, tremendously brilliant men." This atmosphere of the Place d'Armes, Manners continued, challenged that of Washington Square in New York, for the Vieux Carré throws down the gauntlet to Greenwich Village, the Rue Royale takes issue with MacDougal Alley, a hundred buildings and dark dank passageways spell out the Southland's embroidered coverlet of romantic and historic atmosphere. "New Orleans," Manners warned, "has preserved where New York City has destroyed."[97]

"The battle of New Orleans," which took place in 1815, could be said to have lasted most of the nineteenth century. It was an imaginary struggle that pitted two cultures and two towns, that of the Creole French and the materialistic Americans, against each other until the Americans succeeded in dominating and appropriating even the memory of the Vieux Carré. New Orleans had something to sell: its "atmosphere," the ruins of its old architecture, the fragmented myths of its past, its special foods, antique shops, and open-air markets. This Vieux Carré quickly became the prototypical historical tableau, a scenographic arrangement displaying its objects in a neutralized stage set for the tourist to explore. Travel narratives arose to map the itinerary, illustrations of the city marked its important spots, its special locations were named and its commerce celebrated. New Orleans after all had been the commercial capital of America, the trade of its port exceeding that of New York, Philadelphia, or Boston until the mid-nineteenth century.[98] Why not offer its image for sale?

President Jefferson had declared in 1804 that New Orleans, because of its geographical position, was destined to become the greatest city the world had ever experienced.[99] But the development of territories to the west of the Mississippi would not hold back nor be dependent on trading with the port of New Orleans. There were more direct routes to be exploited connecting the west with the east, and with the coming of the transcontinental railroad in the 1860s, New Orleans was left as a backwater route. By the end of the nineteenth century, George Washington Cable would be critical of what he called the lethargy and traditional ways of the New Orleans Creole. He complained that while manufacturing and steam-built cities had expanded in the north, the Creoles with their easy cash crops of sugar, cotton, and tobacco arrogantly waived away the benefits of manufacturing. Americans, he claimed, were thought to be foreigners by the unaspiring, satirical Creole.[100] But even an early guidebook of 1845 captured the same stereotypical view that New Orleans was closed to Americans and considered them outsiders. Seen from the dome of the St. Charles Hotel/Exchange in the American sector, this guidebook reported, New Orleans presented "a panorama at once magnificient and surprising. . . . [although] the stranger finds a difficulty in believing himself to be in an American city. The older buildings are of ancient and foreign construction, and the manners, customs and language, are various—the population being composed, in nearly equal proportions of Americans, French, Creoles, and Spaniards, together with a large proportion of Germans, and a good sprinkling from almost every other nation upon the globe."[101]

Pride in one's city often grows out of the successes of its commercial ventures. It is not surprising, then, to find that early illustrated guidebooks to

American cities were either commercial city directories or promotional books instilled with civic pride: James Mease's *The Pictures of Philadelphia* (1811) being the prototype. Lithography was used extensively in the burgeoning art of advertising during the nineteenth century, and New Orleans was one of its American centers. City views, trade cards of all sorts, posters advertising the wares the city manufactured, its factories, and businesses were common sources of visual information about the city of New Orleans. Originally intended to convey information, to explain what a place looked like, and how successful its businesses were, city views and illustrated guidebooks developed from this commercial base into an art aimed not only at transforming the pleasure of travel into a vicarious entertainment, but intending to turn the city's historical past, recorded in its architecture and sites, into a visual experience. As we have seen, Karl Baedeker of Leipzig was among the early experimenters of guidebooks with his book on Koblenz in 1829; he characterized the town by its visual appearance, outlined the route for tourists to follow, told them what to expect and how to manage their travels.[102] Architectural views soon became popular items on their own right, not just as a guide for tourists: trade cards were often adorned with an image of factories, storefronts, and the facades of hotels, or cards were embellished with an illustration of the home of an important person such as the "Hermitage" or "Arlington House." These were soon followed by lithographic bird's-eye views, and winter and summer genre scenes that captured stereotypical images of a city.[103] Reflecting a newborn pride among city boosters, this American art of city views and panoramic maps became a craze used to advertise a city's commercial and residential potential, helping to sell a culture and town supposedly as developed and ready for settlement as its illustrated portrait conveyed.[104]

Daniel Boorstin in *The Image* claims that tourists look for caricature, surveying cultural views and cityscapes as so many items to purchase and consume.[105] New Orleans in the nineteenth century was a commercial capital, and so its leisure specialists and graphic artists responded to this market by reproducing the synthetic codes they knew would please the visiting tradesman, creating stereotypical images of the city's commerce, entertainment, and architectural atmosphere.[106] It began with travel accounts such as the following, that called New Orleans of 1826

> the wet grave, where the hopes of thousands are buried, for eight years the asylum for outcasts of France and Spain, who could not venture one hundred paces beyond its gates without utterly sinking to the breast in mud, or being attacked by alligators; has become in the space of twenty-three years one of the most beautiful cities of the Union, inhabited by 40,000 persons who trade with half the world.[107]

Even though, as a traveler noted in 1834, there were considerable "commercial advantages which the place affords, the position of the city having rendered it the present emporium of this part of the world; . . . it appeared evident . . . that a man who had no business to transact would find no temptation to remain long, . . . for the only object men can have in coming to reside in a town so fatal to health and life in the summer, and so uncomfortable to reside in winter, must be the accumulation of money. That I am sure is every man's object who comes to New Orleans."[108] Still, in the 1850s A. Oakey Hall would characterize New Orleans as "the Calcutta of America," a panorama of trade and a wilderness of ships and steamboats. On the city's levee a heterogeneous jumble of cotton bales and sugar hogsheads, molasses casks and corn sacks, packages of hemp and tobacco, oat bags and hay bales could be seen. Across from this melee along the city's waterfront a series of stores and warehouses stood to harbor the merchandise. New Orleans, Hall surmised, was the caldron in which commerce came to a boil.[109]

New Orleans described by the gazetteers of urban signs and chroniclers of its commercial traffic was a landscape composed of three separate towns: the Vieux Carré or the original quarter laid out by Adrien de Pauger in 1721, which was the bastion of Creole families; the upstream Faubourg Saint Mary, quickly becoming the American center; and the downstream Faubourg Marigny, planned to rival its American competitor.[110] It would not take long for travelers to New Orleans in the early nineteenth century to order its spatial forms and detail its sites, beginning to stake out the route over which other visitors eventually would follow. By 1834 the makings of a picturesque and melancholic townscape was being formed, a perspective already marked by distance, allowing nostalgia to escape through its gap. Featherstonhaugh, who roamed the old French Quarter at night at this period of time, depicted this autumnal landscape as

> a dirty confined town with narrow unpaved streets often impassable with mud, the principal Rue de Chartres, is only forty feet wide. . . . [A] piratical-looking population. . . . Dark, swarthy, thin, whiskered, smoking, dirty, reckless-looking men; and filthy, ragged, screaming negroes and mulattoes, crowded even Rue de Chartres, where our lodgings were, and made it a very unpleasant quarter to be in. . . . The old city, . . . is already becoming gloomy and partially deserted. Rue de Chartres is less so because the shops are situated there, but in the other streets you only meet with a few anxious Jewish-looking faces going up and down the narrow streets that run at right angles to the principal one . . . but the well-dressed, gallant, careless and cheerful Creole gentleman is no more seen. His day has already passed by. Rue Royale is the next best street running parallel with Rue de Chartres, and is less disagreeable, because there are but a few persons to be seen on it.[111]

The catalog of discrete things to collect and recollect soon would include its side streets, for the Vieux Carré encouraged straying. The nostalgic pencil of A. Oakey Hall bid the visitor in 1851 to enter Condé street (now called Chartres Street) and one, he claimed, had arrived at the St. Giles of New Orleans with all its poverty and vice: here could be found picayune dram-houses (cabarets), high brick buildings with "apartment lodgers," old clo'shops, junk shops, shoe shops; and here could be seen an assortment of nonessential wares in odd juxtaposition such as tea-kettles and bananas, bunches of keys and red and yellow kerchiefs, soap and straw hats, knives and flageolets. By 1885, Chartres Street, part of the latent mythology enticing a stroller to wander, had become a picturesque street. Developing a lens through which to see such profundity of local details, Coleman tells the viewer to peer into its doorways, where smiling inhabitants sit in courtyards filled with flowers, amid great earthen and yellow water jars and battered bronze statues and marble figures. As architecture can be the clearest index of latent mythology, windows and doors had become noteworthy sights: round or peaked in shape, the windows were filled with tiny panes of stained glass while the doors, half wood and half glass, had beautiful latticework.[112]

The Vieux Carré, as originally planned, was a parallelogram fifteen streets broad and eight streets deep, lying along the banks of the Mississippi River. In the center of the Levee was the Place d'Armes (today's Jackson Square), the focal point for the colony's religious, military, and commercial activity. A fortified city until 1804, the margins of the Carré carried military titles—Esplanade where troops drilled, Ramparts like the boulevards of Paris, and Canal Street, where a defense channel had been planned.[113] Walter Benjamin would note that in the meandering streets of a foreign city, "every step one takes . . . is on named ground. And where one of these names happens to fall, in a flash imagination builds a whole quarter about the sound."[114] Sometimes all that remains of the past is a name—it becomes the connective space, the passage to other experiences. "Through their street names the city becomes the likeness of a linguistic universe . . . It is above all the encounter of two different street names that makes up the magic of the 'corner'."[115] Names endow the city with the features of a face, for "the name is the object of a mimesis," simultaneously preserving and prefiguring "the habitus of a lived life'."[116] And street guides reveled in the lore of the Vieux Carré's old-fashioned names, for the original explorers, by dubbing places with titles—of French dukes, princes and saints such as Chartres, Conti, Burgundy, Condé, Toulouse, Royale, Orleans, the Duc du Maine (or Dumaine), the province of Dauphiny (Dauphine)—therein appropriated the territory as their own.[117]

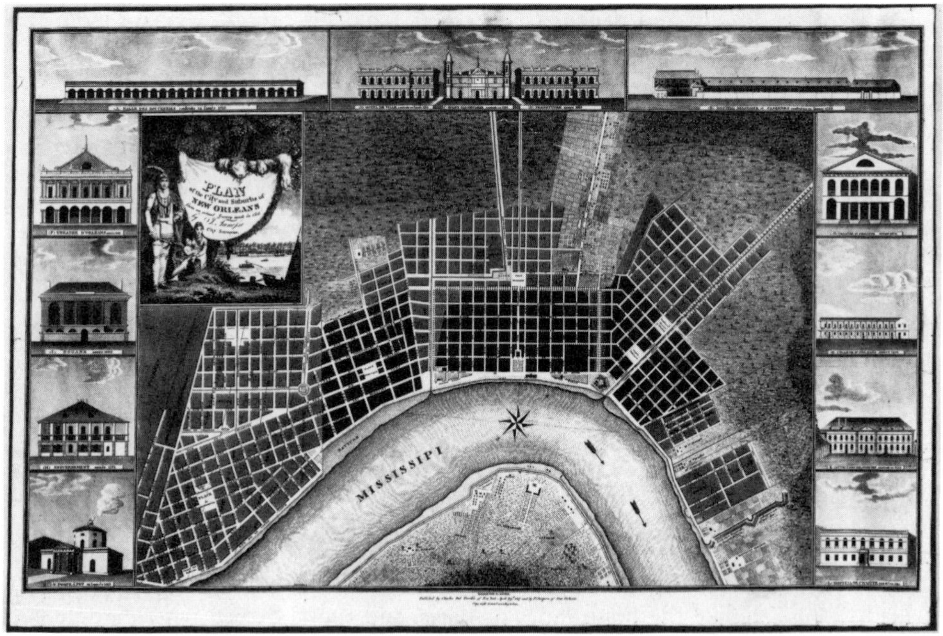

Plan of the City and Suburbs of New Orleans, *Tanesse, Robinson et al., engravers (1815).*

The city of New Orleans expanded in size by superimposing different grid patterns on the plantations, which lay perpendicular to the curving river's edge, creating one of the most beautiful city plans in America, rivaled only by that of Savannah. Among the earliest monuments celebrating the rivalry between the American and Creole communities was the creation of the Faubourg Marigny on a estate that lay downriver from but contiguous to the Vieux Carré. Here, where the river was deep enough to allow the building of docks, in the early 1800s Bernard de Marigny considered an excellent location for a new commercial center. Two open squares were planned, one for the plantation's residence and outbuildings, and the other for a public plaza to be called Washington. Choosing romantic names such as Streets of History, of Peace, of the Poets, Music Street and Champs Élysées (which became Elysian Fields). He waited patiently for real estate investors to arrive, but the lucrative Americans decided to establish a district of their own, the Faubourg Saint Mary on the upriver side of the Vieux Carré. Disappointed over losing these developers, Marigny subdivided his blocks into smaller lots, eventually attracting the less wealthy Creole investor.[118] The American district by the 1830s was both a garden district of Greek Revival homes as well as the location for cotton presses, warehouses, markets, churches, hotels, and theaters.[119] In this quarter, Featherstonhaugh noted, the streets were wider, the houses better built, and the more substantial improvements were located. So he foretold, within fifty more years everything French in New Orleans would be absorbed by the energetic Americans.[120]

Meanwhile the two communities competed, the American and the French, until Saint Mary's eventually became the commercial center of modern New Orleans while the Vieux Carré submitted to the fate of the commodity falling out of style at an ever accelerating pace. Each district would have its grand hotel both financed and promoted by large banks: the American St. Charles Hotel/Exchange and the Creole St. Louis Hotel. The St. Charles Hotel (finished in 1836), designed by James Dakin and James Gallier, Sr., and located on St. Charles Street, was a gigantic structure adorned with a portico six Corinthian columns wide and four

St. Charles Hotel, New Orleans (c. 1900).

deep on a granite base fourteen feet high. A huge octagonal barroom, seventy feet in diameter, was located near the center of the hotel with an interior circle of Ionic columns from which sprung a grand spiral staircase winding up to the dome. Each of the six upper galleries gave access to six different bedrooms. The side wings of the rotunda contained a gentlemen's dining room that could seat at least 400, plus sitting rooms, private parlors, and 350 bedrooms.[121] A. Oakey Hall called the St. Charles Hotel a combination of the type of palaces that could be found in St. Petersburg, plus the colleges of human nature like those located in Boston, and an exchange for money and appetites similar to those situated in London. But no one, he commented further, would ever imagine the St. Charles to be a hotel, unless first told it was built by P. T. Barnum, the circus entrepreneur. Hemmed in by lofty stores and narrow streets, garnished on all sides by oyster saloons, fruit shops, and billiard rooms, and overshadowed by balconies on adjacent structures, "one is as long in finding out its value to a city where fine edifices are yet exceptions. . . ."[122] Of course the Creoles soon erected their own magnificent hotel in the Vieux Carré, protesting the drift of commerce toward the American sector. The St. Louis Hotel, designed by De Pouilly in 1837, was equally difficult to view in spite of its magnificent intentions and gigantic plan. It too sported an interior rotunda, and a spiral mahogany staircase, but its dazzling copper-plated dome could only be glimpsed from courtyards within the hotel itself or from the upper windows of neighboring houses.[123] Surrounded by dirty streets, dirty faces, and dirty moustaches, with cafes and casinos its elbowing neighbors, Hall complained, this hotel, which opened in 1838, remained part of the unwanted wealth of the city and the headquarters of Creole loaferism.[124]

There is something almost primordial and fertile about food markets, and every visitor to nineteenth-century New Orleans was enamored of its French marketplace, impressed by the sheer abundance and sensuousness of its produce and the urbanity of its milling crowd. In a long brick structure supposedly modeled after the Athens Propylea, a melee of meat, vegetables, and fish were sold. Black women at makeshift stalls sold coffee, hot chocolate, and smoking dishes or rice

Aerial View of the Old French Market, New Orleans (c. 1930).

along with gumbo—foods that were already established favorites among visiting tourists.[125] St. Mary's district built two markets of its own, the Tshoupitoulas market in 1836 and the Poydras Street market in 1837, but neither could rival the primacy of the French Market in the Vieux Carré. In 1830, J. Pilé designed a vegetable market in the Roman Doric order, copying the earlier 1817 meat market; and between these two Greek structures, a Bazaar Market with two tin cupolas was added for the sale of dry goods.[126] Coleman told the readers of his 1880s guidebook that a man might study the world in the French Market, for it offered an abundance of oddly cohabitating images. Enter it near Jackson Square, he advised, and one would find

> the dresses are as varied as the faces; the baskets even are of every race, some stout and portly, others delicate and adorned with ribbons and ornaments; some, again, old, wheezy and decayed, through whose worn ribs might be seen solemn and melancholy cabbages, turnips, and potatoes, crammed and jostled together in ruthless imprisonment. The butchers scorn to use those blandishments that the lower grades of market society make use of to attract purchasers. Like Mahomet, the mountain must come to them. From the ceiling hang endless ropes of spider's webs, numberless flies, and incalculable dirt. . . . Through the crowd lurk some skeleton-dogs, vainly hoping . . . to secure a dainty morsel[127] . . . Several marble-top tables [stand] about in different parts of the market; [with] four- legged stools in rows alongside. Many little white cups and saucers are in a line near the edge of the tables. These are the coffee stands. A big steaming urn, with a faucet to it is in the centre of each table, while various dishes, containing bread, beefsteaks, even bacon and greens are scattered over the marble top. These are not very neat looking tables. . . . They are streaked with grease, or the polish is worn off . . . where the stools are placed. . . . stray cabbage leaves and other waste material scattered about their feet, give these legs a half-unclean, negligent appearance that borders on depravity. But then this is the market and the wilted cabbage leaves are part of the place.[128]

Of course the visitor also needed a restaurant guide because New Orleans with its abundant market supplies, its special blend of French, Spanish, West Indian, and Mexican cuisines, produced many savory dishes. Jambalaya, crayfish bisque, gumbo filé, bouillabaisse soon became legendary pleasures of the place. Coleman's guide advised that a soup, a dish of soup meat, followed by a fish dish offered at least twice a week (or a roast the choice of which changed every day), and a medley of five or six vegetable dishes, salad, and desert could be obtained in the city for only thirty cents.[129] The so-called free lunch became a famous New Orleans speciality, after it was first offered at the St. Louis Hotel. Gentlemen conducting business in the Vieux Carré found themselves too far from home at lunchtime yet appeared unwilling to pay for the price of a meal. Consequently first-class barrooms offered a free lunch for their customers, who only had to pay for their drinks. On a narrow tablecloth running the length of the bar, soup, a piece of ham or beef, potatoes, meat pies, and oyster patties were liberally arrayed before the thirsty patron.[130]

These leisure guides, repetitively listing the pleasures of New Orleans streets, architecture, and foods, slowly detailed and exhibited over time the appropriate manner by which the tourist even until today can appropriate the physiognomy—its imagery and memory, the tastes and sounds—of the entire Creole era. Reinforced by comparison and contrast with the more dynamic and developing American sector, almost as if the stage set was spatially divided in two, a composed and static picture of the Vieux Carré was juxtaposed against its antipode, the supposedly superior view of the dynamic and materialistic American sector. This device of absolutizing the division between the city of business and work and the city of leisure and lethargy allowed the south's stereotypical coverlet of romantic and historic themes to be thrown into place, passing down through time street images from the Vieux Carré recomposed into a city tableau. A close-up view of the French Quarter was distilled for the spectator through the use of old lithographs and photographs, the important scenes cross-referenced and reiterated in folktales, stories, and street names. Its foods, smells, and sounds were assembled and cataloged as if these special effects helped to freeze the frame of what in reality was a rapidly transforming picture. By static views and illustrated reference points, the viewer's memory was externalized onto visual surface indicators, architectural forms and atmospheric details, which repetitively shown as a series eventually fabricated a conventional portrait of the town. From that time forward, the anecdotal characterizations of New Orleans, having been placed in the archive of America's collective memory, were easy to recognize and recall. What once was a bizarre landscape and set of mythological hieroglyphs beckoning the wanderer to stray had become a fixed and purchasable commodity.

Rhetorical *Topoi*

Civic art is both a dramaturgical as well as a territorial act; it is the point where a national or municipal ideology leaves its imprint on a city's topography. The physical form and shape of a city, its official plan and ceremonial places are articulated by political and social configurations that a nation or municipality wants to instill within its public. Monuments and civic spaces of the city designed as emblematic scenes are the sites of rhetorical meaning. As staged events they are studied representation of civic authority, becoming the official memory book of significant events or the metaphors of national life.[131] Monuments are really mnemonic devices intended to stir one's memory, they are calendar spaces set aside to commemorate important men and women or past heroic events. Yet how was it possible to create a representative tableau in honor of the birth of a democracy and the formation of the United States of America? This problem has vexed the designers of monuments in America ever since Major Pierre Charles L'Enfant presented his original scheme in 1791 for a city of monuments to be called the District of Columbia and located between Maryland and Virginia.[132] As Alexis de Tocqueville noted as he toured the United States in the late 1830s, "In democratic communities the imagination is compressed when men consider themselves; it expands indefinitely when they think of the state. Hence it is that the same men who live on a small scale in cramped dwellings frequently aspire to gigantic splendour in the erection of their public monuments."[133]

In celebration of democracy and eulogizing the birth of a nation, Americans wanted to build an ideal city, a civic monument to guide their collective memory, reminding them of the heroic deeds of the past and prompting them to accept the challenges and responsibilities of the present. But where in the landscape of the eighteenth-century wilderness called America should they locate their monument to liberty? And how could they represent in spatial terms and symbolic forms the ideals and exemplary acts that sprang from the country's very foundation, so that this monumental spectacle could become the memory book for a nation? Its figurative and emblematic language must be fittingly composed if the spectator was to read from these pages of history, if scenic architecture was to be the authority controlling its civic message. But even more important, this urban theater or city of monuments had to retain over time the static framework its civic idealization required, even though this paradigmatic city would always be transformed by time. If its message was to ring out across the generations and represent the "history" of a whole nation, with all of its diverse peoples, then the coherence of its framework must be maintained against any number of paradoxes and changes. Somehow in this theater of history, both imagination and reality must merge, turning the city into a public spectacle that constantly kept the ideal city and its civic message before its citizens' gaze.[134]

Based on the selection of a few heroic citizens, their deeds reduced to simplistic expression, the imaginary framework of this national city was carefully composed. The heroic acts and patriotic deeds of these figures had to be not only emblematic of but the justification for the foundation of a new nation. They must symbolize its very collectivity. George Washington, Thomas Jefferson, then Abraham Lincoln after the near-sundering of the nation by the Civil War, were selected as the pillars of democracy, patriotism, and virtue on which the city would rise. Techniques of eulogy and allegorical narration helped to establish the uncritical worship and near-sanctification of these founding fathers. Already during the

Revolutionary War, as we have seen, the image of George Washington had been imbued with heroic features, representing the epitome of classical nobility, natural gravity, and prudent rationality. The nation needed a hero of noble stature and dignity around which its citizens could rally, a father symbol who could crystallize and establish its national patrimony. And so the legend of Washington as commander in chief was reformulated in heroic and classical proportion. By 1775, and increasingly thereafter, illustrations of Washington appeared in books and magazines, on sheet music and textiles, adorning china and glassware until his Romanized features quickly passed into the iconography of America and with it the allegorical representation of the nation.[135]

It was Thomas Jefferson, instrumental in formulating ideas for the original plan and layout of a federal city, who initially sought a commemorative act to eulogize and symbolize the common sovereignty of the thirteen original colonies as they formed the United States. Jefferson knew that sovereign power if tyrannically deployed would destroy the delicate balance of republic powers, so he wanted a monument in stone—a memory theater—to remind the nation of its historic albeit wholly experimental cause and its unique constitutional arrangement. But new traditions would have to be invented, symbolizing a national cohesion that had yet to congeal and metonymic devices created in which the emblematic part would stand for the values of freedom and liberty not yet achieved. As commemorative architecture usually dreams of glory and honor, most often conceived in classical garb, how could the everyday American realities of plain values and simple men be adequately represented? And how could classical monuments as a culminating sign of heroic achievements distilled from the past be used to inspire the nation's imagination to look toward the future?

In time, the city plan of Washington, D.C., itself became this commemorative monument. Jefferson was pleased when in 1791 President Washington asked Major Pierre Charles L'Enfant to develop a concept for the new federal city.[136] L'Enfant adopted but amplified Jefferson's initial scheme: the old Babylonian ideal of an enclosed parallelogram containing sites for temples and palaces surrounded

Plan of the City of Washington in the Territory of Columbia. *Line engraving by Thackara and Vallance, Philadelphia (1792).*

with terraced and hanging gardens.[137] The ten-mile-square Territory of Columbia would become the garden spot of the Republic, for its surrounding amphitheater of hills offered picturesque views at every turn of the head.[138] L'Enfant was sensitive to the topographic arrangement that underscored his monumental approach. His first act was to select three principal nodes. Because the west end of Jenkins Hill appeared to be a pedestal waiting for a monument, here L'Enfant located the Congressional Building (Capitol). On another elevated prospect a mile and a half toward the northwest, he placed the Presidential Palace (later referred to as the President's House, and now the White House). To the north of the Palace, diagonal boulevards led outward to the countryside, while to the south the Palace's lawns sloped gently downward toward a Presidential Park. Not only would the spectator gaze from below on these wondrous monuments raised on their natural bluffs and silhouetted against the sky, but each promontory commanded open vistas—one leading westward from the Capitol across broad parklands toward the horizon of the Virginia hills and the other south from the President's House across a park and then down over the waters of the Potomac River. Around both monuments L'Enfant allocated open space to be filled in with executive departments and governmental buildings. Having selected the site for these two principal places, which were isolated intentionally from each other in order to serve the *tout ensemble,* L'Enfant drew twenty-one diagonal and grand boulevards (all planned to be from 80 to 160 feet in width), visually tying his principal points together by "a reciprocity of sight" and therefore making them appear to be connected at least in plan.[139] A Grand Avenue 400 feet wide allowed amble room for state processionals and was to be embellished with gardens and the houses of diplomats, and in plan stretched a mile westward from the foot of Jenkins Hill to intersect near the high-water mark of the Potomac River, with a swath of open space that reached northward to the President's House. At this third focal point, where vistas converged from the Capitol and the President's House, L'Enfant placed an equestrian statue of Washington as his tribute to the founding father.

Near the middle of the Grand Avenue, L'Enfant set aside a site for a National University. In addition he planned fifteen different squares distributed across the city and reserved some 15,000 lots, or half of the city, for civic use. The squares were linked reciprocally to each other along visual corridors that the spacious diagonal boulevards provided. It was L'Enfant's intention that each state should be given a square and each religious society a free donation of land so that the city would be quickly adorned by these benefactors. In the center of the square, L'Enfant expected that each state would erect an obelisk, column, statue, or commemorative monument not only to perpetuate the memory of their contribution to the achievement of American liberty and independence, but also as memory tokens to prompt the viewer's imagination to recall the deeds and actions that were worthy of general emulation.[140] The diagonal route, Pennsylvania Avenue, directly linking the Capitol with the President's House, passed through marshland, but once graded and raised above the bog it would be suitable for commerce, for places of amusement and culture. And further eastward from the Capitol, where three great diagonal boulevards were drawn, L'Enfant reserved the middle one for an avenue of bazaars, planning an arcade of shops along each side.[141] On top of this monumental plan of focal points and connecting diagonals, at least sixteen of which descended on the Capitol itself, L'Enfant superimposed a gridiron pattern of streets. He assumed that these rectangular blocks would yield to private development once each state's square became a settlement node spreading out to connect with the others.[142] Fountains and water views were also to be important ingredients of the plan, for both commercial and pleasurable purposes. A Canal formed the northern border of the Grand Avenue, turning south to pass under a grand cascade where the Tiber River flowed over Jenkins Hill and poured into the water below, before both the canal and the river streamed southward to the port along the Anacostia River.[143]

Even though the Federal City was based on a simply and clearly drawn city plan, this "city of magnificent intentions," as it was perjoratively called in the nineteenth century, nevertheless was defaced and obscured from its very beginning, eventually being forgotten with time. Even the location of the capital was hotly contested, and at every national setback capital-movers raised their voices attempting to relocate its site. Someone supposedly named "Crito" wrote "Letters on the Seat of Government" in 1807, suggesting that the capital be moved to Philadelphia and noting that

> . . . the national bantling called the City of Washington remains, after ten years of expensive fostering, a rickety infant, unable to go [it] alone. Nature will not be forced. . . . This embryo of the state will always be a disappointment to its parents, a discredit to . . . its worthy godfathers and godmothers, and an eyesore to all its relations to the remotest degree of consanguinity.[144]

By 1869 western senators and representatives could find reasons why the capital should be relocated to St. Louis, for now the great American empire ran westward beyond the Mississippi. Expressed animosity to the selected site and general public indifference left the ". . . District [like] the apothecary's cat, to be dosed experimentally with each dubious compound before it can safely be offered to the public."[145] Thus when Anthony Trollope visited Washington in 1862, he saw

> but a ragged, unfinished collection of unbuilt, broad streets, as to the completion of which there can not, I imagine, be but little hope. . . . Massachusetts Avenue runs the whole length of the city, and is inserted on the maps as a full-blown street about 4 miles in length. Go there, and you will find yourself not only out of town. . . . but. . . . beyond the fields in an uncultivated, undrained wilderness. . . . [and] you will be out of reach of humanity. . . .[146]

It was not just the hostile capital-movers who retarded the development of the city, but also its neglectful congressional guardians who kept the large straggling village in an impoverished state of financial support until the end of the nineteenth century. L'Enfant had planned Pennsylvania Avenue to be the great boulevard

View of Washington, 1850. *Drawn by Robert P. Smith.*

visually connecting the White House with the Capitol, but one of the first intrusions on the avenue was the erection in 1801 of a Central Market at the south corner of 7th Street close to the Capitol, a site it retained until 1904. Commerce quickly moved close to the market: and by the following decade all the principal hotels and stores plus a series of schools and offices found this street as it stretched toward the White House to be an ideal position. So Pennsylvania Avenue, even though it remained ungraded and contended on its southern side with boggy land, became the Main Street of town.[147]

In 1800, both the Capitol and the President's House stood out like shining white objects in a desolate wilderness of thickets, shrub-oak bushes, and marshy, impassable land.[148] Architectural competitions had been held in 1792 for both the Capitol and the President's House. Washington, Jefferson, and the commissioners of the Federal City gave William Thornton the prize for the former and James Hoban the bid for the latter. By 1800 only the Senate wing of the Capitol had been completed and the future of the rest remained unclear. Benjamin Latrobe was put in charge in 1803 to reorder Thornton's "mistakes." Thornton had planned to follow L'Enfant's intentions by designing the western facade of the Capitol as the elaborated facade. Latrobe omitted the semicircular portico planned for the western side and completely ignored L'Enfant's gardens and reciprocal vistas, replacing these with an imposing eastern portico and an ascending flight of steps. A few years after a disastrous fire in 1814, Charles Bulfinch was called on for help. He would try to reawaken Thornton's original scheme but to little avail, for Latrobe's design was triumphant and L'Enfant's intent forgotten. By this time other forces were turning the plans for the Capitol into something quite pretentious. Proposing a wooden dome with copper sheathing, Bulfinch preferred that it be slightly higher than the one originally designed by Latrobe, but the cabinet overruled him and selected what Bulfinch thought was an absurd scheme 145 feet high—a scheme he had drawn only to demonstrate how superior a more modest dome might be. Symbolic of the instability and incomplete state of the nation itself, Bulfinch's circular rotunda by the 1850s contained not only a flea market but the entertaining "Panorama of Paris" as well. The architect Thomas U. Walter was soon hired in 1851 to extend the Capitol and to establish a unifying theme. As the Capitol grew in stature and girth, even the oversized Bulfinch dome appeared to be dwarfed and so was demolished. Utilizing the scheme for the great dome of St. Peter's in Rome, Walter erected on top of Latrobe's original base a drum-shaped masonry and cast-iron structure with thirty-six marble surrounding columns representing each state. The cast-iron dome, to be painted white, had a circular lantern errected at its top surrounded by thirteen columns representing the original colonies. Although Walter's extending wings were completed by 1859, the building of the dome languished with piecemeal appropriations and then was delayed still further by the outbreak of the Civil War. Lincoln finally ordered that work be continued until its completion in 1865/1866 as a symbolic gesture recapitulating the fact that the Union prevailed.[149]

The President's House would fare no better, being rebuilt at least three different times. Although still fronting on Pennsylvania Avenue but set back a bit from L'Enfant's original site, James Hoban's original simple and classic design called for a structure three stories high and built of stone. But funds were meager, so two stories would suffice and wood would be cheaper. When President Adams took up residence in 1800, only six rooms were finished and shacks for the workmen were the prevailing view. Benjamin Latrobe was appointed by Jefferson to finish the structure, and he had completed twenty-three rooms before it was burned by the British in the War of 1812. Hoban would be rehired by president Madison to complete the north and south porticos as we know them today.[150] As early as 1796, President Washington decided that L'Enfant's reservation of open parkland expected to highlight this monument node should be used instead for executive offices, and four such structures surrounded the site by 1821: the Department of State and the Treasury Building to the east, the War and Navy Departments to the west.[151] President Jackson requested the architect Robert Mills to compose a gigantic new Treasury building in 1836, straddling the monumental axis leading to the Capitol on the eastern side of the White House. Both its monumental size and its siting completely closed L'Enfant's masterly reciprocal views between the White House and the Capitol.[152]

> By the Civil War a visitor to the city could complain that not one street was paved for any great consecutive distance; there was not a street car in the city; the Capitol was without a dome and the new wings were filled with workmen. No fire department worthy of the name was to be seen, and a mere constabulary comprised the police. . . . The water supply was wholly afforded by pumps and springs. Gas had been in partial use for several years, but little else was lighted except Pennsylvania Avenue and the public buildings. . . . Nearly one-half of the city was cut off from the rest by a ditch [The Canal] and called the Island, while an intervening strip of mall and park was patrolled by outlaws and outcasts, with only a bridge here and there for outlet. The riverside was a mass of earthern bluffs pierced by two streets, and scarcely attainable for mire and obstructions.[153]

L'Enfant's Grand Avenue (the Mall) had been transformed as well into another shabby tragedy of unfulfilled promises. Streets were driven across it at 7th, 12th, and 14th Streets in 1832; the Botanical Gardens was given a site in 1820 at the foot of Capitol Hill, although its building was not erected for several more decades; and in 1846 the Smithsonian Institution was offered a site on the southern edge of the Mall between 9th and 12th Streets.[154] When finally it was decided in 1851 to improve this melancholy tangle of land once proposed by L'Enfant to be a grand processional way, a picturesque scheme was adopted instead. Although this new plan beautifully ornamented the site with a variety of landscape scenes, different flower beds, fountains, gravel walks, and groups of shade trees, it lacked any civic ideals. The great American landscape gardener, Andrew Jackson Downing, took the opportunity created when the low and marshy grounds surrounding the White House were drained to develop a scheme for the two axial parks that L'Enfant had originally set aside, extending south of the President's House and then eastward to the Capitol. But Downing had no desire to implement L'Enfant's civic ideals—he probably had no knowledge of them, for they were by this time lost in somebody's files—but instead he saw this project as a marvelous opportunity to teach Americans the value of picturesque parks. So large an expanse of land offered Downing the chance to show off his art of the picturesque through a variety of shapes and irregular groupings.

As Downing was no champion of the grand and monumental, he divided this park into six distinct landscape scenes, believing nature to be the appropriate antidote for the city's classical structures and straight-lined axial routes. His major formal space was a large circular parade ground whose entrance was marked by a marble arch directly to the south of the President's House. Downing surrounded this ground for military reviews and public spectacles with an immense carriage drive shaded by American Elm trees. Along the outer ring of this drive, he composed a promenade of footpaths winding through thickets of trees and shrubs. Further south, at the site where the Washington Monument was planned, Downing proposed that clumps of large American trees be planted, irregularly grouped so some unobstructed views to the Potomac would remain. Moving eastward down the Capitol's axis, he next placed a sixteen-acre Evergreen Garden, laid out with walks that visually foregrounded his didactic display of 130 different species of evergreen trees and bushes. For as much as L'Enfant may had wanted his vistas and monuments to teach the values of American democracy, Downing's landscape museum was a tribute to the variety and growth of native American vegetation. Next came the grounds of the Smithsonian Institution, where stood the medieval castle of red-brown sandstone designed by James Renwick in 1846. Its site would be naturally landscaped with clumps of rare and exotic trees. To the east Downing placed his scenes of water by diverting the Canal that lay along the northern edge of these grounds and allowing it to flow into the grounds, where it filled fountains and a small but picturesque lake. Finally the triangular remnant of land at the foot of Capitol Hill was composed as a gateway marking the formal exit from Downing's picturesque park. In 1852 Downing drowned in a tragic accident on the Hudson

River, and consequently his plan was left to suffice for itself without a knowledgeable advocate. So it too, like all of the other schemes before it, suffered the trials and tribulations of the larger city's growth, so that in 1867 only one part of his plan, the section near the Smithsonian, had been implemented and developed.[155]

Instead the District of Columbia lopsidedly grew toward the northwest, leaving the land to the south of the open sewer called the Canal cut off from development. It soon became an unsavory location named "Murder Bay." During the Civil War the Armory was placed on Downing's grounds near 7th Street, and the area near the Washington Monument used by troops so that stables, slaughterhouses, hay sheds, mess halls, and bunk houses became the everyday scene. By the end of the Civil War, the swampy land around this was called "murderer's row." Further incursions were made to L'Enfant's grand scheme when the B & O Railroad tracks were allowed to invade the park grounds at the eastern end in the 1870s, while the Pennsylvania Railroad crossed from north to south and erected its depot on the northern part at 6th Street. A glimmer of improvement appeared in 1876 when the Corcoran Art Gallery located on the border of these grounds, followed in 1882 by the draining and reclamation of the marshland near the Potomac River.[156]

Tributes to the nation's founding fathers—Washington, Jefferson, and Lincoln—received the same dubious honor as had been given the city plan and its entire architectural scheme. Monuments, whether in the form of a city plan or civic architecture and public sculpture, seem to be arrogant objects out of place in a democracy. More inspired by the challenges of urban development and the awesome building of monumental bridges, railroads, and skyscrapers, commemorative monuments seemed to be isolated gestures, perhaps appearing insignificant and unnecessary when juxtaposed against the astonishing feats of development Americans experienced daily as they reached westward to the Pacific and grew upward toward the sky. It could be claimed that other countries could cause to leap from their native quarries stones and monuments to immortalize their patriotic men who had distinguished themselves for the sake of their country. Nelson, Wellington, and

Napoleon had each been honored in their countries by monuments that would transmit down through the ages their names and heroic deeds. Could it be that a republic was an ungrateful institution?[157]

The Washington Monument, originally planned to be an equestrian statue, was supposed to be located on a site selected by the General himself in 1783 near the Potomac River, a site that marked the axial cross point of L'Enfant's Grand Avenue where it met the President's Park. Placed almost on the line of the first meridian of the United States, this monument suffered from lack of funds, its design was challenged and altered, its location shifted, and its high cost continuously debated. A controversial statue of George Washington sculpted by Horatio Greenough and placed on the east side of the Capitol grounds fared no better. One nineteenth-century visitor to the city proclaimed that the colossal statue was "supposed to be in imitation of the ancients, who made their statues naked above and clothed below, as being visible to the gods, but invisible to men—[but Washington was] scarcely recognizable in this garb to his countrymen."[158] The trouble began as soon as Washington died. Eight days after his death in 1799, Congress suggested that a marble monument be erected to commemorate his heroic deeds. A pyramidal granite and marble mausoleum 100 feet at its base and of proportional height was proposed the following year, but the Senate rejected the design. In 1816 Congress wanted his tomb to be placed within the Capitol's interior.[159] Even though the Washington family refused to release his remains, a crypt for his body was built underneath the central dome.[160] Out of desperation and in hopes of breaking the deadlock, the Washington National Monument Society was formed in 1817.

Perhaps inspired by France's Arc de Triomphe, which was itself completed only in 1833, the Society decided to advertise for an appropriate architectural design for a monument to Washington that would be durable, simple, and grand. Robert Mills's circular temple-like building was selected, a pantheon of Egyptian, Babylonian, and Greek architectural forms from whose center a four-sided tapering obelisk 600 feet high rose. Around the outer ring, Mills placed the signers of the Declaration of Independence as well as Revolutionary War heroes, while thirty

Robert Mills, Design of the Washington National Monument to be Erected in the City of Washington. *Printed by Charles Fenderich (1846).*

stone columns 30 feet high and 12 feet in diameter supported the pantheon's roof. On this roof a statue of Washington was located, a heroic figure dressed in a toga and driving a horse-drawn chariot. Having decided on this design, under the auspices of the Society, the building of the Washington Monument began. In 1848 soil tests showed that L'Enfant's original cross-point site had to be moved 100 feet eastward in order to find a base that could carry the weight of the structure. Consequently its cornerstone was laid at this new site on July 4 of that year and filled with mementos and memorabilia of the day: all the national coins of the times, an American flag, newspapers from cities in all fourteen states, the bylaws of Powhatan Tribe Number 1, copies of the Declaration of Independence, the United States Constitution, and the constitution of the first American temperance society. Mills's pantheon, however, would have to wait, for there was no money to erect such a grandiose monument even though school children were asked to "give a penny"; states and foreign countries were offered the chance to buy a block of marble; and in New York, in the hope of attracting individual subscribers, a $110 block was displayed in Tiffany's windows. By the outbreak of the Civil War, the obelisk stood only 176 feet high, and for decades appeared more as a ruin than as a tribute to the heroic father of the nation. Finally, as part of the centennial celebration in 1876, Congress undertook the responsibility for the monument's completion, seeing the final stone put into place on December 4, 1884. A pyramidal capstone was designed with three of its sides inscribed with names and events detailing the monument's progress, and the fourth with "Laus Deo." But the name of Washington—perhaps a symbolic tribute to the monument's struggle to be built at all—never appears on the structure.[161]

L'Enfant's original plan for the Federal City ended just west of the nodal point reserved for Washington's equestrian statue, because the high-tide watermark came close to this site and there was at that time no idea of reclaiming any of this marshy tideland. Only after some 1,100 acres had been filled in during the late nineteenth century did the opportunity appear for rethinking the original city plan. It was either Colonel T. A. Bingham or Glenn Brown who found L'Enfant's old plan in the archives where it had lanquished for nearly a century. They began to draw attention to the unfortunate fact that many of L'Enfant's original ideas had been entirely eclipsed. As the country approached the centennial celebration of the government's removal to the District of Columbia in 1800, the American Institute of Architects recommended that an appropriate gesture would be to develop a new plan for the nation's capital. As a result the McMillan Commission of 1901 was formulated and given the task of planning for the artistic improvement of the city and drawing up new schemes for the barren and unimproved acres of land. Thoroughly trained in the lessons of the Ecole des Beaux-Arts and triumphant from their success as designers of the Chicago World's Fair of 1893, the commissioners Daniel Burnham, Charles F. McKim, Augustus Saint-Gaudens, and Frederick Law Olmsted, Jr. (the latter a newcomer to the Chicago triumvirate) decided to give, in their fashion, new life to the spirit of the long-forgotten L'Enfant plan. They were presented, or so the commissioners believed, with the wonderful possibility of improving the architectural and civic setting for the grandest set of public buildings ever erected in America.[162]

By this time the grounds that would become the Mall were a tangle of trees and unrelated and intrusive buildings and train tracks obscuring the view. Burnham had a marvelous idea for this site: a green carpet extending a mile and a half from the foot of Capitol Hill to the Washington Monument, with roadways pushed to its side and four rows of American Elm trees shielding them from sight. This axis then would continue across reclaimed land to the Potomac River, where a newly proposed Lincoln Memorial would rise. Between this monument and the Washington Monument a 200 foot wide reflecting pool immersed in its own parkland was planned to shimmer in the sun and bask in the majestic mirror images of power. L'Enfant's second axis from the President's House was moved nearly 400 feet west of the Washington Monument, and extended southward across new land where it terminated in a new monument to the makers of the Constitution. And finally, at the eastern end of the Mall, it was hoped to reinstate L'Enfant's terraced and hanging gardens with its series of cascades flowing over Capitol Hill. One of the great successes of the McMillan plan was the removal of all the train tracks from the Mall, including the Pennsylvania Railroad depot and the design of a new Union Station and plaza. As a formal gateway to the city, Daniel Burnham copied from the Baths of Caracalla and located this majestic structure just north of the Capitol.[163] It would be several decades more before either the Lincoln or Jefferson memorials were erected, the 1,100 barren acres of new land planted and improved, and the Tidal Basin to the south of the Mall constructed. Nor would these be accomplished without plenty of controversy!

There were several proposals offered in the early twentieth century for a suitable monument to Lincoln, a design one advocate said should be as "simple as his life, as beautiful as his character, as refined as his nature, as dignified as his bearing, as pure as his thoughts, and as noble and great as his life work."[164] One designer advocated that the monument to Lincoln be a peristyle encircling the plaza of Union Station, with a memorial to Columbus placed in its center. Thus Lincoln's memorial would be absorbed as part of the grand railroad station already designed by Burnham and a mere backdrop foil for the statue of Columbus. Perhaps this was modest enough for some advocates, but others decried that the hurry and bustle of the station, the whirr and clash of electric streetcars and the toot of motor horns, meant that this location was not reposeful enough for a marvelous monument, nor did the site carry out the proclamation made by Secretary Hay that "No [other] monuments or buildings shall be near the Immortals."[165] A bill presented to Congress suggested that an appropriate Lincoln memorial would be a highway two hundred feet wide leading from Washington to Gettysburg. This stretch spanning more that fifty miles would enable one hundred miles of stately structures to line its monumental approach.[166] Another suggestion placed an obelisk to Lincoln north of the President's House, although it was quickly pointed out that by copying the Washington monument, this act would degrade both monuments and potentially create a "cyclopean stockade of obelisks bristling from the Capitol to the Potomac."[167] Finally in 1911, the Newlands Bill agreed with the 1901 commissioners plan that a great classic portico on an awe-inspiring pedestal be sited on the new landfill on the western axis of the Mall. So it was proclaimed, "the principal axes of the city as left us by Washington are not mere imaginary lines. The capitol was one important focal point, the Washington Monument another. There is only one site on this. . . . axis, vacant, and this point is selected . . . for a memorial to Lincoln."[168]

The Jefferson Memorial had similar controversies surrounding its proposals. Locating it to the south of L'Enfant's original scheme, on a site the commissioner's had set aside for a monument to the makers of the Constitution, allowed no visual connection to the Washington and Lincoln memorials and added to the destruction of the spirit and intent of L'Enfant's scheme. During the thirty-five years since improvements to the Tidal Basin had begun, this parkland had become a playground for many visiting tourists. The area was planted with cherry trees, a gift from the Japanese Government; hotel owners were alarmed that the destruction of these trees might cause a loss to their industry. Many believed that the proposed design by John Russell Pope and the subsequent smaller scheme by Eggers and Higgins (actually built), by "picking out the domed center of the National [Corcoran] Gallery of Art, and reproducing it as the Thomas Jefferson Memorial," was a decided disappointment.[169] "To copy anything already done as a memorial to Thomas Jefferson would be quite unworthy, and this Congress [the 75th, meeting in 1938], as a representative of the American people, should permit no such travesty. . . . This Pantheon design with its low dome would have much the appearance of a toadstool on the meadow. . .".[170]

No matter how later additions destroyed or ignored L'Enfant's original plan, quite clearly the city of Washington was constructed as a rhetorical device endowed with power and efficacy, hierarchy and significance, to be read as a visual text. Hardly dwelling on the fact that the city of Washington would be as well an inhabited residential place, this city of "sacred" civic spaces was intended to speak to the awestruck suppliant of the values and memories with which its monuments and plan had been inscribed.[171] It seems that L'Enfant utilized a simple rhetorical device, a spatial emblem drawn from the oblique perspectives of baroque scenography, to call forth the nation's identity, coherence, and political legitimation. Perhaps this still remains the theatricalized drama of L'Enfant's planned right-angled triangular space: for he held the silhouettes of the Capitol and the President's House in balance along the oblique perspectival line of the hypotenuse, thus heightening their visual effect, while allowing their frontal perspectives, actually magnifing their isolation, to cross at right angles where L'Enfant's tribute to Washington was placed. Here the powers of the executive and legislative branches of government were mediated by the memory and example of the founding father. Now distances were large and differences great in this spatial composition, so "reciprocity of sight" was fundamental; it was emblematic of the openness and scrutiny, the enlightened critique and rational judgment that must prevail in the public sphere of a democracy. Power and authority lay with what could be seen. Appropriately L'Enfant left opened vistas toward the west and the south, for there were many ambivalent places in nineteenth-century America where licentious behavior and uncouth manners, exploitative and ruthless individualism, were the order of the day, spaces where the liberties and freedoms, the national unity and collective interests that must appear in a democracy, could scarcely be seen. But these spaces lay outside the invisible walls of L'Enfant's imaginary city and were located in the wild west or rebellious south, in the Indian territories and wilderness beyond the horizons of his projected views. National unity had to be maintained against a series of paradoxes, and in this sense the classical forms of antiquity so resistant to innovation, so available for their commemorative sentiments, and so silent in their magnificent appearance were ideal icons masking the chaos of ill-arranged civic duties and misplaced national loyalties. As translated by the architects of America's federal city, antique monuments articulated the language of its civic spaces as free-standing temples sited in vast expanses of space that simulated the breath of the nation.[172]

Apparently the nineteenth century had difficulty reading L'Enfant's city as a rhetorical device, so it was not until the twentieth century that this ritual play of civic pageantry took on a new and inflated appearance. In the early 1900s, it suddenly became a matter of national interest—as well as a reponsibility of wealth and a professional concern for American architects—to embellish the federal city. America had just embarked on its imperial voyage, it had just experienced the first taste of grandeur and power. Aware of its cities' chaotic impression and visual disorder, it desired new settings for civic pomp and national decorum. Besides, the cities of Europe—Vienna, Paris, Berlin, and even Rome—had recently undergone major restructuring as they became the modern capitals of their nations. With the advent of the mass media, and especially film, no capital city dared to stay in the background, but each must seize the center of its public stage with all the representations of power that it could muster. And now the newfangled movies and the camera's traveling eye enabled every nation to export its ceremonial spectacles, carrying them to the far corners of the world where they could impress and inspire. For evidence, we only have to recall the image of Theodore Roosevelt as he marched up San Juan Hill in the Spanish-American War (1898/99), stopping to strike a pose before the moving cameras, or the fact that the British Museum decided in 1897 to collect films of all its recent public events and ceremonies.[173]

In the prenarrative cinema, the early years of experimentation between 1898 and 1903, which coincided with the refurbishing of L'Enfant's designs, movies were used as travelogues and visual newspapers, recording military actions and presidential inaugurations (for example, Theodore Roosevelt's inauguration in 1901/2), parades, street scenes, and "local actualities," recapturing as a moving image the sterotypical places and architectural forms that had already become common sites in postcard views and magazine illustrations. Recreation and all types of leisure-time activities were on the rise in the 1890s, prompting cities to expand their public parks, civic centers, amusement parks, and beer gardens. In this climate, fortified by the legitimation that classical architecture had obtained in the eyes of Americans who viewed the Court of Honour at the Chicago World's Fair, it seemed inevitable that the McMillan Commission would try to amplify the monumental pretensions that the city of Washington offered. And so this scenographic composition of the federal city, heightening the architectonic effect of its monuments and extending its pantheon to include the Lincoln and Jefferson Memorials, became America's way of looking at public space through a mythic enactment of its dramatic foundations that eclipsed L'Enfant's rhetorical devices.

P A R T

Contemporary Forms of the City of Collective Memory

T W O

s e v e n

The Instruments of Memory

Like those birds that lay their eggs only in other species' nest, memory produces in a place that does not belong to it. It receives its form and its implantations from external circumstances, even if it furnishes the content (the missing detail). Its mobilization is inseparable from an alteration. *More than that, memory derives its interventionary force from its very capacity to be altered—unmoored, mobile, lacking any fixed position. Its permanent mark is that it is formed (and forms its "capital") by* arising from the other *(a circumstance) and by* losing it *(it is no more than a memory). There is a double alteration, both of memory, which works when something affects it, and of its object, which is remembered only when it has disappeared. Memory is in decay when it is no longer capable of this alteration. It constructs itself from events that are independent of it, and it is linked to the expectation that something alien to the present will or must occur. Far from*

> *being the reliquary or trash can of the past, it sustains itself by* believing *in the existence of possibilities and by vigilantly awaiting them, constantly on the watch for their appearance.*
>
> MICHEL DE CERTEAU[1]

City Tableaux

If we look across the surface of many cities in the contemporary Western world, we find that a peculiar public place is making an appearance. Essentially a twentieth-century city tableau, this urban scene is a particular kind of aperture focused on the contemporary cityscape. It is not unlike Magritte's painting *In Praise of the Dialectic* (Eloge de la Dialectique), in which we peer through a window on the facade of a house into its interior, where we see the facade of yet another house erected within the enframing one. Magritte traps our view in a double cipher and so does the city tableau: an imaginary redoubling of enclosing and enframed space that disturbs the inside and the outside, the public facade and the private interior, the work of art and the ideal projection. By enfolding a copy of the same facade within the interior, Magritte's painting becomes in addition a displacement of the end and the beginning of representation. A window is a metaphorical device for realistic representation—that is, the perspectival view of empirical reality. Consequently, this irrational juxtaposition of images, which locates a public facade where the viewer expects a domestic interior, comments on the limits of rational thought and the spectator's judgment of reality. What is important is what lies beyond the compositional arrangement, what the painting does not show, and in this sense Magritte's work alludes to the unrolling indeterminacies of current-day cities. Beyond the picture frame, the city remains in chaos; every effort to stabilize its structure seems thwarted where no central authority arises to govern its compositional form. Because the contemporary city appears to be fragmented and decomposed, the only way to overcome this unraveling and indeterminacy is to re-present in the interior of a house, or restage in the aporias of the city's fabric, a centered composition.[2]

The fantastic art of Magritte and the city tableaux of historic preservation and urban design graft the illusionary onto the real, thereby underscoring the theatricality of their imagery. They are a play inserted within a play, or a house within a house, which foreground theatrical conventions and artistic activity. The function of the spectacle, acting through the richness of its forms, is to draw attention to itself as pure art and not as a believable image of the world. Framed by an open window or enclosed within the curtains of a theatrical stage, these scenic views focus on the artistic or architectural process of image construction. "Just putting on a good show," becomes a bracketed moment of time that stands outside narrative coherence, for the spectacle bears little relationship to the overall compositional order, nor does it arrange an easy transition between disparate views.[3] City tableaux are cut-outs, displayed in frontal perspective. They are visual performances that please the admiring eye, for this is the expected and comforting view of the world presented as a theatrical scene. Their lenslike surfaces, however, reflect a projected point of view, an observed order of things. Banishing all that lies beyond their focus, they are instantaneous pictures whose meaning is readily apparent. The tableau is after all a picture that speaks; it knows how to present what it wants to say, it privileges a particular message. As flashbacks that reference traditional cityscapes, this art of delineating views knows how to organize and present its projected ideal.[4]

Originally tableaux vivants were popular eighteenth- and nineteenth-century amusements in which live performers recreated static scenes drawn from famous paintings or sculpture. Viewed through elaborate picture frames, these "living pictures" in color and three-dimensional depth were close enough to the original that spectators were struck with wonder. So it has been claimed, the power of these tableaux lay in their ability to move the spectator to associate the static fragment with an ideal scene drawn from the repertoire of an imaginary theater,

Rene Magritte, Eloge de la Dialectique
(In Praise of the Dialectic) (1936).

and to arouse in the viewer the taste for history and biography, art and literature.[5] Popular as amateur entertainment by the late nineteenth century, manuals were published showing how a parlor could be converted into a suitable stage, how a large picture frame could be constructed, lighting arranged, props, makeup, and costumes composed. As theatrical spectacles, tableaux vivants were generally displayed between acts, after a play, opera, or ballet, and as part of variety shows.[6] The frozen images of these tableaux vivants, as bracketed moments of space and time, were really studied compositions and intentional arrangements copying and imitating art, not reality. It was the tour de force of artistic activity that these inserted scenes displayed.[7] A series of small spatial fragments, set off structurally by theatrical devices such as parting curtains or gilded frames, these tableaux were centered around a single point of view and composed at right angles to the viewer. It was assumed that this frontal vision assured a well-composed, perfectly coherent, and conventional pictorial view, one that conserved and relied on traditional visual conceptions already formed in the past.[8]

In an analogical manner within the historic preserves and some leftover remnants of our cities, the visual imagery of a city's past has been literally reconstituted through the use of old photographs, paintings, lithographs, and former architectural styles, and regulated through design codes and compositional plans. Pictures and traditional architectural arrangements have come to be the standard by which many contemporary cityscapes are judged. Even though the city constructed in reality out of heterogeneous fragments and fortuitous juxtapositions is in fact alien to such formal and orderly scenery, the traditionalist conceives of this regulated re-presentation as an ideal return to the original, claiming that this replication of place is a fantastic duplication and perfect modeling of traditional compositional forms. Albeit in a derivative manner, the nostalgic arts of contemporary architecture and historic preservation have borrowed heavily from the nineteenth-century genre of the tableaux vivant. Presenting a particular cut on or reframing of urban reality, they too are the arts of commercial entertainment and imaginary travel. They as well have confused and even turned upside down the relationship between fine and popular art. As image spectacles, they are scenographic visions relying on an art of verisimilitude and the serial. And they likewise derive from the fate of the public sphere that has been fragmented into the privatized visual environments of mass entertainment. The efforts of contemporary urban design and historic preservation, witnessed in the repetition of historic districts, revitalized waterfronts, recycled monumental structures, restylized public places, rebeautified Main Streets, and gentrified neighborhoods, appearing in almost every major city of the Western world, imply that these gestures capture some popular fantasy. No matter how historically posed and trivialized these efforts may sometimes appear, these historical tableaux have established our perception of what late twentieth-century city space appears to look like. A strange sense of urbanism now invades this city of deconstruction full of inconsistencies, fractures, and voids. Homogenized historic zones protected for their architectural and scenographic value are juxtaposed and played off against areas of superdevelopment, while monumental architectural containers are designed intentionally to turn the urban street inward and internalize their own set of public spaces and services within privatized layers of shops, restaurants, offices, and condominiums. In between and beyond lie the areas of the city left to decay, until the day when they too will be recycled and redesigned for new economic and cultural uses.

A City Promenade

On every city ramble the spectator of today is confronted with a huge parade of city tableaux—blown-up chromolithographs or billboards, skyscraper ready-mades, historic preserves and monumental public places. By emphasizing the pictorial genre of city tableaux, the contemporary arts of city building utilize a standard of perception that reflects a nineteenth-century aesthetic. A gesturing hand reaches out over the twentieth-century era of modernist visual sensibilities to manipulate architectural fragments and city traces for new scenographic effects. These city tableaux become reference points and sites connecting the past to the present, but they are imposed scenes not part of a living memory, and like the popular panoramas of the nineteenth-century, they too are devoid of a host of unsavory and unpleasant visions that their imagery refuses to show. The material forms of a city landscape, once reflecting our pride in the look of a city, have been reduced to mere decoration. Instead they now display a mastery over cultural and architectural expression that subordinates a more spontaneous reaction and covers a wild profusion of unrecovered and jagged remains.[9] In this desire to solidify the traces of the past into a unified image, to restore an intactness that never was, the designer focuses on the context of a landmark or a historic district, thus becoming the architect of theatrical stage sets that have little to say about the memory of place. By borrowing art forms molded in the nineteenth and early twentieth-century, the structure of repetition becomes more important than innovation. The reproductive mold rises above the production of city space: a mold that now incoporates hollowed-out pieces of the city recently deprived of their usefulness and patiently waiting to be filled with contemporary fantasies and wishful projections.

Suppose we say instead that "history" is the weave of difference, the folded-over edge of paper onto which images are traced in another form. Then traces of the past would open on difference. They would be the memory of rejected parts, the supplementary other, the play of citations and allusions. Memories would become fragments reinscribed into other fields and given new meaning according to the constraints of these new contexts. The mark of the past would be only a trace, not a literal re-collection: either a borrowed element graphed onto another context or a condensation point where two incompatible images collide and coalesce. Just as the movie camera destroyed the thrill of the tableau vivant by adding movement to the latter's static frontal perspective and by varying its point of view, so our travels across the contemporary cityscape impose a horizontal linking of a sequence of images, a spatial series of heterogeneous representations and contingent associations that lack any sense of a compositional whole.[10] Michel Foucault suggested that the modern era is exemplified by the archive where books are written to be linked to other books, stored in libraries and museums as collections of incompatible ideas from which only fragments are borrowed. In this indeterminate and undecidable period of time, it is assumed that no metaphors of origins or belief in past covenants guide the present and no subject controls the future or determines the meaning of the past.[11] In a similar manner, we find that displacement reigns in the contemporary city, where we pass from one image to another, shifting focus and meaning, for the very definition of place is composed of fragmented strata and moving layers. In time and place this play of intervals joins or separates disparate images, enabling each spectator to construct his or her own story and form memories of place. Since we have all become wanderers among the vestiges and debris of the city's fabric, it is these scattered images that carry us along a memory walk as either distracted tourists or sympathetic observers.[12] In our accounts of the City of Collective Memory, however, it is the tourist who takes notes, catalogs experiences, follows guidebooks and itineraries, searching for synthetic city tableaux and official narratives; to the contrary, the observer travels through space and time, alternating perspectives, experiencing fragmentations and permutations that may never coalesce into a coherent view.

Perhaps the real trouble lies not with the spectator's mode of observation, but with the conventional quest for representational meanings, hidden truths, underlying messages, grammatical or psychological deep structures that plunge the viewer vertically into the depths of historic urban form, its monuments and memories, in order to return with archetypal forms, normative values, and overriding goals. If we give up this representational quest and move into the realm of poetics, we might begin to examine the figural forms of this deconstructed city. There seems to have occurred a slippage of grids superimposed one upon another, a proliferation of mirrorings and a horizontal blurring of effects, so that here images begin to work at the crossroads of others. The troubled phrase "the presence of the past" tends instead to draw our attention to the contextual and linear relations of new architectural forms as they relate to past urban images, rather than stressing the differences, the rupture between then and now, here and there, and the memory of things and events that have never and can never reoccur in the present. Instead figural forms involve the spectator in the open possibility of displacement and difference. Applied to the contemporary city of deconstructed images, the viewer finds that the citation of past fragments may take place in an infinity of new contexts. Released from the control of an overriding and controlling order, the viewer becomes involved in what has been called the "lateral dance" of interpretation. Searching to retrieve the trace of past events, the spectator simultaneously deconstructs by calling into play a chain of substitutions and displacements.[13]

Because there are only traces of the past to grasp—some old photographs, a few drawings, the residue gathered from diaries and newspaper accounts, familar stories told and repeated—memories are always fragmented, uncertain, even contradictory. Because the past returns in this piecemeal and imaginary form, the problem is necessarily one of reconstruction. We can in our cities continue to puncture holes in their fabric, windows that look back to the past. In these focused and centered apertures we can simulate the art of travel in space and time though architectural compositions and historic preservation. But something will be missing, something closed off, something left out of focus as it has been in every city tableau and in all the arts of verisimilitude. On the contrary, walking through the city of deconstructed images, we are no longer offered a synthetic order that we can readily grasp, nor a reconstruction of a history we can collectively assume. Our sense of an urban totality has been fractured long ago. Thus our personal memories of places visited actually arise from a horizontal juxtaposition of different images, not one of synthetic wholes. They are the memory of rejected parts, the supplementary other, the oscillating play of citations and allusions. It is these forms that must be used to give new meaning to the contemporary city by literally reading concrete images in new ways, tracing them back to their origins as city tableaux, drawing out their associations and projected ideals, and constructing our own story line as we travel from picture to picture. We must learn how to mark with our own desires this visual order already manipulated by stereotypical forms and handed down ceremoniously for our passive consumption. The triumphal coherence of city tableaux act on the other hand like fantastic shop windows lining the streets of the contemporary

Robert Mango, Return to the City *(1985).*

city. As stage sets for other illusions, they dramatically direct our acts of consumption and our territorial explorations. We need to reappropriate these city images and spaces, to create a layered personal record of travels and explorations that can puncture these scenographic compositions of place and transform these spectacles of might.[14]

National Heritage

Because most city spectators prefer the safety of representational order, they cannot tolerate for long open-ended site plans and abstract symbol systems, the disjunctive view and the chaotic disarray of city spaces. Consequently certain pockets of the city have been preserved intact or redesigned intentionally as narrative tableaux utilizing imaginary architectures and historical allusions. Yet viewing history as a series of narrative representations necessarily implies that "history" will be rewritten and realligned for specific concerns. "To write history [Walter Benjamin said] therefore means to quote history. But the concept of quotation implies that any given historical object must be ripped out of its context."[15] So Benjamin warned: we should always be aware that "history" is in need of redemption from a conformism that is about to overpower it in order to erase its differences and turn it into an accepted narration. Historical phenomena portrayed as "heritage" are cultural treasures of art carried by the authorities in every triumphal march, and these treasures reek of omissions and suppressions.

Since a return to history most often occurs in moments of crisis, it is not surprising to find that city tableaux repeat visual ideals and normative views conservatively sanctioned by public authorities, who attempt in this manner to regain a centered world or a concrete system on which moral, political, or social foundations can stand. When England, for example, first established an official King's Antiquary in 1533, this was the same year that Henry VIII declared himself to be head of the Church of England. Surveying the antiquities of England was consequently a political strategy intended to secularize and localize that heritage and thus gain popular support and legitimation for the Crown's usurpation of religious authority.[16] In France, a slightly different effort was begun in 1794 by the abbé Gregoire, who called for the preservation of monuments as national treasures capable of teaching and morally elevating the people but endangered by vandals and revolutionaries all too eager to destroy and deform the booty of war. When Louis Philippe took over the throne in 1830, he too saw the preservation of French antiquities as a way to stabilize and legitimate his regime and thus established a Commission of Historic Monuments.[17] And in Germany as well, an early preservation decree had nationalistic intent: Ludwig I of Hesse proclaimed in 1818 that "The surviving monuments of architecture are among the most important and interesting evidence of history, in that from them may be inferred the former customs, culture, and civil conditions of the nation, and therefore their preservation is greatly to be wished."[18]

During the nineteenth century, however, a separate view of antiquities developed, for suddenly they became symbolic of a dying past that should be recorded and cataloged. As industrialization progressed, a romantic interest in vernacular artifacts, pastoral folklore, and oral traditions arose. These tokens from a nation's childhood and origin were seen from a position of superior development and were intended to enhance and bolster the mature and rational evolution of the bourgeois and bureaucratic state.[19] The movement to preserve monuments and artifacts as national heritage, as well as the search for "medieval" and ancient models on which the art of city building could be based, were related symbolically to the spiritual strength and collective identity new nations garnered from romantic and picturesque images drawn from their "golden age."[20] At the same time, the movement to preserve a nation's "heritage" involved transformations within the public sphere—that is, the arena in which private individuals during the nineteenth century attempted to subordinate public authority to their own interests by fictiously creating an impression of public unity and collective will. The concept of "national heritage" that stems from that period assumes an imaginary good citizen without gender, race, class, or regional identification who acknowledges the representations of a nation's past as they are presented but has no involvement or say in how they are constructed or handed down by authority.[21]

By the mid-nineteenth century it was obvious that industrialization was ransacking the physical environment, disrupting traditional settings and architectural views and causing the visual beauty of landscapes and cityscapes to vanish with alarming speed. Consequently certain elements of a nation's architectural and environmental heritage were granted public status because they belonged to its collective past and cultural heritage. In England, the Ancient Monuments Protection Act of 1882 placed sixty-eight monuments of national interest (i.e., prehistoric ruins and earthworks) under the protection of the state. In 1898 London County Council was given the power to purchase buildings and places of historic or architectural interest. They also paid for the publication of the Survey of London by the architect C. R. Ashbee, and began as well their own protective listing of buildings.[22] With the advent of modern architecture, new building materials, the automobile, functional zoning, and rational city plans in the twentieth century, the pace of disfigurement accelerated. Attempts to preserve monuments and historic landscapes because they belonged to a nation's patrimony increased in number. Slowly the concept arose that particular historic views and cityscapes, even though private property, might be preserved for public display and regulated by public authority if the latter were contained within well-defined limits.[23] In England, however, even though Parliament continued until 1947 to discuss the possibility of listing inhabited buildings and historic properties of less than monumental worth and protecting these from wanton destruction, nevertheless the answer was always a conservative upholding of individual property rights. By 1932 local authorities could halt demolition of noteworthy structures by imposing a "building preservation order," but if the owner contested and the order was not upheld by the courts, compensation had to be paid by the government. The fear of having to pay retroactively for their preservation order meant that this power of preservation to halt demolition was rarely invoked. Consequently the Town and Country Planning Act of 1947 proposed that properties be surveyed throughout England and a list of historic structures (i.e., older than the cut-off date of 1840) be composed. This would enable local authorities to halt the demolition of listed properties with some sense of security.[24]

The preservation process in France took a more radical approach starting in 1835, when the Commission of Historical Monuments began to list and to protect worthy monuments. Yet under the pressure of property owners and local authorities any structure impeding urban development could be quickly erased from the list. It was only in 1913 that the visual setting, a tightly defined perimeter of 500 meters around a classified monument, was allowed protection. And in 1930, groups of buildings and adjoining structures of historical, artistic, picturesque, or scientific importance were added to a list or "inventory of sites."[25] Because preservation attempts in Italy stemmed from the enabling Lex Pacca of 1819, a law that protected archeological artifacts, consequently only urban monuments of universal value, outstanding archeological or artistic specimens, were preserved; everything else being merely a barrier to development and progress. And so it remained until after World War II.[26] And similarly in Greece, the law protected only antiquities and archeological sites, isolated churches, and listed buildings erected before the founding of modern Greece in 1830, and a few traditional settlements of exceptional beauty.[27] In general, throughout Europe by the end of the nineteenth century monuments of outstanding architectural merit were protected by legislation, but the line separating the preservation of monumental artifacts from the restoration of more mundane and colloquial expressions, the architectural or vernacular context in which a monument might sit, was a barrier that few restorers would cross. The Belgian Louis Cloquet seems to have set the formula for preservation work throughout most of the twentieth century when in 1893 he divided monuments into two categories: dead monuments, the documents of history such as pyramids, temples, and ruins that should not be touched, but only preserved; and living monuments, to which architects were given freer rein to restore.[28]

Preservation of the context or ensemble of buildings that support a single monument, or deliberations over the visual relationship that should exist between a monument and its site—these considerations were developing elsewhere outside of the movement for historic preservation. No doubt the Eiffel Tower, certainly the symbol of a modern visual sensibility, is also emblematic of the rise of architectural contextualism. The group of artists protesting its erection in 1887 decried:

> Writers, painters, sculptors, architects, passionate lovers of the heretofore intact beauty of Paris, we come to protest with all our strength, with all our indignation, in the name of betrayed French taste, in the name of threatened French art and history, against the erection in the heart of our capital of the useless and monstrous Eiffel Tower, ...[29]

And two years later, the Viennese city planner Camillo Sitte in *Der Städtebau* (1889) would advocate and clarify the visual harmony that should exist between a monument and its contextual environment. For Sitte, the spread of the modern metropolis, its gigantic size, wider streets, and open vistas had spoiled the traditional framework of the city and destroyed its artistic form. The modern city simply repeated identical and standardized forms, which dulled the spectator's senses.[30] What counted most was how the spectator was located and positioned in public space and the direction in which the architectural forms oriented his or her vision, because the civic tableau should be an art of pure visual and spatial arrangement.[31] Sitte believed that irregularly shaped, moderately sized, and enclosed plazas could act like "islands in the endless sea of buildings" and provide spatial unity across the repetitious patterns the modern city produced. This unity could even be enhanced by cleverly overlapping these containers and creating undulating patterns out of these spaces so that a spectator's visual impression was constantly varied.[32] Traditional architectural forms and colors, greenery and nature, perspective vistas and natural panoramas, the rhythmic relationship of solids to voids, picturesque and curvilinear meanderings, all these became the dramatic elements out of which Sitte proposed his urban stage sets.[33] His work fell among sympathetic friends, for many European architects in their annual meetings were already discussing by 1900 the correct procedures to accept in preserving historic monuments as well as the principles of place and traditional models to follow for new urban development.[34]

Sitte's emphasis on the theatrical nature of public space was a strategic move intended to block the modern sensibility of his Viennese colleague Otto Wagner, who proposed instead that modern city expansion should not be restricted. Unlimited growth could be achieved, he argued, if cellular neighborhood plans were located on an open-ended grid of streets that could be extended indefinitely in all directions. The modern individual praised the city for its anonymity and monumentality because the modern eye, Wagner claimed, found solace in long and unimpeded lines, large open spaces and great masses, and the serial repetition of forms and surfaces.[35] Perhaps then it is only the inevitable recyclings of aesthetic taste swinging back and forth between abstract city plans and traditional cityscapes that found architects and city planners once again after World War II, as they had in the 1900s, reconsidering the artistic relationships among a medley of buildings and savoring the visual pleasure collective space yielded, yet which no one architectural structure alone could provide. City streets, covered passageways, terraces, the promenades and places of exchange, *rond points*, squares, and all the arts of city building that Sitte had advocated were called on once more to heal the fragmented city that modernism had created, in a renewed attempt to rebuild an organic and humane city through a series of satisfying visual arrangements.[36]

Damaged by the bombs of World War II and inviscerated by the bulldozers of renovation, the centers of cities in the 1950s and 1960s seemd just as endangered as ruins and antiquities had been in the nineteenth century. And so it evolved that traditional city centers began to be looked upon as complex monuments that needed protection. In 1962, with the passage of the Malraux Law in France and the creation of a master plan for Rome, the carefully defined archeological and fine arts view of national heritage gave way to a new aesthetic involved in protecting from large-scale renewal and redevelopment the everyday habitats of historic districts and the architectural collages of city streets. The concept of monument was redefined and juxtaposed against the contextual appearance of a "historic district."

No longer to be considered as an isolated structure, a monument was now seen as part of a historic milieu that was often older than the monument itself. The fabric of a historic city was liken to a palimpsest or a layered series of writings and rewritings in which every element lent support to the whole; eradicate part of this ambience or *tout ensemble* and the meaning of the monument was lost as well. It soon became popular to undertake structural analyses of historic building typologies and urban morphologies, as well as surveying, classifying, and listing the building stock in large areas of the city. Suddenly it seemed, as other countries followed France's and Italy's direction, that the entire architectural heritage of Europe would be preserved as outdoor museums. But progress was slow. The Malraux Law, for example, placed architects in charge of the development of preservation plans and they naturally gave conservation and archeological projects priority. Consequently, fifteen years later only sixty historic districts had been created throughout France and only four of these had approved preservation plans. It was generally feared that if the restoration work on one block of a historic center was approved and financed by the central government, then that would be sufficient to convince the local administrators that the entire town should be preserved. Hence historicized zones of luxury development would soon turn towns into frozen museums: such already had been the case in the small town of Sarlat in the Périgord; in Uzes in the south of France, and even in Chartres, Périgueux, Pegenas, and Besançon. As the restoration of monuments was no longer seen as an issue that could be separated from the complex problems of urban development, nor from the living fabric of cities, consequently the job of safeguarding the patrimony of France was transferred to the ministries charged with the problems of "urbanism."[37]

It also became apparent that most European historic centers had lost to their peripheries at least 30 percent and sometimes as much as 90 percent of their residential population, especially expelling their lower-income groups. So a concept of "deep social conservation" arose in order to ensure, if public monies were involved, that buildings in the historic center of cities be restored for the working class, that rents be controlled and services and amenities updated and modernized.[38] In England, the Civic Amenities Act of 1967 created conservation areas of special architectural character and merit—this being the first time for that country that "place" and "townscape" were offered protection.[39] The concept of "historic" was widely extended as well and the entire country resurveyed because preservation interest now had been expressed for Victorian architecture, historic towns, and the hybrid architecture of inner cities. By the 1980s, "historic" even included architecture between the wars and some fine examples from the 1950s. In England as well as Europe in general, the intent behind preservation was not only to protect the townscape and character of historic cities, but to increase the housing stock close to the centers of employment. By allocating "a central activities zone" for nonresidential uses important to the vitality of the city such as headquarter offices, entertainment, and tourist facilities, and "an outside the central activities zone" for residential and compatible uses, London, for example, attempted to preserve not only its architectural patrimony but the residential character of its historic center as well.

Instrumental Memory and American Cities

Whereas the European process of safeguarding its architectural heritage tended to cross over and to join the path of city planning, the American development of preservation planning remained in its infancy, often held hostage by private property and development rights. Preservation activity, supported and implemented through regulatory controls, tax incentives, and city plans was a relatively new field for public policy in American cities during the 1970s and 1980s. Because its roots were grounded in diverse backgrounds, the process of American preservation appeared to have an ad hoc nature, often its procedures were enveloped in vagueness, and many times its advocates expressed contradictory concerns. The architect, the historian, the real estate entrepreneur, the conservator, the planner, and the community resident all held separate, even conflicting expectations of preservation programs. Their implicit desires, which penetrated the process, gave preservation activity a special randomness and complexity. As America is the land of diversity, the standards that different places or people used for saving a building or a historic district varied from state to state and city to city, in turn reflecting different architectural, economic, social, and cultural values, representing individual analyses of the historical past, and using separate instrumental measures to recapture this past. Moreover, the public powers that can be used to protect private property (i.e., the police power, the power of taxation, and the power of eminent domain) reside in the state and hence add to the complexity. Even though each of the fifty states would agree that the preservation of great architectural monuments and historic places is an essential ingredient to the quality of life in the contemporary city, still the relationship between "history" and its instrumental use has often been questioned.

In spite of the fact that both historic preservation and city planning in America originally descend from the profession of architecture, during the twentieth century sustained communication with their architectural base has been broken. The supporters of preservation, abetted by private interest groups, have become the staunchest protectors of American architectural heritage, while planners have drifted away from involvement with the physical form of the city and have fragmented into diverse specializations and abstract policy formulations. Left alone, architects often rise and fall on the basis of pure design and high style. Three points of a triangle under tension—the preservation purists, the abstract policy planner, and the architectural artist—mean that most American cities lack any professional or institutional arrangement to mediate between these extremes. Consequently there is often no entry point into the planning process of historic preservation, of real estate development, of neighborhood conservation, of architectural design, or of tourism and educational policy until after the fact, until after different interests and values have finally broken out into political dispute. But the roots of this American inheritance that pits historic preservation against the rights of private property takes us back into the nineteenth century.

America in that century was a young country not weighed down by the past. It seemed intent to settle and to improve without restraint the vast expanse of land that stretched westward to the Pacific. Anything that inhibited the free exchange of private property, its acquisition, enhancement, and subsequent resale at market value would as well hinder the country's development. In consequence there was little public interest in protecting historic properties from demolition or from renovations that might destroy their integrity: whatever stood in the path of progress could simply be wiped away. Many private citizens, however, thought that some Americans were rather uncouth and uneducated and could benefit from the wise example of the country's founding fathers: filio-piety, it was felt, was not without its virtues of patriotism, morality, and restraint. Thus the historic value of buildings associated with the founding fathers was sporadically expressed and attempts were made to restore some fine examples. In Philadelphia, the architect William Strickland was involved with restoring parts of Independence Hall and rescuing it from neglect in 1816 and 1824, while John Haviland developed a complete restoration plan for the entire structure in 1828. Even the Capitol building in Washington was recognized by 1850 for its associative value, and an architectural competition was held for its completion.[40] But most preservation efforts were sponsored by citizen groups such as the Mount Vernon Ladies' Association of the Union, with Ann Pamela Cunningham at its head, which set about in 1853 to buy and to preserve the endangered home of George Washington and turn Mount Vernon into a national shrine. Even this worthy project was debated, however, for there were others who felt there was nothing sacred or important about Mount Vernon's architectural form. The editor of *Sloan's Architectural Review and Builder's Guide,* for example, visited the house in 1856 and found it in a deplorable state of decay caused not only by neglect but by too many tourists. Hence he suggested that it would be far better to tear the wreck down and erect in its place a new building out of modern materials to house its excellent interiors.[41]

The Civil War, however, proved to be a watershed for historic preservation efforts in America. After so many years of contention, Americans began to seek solace in their country's past, nostalgically desiring a golden age when life was simple and pure. Suddenly "Colonial America" took on a new meaning: it was the perfect refuge for all sorts of ills—from sectional devisiveness, material acquisitiveness, and political corruption; from industrialization, commercialization, and urbanization.[42] In 1864 America, or so art historians have claimed, had no antecedent art, no abbeys in picturesque ruins, no aristocratic mansions, no ancestral homes providing a narrated picture about the past.[43] It was a country too new to have found a path to monumental architectural expression, and the simply hewed and truthful New England architecture was taken to be its only admirable form. Typified by a wide hearth, broad beams, and a spinning wheel, this mythological colonial structure seemed to represent the only true American architecture and it was expected that through its forms the spectator might learn the values of a simple home life that his or her "ancestors" had shared. The pure form of colonial architecture located around a quiet New England village green was the perfect townscape to juxtapose against the raw open landscapes and economic crassness of American urban development. No one seemed worried about authenticating America's "Puritan" heritage nor developing a historically accurate colonial image, instead the Colonial Revival, at least in its architectural expression, represented a return to order and restraint, and was a model of good breeding and refinement. In time, it would even allow for the expression of more monumental and pretentious forms that underlay its simple appearance.

Thus when the country turned to celebrate the centennial of its independence, not surprisingly there arose a nostalgic cry for all things colonial. The old-fashioned New England pavilions erected at the Philadelphia Centennial Exhibition of 1876 by Connecticut and Massachusetts were among the most popular displays. A craze for ancestor worship was heard around the nation. Not only was there a good deal of invention of fictitious relatives in brave attempts to shore up one's social status and secure one's position, but it became a patriotic expression to restore colonial buildings or to build new ones in a Colonial Revival style. The old New England town on the hill with its white clapboard houses and stately elm trees was a symbolic refuge from an uncertain future that promised more urbanization, industrialization, and immigration. Stereotypical images completely restored Stockbridge and Deerfield, Massachusetts, and Old Lyme and Litchfield, Connecticut. These villages became by the early 1900s the visual icons perpetuating the myth of the New England colonial town. Village improvement societies, which sprung up in the 1880s and maintained a vigilant status until World War I, would see to the restoration of other towns by planting rows of elm trees, conjuring up new kinds of colonial gardens, and reconstructing ideal village greens; by repainting everything, including polychromed Victorian structures, in a mythical colonial appearance that dictated white clapboard houses with black or green shutters; and generally by transforming or veiling anything that smacked of industrialization or modernization (e.g., a railroad depot or up-to-date shopfronts).[44]

The dramatic influx of the automobile plus an uncontrollable real estate boom in the 1920s brought a new realization to the preservation movement. From this time forward the unregulated manipulation of the historic centers of American cities was a thing of the past. The first city to take such a stance was Charleston, South Carolina, in 1931.[45] Commercial development pressure on the old Battery district brought numerous requests for permits to build parking lots and gas stations, while scavangers began to destroy the interiors of many of the old houses for their paneling, ironwork, and fireplaces. Protective measures for this historic center were subsequently embedded within a new citywide zoning ordinance. For the first time in America a historic zone of a city, under threat of existence from development pressure, was secured behind the fortified boundary lines of a historic district, regulated by design guidelines that required that all exterior alterations on structures erected before 1860 conform with the general architectural "style" of early Charleston, and protected by a Board of Architectural Review empowered to issue certificates of appropriateness for approved alterations and additions. This innovative use of historic area zoning gingerly transferred control over the architectural wall or the streetscape from the private to the public domain. The characteristic qualities of this historic place were felt to be condensed in the traditional pattern of architectural motifs such as doors, windows, building heights, and roof pitches, and the protection of the district's architectural facades was accepted as part of a city's heritage as well belonging to its collective memory.

From these initial assumptions, however, historic area zoning tested the concept of public control that both regulated private property for purely aesthetic reasons and forced new architectural designs to be consistent with specified historic standards. By singling out a specific area of the city to be preserved as a historic district, moreover, these regulations could in effect be seen as an attempt to stop development pressure by protecting only certain properties and thus could be an unfair taking of private development rights. In addition there was trouble in trying to squeeze preservation concerns onto traditional zoning controls, for the latter was originally created as a mechanism to guide the future development of land. Its projected goal was the city in twenty years or more, and thus it laid out large enough commercial, residential, and industrial zones, often on undeveloped land, to accommodate and channel this estimated growth. Thus historic area zoning by piggybacking on top of a prodevelopment ordinance led to a wealth of confusion.

Out of the problems of aesthetic controls and zoning regulations a separate movement developed to establish historic districts and landmarks based on state enabling legislation authorizing towns and cities to create preservation ordinances. The first city to use this route to preservation was New Orleans in 1937, creating the Vieux Carré Historic District through a Louisiana constitutional amendment. Nevertheless, public control over private property—even if deemed historically valuable—was still controversial and owners of property in the Vieux Carré brought suit. By upholding these regulations, however, the courts eventually described and expanded the legitimate terrain for historic or aesthetic control over private property.[46] Regulations were first legally extended to cover exterior architectural features, even if these were hidden from public view. Consequently inner courtyards, the backsides of structures and rooftops—the three-dimensional and morphological form of the Vieux Carré—were protected from change. Next came a battle over advertising on both modern and historic structures in the district,

Cartoon on the process of "Urban Renovation" by J. F. Batellier, illustrator (1979).

which the preservation commission eventually won. By giving the commission control over the visual appearance of the Vieux Carré, the importance of "streetscape" already outlined in Charleston was now extended to the *tout ensemble*, and consequently the distinct ambience created by the spirit of place or genius loci came under regulatory control. While the constitutionality of the entire ordinance based on aesthetic provisions was eventually upheld, the courts took a sidestep around this sensitive issue, showing that other than aesthetic values were at the heart of preservation activity, that the spirit of place enhanced tourism, protected property values, and supported the urban economy.

Because historic preservation activity represents a movement away from a strict concept of private property and a step toward the public ownership of some rights of development and uses of land, many preservation efforts in the 1960s began to experiment with historic easements.[47] In spite of these gentler attempts to avoid the onerous invasion of preservation controls into the territory protecting sacred property rights, a new alliance was formed in the 1960s. Preservation groups across the nation were outraged when they became aware that one half of the 12,000 structures recorded on the Historic American Building Survey (HABS) had been demolished, many of them through federally financed urban renewal projects in the 1950s and 1960s. Social and architectural critics such as Jane Jacobs and Ada Louise Huxtable became identified with the protest. So did real estate developers and bankers in areas where it was realized that historic preservation activity paid for itself by increasing tourism and by attracting new investment money into the purchase, restoration, and reselling of old and historic properties.

In spite of this new coalition calling for public and private ventures to preserve the architectural heritage of American inner cities in the 1960s and 1970s, nevertheless it was only with reluctance that the federal government joined the preservation game. Federal legislation had extended limited protection to historic properties that the government owned, venturing into the preservation arena with the acquisition of the Gettysburg battlefield in 1895. Under the Antiquities Act of 1906 certain historic landmarks and prehistoric structures were placed under federal ownership and controlled as "national monuments." And no doubt swayed by the important role that "heritage" played in establishing a sense of continuity between the past and the future, Congress during the Depression authorized the secretary of the interior in 1935 to make a survey of historic and archeological sites and to acquire, restore, and maintain them. But these restrictions did little to protect privately owned historic properties or to restrain the federal government from demolishing such properties in their own urban renewal and redevelopment plans. It was decades later that Congress finally declared ". . . that the historical and cultural foundations of the Nation should be preserved as a living part of our community life and development in order to give a sense of orientation to the American people" and so passed into legislation the National Historic Preservation Act of 1966.[48] This act required the secretary of the interior to maintain an expanded National Register of Historic Places and it offered grants-in-aid to the National Trust for Historic Preservation (federally chartered in 1949) and to states for the preservation of their historic properties. Most important, however, many states used these grants to survey their own historic properties, producing long lists of nominations for the National Register.[49]

One of the earliest cities to initiate new public-private ventures in historic preservation and neighborhood revitalization was Philadelphia, and its fantastic success in turning a decayed and forlorn slum area into a new luxury residential enclave would influence subsequent redevelopment policies in other American cities. Beginning to account for its historic past as early as the 1920s, Frances A. Wister as president of the Civic Club of Philadelphia promoted the "Philadelphia Survey," hoping in this manner to guide rehabilitation work into greater architectural harmony with the city's traditional forms. The study of "Old City" near the Delaware River, with measured drawings of some 407 structures, was completed in 1931 by the Philadelphia chapter of the American Institute of Architects.[50] By 1941, however, historic preservation had been pushed to the background as city fathers, looking ahead to postwar reconstruction, began to fear that unless Philadelphia developed a comprehensive city plan it would lose its share of federal redevelopment money. Already in 1938, Washington had rejected Philadelphia's request for $59 million in water and sewer improvement funds because the city had failed to develop a systematic account of how and where and on what it would spend the appropriation. A free-floating group of interested citizens formed a "City Policy Committee" to pressure for needed reforms. In response the mayor appointed a Joint Committee on City Planning, and this group in turn proposed the development of a nine-member Planning Commission. Passed into law, the Planning Commission was established and funded in 1943 along with an unofficial Citizens' Council on City Planning. Philadelphia had put into place a curious mixture of public and private organizations that over the next several decades would guide urban renewal and neighborhood redevelopment in line with the policies of historic preservation, inner city gentrification, and tourist and market development.[51]

The commission's agenda for 1944 was to modernize downtown Philadelphia by making it accessible to the automobile. Not suprisingly, there were proposals to construct off-street and underground parking facilities, to build new bridges over the Schuylkill River and new approaches to the Delaware River Bridge, to construct an elevated highway along the Delaware (thus forming a loop around the center city), and to demolish the Chinese Wall, the great viaduct that brought the Pennsylvania railroad tracks from the Schuylkill River straight down to 15th Street and the old Broad Street Station. But Philadelphia had other problems as well: its center city residential property values were rapidly declining, its banks were disinvesting in properties, its manufacturing base was faltering, and its wealthy population was disappearing into the suburbs. By 1948 nine inner-city areas were certified for redevelopment. Consequently it was proposed that in these areas the city acquire through eminent domain the so-called worn-out structures as well as badly planned areas of land and then clear and prepare them for rebuilding or redevelopment. Among the nine districts first selected were the Historic Independence Hall District in the Old City and the Triangle between the Parkway and Market Street where the Chinese Wall was located.[52]

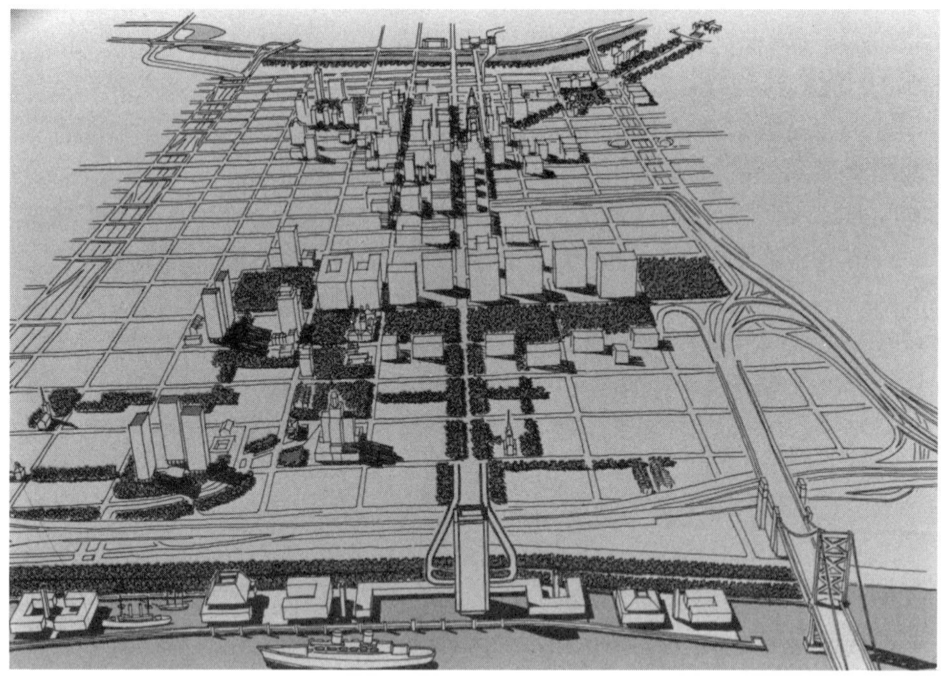

Edmund N. Bacon, Philadelphia Greenways Plan.

Of course Philadelphia was the preeminent colonial city and it had taken great pains to retain its architectural heritage. Consequently redevelopment would be planned step by step with historic preservation. In 1944, the Fairmount Park Art Association had proposed, with the aid of architect Roy F. Larson, that a formal setting be arranged for Independence Hall. This would be the "first major surgical operation" in downtown Philadelphia since 1909, when the Benjamin Franklin Parkway was cut diagonally through unseemly "slums," thus exposing a magnificent view from City Hall to the Art Museum. "History," it was argued, now would take its place beside the modern needs of automobiles. Thus the park was seen not only as an appropriate foreground for Philadelphia's historic shrine, but as a practical link with the proposed downtown highway loop and a graceful transition from an automobile to a pedestrian scale. Larson suggested as well that an eastward park be created, linking three other important historic structures and removing from that three-block area all non-historic and non-noteworthy structures. Not leaving things to fate, the Citizens' Council in 1947 organized an exhibition on "Better Philadelphia" that showed the public what Independence Hall would look like if the surrounding blocks of dilapidated and worn-out structures, factories and warehouses from the late nineteenth century, were swept away and a grand L-shaped park was created instead. This park would lead to a reconstructed waterfront and marina across a great swath of restored historic and colonial homes called Society Hill, an area lying between Front and Eight Streets, Walnut and Pine.[53] In 1947 the city planner Edmund Bacon proposed a series of greenways—really inner-block parks and footpaths centering on and connecting the various historic structures scattered about the venerable but blighted Society Hill. Not taken seriously for another ten years, this Greenway Plan was eventually expanded by Vincent Kling, Roy Larson, and Oskar Stonoror, who enlarged the zone until it extended from the Delaware riverfront to Broad Street along the Market Street axis. Although it took until the mid-1960s to complete the entire Society Hill—Washington Square Redevelopment plan, from its very inception this greenway system became the design framework for the entire center city's revitalization.

I. M. Pei, the winner of an important 1958 architectural competition, designed three skyscraper apartment towers near the southeastern edge of Society Hill and another two towers near Washington Square. These towers were intended to bind a perceptual sequence of views as well as visually terminate the greenway paths and serve as visual linkages between the pedestrian and automobile systems.[54] It had become obvious to the reform coalition as early as 1956 that private capital must become involved if the revitalization of historic Philadelphia was to be a success, and that meant attracting middle- and upper-income residents and jobs back to the center of the city. Consequently an Old Philadelphia Development Corporation was formed, with representatives drawn from the large downtown banks, insurance companies, and corporations to spur the private rehabilitation of hundreds of old houses in "America's Most Historic Area." They contracted with the Redevelopment Authority, which held the power of eminent domain, to condemn slum properties in the urban renewal area, to rehabilitate them, and to fill in some vacant lots with contextually pleasing development. Previous residents could remain in the area if they were able to buy their condemned homes back from the Authority and if they agreed to and could afford to implement the Authority's imposed rehabilitation timetables, authentically "historic" rehabilitation standards, and maintenance requirements. After much hesitation, because it feared that I. M. Pei's residential towers would be isolated outposts on a frontier of delapidated housing far away from other luxury development, the Federal Housing Administration decided to release the funds for their construction. But the reform team was more optimistic, and slowly a plan for the entire revitalization of Society Hill as a luxury residential enclave and the first step in a comprehensive policy to revamp the center city of Philadelphia fell into place.[55]

There were attempts in other cities to revitalize neighborhoods for low-income residents by inserting historic preservation step-by-step into the process of community revitalization. Dating back to 1968, The Pittsburgh History and Landmarks Foundation, headed by Arthur Ziegler, began to focus attention on two clusters of historic homes on its industrial Central North Side, the Manchester district and the Mexican War Streets. Although the area was considered to be a "slum" with declining residential population and a deteriorating housing stock, and consequently threatened with wholesale demolition or industrial expansion, nevertheless the Pittsburgh Foundation began surveying the architectural and socioeconomic characteristics of Manchester, a section gridded with streets in 1832 and developed with late Victorian middle-class homes between 1880 and 1890. And preservation work was also begun on the homes along the Mexican War Streets, an area developed between the 1840s and 1880s. Still the question remained of how to relate historic preservation to urban renewal and how to change the latter's bulldozer mentality to one of community rehabilitation. By the late 1960s, the foundation decided to create the Neighborhood Housing Service Inc. Backed by money from private foundations, the Neighborhood Housing Service set up a low-interest revolving fund for rehabilitation work, and within six years had funded 300 high-risk loans to neighborhood homeowners. Acting as a developer as well, the foundation bought historically noteworthy structures in the area, rehabilitated them, and either rented these apartments at subsidized rentals or put the rehabilitated properties up for resale. In cooperation with the Urban Renewal Authority, the foundation also embarked on a facade easement program and interior rehabilitation efforts. Although Manchester was placed on the National Register in 1975, nevertheless nearly 300 out of the 1,000 residential properties remained abandoned in the late 1970s, with 60 percent of its population elderly residents renting, not owning, their apartments. Thus an attempt was made to advertise the neighborhood and to draw new investment money and the middle class into the preservation game. In addition, private developers began to construct suburban-type single-family homes in the area, hoping that this might be an appropriate catalyst.[56]

In 1972 the Federal Home Loan Bank Board decided to use the Pittsburgh program as a model, establishing Neighborhood Housing Services in other cities such as the Madisonville area of Cincinnati, Southeast Baltimore, and Inman Park in Atlanta. The neighborhoods they targeted for attention generally contained sound housing with early signs of deterioration and faltering maintenance, and although more than 50 percent of the homes were owner-occupied, still these were areas where mortgage and home improvement loans were difficult to obtain. In addition, the areas selected had to be large enough to excite the imagination of future investors, yet small enough so that results would be highly visible. It was assumed that inner-city neighborhoods experienced a "natural life cycle," and that deterioration and downgrading were both inevitable without public or private intervention. As the economic base of these neighborhoods eroded, so the argument went, both property values and return on investment declined and homeownership and rental demands decreased. Consequently lending institutions found these neighborhoods too risky to invest in and began to withdraw their capital. But a self-help effort drawing on the commitment of local citizens, financial institutions, plus the city government, could stem a neighborhood's natural decline. For example, a most dramatic turnaround from slum to historic district took place in Inman Park, Atlanta, between 1969 and 1976. Once an upper-income garden suburb developed in the late 1880s and connected to the center of the city by a streetcar line, this neighborhood had become a slum by the 1950s. In 1970 Inman Park Restoration Inc. was established to help promote neighborhood conservation by homebuyer-renovators. A consortium of banks, savings-and-loan associations, the Central Atlanta Progress Committee, and the National Mortgage Association decided in 1975 to pledge $62.5 million to the area by 1980. One year later 75 percent of the 311 structures were undergoing or had undergone rehabilitation, while property values had soared from a low in 1969 of $20,000–$50,000 to a range of $75,000–$150,000. Placed on the National Register of Historic Places in 1973, Inman Park became Atlanta's first historic district, but it also witnessed the displacement of lower-income and semiskilled residents by white urban professionals.[57]

It appears that 1969/1970 marked the beginning in many large American cities of private market rehabilitation that drew middle-class homeowners back to the city. Fueled by cutbacks in new housing expenditures after 1972, the movement to upgrade inner-city housing had caught fire by the mid-1970s.[58] Undertaking a survey of 260 central cities with population greater than 500,000, the Urban Land

Institute found that some privately sponsored residential rehabilitation work was occurring by 1976 in at least three-quarters of these cities. The residential rehabilitation game would soon become a multi-billion-dollar industry.[59] But displacement of the elderly, of poorer long-time residents, of local services and stores would inevitably be the result, although at first no one seemed clear about just what the extent might be or impact it might have. The same year, The National Urban Coalition decided to study forty-four cities that had significant amounts of renovation and historic preservation occurring in tandem.[60] Finding that renovation activity was widespread but varied, the coalition surmised that historic district designation was a crucial drawing point for private reinvestment, most of which climbed to significant levels only in the mid-1970s. Of the nine Atlanta inner-city neighborhoods undergoing renovation, for example, five were historic districts; Denver had five renovation neighborhoods, two of which were historic districts; and Houston had two historic districts in four renovation areas. When restoration activity was small in scale and undertaken by new homeowners, the rate of "gentrification" and displacement was not alarming. But where real estate speculators had joined the process, in cities such as Washington, D.C., San Francisco, Baltimore, and Houston, then the complete turnaround of neighborhoods that once took five or six years could be accomplished in two years or less. In these neighborhoods dramatic shifts could be seen as the working class, minorities, and renters were replaced by the "gentrifiers" who tended to be middle class, white, and property owners.[61]

There were many causes for private residential reinvestment in the central cities of America during the 1970s: the withdrawal of federal subsidization of inner-city redevelopment projects, the collapse of new housing construction between 1974 and 1976, inflation in the costs of new construction, as well as the influx of postwar baby boomers looking for their first homes to buy, willing and interested in moving "back to the city." When the Community Development Block Grant program (CDBG) of 1974 not only cut the amount of federal money available to cities but shifted the focus of urban renewal away from areas of the city deemed blighted and obsolete and brought the entire city into the redevelopment game, the question arose of how limited federal funds could be spent to achieve maximum benefits. Anthony Downs, a real estate adviser, suggested that community development funds be used to "leverage" private investment dollars by spending the government's money in "moderately or marginally" deteriorated neighborhoods that displayed the following strengths: historic inner-city areas that could attract middle-class residents back to the city, or zones near the downtown districts that had already undergone renewal activity and that now could support nearby residential recycling, or districts surrounding hospitals, universities, museums, and other institutions that might create local housing markets for their employees as well as attract other reinvestors. City after city followed Downs's advice, and in many areas private reinvestment and gentrification grew out of control.[62]

Utilizing federal monies to leverage private reinvestment became a new game in which historic preservation played an unwitting role. When the Urban Development Action Grants (UDAG) were first awarded in 1978, 1979, and 1980, millions of dollars were allocated to neighborhood recycling, adaptive reuse, and historic preservation projects in cities that could demonstrate firm financial commitment from the private sector. Another form of leveraging was the creation of special tax incentives for inner-city neighborhood recycling. In the Tax Reform Act of 1976, Congress recognized the potential of the burgeoning rehabilitation industry. Now private capital invested in the rehabilitation game could be recovered by deducting, on an accelerated schedule, depreciation expenses accumulated on substantial rehabilitation of income-producing certified historic structures, or structures certified to be important to a historic district. The Economic Recovery Act of 1981 simplified this public policy of preserving national heritage enshrined in old or historic structures by continuing to offer tax incentives to compensate for the "costly risks" involved in rehabilitation work. An investment tax credit was offered against the cost of substantially rehabilitating any certified historic structure, or nonresidential income-generating property greater than thirty years old.[63] Once again when tax shelters were reshuffled in the Tax Reform Act of 1986, the public policy remained, although weakened. Instead of receiving a 15 percent investment tax credit against the cost of rehabilitating thirty- to forty-year-old structures, 20 percent on older than forty-year-old structures, and 25 percent on certified historic structures, these credits were lowered to 10 percent against the rehabiliation costs of structures over fifty years old and a 20 percent credit against historic structures.[64]

As revitalization activity gathered speed, so real estate values began to rise in inner-city neighborhoods, taxes were reassessed, rents started to climb, and once questionable neighborhoods suddenly seemed to be socially, racially, and economically stabilized. At some point along this chain of recycling events a gentrified or revitalized neighborhood often received historic district designation, and then the full range of tax incentives, rehabilitation benefits, and regulatory protections applied. But as these protective walls increased, protests occurred in tandem: from poorer old-time residents and local community services being displaced, from private developers, real estate interests, and local architects seeking permits and permission for new development and designs, from city planning authorities who raised equity issues and called for broader-based housing programs. The economic and property values at stake often covered over the reality that certain social and cultural values were being erased from American cities. Once upon a time, before these older neighborhoods had been colonized by new property interests, they had been provincial enclaves, entry points for new arrivals to the cities and breeding spots for colorful folklore, music, poetry, and art—essential ingredients to any urban cultural heritage. At the end of a long period of economic expansion, which began shortly after World War II with the rise of suburban development, pockets of devalued and abandoned central city property, especially if deemed "historic," presented in the 1970s opportunities for massive reinvestment and profitable gains. Not surprisingly "heritage" and historic preservation became an instrument of real estate capital, a form of protection for "risky" ventures seeking to reinvest in and revalue fragments of the inner cities. As this took place, American cities underwent massive spatial restructuring.

Even though all fifty states and over 500 cities by the 1970s had some type of historic preservation statute, running from strong regulatory controls to weakly specified intentions, still the issue of aesthetic controls remained unresolved. If "heritage" was to become a drawing card for reinvestment, even though its regulatory controls invaded the rights of property owners, it had to be backed by legal and financial guarantees minimizing the risks involved. As in the case of England, however, the diminution of property rights would be zealously and contentiously observed. No matter how hard a community might try, it was difficult to claim that "bad or ugly architecture" was a nuisance or harmful to the public if its location was not carefully controlled, or that the loss of our architectural heritage caused a grevious disturbance to the public well-being and justified its protection. A New Jersey court in 1978, for example, ruled that it was invalid to regulate architectural design and visual harmony, yet on the other side of the United States in the very same year, a Washington court enabled the City of Seattle to deny a building permit for a thirteen-story condominium because of the negative aesthetic impact it would have on its surrounding environment.[65]

Preservation and aesthetic regulatory controls received a strong defense when the Supreme Court of the United States ruled in favor of the New York City Landmarks Commission in July 1978, accepting their refusal to allow a skyscraper tower designed by architect Marcel Breuer to fill the air space over the Waiting Room of the landmarked Grand Central Railway Terminal. Indeed New York had been slow to challenge commercial office development that constantly tore down and rebuilt older obsolete structures, and in 1978 only three skyscrapers, the Woolworth Building, the Flatiron Building, and the American Radiator Building, had been designated as landmarks and protected from redevelopment. But now the ability of a city to regulate urban space in its three-dimensional envelope was legally recognized: the hole in the sky created by the low ceiling boundaries of the station and the tower walls that surrounded it came under public control. Besides encouraging the developing preservation movement, the Grand Central Station case also accepted the constitutionality of Transferable Development Rights (TDRs) as a compensatory measure in support of a preservation policy. Thus the unused but allowable development potential standing over a historic landmark or public space could be transferred to another development site somewhere else in the city. Every suggested use of transferable development rights is, however, by definition a response to development pressure. Indeed they make no sense unless there is interest in developing low-rise historic structures, and as a result they always represent a compromised strategy.[66]

The landmarked Grand Central Station was back on the development scene in 1986. This time, incredulously, its owners were proposing to transfer its unused development rights along its underground tracks or "surface rights" over which it still retained control. Development rights would thus be transferred over connecting properties that led to a site four blocks to the north between 46th and 47th Streets. On that small site, First Boston Corporation planned to squeeze a gigantic seventy-four-story retail and office tower. The building would be twice the size that zoning otherwise allowed, but the developers argued that New Yorkers cannot have it both ways: if they want to save the low-scale ambience of historic landmarks such as the Grand Central Station, then they have to expect in the supercharged atmosphere of Manhattan real estate in the 1980s, superdevelopment in other locations. Such has become the case all around the city, where development after development has seen gigantic towers sprouting above the base of historic landmarks.[67]

There were other lessons to learn from the Grand Central Terminal case, where the "rational" use of preservation controls, or so the court deemed, depended on a prior question of whether there existed a plan against which these apparently ad hoc regulations could be tested. If the answer was yes, and the court felt that the selection by the commission of thirty-one historic districts and over 400 individual landmarks constituted planned forethought, then preservation regulations were not an unfair taking of private property irrationally applied to isolated properties because the properties were simply "historic." The trouble has been, however, that real estate developers and property owners do not necessarily accept that inventorying historic resources, setting aside landmarks and historic districts, and specifying the public purposes embodied in a preservation policy constitutes a preservation plan. Controversy erupted in New York City again in 1984 when real estate developers decided that landmarking procedures—far from constituting a plan well know in advance—were instead ad hoc and irrational, and consequently they requested a procedural review to bring some certainty into the historic designation and development contest. The mayor appointed a Landmarks Committee in 1985 to accomplish this review. Reporting within the year, the committee proposed an elaborate reshuffling of the process by which potentially landmarkable structures were listed. They suggested instead that a comprehensive list of the city's "potential landmarks" be completed and then frozen, thus enabling developers to know that if a building was not on that list it could not be added for three to five years, and that under threat of immediate demolition a structure could not be landmarked if not on the list.[68] Although these proposals were modified and reorganized, still development interests continued to pressure the mayor in the late 1980s for greater protection against "irrational" landmark controls. "Study areas" were proposed in the spring of 1988, where the entire built fabric would come under the jurisdiction of the Landmarks Preservation Commission for at least a year. After that period of review, the commission would publish a "protected-buildings list" from which it could designate "landmarks," yet it would forfeit control over the nonlisted structures, which would remain ineligible for reconsideration for at least five to ten years. In addition, any owner of a listed property could demand a landmark decision within a period of ninety days. These procedural maneuverings once again revealed the delicate balance that could easily be upset between the desire to protect collective heritage as a public right and the development rights of private property.[69] By 1989 this debating contest over the historic image of the city, claiming that it was either a private or public view to be developed or protected, produced yet another suggestion. A special panel, "The Historic City Committee," proclaimed that the Landmarks Commission should published a list of potential landmarks and historic districts four times a year. It should in addition hold public hearings on controversial sites within three months and move to landmark a single structure within a year's time, and an entire historic district within two years.[70] Adding to this preservation planning dilemma, the Supreme Court chilled preservation enthusiasts by suggesting, through the reasoning of its June 1987 land use ruling, that property owners might receive compensation from historic regulations if the courts decided such regulations retroactively deprived the landowners of a reasonable use of their land.[71]

Although city planners may have left behind the question of physical planning in the upheavals and dust of the 1960s, the preservation concern for the physical environment surrounding historical and cultural artifacts reawakened a notion of some kind of planning. The courts, as we have seen, simply strengthened this interest by recommending that the normally ad hoc process of land use development be guided by a clearly stated public policy best embodied in a physical plan. And it appeared, if we use New York City as a bellwether, that even development interests during the building boom of the 1980s seem to think that some mediating procedure would offer them more investment security where potentially landmarkable structures were concerned. The courts seemed to follow the advice of Harvard land use law professor Charles Haar, who pointed out as early as 1950 that planning could control the ad hoc nature of zoning, which market pressures bent out of shape. The welter of zoning amendments, variances, and special exceptions could all be managed, he suggested, if measured against a separate document, a long-range development plan. This plan would be able to withstand the pressure of property owners requesting zoning changes if these changes had not been foreseen or allowed by the plan. Along the environmentally sensitive west coast of America, there was a general acceptance by the 1970s that a plan was a separate legal document against which development pressures could be compared.[72] Thus for example the struggle that generally pits real estate development against historic preservation was mediated in San Francisco by the creation of a legal development plan in 1985 protecting the visual environment and scale of its commercial downtown.

Until quite recently, San Francisco's downtown had been a relatively cohesive area, with most of its commercial structures erected shortly after the earthquake and fire of 1906. Yet by the 1970s many of these structures had already been lost to development pressure. Just as important as its threatened architectural heritage, the visual topography of San Francisco's hills and ridges and their relationship to the Bay and to ocean views seemed endangered as well by tall urban structures that were out of scale with the traditional form of the city. Sensing the imminent threat of development, the Foundation for San Francisco Architectural Heritage undertook an architectural survey of the commercial downtown in 1975. They proposed subsequently that among nearly 800 structures located in the financial-retail district and the Market Street area, 272 buildings were worthy of protection (later upgraded to 289) and another 279 were of contextual importance.[73] They decided in addition to develop a preservation strategy for downtown San Francisco that centered on the use of transferable development rights. This instrument, the foundation argued, was the only preservation control that allowed for development supportive of economic growth, met property owner's expectation of reasonable return on a real estate investment, yet guaranteed that the historically and architecturally important commercial structures would be preserved. Consequently they suggested that special development districts be set aside within the general downtown area where unused development rights could be transferred from landmarked structures. Furthermore these development rights could be stored in a land bank to be traded and sold when needed, and additional bonus transfers from the bank could be made available to developers intending to rehabilitate significant structures.[74] The 1985 San Francisco Plan carried these suggestions even further. Focusing on the downtown, the plan lowered the allowable density (by lowering floor area ratios, or FARs) and imposed height restrictions on new development. Through regulations that explicitly called for tapered buildings and more expressive building "tops" instead of the ugly box structures that were a common occurrence, plus a design review for all new proposals, the Planning Commission hoped to force the construction of smaller, thinner, and more detailed buildings and thus enable sunshine and views of the sky to reach the streets. Allowing transferable development rights from 266 significant structures and creating several conservation districts where the preservation of contextual structures sited near more valuable buildings would be encouraged, and in addition by developing open space, public arts, and new housing programs, it was believed that a modicum of development combined with selected preservation would secure a visually cohesive and livable city.[75]

The Spectacle of Spatial Restructuring

Increasingly in the 1970s and 1980s, the centers of American and European cities were seized with nostalgia for past architectural styles, transforming enclaves of their architectural patrimony into city tableaux arranged for visual consumption. Although these tableaux turned public spaces into a kind of spectacle and seemed to be coming to terms with the styles of popular culture and the tastes of mass consumption, nevertheless this reformulation, in which certain images of the city appear to stand still as though in a static painting or photograph, should be understood and explored as only one facet of a much larger story. Historic preservation and traditional images of the city became major instruments involved with the massive restructuring of city spaces, and as this occurred the right to own the historic image of the city was transferred from the private to the public realm, where it could be guarded safely by municipal authorities. Although the public appropriation of a formerly private image has been accepted as necessary if we are to protect our collective heritage, still the political economy of the last two decades provided a new twist to these historic tableaux when positioned against the backdrop of an entire city's land use base being restructured as well. Because these city tableaux, moreover, diverted the spectator's attention into pockets of amusement and scenographic display, they drew the curtains closely around their protecting frames in order that abandoned and neglected areas were no longer visibly apparent.

There are many reasons why cityscapes of the 1980s were filled with civic gestures and grand discourses on history, drawing the spectator's gaze away from its seamier underside. American leaders, for example, having suffered the protests of students, environmentalists, women, and civil rights groups during the 1960s, still painfully aware of the failures endured during the Vietnam War, and concerned about the dissolution of family values, sensed in the 1970s and 1980s a deep cultural crisis and a loss of order. One culprit to blame resided in the cultural reformulations of modernism: for modernism rejected the stability of the past; it destroyed the preserving strength of tradition, and it believed that the center could no longer hold.[76] In Europe as well as in America, the postmodern return to history and the evocation of past city tableaux in the 1970s and 1980s can be viewed as an attempt by political and social authorities to regain a centered world, a concrete system on which moral, political, social, and economic foundations could stand. A past connected to the present across the gaping maw of modernism, visual memories sweetened and mystified by the haze of time and codified as fashionable styles and images—these could be manipulated to release the tensions that social change and political protests, uneven economic and urban development had wrought, and instead these styles and images could be used to recapture a mood of grandeur, importance, heroism, and action that appeared to have been lost forever.[77]

But there was more than nostalgia involved in the restructuring of the contemporary cityscape. Henri Lefebvre has taught that city space is a product, marked, measured, marketed, and transacted; like any capitalist tool the efficiency and functionality of its performance is studied and perfected, and as a commodity its representational form is restylized and reformed.[78] City space in the last half of the twentieth century has been homogenized at the global level: every traveler knows that airports, highway systems, downtown skyscraper centers, and suburban sprawl look the same the world around. At the local level, however, space is fragmented into separate districts of work, leisure, and living; hierarchicalized with respect to property values, revitalized and restructured with the movements of capital. In the long wave of economic prosperity that lasted from 1945 until the late 1960s, large corporations began to centralize their managerial headquarters but decentralize their production and administrative units into many locations and countries. Center city capital investments in low-income residential areas, in manufacturing zones, in warehouse and waterfront districts, in old-fashioned food markets and retail districts withered and shrunk. The middle class fled to the suburbs, manufacturing jobs flowed where employment and expansion were cheaper, center city tax bases faltered, and land values plummeted. In America, the state stepped in with urban renewal and community revitalization projects to offset the risks of center city real estate investments in cultural and educational facilities, in government and commercial office centers, in low-income housing and community facilities. In certain segments of the city they tried to stabilize real estate values, increase the tax base, and draw the middle class back to the city, but in the end these public interventions simply cleared the path for massive recapitalization of inner-city real estate by the private sector in the 1970s and 1980s.[79]

A flexible flow of capital relocating from the center of cities to the periphery during the 1950s and 1960s, followed by the reinvestment in luxury and upmarket real estate developments in the center of cities during the 1970s and 1980s, and including new investments in smaller cities and towns, slowly produced a restructured network of cities around the globe. New York, London, Tokyo, Paris, Chicago, and Los Angeles, among others, became so-called command and control centers where international banks and transnational corporate headquarters located; where accounting, legal, and informational services concentrated; where office development and shopping, convention, entertainment, and hotel districts multiplied. Some cities developed as specialized, or state and regional, command centers, concentrating the headquarters of certain manufacturers or the offices for regional and national governments. In the first-tier cities holding the network together, white-collar and service employment expanded and office, residential, and consumption spaces for the wealthy elite became profitable investments. Fixed capital—finding itself invested in outmoded industrial plants and devalued residential and manufacturing properties—no longer produced a profitable return, so plants began to close, manufacturing employment declined, and inner-city middle- and low-income residential areas were abandoned and ignored.[80]

"Hot Cities," cover of Newsweek *(February 6, 1989).*

Real estate capital came to the fore in these command and control centers, and in the second-tier smaller regional cities as well, exploiting profitable opportunities in housing for the well-to-do and young professionals; consumption spaces for food, clothing, and entertainment; office towers for corporate identification and possession. These all became important new investment areas attracting capital from all over the world. And as they did, local space was fragmented still further: space being utilized to draw distinctions between the luxury classes and the rest of the city's inhabitants. "Style of life" took on a normalizing and representational form that veiled massive spatial reorganization: the spread of gentrifying neighborhoods, the emergence of media and high-technology electronic centers, expanding swaths of luxury housing, new entertainment and consumption zones, and even the spread of low-skilled and underemployed food and garment support industries. An aesthetic discourse erupted in these cities that furthered the distinction between outmoded spaces and revitalized forms, for this regenerated city had to appear secure, fun, upbeat, and innovative if it was to compete successfully against other cities attracting capital investment.[81] Historic preservation and architecture became the two directors of this spectacular performance: they constantly rebuilt, restored, relocated, recycled, and revalued what was once redlined and abandoned, neglected and ignored, inefficient and nonfunctional. And they did so without drawing attention to the dynamics of the real estate industry that left in its wake areas of uneven development and disinvestment, positing this recycling as a normal and natural occurrence that simply stemmed from the ebb and flow of "natural neighborhood life cycles" and reflected only the aesthetic autonomy and enduring value of historic architectural styles.

Thus architectural expansionism employed against isolated fragments of the city, the better able to normalize its aesthetics of distinction, set up boundaries that maintained a distance from the unemployed, impoverished, and outmoded. The preservation of traditional architectural forms and the social stability and security to be garnered from the permanency of architectural styles, the manufacturing or resuscitation of a city's original site, its historical and generative roots, or the updating of plans drawn from the heroic pages of a city's architectural history books operated on isolated and bounded fragments of the city, turning them into containers for new economic and real estate activity. But no overall structural plan drew this combinatorial play of autonomous elements into a whole, and no one appeared to look beyond the gilded frame of the city tableaux to observe the violent conflicts left out of the picture. The spectator's vision was lured by the aesthetic architectural object, by the pleasures and refined gestures it referenced, until finally the homeless, the dispossessed and displaced, the downgraded, devalued, and disturbing became an aesthetic and social nuisance to be pushed still further away, until they were expelled entirely from both sight and social sensibilities.

When juxtaposed against economic restructuring, it is possible to understand from a different perspective why the residential areas in the center of London since the late 1960s, for example, have been placed behind the protective walls of so many conservation districts. Until that time central London's residential buildings were owned by a few large real estate companies and other institutions as high-income or luxury rental properties.[82] Starting in the mid-1960s, however, a few years before the movement for historic preservation really took hold, London's residential housing market began to be restructured. After witnessing the 1950s' and early 1960s' building boom in both commercial and office structures, real estate investors and estate landlords sensed that capital tied up in residential property no longer was a good investment. With long-term leases running between five and nine years or more, these residential rental properties were low-yielding investments when compared to the more lucrative commercial properties. Owners held off necessary repairs, squeezing their profits as much as possible. Consequently, at the point where an increasing demand for apartments caused by the influx of white-collar professionals and managerial classes flowing into the command and control center of London crossed over with the decision among many large real estate companies to disinvest in residential ownership, these companies began to rapidly release their holdings, transferring their ownership, with substantial profits gained, to long-leasehold owner occupation. On the backs of these new leasehold owners all the problems of long-delayed maintenance and revitalization eventually fell.[83] As a result of this restructuring of Central London real estate, there were many who began to deplore the new commercial development wantonly destroying historically valuable properties and sought some kind of preservation control. There were also the new owner-occupiers of residential units, now bearing the costs of maintenance and renovation, who sought investment protection behind historic facades. Consequently, as is the case in many other cities of the western world, all the regulatory controls of historic preservation covering maintenance, structural changes, and demolitions of valuable historic properties were put into place.

Another instrument of spatial restructuring has been the enchancement of national imagery in monumental and free-standing architectural developments. So for example during a time of economic crisis in the 1970s, the government of Francois Mitterand embarked on an ambitious program to transform the center of Paris and parts of its periphery into new cultural and entertainment zones, laying the foundation for an urban civilization to extend into the twenty-first century. At an estimated expense of $3 billion, the nine Grand Projets include the recycling of the Gare d'Orsay into a museum of the nineteenth century, a great Museum of Science and Industry plus a Center for Music at la Villette, a renovated Grand Louvre, a new opera house at the Place de la Bastille, the Arab World Institute on the Left Bank, a Great Arch at La Defense, and the Ministry of Finance on the periphery. Together with the Pompidou Center in the heart of Paris, these public projects have revitalized older neighborhoods, spurred on gentrification, and continued the 1962 policy of André Malraux to turn the center of French cities into living outdoor museums.[84] The old Marais, for example, a 320 acre district lying adjacent to the Pompidou Center, became one of the largest conservation districts in the historic center of Paris, one that has been turned into a luxury residential and tourist enclave over the last three decades.

Bordered by large roads, the Marais's interior nevertheless is a maze of narrow streets and its architecture a medley from different periods of time. Since the end of the nineteenth century, the Marais had been a working-class district and was still in the mid-1960s the location of thousands of small businesses and wholesale establishments. In 1965/67 a preservation plan for its protection was drawn up, attempting to restore the architectural look of the Marais to approximately the state represented on the 1739 Turgot Map of Paris and before there were so many nineteenth- and twentieth-century intrusions. This restoration would involve considerable demolitions and reconstructions, but the opportunity was at hand, or so it was argued, for the Marais was the most congested residential district of central Paris with the worst conditions of living. The preservation plan proposed to regroup many of the Marais's small businesses such as jewelery, optical work, and leather goods, transferring these activities to other locations within the district of lesser architectural importance. But the slow process of preservation and restoration, removal and relocation was soon captured by avid real estate entrepreneurs. Subsequently property values spiraled, causing wholesale demolitions and reconstructions proposed in the initial plan to become economically infeasible. "Spontaneous" restoration activity, moreover, encroached on traditional workspaces, eventually overtaking these places and quickly transforming the Marais, in spite of its preservation plan, into a luxury residential district and a tourist attraction filled with restored architectural monuments, criss-crossed by heritage trails, and peppered liberally with art galleries and museums, boutiques, antique shops, and restaurants.[85]

Part of the story of spatial restructuring lies, as well, in the formation of new forms of public and private cooperation promoting capital reinvestment in the center of cities. In America, the Rouse Company, for example, has received major support from the city governments of Philadelphia and Boston, making reinvestment in those cities palatable: Philadelphia allocated $12 million for the Gallery at Market East and Boston provided $40 million for the Faneuil Hall Marketplace. Both development projects, however, extend backward by twenty years and thus reflect even greater public involvement. Philadelphia already had acquired through eminent domain and subsequently restructured a good deal of the surrounding land where the Chinese Wall once stood. As well the city had convinced two major department stores, Gimbels and Strawbridge & Clothier, to remain at their downtown locations. Consequently when Rouse proposed Market East as a series of small boutiques linking these two department stores and revitalizing the area once known as the Chinese Wall, the pieces for this inner-city shopping center quickly fell into place. The Boston Redevelopment Authority, on the other hand, had begun the revitalization of its waterfront area in the 1960s, primarily focusing on office and mixed-use development, but a catalyst for successful private investment was missing. In the mid-1970s, however, the Fanueil Hall Revitalization Project leased the old granite Quincy Markets to the Rouse Company for 99 years in return for an eventual share of the profits that this recycled historic shopping mall and food emporium would earn. These markets, built in 1826, were located next to Boston's City Hall Urban Renewal project of the 1950s and 1960s and linked to its waterfront and historic North End. Extending its commitment to the area, the city spent more than $2.5 million on structural improvements of the market buildings before the Rouse Company undertook the rehabilitation and redevelopment "risks." Even these were backed up with loans from Chase Manhattan Bank and twelve local banks covering the construction costs, while Teachers Insurance and Annuity provided the long-term financing.[86]

In a number of cities quasi-public development corporations were granted special authority to overrule local regulatory controls. They held discretionary power over the allocation of their public funds and were offered special tax concessions and infrastructure support. These development corporations were appealing to cities because they assumed or appeared to assume the financial risks involved in revitalizing declining zones of the city. The city, on the other hand, by streamlining land use decisions, could ease the way for redevelopment, allowing spatial restructuring to move easily over the heads of those who raised objections. So, for example, the Charles Center–Inner Harbor Management Office has been the nonprofit corporation in charge of Baltimore's Inner Harbor redevelopment since 1965. These efforts have linked 240 acres of so-called abandoned waterfront with the Charles Center redevelopment project, a thirty-three-acre downtown urban renewal adventure of the early 1960s. Following the creation of an Inner Harbor Plan in 1964, the government spent $200 million to acquire and clear land adjacent to the southern border of Charles Center and to make infrastructure improvements along the waterfront. The centerpiece of this development has been the Rouse Company's 1980 Harbor Place, two retail pavilions and a more recent hotel-retail addition called Gallery. These projects are now surrounded by a convention center, hotels, luxury housing, parks, walkways, marinas, an aquarium, a science museum, and an indoor historic theme park in a recycled power plant. By the late 1980s, private reinvestment in waterfront condominiums, restaurants, and marketplaces had turned the U-shaped Baltimore harbor into a new focus for the broader metropolitan district and a cultural and recreation zone whose extent defies the imagination.[87]

The Transformed Public Sphere

Slowly over the years, historic preservation has gained a degree of instrumental control over the aesthetic and visual look of the city. In a one-dimensional manner that ignores many cultural and social concerns, it has been able to transfer through ad hoc or comprehensive procedures some private development rights to the public realm of regulatory controls. But slashing across these advances, other forces have colonized the consciousness of those involved with preservation or urban design and transformed the public sphere into a less than neutral mediator of historical patrimony and national heritage. Perhaps the rhetoric and ideology embedded in the concepts of "patrimony" and "heritage" need to be understood more clearly by reconsidering the historic changes that have taken place within the so-called public sphere. Originally in the late seventeenth and early eighteenth centuries, the "public sphere," where today historic preservation and scenographic architectural compositions play an increasing role, referred to the emergence of a series of discursive spaces and sites for conversational and written exchange—spaces such as clubs, coffeehouses, pleasure gardens, and leisure-time resort areas plus sites such as newspapers, periodicals—even theatrical plays and the realist novel. In these new spaces and sites, the European bourgeoisie met to exchange opinions, develop rational judgment, and express enlightened critique. There was, however, nothing "natural" about this democratic process of reasoned discussion and the expression of a mannerly public opinion, because both had to be constructed through a series of bodily and territorial negations and through the regulating control of norms and moral constraints. Over time and with practice, eventually unruly crowds and disruptive behaviors congealed into a refined and regulated political force that could both oppose the ruthless authority of the absolutist state and mediate the steps between the private sphere of domestic life and the public arena of business and state.[88]

Since the nineteenth century, this autonomous and mediating public sphere has disappeared and its critical functions have been destroyed. With the rise of the mass media in the mid-nineteenth century, private interests and commercial concerns have invaded public opinion, limiting the access of alternative voices and controlling allowable discourses. In place of the "public sphere" a fictitious and "universal" public has been constructed. On the other hand, group needs that could not be satisfied by the private market increasingly turned to the state for retribution, asking it to regulate and reform the offense or provide the necessary concessions. The resulting competition among private interests for state regulation and control distorted the supposed neutrality of public reasoning in its deliberative weighing of social problems, while a constructed public opinion weakened any critical force to the "public sphere."[89] Perhaps this was an inevitable process, reducing irreversibly the contemporary "public sphere" to an arena where private interests compete and consumer choices are displayed, as well as to a space where public debate and critical reasoning no longer take place.

As private interests sponsoring historic preservation and urban scenographic designs have reached out for public controls and regulations, as if in tandem, the commercialized public sphere as well has sought direct access to the private sphere of fantasy and imagination, diverting it toward consumption. With respect to historic preservation and architectural compositions, then, we might expect to find that the "past" as it has been represented in the contemporary "public sphere" has been colonized by commercial interests and reconstructed for special purposes. But if there is a possibility that we might be able to gain a critical perspective over the instrumental aspects of historic preservation and urban design with their associated fictional constructions and universalized narratives, then we need to examine more carefully the shifting relationships between the public and private spheres within present-day consumer society and understand the links that bind styles and forms of architecture to the productions of collective memory that have little to do with lived experiences and emerging decentered formations. Almost all the forms of commercial entertainment that have focused at one time or another on either the image of the city or exotic architectural forms, be they in panoramas, illustrated travelogues, the cinema, and industrial exhibitions; or the inventions of traditions that project a universal and official narration when fragmentation and diversity are the reality; or structures of feeling and staged image-sets that insert the spectator into predetermined arrangements that habitually transform the present that is moving and partially formed into a past where it can be safely assumed to have achieved a fixed and final form—these are all aspects of the shifting relationship between the public and private spheres that remain to be examined and explored.[90]

Justifiably, preservation interests feel that regulatory controls are a legitimate use of public power, for they have been able at times to block the wanton destruction of historic properties, they have provided recycled housing and revalued neighborhoods in the face of an energy and environmental crisis, they have even added to the economic base of the city by attracting more tourists and middle-class residents, and they have generally expanded the quality of life when urban riots and city abandonment once were the norm. But there have been wider societal movements utilizing historic preservation and symbolic images of the city for other purposes. Commercial real estate firms have obviously taken notice that traditional architectural forms, materials, and ornamentation sell because they answer sensuous and emotional needs that modern styles never could fill. So they

"Do You Know Brooklyn?" Poster for Nike.

have plundered to their advantage the grab bag of historical styles and nostalgic motifs until these picture-makers and scene painters have turned nearly every Main Street and city center into historicized stage sets. But the market shifted in other directions as well: if high-volume, low-cost mass consumption was the objective of retailers in the 1950s and 1960s, then low-volume, high-cost conspicuous consumption became the lucrative target in the 1970s and 1980s. And these transformations were paralleled by declining interests of city governments in poverty and social welfare issues, which they expressed during the 1950s and 1960s, and their increasing concern in the 1970s and 1980s to attract and retain businesses that offered white-collar employment and generated affluent middle-class residents. Restructuring markets and issues until they privileged the well-to-do had important effects on urban space and consumer choices within the "public sphere." And it did not take long for advertising agents to realize that atmospheric milieus or historic image-sets, which presented the spectator with a packaged array of commodities and showcased specific styles of life, offered effective commercial environments for the selling of goods. In the end, the elite and urbane spectator seeking entertainment and education became the contemporary explorer of a city's architectural promenades, desiring nostalgically to reside in places that reeked with historical allure or to be clothed in the outfit of safari adventurers, Scottish pheasant hunters, or Victorian maidens—to name just a few of the choices. The discourse of advertisement and the fictive constructions that often accompany historic preservation and architectural compositions, at least in America, found their mark where private fantasies and public sites intertwined: 67 percent of Americans, so a "values and lifestyle" typology proclaimed in the early 1980s, were outer-directed consumers seeking to emulate the various styles of life that consumer society constructed. And historic compositions and city tableaux, as we shall explore, were one of the ways lifestyles were constructed and sold.[91]

e i g h t

Manhattan Montage

By what then are montage and its embryo—the frame—characterized? By collisions. By the conflict of two fragments placed side by side. By conflict. By collision.[1]

SERGEI EISENSTEIN

Just Looking at Cities

The landscape of the contemporary city seems to be composed of conflicting fragments, slices or framed views first cut out and extracted from the city fabric, then set up and juxtaposed against each other. Suddenly in Manhattan, as well as in most global or first-tier cities that experienced explosive real estate growth in the 1980s, it appeared as if someone had twisted Alberti's beautiful dictum that called for the design of a city and a house to be considered as one, and instead said, "make of the city a large museum, and a museum a small city." Tradition in public places, the showcasing of its architectural and urban heritage, returned with a vengeance, transforming isolated fragments of the city into open-air museums, celebratory promenades, and scenographic events. These public spaces became collections of architectural styles and materials, arcades of shops and restaurants, mixtures of residential and office spaces, and labyrinthine arrangements of pathways, parks, and esplanades. What used to be underdeveloped edges of the city, its waterfront and railway tracks, have either been reclaimed and redeveloped or have visionary plans to do so in the future. We have only to pass along the waterfront of Manhattan, for example, following a rhythmic sequence of visual enclosures, both real and imaginary, from Riverwalk on to South Street Seaport, South Ferry, Battery Park City, the Hudson River Center, Riverside South or some facsimile to come, and a grand ribbon of green stretching between Riverside and Battery Parks, to experience a surprising compositional effect that pulls these diverse scenes together, yet sets one off against the other.

Each fragment becomes a static tableau of the city, representing contrasting views made more potent by their proximity to each other. Some capture the fads and fashions of architecture and urban design, others comment on the public and private notions of space, yet each conveys some nuance of contemporary times. With the return of tradition, the city was folded back on itself, celebrating its grandiose past with renewed enthusiasm and basking in the security evoked by the memory of bygone times. For what was being highlighted in these public places was a city's civic heritage or patrimony embedded and engendered by the physical form of the city. To stop the unravelings of the modernist aesthetic, a historicized discourse on the city reached out to gain instrumental control over its past. Yet resemblance has a model that it inevitably reorders and hierarchicalizes for its own effect. Duplication and repetition as the prevalent mode of spatial organization isolate the fragment and highlight only its surface appearance. They draw our attention to the image capitalized in a few privileged sites, yet they ignore all the interstitial spaces. The nostalgic mode so prevalent in these world-class cities since the late 1960s has mystified and mythified our collective memory of the city, sweetened and distilled our spatial sensibility into the look and the feel of cherished times and places. Although we might disclaim that historicist precision and styling cover a vagueness in historical reasoning, this is only its simplest effect because the image is inscribed in the more complex logic of the 1970s and 1980s, restructuring urban space.

To explore these new city tableaux, let us hold up the picture of South Street Seaport, or an equivalent historic district such as Quincy Market in Boston or the Place Beaubourg in Paris, and look through their redoubling frames. These areas represent holes in the heart of our cities and gaps in our present concept of history, which can be filled with true or false visions. If once the picture frame was essential for a well-composed tableau, now the invisible boundaries that enframe the historic district must provide an equivalent allusion. The spectator enters these centered districts from City Hall or Wall Street, or unexpectedly stumbles on them upon emerging from underneath an elevated highway or inadvertently discovers them when exiting from narrow and meandering streets. Suddenly the spectator is plunged into a totally constructed space. The surprise is enhanced, perhaps, because only a few years before these areas had been the remnants of the city that modernist town planning ignored. Now they have been recycled as gigantic image spectacles to enhance the art of consumption. Spectators have responded positively to the bland and fictive pleasures offered in these new public theaters of late capitalism. As recycled remnants of the past, they have become monumental tourist and shopping containers. Perhaps it all began in San Francisco with the restoration of Ghirardelli Square (1962), then the Cannery (1964) and all of Fisherman's Wharf. But the movement has spread: Paris has its Place Beaubourg, with an underground shopping mall built where its nineteenth-century food markets (Les Halles) once stood; London has its Covent Garden, another recycled food market; New Orleans its Old French Market; Portland, Maine, its Customs House Wharf; Boston its Quincy Market; New York its South Street Seaport; and so on in countless cities. These open-air bazaars and storehouses of heterogeneity, where one can buy anything from anywhere, have so concentrated geographical space and historical time that the uniqueness of place and the specifics of context have been erased completely.

Guy Debord has written that "the spectacle is capital accumulated until it becomes an image," and T.J. Clark has used this concept of spectacle in referring to the changes Baron von Haussmann wrought to the Paris of Napoleon III. The spectacle was an attempt to colonize the realm of everyday life, to extend the capitalist market into the private arena of leisure time and personal styles and into the public scenery of boulevards and architectural landscapes. As the consumer market developed the new world of the giant boulevards and department stores, it altered the space of the nineteenth-century city, producing new urban forms and new building types.[2] Late capitalism has replaced the boulevard with the pedestrian plaza of a historic district, and the department store with refurbished markets. These open-air shopping emporiums are bound to proliferate for they represent, as one enthusiast claims, "the happy marriage of a number of phenomena in American culture—a new style of business, a newly discovered interest in food and an informal festival, and a recently aroused passion for making what is historically significant useful."[3]

Most of these city tableaux are marketplaces, and their architectural compositions set the stage for a particular kind of experience. Marketplaces from the beginning of time have always been those interstitial spaces where go-betweens gather and contracts are negotiated. Often located on the edges of town or at crossroads and border lands—just beyond the control of regulated zones—they were places of exchange and movement between people and goods. They were liminal places, in the sense that they epitomized the betwixt and between in space and time. Brought face to face in the marketplace, the known and ordinary everyday world met the exotic sphere of faraway places.[4] In addition, the market was a space where "just looking" represented that moment of hesitation before one purchased an item for sale, when one calculated the character of the seller and the worth of an object, yet it was the same moment in which the buyer experienced pure desire and conjured up in his or her imagination the images of a fantastical world that the possession of that object seemed to promise. A marketplace, then, was a container of desires and yearnings; and ships and sailors, waterfronts and seaports—what else are they but markers of that desire, which propelled men and ships to voyage thousands of leagues around the world for that pinch of Madagascar pepper for seasoning meat or coffee from Mocha to stimulate spirits?[5]

In every town the story appeared to be similar: either city authorities decided the working market—a term for the wholesale vegetable, fish, or meat market—was an obstacle to efficient city planning and so banished its presence to the city's periphery, sometimes as long ago as the 1950s; or private interests discovered that rehabilitated Victorian building facades, reconstructed market stalls, and trendy shops and restaurants returned more revenue on their investment than smelly fishmongers and boisterous vegetable hawkers ever could pay. The consequences were clear: every city began to revalue and recycle its leftover "working" districts, its warehouses, its waterfronts, its Main Streets, and its commercial centers, and every city began to look like everywhere else. Serial replication followed well-established rules: the pioneers with their arts-and-crafts appearance began the recycling, but soon the trendier and higher-priced merchants arrived. They started to rehabilitate and refurbish in a grander style. Rents rose and speculators descended, while federal, state, and local monies advanced. Cultural centers were built, theatrical backdrops rearranged, special regulatory zoning and historic district status was granted, historic signs and descriptive labels prescribed, and guided tours and educational programs developed. The battle strategy was apparent: the old ways must go. To assure the rapid circulation of goods, people, real estate, and fashionable styles, pedestrian zones banned the automobile from these sacred enclaves, speculators evicted local businesses and services, and invitations were sent to national retailers. The regional and local sense of place changed entirely.

In the economy of late capitalism, the emphasis is most often placed on the individual consumer of goods and services. As a result, packaged tours, museum extravaganzas, and food emporiums become the consumer arts of mass entertainment, while the city landscape itself is transformed into a background prop for the graphic display of billboards, neon signs, and advertisements. A new visuality is introduced into the cityscape by reducing the language of architecture to a serial experimentation with pure signs, media codes, styles, or fashions. But a language dependent on the commercial image, the perfect lure, conflates artistic and popular imagery and removes the border line that once separated the observant and sensitive traveler along city streets from the promenader and consumer of commodities and scenographic spaces. The self-consciously drawn boundary carefully marking the distinction between tasteful art forms and the popular arts has been rearranged, and the critical art forms of modernism that refused to surrender to "easy seductions and collective enthusiasms" have been negated in the contemporary art forms of popular participation.[6] Hence the flux of constant revivals, rediscoveries and reinterpretations of outmoded styles, acts as one more spur for consumption. Popular art forms and images are designed to be consumed: they are drawn close in order to be totally devoured, jostling the viewer against what once were considered vulgar and distasteful.[7] By turning the values of high art upside down, tourist experiences in combination with historic districts of our cities—areas such as New York's South Street Seaport, Boston's Quincy Market, or the Baltimore Harborplace—become food-oriented and clothing emporiums packaging a specific style of life. These sites are culinary and ornamental landscapes through which the tourist now grazes, celebrating as she or he goes the consumption of places, art, and exotic stuff.

Producing the Show

South Street Seaport's story is typical of waterfront restructuring projects where the dynamics of buying and selling not only determined its origin but controlled its future as well. An elaborate and detailed series of real estate transactions has been set into play in order to gain instrumental control over the saving of history and the production of place. But in the process, these arts of building city spaces have been inhibited from attaining their original goal. The last vestiges of New York's

"South Street Seaport," cover for Advertising Supplement to the New York Times, *1984.*

mercantile history, an eleven-block area of four- and five-story late eighteenth- and nineteenth-century commercial structures in Lower Manhattan, seemed imperiled in the 1960s by a Wall Street building boom encroaching from the south and by the threatened relocation of the Fulton Fish Market, which had held to this spot since 1822. From an urban redevelopment viewpoint, the area contained only shabby structures, dilapidated piers, marginal enterprises, and squatters that entitled it to be officially designated a "slum." But the Lower Manhattan Plan of 1966, noting that the financial district was running out of space in which to expand, proposed that office and luxury residential towers be built on landfill extending out to the pier line along the entire waterfront from the Brooklyn Bridge on the East River to Battery Park on the Hudson River. If the financial district was to retain its national and international supremacy, the report argued, it must not only be given the opportunity to expand but it must be sustained as well by at least six residential communities within walking distance, containing somewhere between 10,000 to 15,000 people. Each one of these communities would be centered around a waterfront plaza located at the end of the axis of Wall Street, Broad, Chambers, Fulton, and the World Trade Center. Already in 1964 the Port Authority had announced plans to build the World Trade Towers, and proposed two years later to use the earth dug up for its construction as landfill along the derelict piers on the Hudson River, creating the area on which Battery Park City would rise. So the opportunity seemed ripe for the fulfillment of a dream that reached back to the 1930s and envisioned luxury residential communities developed within walking distance of the Wall Street financial district.[8]

Not everyone shared this dream. There would be protracted debates over the amount of subsidized housing to be offered in each new residential community, and there were alternatives to be considered for waterfront redevelopment as well. As shipping activity was fading along the waterfront, what better way to commemorate its contribution to New York's economy then to create a Maritime Museum? Consequently the state passed a bill in 1966 to locate such a museum in Schermerhorn Row. These twelve old counting houses had been erected in 1810–12 by Peter

Schermerhorn on landfill along the south side of Fulton Street and the corner of South Street, a site right in the center of one of the proposed waterfront communities. Here in these buildings during the heyday of South Street's mercantile past, a merchant received goods from his ships, counted, stored, sold, and later distributed the merchandise, and so these buildings, it was argued, must become the commemorative focal point for a maritime museum. So vehemently did downtown real estate interests pressure the state to withdraw this bill, however, that funding was delayed for at least a year.[9] Meanwhile another interest group arose, "The Friends of South Street," with Peter Stanford as its head, which proposed to create a living outdoor museum recreating the ambience of a "street of ships" out of four blocks of the old mercantile district along the East River, with the Schermerhorn block as its centerpiece. Their plan called for a pedestrian plaza and a mixture of low-scale retail, office, residential, and museum spaces located in restored and reconstructed buildings between Burlington Slip and Peck Slip, Water Street and the East River.[10]

To implement something from each of these redevelopment and preservation plans, the City Planning Commission created the Brooklyn Bridge Southeast Urban Renewal Plan in 1968 (approved 1969), intending through its power of eminent domain to condemn some derelict blocks, create pedestrian promenades, preserve certain structures, and build new housing and office spaces.[11] Instead the city entered into long negotiations, acquiring and reselling parcels of South Street Seaport and allocating them to different interests as the development game unfolded. Designating the area around South Street to be a Special District within the larger renewal district, the city named the Friends of South Street, incorporated as the South Street Museum in 1967, as the official sponsors of this newly created district. This would allow the district to remain open to the waterfront, to set aside several of its streets as pedestrian walks, to ensure the preservation of some of its valuable historic properties, and to guarantee through its design guidelines that in the midst of high-rise development, South Street Seaport would eventually become a special retreat. Not waiting for the uncertain and lengthy process of city planning, however, the Seaport Museum created Seaport Holdings, Inc., directed by Jakob Isbrandtsen, who was also chairman of the museum's board, and this corporation began to negotiate the purchase of the Schermerhorn block. But so did a real estate development company headed by Sol G. Atlas and John P. McGrath, who already owned one-third of a neighboring block and now convinced the owners to sell them Schermerhorn Row. Isbrandtsen immediately bought the rest of that block, hoping to stop their assemblage and knowing that if this historic centerpiece was lost, so was the whole concept of an outdoor South Street museum. Consequently another route was taken, and he mounted a successful public campaign in December 1968 to convince the New York City Landmarks Commission to designate Schermerhorn Row a landmark within forty-eight hours, and so stop the threat of its immediate destruction. This landmark action prodded Atlas and McGrath to sue the city for depriving their company of its development rights.[12]

Meanwhile the Museum's Seaport Holdings, Inc., gained title to the block north of Schermerhorn Row and two historically valuable blocks across from the Row, where the future market and museum buildings would eventually be established, placing these properties in escrow for the museum until the latter could raise the money for their purchase. It was hoped that an innovative and untried use of zoning would permit the allowable development rights over these valuable historic structures to be sold by the museum and to be allocated to seven different transfer sites in lower Manhattan, and that this sale would enable the museum to buy back the properties from their own Seaport Holdings, Inc. Cooperating with this idea, the city created an enlarged development district around Schermerhorn Row, including some of the public street from which development rights could be transferred. Because the gap between the four- or five-story historic structures and the large towers that zoning allowed was so great (i.e., Floor Area Ratios [FARs] between 10 and 18), acquisition of these properties through eminent domain was not justifiable. Thus some other compromise had to be arranged between preservation interests and development pressures. It was hoped that if development rights were sold to Atlas and McGrath from the Schermerhorn Row block and the two historically valuable blocks that Seaport Holdings owned, they in turn would be allowed to build a far taller structure on the nonhistoric westward block adjacent to Schermerhorn Row. In return for additional development rights, it was expected that Atlas and McGrath would give Schermerhorn Row to the museum as a special gift.[13] To facilitate this compromise, the city designated a Special South Street Seaport Zoning District in 1972 within the Urban Renewal District, planning through its design guidelines to preserve the architectural quality of this historic enclave, yet through its zoning provisions to facilitate nearby office development where transferable development rights could be used.[14]

By 1972, however, office space in lower Manhattan was overbuilt, and the city was beginning to slip toward a fiscal crisis, so development pressure subsided, giving the South Street Seaport Museum time to develop its plans but transforming the compromise transactions into an issue that now was dead. Because Atlas and McGrath were in financial trouble, they decided not to build on Schermerhorn Row and instead sold the property to the city and transferred their development rights to Chase Manhattan Bank, one of a consortium of banks enabled to receive such land and air rights. Meanwhile the museum's Seaport Holdings, Inc., fell behind in both its tax and mortgage payments, because no development rights had been sold from the properties it controlled and consequently the banks moved to foreclose. Other complex negotiations ensued in which the city eventually acquired the entire four-block nucleus on which the museum was focusing, along with several waterfront piers. The city paid the mortgages that Seaport Holdings held on the blocks across from Schermerhorn Row, while the latter relinquished all of its property claims and transferred to the consortium of banks the development rights it was holding in lieu of the rest of the purchase money that the museum owed.[15] In 1974 the city sold Schermerhorn Row to the museum, and they promptly sold it to the state for its Maritime Museum. As the property passed through the ownership of the Seaport, however, convenants were attached guaranteeing that it be restored by the state in a manner specified by the museum, and that its development plans be coordinated in tandem with those of the Seaport Museum.

Within a few years, however, as the Seaport Museum was searching for more retail space that would allow it to enter an entirely new restructuring game, two museums seemed incompatible and so the Maritime Museum was terminated even though the state, through its Urban Development Corporation, would see that the restoration of Schermerhorn Row went ahead as planned.[16]

In 1977, as the entire ten-block area surrounding South Street Seaport south of the Brooklyn Bridge to John Street, including several piers, became a historic district, a new public-private partnership arose, and now the meaning of "historic" was stretched beyond preserving the rich history of New York's nineteenth-century maritime development to a concept that hopefully would reintroduce economic vibrancy to the area as a twenty-four-hour tourist, residential, and commerical district and would produce an income base from which the museum could subsidize its cultural programs. By this time the Seaport Museum was under a barrage of criticism: it had not paid rent to the city for at least two years, it had mismanaged several million dollars on shoddy restoration work, it was pressuring for the removal of the politically sensitive Fulton Fish Market, and it had spent money allocated for relocating artists who lived in Schermerhorn Row on administrative expenses. In 1977 John Hightower, the former director of the Museum of Modern Art, was appointed president of the Seaport Museum while James Shepley, the president of Time, Inc., was made chairman of the board. They began to discuss the idea of restructuring the Seaport into a retail shopping center with a historic maritime theme.[17]

Commercial development gained an advantage in 1979, when the Rouse Company joined the city, the Seaport Museum, and the Urban Development Corporation in an agreement to turn South Street Seaport into a specialty retail center similar to its successful projects in Boston's Faneuil Hall and Baltimore's Harborplace. The first phase of the project would see Fulton Street and Front Street set aside as the pedestrian crossroads of the new marketplace, and the museum block developed with small specialty retail shops, in a nautical mode to complement its seafaring exhibits. In addition the old Fulton Market block where food sheds had stood since 1822 would be the site of a new festival food market, designed by Benjamin Thompson & Associates to simulate the old tin sheds of earlier times. This new market shed was arranged so that the street-level fish-market stalls along South Street would remain as part of the Fulton Fish Market, but four levels entered from the Fulton Street market axis would be dedicated to specialty foods, fast food stands, and restaurants. The second phase would see the site at the Water Street entrance to the Seaport privately developed as office space, with shops and restaurants along its Fulton Street facade. In conjunction with this commitment of private development money, the city received a $20.4 million Urban Development Action Grant (UDAG) from the federal government in 1981 to enable it to reconstruct Pier 17 and to improve the infrastructure in the entire urban renewal area, including a waterfront promenade. The third phase would develop the retail areas of Schermerhorn Row as small nautical theme shops yet guarantee the continuation of two historic restaurants, Sweets (established in 1842) and Sloppy Louie's (established in 1930). Meanwhile the Rouse Company would build a three-story pavilion simulating nineteenth-century entertainment piers lying adjacent to the museum's ships with restaurants, cafes, and clothing shops lining this great hall of commerce.[18]

As real estate development and commercial retailing became more important than museum activities, an independent nonprofit South Street Seaport Corporation was established in 1982 to shelter the museum, with its interest in public education and historic preservation, from it profit-making ventures in real estate development. Christopher Lowery became president of South Street Seaport Museum, with real estate development his obsession.[19] Nevertheless there were snares in mixing culture and commerce, and the recycling machine did not always run smoothly. The gradual and piecemeal instruments of historic preservation took a backseat as development forces rapidly rose. By the time South Street Seaport officially opened in 1983, three-quarters of its museum exhibition space had been reassigned to Cannon's Walk, an interior space lined with retail shops, while 95 percent of the material acquired for Seaport exhibits remained in storage. In

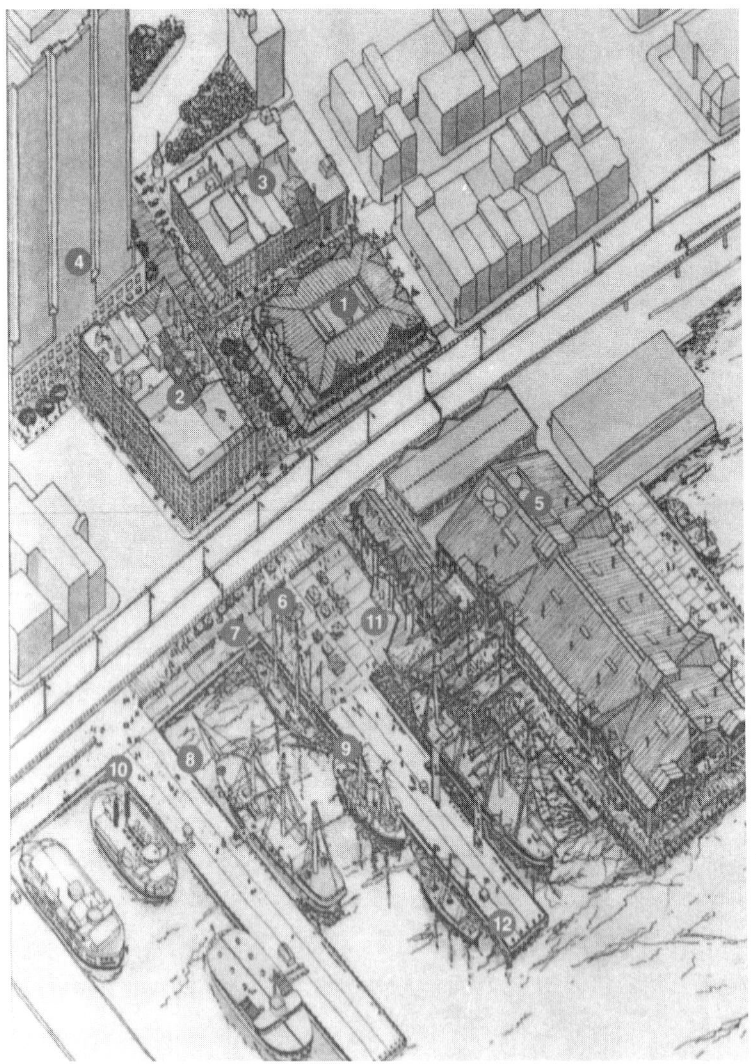

"South Street Seaport Plan," from Advertising Supplement to the New York Times, *1984. [Key: 1. Fulton Market, 2. Schermerhorn Row, 3. Museum Blocks, 4. Seaport Plaza, 5. Pier 17, 6. Pier 16, 7.–12. Historic Ships.]*

addition, the museum's ability to raise money for cultural activities was weakened and its membership interest tarnished by so much commercial activity. South Street Seaport's revitalization of "the street of ships" may have begun with a desire to preserve seedy taverns, fish stalls, and its Schermerhorn Row as a commemorative monument to its great maritime past, but it was also hoped that historic preservation could facilitate the creation of a twentieth-century outdoor museum. Besides a museum whose cultural programs had yet to be financed, a few ships rehabilitated and rebirthed at its slips, and a multiscreen adventure film "The Seaport Experience" in which the sights, sounds, and smells of clam hawkers, the clatter on cobblestones and clamor of bells, and the feel of fog, mist, and sea spray were cleverly simulated, cultural resuscitation and exhibition development seemed to have stalled. Economic restructuring as a festival marketplace gained the advantage: Benjamin Thompson's specially designed New Fulton Market Building opened in 1983 and the new Pier 17 Pavilion in 1985, in addition to the Seaport Plaza, a thirty-four-story office tower. In all, the public spent $61.05 million for the restoration of the museum block, improvements to the Fulton Fish Market, the restoration of Schermerhorn Row, and a waterfront promenade and pier construction. Private enterprise added another $289.5 million for the development of the Fulton Market block, the Pier Pavilion, retail improvement on the two blocks along Fulton Street and in the museum block, and Seaport Plaza.[20] Even in the slowed-down economy of the early 1990s, it is expected that still more real estate development will come, because South Street Seaport stands as the successful emblem or flagship project of Manhattan's waterfront restructuring.

Although the four-block centerpiece, the city tableaux of South Street Seaport, has been in operation since 1983, the entire urban renewal and historic district projects are far from being complete. The museum's real estate wing leased a total of thirty-five acres from the city, roughly half of which comprise the four blocks on which the marketplace is focused. The rest are 13 buildings, some vacant and some containing wholesale fishing concerns. In 1986 the museum began to study the feasibility of converting these structures into retail and residential uses more in line with its festival theme. Luxury residential development was becoming increasingly important, not only to support the retail concessions that still seemed to bloom in the summer and wither by the fall, but to establish as well a twenty-four-hour downtown residential community. In addition, the planned marina and hotel facilities have yet to materialize, and public money to leverage further private investment has failed to appear. Because property values spiraled upward during the 1980s, turning a dilapidated four-story brick building whose market price might have been $350,000 in 1982 into property valued at $1.5 million by 1986, it has made even five- or six-story new construction projects financially unfeasible. And the Landmarks Commission has been zealous in maintaining its curatorship over the ten-block historic district, and in spite of real estate economics has rejected every proposal for large-scale development.[21] In addition, much to the distaste of redevelopers, the Fulton Fish Market has stubbornly refused to be moved even though the Port Authority's recently constructed Fishport in South Brooklyn stands open and waiting. Still, every day in the early hours of the morning more than 350,000 pounds of fresh fish are distributed to restaurants and fish markets from South Street's crowded and antiquated market sheds, and the city seems to have no plans to prod it to abandon its South Street location.[22]

As the economic value of land in the South Street Historic District continued to climb, however, a potential problem arose over the privately owned blocks to the north of the Seaport Marketplace lying along Peck Slip and Pearl, Beekman, and Water Streets. At least one of these blocks, the northwesterly one along the Brooklyn Bridge, was excluded from the designated historic district in 1977. Ten years later, however, its property owners and the consortium of banks began to pursue plans for developing the site, while others sought to place the block under landmark control. The consortium originally had purchased 1.4 million square feet of air rights from the low-rise structures along Fulton Street, and in 1987 half a million of those air rights still remained to be sold and the contested block the only "receiving" site left as originally proposed. If the block was landmarked as preservation required, then the banks would be left with unusable air rights valued in the range of $15–$25 million. At this cost it seemed inevitable that a compromise would be negotiated and some high-rise development sure to succeed.[23] Consequently, in the early hours of 1989 the city and two developers announced a new scheme for the development of Front Street between Beekman Street and Peck Slip, where a row of red-brick nineteenth-century structures still stood, containing among its former uses the "House of Fillet," "Rupert Fish Company," and the "Fishermen's Federation." The developers were proposing to lease the property from the city for forty-three years, in order to erect a $40 million mixed-use complex with ground-level shops and offices and 130 apartments on the upper floors. The project was in keeping with the historic ambience of the district, or so the developers said, because it would renovate the existing structures and only construct new buildings six or seven stories in height on two vacant lots on the block.[24]

In spite of this long, drawn out compromise, however, taller structures inevitably were encroaching on the edges of the historic area. Seaport Tower, for example, pushed a slender twenty-eight story structure onto the corner of Fulton and Pearl Streets with its design, or so it was claimed, based on the red-brick historic structures of Schermerhorn Row. And at least six different projects had been planned for the parcels assembled at 250 Water Street before approval finally was given in 1991 to the seventh proposal, a ten-story building designed by Charles A. Platt and Paul Spencer Byard. Since 1983, however, when a starkly modern twenty-three story structure with a concave glass facade was proposed for the site, preservationists have battled against the developers, demanding a more sensitive design. With the aid of a zoning bonus plus the application of transferable development rights, the developers had the right but not the permission to erect such a tall and overwhelming building. Over the ensuing years, as the battle raged on, it raised but did not answer the important question of whether new designs for sites on the edge of a historic district must take into consideration all of the distinguishing architectural characteristics—such as the low-scaled height, small bulk, materials, and ornamental treatment—that define the historic ambience of the *tout ensemble*, or whether they might be considered transitional structures and address the general context of buildings erected on the other side of the imaginary frame that outlines a historic preserve.[25]

Brokering Desire

There are other stories belonging to mercantile memories that these real estate developments may not allow. Gaddis Smith, for example, wrote in *The American Neptune:* "One of the great delights of maritime history is the scope it grants for operating across the full scale of human experience. At one end of the scale we can examine specific vessels, trace voyages moment by moment, and probe the character of particular people. At the other end, we can grapple with the most fundamental forces in our history—chronicling the mass movement of commodities and population, the spread and impact of technology, the rise and fall of empires."[26] Can a better stage set be found for a marketplace spectacle than recycling old mercantile areas that reek with the history of commerce and establish associative links in our mind?

From its earliest conception the Seaport was intended to be a twentieth-century outdoor museum stressing involvement, not contemplation, and acting on behalf of people, not simply preserving artifacts.[27] But this contemporary museum has consuming at its very core, for the money used to preserve its historic structures and maintain the ambience of its street of ships comes from its share of the revenues that this street of shops can produce. Consequently the Seaport is in reality an outdoor advertisement that narrates a story about trade and commodities stretching far beyond the ordinary shopping mall. This mode of advertising blurs the distinction between the atmospheric stage set and the commodities being sold, for its well-constructed historic tableau not only enhances the products displayed but locks the spectator into a consuming mode. Because the Rouse Company and the Seaport Museum depend on the income generated from retail rentals and sales, they must produce consumers in the mood to purchase the particular commodities the Seaport sells. Their advertising, which is the entire historical milieu, must be pleasurable, mildly educational, and definitely entertaining if it is to establish popular appeal. What they sell to the retailers is access to a particular clientele delivered in the right frame of mind. Within the space of the South Street Seaport's historic tableau and through its museum's interpretative programming, the consumer is drawn into a special network of associated meanings, enabling a transference to take place between the context and the commodities for sale. In today's advertising world, after all, it is the atmosphere that sells; and in South Street Seaport, it is the compensating narratives of adventure and conquest that fill the spectator's nostalgic desires and prompt him or her to consume.[28]

From time immemorial, women and men have been appropriators of nature for food, clothing, and shelter, and explorers and voyagers have traveled the endless oceans and plundered the farthest continents for raw materials and exotic stuff. With scientific instruments and technical knowledge, humankind has sought to conquer nature, to deny its supremacy, and bend it to human needs. But in the postindustrialized world of the present, an intimate link with nature has been severed, giving rise to a set of nostalgic desires to reexperience the time when man confronted nature directly, mastering the perils at sea and the dangers on land. Any seaport symbolizes this world of mercantile exploration that launched a thousand ships around the world. That mercantile world of goods and trading, of horsepower and reefed sails, of ropes and pulleys, wheels and weights came to an end in the late eighteenth-century, supplanted by the industrial power of fire, the steam engine, the factory, and the railroad. And with it died a view of the world that could be measured and counted, drawn and mapped by the knowledge of geometry and mechanics.[29] This is the same visible and demonstrable mercantile world that Diderot's encyclopedic mind reached out to captured as it slid away from his view: he visited workshops and built models of machines, he studied documentary images and artisan drawings, trying to reassemble a harmonious tableau of commerce and trade, to dignify manual labor, and to praise the mechanical arts.[30] And it is just this measurable and controllable mercantile world that South Street showcases and nostalgically extols.

Henry Adams may have said "that every trader's taste smelt of bric-a-brac," and indeed merchant collections of exotic stuff always defied a unifying principle. Yet unbridled eclecticism with its mobile categories and slippery boundaries was often viewed as a threat to more conservative taste.[31] In a similar manner, the Seaport Museum was concerned with visual disarray and attempted to retain instrumental control over the scenographic displays of New York's mercantile tradition by developing streetscape programs in its weekly meetings with the Rouse Company merchants, thereby ensuring the success of its historical mission. Approval must be obtained for all street vendors, outdoor entertainment, and seasonal decorations, and permission is refused to any retail or festival activity if deemed inappropriate to the overall maritime and historical theme. As well, the museum controls the types of signs and advertising used by the merchants. A painted wall sign on Water Street, for example, reminding the spectator to "Visit the South Street Museum," recreates a nineteenth-century style of advertising. Vista markers as well as labels and signs on shops and on the museum's ships and historic buildings are carefully planned and controlled. Guided architectural tours, performing events, and historical pageants are also closely supervised by the museum for fear that eclectic disorder and randomness would endanger and diminish the meaning of this historical tableau.[32]

A well-composed city tableau is itself an incomplete and impoverished picture that can be sustained only by inventing traditions and narrative stories that it calls to its support. Its real value is that of display, enabling the spectator—at South Street Seaport, for example—to travel vicariously and imaginatively into the mercantile past through its architectural traces, its exhibitions, and its commodities for sale. This distilled and composed picture, actually estranged and removed from the contemporary city, can be considered a collective souvenir drawn from the city's historical past. As a possession on display, every souvenir generates a travel narrative, for it is a visible reminder of past journeys whose distance reawakens the longing for more adventures and explorations. Yet it envelops a predatory urge as well, swelling on the desire to return home with bags filled with the latest trophies and exotic remnants discovered on every voyage.[33] So for example, trinkets can be bought throughout South Street Seaport but especially at Captain Hook's in Schermerhorn Row, a simulated pirate's cave where seashells and ship's bells, scrimshaw and nautical antiques are sold. These offer the spectator a second-hand and partial experience of the sea and later, when displayed in one's home, narrate for the viewer a story of that long-ago visit to South Street Seaport.

A sign on the South Street Seaport Museum claims that "The Museum is around you" in the restored mercantile architecture, in the tall ships docked at its slips, in the morphological plan and names of its streets. This mildly educative and entertaining tableau constitutes the scenographic milieu and works in the following manner. It was common practice along the East River waterfront in the eighteenth century to locate slips for merchants' ships between the streets. One of the earliest was Beekman's Slip, which lay between Pearl and Water Streets below Fulton Street in 1720. In addition, the Beekman family in 1807 gave the city a plot of land to be used as a public marketplace. In the contemporary South Street Seaport, the name of the Beekman Market pushcarts is therefore not only a reminder of these city benefactors who donated the original market site, but as well it is a symbolic marker of earlier modes of merchandising. Always in need of extra warehouse space as commerce expanded during the eighteenth century, merchants along the East River harbor continuously pushed the mercantile district out into the river, filling in the old slips and building new wharves and piers. One of the earliest entrepreneurs was John Cannon, who filled in his waterfront lots in 1721 and built a wharf along Water Street. Today the interior street of the museum block is called Cannon's Walk, in memory of this early entrepreneur. New York as an entrepot lagged behind the growth of other east coast cities until 1774, when shipping activity suddenly doubled, and then redoubled again by 1795. Consequently Water Street soon lay inland as landfills continued and shipping activity expanded. Only two generations after Cannon, we find his grandson Peter Schermerhorn filling in water lots along Fulton Street between Front Street and South Street and building Schermerhorn Row.[34] Consequently, South Street Seaport presents itself as the contemporary and inevitable continuation of this age-old mercantile practice of commercial expansion in which landowners constantly developed and redeveloped their waterfront on land reclaimed not only from the sea, but from the "natural" process of decay and decline. For with the advent of the steamship and large oceangoing vessels requiring a deep-water port, South Street Seaport by the late nineteenth century began to slide into a long decline. A seedy derelict waterfront arose by the mid-twentieth century with underutilized warehouses and marginalized activities. A once vital and diverse area diminished by neglect and the forces of urbanization found only its produce and fish markets standing vigilant over its maritime and commercial past. Surprisingly, it would be this food and fish motif that would become the center of South Street Seaport's revitalization, the "natural" vehicle, as we shall see, through which the narrative stories of this marketplace could be recovered and renewed.

In industrial exhibition halls and department stores of the nineteenth century, spectators went "to just look" at the merchandise, not necessarily to buy but to see what wondrous marvels modern techniques had produced and what exotic novelties had been sent from faraway places. The commodity became a spectacle, a series of beautiful images enveloped by fantastic and pleasurable allusions. And "just looking" was that moment of hesitation before purchasing a commodity when the shopper reflected on an idealized image that might be achieved if she or he were to purchase the item offered for sale. A kind of montage effect operated in this act, juxtaposing and blending real and illusory images.[35] "Just looking" at the architecture and historical displays of South Street Seaport as a backdrop for contemporary consumption is a spectator act inscribed in a similar image system, which extends the scene and initiates complex trains of thought. The image of the city is narrowed to the aesthetic experience of pure visual contemplation and to the physical configuration of place. Such a pleasurable and rationally composed cityscape, with its carefully drawn nodes, pathways, and edges, can be readily consumed by the tourist or spectator.

In the late eighteenth century, for example, the ideal cityscape was one of varied surprises and theatrical effects, expressly designed for the pleasure of viewing. Abbé Laugier, a historican and member of Diderot's circle, in his *Essai sur l'Architecture* (1753) suggested that a city could be conceived as an analogical wilderness transformed by the gardener/planner into a landscaped park through the proper subdivision and location of its streets and squares. It was essential to secure the aesthetic effect that nature held over man by allowing lush vegetation and shaded greenery to invade the city, thus inviting—as contact with nature inevitably did—associations with noble thoughts and melancholic or innocent sentiments.[36] South Street Seaport borrows metaphorically from the garden effects of a landscaped city. Certainly a curious aggregation of architectural styles, the Seaport's historic district stands as an open-air equivalent of the curio cabinets and gardens filled with natural and artificial wonders that merchants constructed to display the bric-a-brac they brought back from the corners of the world. But South Street Seaport is as well a bounded and enclosed marketplace centered around the crossroads of Fulton and Front Streets and focused along the pedestrian axis of Fulton Street onto the East River and its line of tall ships. A hybrid place if ever there was one, to the right the image of Wall Street's financial towers arrests the view, to the left the scene is redoubled by a trompe l'oeil wall painting by Richard Haus, while straight ahead the prospect opens on the waterfront and beyond to the outside world. Perhaps the symbolism is clear: the financial mechanisms that orchestrate the scenery; the river that not only represents the mysteries of nature but as well the great unifying element opening up the world in space and time and bringing every product to town; and the trompe l'oeil painting that is a playful gesture never taken for reality, but always reeking of déjà vu and deception, ridicule and mockery. It is an effective boundary or limit, pushing the spectator's view back from the boondocks where development raises its head and returning the viewer's sight to the focused tableau. Parodying architecture and the South Street Seaport's tableau, the trompe l'oeil wall painting is suggesting perhaps that this reconstructed marketplace is but one of the tricks of perspective that those in power can play.[37]

Nature as the great storehouse of raw materials and wondrous secrets seems to be a central theme of South Street Seaport, symbolized by The Nature

South Street Seaport, *Richard Haas trompe l'oeil wall mural (Winter 1993).*

Store in Schermerhorn Row, which carries an electic list of items that teach about birds, fish, dinosaurs, and crystals; sells books about the stars, wild animals, and mushrooms; offers atlases and globes, prints of wildlife and landscapes, telescopes and binoculars, pedometers, thermometers, travel watches and clocks. Because nature is the repository of great secrets into which the adventurous explorer delves, then another store on Schermerhorn Row, Brookstone's, becomes a modern-day outfitter, offering every type of travel equipment, including cases that protect cameras, films, cassettes, and compact disks against security x-ray devices; carrying wheels and carrying cases; all kinds of nineteenth-century games and entertainment, both indoor and outdoor, such as sets for croquet and badminton; and garden hoses and tools, planters and watering cans. Of course no monument to the sea would be complete without a supply of charts and maps aiding man in his confrontation with nature and enabling him to plot out his course on a spatial grid. The Book & Chart Store stocks an array of treatises on the sea and sailing charts and maps for the real and imaginary sailor.

Not only is there an attempt at South Street Seaport to nostalgically record the pure forms of landscape and the presence of wildlife untouched by civilization and industrialization, but there is also great pride displayed in recording the presence of man in this landscape, including the instruments of knowledge developed and perfected in the late eighteenth century such as the clock, thermometer, barometer, and telescope—tools that enabled man the explorer to accurately measure, survey, and territorialize nature's wild and savage appearance. And clothing too reflects this desire to return to simpler and more innocent times: pure natural fibers, Irish linens and woolens can be purchased at Williamson's of Schermerhorn Row; Laura Ashley sells Victorian-styled clothing that speaks of a higher morality and domesticity; and Pier 17 has its fill of trading posts selling clothing and equipment for contemporary explorers and travelers. This nostalgia for colonial attire deflected onto "the once-upon-a-time," veils any awareness of how we modern-day colonizers comply with contemporary modes of economic exploitation and territorial appropriation. Past and present forms of colonization, both economic and spatial, are quickly inverted into amusement and displaced by a discourse that locates fashion and style within a discussion of natural beauty and raw materials, of exotic places and travel.

Space, clothing, and food are discriminating values, and their finely tuned classifications set up a hierarchy of tastes and distinctions. Consequently the theme of "fish" at South Street Seaport represents another natural and symbolic marker. At first appearance, Fulton Market seems to display two different food cultures: the "shirt-sleeve" wholesale fish market along the river's edge, which comes alive at the crack of dawn when fresh supplies of fish are sold to Manhattan chefs and restaurateurs, and the Festival Market Hall, which opens in the lazy hours of mid-morning and caters not only to gourmets shopping on its first-floor level for a range of delicacies such as Madagascar vanilla, Mississippi crayfish, or hazelnut coffee, but as well to tourists who may be satisfied on an upper level by assorted facsimiles of Coney Island refreshment stands such as the New York Pastrami Factory or the Burger Boys of Brooklyn. There are as well more refined dining spots, such as Roebling's Bar and Grill or the Ocean Reef Grill, carrying on the tradition of man and the sea. Now obstensibly the two different food cultures seem to clash, but in reality they cater to different tastes in order to generate more tourists. Tastes in food, Pierre Bourdieu describes in *Distinctions*, are discriminated by class attitudes toward the body, and fish in particular is deemed by the working class to be an unsuitable food for robust men for it must be eaten delicately to avoid choking on the bones, and it appears to be insubstantially light nourishment, feminine, almost medicinely "healthful."[38] Fish is consequently the perfect food for health-conscious natural food devotees found among the upper classes, and the perfect advertising emblem to capture the imagination of consumers already concerned with appearance and form. By calling on the tradition of Coney Island known as the "Mecca of the Millions," however, this spectacle of food and the pleasures that surround it establish yet another classification: that of popular taste. Because the Rouse Company is under agreement with the Seaport Museum and the city to attract large numbers of customers to the Seaport to eat and shop, it must produce not just a food show for the monied elite, but low-brow popular exhibits as well.[39] And mass taste tends, or so Bourdieu has claimed, to prefer a mouthful of beef.

All of this discourse on nature, on colonization, on adventures at sea, spirals inward and downward toward the central preoccupation of South Street Seaport: the "natural" recycling of degraded and devalued territory unrelated to the rest of the city. Of course the "return to nature" and the adventures of travel can be looked upon as a critique of the flawed project of modernism, which attempted to deny the power of nature through its faith in science and technology. But Neil Smith has noted that pitting the individual against nature in the urban theater has another meaning as well. He claims that the image of the "urban pioneer" who moves into downgraded neighborhoods and begins the cycle of gentrification assumes that these adventurers are the first settlers on the frontier, populating abandoned districts of the city uninhabitated except for a few straggling "natives," and claiming land that stands as a virtual wilderness waiting to be conquered and won.[40] But there is in fact nothing "natural" about this process of spatial restructuring that leaves parts of the city to decline while others are revitalized through massive flows of capital investment, regulatory land use controls, real estate transactions, and tax concessions. In particular, South Street Seaport, through its illusion of natural landscapes and travel adventures, pre-industrial market conditions and artisan production, masks other conditions of dominance. Part of New York's revitalized garment industry depends on sweatshop employment, many of the specialty food providers pay workers minimal wages and often violate health codes and safety requirements, and the upscaled marketplace for tourists, shoppers, and financial employees has displaced residential uses and marginal businesses, and banished from view every unregulated clown and spontaneous street performance.

In spite of all the plans and preparations for festival marketplaces, including those executed for South Street Seaport, these places have not always been successful at attracting tourists and customers. In the first few years of its operation the Seaport failed to draw the expected number of customers, and consequently many of the original small-scale retail and food enterprises pressured for reductions in rent. Changes in retailing inevitably occurred and now many of the more successful stores, such as Banana Republic, Brookstone's, The Nature Store, and Laura Ashley, are national retailers who showcase their line of products in upscaled historic marketplaces such as South Street Seaport, but who rely on catalog sales to generate their profits. These highly verticalized contemporary colonists import their products from production zones in developing countries where labor and materials are cheap and then distribute these from automated mailing centers within the United States. They rely, however, on the historic ambience of festival marketplaces for advertising a particular arrangement of commodities and underwriting a pleasurable and valued style of life.[41] Modern consumption depends on remarkable sites and image displays, sparking a desire for travel and adventure, for change and novelty, hence "selling" has developed intimate tie-ins with cultural tourism and leisure-time activities. What counts is the style, the look, or the image and how it is linked to a structure of feeling and incorporated into the marketing of furnishings, clothing, food, and holiday expenditures. The production of South Street Seaport is coextensive with the creation of such a market, and nostalgia the choreographer for its set of desires. It is a continuous advertisement, a theater stage for the business of selling with all of its hype and role playing, dissimulation and allure. Advertising in South Street Seaport places the spectator inside a specific historical and narrative milieu and plays with a series of references that the consumer must be able to read. Linked to advertising, the preservation of historic architecture and the reconstitution of past urban landscapes generate through their image-sets an emotional mood and style of life and thus become an integral part of production. In the 1970s and 1980s, it was after all not the choice between different products that was being advertised as much as it was alternative lifestyles and the staging of a particular set of goods.

The contemporary spectator of city spaces inevitably finds that the public spaces of her or his present-day promenades are none other than recycled and revalued territories like South Street Seaport that have been turned into gentrified, historicized, commodified, and privatized landscapes. They represent one of the many cultural spheres that once existed outside of the marketplace, but now survive only through the support of advertising and consequently display an aesthetic controlled to produce an environment that sells. "Just looking" at city spaces and traveling along their architectural promenades, although still pleasurable public experiences, increasingly tend to represent that moment of association when private desires take flight and become linked to future promises offered by items for sale. On one register, South Street Seaport narrates a partial story about the instrumental reproduction of a public marketplace where communal celebrations and festivals still take place, albeit in truncated and modified form. On another register, however, the spectator is targeted by the narrative "style of life" advertising that the Seaport represents, and finds her- or himself inscribed within a historic tableau appealing directly to fantasies of private identification. Shifting modes involving the public and private spheres are turning streets and spaces of our cities inside out, internalizing public ways and communal spaces behind the walls of privatized market development, while externalizing the private sphere of nostalgic desires and historic imagination within the scenographic stage sets of these reconstituted public places.

So finally it is here in South Street Seaport that present-day realities and nostalgic desires collide, for there is nothing "natural" about the uneven development of urban America that the market actually sustains. Wall Street financial interests desired to find new territory in which to expand, but they were concerned with the preservation of the city's historic waterfront and the reconstruction of its former marketplace only as stage props supporting a cast of more lucrative ventures. The urban voyager setting his or her sails against the howling forces of nature—a theme reiterated over and over again at South Street Seaport—is none other than a metaphorical device that situates the memory of historical voyages to uncivilized terrains against the contemporary appropriation of the city's undervalued and marginal wastelands and through this juxtaposition (or montage) legitimizes their conversion into profitable leisure-time places.[42] But a city of increasing spatial differentiation results and the gap looms larger between neglected land and revalued places, between the poor that the market ignores and the well-to-do that it privileges. The use of historic preservation and the creation of atmospheric milieus to stabilize this difference between types of public space may not change in the future, for we are only beginning to witness this process of spatial restructuring and to understand the manner in which the market draws on and sustains our historic imagination and plays with our desire to experience the present as a time and place retreating every day into the past.

Images of Battery Park City

From South Street Seaport, the spectator of city places seeking the Hudson River can either meander along the passageways that lead through the skyscraper canyons of Wall Street or follow a more direct route across Fulton Street. On either voyage the traveler is blocked from the river by streams of roaring traffic on West Street or arrested in the subterranean maze of the massive platform that serves as the base for the twin towers of the World Trade Center. Just beyond reach, jutting out from the Hudson River waterfront, lies the new development called Battery Park City.[43] The pedestrian is really not welcomed to this new public space, for she or he has to painstakingly and cautiously cross lanes of highway traffic with no obvious point of entry in sight. Or the traveler may select one of two elevated skywalks over West Street that unexpectedly lead from within the general confines of the World Trade Center's platform into the interior corridor of the megacomplex known as the World Financial Center, and suddenly plunge to earth over cascades of stairways and elevator banks.

This project was conceptually linked to six other waterfront communities in the original 1960s development plan proposed for Lower Manhattan. Today, however, Battery Park City stands as yet another isolated city tableau in the contemporary game of spatial restructuring. On ninety-two acres of landfill at the southern tip of Manhattan, this idealized New York neighborhood was put in place during the 1980s. Here one can find the look of prewar apartment houses combined with the views and atmosphere of Brooklyn Heights, the reproduction of Central

Park lampposts and benches, the inspiration drawn from the private enclave of Gramercy Park, as well as the great landscape inheritance of Olmsted's parks. This "urban dream" is based on a master plan created in 1979, which embodied design guidelines specifying architectural elements and styles borrowed from the city's best residential streetscapes such as Central Park West, West End Avenue, and Riverside Drive. But the plan as well was informed by the memory of Manhattan's gridiron street pattern and the more subtle effects of its lighting, signage, and colors. No single-use projects such as the modern movement's red-brick housing complexes that dot the East River side of Manhattan or the node of culture at Lincoln Center, Battery Park City was to be instead a multi-use minicity incorporating within its boundaries apartments and offices, museums and schools, parks and marinas, hotels and restaurants, theaters and shops.

In this new exchange place dedicated to financial capital, we are given a view of how New York in the 1980s envisioned itself. Like South Street Seaport, Battery Park City is a historically constituted and compositionally structured place. But the story of its spatial production reveals a different set of tensions and conflicts. As a business center of worldwide importance, New York's financial district in the 1950s needed room to expand and places to house its workers if it was to compete successfully against the development of midtown Manhattan. This had been a dream of New York planners for Lower Manhattan since the 1920s and 1930s, when office developments around both Grand Central Station and Rockefeller Center were accepted as clear setbacks to the unchallenged supremacy of the financial district.[44] The dream was reaffirmed by David Rockefeller and the Lower Manhattan Association in their first proposal of 1958. Calling for a plan to save the financial district from slow strangulation, their report noted that sixteen new office buildings located in the hard core of the Wall Street district were forced to reach skyward, choked on all edges by ninety-seven acres of obsolescent, deteriorating, and economically wasteful land uses comprised of old fish stalls, vegetable and butter markets, old piers, ships' chandleries and light industries, and rows of small buildings—some more than one hundred years in age.[45] In addition, circulation was a major problem, and the possibility of a Lower Manhattan Crosstown Expressway had been under study since 1948. But most important, the district had fewer than 4,000 residents, and the argument was made that if the financial district was to compete with midtown, it must develop new luxury residential spaces. The logical areas into which the financial district might expand, or so the Plan suggested, were the congested blocks surrounding the old West Side Produce Market below Canal Street and the East River Fulton Fish Market below the Brooklyn Bridge. These newly "prized" waterfront areas offered sufficient "fallow" land not only for office towers to sprout and expand but for residential communities to grow, housing in their turn leagues of white-collar office workers.

During the 1960s, the Manhattan waterfront continued to decline, being supplanted as an important cargo and shipping center by modernized container facilities in New Jersey and Brooklyn. Consequently many plans for waterfront restructuring were in place by 1966. The Washington Market Urban Renewal project took care of eradicating the produce market on the west side during the 1960s, subsequently clearing twenty-four blocks along the waterfront from its "encumbering" historic structures. And already the World Trade Towers development project, announced in 1964 and actively sponsored by both David and Nelson Rockefeller, suggested that the financial district might shift toward the Hudson River. Alongside these plans, waterfront restructuring proposals were offered by Mayor Lindsay, the Parks Department, and the Marine and Aviation Department. The latter had requested in 1958 that the Hudson River waterfront be revitalized with new cargo facilities; by the late 1960s, however, only two out of the entire seven miles of the Hudson River waterfront remained devoted to shipping uses, and it was expected in the future that these activities were doomed to wither and die. Thus Mayor Lindsay proposed to transfer jurisdiction over the waterfront to the Parks Department; not surprisingly the Parks Commissioner, Thomas Hoving, wanted to redevelop the decaying piers along the waterfront with swimming barges, strips of parkland, entertainment facilities, and residential communities. A hastily drawn up plan by the architects Harrison & Abramowitz for Governor Rockefeller

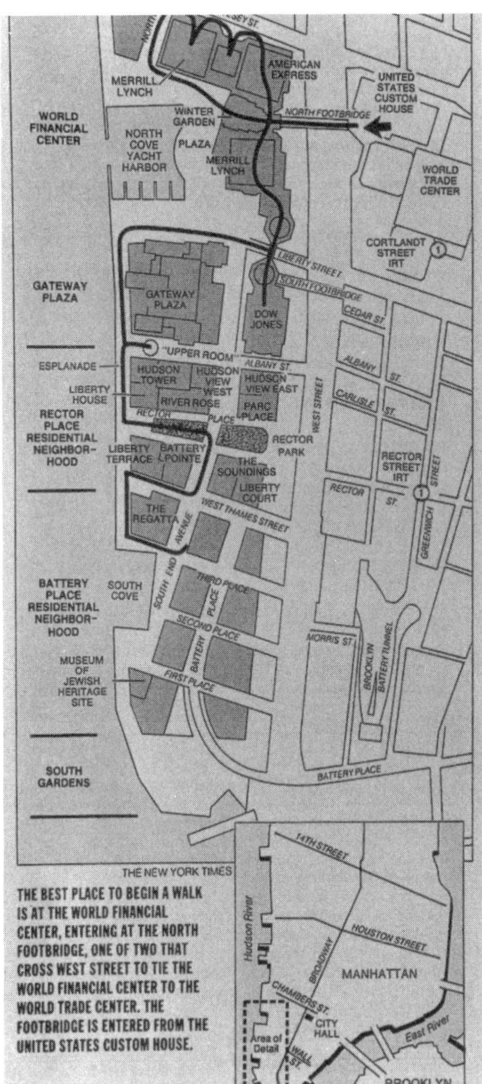

"Battery Park City Plan and Walking Tour,"
The New York Times Magazine
(November 20, 1988).

proposed a row of high-rise mixed-income residential towers standing in parks of green on landfill along the waterfront.[46] Mayor Lindsay's Office of Lower Manhattan Development offered their own plan for luxury housing by the team of Wallace, McHarg, Roberts & Todd; Whittlesey, Conklin & Rossant; and Alan M. Voorhees & Associates, Inc. Discussed above with respect to South Street Seaport, this plan located mixed-income residential communities at the ends of the axes of Wall Street, Broadway, Chambers Street, Fulton Street, and the World Trade Center. Each community was designed around waterfront plazas, and they were linked by a string of parks and an esplanade.[47] Eventually a new development scheme with a smaller amount of low-income housing was proposed as a compromise between the city's and the governor's plans. But commitment to develop even this compromise remained a debatable issue.[48]

Then a dramatic new restructuring effort suddenly joined the development game. Following by two years the announced plans for the World Trade Towers, it was proposed to use the soil excavated in the development of those towers for landfill along the derelict Hudson waterfront. Unlike South Street Seaport, however, the key to this new development would lie in the creation by 1968 of the quasi-public Battery Park City Authority, empowered by the state to sell $200 million worth of bonds to finance its landfill operations, the removal of decaying piers, and all of its public infrastructure improvements. Operating under a ninety-nine-year lease from the city, with an approved development plan that overrides any local land use review and remains but a gentleman's agreement, the authority was granted the right to sublet this landfill to private developers.[49] Development remained a dream, however, for Battery Park City was in 1976 just a barren landfill unable to attract development interest. The mid-1970s were of course exactly the years in which New York City slid toward bankruptcy during its fiscal crisis. In such financially gloomy times, plans for waterfront restructuring were forgotten, and the Battery Park City Authority was unable to sell additional bonds and thus could not raise the money for loans to support its residential developments. Meanwhile the market for office space declined all over Manhattan, in part due to a glut of overbuilding in the early 1970s but also because New York had lost its allure as a business center, causing some corporate headquarters to relocate outside of the city. So plans to expand the financial district and underwrite its future with waterfront residential communities came to a halt.

The original site plan for Battery Park City located a huge, self-contained megastructure along the entire spine of a suppressed West Street roadway. The superstructure would then spin off an entire network of subterranean connectors, access ramps, and parking lots and lead to the financial district across a series of elevated pedestrian walkways. Megastructures, a technological framework combining the visually rich scenery of industrial piping, catwalks, and ramps with internalized multifunctional spaces for work, leisure, and movement were the rage of the 1960s. The architect Paul Rudolph's intended Lower Manhattan Expressway (1970), or the air rights development above the Port Authority near the George Washington Bridge (1965), were exemplary of this type of structure.[50] Battery Park City's site plan also included mixed-income government subsidized housing projects as isolated towers along the Hudson River waterfront. By the late 1970s, however, government subsidies for low- and moderate-income housing no longer existed, and so it was argued without any need to resort to issues of equity or social justice that if housing was to be part of the future Battery Park City, it must respond to the demand increasing throughout Manhattan for luxury housing at market prices. In addition, the total architectural outlook of the modern movement was under serious debate by the mid-1970s, and superstructural containers or residential towers in parks of green as part of this aesthetic approach suddenly looked as outmoded as last year's fashion designs.

In the late 1970s, New York's office market began to recover, and its image as a glittering world city reemerged. So the need arose, once again, not only for new office spaces but for corporate support services and communication centers, for entertainment spaces and for luxury housing to complement its expanding base of white-collar employment.[51] By this time the World Trade Center had become a dominant force restructuring the shape of Lower Manhattan. This new transportation, office, tourist, and commercial hub lay directly opposite the Battery Park City site and was pushing the office center of Lower Manhattan toward the west and the river. To the northeast of Battery Park City, the old wholesale district and manufacturing area of Tribeca (Triangle Below Canal) experienced in the late 1970s a lively pace of residential loft conversions. It contained the Washington Market Urban Renewal project toward its southern end, where Manhattan Community College and Independence Plaza, a middle-income residential development, had been erected in 1975. However, this urban renewal project stood out as a dramatic reminder of the problems that megastructure planning had posed. Designed as a huge complex raised on a platform, this project would have been connected to the World Trade Center and to Battery Park City by elevated pedestrian passageways. New York's fiscal crisis brought all of these development plans to an abrupt end, leaving the community college only 20 percent completed. With renewed development interest, however, the open areas of land surrounding the Washington Market Urban Renewal site plus the vacant landfill of Battery Park City were the only places for real estate expansion in close proximity to the World Trade Center. In addition, the middle-income project of Independence Plaza was now called a failure, because the city eventually bailed out the project by subsidizing rentals and thus brought their prices down to at least moderate-income levels. So it was easy to argue that if the master plan for Battery Park City was reorganized to allow more flexible and smaller-scaled development, and if the ideal of middle- or mixed-income residential communities in Lower Manhattan could be abandoned once and for all, then the barren landfill of Battery Park City might appeal to local developers as a luxury office and residential community. As it also appeared to be possible that the authority might default on its bond payments due in 1980, profitable development became more appealing than any form of subsidization. Of course this action under the duress of default and bankruptcy may have been only a sleight of hand, for implicit subsidies hidden from public awareness and accountability always underwrite private development through the provisions of public parks and public arts programs, corporate and financial tax abatements, or zoning and planning allowances. Nevertheless, with the twist of these events the dream of a luxury minicity in Lower Manhattan was almost a reality, and as the rhetoric proclaimed, private enterprise now would build a new prestige community to house and entertain the expanding financial service workers, accountants, corporate lawyers, management consultants, public relations and communication experts, advertisers, and insurance agents that kept rising in number on the tide of New York City's renewed prosperity.[52]

The time seemed ripe for restructuring the plans for the Hudson River waterfront as well. Disgarding the superblock megastructure mentality of the original plan, the revised master plan developed by Alexander Cooper Associates in 1979 believed that there was nothing wrong with Manhattan's street pattern of small rectangular blocks. Thus the new plan, either literally or figuratively, enabled the memory of this grid pattern to connect the northern and southern ends of Battery Park City to the rest of Manhattan. Conventional building lots and streets with sidewalks would enable the normal rules of Manhattan block and lot development to prevail and this ordinariness, or so it was argued, would appeal to the average New York developer. Abandoning the modernist concept of total design, Battery Park City would be developed incrementally over time as different areas of landfill were opened for development, thus simulating the manner in which a city actually develops. Emblematic residential places of Manhattan, such as Central Park West, Tudor City, Gramercy Park, and Riverside Drive were the designs against which Battery Park City's residential development guidelines were placed. The street would once again become the major organizing device, reintroducing shopping arcades, street-level crossings, and vehicular traffic. In addition a variety of park and landscape designs, public amenities, and street furniture would fully exploit the scenic potential of this waterfront property where landscape and riverscape merged. Because the success of the new plan lay dependent on commercial development, the business district of this new town was shifted to the center of the site just opposite the World Trade Towers. Here transfer of development rights from site to site would enable a large-scale office complex to arise—albeit a modernist megastructure—while leaving the waterfront edge free for smaller-scale residential development and preserving riverscape views.

With these new plans in hand, developers responded and construction began. A remnant from the older plans, Gateway Plaza would be the first residential development of Battery Park City when it opened in 1982. Meanwhile Olympia & York Properties from Canada leased substantial areas of Battery Park City in 1981 and began to construct, at an estimated cost of $1.5 billion, the four-tower complex designed by architect Cesar Pelli and henceforth known as the World Financial Center. And finally, the Battery Park Authority designated eight development teams for its Rector Place residential community. By 1983 the first segment of the waterfront esplanade was opened and within a few years followed the second esplanade section, Rector Park, South Cove Park, the glass-enclosed Winter Garden, and a 3.5 acre plaza surrounding North Cove. And of course there was more to come: North Cove Yacht Harbor, Vesey Place ice skating rink, the North Park and North End Parks, South Gardens, hotels, museums, and schools.

Battery Park City and the Rhetoric of "New York Ascendant"

Alongside the real estate and architectural producers of Battery Park City, there developed a series of postproduction artists such as advertisers and newspaper journalists who have manipulated and rearranged the images of place and showcased "history" for specific effects. One of their claims located New York among the ascendant world-class cities in the 1980s, perhaps the preeminent command and control center of the entire global economy. In this powerful media performance, Battery Park City, where the World Financial Center is located, played an important rhetorical role. New York, this play proclaimed, was the commercial capital of the world's largest market-oriented country; it was a major exporter and distributor of images and information in the business, financial, political, and cultural spheres of influence. And since the fiscal crisis of the mid-1970s, the city and state in the interest of the public good had focused their attention on the

Aerial View of The World Financial Center at Battery Park City.

direction in which this international economy was moving, and attempted to capture the benefits that an expanding world financial exchange and its telecommunications support might generate.[53]

One result of this framing narration of "New York Ascendant" has been the dismantlement of programs designed in the 1950s and 1960s to aid the poor and putting in their place an increasingly market-oriented set of urban policies that have transferred resources instead to the privileged and private sector. To no one's surprise uneven development has been the result, with expanding growth at the top where the well-to-do white-collar workers reside, and swelling ranks at the bottom where the marginally employed and ill-educated poor may dwell. Thus a breach continuously widens, placing the city of the rich on one side and that of the poor on the other. In this gap between the rich and the poor, an antagonistic "war of positions" pitting "them" against "us" might have been the response if the 1970s and 1980s had remained as politically volatile as the 1960s had been. But a dialogue of confrontation was artfully contained and neutralized in the 1980s' media performances that spoke of a new public spirit and civic grandeur overriding existing social and political tensions. Banished from our memories were values of mutual support, cooperation, and sharing that demand within a fractured metropolis that affinities be made across racial and economic differences.[54] By concentrating on corporate power, however, and all the glamor and glitter that a world-class city may reveal, media support for these other affinities was nowhere to be found. Disassociating the images of uneven development from those of place and privilege allowed unmentionable inequities to be sustained as normal and inevitable consequences of economic growth and global preeminence.

Noam Chomsky has critically observed that the media, as an adjunct of government, is expected to educate the public in the interests of those who manage state policies at any given moment in time, and to do so with enthusiasm and optimism about the causes in which the state is engaged. If one of those causes is the concentration of private power concomitant with the manufacturing of consent to its set of priorities and privileges, then in order to act as vigilant guardians protecting privilege from the threat of public understanding and participation, the media may resort to "necessary illusions" by carefully selecting the general framework in which topics are discussed, issues raised, and premises left unmentioned.[55] The images of Battery Park City and the media performances that surround them are steeped in the invention of "necessary illusions." They legitimate the privileging of private interests through the construction of an optimistic media consensus telling the reader in a repetitious manner that the architectural productions of Battery Park City enhance the public welfare, demonstrate a new civic pride in the city, and through a backward-binding sense of tradition guarantee the illusion that these images belong to New Yorker's rightful and collective inheritance. In these media performances, our sense of collective identity is experienced aesthetically and noncritically through images that foreground the pleasurable look of the city while obscuring the agents of re-presentation and those that compose consensus.[56]

One *New York Times* writer noted, "If this newest part of Manhattan called Battery Park City were a movie set, New Yorkers would laugh at its impossible concentration of city landmarks in reality."[57] And indeed Battery Park is a cinematographic setup, or a fabricated city tableau, that congeals into a universal generalizing theme. Starting with the impression they wanted to convey, its architectural directors carefully selected the views that would enhance this feeling. By drawing from a set of images that both exist and are valued in New York City, they meant to refigure the way that the spectator would perceive this new architectural assemblage. Through the juxtaposition of disparate images this montage is meant to evoke analogical associations that bind the new to the old, the fragment to the whole, the past to the present. As an advertising campaign proclaims, Battery Park City is just "More New York New York." And like the line in the song, "New York, New York, it's a wonderful town, the Bronx is up and the Battery down," this media narrative links the territory of the new city to the map of the old and merges high art with popular forms. Another journalist simply underlined these same themes as he eavesdropped on a fictitious conversation between "Weekend Walker" and "City Stroller" on a ramble around the landfill:

> And all this talk of new lands: we're not opening up Oklahoma. Everything around the rim of Manhattan, downtown anyway, was a new land. Why do you think we have Front Street and Water Street inland from South Street on the East Side? Landfill, landfill. Even Greenwich Street, two blocks in, was on North River waterfront and, later the Battery was sticking out in the harbor.

Supposedly there is nothing unnatural or unusual that the stroller might encounter about the creation of Battery Park City, situated as it is in the historical record of how the cityscape of New York was created in the past.[58]

Paul Goldberger, the upbeat architectural critic of the *New York Times*, was a major orchestrator of the media constructions that bind Battery Park City to the architectural heritage of New York. He claimed that this triumph of urban design was "close to a miracle," being "the finest urban grouping since Rockefeller Center."[59] Based on what he referred to as a radical notion, the 1979 master plan decided and most New Yorkers agreed that there was nothing wrong with Manhattan as it appears and that "most of the attempts by architects and planners to rethink the basic shape of the city have resulted in disaster."[60] In its initial form, Battery Park City was designed as a series of vast modernists "superblocks" and unfortunately, or so Goldberger felt, a remnant of these "eastern European housing complexes jazzed up by Buck Rogers" remained as Gateway Plaza in order to disturb the ensemble's historicist totality.[61] But after the new master plan had been placed firmly in control of the look of the place, it was able to negotiate the architectural styles, historical allusions, and meaning of its public places in return for giving a private developer permission to build. The master plan symbolically located the major office building complex in the center of the plan—making the World Financial Center the new city's downtown—"the place to go for a special meal, dancing or a cabaret."[62] Four gigantic towers designed by Cesar Pelli for Olympia & York, with their varied tops and different heights yet identical facades, "constitute a serious essay in romantic modernism," an attempt that combines the look of the past with modern materials.[63] The ten residential buildings of Rector

Place, a simulated Gramercy Park, provide a coherent sense of place and will act as a neighborhood template for future development in the northern and southern edges of town. Tying the entire ensemble together are the fifty acres of parks and promenades, a public gesture of magnificence, avidly celebrated by politicians who see Battery Park City as emblematic of the renewed energy and dynamism of New York as a great world financial center and the commitment of its government to the "public realm."[64]

As a form of melodrama, this glorification of Battery Park City pitted the modernist aesthetic against the postmodern, innovation against tradition, an impaired city against its ideal form—a gesture in which "history" was constantly evoked as a reassuring device and traditional urban spaces were as welcome as a hero's return. By drawing on the tensions envisioned by good and bad architectural forms, this city tableau and its verbal hyperbole displaced the contradictions of spatial production onto an emotional and visual level. Constantly reenacting the same formula, this melodramatic performance created a sense of living tradition and mythology to be judged by its collective energy and nostalgic effect. Although Battery Park City did not depend on or borrow from the instinct of historic preservation, it was moved instead by the extraction and seriality of images drawn from New York's heroic commercial architecture as well as its liberal record of public and private parks. The organizing principle of this collection of architectural and urban forms was a backward-binding nostalgia that longed to repossess and return to New York's commercial heyday in the 1920s. For we have been told by architectural historians that American architecture in this interwar period finally created a style of its own when the city was catapulted into being a world-class financial capital. New York, *The Nation* proclaimed in 1929, became the "mecca and the model" for all of America.[65] Its spectacle of power could be viewed by every passenger who entered the harbor of the city, for its skyscraper towers were a vision "prophetic of modernity, of immense mechanical superiority, of intolerance of all that is not the newest, the latest and best."[66] Public grandeur became a by-product of America's commercial architecture whose tone was established in the 1920s. As corporate skyscrapers replaced the lower profile of public buildings, they became the new symbol of the city's civic pride. Commercial buildings defined the cutting edge of architecture, setting procedents that others would follow.[67]

Consequently the images collected in Battery Park City become metaphorical carriers of a special kind of history and defenders of a set of values established in earlier times. Through the recreations of traditional New York spaces and architectural forms—historical examples all built by private enterprise such as Gramercy Park, or Central Park West, Tudor City, or Rockefeller Center—the present is filled with a sense of grandeur and self-importance, or pleasure and excitement, that many modernist places in the city apparently failed to achieve. Battery Park City teaches us how to feel, not think, about the past, how to overcome the sense of failure and crisis that modernism provided, that the near bankruptcy of the city's fiscal crisis congealed, and that the decline of American international supremacy revealed.[68] The citation of these few images drawn from New York's commercial heritage seemed to justify the entire outdoor museum of Battery Park City. Some might question whether the city and the state should have been involved in helping financially to underwrite a $4.5 billion, fundamentally upper-class project. But then, this is the intention of nostalgia, to invert and gloss over reality and twist and turn the dividing line that separates public and private space. And this seems to be New York's inheritance from the 1920s as well, a time when commercial architecture developed a truly American style and by this gesture alone turned the "image" of New York into that of a world-class city. As the boomtown mythology of the 1920s is carried over into the 1980s, Battery Park City's development energy, it was argued, might simply spill over and push the project thirteen blocks northward from Chambers Street as far as Canal Street. And some of the residential assignments, furthermore, might be transferred instead to more lucrative commercial development.[69]

As the New York Regional Plan proclaimed during the 1920s, New York's ". . . most striking architectural feature is its mass of high buildings as seen from the surrounding areas of open water, which give it the benefit of open space from which buildings can be seen. It is on the frontage of these water areas that its greatest opportunity lies for creating beauty of building."[70] Reiterated by a Mayor's Task Force on the Design of the City of New York in 1967, this group of elite New Yorkers noted that "New York needs—and could have—closer connections with nature . . . The city's largest sweep of nature by far is its harbor and rivers. The city is almost 25% water, with no less than 578 miles of waterfront within the city limits. This presents opportunities for both lyricism and liveliness which has largely been ignored."[71] So the waterfront of Manhattan, that fallow landscape of decaying piers and underutilized spaces that has been described "as being like an unhemmed dress"—this too might follow the path outlined in the 1920s, and again in the late 1960s, and be restructured and recycled with monumental commercial developments.[72] As if she were a stereotypical woman standing before her mirror, New York City seems addicted to a flawless perfected image of herself, always a younger image drawn nostalgically from her past.

This collection of city images, drawn from the memory of New York's heroic past, are situated quotations. They are public images appropriated for private means, underscoring the political message of "New York Ascendant," but they are also a way of giving form and expression to the invisible financial transactions and monetary exchanges of the World Financial Center. Susan Stewart, in her book *On Longing,* has noted that a collection replaces history with classification, formally ordering and arranging each item as a member of a set of objects and displaying them serially in its arrangement of boxes, shelves, cabinets, or museum rooms. Once upon a time the collection of bric-a-brac captured the aesthetics of mercantilism—a trader's possessions gathered from around the world, valued and displayed for their curiosity, monetary value, or for their uniqueness among a set of things. In every one of these prototypical collections, the world of things was given to the collector as if she or he were its rightful inheritor. "And this scene of acquisition is repeated over and over through the serial arrangement of objects in display space. . . . if they [the objects] are 'made,' it is by a process that seems to invent itself for the pleasure of the acquirer."[73] Now there were as well open-air equivalents to these curio collections of appropriated objects—landscaped gardens surrounded by a perimeter belt of trees that turned the perspective toward the interior of the site, which in turn was composed as a series of walks and vistas with a sequence of architectural curios and facsimiles representing "our possessions" from India, China, or Greece. So it has been claimed, the aesthetics of eclecticism depended on "an extrapolation of the best that has been thought and said in the world by a Citizen of the World."[74]

Drawing on these analogies, we find that the images of Battery Park City are presented to the spectator as a series of views, classified and arranged within the interior of an outdoor architectural museum for his or her amusement, ripped out of their original context and displayed for the pleasures of possession and inheritance. The most emblematic space of this type, actually simulating a cabinet of curiosity with items selected from a thousand years of garden design, was the planned but rejected composition for South Garden. A collaborative effort between architect Alexander Cooper and landscape architect Jennifer Bartlett, this three-acre park at the southern tip of Battery Park City was designed as a grid of twenty-four cellular divisions, each 50 by 50 feet in size. Since New York's climate is hot in the summer and cold in the winter, a ten-and-a-half-foot concrete wall would have enclosed the entire garden, allowing only one small entry point in the middle of its eastern side. From within this enclosure, a spectator could ramble at his or her leisure amid the cells of the grid, each one composed of a different type of garden such as an evergreen winter garden, a serpentine garden, an orchard of apple trees, a lily pond, a rose garden, and more.

In addition to these staged landscapes meant for the pleasure of looking, Battery Park City's $4.5 billion display of architectural might is contaminated with commercialism and like all commercial architecture, its scenographic compositions invoke the art of advertising. These public forms of communication influence still further the manner in which the spectator links Battery Park City to a network of other city views and spaces. Because it is difficult to give the boundless and abstract market transactions that surround the World Financial Center an image, this might have led to a crisis in representation. Fredric Jameson, in *Postmodernism or, The Cultural Logic of Late Capitalism,* claims that the rise of the British colonial system in the late nineteenth century created such a crisis, for imperialism was a global reality no longer visualizable, mappable, or representable. Man in the center of London, for example, experienced a gap between his bounded and centered everyday reality and this new global reality, and hence his world was haunted by a sense of alienation and filled with vacancies and voids. Jameson also suggests that a similar crisis has erupted under late capitalism with its global network of multinational corporations. In this worldwide system, he argues, the individual is thrown against an unmappable and bizarre juxtaposition of multidimensional spaces and discontinuous realities. So, he proclaims, a world that is not mappable is a world that cannot be critically transformed.[75]

But instead of Jameson's unmappable world, this crisis of representation has been met in the contemporary city by the construction of new theatrical tableaux. In each of these stage settings the spectators are presented with well-established and valued views that showcase special styles of life, underscore social norms and moral structures, and offer entertaining and pleasurable events. On these stages, which ignore all the spaces and affinities that exist outside of their prosceniums, the new social norms and moral relationships that pertain in the global economy are given a show. Borrowing analogically from the *theatrum mundi* metaphor, claiming that all the world's a stage, these city tableaux are reminiscent of the seventeenth century, when the local customs and bartering practices of traditional fairs and marketplaces were transformed by the more abstract, invisible, and infinite processes of commodity circulation and money exchange. The theater became the terrain on which new relationships were defined and explained to spectators, who now resided within a strange and perplexing economy. "What made the theatrical metaphor so resilient [in the face of the powerfully transformative effects of commodity exchange] was no doubt its capacity to evoke the sense of a lived abstraction of distinctively human contrivance, ..." In this theatrical metaphor, willful individuals were given a role to play in a predetermined world. Their duty was then to act out the part allotted to them as perfectly as possible without questioning the assignment of roles.[76]

And so we are brought full circle to the entertaining city tableaux that the world's financial capital has constructed before the spectator's eyes and to the concept of the "public sphere," which has been cleverly contrived. When the World Financial Center was inaugurated in October of 1988, five days of fairs and celebrations were staged by Drenttel Doyle Partners, the advertising agents hired by Olympia & York to celebrate the event with appropriate fleets of boats, puppet shows, banners, balloons, and carnival floats. In addition, a series of theatrical performances and art exhibitions were showcased in the glass and marble agora of the Winter Garden: events that tried to create the impression that this "new-generation Rockefeller Center" was the latest addition in a line of projects that inevitably link corporate sponsorship to the cultural life of the city. The World Financial Center's advertising campaign included a series of full-page, two-color advertisements entitled "City Tales." Each one of these advertisements was placed in prestigious New York publications such as the *New York Times Magazine*, the *New Yorker*, the *New York Magazine*, and *Vanity Fair*. These city tableaux, really photo-essays commissioned by the advertisers, asked twelve different poets, writers, and humorists to describe in their own words something characteristic yet special about Manhattan, some event or place that they encountered every day in the life of the city. Geared to the users of the World Financial Center, or so the advertisers claimed, "Everything about the Center is influenced by a progressive understanding of the uses of public space, and it's skewed toward the tastes of a younger, downtown crowd. The objective of DDP's campaign, Mr. Drenttel said, is to present the Center as a part of the fabric of New York," and hence the advertisements were actually "short on sell, long on creating a special look and feel of city life."[77] Intended to be twelve in number, after protests by the retailers who wanted a more direct selling campaign and less literary and artistic allusion, the campaign took on a more traditional bent. But the series of "City Tales" that did appear, however, reveal not only the type of "public" that Battery Park City was designed for, but the legitimating rhetoric that its imagery instills. Around the edges of each photo-essay in tiny print are the list of stores, businesses, and restaurants located in the World Financial Center. And at the bottom, on either side of the four-square logo of the World Financial Center—a kind of medieval *mappa mundi* dividing the globe into four continents—is the major advertising theme: "At Battery Park City it's more New York New York." This graphic display and the stories narrate the obvious message of work and play in a city whose architectural and public heritage is shared and extolled by all groups who supposedly make up the public.

The "City Tales" read something like this: Poet Dana Gioia's "City Tale of Destinations: Arrivals & Departures," takes Grand Central Station as a theme. Although claiming that most contemporary travel feels more like commuting, he noted that one experience, that of Grand Central Station, still actually feels like travel as one enters into or departs from New York's greatest indoor public space. In this "democratic precinct," really a theater stage, one can meet people from all walks of life, each with his or her own compelling story. Grand Central's architectural triumph, moreover, lies in its ability to blend functional and impressive forms that "not only are unintimidating but inviting. This is a place which recognizes the importance of each arrival." The obvious associative linkages with Battery Park City are not difficult to draw, but not one mention is made throughout this essay that Grand Central Station is simultaneously a magnificent landmark structure from New York's historic heritage, and it was at that time also a shelter for hundreds of homeless; that every arrival was greeted not only with the view of its cavernous lobby, but with the outstretched hands of panhandlers and the wretched faces of poverty; that a war over public space had its seamiest sites in the station.

Humorist Mark O'Donnell's tale was about "Eavesdropping: Fragments of the Perambulation." Juxtaposing snippets of conversation, he allows the unexpected to puncture the obvious and celebrates the contradictory montage that is New York. Here the conflicts and tensions of uneven spatial development that currently hound New Yorkers are released through laughter in the following manner: ". . ."Spare change? I'm trying to buy a condo". . . . "Did whoever wrote

City Tales:
DESTINATIONS

Arrivals & Departures

by DANA GIOIA

photograph by Elizabeth Zeschin

Today most travel feels like commuting. Distant airline journeys begin and end by waiting in line. Cars find the traffic in exotic cities drearily familiar. The same bored faces look up from bus station benches from Antwerp to Alabama. There is no poetry in reaching a public garage, a bus stop or luggage carrousel. Just the flat, minimal prose of baggage claims and parking meters. But there is one commute that actually feels like travel –coming into Grand Central Terminal. Entering its vast main lobby either by descending from the noisy street or by rising from the steamy train platforms underground, one walks into Manhattan's greatest indoor public space, an area all the more exciting because unlike its closest contenders– Carnegie Hall, the Stock Exchange, the Palm Court at the Plaza–Grand Central is neither elitist nor exclusionary. In its democratic precincts investment bankers in snug italian suits line up for coffee behind Hawaiian-shirted street vendors and elderly nuns on a shopping spree share waiting room benches with honeymooners from Osaka. Stepping onto Grand Central's smooth marble floor is always like walking onstage but whether into a stark social drama or screwball screen comedy one can never quite tell in advance. Hundreds of lives hurry by, each one starring in its own compelling story. Charged by their sheer energy, one feels that particular rush of excitement that only great cities give. This almost delirious feeling that anything is possible represents the unacknowledged triumph of Grand Central's architecture. Utterly functional, this station is also truly grand. Its one vast central chamber stands impressively surrounded by teeming platforms, passageways, tunnels, balustrades, and antechambers, the air above crisscrossed by huge shafts of filtered sunlight rising to the high arched ceiling decorated astonishingly –as if to say that this one room is indeed its own universe– by the stars and constellations of the zodiac. Yet even to a gaping first-time visitor, a lone pedestrian clutching a battered suitcase on the swirling concourse below, all this grandeur seems not only unintimidating but inviting. This is a place which recognizes the importance of each arrival. Nervous, giddy, even inspired, one steps into the crowd ready to begin.

Over 30 thousand people come to work or play at The World Financial Center every day. They come by cars, boats, trains and planes. Once they come, they stay till all hours. Come and see what all the fuss is about.

Dana Gioia, "Arrivals & Departures," "City Tales" Advertisement, Agency Drentell Doyle Partners (November 1988).

the Internationale make any money off it?" . . . "Ya, I have been riding the subway all week, I feel very homely on it". . . ." In another photo-essay entitled, "Business Day: Work Study," Guy Martin humorously claimed that New York was "a great concentration of people with aberrant jobs." No other place would offer a detective, for example, the opportunity to specialize in scuba diving for discarded weapons; or develop a whole specialty around insomniacs; or offer a market for fleet-footed venture capitalists, who hawk their wares to trapped drivers en route to the airports. "Work give us an idea of what New York requires and, more importantly, just how much you can get away with here." And David Rieff's "Feeding Patterns; All Night Fruit" noted that New York had become a special space for single people, who by some magical law all become hungry around midnight. Thank heavens for the Korean fruit stands that began to appear all over town about fifteen years ago, a group of newcomers who made New York an all-night city the way it used to be. "It was the greatest event in the lives of single people since the invention of the VCR."

Wondrous Images

Seductive images in the camera obscura always turn reality on its head. In a similar manner these visual narratives of South Street Seaport and Battery Park City mix theater play with actuality, publicize private space as public terrain, and push every neglected space of the city through the sieve of an imaginary matrix whose nodes are none other than well-designed city tableaux. The contemporary spectator envisions isolated city worlds as if they were framed within a frame—they appear as scenographic stage sets of different lifestyles to try and different voyages to take. Searching for exotic unreality, realms that lie beyond our everyday life, the stroller meanders through the corridors and containers of city places hoping to encounter the strange effect where reality and illusion collide. We travel on, lured by legendary accounts that fill our imagination. So it has been since the fragmentary travelogues of antiquity first publicized the Wonders of the World, lost somehow in time but residing somewhere on the geographical edge of the world. Astonishing monuments

Advertisement for Donna Karan Eyewear.

Advertisement for Yamamoto Men's Suit, Charivari Store, New York.

suspended above reality, marvels that distance only intensified, the mythological picture stories of the Colossus of Rhodes, the Faros of Alexandria, the Mausoleum of Halicarnassus, the Hanging Gardens of Babylon, spread their reknown around the world. Unforgettable across the ages, the Seven Wonders were incomparable—they had to be seen to be believed. Perhaps they were only imaginary constructions, but reality remained deficient in comparison, and their mirage convinced many a traveler that somewhere in the fabulous East these marvels could be experienced. Wonders confuse fact and fiction, they lie beyond the documented and charted, in the land of the bizarre and unknown just off the map. If we knew all there was to known about cities, we would not travel nor find their scenographic and nostalgic arrangements alluring.

We used to wonder about the future of the city in spatial terms; it was a place toward which we were progressing, full of hope and expectation that a better world might someday be accomplished. In the contemporary city, we have lost this hope and critical engagement and are offered no alternative to the flattened, absorbing present. Immersed in its awful sublimity and laced with autarchic anxiety, the spectator as Fredric Jameson accounts can no longer make sense of nor question nor cognitively map the meaning of existence. But beyond the denials, outside of the carefully composed prosceniums, still there lies an enchanted kingdom of wonder, a future land toward which we travel. Pushed to the margins and the preface of the contemporary city, there nevertheless lies a carnival of possibilities and critical discriminations that every city provides, liminal spaces just outside the "city walls" enclosing official reality, just beyond the stretch of the hand that rushes to replicate the sensational. A myriad of details swarm up—the smells, colors, textures, and signs of a city or the rare and the peculiar incident. Nothing is intentionally or artificially configured about these unexpected city landscapes, nor is there a guided tour of their wondrous terrain; they arise naturally, imprinted with the customs of time and the claims different uses pronounce.

Besides these compelling adventures, there are as well egregious city images that spectators no longer wish to speak of, yet can not keep from spilling over into their everyday lives, pricking their consciousness and demanding attention. On every city encounter, there suddenly bursts forth a vibrant parade of excess and waste—neighborhoods stand before our eyes pockmarked with the upheavals of economic and social advance, drug wars wreack their devastation and whirl out of control, the homeless wander about with no hope nor relief in sight. Brought face-to-face with the underside of the city where scenes of calamity reside, the spectator's compassion and inquiry arise. Passages through the city must lead the traveler in both directions: forward toward the city of hope and the future, and backward toward the mire of decay and neglect. In the city of collective memory, we cannot stop to admire the spectacles of a city tableau yet ignore the bridges that link the high with the low life, that close the gap of indifference and distance, for they alone prod our steps along the unfinished path of anticipation where an undisputably better and more wondrous city may be discovered one day.

It is not good enough to remind the spectator of city spaces, as the architectural critic Paul Goldberger has done, that rich and poor traditionally have shared the turf of the city, that the homeless and downtrodden always have been part of the harsh and dirty cityscape, loitering under its bridges, settling in the crannies of its architectural monuments, staring at the spectator across the blank spaces of wide city streets. Our indifference to the affinities that bind citizens in common cause, Goldberger recognizes, is the product of a devalued public realm and the effect of allowing the private sector to plan and design our public spaces. For they have built corporate structures but not low-income housing, shopping arcades but not parks and promenades, until the quality of both the built environment and urban life have been diminished and impoverished. Yet the lesson that Goldberger draws from these failures is the realization that "there is no utopia," and he acknowledges "the wisdom of accepting what is there, of accepting certain social patterns and certain aspects of the physical form of cities as they exist . . . . We realize now, [he surmises] far more than in the last generation that architecture must be evolutionary, not revolutionary, that it can not make the world anew."[78] Yet this new realism uplifting the city's facade bit by bit, tableau by city tableau, still holds a veil over the spatial politics restructuring the heart and fallow fringes of the contemporary city and declines to challenge the process of colonization that has appropriated the image and representations of the city for private concerns. If the spectator is mired in realistic narrations and offered no utopic visions, what will produce a disposition for social change, an inclination to draw affinities across all the spaces and peoples of the city? What moral authority can be drawn on to challenge the private claims that have distorted the public sphere? What will move us along the path toward collectively shared memories and values that cross over and involve the beliefs and needs of different groups and unrepresented places, allowing more ambiguous and open-ended expressions and less constructed spatial enactments? In the last decade of the twentieth century, it is these questions that must be addressed.

Epilogue

nine

The City as Radical Artifice

An important difference exists between the palimpsest manuscript that superposes, one upon the other, a Greek tragedy, a monastic legend, and a chivalric tale, and the divine palimpsest created by God, which is our incommensurable memory: in the first there is something like a fantastic, grotesque randomness, a collision between heterogeneous elements; whereas in the second (memory) the inevitability of temperament necessarily establishes a harmony among the most disparate elements. However incoherent a given existence may be, its human unity is not upset. All the echoes of memory, if one could awaken them simultaneously, would form a concert—pleasant or painful, but logical and without dissonance.

CHARLES BAUDELAIRE[1]

> *Today's antiabsorptive works are*
> *tomorrow's most absorbing ones, & vice*
> *versa: the absorbable, accommodationist devices*
> *of today will in many cases fade into arcanity.*
> *The antiabsorptive, insofar as it is accurately*
> *understood as essentially transgressive, is*
> *historically & contextually specific. Understood*
> *as a dynamic in the history of a work's reception,*
> *absorption & repellency will shift with new contexts*
> *of publication, new readers, & subsequent formal &*
> *political developments. For this reason,*
> *the acknowledgment from the first of a work's*
> *status as artifice may better prepare it*
> *for its long journey through time. . . .*
>
> CHARLES BERNSTEIN[2]

Our contemporary time affirms an unstable logic of ruptures and ambivalences. It celebrates contingency and expels necessity, it focuses on the fragment and fractures all totalities, it praises singularity and avoids universality, it values otherness and decries sameness. As "reality" or experience can never be grasped nor truthfully depicted, postmodernists hope to avoid inevitable errors by maintaining an open position. Yet the discontinuities and ruptures, difference and otherness they uncritically celebrate impose severe consequences on the public realm of the city.[3] They have caused any sense of collectivity to disappear and undermined any attempt to take a critical stance. Driven by negativity, by being against and not being for, postmodern times have discredited all discourses on history and memory, liberating the age from fearful and oppressive narrations that transcend time and place. In place of remembrance, parts of our collective past have been either so historicized or so completely repressed that they can never be recalled, while memory—instead of keeping track of these erasures and suppressions—has fallen prey to mythical narrations and nostalgic recollections. Not concerned with the consequences of their negations nor the effects of amnesia they produce, postmodernists hold no compassion for the whole nor sympathetic attachment to others. Compassion, the glue that once held society together, has been reduced to a numb and distanced experience. In another century, as the passage quoted above reminds us, Baudelaire found memory, the great generator of representation, to be governed by a metadiscourse of unification that closed the play of difference. No matter how unconstrained postmodernists wish the play of codes, writing, and textual readings to be, in the end the latter find their ground in social relations and collective consensus. It is these that form the essence of language and communication.[4]

Then what, we might ask, has created this retreat from history and fostered a blasé indifference to collective experience? What has erased the tissue of relations on which community and compassion must rest? And how has this decline and numbness affected the public realm of the city? What seems to be at issue here is the impact of critical theory on the perception of urban experience, and the effect of technology on artistic expression that entails liberating or reifying potential. This brings to mind Walter Benjamin's 1935/6 essay, "The Work of Art in the Age of Mechanical Reproduction," and his warning that to "aestheticize politics" by removing it as far as possible from the realm of truth or falsehood, as postmodernists have tried to do, is to fall back into a ritualistic dimension or elitist nostalgia. Instead, Benjamin proclaimed in the 1920s and 1930s, such philistine conceptions of art were completely foreign to the new technology of photography and film.[5] This new technology spoke directly to the senses in a different manner: on one hand it extended the eye, allowing it to perceive the minutest details, but at the same time it left the eye exposed to traumatic overstimulation without protective defenses.[6] So he argued

> For it is another nature that speaks to the camera than to the eye: other in the sense that a space informed by human consciousness gives way to a space

> informed by the unconscious. . . . Photography, with its devices of slow motion and enlargement, reveals the secret. It is through photography that we first discover the existence of this optical unconscious, just as we discover the instinctual unconscious through psychoanalysis. Details of structure, cellular tissue, with which technology and medicine are normally concerned—all this is in its origins more native to the camera than the atmospheric landscape or the soulful portrait. Yet at the same time photography reveals in this material the physiognomic aspects of visual worlds which dwell in the smallest things, meaningful yet covert enough to find a hiding place in waking dreams, but which, enlarged and capable of formulation, make the difference between technology and magic visible as a thoroughly historical variable.[7]

Borrowing from Freud, Benjamin found that the function of consciousness was to protect against the stimuli and shocks of everyday existence, to make sure that they did not register memory traces.[8] "Rather, memory fragments are 'often most powerful and most enduring when the incident which left them behind was one that never entered consciousness . . .'"[9] Thus Buck-Morss has recently argued in her reconsiderations of Benjamin's "Work of Art" essay that the phantasmagorical effects of magic lantern shows, panoramas, Paris shopping arcades, department stores, and World's Fairs, so evident as the nineteenth-century's artificial shows of mass entertainment, acted as a protective shield to the vulnerable overstimulated senses of the spectator, altering consciousness through sensory distraction.[10] These spectacular technoaesthetical displays, or ecstatic blinkers, anaesthetized spectators' visual perception, allowing them to retreat from experience. They thus inhibited the recording of memory traces. So, Buck-Morss concludes, "the development of the machine as tool has its correlation in the development of the machine as armour [providing protection against fragmentation and pain]. . . ."[11]

Yet Benjamin saw both positive and negative potential in this form of retreat and indifference. On one hand he realized that time and space in the nineteenth-century industrial city no longer offered a reassuring correspondence between external experience and interior perception, and hence exterior events no longer entered directly into memory. That is why Benjamin believed that Baudelaire never described the crowd explicitly and made only an implicit connection between shock and contact with this throng in the street. Because Baudelaire was more absorbed with planting the impact of this amorphous swelling multitude in his memory than he was in describing and depicting its exact form and shape, it lay as a "hidden figure" or psychic concept concealed in the fragments of his prose poems.[12] Although intoxicated by the crowd, he held his distance and refused to be blinded by the horrible social reality that metropolitan existence entailed.[13] Similarly, Benjamin found that Proust's *memoire involontaire* lay closer to forgetting (unweaving) experience and consequently nearer to the act of recollection (weaving together life's threads). Rather than consciously describing the details of life as they unfurled, Proust allowed unconscious associations or images to intervene absent-mindedly in the act of recall.[14] In contrast to this involuntary memory that relied on distance, conscious remembering was drawn close to reality. It froze images into concrete forms, placing them within already interpreted narrative molds as the phantasmagorical displays of nineteenth-century mass entertainment had invariably done. This attempt to reconstruct things exactly as they were was for Benjamin the strongest narcotic of the nineteenth century.[15]

So too with history, Benjamin would note: "To articulate the past historically does not mean to recognize it 'the way it really was' (Ranke). It means to seize hold of a memory as it flashes up at a moment of danger."[16] Because the image of the past moves by in instantaneous time periods, it can be seized only at the point when it appears and just before it disappears forever.[17] Thus fleeting images of the past, isolated as moments of time and grasped as astonishing and important for the present, are too instantaneous to be called conscious or archeological retrieval, but as involuntary recollections closed off from explanation and historical reconstructions they can become useful for the present. As memory traces they enabled the spectator to come to terms with the shocks and surprises for which the latter remained unprepared, yet by displacing literal experiences they seemed to gain entry to the unconscious.[18] Drawing a relationship between memory traces and "involuntary recollection," Benjamin made reference to moments of sudden transference between the viewed object and the viewer that he defined as auratic experience. But this is a highly ambivalent reference: on one hand the decline of aura allowed hidden figures and secret affinitites to come into view, but on the other it led to a preference for mythical images and illusory distractions.[19]

Both perception and auratic experience were in crisis, and as Benjamin notes their decline was related to the rise of photography and the promise of technical reproduction. "If the distinctive feature of the images that rise from the *memoire involontaire* is seen in their aura, then photography is decisively implicated in the phenomenon of the decline of the aura. What was inevitably felt to be inhuman . . . in daguerreotypy was the (prolonged) looking into the camera, since the camera records our likeness without returning our gaze." [20] The aura of an object rested in its ability to look at the perceiver in return, a phenonenon the photograph had decisively ruptured. But this auratic experience corresponded in turn to the data of the *memoire involontaire.*[21] Adding to these crises, Benjamin noted that "the technique of reproduction detaches the reproduced object from the domain of tradition. By making many reproductions it substitutes a plurality of copies for a unique existence."[22] Once torn from the fabric of tradition, a work of art's auratic uniqueness is destroyed.[23] Given a photographic negative, any number of prints can be made, and thus it no longer makes sense to ask for the authentic print. The moment this reversal occurs, art no longer finds its base in the rituals of tradition and the ceremonial procedures of cults, but in the practice of politics.[24] Thus, he optimistically professed, both the photograph and film had a liberating potential. As politicized art devoid of auratic performance they broke the phantasmagorical chain of illusions that mass entertainment instilled and led, he hoped, to the critical decipherment of reality's illusions.[25] Film cut "reality" like a surgeon's knife into a series of images that mimicked the fragmentary perceptions of modern existence and blew apart an absorbed or concentrated gaze. Subsequently the camera liberated these fragments, allowing them, through editing procedures, to be recontextualized into new constellations. By offering a mode of distracted viewing, therefore, film copied the neutralizing habits of shock perceptions that metropolitan life entailed and enabled the individual to parry a vast array of incongruous visual data into new meanings and forms.[26]

On the negative side, however, both the photograph and cinema were primary agents for expanding the archive of *voluntary memory* and reducing the play of *involuntary recollection.* By contributing massively to the power of voluntary memory, they became destructive devices eradicating the fragile inner connections linking experience to perception. The photograph, for example, opened up an abyss between the moment of looking and the moment of recording; henceforth these fragments of time held only tenuous links with the present and with each other. The cinema, through its editing and framing procedures and its artifical manner of replicating reality in travelogues and historicized epics, for example, radically restructured spatial and temporal relations. Thus it added to the proliferation of visual shocks and helped to force perception into a state of permanent psychic defense.[27] "When a visual image is too bright, one shuts one's eyes defensively against it; similarly, when reality is overwhelming, one turns defensively away from it."[28]

Benjamin claimed that images offered by the illustrated press and by newsreels were different from images seen by the unarmed eye. The latter carried with them a sense of uniqueness and permanence, whereas transitoriness and reproductivity were the essence of the former. "Thus is manifested in the field of perception what in the theoretical sphere is noticeable in the increasing importance of statistics."[29] Benjamin seemed to acknowledge the spread of a cold, abstract, rational look over the surface of things, not necessarily a positive effect of photography but one that weakened the image and lessened its contribution to involuntary memory. Nevertheless he believed that Eugene Atget's distilled empty streetscapes of Paris in the early twentieth century opened the field for a politically educated sight.[30] These serial arrays of images photographed views of the city as if they were scenes of a crime. "The scene of a crime, too, is deserted; it is photographed for the purpose of establishing evidence. With Atget, photographs become standard evidence for historical occurrences, and acquire a hidden political significance. They demand a specific kind of approach; free-floating contemplation [i.e., auratic] is not appropriate to them. They stir the viewer; he feels challenged by them in a new way."[31] By cleansing the photograph of its fuzzy atmosphere, Atget liberated the image from its aura.

> He looked for what was unremarked, forgotten, cast adrift, and thus such pictures too work against the exotic, romantically sonorous names of the cities: they pump the aura out of reality like water from a sinking ship. . . . The stripping bare of the object, the destruction of the aura, is the mark of a perception whose sense of the sameness of things has grown to the point where even the singular, the unique, is divested of its uniqueness—by means of reproduction.[32]

The photograph and film also affected the way the spectator looked at architecture, sculpture, and painting in a somnambulant manner. Benjamin wrote:

> It is all too tempting to blame this squarely on the decline of artistic appreciation, or failure of contemporary sensibility, But one is brought up short by the way the understanding of great works was transformed at about the same time the techniques of reproduction were being developed. They can no longer be regarded as the work of individuals; they become a collective creation, a corpus so vast it can be assimilated only through miniaturization. In the final analysis, mechanical reproduction is a technique of diminution that helps men to achieve a control over works of art without whose aid they could no longer be used.[33]

But film also changed the reaction of the masses to art in a negative manner that resisted the de-auratization of art.

> [In the cinema, t]he conventional is uncritically enjoyed, and the truly new is criticized with aversion. With regard to the screen, the critical and the receptive attitudes of the public coincide. The decisive reason for this is that individual reactions are predetermined by the mass audience response they are about to produce, and this is nowhere more pronounced than in the film. The moment these responses become manifest they control each other.[34]

Large panoramic paintings of the nineteenth century began this crisis by conflating critical and receptive attitudes; these were objects produced for the simultaneous collective experience of uncritical followers, and they erased the distance necessary for rational thought.[35] Here lay the origin of reception in a state of distraction, and while the public could be a critical examiner of both photographic details as well as the editing and framing techniques of film construction, it was also seeking entertainment, escape, and gratification. This alienated audience most often absorbed the film in an absentminded manner, protecting itself from the shocks of everyday life or the contradictions and social consequences of urban and industrial life.[36]

If the photograph and the cinema as mechanical means of reproduction affected aesthetic perception and rendered auratic reception obsolete, thereby creating a crisis in critical reception and involuntary memory and consequently enabling many different types of historicized cityscapes to be absorbed in a somnabulant manner, then today we need to turn to the issue of electronic reproduction and to Charles Bernstein's claim in the poem quoted above that the anti-absorptive artifice will be the one that leaves behind memory traces. Bernstein reminds us that

> . . . 'Artifice' is a measure of a poem's
> intractability to being read as the sum of its
> devices & subject matters. In this sense,
> 'artifice' is the contradiction of 'realism' with

> its insistence on presenting an unmediated (immediate) experience of facts, either of the 'external' world of nature or the 'internal' world of the mind;. . . .[37]

As performed by Bernstein, the anti-absorptive artifice produces self-consciousness in the reader. By theatricalizing or conceptualizing the text, it destroys absorption, and by removing the text as far as possible from the experiential realm, it allows the techniques of its construction to be exhibited—for it is these framing devices and processes that shift attention and affect perception.[38]

In her book, *The Radical Artifice: Writing Poetry in the Age of Mass Media,* Marjorie Perloff claims that writing has to be recognized as a performative practice engaged with and shaped by the material reality of the everyday world, a practice intended to transform the reader's perception of meaning and experience. She argues that contemporary media and computer technology have deeply affected our sense of language. For Perloff, the artifice is a contrived, constructed, designed, made thing. It focuses on the materiality of writing and the contamination of meaning and must be understood in the context of postmodern information systems that have taught us to snip, to cut, to rearrange lines on the page, to shift about fonts and letter sizes. Written in the age of computer networks, laser printers, and fax machines, therefore, the more radical poetry carries traces of this electronic environment. Since writing, advertising, and art feed back on each other in circulating patterns of invisible data structures and information banks, making each the artifact of the other, many poets, Perloff notes, have turned toward some form of "artifice," trying to overcome the endless glut of information that constantly surrounds and bombards them.[39]

In the strange worlds of computerland, to be involved no longer means to participate in community affairs, to communicate face to face, or to expect language to bear uncontaminated meanings, but as Perloff points out, to be involved now means to be connected to the right computer network with its online lifeline, to passively accept that the computer "systems that control the formats that determine the genres of our everyday life are inaccessible to us."[40] Perloff found a wonderful synecdoche for our contemporary denial of complicity in the construction of everyday life in Steve McCaffery's poem "Lag," where he writes "You check the map I must have brought," for even if I didn"t bring a map, it is up to you to make sure we get where we want to go.[41] So, the argument goes, postmodern technologies remove from consciousness our complicity in the suffering or exploitation of others. There is always an available escape key, a control button to abort or ignore a command. But no matter how far critical engagement is deferred or critical awareness numbed, it still remains an issue of agency, of human responsibility and action, for the computer is yet another technology with beneficial and catastrophic capacities that remain within our control. Rather than worry over their inherent and multilayered opacities, we need to find out how these technologies work and how they alter perception.[42]

Bernstein and Perloff, like Walter Benjamin before them, call us to wake up from the hypnosis of absorption and from the somnambulant manner in which we experience the fabricated artifacts of our everyday lives, including the construction of contemporary cityscapes. We are asked, in addition, to understand both the liberating and controlling potential of the new technologies through which mass culture is and has been disseminated. Postmodern electronic technology has transformed everday activites, leisure time, and urban space much the way the photograph and the cinema inaugurated and reflected a modernist point of view. Both modern and postmodern technologies destabilize the relationship between experience and perception, offering images that quickly turn into the cliché and the stereotypical, yet erecting others that prod the viewer to account for what is absent or may be suppressed but nevertheless uncannily felt to be there. Thus what becomes important to examine is how these technologies erect an order that can be seen as both critical and contesting, even if they are simultaneously passive and entertaining. In this project we have only begun to understand how our new electronic technologies affect visual perception, spectator reception, and empathy at a distance.

D. N. Rodowick has claimed that "electronic and digital arts are rapidly engendering new strategies of creation and simulation, and of spatial and temporal ordering, that linguistic philosophies are ill-equipped to understand."[43] In the electronic and digital arts, the boundaries between the word and the image have collapsed, replaced by new modes of spatial and temporal ordering. This new technology allows the viewing collectivity to be separated in discrete and discontinuous space while sharing a temporal continuum. And while Siegfried Kracauer, a contemporary of Walter Benjamin, may have worried over the spatial image of collective life externalized as the mute and self-alienated "mass ornament," this primacy of the visual image and the spatial hieroglyphics of the public sphere have been transformed by randomly sampled public opinion polls and replaced by a serial mass of aggregated entities. There is no hidden meaning or preconceptual layer to decipher or translate that gives this contemporary public sphere coherence or closure. It is decentered and multiple, compartmentalized and reassembled by the technologies of information that condense and abstract reality. Thus Rodowick claims that "[w]herever analog information is replaced by the digital, the copy is disordered by simulation, and wherever physical distribution is replaced by electronic storage, retrieval, and transmission, there one will find the figural."[44] "The technologies of figural expression offer unprecedented control over the strategies of divide in space, order in time, and compose in space-time. This is not simply a question of what happens on the screen (cinematic, televisual, or computer), but how these technologies serve to define, regulate, observe, and document human collectivities."[45]

Alan Liu calls these figural expressions an aesthetic of detailism that myopically displays a picture of local knowledges, regionalisms, historicisms, anecdotalisms, or contextualisms.[46] These endless listings of discretely perceived items never congeal into a totality or a unified order and remain indeterminate and open to innumerable recombinations and reaggregations. The apparatus that best displays this virtuosity of diverse things is a matrix, grid, or network—with its cuts and disconnections, its blank spaces and intervals inserted between the serial entries of its rows and columns. This is the instrument to screen, cover, and master the multiple, it is the hyperspace that simulates the whole from the characteristics of its parts, and it is of course the replica of a computer memory.[47] A grid offers no singular focus, clear image, or master plan but multiple scannings, spatial interruptions, fractures, and lags. These disjunctive sequences of intensively realized spots form the generating matrix of contemporary city plans—they represent the literal re-membering and re-collecting of urban parts when the whole has gone to pieces. And it is just such figural expressions that electronic technologies enhance: the pleasure of detail dependent on the quality of technical reproduction or the aesthetics of fragmentation, allowing the erasure of contextual memory to facilitate immersion into small zones and parts.[48]

To return to the City of Collective Memory, we have noted that this city is an artifice that is meant to be looked at, it is a city on exhibition flaunting its image as if in the theater, the museum, the photograph, or the cinema. The spectator travels across the city's surface by following routes on the map, guided tours both fictional and virtual, studying its imagery in folios and reality. Perloff and Bernstein seem to suggest, however, that if this city were treated as a radical artifice with its materiality kept constantly in mind, then it might reveal the rules of its own construction, allowing the spectator to experience "what" is being re-presented in its visual tableaux and architectural scenes, or "what" is unfolding in its travelogues and narrations.[49] It might also expose a contaminated view that retreats in indifference from the gaps its neutrality supposedly sustains. Perhaps it is through the play of a radical and anti-absorptive artifice that we can reclaim responsibility for constructing the city, a gesture that may lessen the impulse to erect banal images and impose abstract grids over its surface. It may as well enable us to cease treating the pain and exclusion of others as illusions and fictional narrations we no longer desire to hear.

Modernism, as Walter Benjamin explained, attempted to describe the crisis in perception that everyday experience created: whether it was through the loss of aura and historical uniqueness that mechanical reproduction caused, or over the rise of a cold and abstract outlook that turned every scene into statistical evidence, or in the strange juxtapositions and fragmented display of newspaper "stories" that arranged time and place in odd montages, or because of the jostlings and bombardments of the crowd that caused the senses to retreat and memory to cease being recorded. Retreat was the problem and authenticity the issue, for experience required interpretation and critical awareness was necessary to decode the distortions of communication. But these epistemological problems of perception, interpretation, and authenticity are no longer the dominant issues controlling postmodern thought in the era of electronic communication. Instead the contemporary focus involves multilevel thinking, where the collisions and contradictions of parallel albeit imaginary possible worlds, paraspaces, or heterotopias raise ontological questions. Now it seems important to determine what happens when inserted "worlds" occur within metaworlds, to define how one "world" differs from others, to outline the rules and codes that constitute or construct such simulated worlds, and to understand what happens when a subject passes from one world to another. To see the world as a figural construct is a way of seeing double: both its structure and its affects. As the distinction between reality and fiction becomes an artifice, just one manner of constructing a series of things, "we depart from the Euclidean universe of unity, identity, center, and enter the non-Euclidean universe of pattern, superimposition, and differential function. Instead of continuity we have leaps in space, instead of linear time we have time warps that 'superimpose one part of the pattern upon another'."[50] So Jean Baudrillard claims

> There is no real and no imaginary, except at a certain distance. What happens when this distance, even the one separating the real from the imaginary, begins to disappear and to be absorbed by the model alone? Currently, from one order of simulacra to the next, we are witnessing the reduction and absorption of

> this distance, of this separation which permits a space for ideal or critical projection.[51]

Not only is it impossible to speak of an artwork's aura in these imaginary worlds of simulation from which the real has receded, but the distance assumed to facilitate a critical perspective has dissolved as well.[52] Because "reality" or the world now seems to be a cybernetically organized continuum of kinetic images, information, and technological artifacts, it appears that value and meaning also have been lost in the transformation. Or are these simply rhetorical tactics of disruption, just like the matrix we impose on the surface of the city that allows us to focus on well-designed nodes and ignore in-between gaps? Sitting at our computer monitors, we can turn off this hyperreality, make the real city disappear with the flick of a switch, for it occupies a different world of time and space on the other side of the screen. Perhaps it is only a fictive construction of various proliferating codes and ambiguous language games, not really a lived experience. Quite clearly an unbridgeable "reality gulf" divides and separates the fablelike quality of the forgotten city from the space of electronic transmissions. Not wanting to listen to these tales of terror or look at these visions of violence is an attitude of privatization that effaces our complicity in the perpetuation of public acts that hold the power to control narrations, to define subjects, to switch channels and codes.

In this exit essay, we are drawn inevitably to describe the "destructive character" that Walter Benjamin told us is a sign to be read—he "knows only one watchword: make room; only one activity: clearing away. His need to fresh air and open space is stronger than any hatred."[53] Constantly at work, the destructive character clears away the traces of an age with no thought to what will replace it in the future, reducing and eradicating even the traces of destruction.

> The destructive character stands in the front line of the traditionalists. Some pass things down to posterity, by making them untouchable and thus conserving them,

> others pass on situations, by making them practical and thus liquidating them. The latter is called destructive.[54]

Benjamin offers us yet another unstable constellation of centrifugal forces in which the materialist historian becomes a destructive character in order to clear the ground for emancipating construction. So we remain today, unable to escape the ambivalent tensions between the new and the traditional: bound either way in double suspension, to construct and consequently to erase by clearing a path for a new age of technoartifacts, or to destruct and thus to forget by committing to a historicized and conscious memory the discarded remnants from this emptied field, not recognizing them as the ruins of progress.[55] Even if Benjamin prophesized that it would be only through mechanical reproduction that "what has traditionally been called art can be superseded, politicized, resocialized, and the unstructured 'public' transformed into a collective subject. . . .", nevertheless a warning raised by Benjamin still remains to be examined: the cult of technology in the 1920s and 1930s, the history of positive barbarism and technology-enabled power, did not lead to progress in a broader cultural, political, and social sense, but to catastrophe and war.[56]

Notes

Chapter 1

1
For a discussion of "The Matrix of Detail," see Alan Liu, "Local Transcendence: Cultural Criticism, Postmodernism, and the Romanticism of Detail," *Representations* 32 (Fall 1990): 75–113.

2
Jean-Paul Sartre paraphrased without citation by Fredric Jameson, *Postmodernism or, The Cultural Logic of Late Capitalism* (Durham: Duke University Press, 1991): 332.

3
Michael W. Jennings, *Dialectical Images: Walter Benjamin's Theory of Literary Criticism* (Ithaca: Cornell University Press, 1987): 49–51. For an extended discussion on the ambiguous positions of postmodern thought, see Terry Eagleton, "From Polis to Postmodernism," *The Ideology of the Aesthetic* (Cambridge: Basil Blackwell, 1990): 366–417.

4
Michel de Certeau, *The Writing of History.* Translated by Tom Conley (New York: Columbia University Press, 1988): vii, 3–5.

5
Steven Mullaney, *The Place of the Stage* (Chicago: University of Chicago Press, 1988): 10–14.

6
Jurgen Habermas, *The Structural Transformation of the Public Sphere.* Translated by Thomas Berger (Cambridge: MIT Press, 1989).

7
Jose B. Monleon, *A Specter is Haunting Europe: a sociohistorical approach to the fantastic* (Princeton: Princeton University Press, 1990): 24–30.

8
Ibid.: 49–80, 94; and Jon Stratton, *Writing Sites* (Ann Arbor: University of Michigan Press, 1990): 191–202.

9
Report of the Committee on Civic Centers, Bulletin No. 15 *Municipal Art Society* (New York: 1905): 8.

10
Stuart Hall, *The Hard Road to Renewal* (New York: Verso Press, 1988): 138–146.

11
Stephen Tyler, *The Unspeakable* (Madison: University of Wisconsin Press, 1987): 36.

12
Michel Foucault, *Discipline and Punish.* Translated by Alan Sheridan (New York: Pantheon Books, 1977).

13
Georges Canguilhem, *The Normal and the Pathological.* Translated by Carolyn R. Fawcett (New York: Zone Books, 1989): 250.

14
Michel Foucault, "On Governmentality," *Ideology and Consciousness* [referenced below as *I & C*] no. 6 (Autumn 1979): 5–22; Michel Foucault, "Politics and Reason," in Lawrence D. Kritzman (ed.), *Michel Foucault, Politics, Philosophy, Culture—Interviews and Other Writings, 1977–1984* (New York: Routledge, 1988): 57–85; and Michel Foucault, "An Ethics of Pleasure" [Translated by Stephen Riggins] *Foucault Live* (New York: Semiotext(e), 1989): 257–277.

15
A. Perreymonde, "Deuxième Etude sur la Ville de Paris," *La Revue Générale de l'Architecture et des Travaux Publiques; Journal des Architectes, des Ingénieurs, des Archeologues, des Industriels et des Propriétaires sous la Direction de M. César Daly Architecte* [abbreviated as *RGA*] III (1842): 571. Quoted in and translated by Richard Becherer, *Science plus Sentiment, César Daly's Formula for Modern Architecture* (Ann Arbor: UMI Research Press, 1975): 203.

16
Becherer, *Science plus Sentiment:* 203–209.

17
Ibid.: 169–246.

18
César Daly, "De la Locomotion Aérienne," *RGA* IV (1843): 17. Quoted in and translated by Becherer, *Science plus Sentiment:* 176.

19
Becherer, *Science plus Sentiment:* 204.

20
César Daly, "Vue Intérieure d'un Tombeau Etrusque à Corneto (Paris: J. Claye, 1862): 8. Quoted and translated by Becherer. *Science plus Sentiment:* 253.

21
Aldo Rossi. *Architecture of the City.* Translated by Diane Ghirardo and Joan Ockman (Cambridge: MIT Press, 1984): 50–55.

22
Marcel Poëte, "L'Évolution des Villes (1935–1936)" (Université de Paris, Institute d'Urbanisme, mimeographed notes located in Avery Library, Columbia University, New York); and Marcel Poëte, *Bulletin de la Bibliothèque de la Ville de Paris,* Vol. 1 (1906) and Vol. 4 (1909).

23
Tyler, *The Unspeakable:* 205–207; and Hayden White, *Metahistory: The Historical Imagination in Nineteenth-Century Europe* (Baltimore: Johns Hopkins University Press, 1973): 381–382.

24
De Certeau, *The Writing of History:* 6.

25
Reinhart Koselleck, *Futures Past* (Cambridge: MIT Press, 1985): 28, 48, 58, 201.

26
Quoted and translated by Marie Maclean, *Narrative as Performance* (London: Routledge, 1988): 52.

27
Walter Benjamin, *Illuminations*. Translated by Harry Zohn (New York: Schocken Books, 1969): 83.

28
Ibid.: 89.

29
David Frisby, *Fragments of Modernity* (Cambridge: MIT Press, 1986): 261.

30
Susan Buck-Morss, *The Dialectics of Seeing* (Cambridge: MIT Press, 1989): 278–279; Frisby, *Fragments of Modernity:* 260; and Richard Wolin, *Walter Benjamin: An Aesthetic of Redemption* (New York: Columbia University Press, 1982): 219, 221–222.

31
Frisby, *Fragments of Modernity:* 261; Jennings, *Dialectical Images:* 82–83; and Wolin, *Walter Benjamin:* 226–230.

32
Burkhardt Lindner, "The Passagen-Werk: the Berliner Kindheit, and the Archaeology of the 'Recent Past'," *New German Critique* [abbreviated *NGC*] 39 (Fall 1986): 45; Winfried Menninghaus, "Walter Benjamin's Theory of Myth," in Gary Smith (ed.), *On Walter Benjamin* (Cambridge: MIT Press, 1988): 292–325.

33
Richard Terdiman, "Deconstructing Memory: On Representing the Past and Theorizing Culture in France Since the Revolution," *Diacritics* (Winter 1986): 13–36.

34
Michael S. Roth, "Remembering Forgetting: Maladies de la Mémoire in Nineteenth-Century France," *Representations* 26 (Spring 1989): 49–68.

35
Michel de Certeau, *Heterologies: Discourse on the Other.* Translated by Brian Massumi (Minneapolis: University of Minnesota Press, 1986): 29.

36
Gilles Deleuze, *Bergsonism.* Translated by Hugh Tomlinson and Barbara Habberjam (New York: Zone Books, 1988): 22–24, 39.

37
Quoted by Deleuze, *Bergsonism:* 56.

38
Mary Douglas, "Introduction" to Maurice Halbwachs, *The Collective Memory.* Translated by Francis J. Ditter, Jr., and Vida Yazdi Ditter (New York: Harper Colophon Books, 1980; originally published 1950): 1–21.

39
Maurice Halbwachs, *La Mémoire Collective:* 167. Translated and quoted by Suzanne Vromen, "The Sociology of Maurice Halbwachs" (Unpublished Ph.D. diss., New York University, 1975): 198.

40
Gilles Deleuze, *Cinema 1 The Movement-Image.* Translated by Hugh Tomlinson and Robert Galeta (Minneapolis: University of Minnesota Press, 1986); Gilles Deleuze, *Cinema 2 The Time-Image.* Translated by Hugh Tomlinson and Robert Galeta (Minneapolis: University of Minnesota Press, 1989); and Vromen, "The Sociology of Maurice Halbwachs."

41
Roth, "Remembering Forgetting."

42
Jean-Louis Comolli, "Machines of the Visible," in Teresa de Laurentis and Stephen Health (eds.), *The Cinematic Apparatus* (New York: St. Martin's Press, 1980): 121–142.

43
De Certeau, *The Writing of History:* 79.

44
Roy Boyne, *Foucault and Derrida: The Other Side of Reason* (London: Unwin Hyman, 1990): 90–122.

45
Gilles Deleuze, *Foucault.* Translated by Sean Hand (Minneapolis: University of Minnesota Press, 1986): 97.

46
Deleuze, *Foucault:* 107.

47
Ibid.: 119.

48
Deleuze, *Cinema 2:* 251, 277; and Terdiman, "Deconstructing Memory."

49
For the aporia of postmodern philosophy, see Alan D. Schrift, "The Becoming-Postmodern of Philosophy," in Gary Shapiro (ed.), *After the Future: Postmodern Times and Places* (Albany: State University of New York Press, 1990): 99–113.

Chapter 2

1
This book was initally inspired by the work of Marcel Poëte as referenced by Aldo Rossi, and of course by Aldo Rossi, *The Architecture of the City.* Translated by Diane Ghirardo and Joan Ockman (Cambridge: MIT Press, 1981). See also Marcel Poëte, *Une Vie de Cité, Paris* (Paris: August Picard, Editeur, 1924); and Marcel Poëte, "L'Evolution des Villes," (Unpublished lecture notes from the Université de Paris, Institut d'Urbanisme, 1935–36).

2
Stephen Kern, *The Culture of Time and Space, 1880–1918* (Cambridge: Harvard University Press, 1983): 96–97.

3
Michel Foucault, "On Governmentality," *I & C* 6 (Autumn 1979): 5–22; Michel Foucault, "An Ethics of Pleasure," *Foucault Live* (New York: Semiotext(e), 1989): 257–277; and Lawrence D. Kritzman (ed.), *Michel Foucault Politics Philosophy Culture.* Translated by Alan Sheridan and others (New York: Routledge, 1988): 57–85.

4
Jurgen Habermas, *Philosophical–Political Profiles.* Translated by Frederick G. Lawrence (Cambridge: MIT Press, 1983): 140.

5
Donald David Schneider, *The Works and Doctrine of Jacques Ignace Hittorff (1792–1867): Structural Innovation and Formal Expression in French Architecture* (Ph.D. diss., Princeton University, 1970; New York: Garland Press Inc., 1977); Henry-Russell Hitchcock. *Modern Architecture Romanticism and Reintegration* (New York: Payson & Clarke, Ltd., 1929): 32–33; and *L'Exposition Hittorff (1792–1867) Un Architect du XIXeme Siècle* (Paris: Musée Carnavalet, 20 October 1986–January 1987).

6
Unfortunately a technical fault occurred so that the obelisk on the day of its unveiling was actually raised by manpower, using ten different winches. Peter Tompkins, *The Magic of Obelisks* (New York: Harper and Row, 1981): 243–245.

7
Schneider, *Hittorff:* 431–493; and *L'Exposition Hittorff.*

8
Schneider, *Hittorff:* 494–565; and *L'Exposition Hittorff.*

9
Similar themes have been developed by Dolf Sternberger, *Panorama of the Nineteenth Century* (New York: Urizen Books, Mole Editions, 1977); and Wolfgang Schivelbusch, *The Railway Journey: Trains and Travel in the Nineteenth Century* (New York: Urizen Books, 1979).

10
Kern, *The Culture of Time and Space:* 235.

11
Siegfried Giedion, *Architecture, You and Me* (Cambridge: Harvard University Press, 1958): 106–119, 178–199; and Siegfried Giedion, *Architecture and the Phenomena of Transition* (Cambridge: Harvard University Press, 1971).

12
Blaise Cendrars, "La Tour Eiffel: A Madame Sonia Delaunay," quoted by Marjorie Perloff, *The Futurist Moment* (Chicago: University of Chicago Press, 1986): 195–213.

13
Stanislaus von Moos, *Le Corbusier Elements of a Synthesis* (Cambridge: MIT Press, 1983): 197.

14
Le Corbusier, *The Radiant City* (New York: Orion Press, 1964 reprint of 1933 edition): 79.

15
Le Corbusier, *The Four Routes* (London: Dennis Dobson, Ltd., 1947): 97, 111.

16
Ibid.: 108.

17
Hubert Damisch, "Les Treteaux de la Vie Moderne," in *Le Corbusier une encyclopédie* (Paris: Centre Georges Pompidou, 1987): 252–259.

18
Ibid.

19
Le Corbusier, *Concerning Town Planning* (New Haven: Yale University Press, 1948): 72; and Damisch, "Les Treteaux."

20
Le Corbusier, *The Four Routes.*

21
Ignasi de Sola-Morales, "Nouveaux Espaces dans la Ville Moderne," in *Le Corbusier une encyclopédie:* 136–139.

22
Le Corbusier, *The City of Tomorrow.* Translated by Frederick Etchells (Cambridge: MIT Press, 1971): 287–288.

23
Les Immateriaux Album (Paris: Centre Georges Pompidou, 1985).

24
John Rajchman, "The Postmodern Museum," *Art in America* (October 1985): 111–117, 171.

25
Hal Foster, "Wild Signs: The Breakup of the Sign in Seventies' Art," in Andrew Ross (ed.), *Universal Abandon? The Politics of Postmodernism* (Minneapolis: University of Minnesota Press, 1988): 251–268.

26
Sergei Eisenstein, *The Film Sense.* Translated by Jay Leyda (New York: Harcourt Brace, Inc., 1942): 14–15, 98–99.

27
Ibid.: 100.

28
Guy Debord, *Society of the Spectacle* (Detroit: Black & Red, 1983): 34.

29
Giedion, *Architecture, You and Me:* 125–137.

30
J. Tyrwhitt, J. L. Sert, and E. N. Rogers, *The Heart of the City: Towards the Humanisation of Urban Life* (London: Lund Humphries, 1952): 73.

31
M. Doublet, "Paris: Les Halles," *L'Architecture d'Aujourd'hui* 132 (Juin–Juillet 1967): 23; Pierre Faucheux, "La Platform du XIXe Siècle," *L'Architecture d'Aujourd'hui* 138 (Juin–Juillet 1968): 54–58; and Jacques Herbert, *Sauver Les Halles: Coeur de Paris* (Paris: Denöel, 1971).

32
Alison and Peter Smithson, *Ordinariness and Light: Urban Theories 1952–1960 and Their Application in a Building Project 1963–1970* (Cambridge: MIT Press, 1970): 86.

33
Alison and Peter Smithson, *Without Rhetoric: An Architectural Aesthetic 1955–1972* (London: Latimer News Dimension Ltd., 1973): 92.

34
Kenneth Frampton, "New Brutalism and the Welfare State: 1949–1959," *Modern Architecture: A Critical History* (New York: Oxford University Press, 1980): 262–268.

35
Reyner Banham, "Throw-Away Aesthetic," in Reyner Banham, *Design by Choice* (New York: Rizzoli, 1981): 90–93.

36
John McHale, "The Expendable Icon *1," and "The Expendable Icon *2," *Architectural Design* 29, nos. 2 and 3 (Feb. and March 1950): 82–83; 116–117.

37
Lawrence Alloway, "Junk Culture," *Architectural Design* 31, no. 3 (March 1961): 122.

38
Denise Scott Brown, "Learning from Pop," in Robert Venturi and Denise Scott Brown, *A View from the Campidoglio* (New York: Harper and Row, 1984): 28.

39
Robert Venturi, "A Definition of Architecture as Shelter with Decoration on It and Another Plea for a Symbolism of the Ordinary in Architecture," *A View from Campidoglio:* 63.

40
Scott Brown, "Learning from Pop": 32–33.

41
For comments on "the city observed," see Rosalynn Deutsche, "Krzysztof Wodiczko's Homeless Projection and the Site of Urban Revitalization," *October* 38 (1986): 63–98.

42
Russell A. Berman, "The Routinization of Charismatic Modernism and the Problem of Post-Modernism," *Cultural Critique* 5 (Winter 1986/7): 49–68.

43
Arno Mayer, *The Persistence of the Old Regime: Europe to the Great War* (New York: Pantheon Books, 1981).

44
Theodor Adorno, "Letters to Walter Benjamin," *Aesthetics and Politics* (London: New Left Books, 1977): 123.

45
This rhetoric comes from the advertising brochure mailed to likely conferencegoers for the "Remaking Cities Conference," sponsored by the American Institute of Architects and the Royal British Institute of Architects (Pittsburgh, March 2–5, 1988); for details on the restructuring of cities in the 1970s and 1980s, and the shift from social welfare to fiscal welfare policies in particular, see Michael Peter Smith, *City, State & Market: The Political Economy of Urban Society* (New York: Basil Blackwell, 1988).

46
Herbert I. Schiller, *Culture Inc. The Corporate Takeover of Public Expression* (New York: Oxford University Press, 1989).

47
Umberto Eco, "Innovation and Repetition: Between Modern and Postmodern Aesthetics," *Daedalus* (Fall 1985): 161–184.

48
Maurice Halbwachs, *The Collective Memory.* Translated by Francis J. Ditter, Jr., and Vida Yazdi Ditter (New York: Harper Colophon Books, 1980): 78–79.

49
Ibid.: 78–80.

50
Michel de Certeau, "The Theater of the Quidproquo: Alexandre Dumas," *Heterologies:*

Discourse on the Other. Translated by Brian Massumi (Minneapolis: University of Minnesota Press, 1986): 150–155.

51
Halbwachs, *The Collective Memory:* 140.

52
Michel de Certeau, *The Practice of Everyday Life.* Translated by Steven F. Rendall (Berkeley: University of California Press, 1984): 87, 89, and 109.

53
De Certeau, "Walking in the City," *The Practice of Everyday Life:* 91–110.

Chapter 3

1
Quoted by Mark Jarzombek, *On Leon Baptista Alberti* (Cambridge: MIT Press, 1989): 117.

2
Edward Gordon Craig, "The Steps I" (1905). Quoted by J. Michael Walton (ed.), *Craig on Theatre* (London: Methuen, 1983): 108.

3
Denis Bablet, "La Remise en Question du Lieu Théatral au Vingtième Siècle," in Denis Bablet and Jean Jacquote (eds.), *Le Lieu Théatral dans la Société Moderne* (Paris: Editions du Centre National de la Recherche Scientifique, 1978): 13–25; and Victor Turner, *The Anthropology of Performance* (New York: P & J Publications, 1986).

4
Johannes Birringer, "Invisible Cities/Transcultural Images," *Performing Arts Journal* 33/34 (1989): 120–138; Karen Hermassi, *Polity and Theatre in Historical Perspective* (Berkeley: University of California Press, 1977): 3–24; and Steven Mullaney, *The Place of the Stage: License, Play, and Power in Renaissance England* (Chicago: University of Chicago Press, 19£8): 7–10.

5
Jean Baudrillard, *Seduction.* Translated by Brian Singer (New York: St. Martin's Press, 1990): 53.

6
Cheldon Cheney, *Stage Decoration* (New York: Benjamin Blom, Inc., 1966. Reprint of 1928 Edition): 11–31.

7
James Laver, *Drama, Its Costume and Decor* (London: Studio Publications, 1951); and Vitruvius, *Ten Books on Architecture.* Translated by Morris Hicky Morgan (New York: Dover Publications, Inc., 1960): 146–151.

8
Samuel Y. Edgerton, Jr., *Alberti's Optics* (Unpublished Ph.D. diss., University of Pennsylvania, 1965): 102; and Vitruvius, *Ten Books:* 198.

9
Printing was introduced in Italy in 1464. William Bell Dinsmoor, "The Literary Remains of Sebastiano Serlio," *The Art Bulletin* 24, 2 (June 1942): 155–191.

10
A. W. Eden, "Studies in Urban Theory: The De re Aedificatoria of Leon Baptista Alberti," *Town Planning Review* 19, 1 (1943): 10–28.

11
Jarzombek, *Alberti*: 113, 144.

12
Franco Borsi, *Leon Baptista Alberti* (New York: Harper and Row, 1977): 294.

13
Eden, "Urban Theory."

14
Jarzombek, *Alberti:* 117.

15
Ibid.: 151–159.

16
Ibid.: 182.

17
Ibid.: 158.

18
Norman Bryson, *Vision and Painting: The Logic of the Gaze* (New Haven: Yale University Press, 1983).

19
Rudolf Wittkower, "Brunelleschi and 'Proportion in Perspective'," *Idea and Image* (London: Thames and Hudson, 1978): 125–135.

20
Guilio Carlo Argan, "The Architecture of Brunelleschi and the Origins of Perspective Theory in the Fifteenth Century," *Journal of the Warburg and Courtauld Institute* 9 (1946): 96–121.

21
Argan, "Brunelleschi": 104.

22
Eugenio Battisti, *Filippo Brunelleschi. The Complete Works* (New York: Rizzoli, 1981): 102–103; and Wittkower, *Idea and Image:* 125–135.

23
Bryson, *Vision and Painting:* 106.

24
Charles Burroughs, *From Sign to Design: Environmental Process and Reform in Early Renaissance Rome* (Cambridge: MIT Press, 1990): 1–19, 217–222.

25
John A. Pinto, "Origins and Development of the Ichnographic City Plan," *Journal of the Society of Architectural Historians* 35 (1976): 35–50.

26
Borsi, *Alberti:* 1–58.

27
Dinsmoor, "Remains of Serlio": 155–191.

28
John Orrell states that it was Inigo Jones who replaced Serlio's flat-angled frame with three-dimensional *periaktoi.* John Orrell, *The Theatres of Inigo Jones and John Webb* (Cambridge: Cambridge University Press, 1985).

29
Gosta M. Bergman, *Lighting in the Theatre* (Totowa, New Jersey: Rowman and Littlefield, 1977): 57–59; and Barnard Hewitt (ed.), *The Renaissance Stage Documents of Serlio, Sabbattini and Furttenbach* (Coral Gables, Fla.: University of Miami Press, 1958): 18–36.

30
George Kernodle, *From Art to Theatre: Form and Convention in the Renaissance* (Chicago: University of Chicago Press, 1944): 188–200.

31
For a similar treatment in the late Renaissance theater, see Timothy C. Murray, "Richlieu's Theater: The Mirror of a Prince," *Renaissance Drama* n.s. 8 (1977): 275–298.

32
Hewitt (ed.), *Renaissance Stage Documents:* 190.

33
Kernodle, *From Art to Theatre:* 216.

34
Walter Cohen, *Drama of a Nation: Public Theater in Renaissance England and Spain* (Ithaca: Cornell University Press, 1985): 136–185.

35
Jean-Christophe Agnew, *Worlds Apart: The Market and the Theater in Anglo-American Thought, 1550–1750* (Cambridge: Cambridge University Press, 1986): 60.

36
Agnew, *Worlds Apart:* 12, 16.

37
Ibid.: 97.

38
Ibid.: 98.

39
Cohen, *Drama of a Nation:* 188–189, 202–203.

40
Mullaney, *Place of the Stage:* 24.

41
Ibid.: 30.

42
Stephen Gosson, *Plays Confuted in Five Actions* (1582). Quoted in Mullaney, *Place of the Stage:* 51.

43
Stephen Orgel, "The Poetics of the Spectacle," *New Literary History* 2 (1971): 368–389; John Harris, Stephen Orgel, and Roy Strong, *The King's Arcadia: Inigo Jones and the Stuart Court* (London: Arts Council of Great Britain, 1973); and John Peacock, "Inigo Jones' Stage Architecture and Its Source," *The Art Bulletin* 64, no. 2 (June 1982): 195–216.

44
Peter Stallybrass and Allon White, *The Politics & Poetics of Transgression* (Ithaca: Cornell University Press, 1986): 27–79.

45
Harris, Orgel, and Strong, *Arcadia:* 84–89.

46
Ibid.: 127.

47
Ibid.: 127, 165; and Orgel, "Poetics": 389.

48
Agnew, *Worlds Apart:* 146–148; and John Peter, *Vladimir's Carrot: Modern Drama and the Modern Imagination* (Chicago: University of Chicago Press, 1987): 302–303.

49
Quoted by Stephen Orgel, *The Illusion of Power: Political Theater in the English Renaissance* (Berkeley: University of California Press, 1975): 42.

50
Cohen, *Drama of a Nation:* 256, 264–281.

51
Quoted by Daniel Rabreau, "The Theatre-Monument: A Century of 'French' Typology," *Zodiac* 2 (1988): 47.

52
Pierre Lelievre, "Théatre et Scenographie Urbaine en France au XVIIIe Siècle," *Victor Louis et le Théatre* (Paris: Editions du Centre National de la Recherche Scientifique, 1986): 97–105.

53
Quoted by Lelievre, "Théatre Urbaine": 50.

54
Lelievre, "Théatre Urbaine": 60.

55
Michael Hays, "Theater and Mass Culture: The Case of the Director," *New German Critique* 29 (Spring/Summer 1983): 133–146.

56
Raymond Williams, "A Lecture on Realism," *Screen* 18, no. 1 (Spring 1977): 61–74.

57
John Hope Mason, *The Irresistible Diderot* (London: Quartet Books, Ltd., 1982): 126.

58
Michael Fried, "Toward a Supreme Fiction: Genre and Beholder in the Art Criticism of Diderot and His Contemporaries," *New Literary History* 6 (Spring 1975): 543–585.

59
Jay Caplan, *Frame Narratives: Diderot's Genealogy of the Beholder* (Minneapolis: University of Minnesota Press, 1985): 543–585.

60
Bamber Gascoigne, *World Theater: An Illustrated History* (Boston: Little, Brown and Company, 1968): 233–264.

61
Richard Altick, *The Shows of London* (Cambridge: Harvard University Press, 1978); and Fried, "Toward a Supreme Fiction": 564–565.

62
Catherine Join-Dieterle, "Ciceri et la decoration théatrale à l'Opera de Paris pendant la Premier Moitié du XIXe Siècle," in *Victor Louis:* 141–151; and Denis Bablet, *Esthétique Generale du Décor de Théatre de 1870 à 1914*

(Paris: Editions du Centre National de la Recherche Scientifique, 1975): 18.

63
Gascoigne, *World Theater:* 233–264.

64
Eva Borsch-Supan, "Schinkel as a Universal Man," *Apollo* 106, no. 186 (August 1977): 134–141.

65
Hermann G. Pundt, *Schinkel's Berlin: A Study in Environmental Planning* (Cambridge: Harvard University Press, 1972).

66
James Allen Vann, "Karl Friederich Schinkel: Berlin as the City Beautiful," *Classical America* 4 (1977): 174–182.

67
Quoted by Julius Posener, "Theater Construction in Berlin from Gilly to Poelzig," *Zodiac* 2 (1988): 10.

68
Hermann G. Pundt, "K. F. Schinkel's Environmental Planning of Central Berlin," *Journal of the Society of Architectural Historians* 26, no. 2 (May 1967): 114–130.

69
Posener, "Theater Construction in Berlin": 15.

70
Pundt, "Schinkel's Environmental Planning."

71
Kurt W. Forster, "Schinkel's Panoramic Planning of Central Berlin," *Modulus* 16 (1983): 63–77.

72
Bablet, *Esthétique Generale du Décor:* 7; and Bablet, "La Remise en Question."

73
Théophile Gautier, "Nouvel Opera," *Moniteur* (May 13, 1883). Quoted in Michael Hays, *The Public and Performance: Essays in the History of French and German Theater, 1871–1900* (Ann Arbor: UMI Research Press, 1981): 4–5.

74
Charles Garnier, "Le Théatre" (1871). Quoted by Christopher C. Mead, *Charles Garnier's Paris Opera and the Renaissance of Classicism in Nineteenth Century French Architecture* (Ann Arbor: UMI Research Press, 1986): 611.

75
The staircase of honor, only leading in turn to the parterre and étage noblier, gave the bourgeoisie their own room for being part of the spectacle. A series of smaller less well appointed stairways led to the upper balconies, offering the lower-middle-class spectators prospective views over the staircase of honor and the parterre and étage noblier below, enabling them to watch the social drama and if they wished to emulate and restage it. Hays, *The Public and Performance:* 3–11, 63; Anne, Margaret, and Patrice Higonnet, "Facades: Walter Benjamin's Paris," *Critical Inquiry* 10, 3 (March 1984): 391–491; and Mead, *Charles Garnier:* 615.

76
Hays, *The Public and Performance:* 61–77.

77
Michael Hays, "Theater and Mass Culture; The Case of the Director," *New German Critique* 29 (Spring/Summer 1983): 133–146.

78
Bablet, *Ésthetique Generale:* 109–110.

79
Hays, *The Public and Performance:* 70–118.

80
Bablet, "La Remise": 17; and Arthur Feinsod, "The Origins of the Minimalist Mise-en-Scene in the United States" (Unpublished Ph.D. diss., New York University, 1985).

81
Quoted by Bablet, "La Remise": 16.

82
Adolphe Appia, "Introduction," in Walter R. Fuerst and Samuel J. Hume, *Twentieth Century Stage Decoration,* 2 vols. (London: Alfred A. Knopf, 1927).

83
Quoted in Fuerst and Hume, *Stage Decoration,* vol. 1: 28.

84
Bergman, *Lighting in the Theatre:* 325–326.

85
Emile Jacques-Dalcroze, *Rhythm, Music and Education* (New York: Arno Press, 1976 reprint of 1921 edition): 149.

86
Marco De Michelis, "Modernity and Reform, Heinrich Tessenow and the Institute Dalcroze at Hellerau," *Perspecta* 26 (New York: Rizzoli, 1990): 143–170.

87
Fuerst and Hume, *Stage Decoration:* 50.

88
Ibid.: 51.

89
E. Gordon Craig, *Scene* (New York: Benjamin Blom, 1923): 22.

90
Fuerst and Hume, *Stage Decoration:* 55–66.

91
Craig, *Scene:* 20.

92
Brian Arnott, *Edward Gordon Craig's Hamlet* (Ottawa: National Gallery of Canada, 1975); and Bergman, *Lighting in the Theatre:* 323–339.

93
Denis Bablet, "D'Edward Gordon Craig au Bauhaus," in *Le Masque: Du Rite au Théatre* (Paris: Editions du Centre National de la Recherche Scientifique, 1985); Christopher Innes, *Edward Gordon Craig* (New York: Cambridge University Press, 1983); and J. Michael Walton (ed.), *Craig on Theatre* (London: Methuen, 1983): 21–23.

94
Walton (ed.), *Craig on Theatre:* 23.

95
Innes, *Craig:* 133–134.

96
Peter, *Vladimir's Carrot:* 275.

97
Ibid.: 16, 278–282.

98
Manfredo Tafuri and Francesco Dal Co, *Modern Architecture* 1 (New York: Electra/Rizzoli, 1986): 130–136.

99
Kasimir Malevich, *From Cubism and Futurism to Suprematism: The New Painterly Realism* (1918): 118. Quoted by Marjorie Perloff, *The Futurist Moment* (Chicago: University of Chicago Press, 1986): 118.

100
Malevich, *From Cubism:* 134. Quoted by Perloff, *The Futurist Moment:* 121.

101
E. Prampolini, "Futurist Scenography" (1915), in E. T. Kirby, (ed.) *Total Theatre: A Critical Anthology* (New York: E. P. Dutton, 1969): 95–99; Michael Kirby and Victoria Nes Kirby, *Futurist Performance* (New York: P & J Publications, 1986): 71–90; and Håkan Lövgren, "Sergei Radlov's Electric Baton: The 'Futurization' of Russian Theater," in Lars Kleberg and Nils Åke Nilsson, *Theater and Literature in Russia 1900–1930* (Stockholm: Almqvist & Wiksell International, 1984): 101–112.

102
Joseph Cary, "Futurism and the French Theatre d'Avant-Garde," in Kirby, *Total Theatre:* 99–114.

103
Quoted by Kirby and Kirby, *Futurist Performance:* 43.

104
Michel Aucouturier, "Theatricality as a Category of Early Twentieth-Century Russian Culture," in Kleberg and Nilsson, *Theater and Literature:* 9–21.

105
Futurist Manifestos (New York: Viking Press, 1973): 194–195. Quoted by Perloff, *The Futurist Moment:* 102.

106
Thomas Elsaesser, "Dada/Cinema?" in Rudolf E. Kuenzli, *Dada and Surrealist Film* (New York: Willis Loxker & Owens, 1987): 13–27.

107
Kirby and Kirby, *Futurist Performance:* 47, 80.

108
Sergei Eisenstein, "Through Theater to Cinema," in James Hurt (ed.), *Film and Theatre* (Englewood Cliffs, New Jersey: Prentice-Hall, 1974): 126–127; and Marie Seton, *Sergei M. Eisenstein, A Biography* (London: Dennis Dobson, 1978): 44.

109
Seton, *Eisenstein:* 66–67, 115.

110
J. Garret Glover, "Fernand Leger and the Theatre of Spectacle," *The Cubist Theatre* (Ann Arbor: UMI Research Press, 1983): 91–99.

111
Standish D. Lawder, *The Cubist Cinema* (New York: New York University Press, 1975): 94–95, 161.

112
Glover, *Cubist Theatre:* 93.

113
Ibid.: 95.

114
Lawder, *Cubist Cinema:* 167.

115
Steven A. Mansbach, *Visions of Totality* (Ann Arbor: UMI Research Press, 1978): 23.

116
Laszlo Moholy-Nagy, "Theatre, Circus, Variety," in E. T. Kirby, *Total Theatre:* 124.

117
Laszlo Moholy-Nagy, "Letter to Frantisek Kalivoda," (1936) in Kisztina Passuth, *Moholy-Nagy* (New York: Thames and Hudson, 1985): 333–335.

118
Joseph Harris Caton, *The Utopian Vision of Moholy-Nagy Technology, Society, and the Avant-Garde* (Ann Arbor: UMI Research Press, 1980): 70.

119
Laszlo Moholy-Nagy, "Space-Time and the Photographer," in Passuth, *Moholy-Nagy:* 349.

120
Passuth, *Moholy-Nagy:* 352.

121
Peter, *Vladimir's Carrot:* 19.

122
Thomas Elsaesser, "Cinema—The Irresponsible Signifier or 'The Gamble with History'," *New German Critique* 40 (Winter 1987): 65–89; and David Frisby, *Fragments of Modernity* (Cambridge: MIT Press, 1986): 148–151.

123
Karsten White (ed.), *Siegfried Kracauer, Schriften* 1 (Frankfurt: Suhrkamp, 1970): 286–287. Quoted in Elsaesser, "Cinema": 74.

124
Frisby, *Fragments:* 157, 170.

125
Elsaesser, "Cinema": 74; and Frisby, *Fragments:* 184.

126
Frisby, *Fragments:* 135–136.

127
Sabine Hake, "Girls and Crisis—The Other Side of Diversion," *New German Critique* 40 (Winter 1987): 147–164; and Siegfried Kra-

cauer, "Cult of Distraction: On Berlin's Picture Palaces," *New German Critique* 40 (Winter 1987): 91–96.

128
Michael Fried, "Art and Objecthood," *Artforum* (June 1967): 13–23; and Michael Fried, *Absorption and Theatricality: Painting and the Beholder in the Age of Diderot* (Berkeley: University of California Press, 1980).

129
Richard Schechner, *The End of Humanism: Writings on Performance* (New York: Performing Arts Journal, 1982): 52.

130
Schechner, *The End of Humanism:* 53.

131
Tim Benton, "Urbanism," in *Le Corbusier, Architect of the Century* (London: London Arts Council, 1987): 200–207.

132
Dana Polan, *Power and Paranoia: History, Narrative, and the American Cinema, 1940–1950.* (New York: Columbia University Press, 1986): 234–236.

133
Dana Polan, *The Political Language of Film and the Avant-Garde* (Ann Arbor: UMI Research Press, 1985): 24, 29.

134
Schechner, *The End of Humanism:* 52, 102.

135
Janny Donker, *The President of Paradise: A Traveller's Account of Robert Wilson's The CIVIL warS* (Amsterdam: International Theatre Bookshop, 1985).

136
Colin Rowe and Fred Koetter, *Collage City* (Cambridge: MIT Press, 1978): 14–15.

137
Stanislaus von Moos, "The City as Stage," *Venturi, Rauch & Scott Brown* (New York: Rizzoli, 1987): 60–69.

138
Ibid.: 47–59.

139
John Walker, *Art in the Age of Mass Media* (New South Wales, Australia: Plout Press Ltd., 1985).

140
Robert Venturi and Denise Scott Brown, *A View from the Campidoglio* (New York: Harper and Row, 1984): 32–33.

Chapter 4

1
Henry James, *The American Scene* (Bloomington: Indiana University Press, 1968): 253. Quoted in Michael North, *The Final Sculpture* (Ithaca: Cornell University Press, 1985): 28–29.

2
Quatremère de Quincy, Lettres sur le préjudice qu' occasionneraient aux Arts & à la Science le déplacement des monuments de l'art de l'Italie, le démembrement de ses écoles et la spoliation de ses collections, galeries, musées, etc. (Paris: 1796): 22. Quoted by Yve-Alain Bois, *Susan Smith's ARCHEOLOGY* (New York: Margarete Roeder Gallery, 23 March to 29 April, 1989): 8–9.

3
Irving Wohlfarth, "On the Messianic Structure of Walter Benjamin's Last Reflections," *Glyph* 3 (1978): 148–212. A similar argument about the crisis of history in the ninteenth century is developed by Richard Terdiman, "Deconstructing Memory: On Representing the Past and Theorizing Culture in France Since the Revolution," *Diacritics* (Winter 1985): 13–36.

4
Irving Wohlfarth, "Re-fusing Theology. Some First Reponses to Walter Benjamin's Arcades Project," *New German Critique* (*NGC*) 39 (Fall 1986): 16.

5
Jean Baudrillard, "Revolution and the End of Utopia." Translated by Michel Valentin, in William Stearns and William Chaloupka, (eds.) *Jean Baudrillard: the Disappearance of Art and Politics* (New York: St. Martin's Press, 1992): 233–242.

6
Michel Foucault, "Fantasia of the Library, " in Michel Foucault *Language, Counter-Memory, Practice.* Translated by Donald F. Bouchards and Sherry Simon (Ithaca: Cornell University Press, 1977): 92.

7
Eugenio Donato, "The Museum's Furnace: Notes toward a Contextual Reading of Bouvard and Pecuchet," in Joseph V. Harari (ed.), *Textual Strategies* (Ithaca: Cornell University Press, 1979): 216.

8
Paraphrase from Hegel's *Aesthetics* (1828) in Michael Podro, *The Critical Historians of Art* (New Haven: Yale University Press, 1982): 18.

9
Donato, "The Museum's Furnace": 213–238.

10
Francis A. Yates, *The Art of Memory* (Chicago: University of Chicago Press, 1966): 1–26.

11
Maurice Halbwachs, *The Collective Memory* (New York: Harper Colophon Books, 1980): 78–79, 80, 82, 84.

12
Walter Benjamin, *Gesammelte Schriften* 1, 637. Quoted by Andrew Benjamin in Andrew Benjamin (ed.), *The Problems of Modernity* (London: Routledge, 1989): 132.

13
Wohlfarth, "Messianic Structure": 153, 167.

14
Burkhardt Lindner, "The Passagen-Werk, the Berliner Kindheit, and the Archaeology of the "Recent Past" *NGC* 39 (Fall 1986): 33–34.

15
Richard Wolin, *Walter Benjamin, An Aesthetics of Redemption* (New York: Columbia University Press, 1982): 254; and Lloyd Spencer, "Allegory in the World of the Commodity," *NGC* 34 (Winter 1985): 59–77.

16
Walter Benjamin, "The Work of Art in the Age of Mechanical Reproduction," *Illuminations.* Translated by Harry Zohn (New York: Schocken Books, 1965): 239.

17
Walter Benjamin, *Gesammelte Schriften* 1,698; IU 258. Quoted by Irving Wohlfarth, "On Some Jewish Motifs in Benjamin," in A. Benjamin (ed.), *The Problems of Modernity:* 162.

18
Walter Benjamin, *Gesammelte Schriften:* 11, 154; O 121. Quoted in Wohlfarth, *The Problems of Modernity:* 162.

19
Halbwachs, *Collective Memory:* 23–24, 131.

20
Ibid.: 140.

21
Lloyd Spencer, "Allegory": 73; and Joel Synder, "Benjamin on Reproducibility and Aura: A Reading of 'The Work of Art in the Age of its Technical Reproduction,'" *The Philosophical Forum* 15, 1–2 (Fall–Winter 1983/4): 130–145.

22
Carlos Ginzburg, "Clues: Roots of an Evidential Paradigm," *Clues, Myths, and the Historical Method.* Translated by John and Anne C. Tedeschi (Baltimore: Johns Hopkins University Press, 1989): 96–125.

23
Wohlfarth, "Messianic Structure": 172.

24
Walter Benjamin, "The Task of the Translator," *Illuminations:* 69.

25
Benjamin "The Task of the Translator": 79. "While content and language form a certain unity in the original, like a fruit and its skin, the language of translation envelops its content like a royal robe with its ample folds. For it signifies a more exalted lanaguge than its own and this remains unsuited to its content, overpowering and alien." Ibid.: 75.

26
Tejaswini Niranjana, *Siting Translation* (Berkeley: University of California Press, 1992): 148. Likening the act of translation to restoration, Benjamin found that:

> Fragments of a vessel which are to be glued together must match one another in the smallest details, although they need not be like one another. In the same way a translation, instead of resembling the meaning of the original, must lovingly and in detail incorporate the original's mode of signification, thus making both the original and the translation recognizable as fragments of a greater language, just as fragments are part of a vessel. For this very reason translation must in large measure refrain from wanting to communicate something, from rendering the sense, and in this the original is important to it only insofar as it has already relieved the translator and his translation of the effort of assembling and expressing what is to be conveyed. Benjamin, "The Task of the Translator": 78.

27
Walter Benjamin, *Gesammelte Schriften* V, N, 15a, I. Quoted by Michael W. Jennings, *Dialectical Images — Walter Benjamin's Theory of Literary Criticism (Ithaca: Cornell University Press, 1987): 147.*

28
For general English references to Aloïs Riegl, see Alan Colquhoun, "'Newness' and 'Age-Value' in Aloïs Riegl," *Modernity and the Classical Tradition* (Cambridge: MIT Press, 1989): 213–221; Kurt W. Foster, "Monument/Memory and the Mortality of Architecture," *Oppositions* 25 (Fall 1982): 2–19; Ignasi de Sola-Morales, "Toward a Modern Museum: From Riegl to Giedion," *Oppositions* 25 (Fall 1982): 69–77.

29
Of course Benjamin's close reading of Riegl has to do with Benjamin's own revaluation of seventeenth-century German tragic drama, the *Trauerspiel.* See Thomas Levin, "Walter Benjamin and the Theory of Art History," *October* 47 (Winter 1988): 77–83, and Jennings: *Dialectical Images:* 151–163.

30
Walter Benjamin, *Passagenwerk* 533, 1051. Quoted by Lindner, "The Passagen-Werk": 45.

31
Walter Benjamin, "Rigorous Study of Art," *October* 47 (Winter 1988): 84–90.

32
Quoted by Michael Ann Holly, *Panofsky and the Foundations of Art History* (Ithaca: Cornell University Press, 1984): 77.

33
Aloïs Riegl's first important book, *Stilfragen* (Problems of Style) was published in 1893. The work follows patterns of ornamentation from the time of Egyptian through to classical antiquity. Jennings, *Dialectical Images:* 152.

34
Jennings, *Dialectical Images:* 154.

35
Margaret Rose Olin, "Aloïs Riegl and the Crisis of Representation in Art Theory" (Unpublished Ph.D. diss., University of Chicago, Dec. 1982).

36
Aloïs Riegl, *Le Culte Moderne des Monuments* (Paris: Éditions du Seuil, 1984).

37
Olin, "Aloïs Reigl" and Riegl, *Le Culte.*

38
Philip Fisher, "The Future's Past," *New Literary History* 6, No. 3 (Spring 1975): 587–606; and Francis Haskell, *Rediscoveries in Art: Some Aspects of Taste, Fashion and Collecting in England and France* (Ithaca: Cornell University Press, 1976): 24–44.

39
Ginzburg, "From Aby Warburg to E. H. Gombrich . . . A Problem of Method," *Clues, Myths:* 17–59.

40
Gottfried Semper, *Der Stil,* Vol 1. 1. Quoted by Podro, *The Critical Historians:* 52–53.

41
Irving Babbitt, *The New Laocoon: An Essay on the Confusion of Arts* (New York: Houghton Mifflin Company, 1910): 196.

42
William Spanos, "The Apollonian Investment of Modern Humanist Education: The Examples of Matthew Arnold, Irving Babbitt and I. A. Richards," Part I, Part II *Cultural Critique* 1, 2 (Fall 1985; Winter 1985/6): 7–72, 105–134.

43
Babbitt, *The New Laocoon:* 202.

44
"No matter how clever he may be, an eclectic is but a feeble man . . ." Prescient of postmodernism but reminiscent of Baudelaire, Giedion continued "an eclectic is a ship which tries to sail before all winds at once." "Experiment with contradictory means, the encroachment of one art upon another, the importations of poetry, wit, and sentiment into painting—all these modern miseries are vices peculiar to the eclectics." Siegfried Giedion, "The Tragic Conflict," *Architecture, You and Me* (Cambridge: Harvard University Press, 1958): 18.

45
Gerald Gillespie, "Scientific Discourse and Postmodernity," *Boundary 2 7,* 2 (Winter 1979): 119–148.

46
Olive Cook, *Movement in Two Dimensions* (London: Hutchinson & Co., 1963): 19; and Martin Quigley, Jr., *Magic Shadows, The Story of the Origin of Motion Pictures* (New York: Quigley Publishing Co., 1960): 48–60.

47
Geoffrey H. Hartman, *Saving the Text* (Baltimore: Johns Hopkins University Press, 1981): 49.

48
Henry Fuseli's English translation in 1765 of Winckelmann's *The Imitatation of the Painting and Sculpture of the Greeks* (1755). Quoted by Robert Eisner, *Travelers to an Antique Land* (Ann Arbor: University of Michigan Press, 1991): 76.

49
Spanos, "The Apollonian Investment": 120–121.

50
Marguerite Iknayan, *The Concave Mirror, From Imitation to Expression in French Esthetic Theory, 1800–1830* (Saratoga, Calif.: Anma Libri & Co., 1983).

51
Spanos, "The Apollonian Investment": 37.

52
Quoted in *Paris-Rome-Athènes: Le Voyage en Grèce des Architectes Français aux XIXe et XXe Siècles* (Paris: Ecole Nationale Superieure des Beaux-Arts, 1982).

53
Michael Herzfeld, *Anthropology Through the Looking-Glass* (Cambridge: University of Cambridge Press, 1987).

54
Homi Bhabha, "DissemiNation," in Homi Bhabha (ed.), *Nation and Narration* (London: Routledge, 1990): 291–322.

55
"Athens," *Harper's New Monthly Magazine* 62 (May 1881): 819–833.

56
Lya Matton and Raymond Matton, *Athènes et Ses Monuments du XCIIe Siècle à Nos Jours* (Athens: Institute Français d'Athènes, 1963): 51–60.

57
Richard Altick, *The Shows of London* (Cambridge: Harvard University Press, 1978): 99–116.

58
Fisher, "The Future's Past": 591.

59
Matton and Matton, *Athènes:* 51–70.

60
Richard Stoneman, *Land of Lost Gods* (Norman: University of Oklahoma Press, 1987): 116–119.

61
Lionel Cust, *History of the Society of Dilettanti* (London: MacMillan & Co., 1914); and "Historical Notes of the Society of Dilettanti," *The Edinburgh Review* 60 (Jan.–April 1857): 493–517.

62
Eisner, *Travelers:* 71.

63
Stoneman, *Land of Lost Gods:* 123.

64
Cust, *History of the Dilettanti.*

65
Eisner, *Travelers:* 74.

66
Matton and Matton, "Athènes": 51–70.

67
Quoted by Herzfeld, *Anthropology:* 81.

68
Quoted in Eisner, *Travelers:* 80.

69
Herzfeld, *Anthropology:* 18–19.

70
Ibid.: 21.

71
The Doric order, as Edmund Aikin defined it in 1810, displayed a column without a base terminated by a capital consisting of a square abacus; an entablature of three parts consisting of a plain architrave, a frieze ornamented with triglyphs, and a cornice with mutules. The column, Aikin noted, "ought" to be fluted. Edmund Aikin, *An Essay on the Doric Order of Architecture, Containing a Historical View of its Rise and Progress among the Ancients, with a Critical Investigation of its Principles of Composition and Adaptation to Modern Use* (London: The London Architectural Society, 1810).

72
George K. T. Aberdeen, *An Inquiry into the Principles of Beauty in Grecian Architecture; with an historical view of the rise and progress of the art in Greece* (London: John Murray, 1822). This essay was originally the "Introduction" to William Wilkin's English translation of Vitruvius' work (January 1812).

73
Ibid.: 36.

74
Ibid.: 26, 46.

75
Ibid.: 216.

76
Richard Jenkins, *The Victorians and Ancient Greece* (Cambridge: Harvard University Press, 1980): 17.

77
Richard Terdiman, "Ideological Voyages: On a Flaubertian Dis-Orient-ation," *Discourse/*

Counter-Discourse (Ithaca: Cornell University Press, 1985): 227–257; and Edward W. Said, *Orientalism* (New York: Random House, 1978).

78
Matton and Matton, *Athènes:* 56.

79
Walter Thornbury, "Athens under King Otto," *The Gentleman's Magazine* (Jan.–June 1879): 84–92; and A. M. Raoul-Rochette, "Athènes sous le Roi Otton," *Revue des Deux Mondes* 16, No. 2 (Oct. 15, 1838): 179–192.

80
William Croswell Doane, "A Visit to Athens," *Harper's New Monthly Magazine* 43 (June, 1896): 3–14.

81
Amèdée Britsch, *La Jeune Athènes: Une Démocratie en Orient* (Paris: Librairie Plon, 1910).

82
Matton and Matton, *Athènes:* 188–200.

83
Christopher Wordsworth, *Athens and Attica: Journal of a Residence There,* 2nd Edition (London: John Murray, 1837): 51.

84
Ibid.: 52.

85
Ibid.: 52.

86
Jean Travlos, *Athènes au fil du Temps.* Translated by Michel Saumier (Paris: Editions Joel Cuenot, 1972).

87
Count Forbin, *Revels in Greece, Turkey, and the Holy Lands in 1817–18* (London: Sir Richard Philips, 1820). Quoted by Herzfeld, *Anthropology:* 87.

88
Herzfeld, *Anthropology:* 80–81.

89
In 1818 Ludwig I of Hessen established the first preservation decree, noting that "the surviving monuments of architecture are among the most important and interesting evidence of history, in that from them may be inferred the former customs, culture and civic conditions of the nation and therefore their preservation is greatly to be wished." Quoted by David Lowenthal in *The Past is a Foreign Country* (Cambridge: Cambridge University Press, 1985): 393.

90
Demetrios Sicilianos, *Old and New Athens.* Translated by Robert Liddell (London: Putnam, 1960): 325.

91
Travlos, *Athènes.*

92
Hermann G. Pundt, *Schinkel's Berlin: A Study in Environmental Planning* (Cambridge: Harvard University Press, 1972): 88–90.

93
Matton and Matton, *Athènes;* and Sicilianos, *Old and New Athens.*

94
A. M. Raoul-Rochette, "Athènes sous le roi Othon," *Revue des Deux Mondes* 16, 2 (Oct. 15, 1838): 185.

95
William Miller, "The Early Years of Modern Athens," (lecture delivered before the Anglo-Hellenic League in Athens, March 27, 1925): 14.

96
Matton and Matton, *Athènes:* 188–200.

97
Stoneman, *Land of Lost Gods:* 243.

98
Matton and Matton, *Athènes:* 188–200.

99
Charles H. Bracebridge, *Notes Descriptive of a Panoramic Sketch of Athens Taken May 1839* (London: W. H. Dutton, 1839): 1.

100
"Notes from a Tour of 1839 by Henry J. G. Herbert, Earl of Carnarvon," *Reminiscences of Athens and the Morea* (London: John Murray, 1869): 1–86.

101
Herzfeld, *Anthropology:* 51–53.

102
Ibid.: 118.

103
Raoul-Rochette, "Athènes."

104
Britsch, *La Jeune Athènes.*

105
Britsch, *La Jeune Athènes.*

106
Thornbury, "Athens under King Otto": 86.

107
Raoul-Rochette, "Athènes": 192.

108
David Carroll, *The Subject in Question* (Chicago: University of Chicago Press, 1982): 88–118.

109
Quoted by Britsch, *La Jeune Athènes.*

110
Quoted by David Watkin and Tilman Mellinghoff, *German Architecture and the Classical Ideal* (Cambridge: MIT Press, 1987): 156.

111
Watkins and Mellingkoff, *German Architecture:* 62.

112
Ibid.: 65–69.

113
Le Corbusier, *Towards a New Architecture.* Translated by Frederick Etchells (New York: Praeger Publishers, 1960): 173–175.

114
Herzfeld, *Anthropology:* 30–31.

115
Carroll, *The Subject in Question:* 116, 148.

116
W. Barcham, *The Imaginary View of Antonio Canaletto* (Ann Arbor: University of Michigan Press, 1974).

117
J. G. Links, *Canaletto and his Patrons* (New York: New York University Press, 1977); Burr Wallen, *Catalogue of the William A. Gumberts Collection of Canaletto Etchings* (Santa Barbara: Santa Barbara Museum of Art, 1979).

118
Phillip Dennis Cate, "Piranesi's Imperial Vision of Rome," *Art News* 72, 3 (Sept. 1973): 40–44; and Manfredo Tafuri, *The Sphere and the Labyrinth: Avant-Gardes and Architecture from Piranesi to the 1970s.* Translated by Pellegrino d'Acierno and Robert Connolly (Cambridge: MIT Press, 1987); and Phillip Duboy, *Lequeu: An Architectural Enigma.* Translated by Francis Scarfe (Cambridge: MIT Press, 1987): 47–53.

119
Roman Jakobson, "A Few Remarks on Pierce, Pathfinder in the Science of Language" *MLN* 92 (1977): 1029. Quoted by Ronald Schleifer, *Rhetoric and Death* (Urbana and Chicago: University of Chicago Press, 1990): 126.

120
Manfredo Frank, "On Foucault's Concept of Discourse," *Michel Foucault Philosopher.* Translated by Timothy J. Armstrong (New York: Routledge, 1992): 115–116.

121
Michel Foucault, "Life, Labor, Language," *The Order of Things* (New York: Pantheon Press, 1973): 250–302.

122
Michel Foucault, "Introduction," *The Archaeology of Knowledge*. Translated by A. M. Sheridan Smith (London: Tavistock Publications, Ltd., 1972): 3–17.

123
Frank, "On Foucault's Discourse": 105; and Thomas Pavel, *The Feud of Language* (Boston: Basil Blackwell, 1989): 87–90.

124
Pavel, *The Feud:* 94.

125
Iknayan, *The Concave Mirror:* 107–128.

126
Aldo Rossi, *The Architecture of the City*. Translated by Diane Ghirardo and Joan Ockman (Cambridge: MIT Press, 1985): 36.

127
Ibid.: 40.

128
Rossi was paraphrasing Quatremère de Quincy, in Rossi, *Architecture of the City:* 41.

129
David Summers, " Conditions and Conventions: on the disanalogy of art and language," in Salim Kemal and Ivan Gaskell (eds.), *The Language of Art History* (Cambridge: Cambridge University Press, 1991): 183.

130
Rossi, *Architecture of the City:* 42.

131
Bernard Huet, "Aldo Rossi or The Exaltation of Reason," in *Aldo Rossi, Three Cities, Perugia, Milano, Mantova* (Electra/Rizzoli: 1984): 9–22; Rossi, *Architecture of the City:* 35; and Aldo Rossi, *Selected Writings and Projects* (London: Architectural Digest, 1983): 15–25.

132
This statement refers to Saverio Muratori's work cited by Luciano Semerani, "Why Not?" *The School of Venice Architectural Digest* 55 5/6 (1986): 11.

133
Rossi refers to this work of Aymonino's in Footnote 12 in Rossi, *Architecture of the City:* 182.

134
Ibid.: 47.

135
Ibid.: 48–51.

136
Viollet-le-Duc in his encyclopedic analysis of building types in the nineteenth century was one exception among typologists that Rossi noted, for Viollet-le-Duc sometimes understood the historical relationships that engendered the architectural forms of the city. By studying the plans of French houses, for example, Viollet-le-Duc was able to reconstruct the formation of urban centers, while his studies of the block and lot morphology of towns built by French kings enabled him to describe the history of social classes in France. Ibid.:, 189.

137
Philippe Panerai, "Typologies," in Philippe Panerai, Jean-Charles Depaule, Marchelle Demorgan, and Michel Veyrenche, *Éléments d'Analyse Urbaine* (Paris: Éditions, Archives d'Architecture Moderne, 1980): 73–108.

138
Rossi, *Architecture of the City:* 118–126.

139
Ibid.: 120.

140
Ibid.: 123–124.

141
Ibid.: 58–69; 86–101.

142
Summers, "Conditions and Conventions": 193.

143
Stephen Tyler, *The Unspeakable: Discourse, Dialogue, and Rhetoric in the Postmodern World* (Madison: University of Wisconsin Press, 1987): 31.

144
Yuri Lotman, *Universe of the Mind: A Semiotic Theory of Culture.* Translated by Ann Sukman (Bloomington: Indiana University Press, 1990): 37.

145
Ibid.: 44.

146
Ibid.: 38.

147
Gilles Deleuze, *Cinema 2.* Translated by Hugh Tomlinson and Robert Galeta (Minneapolis: University of Minnesota Press, 1989): 88.

148
Ibid.: 89.

149
Quoted and translated by David Frisby, *Fragments of Modernity* (Cambridge: MIT Press, 1986): 223–227.

150
Walter Benjamin, *Das Passagen-Werk:* 272. Translated by David Frisby, *Fragments:* 228.

151
Walter Benjamin, "On Some Motifs in Baudelaire," *Illuminations:* 157–158. In general see Ackbar Abbas, "Walter Benjamin's Collector," in Andreas Huyssen and David Bathrick (eds.), *Modernity and the Text: Revisions of German Modernism* (New York: Columbia University Press, 1989): 216–239.

152
Abbas, "Collector,": 229.

153
Ibid.: 230.

154
Benjamin, *Illuminations:* 60; Quoted in Abbas: 232.

155
Ibid.: 234.

156
Quoted by Frisby, *Fragments:* 236.

157
Irving Wohlfarth, "Et Cetera? The Historian as Chiffonnier," *NGC* 39 (Fall 1986): 145.

158
Aldo Rossi, *A Scientific Autobiography.* Translated by Lawrence Venuti (Cambridge: MIT Press, 1981): 35.

159
Phillipe Ivornel, "Paris, Capital of the Popular Front," *NGC* 39 (Fall 1986): 61–84.

160
Ivornel, "Paris": 65.

161
Rossi, *Autobiography:* 23.

162
Ibid.: 23.

163
Ibid.: 19.

164
Ibid.: 6.

165
Ibid.: 5.

166
Ibid.: 78.

167
Ibid.: 26, 29, 30–33, 45, 48, 50–54, 61, 66–69, 78–80.

168
Ibid.: 80.

169
Ibid.: 30, 33.

170
Ibid.: 66.

171
E. H. Gombrich, *Aby Warburg: An Intellectual Biography* (London: The Warburg Institute, University of London, 1970): 239–259; 270–271.

172
Ibid.: 253.

173
Ibid.: 221–227.

174
Theodor W. Adorno, "Valery Proust Museum," *Prisms*. Translated by Samuel and Shierry Weber (London: Neville Spearman, Ltd., 1967): 172–185.

175
Ibid.: 185.

Chapter 5

1
Michel Foucault, *Discipline and Punish*. Translated by Alan Sheridan (New York: Pantheon, 1977): 216–217.

2
Dana Polan, *The Political Language of Film and the Avant-Garde* (Ann Arbor: UMI Research Press, 1985): 53–77.

3
Svetlana Alpers, *The Art of Describing Dutch Art in the Seventeenth Century* (Chicago: University of Chicago Press, 1983): 26–71; and Louis Marin, "In Praise of Appearance," *October* 37 (Summer 1986): 99–112.

4
Peter Mason, *Deconstructing America: Representations of the Other* (New York: Routledge, 1990): 13–38.

5
Ronald Rees, "Historical Links between Cartography and Art," *Geographical Review* 70 (1980): 60–78.

6
George R. Kernodle, *From Art to Theatre: Form and Convention in the Renaissance* (Chicago: University of Chicago Press, 1944).

7
Steven Mullaney, *The Place of the Stage: License, Play, and Power in Renaissance England* (Chicago: University of Chicago Press, 1988): 12.

8
Carolly Erickson, *The Medieval Vision: Essays in History and Perception* (New York: Oxford University Press, 1970): 3–28.

9
John A. Pinto, "Origins and Development of the Ichnographic City Plan," *Journal of the Society of Architectural Historians* 35 (1976): 35–50.

10
P. D. A. Harvey, *The History of Topographical Maps* (London: Thames and Hudson, 1980): 66–83; and Rees, "Cartography and Art."

11
Pinto, "Ichnographic City Plan."

12
Alpers, *The Art of Describing:* 119–168.

13
Barbara Maria Stafford, *Voyage into Substance. Art, Science, Nature, and the Illustrated Travel Account, 1760–1840* (Cambridge: MIT Press, 1984): 1–29.

14
Ibid.: 1–19, 59.

15
Victor Turner, *The Anthropology of Performance* (New York: Performing Arts Journal, Inc., 1986): 99–107.

16
Ibid.: 102.

17
Mullaney, *The Place of the Stage:* 12–17, 73–75.

18
Patrick Geddes, "The Survey of Cities," *Sociological Review* (January 1908).

19
Amelia Defries, *The Interpreter Geddes: The Man and His Gospel* (New York: Boni and Liverwright, 1928): 78–79.

20
Philip Mairet, *Pioneer of Sociology: The Life and Letters of Patrick Geddes* (London: Lund Humphries, 1957).

21
Patrick Geddes, *City Development; A Report to the Carnegie Dunfermline Trust.* Reprint of a 1904 Report. (New Brunswick, N. J.: Rutgers University Press, 1973).

22
Helen Miller, "Cities and Evolution: Patrick Geddes as an International Prophet of Town Planning before 1914," in Anthony Sutcliffe (ed.), *The Rise of Modern Urban Planning, 1800–1914* (New York: St. Martin's Press, 1980): 199–233; and Alessandra Ponte, "Thinking Machines: From the Outlook Tower to the City of the World," *Lotus* 35 (1982): 47–51.

23
Defries, *The Interpreter Geddes:* 90.

24
Mairet, *Pioneer of Sociology.*

25
Paddy Kitchen, *A Most Unsettling Person: The Life and Ideas of Patrick Geddes, Founding Father of City Planning and Environmentalism* (New York: E. P. Dutton and Co. Inc., 1975): 139.

26
Ibid.

27
Gary S. Dunbar, *Élisée Reclus: Historian of Nature* (Hamden, Conn.: Archon Books, 1978): 41, 52.

28
Patrick Geddes, "The Valley Section," in David M. Lewis (ed.), *Urban Structure* (New York: John Wiley & Sons, Inc., 1968): 65–70.

29
Kitchen, *Unsettling Person.*

30
Ponte, "Thinking Machines."

31
Mairet, *Pioneer of Sociology:* 99–108.

32
Geddes, *City Development:* 5–33.

33
Ibid.: 115.

34
Kitchen, *Unsettling Person* and Defries, *The Interpreter Geddes.*

35
Kitchen, *Unsettling Person.*

36
Marshall Stalley (ed.), *Patrick Geddes: Spokesman for Man and the Environment* (New Brunswick, N.J.: Rutgers University Press, 1972): 222–241.

37
Ibid.: 222–241.

38
Geddes, *City Development:* 130.

39
Philippe Duboy, *Lequeu: An Architectural Enigma* (Cambridge: MIT Press, 1987): 22–23.

40
Wilda Anderson, "Encyclopedic Topologies," *Modern Language Notes* (MLN) 100, No. 4 (Sept 1986): 912–929.

41
Eric M. Steel, *Diderot's Imagery: A Study of a Literary Personality* (New York: Haskell House, 1966): 13–32.

42
Michel Foucault, "Fantasia of the Library," in Donald F. Bouchard (ed.), *Language, Counter-Memory, Practice* (New York: Cornell University Press, 1977): 85–100; and Duboy, *Lequeu:* 29.

43
E. T. Cook and Alexander Wedderburn (eds.), *The Works of John Ruskin. Literary Editions* (London: George Allen, 1904): Vol. 9: 411. [Henceforth referenced as *Works of Ruskin*]

44
Ibid.: 8: 225.

45
Raymond E. Fitch, *The Poison Sky: Myth and Apocalypse in Ruskin* (Athens, Ohio: Ohio University Press, 1982): 125–138; and John Ruskin, *The Seven Lamps of Architecture* (New York: Farrar, Straus and Giroux, 1986, tenth printing).

46
Works of Ruskin: 5: 427.

47
Jeffrey L. Spear, *Dreams of an English Eden: Ruskin and His Tradition of Social Criticism* (New York: Columbia University Press, 1984).

48
Works of Ruskin: 6: 69.

49
Gary Wihl, *Ruskin and the Rhetoric of Infallibility* (New Haven: Yale University Press, 1985): 168–182.

50
Works of Ruskin: 10: 114.

51
Wihl, *Ruskin:* 181.

52
Ibid.: 173.

53
Ibid.: 171.

54
Fitch, *Poison Sky:* 5.

55
Ibid.: 113–115.

56
Works of Ruskin: 12: 422–423.

57
Ibid.: 12: 427–428.

58
Ibid.: 12: 314–315.

59
Ibid.: 12: 428.

60
Ibid.: 12: 429.

61
Elizabeth K. Helsinger, *Ruskin and the Art of the Beholder* (Cambridge: Harvard University Press, 1982): 140.

62
Ibid.: 68, 80.

63
Works of Ruskin: 5: 182–183.

64
Ibid.: 5: 381.

65
Ibid.: 25: 451.

66
Ibid.: 12: 314–315.

67
Spear, *Dreams of an English Eden:* 40–51.

68
Helsinger, *Ruskin:* 153; Robert Hewison, *John Ruskin: The Argument of the Eye* (Princeton: Princeton University Press, 1976); and *Works of Ruskin:* 11: 226.

69
John D. Rosenberg (ed.), *The Genius of John Ruskin. Selections from his Writings* (Boston: Routledge & Kegan Paul, 1979): 163–187.

70
Jay Fellows, *The Failing Distance: The Autobiographical Impulse in John Ruskin* (Baltimore: Johns Hopkins University Press, 1975): 158–187.

71
Works of Ruskin: 19: 217.

72
Ibid.: 19: 218; 20: 237.

73
Ibid.: 19: 218.

74
Jay Fellows, *Ruskin's Maze: Mastery and Madness in his Art* (Princeton: Princeton University Press, 1981): 127–153.

75
Works of Ruskin: 19: 219, 221.

76
Ibid.: 34: 247–249.

77
Hewison, *Ruskin:* 183–186; *Works of Ruskin:* 28: 20; 28: 385; 28: 450; 30: 51.

78
E. T. Cook, *The Life of John Ruskin,* vol. 2 (London: George Allen & Co., 1912): 345–360.

79
Hewison, *Ruskin:* 170.

80
Works of Ruskin: 31: xxix.

81
Ibid.: 26: 1.

82
The Educational Series was for undergraduate study and the Rudimentary Series was for classes of general education. *Works of Ruskin:* 16: 440, 451; 31: xxxc. His Standard Series was supposed to be a collection of 400 exemplary images of the best art of the Western world. In actuality only 50 specimens were gathered. The Reference Series overlapped with the Standard Series and were examples used for lecturing purposes. On these two series, the work of his school of criticism would depend: standards in the sense that the student could develop a "sense of right" and specimens for moral, historical, and technical reference. *Works of Ruskin:* 31: xxxi–xxxiv.

83
Helsinger, *Ruskin:* 83.

84
Kim Ian Michasiw, "Nine Revisionist Theses on the Picturesque," *Representations* 38 (Spring 1992): 84.

85
Charles L. Batten, Jr., *Pleasurable Instruction: Form and Convention in Eighteenth-Century Travel Literature* (Berkeley: University of California Press, 1978); and Stafford, *Voyage.*

86
Stafford, *Voyage:* 105.

87
Spear, *Dreams of an English Eden:* 40–51.

88
Stafford, *Voyage:* 320–321.

89
Helsinger, *Ruskin:* 67–68.

90
Ibid.: 69–76; 143–145.

91
Daniel J. Boorstin, *The Image: A Guide to Pseudo-Events in America* (New York: Atheneum, 1971): 106.

92
Francis Haskell, *Rediscoveries in Art: Some Aspects of Taste, Fashion and Collecting in England and France* (Ithaca: Cornell University Press, 1976): 96–117.

93
Bonnie L. Grad and Timothy A. Riggs, *Visions of City and Country: Prints and Photographs of Nineteenth-Century France* (Worchester: Worchester Art Museum and The American Federation of Arts, 1982): 22.

94
C. Nodier, *Voyages Pittoresques et Romantiques dans L'Ancienne France: Normandy,* Vol. 1. (Paris: 1820): 4. Quoted by Grad and Riggs, *Visions of City and Country:* 17.

95
Michasiw, "Revisionist Theses": 88–89.

96
Grad and Riggs, *Visions of City and Country;* and André Jammes and Eugenia Parry Janis, *The Art of French Calotype* (Princeton: Princeton University Press, 1983): 49–51; and Michael Twyman, *Lithography 1800–1850* (London: Oxford University Press, 1970): 226–253.

97
James Borcoman, *Eugène Atget, 1857–1927* (Ottawa: The National Gallery of Canada, 1984): 34–55; and Jammes and Janis, *French Calotype:* 52–56.

98
Eugenia Parry Janis, "Demolition Picturesque: Photographs of Paris in 1852 and 1853 by Henri Le Secq," in Peter Walch and Thomas F. Barrow (eds.), *Perspectives on Photography* (Albuquerque: University of New Mexico Press, 1986): 33–66.

99
Jacquelin Chambord (ed.) *Charles Marville: Photographs of Paris at the Time of the Second Empire* (New York: French Institute/Alliance Française, 1981).

100
Maria Luisa Marceca, "Reservoir, Circulation, Residue," *Lotus International* 30 (1981): 57–65.

101
Borcoman, *Atget:* 10–31; and Maria Morris Hambourg, "A Biography of Eugene Atget," vol. 2, *The Art of Old Paris* (New York: The Modern Museum of Art, 1982): 9–31; Maria Morris Hambourg, "The Structure of the Work" vol. 3, *The Ancien Regime* (New York: The Modern Museum of Art, 1983): 9–28.

102
Borcoman, *Atget:* 10–31.

103
Max Kozloff, "Abandoned and Seductive: Atget's Streets," *The Privileged Eye: Essays on Photography* (Albuquerque: University of New Mexico Press, 1987): 279–304.

104
Roberta Hellman and Marvin Hoshimo, "On the Rationalization of Eugene Atget," *Arts Magazine* 56, 6 (Feb. 1982): 88–91.

105
Hambourg, *The Ancien Regime:* 9–28.

106
Michael Fried, *Absorption and Theatricality: Painting and the Beholder in the Age of Diderot* (Berkeley: University of California Press, 1980): 107–160.

107
Ian J. Lochhead, *The Spectator and the Landscape in the Art Criticism of Diderot and His Contemporaries* (Ann Arbor: University of Michigan Research Press, 1982): 23–68.

108
Bernard Smith, *European Vision and the South Pacific* (New Haven: Yale University Press, 1985): 51.

109
Ibid.: 1–7, 29.

110
Ibid.: 79.

111
Ibid.: 90–99, 133–154.

112
William Hodges, *Travels in India* (London: 1793): 641. Quoted by Partha Mitter, *Maligned Monsters: A History of European Reactions to Indian Art* (Chicago: University of Chicago Press, 1992 paperback of 1977 edition): 125.

113
Christopher Hussey, *The Picturesque Studies in a Point of View* (London: Archon Books, 1967, reprint of 1927 original): 83–127.

114
"De Loutherbourg and Captain Cook," *Theatre Research/Research Theatrical* 4, no. 2 (1962): 198.

115
Michel de Certeau, "Heterologies: Discourses on the Other," *Theory and History of Literature* 17 (Minneapolis: University of Minnesota Press, 1986): 137–149; Steel, *Diderot's Imagery:* 185–186.

116
Smith, *European Vision:* 109–132.

117
Mitter, *Maligned Monsters:* 127.

118
Dipesh Chakrabarty, "Postcoloniality and the Artifice of History: Who Speaks for the 'Indian' Pasts?" *Representations* 37 (Winter 1992): 1–26.

119
Hegels Werke (Berlin, 1832–40). Quoted by Mitter, *Maligned Monsters:* 217.

120
Robert Eisner, *Travelers to an Antique Land* (Ann Arbor: University of Michigan Press, 1991): 76–77; and Mitter, *Maligned Monsters:* 192.

121
Works of Ruskin: 1: 13–15.

122
Ibid.: 1: 67–70.

123
Ibid.: 1: 71.

124
John Ruskin *Modern Painters,* V: 123. Quoted in Mitter, *Maligned Monsters:* 242–241.

125
John Ruskin, *Queen of the Air* II (1869): 383. Quoted in Mitter, *Maligned Monsters:* 242.

126
Paul Coates, *The Story of the Lost Reflection* (London: Verso Press, 1985): 51.

127
One of the most important panoramic wallpapers was "The Royal Fête in the Champs Élysées," produced in 1815. It was a series replicating the landscape view in historic and architectural detail as if seen from one of the balloon voyages of Marie Madeleine Sophie Armant, the wife of the aeronaut François Blanchard. Alexander Watt, "The History of French Panoramic Wallpapers," *Apollo* 51 (1950): 44–47.

128
Another theater of illusion, the Diorama invented by Daguerre opened in Paris in 1822. The following year a replica Diorama designed by Augustus Charles Pugin (the father of Charles Welby Pugin) was located near Regent's Park in one of the London terraces designed by John Nash. The circular auditorium held two hundred people, who were submerged in darkness immediately on entering the building in order to heighten the luminous effects of the show. A second rotunda, the amphitheater at least ten feet wide and balanced on eighteen-foot-high pillars lay entirely within the larger rotunda. A picture-frame aperture mounted on the amphitheater's wall faced the audience and was aligned with two similar apertures mounted on the enclosing wall. A tunnel thirty or forty feet long focused on a giant picture, seventy-two by forty-two feet, painted partly in translucent and partly in opaque colors. No artificial lighting was used; the opaque parts being frontally illuminated by skylights mounted in the tunnel's corridor, and the translucent parts illuminated from behind by tall glass windows at the end of the tunnel. An elaborate system of shutters and curtains could modify the color or intensity of the light or

obscure and overshadow parts of the scenery. After a performance of fifteen minutes, most of the paintings being architectural landscapes or the mountains of Switzerland, the aperture was rotated to align with the second aperture, in which was hung a second performance. The London Diorama became a Baptist church in 1853 and then part of the University of London in 1921. Richard D. Altick, *The Shows of London* (Cambridge: Harvard University Press, 1978): 136, 173–183, 188.

129
This is why Rousseau feared the effect theater might have on Geneva: actors taught deception and artful poses, while the play entertained and its scenery projected artificial illusions. Theater was dangerous because the public learned to adopt a theatrical consciousness, seeing the world from a distance as one gigantic stage. It was there that they learned the exchange of regards and how to make spectacles of themselves. So Rousseau believed, the public eye, the regulator of public opinion and social behavior, was weakened in this artificial milieu, replaced by a world of appearances. David Marshall, "Rousseau and the State of Theater," *Representations* 13 (Winter 1986): 84–114.

130
Altick, *Shows of London:* 147.

131
Quoted by Dorothy Dondore, "Banvard's Panorama and the Flowering of New England," *New England Quarterly* 11 (1938): 819.

132
Curtis Dahl, "Mark Twain and the Moving Panorama," *American Quarterly* 13 (1961): 20–32.

133
Perry T. Ratbone, "The Art of the Mississippi," *Mississippi Panorama* (St. Louis: City Art Museum at St. Louis, 1950): 27–48.

134
Lucien Goldmann, *La Création Culturelle dans la Société Moderne* (Paris: Denoel/ Gonthier, 1971): 111–117.

135
Dana Polan, "'Above all else to make you see': Cinema and Ideology of Spectacle," *Boundary 2* 2 (Fall/Winter 1982/3): 129–144.

136
Philip Fisher, "The Future's Past," *New Literary History* 6, 3 (Spring 1975): 593.

137
Owen Jones quoted in *The Fine Arts' Courts in the Crystal Palace* (London: Bradbury and Evans, 1854): 17.

138
Altick, *Shows of London:* 483–503.

139
Pat Mainardi, *Art and Politics of the Second Empire, the Universal Expositions of 1855 and 1867* (New Haven: Yale University Press, 1987): 128–134.

140
Edward N. Kaufman, "The Architectural Museum from World's Fair to Restoration Village," *Assemblage* 9 (1989): 21–39; and Joseph M. Wilson, *The Masterpieces of the Centennial International Exhibition,* Vol. 3 (New York: Garland Publications, Inc., 1977).

141
The Dewey Decimal System enabled a catalog entry of Water Color Pictures, for example, to be defined as sub-subset 411 and cross-referenced as belonging to the subset 40 of painting, which in turned was contained within the set 4 called art. John Maas, *The Glorious Enterprise: The Centennial Exhibition of 1876* (Watkins Glen, New York: American Life Foundation, 1978): 113–114; and Wilson, *Masterpieces:* lxxxiii–clxxxvi.

142
John Allwood, *The Great Exhibitions* (London: Studio Vista, 1977); and Wilson, *Masterpieces.*

143
"New England Kitchen," in *A Facsimile of Frank Leslie's Illustrated Historical Register of the Centennial Exposition, 1876* (New York: Paddington Press, Ltd., 1976): 87.

144
Joseph M. Wilson, *The History of the Exhibition* (Philadelphia: 1876): clxiii–iv.

145
"New England Kitchen": 87.

146
Reports of the U.S. Commissioners to the Paris Universal Exposition of 1878, vol. 2 (Washington, D.C.: Government Printing Office, 1880).

147
Victor Champier, "Les 44 Habitations Humaines," in F. G. Dumas and L. de Fourcaud, *Revue de l'Exposition Universelle,* vol. 1 (Paris: Librairie d'Art, 1889): 115–125.

148
Eugene Emmanuel Viollet-le-Duc, *Discourses on Architecture.* Translated by Henry Van Brunt (Boston: James R. Osgood and Co., 1876): 515.

149
Eugene Emmanuel Viollet-le-Duc, *The Habitations of Man in All Ages.* Translated by Benjamin Bucknall (Boston: James R. Osgood and Co., 1876).

150
Viollet-le-Duc, *Discourses:* 170–171, 514.

151
Virginia W. Bradford, "Nineteenth-Century Exhibition Architecture" (unpublished masters thesis, Avery Library, Columbia University, 1965).

152
Dumas and Fourcaud, *Revue:* 78–85.

153
Ibid.: 115–125.

154
Paul Bourde, "La Rue de Caire," in Dumas and Fourcaud, *Revue,* vol. 1: 73–76.

155
Albert de Korsak, "Promenade au Panorama de la Compagnie Générale Transatlantique," Dumas and Fourcaud, *Revue:* 51–56.

156
Rosalind H. Williams, *Dream Worlds, Mass Consumption in Late Nineteenth-Century France* (Berkeley: University of California Press, 1982): 3.

157
William Dean Howells, *Letters of an Altruvian Traveller* (Gainesville, Fl.: Scholars' Facsimiles and Reprints, 1961): 20–34.

158
Major Ben C. Truman. *History of the World's Fair* (copyright B. C. Truman, 1893).

159
Rachel Bowlby, *Just Looking: Consumer Culture in Dreiser, Gissing and Zola* (New York: Methuen, 1985).

160
Susan Stewart, *On Longing: Narratives of the Miniature, the Gigantic, the Souvenir, the Collection* (Baltimore: Johns Hopkins University Press, 1984): 139–151.

161
Roger Scruton, *The Aesthetics of Architecture* (Princeton: Princeton University Press, 1979): 16.

162
Stephen Tschudi-Madsen, *Restoration and Anti-Restoration* (Oslo: Universitetsforlaget: 1976): 27–28.

163
Augustus W. N. Pugin, *Contrast,* 2nd Edition (London, 1836): 57. Quoted by Tschudi-Madsen, *Restoration:* 29.

164
Peter Conrad, *The Victorian Treasure-House* (London: Collins, 1973): 151–157.

165
Michael Bright, *Cities Built to Music, Aesthetic Theories of the Victorian Gothic Revival* (Columbus: Ohio State University Press, 1984): 54.

166
Works of Ruskin: 1: 68.

167
Bright, *Built to Music:* 142.

168
Tschudi-Madsen, *Restoration:* 127.

169
Ibid.: 129.

170
Ibid.: 130.

171
Ibid.: 130–131.

172
Ibid.: 15, 37.

173
Ruskin, *The Seven Lamps of Architecture* (New York: Farrar, Straus and Giroux, 1986 reprint of 1849 edition): 184.

174
Ibid.: 186.

175
Ibid.: 187.

176
Ibid.: 169. In 1877 William Morris and eighty-eight others following Ruskin's philosophy established the Society for the Protection of Ancient Buildings, a group opposed to the barbarism of restoration, dedicated to safeguarding all old monuments, and pleading for an architecture of all times and styles. They too believed a monument was a historical document, which should neither be scrapped nor touched. There was much surrounding and contained within a historic structure that was more in keeping with its original style than otherwise. These accretions of time were its historical record; they should be not be stripped away nor should preference be given to the unity of one particular style. The decades of the 1870s and 1880s saw many different countries passing legislation to protect their monuments: Italy in 1872, Spain in 1873, England in 1882, and France in 1887. Finally in the Athens Conferences "La Conservation des Monuments d'Art and d'Histoire," the unity of style advocated by Viollet-le-Duc was formally rejected. "In the case where a restoration seems unavoidable because of degradation or destruction, the Conference recommended that the historic and artistic work of the past should be respected without rejecting the style of any one period." Tschudi-Madsen, *Restoration:* n23, 18.

177
George L. Hersey, "Ruskin as Optical Thinker," in John Dixon Hunt and Faith M. Holland (eds.), *The Ruskin Polygon: Essays on the Imagination of John Ruskin* (Manchester, England: Manchester University Press, 1982): 46; and *Works of Ruskin:* 5: 333.

178
Michael Spencer, *Michel Butor* (New York: Twayne Publishers, Inc., 1974): 124.

179
Tschudi-Madsen, *Restoration:* 139.

180
Bright, *Built to Music:* 39–42, 97.

181
Frederick Lush, "Style in Architecture," *The Builder* 16 (1858): 865.

182
Lawrence Harvey, "The French Mind," *The Builder* 28 (1870): 280.

183
Lush, "Style": 867.

184
"The Adornment of Cities," *The Builder* 37 (1879): 393.

185
Works of Ruskin: 16: 304. Quoted by Mitter, *Maligned Monsters:* 247.

186
Ronald R. Thomas, *Dreams of Authority: Freud and the Fictions of the Unconscious* (Ithaca: Cornell University Press, 1990) 193–203.

187
Henry Mayhew, *London Labour and the London Poor.* Quoted by Jon Stratton, *Writing Sites* (Ann Arbor: University of Michigan Press, 1990): 199.

188
Louis Chevalier, *Labouring Classes and Dangerous Classes* (New York: Howard Fertig, 1973): 222–223. Quoted by José B. Moleón, *A Specter is Haunting Europe* (Princeton: Princeton University Press, 1990): 60.

189
B. Disraeli, *Sybil, or The Two Nations* (Harmondsworth: Penguin, 1954): 73. Quoted by Stratton, *Writing Sites:* 193.

190
Alexander Payne, "London as It Is, and Might Be," *The Builder* 30 (1872): 40–41; 61–63.

191
Nicholas Tyler, "The Awful Sublimity of the Victorian City," in H. J. Dyos and Michael Wolff (eds.), *Victorian City: Images and Realities,* vol. 2 (London: Routledge and Kegan Paul, 1973): 431–447.

192
Gareth Stedman Jones, *Outcast London* (London: Penguin Books, 1971).

193
Blanchard Jerrold, *Life of Gustave Doré* (London: W. H. Allen and Co. Ltd., 1891): 169.

194
Ibid.: 176.

195
Francis Haskell, "Doré's London," *Past & Present in Art & Taste* (New Haven: Yale University Press, 1987): 128–140.

196
Wohlfarth, "Messianic Structure": *Glyph* 3 (1978): 167.

197
Peter Conrad, *The Victorian Treasure-House* (London: Collins, 1973): 65–105; and John H. B. Knowlton, *The Graphic Art of Gustave Doré* (unpublished Ph.D. diss., New York University, 1950): 161–168.

198
Wohlfarth, "Messianic Structure": 155.

199
Peter Stallybrass and Allon White, *The Politics & Poetics of Transgression* (Ithaca: Cornell University Press, 1986): 128.

200
David Woodward (ed.), *Five Centuries of Map Printing* (Chicago: University of Chicago Press, 1975): 77–112.

201
Historical cartography, especially the mapping of military strategies and battles, was another early use of lithographic printing. Arthur H. Robinson, *Early Thematic Mapping in the History of Cartography* (Chicago: University of Chicago Press, 1982): 44–67, 155–188.

202
Michel Foucault, *Discipline and Punish.* Translated by Alan Sheridan (New York: Pantheon Books, 1977): 195–197.

203
For a description of the topographic view of Michel Foucault and its relationship to the rise of city planning, see M. Christine Boyer, *Dreaming the Rational City* (Cambridge: MIT Press, 1983): 59–82.

204
Didier Gille, "Maceration and Purification," *Zone* 1/2 (1988): 227–281; and Rosalind Wil-

liams, *Notes on the Underground* (Cambridge: MIT Press, 1990).

205
Adolph Smith and John Thompson, *Street Life in London* (New York: Benjamin Blom, Inc., 1969 reprint of 1877 book).

206
Ibid.: 9–10.

207
Ibid.: 116–118.

208
Ibid.: 28–29.

209
Ibid.: 49–50, 135.

210
Andrew Benjamin, "Tradition and Experience: Walter Benjamin's 'On Some Motifs in Baudelaire,'" in Andrew Benjamin (ed.), *The Problems of Modernity* (London: Routledge, 1991): 124.

211
Walter Benjamin, "The Storyteller," *Illuminations*. Translated by Harry Zohn (New York: Schocken Books, 1969): 83–109; and Benjamin in Benjamin, *Problems of Modernity:* 122–140.

212
Peter Stallybrass and Allon White, "The City, the Sewer, the Gaze & the Contaminating Touch," in *Politics & Poetics:* 125–148.

213
Robert Alter, *Necessary Angels: Tradition and Modernity in Kafka, Benjamin, and Scholem* (Cambridge: Harvard University Press, 1991): 83.

214
Ibid.: 84.

215
Ibid.: 11.

Chapter 6

1
Hollis Frampton, *Circles of Confusion* (Rochester: Visual Studies Workshop Press, 1983): 178–179.

2
Karl Marx, *The German Ideology* (New York: International Publishers, 1970): 14.

3
W. J. T. Mitchell, *Iconology Image, Text, Ideology* (Chicago: University of Chicago Press, 1986): 160–208.

4
Ibid.: 7–42.

5
Richard Palmer, "Toward a Postmodern Hermeneutics of Performance," in Michel Benamou and Charles Caramello (eds.), *Performance in Postmodern Culture* (Madison: University of Wisconsin Press: 1977): 19–32.

6
Thus the nineteenth-century international expositions are an exhortation of this belief: as immense catalogs and classificatory lists of the mechanical and scientific progress of all nations, they simultaneously became the selective inventories and industrial molds into which that century poured its image of reality. The startling images of the panorama and the popular lithographs, by displaying their virtuoso effects of replication, gained control over contemporary imaginations, forcing them into stereotypical molds. As nationalism rose in America after the Civil War, so too did pride in her majestic landscape and sublime rivers, in her new Capitol and the building of the Washington Monument, all events pictorially replicated again and again. Indeed the many western panoramas, such as Wilkin's "Moving Mirror of the Overland Trail" or Beale and Craven's "Voyage to California and Return" taught spectators how to think pictorially, how to combine local color, amusing anecdotes, and dialect with spectacular scenic effects.

7
Gerald Gillespie, "Scientific Discourse and Postmodernity: Francis Bacon and the Empirical Birth of 'Revision'," *Boundary 2* 7, no. 2 (Winter 1979): 119–148; and James Stephens, *Francis Bacon and the Style of Science* (Chicago: University of Chicago Press, 1975).

8
In one of Warburg's last projects, called Mnemosyne, he tried to demonstrate how pictures alone could be combined to tell a complex story. He left at his death forty screens of nearly 1,000 photographs whose arrangement was expected to tell a story without the aid of captions. E. H. Gombrich, *Aby Warburg: An Intellectual Biography* (London: Warburg Institute, University of London, 1970): 239–250, 283–306.

9
Roland Barthes, *Camera Lucida.* Translated by Richard Howard (New York: Hill & Wang, 1981); Naomi Schor, *Reading in Detail* (New York: Methuen, 1987): 79–97; Gary Shapiro, "To Philosophize is to Learn to Die," in Steven Ungar and Betty R. McFraw (eds.), *Signs in Culture: Roland Barthes Today* (Iowa City: University of Iowa Press, 1989): 3–31.

10
Barthes, *Camera Lucida:* 32.

11
Terry Castle, "Phantasmagoria: Spectral Technology and the Metaphorics of Modern Reverie," *Critical Inquiry* 15 (Autumn 1988): 26–61.

12
"When we build a city, art is not reckoned with. After the city is there, some records, photographic and calligraphic, are taken of it. These records serve but as a laughing-stock and a warning to future ages, recording the folly of blundering at the beginning and taking infinite pains when it is too late; recording how through fear we omit to face facts about nations, cities, people, even our own lives, because it seems so costly—no other reason—and how we are forced in the end a thousand times the price for what we could have had, had we trusted our Imagination and our Emotions." Edward Gordon Craig, *Towards a New Theatre* (London: J. M. Dent and Sons Limited, 1913): 86.

13
Castle, "Phantasmagoria": 59.

14
Ibid.: 48.

15
T. R. Nevett, *Advertising in Britain* (London: William Heinemann Ltd., 1982): 96.

16
W. Hamish Fraser, *The Coming of the Mass Market, 1850–1914* (Hamden, Conn.: Archon Books, 1981): 136.

17
Philip Fisher, *Hard Facts: Setting and Form in the American Novel* (New York: Oxford University Press, 1985): 132–135; Stuart Culver, "What Manikins Want: The Wonderful Wizard of Oz and the Art of Decorating Dry Goods Windows," *Representations* 21 (Winter 1988): 97–116.

18
Jacques Attali, *Noise: The Political Economy of Music.* Translated by Brian Massumi (Minneapolis: University of Minnesota Press, 1985).

19
Michael Chanan, *The Dream that Kicks* (London: Routledge & Kegan Paul, 1980): 143–145, 176–177.

20
Attali, *Noise:* 89.

21
The first English postcards, called Opal Cards were produced in 1889. See Chanan, *Dream that Kicks:* 88; and W. Hamish Fraser, *The Mass Market.*

22
Mariam Klamkin, *Picture Postcards* (London: David & Charles Ltd., 1974): 35, 58–66.

23
Fraser, *Mass Market:* 222.

24
George F. Chadwick, *The Works of Sir Joseph Paxton* (London: Architectural Press, 1961): 153–155.

25
Jean Starobinski, "The Idea of Nostalgia" *Diogenes* 54 (1966): 81–103.

26
Susan Stewart, *On Longing: Narratives of the Miniature, the Gigantic, the Souvenir, the Collection* (Baltimore: Johns Hopkins University Press: 1984): 23, 140–145.

27
Marcel Poëte, the avid collector of Atget photographs for the Bibliothéque des Travaux Historiques de Ville de Paris in 1903, also believed that it was the library's task to collect all the sources that would eventually become the records of the past or the history of an epoch—such everyday items as menus, letters, street cries, and popular songs. He was also interested in understanding the transformations to a city's physical composition by studying the lithographic and photographic record of its streets, buildings, and everyday scenes. These images, Poëte reasoned, reveal to the viewer the physical traces of former times that were now impressed on the city's present physiognomy. And he claimed further that it was only by examining the record of the past that we could develop an understanding of the complex organism called a city. Marcel Poëte, "Le Service de la Bibliothéque," *Bulletin de la Bibliothéque et des Travaux Historique de la Ville,* vol. 1 (1906): v–xxviii; Marcel Poëte, *Une Vie de Cité, Paris* (Paris: Auguste Picard, Éditeur, 1924); and Marcel Poëte "L'Evolution des Villes" (unpublished lecture notes from Cours de Université de Paris, Institut d'Urbanisme, 1935, 1936, and 1937).

28
Chanan, *Dream that Kicks:* 264–318.

29
Lafcadio Hearn, "The City of Dreams," quoted by Jonathan Cott, *Wandering Ghost: The Odyssey of Lafcadio Hearn* (New York: Alfred A. Knopf, 1991): 124.

30
Lafcadio Hearn, *Sketches of New Orleans* (Franklin, New Hampshire: Illside Press, 1964): 60–61.

31
Quoted by Cott, *Wandering Ghost:* 137.

32
Lafcadio Hearn, "Some Fancies about Fancy," (March 28, 1881). Quoted by Elizabeth Stevenson, *Lafcadio Hearn* (New York: Macmillan Co., 1961): 110.

33
Cott, *Wandering Ghost:* 69.

34
Quoted by Cott, *Wandering Ghost:* 138.

35
Ibid.: 228.

36
Ibid.: 229.

37
Alphonse V. Roche, *Provencal Regionalism: A Study of the Movement in the Revue Felbireene, Le Feu and other Rives of Southern France* (New York: AMS Press, 1907; reprint from Northwestern University Press, 1954); and Frederic Mistral, *The Memoirs of Frederic Mistral.* Translated by George Wicker (New York: New Directions Books, 1986).

38
Raymond Williams, *Marxism and Literature* (Oxford: Oxford University Press, 1977): 24.

39
Michael Herzfeld, *Anthropology Through the Looking-Glass* (Cambridge: Cambridge University Press, 1987): 13.

40
Joseph Mali, "The Public Grounds of Truth," *New Vico Studies* 6 (1988): 59–83.

41
Herzfeld, *Looking-Glass:* 32–33, 169–171, 186–194.

42
Michel Foucault, "Two Lectures," in Colin Gordon, *Power/Knowledge.* Translated by Golin Gordon, Leo Marshall, John Mepham, and Kate Soper (New York: Pantheon Books, 1980): 78–108.

43
Herzfeld, *Looking-Glass:* 8.

44
Ibid.: 9.

45
Ibid.: 10.

46
Quoted without reference in Timothy Brennan, "The National Longing for Form," in Homi Bhabha (ed.), *Narration and Nation* (London: Routledge, 1990): 44–70.

47
Eric Hobsbawm and Terence Ranger, (eds.), *The Invention of Tradition* (Cambridge: Cambridge University Press, 1983): 10.

48
Simon During, "Literature–Nationalism's Other? The Case for Revision," in Bhabha (ed.), *Narration:* 145.

49
During, "Literature—Nationalism's Other?": 145.

50
J. B. Jackson, *The Necessity for Ruins and Other Topics* (Amherst: University of Massachusetts Press, 1980): 73, 88–102.

51
Hobsbawm and Ranger, "Introduction," *Invention of Tradition:* 1–15.

52
Oscar George Theodore Sonneck, *Report on "The Star-Spangled Banner," "Hail Columbia," "America," "Yankee Doodle,"* (New York: Dover Publications, Inc. 1972 facsimile reproduction of 1909 edition).

53
Sonneck, *Report of "Yankee Doodle":* 109.

54
Thomas H. Pauley, "In Search of 'The Spirit of '76'," *American Quarterly* 28 (Fall 1976): 445–464; and James F. Ryder, "The Painter of 'Yankee Doodle'," *New England Magazine* (Dec. 1895): 483–494.

55
William Henry Fox Talbot, the inventor of the negative-positive process of photography, reflected this longing as he pondered the act of tracing images through the camera obscura: "This [act] led me to reflect on the inimitable beauty of nature's painting which the glass lens of the Camera throws upon the paper in its focus . . . creatures of a moment, and destined as rapidly to fade away . . . how charming it would be if it were possible to cause these natural images to imprint themselves durably, and remain fixed upon the paper." W. H. Talbot, "The Pencil of Nature," (1844). Quoted by Frampton, *Circles of Confusion:* 188.

56
Peter C. Marzio, *The Democratic Art: Chromolithography, 1840–1900* (Boston: David R. Godine, 1979): 14.

57
John Thomas Carey, *The American Lithograph: From its Inception to 1865* (unpublished Ph.D. diss. Ohio State University, 1954).

58
James Parton, "Popularizing Art," *Atlantic Monthly* (March 1869): 348–357.

59
Marzio, *The Democratic Art:* 95.

60
Ibid.: 96.

61
Louis Prang printed F. V. Hayden's folio book on *The Yellowstone National Park* (1875), which were called "sensation landscapes." He also printed Albert Bierstadt's *Sunset: California Scenery* (1868), Thomas Hill's *Yosemite Valley* (1869). Marzio, *Democratic Art:* 107–115.

62
Norman Bryson, *Vision and Painting: The Logic of the Gaze* (New Haven: Yale University Press, 1983): 158.

63
Ibid.: 159.

64
David D. Van Tassel, *Recording America's Past: An Interpretation of the Development of Historical Studies in American, 1607–1884* (Chicago: University of Chicago Press, 1960): 70.

65
Ibid.: 72.

66
Sergei Eisenstein, *Film Essays.* Edited and translated by Jay Leyda (London: Dennis Cobson, 1968): 144.

67
Richard Moody, *America Takes to the Stage: Romanticism in American Drama and Theatre, 1750–1900* (Millwood, New York: Craus Reprint Co., 1977. Reprint of original: Bloomington: Indiana University Press, 1955).

68
Described by G. O. Seilhamer, *History of the American Theater* and quoted by Moody, *America Takes to the Stage:* 209.

69
Moody, *America Takes to the Stage:* 225–226.

70
Raymond Field, "Hale's Tour: Ultrarealism in the pre-1910 Motion Picture," in John L. Fell, *Film Before Griffith* (Berkeley: University of California Press, 1983): 116–130; and N. Nicholas Vardac, *Stage to Screen: Theatrical Method from Garrick to Griffith* (New York: Benjamin Blom, 1968): 168.

71
Quoted from *The New York Times* (April 24, 1896) in A. R. Fulton, *Motion Pictures: The Development of an Art from Silent Films to the Age of Television* (Norman: University of Oklahoma Press, 1960): 16.

72
Chanan, *Dream that Kicks;* and Joseph H. North, *The Early Development of the Motion Picture (1887–1909)* (New York: Arno Press, 1973).

73
Tom Gunning, "An Unseen Energy Swallows Space: The Space in Early Film and its Relation to American Avant-Garde Film," in John L. Fell, *Film Before Griffith:* 335–366.

74
Lewis Jacobs, *The Rise of the American Film: A Critical History* (New York: Harcourt, Brace & Co., 1939): 16.

75
Robert C. Allen, "Vaudeville and Film: 1895–1915: A Study in Media Interaction" (unpublished Ph.D. diss., University of Iowa, 1977): 134–137.

76
Jacobs, *American Film:* 16.

77
Seymour Stern, "Griffith: The Birth of a Nation, Part I," *Film Culture* 36 (Spring–Summer 1965): 159.

78
Jean Moffet (ed.), *D. W. Griffith Colloque International* (Paris: Editions L'Harmattan, 1984): 283–298.

79
Stern, "Griffith."

80
Victor Burgin, "Diderot, Barthes, Vertigo," in Victor Burgin, James Donald, and Cora Kaplan (eds.), *Formations of Fantasy* (New York: Metheun & Co., 1986): 85–108.

81
Dolf Sternberger, *Panorama of the Nineteenth Century.* Translated by Joachim Neugrochel (New York: Urizen Books, Mole Editions, 1977): 11.

82
Umberto Eco, "Innovation and Repetition: Between Modern and Postmodern Aesthetics," *Daedalus* (Fall 1985): 161–184.

83
Homi Bhabha, "Disseminations," in Bhabha (ed.), *Nation and Narration:* 295.

84
Christian Mertz, *The Imaginary Signifier.* Translated by Celia Britton, Annwyl Williams, Ben Brewster, and Alfred Guzzetti (Bloomington: Indiana University Press, 1982): 159.

85
Louis Marin, *Utopics Spatial Play.* Translated by Robert A. Vollrath (Atlantic Highlands, N.J.: Humanities Press, 1984): 201–232.

86
Illustrated Visitors' Guide to New Orleans (New Orleans: J. Curtis Waldo, 1879): 16.

87
Walter Benjamin develops this symbol of the inversion of Penelope's work when he explains that Proust's "artful and artifical light substitutes night for day, in a web of memory and forgetting." Beryl Schlossman, "Proust and Benjamin," in Rainer Nägele (ed.), *Benjamin's Ground* (Detroit: Wayne State University Press, 1988): 110.

88
Jay J. Jackson, *New Orleans in the Gilded Age: Politics and Urban Progress 1880–1896* (Baton Rouge: Louisiana University Press, 1969): 283–311.

89
Cott, *Wandering Ghost:* 156.

90
Arthur E. Kunst, *Lafcadio Hearn* (New York: Twayne Publishers, 1969): 37.

91
Edward L. Tinker, *Lafcadio Hearn's American Days* (New York: Dodd, Mead & Co., 1924): 239.

92
Parallels can be drawn between Hearn's treatment of New Orleans as non-Western or not American and the colonial construction of images of India in the nineteenth century. Ashis Nandy explores this imposed burden on India of being non-West with its responsibility of stressing subsequently only those parts of India's culture deemed recessive in the West. Ashis Nandy, *The Intimate Enemy: Loss and Recovery of Self under Colonialism* (Delhi: Oxford University Press, 1983): 73–84.

93
Lafcadio Hearn, "Creole Courtyard." Quoted by Cott, *Wandering Ghost:* 139.

94
William H. Coleman, *Historical Sketch Book and Guide to New Orleans and Environs* (New York: W. H. Coleman, 1885): 63.

95
Ibid.: 66.

96
Susan Buck-Morss, *The Dialectics of Seeing* (Cambridge: MIT Press, 1989): 26.

97
Guy Manners, *Atmosphere: The Fact, Place d'Armes, New Orleans; The Fable, Greenwich Village, New York* (New York: Robt. H. True, 1922): 8–10.

98
Benjamin Moore Norman, *Norman's New Orleans and Environs* (Baton Rouge: Louisiana State University Press, 1976. Fascimile reproduction of 1845 edition): xii–xxiv.

99
George Washington Cable, *The Creoles of Louisiana* (London: C. Nimmo, 1885): 240.

100
Ibid.: 240.

101
Norman, *Norman's New Orleans:* 69–70.

102
Daniel J. Boorstin, *The Image: A Guide to Pseudo-Events in America* (New York: Atheneum: 1971): 106.

103
John Thomas Carey, *The American Lithograph from its Inception to 1865* (unpublished Ph.D. diss., Ohio State University, 1954).

104
John R. Hebert (ed.), *Panoramic Maps of Anglo-American Cities* (Washington: Library of Congress, 1974).

105
Boorstin, *The Image:* 106.

106
James Parton, "Popularizing Art," *Atlantic Monthly* (March 1869): 348–357, 355.

107
Quoting Karl Anton Postl, Liliane Crete, *Daily Life in Louisiana: 1815–1830* (Baton Rouge: Louisiana State University Press, 1981): 35.

108
G. W. Featherstonhaugh, *Excursions through the Slave States, from Washington on the Potomac to the Frontier of Mexico,* 2 vols. (London: John Murray, 1841): 259.

109
A. Oakey Hall, *The Manhattaner in New Orleans; Phases of "Crescent City" Life* (New York: J. S. Redfield, 1851).

110
From *Paxton's Directory* (John Paxton publisher, 1822). Quoted by Crete, *Daily Life.*

111
Featherstonhaugh, *Excursions:* 259, 261.

112
Coleman, *Historical Sketch Book:* 65.

113
In the late 1840s, Michaela Baroness Pontalba erected two rows of brick apartment buildings flanking the Place des Armes and remodeled the latter into Jackson Square. This peculiar half-tropical, half-European place became the selected site for a bronze statue of the stern old hero Andrew Jackson, who still salutes every tourist from the back of his rearing horse. Hall, *The Manhattaner;* Coleman, *Historical Guide; Nathaniel C. Curtis, New Orleans: Its Old House, Shops, and Public Buildings* (Philadelphia: J. B. Lippincott, 1933).

114
Walter Benjamin, quoted by Peter Szondi, "Walter Benjamin's City Portraits," in Gary Smith (ed.), *On Walter Benjamin: Critical Essays and Recollections* (Cambridge: MIT Press, 1988): 26.

115
Walter Benjamin, quoted by Richard Sieburth, "Benjamin the Scrivener," *Assemblage* 6 (June 1988): 8.

116
Benjamin, quoted by Sieburth, "Benjamin": 9.

117
Hall, *The Manhattaner,* and Coleman, *Historical Guide.*

118
Crete, *Daily Life:* 36; and *New Orleans Architecture: The Creole Faubourgs,* vol. 4 (Gretna: Pelican, 1974): 9.

119
Crete, *Daily Life.*

120
Featherstonhaugh, *Excursions:* 260.

121
Norman's New Orleans: 138–141. Burnt to the ground in 1851, this hub of the American business section was rebuilt by Isaac Rogers of New York City in 1852 and remained a profitable hotel until the turn of the century. John Smith Kendall, *History of New Orleans,* 3 vols. (Chicago: Lewis Publishing Co., 1922); Curtis, *New Orleans.*

122
Hall, *The Manhattaner:* 9.

123
Curtis, *New Orleans.*

124
The St. Louis Hotel burned in 1841; rebuilt, it was sold to the state in 1874, reopening briefly as the Royal Hotel from 1888–1896/7. It was abandoned and eventually demolished. Hall, *The Manhattaner:* 17; and Kendall, *New Orleans:* 689. Each district as well would have its array of entertainments: the Orleans Theater (1817/1819) in the Vieux Carré, the St. Charles Theater (1835; and 1842) in the American sector. Rising like a colossus over everything in the Vieux Carré, the New Opera House designed by James Gallier, Jr., and the engineer Esterbrooke in 1859 appeared more like a hotel than a music hall, for the entire second story front contained rooms for relaxation, saloons or "crush-rooms," special stockholders' rooms, and a series of rooms for women. Curtis, *New Orleans* and *Norman's New Orleans.*

125
Crete, *Daily Life.*

126
Illustrated Visitors' Guide to New Orleans (1879).

127
Coleman, *Historical Sketch Book:* 258.

128
Ibid.: 262.

129
Ibid.: 88.

130
Ibid.: 87–89.

131
Steven Mullaney, *The Place of the Stage: License, Play, and Power in Renaissance England* (Chicago: University of Chicago Press, 1988): 1–25.

132
A later tribute to the founding father of the nation added the name "Washington" to the District of Columbia.

133
Alexis de Tocqueville, *Democracy in America,* vol. 2. Translated by Henry Reeve (New York: Random House, Vintage, 1945; originally published 1840): 56.

134
In ancient Greece, the Athenians invented an abstract concept of Athens to be the authority over all memory. Every funeral oration, in standardized and repetitive form, was in fact a celebration of this ideal city, raising its glory while they enumerated the deeds and valor of past generations. Through all vicissitudes of time and of war, the city remained triumphant. In analogical form, the scenic architecture and compositional urban forms of Washington were to hold the same role for Americans that oratorical rhetoric held for Athenians. Nicole Loraux, *The Invention of Athens: The Funeral Oration in the Classical City.* Translated by Alan Sheridan (Cambridge: Harvard University Press, 1986).

135
Wendy C. Wick, *George Washington An American Icon The Eighteenth-Century Graphic Portraits* (Washington, D.C.: A Barra Foundation Book, 1982); Van Tassel, *Recording America's Past.*

136
Thomas Jefferson's letter to Major L'Enfant (April 10, 1791). Quoted in *Records of Columbia Historical Society* 2 (Washington, D.C.: The Columbia Historical Society, 1899): 130–131.

137
Mary Smith Lockwood, *Columbia Guide: Historical and Modern Washington* (Harrisburg: Harrisburg Publishing Co., 1897).

138
Force's Pictures of the City of Washington and Its Vicinity for 1848 (Washington: William Q. Force, 1848).

139
"L'Enfant's Reports to President Washington," *Records of Columbia Historical Society* 2 (Washington: Columbia Historical Society, 1899): 26–48.

140
"L'Enfant's Report to President Washington." Quoted by Major General Ulysses S. Grant, 3rd, "Washington—A Planned City in Evolution," *American Planning and Civic Annual* (1943): 63.

141
"Development of the Eastern Section and the Policy of Land Owners," *Columbia Historical Society* 7 (1904): 118–134.

142
Montgomery Schuyler, "The Art of City-Making," *The Architectural Record* 12, 1 (May 1902): 7–26.

143
George J. Olszewski, *History of the Mall, Washington D.C.* (Washington: U.S. Department of Interior, March 1970); Ainsworth R. Spofford, *The Founding of Washington City: With Some Considerations on the Origin of Cities and Location of National Capitals.* (Baltimore: Maryland Historical Society, 1881).

144
Theodore W. Noyes, *The National Capital: Newspaper Articles and Speeches Concerning the City of Washington* (Washington: Byron S. Adams, Printer and Publisher, 1893): 5.

145
Ibid.: 8.

146
Ibid.: 15.

147
W. B. Bryan, "The Central Section of the City," *Columbia Historical Society* 7 (1904): 135–145; Noyes, *The National Capital.*

148
Force's Pictures of Washington: 23–27.

149
Paul C. Ditzel, *How They Built Our National Monuments* (Indianapolis: The Bobbs-Merrill Company, Inc., 1976); J. Dudley Morgan, "L'Enfant's Idea as to How the Capitol Building Should Face," *Columbia Historical Society* 7 (1904): 107–113; Lois Craig (ed.), *The Federal Presence, Architecture, Politics, and Symbols in United States Government Buildings* (Cambridge: MIT Press, 1977).

150
Ditzel, *Our National Monuments.*

151
Bryan, "The Central Section"; and Craig, *The Federal Presence:* 43.

152
The Library of Congress, built in 1897 to the southeast of the Capitol across Pennsylvania Avenue, was another intrusion marring L'Enfant's intended reciprocity of sight. Schuyler, "The Art of City-Making."

153
Noyes, *The National Capital:* 16.

154
Olszewski, *History of the Mall.*

155
George Tatum, "Andrew Jackson Downing, Arbiter of Taste, 1815–1852" (unpublished Ph.D. diss. Princeton University, 1949).

156
Grant, "Washington"; Olszewski, *History of the Mall;* and H. Paul Caemmerer, *A Manual on the Origin and Development of Washington* (Washington: Government Printing Office, 1939).

157
Isaac S. Lyon, *The Washington Monument. Shall it be Built?* (New York: William Olland Bourne, 1846): 4.

158
A Guide to the City of Washington: What to See and How to See it (Washington: Philip and Solomon, 1869).

159
Glenn Brown, *The Development of Washington: With Special Reference to the Lincoln Memorial* (Washington: Chamber of Commerce, 1910).

160
Ditzel, *Our National Monuments;* Rudolph De Zapp, *The Washington Monument* (Washington: Caroline Publishing Co., 1900).

161
Ditzel, *Our National Monuments;* Brown, *The Development of Washington;* Lyon, *The Washington Monument.*

162
Grant, "Washington": 67–68.

163
"Thomas Jefferson Memorial Site," (House of Representatives 75th Congress, lst Session, U.S. Congress, 1937); Brown, *The Development of Washington;* and Olszewski, *History of the Mall.*

164
Brown, *The Development of Washington:* 23.

165
Ibid.: 25.

166
Ibid.: 25.

167
Sal A. Kohler, *The Commission of Fine Arts: A Brief History, 1910–1976* (Washington: Commission of Fine Arts, 1981).

168
Brown, *The Development of Washington:* 39.

169
"Thomas Jefferson Memorial Site": 2.

170
Ibid.: 4; John W. Reps, *Monumental Washington: The Planning and Development of the Capital Center* (Princeton: Princeton University Press, 1967).

171
Mullaney, *The Place of the Stage:* 13–19.

172
Peter Smithson, "Space is the American Mediator: or The Blocks of Ithaca—A Speculation," *Harvard Architectural Review* 2 (Spring 1981): 106–113.

173
Chanan, *Dream that Kicks:* 273–274; Joseph H. North, *The Early Development of the Motion Picture 1887–1909 (New York: Arno Press, 1979. Reprint of Ph.D. diss. Cornell University Press, 1949).*

Chapter 7

1
Michel de Certeau, *The Practice of Everyday Life.* Translated by Steven F. Rendall (Berkeley: University of California Press, 1984): 86–87.

2
An open window also suggests a view into an interior, to the privatized world of inner thoughts. Here Magritte's title, "In Praise of the Dialectic," perhaps refers to three win-

dows of the dialectic: the window on reality, the interior view of self-reflection, and the final synthesis or collision of images forcing the viewer to imagine the impossible. Susan Harris Smith, "The Surealists' Window," *Dada/Surrealism* 3 (1984): 48–69; and John Berger, "Magritte and the Impossible," *About Looking* (New York: Pantheon Books, 1980): 155–161.

3
Dana Polan, *The Political Language of Film and the Avant-Garde* (Ann Arbor, Michigan: UMI Research Press, 1985); and Dana Polan, "Above All Else to Make Your See: Cinema and the Ideology of the Spectacle," *Boundary 2* 11, no. 1/2 (1982/3): 129–144.

4
Roland Barthes, "Diderot, Brecht, Eisenstein," *The Responsibility of Forms.* Translated by Richard Howard (New York: Hill and Wang): 96.

5
Jay Caplan, *Framed Narratives: Diderot's Genealogy of the Beholder* (Minneapolis: University of Minnesota Press, 1985).

6
Jack W. McCullough, "Jack Kilanyi and American Tableaux Vivants," *Theater Survey* 16 (1975): 25–41.

7
Michael Chanan, *The Dream that Kicks* (London: Routledge & Kegan Paul, 1980): 200–204.

8
Jean Mitry, "Le Montage dans les Films de Méliès," in Madeleine Malthête-Méliès (ed.), *Méliès et la Naissance du Spectacle Cinematographique* (Paris: Klincksieck, 1984): 149–155.

9
Chanan, *Dream that Kicks*: 121.

10
Ibid.: 205.

11
Michel Foucault, *The Archaeology of Knowledge and the Discourse on Language.* Translated by A. M. Sheridan Smith (New York: Pantheon Books, 1972).

12
de Certeau, *Practice of Everyday Life*: 108.

13
Vincent Leitch, *Deconstructive Criticism* (New York: Columbia University Press, 1983): 121, 124.

14
Narrative systems utilize imaginary architectures—this is the problem with the parodies of postmodern architecture and the reconstructions of historic preservation. They stop the imagination, drawing the simulated mimetic forms so close to our gaze that we are lost in their literal allusions. Flaubert strenuously objected to illustrating his books, for he felt that "the most beautiful literary description is eaten up by the most wretched drawing. As soon as a figure [type] is fixed by the pencil, it loses that character of generality, that harmony with a thousand known objects which makes the reader say: 'I've seen that' or 'That must be so'. . . . The idea is closed, complete and every sentence becomes useless. . . ." Quoted by Roger Shattuck, "Words and Images: Thinking and Translation," *Daedalus* (Fall 1985): 208. Henry James also refused to allow illustrations in his books, claiming that at most they were "set stage[s] with actors left out; for there was no way that a pictorial representation could get it right." Quoted by Jonathan Mille, "The Mind's Eye and the Human Eye," *Daedalus* (Fall 1985): 185.

15
Walter Benjamin, "N [Theoretics of Knowledge; Theory of Progress]". Translated by Leigh Hafrey and Richard Siebarth, *The Philosophical Forum* 15, no. 1–2 (Winter 1983/4): 24.

16
Susan Stewart, *On Longing* (Baltimore: Johns Hopkins University Press, 1987): 140–141.

17
Hans Huth, "The Evolution of Preservationism in Europe," *JSAH* 2 (1942): 5–17; Anthony Vidler, *The Writing of the Wall* (Princeton: Princeton University Press, 1987): 168–169.

18
Quoted by David Lowenthal, *The Past is a Foreign Country* (Cambridge: Cambridge University Press, 1985): 393.

19
Michel de Certeau, "Les Revenants de la Ville," *Traverses* 40 (April 1987): 75–85; Stewart, *Longing:* 140–142.

20
Camillo Sitte, *The Art of City Building.* Translated by George R. Collins and Christiane Crasemann Collins (New York: Rizzoli, 1986): 32; footnotes n22: 341–342; n37: 346.

21
Peter Hohendahl, "Jurgen Habermas: The Public Sphere," *New German Critique* 3 (1974): 45–55; and Michael Bommes and Patrick Wright, "'Charms of Residence': The Public and the Past," *Making Histories* (Hutchinson: Centre for Contemporary Cultural Studies, University of Birmingham, 1982): 260–267.

22
Greater London Council, *Historic Buildings in London* (London: Academy Editions, 1975).

23
Bommes and Wright, "'Charms of Residence'": 253–301.

24
Interviews with Brian Anthony, Historic Buildings and Monuments Commission for England, Fortress House, London (March 1984) and with Christopher Mason, City Planner, City of Westminster, City Hall (March 1984).

25
Michel Ragon, "Historiques d'un Problem,170 *Monuments Historique. Construié en Quartiers Anciens* 105 (1979): 5–13; Working Paper on "Historic Town Centres," *The Renewal of Historic Town Centers in Nine European Countries* (UNESCO, Federal Ministry for Regional Planning, Building and Urban Development, 1975).

26
Spiro Kostof, *The Third Rome 1870–1950* (Berkeley: University of California Press, 1973).

27
Dionysis A. Zivas, et al. *Plaka: The Old Town of Athens* (Athens: unpublished manuscript, 1978).

28
Besides the countries mentioned above, Sweden had enacted preservation legislation by 1881, Spain in 1873, Hungary and Egypt in 1881, Finland in 1883, Turkey in 1884, Bulgaria in 1889, Rumania in 1892, and Norway in 1897. Stephen Tschudi-Madsen, *Restoration and Anti-Restoration* (Oslo: Universitetsforlaget, 1976): 98, 102.

29
Quoted by Marjorie Perloff, *The Futurist Moment* (Chicago: University of Chicago Press, 1986): 201.

30
Collins and Collins, Sitte, *City Building:* 244.

31
Ibid.: 177.

32
Ibid.: 197.

33
Ibid.: 249, 267.

34
Ibid.: 41.

35
Heinz Geretsegger and Max Peintner, *Otto Wagner: 1841–1918.* Translated by Gerald Onn (New York: Rizzoli, 1979).

36
Collins and Collins, Sitte, *City Building:* 121; Frederick Gibber, *Town Design* (London: Architectural Press, 1953); and Gordon Cullen, *Townscape* (London: Architectural Press, 1961).

37
Restauration et Vie des Ensembles Monumentaux (Nancy: Les Cahiers de la Section Française de L'ICOMOS, 1980).

38
The first city to experiment with a deep-structured restoration policy was Bologna in 1972. Armando Montanari, *Towns: Social and Economic Aspects* (Vienna: International Social Science Council, European Coordination Center for Research and Documentation in the Social Sciences, 1981).

39
More than 3,000 Conservation Areas were established in England by 1975, 29 of which were located in Westminster City (London) alone. George Mansell (ed.), *The Living Heritage of Westminster* (London: Westminster County Council, 1975).

40
William B. Rhoads, *The Colonial Revival* (New York: Garland Publishing Inc., 1977).

41
Charles B. Hosmer, *Preservation Comes of Age: From Williamsburg to the National Trust, 1926–1949.* Vol. 1 and 2 (Charlottesville: University Press of Virginia, 1985): 105–124.

42
Lowenthal, *The Past is a Foreign Country:* 105–124.

43
Rhoads, *Colonial Revival.*

44
William Butler, "Another City upon a Hill: Litchfield Connecticut and the Colonial Revival," in Alan Axelrod (ed.), *The Colonial Revival in America* (New York: W.W. North and Co., 1985): 16–51.

45
Nathan Weinberg, *Preservation in American Towns and Cities* (Boulder: Westview Press, 1979).

46
Thomas J. Reed, "Land Use Controls in Historic Areas," *Notre Dame Lawyer* 44 (1968–1969): 379.

47
When an owner of a historic property sells or donates an easement to a preservation commission, then that owner relinquishes the right to alter the facade or to destroy the environmental setting that surrounds the historic structure. Because an easement restricts the development potential of historic properties and lowers its resale value, it has an economic value. In return the owner is rewarded income tax benefits equal to the value of the easement that has been lost and sometimes property tax abatements based on the property's lower assessed value or on a proportion of the restoration costs that easements incur. *Preservation Easements: A publication of Maryland Historical Trust* (Annapolis: Department of Economic and Community Development, 1977).

48
Quoted by Oscar S. Gray, "The Response of Federal Legislation to Historic Preservation," *Law and Contemporary Problems* 36 (1971): 315.

49
Gray, "Federal Legislation": 315–317; and Paul E. Wilson and H. James Winkler II, "The Response of State Legislation to Historic Preservation," *Law and Contemporary Problems* 36 (1971): 329–347.

50
Richard J. Webster, *Philadelphia Preserved: Catalogue of the Historic American Building Survey* (Philadelphia: Temple University Press, 1976).

51
"City Planning in Philadelphia," *Citizens' Council on City Planning* (Jan. 1944); and Roman A. Cybriwsky, David Ley, and John Western, "The Political and Social Construction of Revitalized Neighborhoods: Society Hill, Philadelphia, and False Creek, Vancouver, " in Neil Smith and Peter Williams (eds.), *Gentrification of the City* (Boston: Allen & Unwin, 1986).

52
The Pennsylvania Railroad announced plans to remove the Wall in 1948. *Citizens' Council on City Planning, Philadelphia* 4, no. 4 (Jan. 1948).

53
Conrad Weiler, *Philadelphia: Neighborhood, Authority and the Urban Crisis* (New York: Praeger, 1974).

54
Edmund N. Bacon, *The Design of Cities* (New York: Viking Press, 1967): 243–271; Edmund N. Bacon, "Downtown Philadelphia: A Lesson in Design for Urban Growth," *Architectural Record* 109, 5 (May 1961): 131–146; and Eleanor Smith Morris, "New Urban Design Concepts: Greenways and Movement Structures in the Philadelphia Plan," in David Lewis (ed.), *The Pedestrian in the City* (Princeton: D. Van Nostrand Company. Inc., 1965).

55
Cybriwsky, Ley, and Western, "Society Hill."

56
Stuart Stein, "A Pittsburgh History and Landmarks Foundation Case Study: Manchester District" (unpublished Cornell University study, 1976); Carol Galbreath, "Conservation: The New World for Old Neighborhoods," *Connecticut Law Review* (1976); and James D. Van Trump and Arthur P. Ziegler, *Landmark Architecture of Allegheny County, Pennsylvania* (Pittsburgh: Pittsburgh History and Landmarks Foundation, 1967).

57
"Private Market Renovation in Older Urban Areas," *Urban Land Institute Report* #26 (1976); and Carl Holman, *The Neighborhood Housing Services Model: A Progress Assessment of the Related Activities of the Urban Reinvestment Task Force* (September 1975).

58
Franklin J. James, *Private Reinvestment in Older Housing and Older Neighborhoods: Recent Trends and Forces* (Washington, D.C.: Urban Institute, 1975).

59
"Private Market Renovation," *Urban Land Institute* #26 (1976).

60
Some of the cities studied were Albuquerque, Atlanta, Baltimore, Bridgeport, Chicago, Cleveland, Columbus, Denver, Detroit, El Paso, Flint, Gary, Houstin, Indianapolis, Los Angeles, Minneapolis, Oakland, Pasadena, Racine, Richmond, St. Louis, St. Paul, San Antonio, San Francisco, Seattle, South Bend, Washington, D.C., and Wilmington.

61
National Urban Coalition, *Displacement City Neighborhoods in Transition* (Washington, D.C., 1978).

62
Anthony Downs, *Urban Problems and Prospects* (Chicago: Markham Publishing Company, 1971).

63
G. Timothy Haight and Deborah Ann Ford, "Renovating Older Buildings: The Recapture Dilemma," *Real Estate Review* 13, no. 4 (Winter 1984): 33–36; Richard J. Roddewig, "'Certified' Rehabilitation of Historic Buildings," *Real Estate Review* 12, no. 3 (Fall 1982): 67–71.

64
Radie Bunn and Franklin J. Ingram, "Rehabilitation Tax Credits: A Surviving Tax Shelter," *Real Estate Review* 17, no. 4 (Winter 1988): 96–99.

65
It obstructed the view, its bulk was out of scale with the surrounding development, it blocked sunlight, and cast huge shadows. Paul Brace, "Comment: Urban Aesthetics and the Courts," *The Urban Lawyer* (Winter 1980).

66
For example, on Fifth Avenue the Metropolitan Club and Saks Fifth Avenue requested new towers (only the latter was granted one), and Central Park West received a flurry of activity when the New York Historical Society, the Towers Nursing Home, the Ethical Cultural School, the Shearith-Israel Synagogue, and the nearby West Side YMCA on 63rd Street all proposed new towers. New skyscraper towers sprang from the head of the Villard Houses on Madison Avenue, from sites adjacent to the Museum of Modern Art and Carnegie Hall, and in back of the Rizzoli-Coty facade on Fifth Avenue, to name just a few. *Penn Central Transporation Company v. City of New York* 438 U.S. 104 (1978); Carrol T. Lippman, "From Zoning to Landmark Preservation: The Grand Central Terminal Decision Signals a Shift in Land Use Regulation," *New York Law School Review* 25 (1979): 39–78; Richard Wolloch, "Penn Central v. City of New York: A Landmark Case," *Fordham Urban Law Journal* 6 (1978): 667–685; and Jerome Rose, "The Transfer of Development Rights" A Preview of an Evolving Concept," *Real Estate Law Journal* 3 (1975): 330–358.

67
Paul Goldberger, "When Air Rights Go Underground," *NYT* (Dec. 21, 1986): 1, 14; Paul Goldberger, "The City's Birthright Sold for Air Rights," *NYT* (June 21, 1987): 32, 33; and Martin Gottlieb, "Zoning Fight Again Imperils Grand Central," *NYT* (Oct. 14, 1986): B1.

68
"The Mayor's Ad Hoc Landmarks Committee Report," (unpublished, May 1986).

69
David W. Dunlap, "Landmarks May Get New Rules," *NYT* (May 1986): B1, B4; and David W. Dunlap, "Rally Protests Proposal to Alter Landmark Law," *NYT* (June 30, 1988): B3.

70
David W. Dunlap, "Panel Urges Deadlines for Votes on Landmarks," *NYT* (Feb. 6, 1989): B3.

71
Stuart Taylor, Jr. "High Court Backs Rights of Owners in Land-Use Suits," *NYT* (June 10, 1987): A1, A26.

72
Richard O. Brooks, "The Law of Plan Implementation in the United States," *Urban Law Annual* 16 (1979): 225–260.

73
Splendid Survivors: San Francisco's Downtown Architectural Heritage (San Francisco: Foundation for San Francisco Architecture, 1979).

74
Sanger Associates, Inc., *A Preservation Strategy for Downtown San Francisco* (San Francisco: Foundation of San Francisco's Architectural Heritage, 1982).

75
The Downtown San Francisco Plan (Department of City Planning, City and County of San Francisco, August 1983); and Dean Macris, Director of Planning, San Francisco, "Outline of Comments," (unpublished presentation at Yale University School of Architecture's Symposium on Middle-Sized Cities, February 6, 1987).

76
For an extended discussion of postmodernism and cultural conservatism, see Jurgen Habermas, "Neo-Conservative Culture Criticism," in Richard J. Bernstein (ed.), *Habermas and Modernity* (Cambridge: MIT Press, 1985): 78–94.

77
Paul Monaco, *Ribbons in Time: Movies and Society since 1945* (Bloomington: Indiana University Press, 1985): 78–94.

78
Henri Lefebvre, *The Production of Space*. Translated by Donald Nicholson-Smith (Cambridge: Oxford University Press, 1991); Henri Lefebvre, *Une Pensée Devenue Monde/ Faut-il Abandonner Marx?* (Paris: Librairie Artheme Fayord, 1990); and M. Gottdiener, *The Social Production of Urban Space* (Austin: University of Texas Press, 1985).

79
Neil Smith, "Gentrification, the Frontier, and the Restructuring of Urban Space," in Smith and Williams (eds.), *Gentrification of the City:* 15–34.

80
Joe R. Feagin and Michael Peter Smith, "Cities and the New International Division of Labor: an Overview," in Michael Peter Smith and Joe R. Feagin (eds.), *The Capitalist City: Global Restructuring and Community Politics* (New York: Basil Blackwell, 1987): 3–34.

81
The brochure advertising the "Remaking Cities Conference" convened by the American Institute of Architects and the Royal Institute of British Architects in Pittsburgh, March 2–5, 1988, noted that "As cities lose their powerful industries, they must rely on non-traditional merits to attract and develop new economic bases. Businesses and individuals—select cities with the finest features and benefits. They look for history, culture, safe neighborhoods, good housing, shops and education, and progressive local governments. Cities are competing, and their edge is livability . . ."

82
In Central London, 80 percent of all households rented in 1961, and 70 percent in 1971. In addition, the Greater London area contained a total of 222,000 rental apartments in 1966, of which 28 percent were concentrated in the central boroughs. Chris Hamnett and Bill Randolph, "Tenurial Transformation and the Flat Break-Up Market in London: The British Condo Experience," in Smith and Williams, (eds.), *Gentrification of the City:* 127.

83
Hamnett and Randolph, "Tenurial Transformation," 121–152.

84
David Wachtel, *Cultural Policy and Socialist France* (New York: Greenwood Press, 1987); and Paul Goldberger, "In Paris, A Face Lift in Grand Style," *NYT* (May 17, 1987): section H: 1,42.

85
Jean-Pierre Babelon, "Le Marais et Ses Problèmes," *Sites et Monuments* 98 (1982); Roger Kain, "Conservation Planning in France: Policy and Practice in the Marais, Paris," in Roger Kain (ed.), *Planning for Conservation* (London: Mansell, 1981): 199–233; Maurice Minost, "Quoi de Neuf au Marais?" *Monuments Historiques. Construié en Quartiers Anciens* 105 (1979): 41–48; and "Le Plan de Sauvegarde et de Mise en Valeur du Marais," *Paris Projet: Revue Preparée par L'Atelier Parisien d'Urbanisme* no. 23/24 (1983): 208–249.

86
"Public-Private Cooperation Called Key to Success," *National Real Estate Investor* 20 (July 1978): 32–33.

87
Harold R. Snedcof, *Cultural Facilities in Mixed-Use Development* (Washington, D.C.: Urban Land Institute, 1985): 236–255; William K. Stevens, "Renaissance Along the Waterfronts of 3 Cities Transform Down-

towns," *NYT* (May 25, 1985): 40; and "Rouse Expands Grip on Harbor, " *NYT* (Oct. 2, 1988): 32–33.

88
Jurgen Habermas, *The Structural Transformation of the Public Sphere.* Translated by Thomas Burger (Cambridge: MIT Press, 1989).

89
Jurgen Habermas, "The Public Sphere: An Encyclopedia Article (1964)," *New German Critique* 3 (Fall 1974): 49–55; Oscar Negt and Alexander Kluge, "The Public Sphere and Experience: Selections," *October* 46 (1989): 60–82; Peter Stallybrass & Allon White, *Politics & Poetics of Transgression* (Ithaca: Cornell University Press, 1986): 80–100.

90
Raymond Williams, "Structures of Feeling," *Marxism and Literature* (London: Oxford University Press, 1977): 253–301.

91
Sut Jhally, *The Codes of Advertising: Fetishism and Political Economy of Meaning in the Consumer Society* (New York: St. Martin's Press, 1987): 125; and Timothy W. Luke and Stephen K. White, "Critical Theory and an Economic Path to Modernity," in John Forester (ed.), *Critical Theory and Public Life* (Cambridge: MIT Press, 1987): 34.

Chapter 8

1
Sergei Eisenstein, "Off-Frame" 1929; quoted by Jacques Aumont, *Montage Eisenstein.* Translated by Lee Hildreth, Constance Penley, Andrew Ross (Bloomington: Indiana University Press, 1987): 40.

2
T. J. Clark, *The Painting of Modern Life: Paris in the Art of Manet and His Followers* (London: Thames and Hudson, Ltd., 1985): 23–78.

3
Elizabeth Hawes, "The Greening of American Markets: Fresh Food and Constant Festivals are the Heart of Our Most Exciting Urban Renovations," *Diversions for Physicians at Leisure* (January 1981): 194.

4
Jean-Christophe Agnew, *Worlds Apart: The Market and the Theater in Anglo-American Thought, 1850–1750* (Cambridge: Cambridge University Press, 1986).

5
Rachel Bowlby, *Just Looking, Consumer Culture in Dreiser, Gissing and Zola* (New York: Methuen, 1985): 18–24; and Philip Fisher, *Hard Facts: Setting and Form in the American Novel* (New York: Oxford University Press, 1985): 133.

6
Pierre Bourdieu, *Distinctions: A Social Criticism of the Judgement of Taste.* Translated by Richard Nice (Cambridge: Harvard University Press, 1984): 35.

7
Ibid.: 485–502.

8
Nancy Bloom and Jo Ellen Freese, "Planning for the Preservation of South Street Seaport," (unpublished term paper, Columbia University, 1977); *The Lower Manhattan Plan* (New York: City Planning Commission, 1966): vii; Hilary Silver, "The Last Frontier, Politics and Redevelopment on the New York Waterfront" (unpublished paper, 1988); and Harold R. Snedcof, *Cultural Facilities in Mixed-Use Development* (Washington, D.C.: Urban Land Institute, 1984): 160–175.

9
Reported by Bloom and Freese, "Preservation of South Street Seaport," from *NYT* (Dec. 17, 1966): 66.

10
Reported by Bloom and Freese, "Preservation of South Street Seaport," from *NYT* (Oct. 15, 1967): Sec. 8, 4.

11
Reported by Bloom and Freese, "Preservation of South Street Seaport," from *NYT* (March 28, 1968): 51.

12
Reported by Bloom and Freese, "Preservation of South Street Seaport," from *NYT* (Dec. 18, 1968): Sec. 31, 1.

13
Reported by Bloom and Freese, "Preservation of South Street Seaport," from *NYT* (June 11, 1970): Sec. 38, 2.

14
Eventually 1,400,000 square feet of development rights were tranferred to the Chase Manhattan Bank and a consortium of banks that it led. Bloom and Freese, "Preservation of South Street Seaport," and Snedcof, *Cultural Facilities:* 160–175.

15
Reported by Bloom and Freese, "Preservation of South Street Seaport," from *NYT* (July 30,1973): Sec. 31, 3.

16
Bloom and Freese, "Preservation of South Street Seaport," and Snedcof, *Cultural Facilities:* 160–175.

17
Snedcof, *Cultural Facilities:* 160–175.

18
"Seaport Market Place," *The Final EIS Statement* (prepared for the Rouse Company by The Erhrenkrantz Group, Sept. 1980); and Snedcof, *Cultural Facilities:* 160–175.

19
Christopher Lowery was relieved in 1985 of his museum responsibilites in order to focus his entire attention on the museum's real estate ventures.

20
Snedcof, *Cultural Facilities:* 172; and Meg Cox, "All at Sea: New York Museum's Problems Show Snares in Mixing Culture, Commerce," *Wall Street Journal* (April 12, 1985). [Article without page reference taken from South Street Seaport Museum's history file.]

21
Lisa W. Foderaro, "At South Street Seaport, The Other Half Beckons," *NYT* (Nov. 28, 1986): B6.

22
Michael Quint, "Only the Fish are Missing at Fishport in Brooklyn," *NYT* (July 27, 1988): B1, B8.

23
David Dunlap, "Seaport May Regain Block City Excised," *NYT* (Dec. 20, 1987): Sec. 8, 24.

24
David Dunlap, "Wave of Growth Planned at South Street Seaport," *NYT* (Jan. 19, 1989): B1.

25
Shawn G. Kennedy, "Seaport Link for a Tower in Manhattan," *NYT* (Oct. 26, 1988): B6 and David Dunlap, "At Last, a Plan Wins in Landmark District," *NYT* (June 9, 1991): Sec. 10, 1, 13

26
Quoted by Ellen Fletcher, "South Street Seaport Museum: Program Plan for 1984" (unpublished memorandum from the files of the South Street Seaport Museum): 5.

27
"South Street Seaport Museum Planning Conference" (unpublished reports from the files of the South Street Seaport Museum, Nov. 7, 1968).

28
Sut Jhally, *The Codes of Advertising: Fetishism and the Political Economy of Meaning in the Consumer Society* (New York: St. Martin's Press, 1987): 130–131; Sut Jhally, "The Political

Economy of Culture," in Ian Angus and Sut Jhally (eds.), *Cultural Politics in Contemporary American Society* (New York: Routledge, 1989): 65–81.

29
Michel Serres, "Turner Translate Corot," in Norman Bryson (ed.), *Calligram: Essays in New Art History from France* (Cambridge: Cambridge University Press, 1988): 154–155.

30
Eric M. Steel, *Diderot's Imagery: A Study of a Literary Personality* (New York: Haskell House, 1966): 98–165.

31
James H. Bunn, "The Aesthetics of British Mercantilism," *New Literary History* 11 (1980): 303.

32
Fletcher, "Program Plan for 1984," and Snedcof, *Cultural Facilities*.

33
Susan Stewart, *On Longing: Narratives of the Miniature, the Gigantic, the Souvenir, the Collection* (Baltimore: Johns Hopkins University Press, 1984): 23, 135, 149–150.

34
Ellen Fletcher Rosebrock, "Walking Around in South Street: Discoveries in New York's Old Shipping District" (New York: South Street Seaport Museum, 1974); and John G. Waite and Paul R. Huey, *A Compilation of Historical and Architectural Data on the New York State Maritime Museum Block in New York City* (New York: New York State Historical Trust, 1972).

35
Bowlby, *Just Looking*.

36
Dora Wiebenson, *The Picturesque Garden in France* (Princeton: Princeton University Press, 1978): 108–121.

37
Jean Baudrillard, "The Trompe-l'Oeil," in Bryson (ed.), *Calligram*: 53–62.

38
Bourdieu, *Distinctions*: 190–200.

39
Snedcof, *Cultural Facilities*: 60–175.

40
Smith, "Gentrification, the Frontier, and the Restructuring of Urban Space," in Neil Smith and Peter Williams (eds.), *Gentrification of the City* (Boston: Allen & Unwin, 1986): 15–35.

41
Paul Smith, "Visiting Banana Republic," in Andrew Ross (ed.), *Universal Abandon? The Politics of Postmodernism* (Minneapolis: University of Minnesota, 1988): 128–148.

42
Neil Smith presents the same argument using the "pioneer" and the "frontier" as the metaphorical devices. Smith, "Gentrification," in Smith and Williams (eds.), *Gentrification*: 15–34.

43
Rosalyn Deutsche, "Uneven Development: Public Art in New York City," *October* 47 (Winter 1988): 3–52; and Silver, "The Last Frontier."

44
Felt and Co., Inc., Voorhees, Walker Foley & Smith, "Recommendation for a Redevelopment Study of Lower Manhattan South of Fulton Street," (June 12, 1958).

45
David Rockefeller, John D. Butt, "Lower Manhattan Recommended Land Use Redevelopment Areas" (New York: Downtown Lower Manhattan Association, Inc., First Report, 1968).

46
"Back to the Waterfront: Chaos or Control?" *Progressive Architecture* 47, no. 8 (August, 1966): 128–139.

47
"The Lower Manhattan Plan" (New York: New York City Planning Commission, 1966).

48
"Manhattan Battery Park City," *Architectural Design* 39 (Dec., 1969): 673–676.

49
So it was projected, when Battery Park City was in full operation by the early 1980s, that the city would receive at least $12 million a year in lieu of property taxes. By 1984 an agreement had been struck to use this left-over portion, after debt service on the Authority's bonds had been paid, for the development of low-income housing somewhere else in the city and at some future time. The first 1,600 units were developed in 1989.

50
Reyner Banham, *Megastructure: Urban Futures of the Recent Past* (New York: Harper & Row, 1976).

51
Emanuel Tobier, "Manhattan Emerges as 'World City'" *Real Estate Review* 14, no. 1 (Spring 1984): 47–49.

52
For the rhetoric of "New York Ascendant," see Alexander Cooper Associates, *Battery Park City Draft Summary Report and 1979 Master Plan* (New York: Battery Park City Authority, October, 1979). Between 1977 and 1987, New York City added 400,000 new jobs. Of these, 342,000 were in the private sector and 70 percent of these in the FIRE (Finance, Insurance and Real Estate) and Business sectors. Manuel Castells, "Social Theory and the Dual City" (unpublished paper written for the New York City Committee, Social Science Research Council, 1989).

53
Regional Plan Association, "New York in the Global Economy: Study the Facts and the Issues," Draft for Discussion (April 1987).

54
Stuart Hall, "Popular-Democratic vs. Authoritarian Populism," *The Hard Road to Renewal* (New York: Verso Press, 1988): 123–149.

55
Noam Chomsky, *Necessary Illusions: Thought Control in Democratic Societies* (Boston: South End Press, 1989): 1–20; quotation on 14.

56
Ibid.: 2–3, 5.

57
Michael de Courcy Hinds, "Shaping Landfill into a Neighborhood," *NYT* (March 23, 1986): Section 8: 1, 18.

58
Richard F. Shepard, "Exploring Battery Park City: A Guided Ramble Around the Landfill," *NYT* (May 19, 1989): C1, C19.

59
Paul Goldberger, "Battery Park City is a Triumph of Urban Design," *NYT* (August 31, 1986): H1.

60
Ibid.

61
Ibid.

62
Michael de Courcy Hinds, "Vast Project Heads for '93 Finish," *NYT* (March 6, 1986): R18.

63
Goldberger, "Battery Park."

64
Paul Goldberger, "Public Space Gets a New Chance in New York," *NYT* (May 22, 1988): H35.

65
"What is American," *The Nation* 128 (June 26, 1929): 755. Quoted in Robert A. M. Stern, Gregory Gilmartin, and Thomas Mellins, *New York 1930* (New York: Rizzoli, 1988): 15.

66
Stern, et al., *New York 1930:* 18.

67
Ibid.: 30.

68
Paul Monaco, *Ribbons in Time: Movies and Society since 1945* (Bloomington: Indiana University Press, 1987): 93–95.

69
Albert Scardino, "Big Battery Park Dreams," *NYT* (Dec. 1, 1986): D1, D10.

70
Thomas Adams, *The Building of the City, The Regional Plan,* vol. 2 (New York: Regional Plan of New York and Its Environs, 1931): 75–76.

71
William Paley, Chairman, "The Threatened City: A Report on the Design of the City of New York by the Mayor's Task Force," (February 7, 1967): 30.

72
Unknown source quoted by Alan Finder, "Developers Named for Hudson Complex," *NYT* (Feb. 11, 1987): B1, B12.

73
Stewart, *On Longing:* 151. Quotation: 165.

74
Bunn, "The Aesthetics of Mercantilism": 303–321; Quotatation: 311.

75
Fredric Jameson, *Postmodernism or, The Cultural Logic of Late Capitalism* (Durham: Duke University Press, 1991): 399–418.

76
Jean-Christophe Agnew, *Worlds Apart:* Quotation: 16, 50–56, 170–171.

77
Anthony Vagnoni, "Here's Why You May Be Hearing, 'It's More New York New York'" *The New York Observer* (Nov. 21, 1988): 9.

78
Paul Goldberger, "Beyond Utopia: Settling for a New Realism," *NYT* (June 25, 1989): Section 2: 1, 30, Quotation: 30.

Epilogue

1
Charles Baudelaire, "Paradis Artificiels," Translated by Richard Terdiman. Richard Terdiman, "On Dialectics of Postdialectical Thinking," in Miami Theory Collective (ed.), *Community at Loose Ends* (Minneapolis: University of Minnesota Press, 1991): 118.

2
Charles Bernstein, "Artifice of Absorption," *A Poetics* (Cambridge: Harvard University Press, 1992): 85.

3
Richard J. Bernstein, *The New Constellation* (Cambridge: MIT Press, 1992): 310.

4
Terdiman, "On Dialectics": 118–119.

5
Christopher Norris, "Image and Parable Readings of Walter Benjamin," *Philosophy and Literature* 7, 1 (Spring 1983): 20.

6
Susan Buck-Morss, "Aesthetics and Anaesthetics: Walter Benjamin's Artwork Essay Reconsidered," *October* 62 (Fall 1992): n80, 22.

7
Walter Benjamin, "A Small History of Photography," *One Way Street.* Translated by Ed-

mund Jephcott and Kingsley Shorter (London: New Left Books, 1979): 243.

8
Walter Benjamin, "On Some Motifs in Baudelaire," *Illuminations*. Translated by Harry Zohn (New York: Schocken Books, 1969): 160–161.

9
Ibid.: 160.

10
Buck-Morss, "Aesthetics and Anaesthetics": 22–24.

11
Ibid.: n80, 22.

12
Benjamin, "Motifs": 165, 168.

13
Ackbar Abbas, "On Fascination: Walter Benjamin's Images," *New German Critique* 48 (Fall 1989): 51.

14
Benjamin, "The Image of Proust," *Illuminations:* 202.

15
Abbas, "On Fascination": 54.

16
Benjamin, "Theses on the Philosophy of History," *Illuminations:* 255.

17
Benjamin, "Theses": 255.

18
Abbas, "On Fascination": 54; and Irving Wohlfarth, "On the Messianic Structure of Walter Benjamin's Last Reflections," *Glyph* 3 (1978): 164–165.

19
Miriam Hansen, "Benjamin, Cinema and Experience: 'The Blue Flower in the Land of Technology'," *New German Critique* 40 (Winter 1987): 188.

20
Benjamin, "Motifs": 187–188.

21
Ibid.: 188.

22
Walter Benjamin, "The Work of Art in the Age of Mechanical Reproduction," *Illuminations:* 221.

23
Ibid.: 223.

24
Ibid.: 224.

25
Hansen, "Benjamin, Cinema": 205.

26
Richard Allen, "The Aesthetic Experience of Modernity: Benjamin, Adorno, and Contemporary Film Theory," *New German Critique* 40 (Winter 1987): 234.

27
Hansen, "Benjamin, Cinema": 203.

28
Walter Benjamin. Quoted by Abbas, "On Fascination": 44.

29
Benjamin, "Mechanical Reproduction": 223.

30
Benjamin, "Small History": 250–251, 256.

31
Benjamin, "Mechanical Reproduction": 226.

32
Benjamin, "Small History": 250.

33
Ibid.: 253.

34
Benjamin, "Mechanical Reproduction": 234.

35
Ibid.: 234–235.

36
Ibid.: 240–241.

37
Bernstein, "Artifice of Absorption": 9.

38
Ibid.: 53.

39
Marjorie Perloff, *Radical Artifice: Writing Poetry in the Age of Media* (Chicago: University of Chicago Press, 1991): 18, 27–28.

40
Charles Bernstein, "Hot Circuits: A Video Arcade," cited in Perloff, *Radical Artifice:* 2, 188.

41
Perloff, *Radical Artifice:* 133.

42
William Chaloupka, *Knowing Nukes: The Politics and Culture of the Atom* (Minneapolis: University of Minnesota Press, 1992): 64–67.

43
D. N. Rodowick, "Reading the Figural," *Camera Obscura* 24 (1991): 12.

44
Ibid.: 14.

45
Ibid.: 35.

46
Alan Liu, "Local Transcendence: Cultural Criticism, Postmodernism and the Romanticism of Detail," *Representations* 32 (Fall 1990): 75–113.

47
Michel Foucault, *Discipline and Punish.* Translated by Alan Sheridan (New York: Pantheon Press, 1977): 148.

48
Omar Calabrese, *Neo-Baroque: A Sign of the Times.* Translated by Charles Lambert (Princeton: Princeton University Press, 1992): 87–89.

49
Bernstein, "Artifice of Absorption": 31.

50
Elizabeth Deeds Ermarth, *Sequel to History: Postmodernism and the Crisis of Representational Time* (Princeton: Princeton University Press, 1992): 166.

51
Jean Baudrillard, "Simulacres et science fiction," *Science Fiction Studies* 55 (November 1991): 180. Quoted in Istvan Csicsery-Ronay, Jr., "The Sentimental Futurist: Cybernetics and Art in William Gibson's Neuromancer," *Critique* 23, no. 3 (Spring 1992): 224.

52
Csicsery-Ronay, Jr., "Sentimental Futurist": 224–230.

53
Walter Benjamin, "The Destructive Character," *Reflections.* Translated by Edmund Jephcott (New York: Schocken Books, 1979): 301.

54
Ibid.: 302.

55
Robert Alter, *Necessary Angles: Tradition and Modernity in Kafka, Benjamin, and Scholem* (Cambridge: Harvard University Press, 1991): 84; Irving Wohlfarth, "Resentment Begins at Home: Nietzsche, Benjamin, and the University," in Gary Smith (ed.), *On Walter Benjamin* (Cambridge: MIT Press, 1988): 242–244; and Irving Wohlfarth, "On the Messianic Structure of Walter Benjamin's Last Reflections," *Glyph* 3 (1979): 168–170.

56
Wohlfarth, "Last Reflections": 175.

Index

Illustration Credits

10 *Imagenie Parisiènne XVIe–XIXe siécle* (Paris, 1977), plate 54; **20, 234, 235** *Papiers Peints Panoramique Paris: Musée des Arts Décoratifs* (Paris: Flammarion, 1990), p. 251; **36** Howard Saalman, *Haussmann: Paris Transformed* (New York: George Braziller, 1971); **39** L. Dubech and P. d'Espezel, *Histoire de Paris,* vol. 11 (Paris: Les Editions Pittoresques, 1931), plate 32; **44** Michel Hoog, *Robert Delaunay* (New York: Crown Publishers, 1976); **49** Dawn Ades, *Photomontage* (London: Thames and Hudson, 1976), p. 98; **55** *La Ricostruzione della Citta* (Milan: Electra, 1985), p. 107, courtesy of Diana Agrest; **62** Stanislaus von Moos, *Venturi, Rauch & Scott Brown* (New York: Rizzoli, 1987), p. 112; **82, 89** W. J. Loftie, *Inigo Jones and Wren* (New York: MacMillan, 1893); **93** Simon Tidworth, *Theatres: An Illustrated History* (London: Pall Mall Press, 1973), plate 95; **98, 166** Mario Zadow, *Karl Friedrich Schinkel* (Berlin: Rembrandt Verlag, 1980); **101** Hermann G. Pundt, *Schinkel's Berlin* (Cambridge: Harvard University Press, 1972); **105** Daniel Couty and Alain Rey, eds., *Le Théâtre* (Paris: Bordas, 1989); **134, 182** Raymon Keaveney, *Views of Rome* (Washington, D.C.: Smithsonian Institute Scala Books, 1988); **139** *Roma in Dagherrotipia* (London: Strand of London, n.d.); **145** *Roma 70 Vedute* (Rome: Ricordo di Roma, n.d.), p. 119; **153** Lya and Raymond Matton, *Athènes et Ses Monuments* (Athens: Collection Institut Français d'Athènes, 1963); **156, 172** Ernest Breton, *Athènes* (Paris: Gide, Librairie-Editéur, 1862); **177** Mole Adriana, *Vedute di Roma*; **190, 194** *The Habitations of Man in All Ages* (Boston: James R. Osgood & Co., 1876); **198** Aldo Rossi, *Three Cities* (New York: Rizzoli, 1984), p. 108; **215** Sir Patrick Geddes, *The Ghent Exhibition*; **242** Andre Balland, ed., *Les Metamorphoses de Paris*; **254, 255** Stephan Oettermann, *Das Panorama* (Frankfurt: Syndikat, 1980); **261** Gilbert Guilleminault, *Grandes Heures Joyeuses de Paris de la Révolution à nos jours* (Paris: Gautier-Languereau); **265, 267** Victor Champier, "Les 44 Habitations de L'Homme," *Revue de l'Exposition Universelle,* vol. 1 (Paris: Librairie d'Art, 1889), pp. 115–125; **283, 286** Adolphe Smith, *Street Life in London* (New York: Benjamin Blom, reissued 1969, p. 37 [first published in 12 monthly parts in 1877, with photographs by John Thompson]; **299, 304** Howard M. Rosen and John M. Kaduck, *Columbia World's Fair Collectibles* (Des Moines, Iowa: Wallace-Homestead Book Co., 1979); **314** James M. Dennis, *Grant Wood: A Study in American Art and Culture* (New York: Viking Press, 1975); **324, 329, 336, 338, 340** Courtesy of The Historic New Orleans Collection; **346, 350, 357** John W. Reps, *Washington on View: The Nation's Capital since 1790* (Chapel Hill: University of North Carolina Press, 1991), pp. 39, 122, 103; **370** *Retrospective Magritte* (Brussels, 27 Oct.–31 Dec. 1978); **376** Advertisement, Neo Personal Gallery, New York. Courtesy of Robert Mango; **390** *Images et Imaginaires d'Architecture* (Paris: Centre Georges Pompidou, 1984), p. 407; **394** Edmund N. Bacon, *Design of Cities* (New York: Viking Press, 1967); **419** Jim Nudo, art director, Nike Design, Portland, Oregon; **459** Publicity package, Battery Park City Authority.